The Role of the Father in Child Development *edited by Michael E. Lamb*

Handbook of Behavioral Assessment *edited by Anthony R. Ciminero, Karen S. Calhoun, and Henry E. Adams*

Counseling and Psychotherapy: A Behavioral Approach *by E. Lakin Phillips*

Dimensions of Personality *edited by Harvey London and John E. Exner, Jr.*

The Mental Health Industry: A Cultural Phenomenon *by Peter A. Magaro, Robert Gripp, David McDowell, and Ivan W. Miller III*

Nonverbal Communication: The State of the Art *by Robert G. Harper, Arthur N. Wiens, and Joseph D. Matarazzo*

Alcoholism and Treatment *by David J. Armor, J. Michael Polich, and Harriet B. Stambul*

A Biodevelopmental Approach to Clinical Child Psychology: Cognitive Controls and Cognitive Control Theory *by Sebastiano Santostefano*

Handbook of Infant Development *edited by Joy D. Osofsky*

Understanding the Rape Victim: A Synthesis of Research Findings *by Sedelle Katz and Mary Ann Mazur*

Childhood Pathology and Later Adjustment: The Question of Prediction *by Loretta K. Cass and Carolyn B. Thomas*

Intelligent Testing with the WISC-R *by Alan S. Kaufman*

Adaptation in Schizophrenia: The Theory of Segmental Set *by David Shakow*

Psychotherapy: An Eclectic Approach *by Sol L. Garfield*

Handbook of Minimal Brain Dysfunctions *edited by Herbert E. Rie and Ellen D. Rie*

Handbook of Behavioral Interventions: A Clinical Guide *edited by Alan Goldstein and Edna B. Foa*

Art Psychotherapy *by Harriet Wadeson*

Handbook of Adolescent Psychology *edited by Joseph Adelson*

Psychotherapy Supervision: Theory, Research and Practice *edited by Allen K. Hess*

Psychology and Psychiatry in Courts and Corrections: Controversy and Change *by Ellsworth A. Fersch, Jr.*

Restricted Environmental Stimulation: Research and Clinical Applications *by Peter Suedfeld*

Personal Construct Psychology: Psychotherapy and Personality *edited by Alvin W. Landfield and Larry M. Leitner*

Mothers, Grandmothers, and Daughters: Personality and Child Care in Three-Generation Families *by Bertram J. Cohler and Henry U. Grunebaum*

Further Explorations in Personality *edited by A.I. Rabin, Joel Aronoff, Andrew M. Barclay, and Robert A. Zucker*

Hypnosis and Relaxation: Modern Verification of an Old Equation *by William E. Edmonston, Jr.*

Handbook of Clinical Behavior Therapy *edited by Samuel M. Turner, Karen S. Calhoun, and Henry E. Adams*

Handbook of Clinical Neuropsychology *edited by Susan B. Filskov and Thomas J. Boll*

The Course of Alcoholism: Four Years After Treatment *by J. Michael Polich, David J. Armor, and Harriet B. Braiker*

Handbook of Innovative Psychotherapies *edited by Raymond J. Corsini*

The Role of the Father in Child Development (Second Edition) *edited by Michael E. Lamb*

Behavioral Medicine: Clinical Applications *by Susan S. Pinkerton, Howard Hughes, and W.W. Wenrich*

Handbook for the Practice of Pediatric Psychology *edited by June M. Tuma*

Change Through Interaction: Social Psychological Processes of Counseling and Psychotherapy *by Stanley R. Strong and Charles D. Claiborn*

Drugs and Behavior (Second Edition) *by Fred Leavitt*

(*continued on back*)

VERMONT COLLEGE

WITHDRAWN

LIBRARY
MONTPELIER, VERMONT

HANDBOOK OF
JUVENILE DELINQUENCY

Please remember that this is a library book,
and that it belongs only temporarily to each
person who uses it. Be considerate. Do
not write in this, or any, library book.

Handbook of Juvenile Delinquency

HERBERT C. QUAY, Editor
University of Miami

A WILEY-INTERSCIENCE PUBLICATION

JOHN WILEY & SONS

New York · Chichester · Brisbane · Toronto · Singapore

Copyright © 1987 by John Wiley & Sons, Inc.

All rights reserved. Published simultaneously in Canada.

Reproduction or translation of any part of this work
beyond that permitted by Section 107 or 108 of the
1976 United States Copyright Act without the permission
of the copyright owner is unlawful. Requests for
permission or further information should be addressed to
the Permissions Department, John Wiley & Sons, Inc.

This publication is designed to provide accurate and
authoritative information in regard to the subject
matter covered. It is sold with the understanding that
the publisher is not engaged in rendering legal, accounting,
or other professional service. If legal advice or other
expert assistance is required, the services of a competent
professional person should be sought. *From a Declaration
of Principles jointly adopted by a Committee of the
American Bar Association and a Committee of Publishers.*

Library of Congress Cataloging in Publication Data:

Handbook of juvenile delinquency.

  (Wiley series on personality processes)
  Bibliography: p.
  "A Wiley-Interscience publication."
  1. Juvenile delinquency—United States.
2. Juvenile delinquents—United States—Psychology.
3. Rehabilitation of juvenile delinquents—United
States. I. Quay, Herbert C. (Herbert Callister),
1927- . II. Series.
HV9104.H24 1987   364.3'6'0973   86-34008
ISBN 0-471-81707-4

Printed in the United States of America

10 9 8 7 6 5 4 3 2 1

Contributors

Jack Arbuthnot, Ph.D.
Professor of Psychology
Ohio University
Athens, Ohio

Arnold Binder, Ph.D.
Professor
Program in Social Ecology
University of California
Irvine, California

William S. Davidson II, Ph.D.
Professor of Psychology
Michigan State University
East Lansing, Michigan

David P. Farrington, Ph.D.
Institute of Criminology
University of Cambridge
Cambridge, England

Leah K. Gensheimer, M.A.
Research Associate
Department of Psychology
Michigan State University
East Lansing, Michigan

Martin Gold, Ph.D.
Program Director
Institute for Social Research
University of Michigan
Ann Arbor, Michigan

Donald A. Gordon, Ph.D.
Associate Professor of
   Psychology
Ohio University
Athens, Ohio

Rand Gottschalk, M.A.
Research Assistant
Department of Psychology
Michigan State University
East Lansing, Michigan

Gregory J. Jurkovic, Ph.D.
Assistant Professor of
   Psychology
Georgia State University
Atlanta, Georgia

Rolf Loeber, Ph.D.
Assistant Professor of
   Psychology
Western Psychiatric Institute
   and Clinic
School of Medicine
University of Pittsburgh
Pittsburgh, Pennsylvania

Raymond P. Lorion, Ph.D.
Professor of Psychology
University of Maryland
College Park, Maryland

Jeffrey P. Mayer, M.A.
Research Associate
Department of Psychology
Michigan State University
East Lansing, Michigan

Gerald R. Patterson, Ph.D.
Director
Oregon Social Learning Center
Eugene, Oregon

Herbert C. Quay, Ph.D.
Professor of Psychology
University of Miami
Coral Gables, Florida

Abram Rosenblatt, M.A.
Graduate Student
Department of Psychology
University of Arizona
Tucson, Arizona

Lee Sechrest, Ph.D.
Professor of Psychology
University of Arizona
Tucson, Arizona

James Snyder, Ph.D.
Associate Professor of
   Psychology
Wichita State University
Wichita, Kansas

Magda Stouthamer-Loeber, Ph.D.
Assistant Professor of
   Psychology
Western Psychiatric Institute and Clinic
School of Medicine
University of Pittsburgh
Pittsburgh, Pennsylvania

Patrick H. Tolan, Ph.D.
Assistant Professor of
   Psychology
DePaul University
Chicago, Illinois

Gordon Trasler, Ph.D.
Professor of Psychology
The University of Southampton
Southampton, England

Robert G. Wahler, Ph.D.
Professor of Psychology
University of Tennessee
Knoxville, Tennessee

Series Preface

This series of books is addressed to behavioral scientists interested in the nature of human personality. Its scope should prove pertinent to personality theorists and researchers as well as to clinicians concerned with applying an understanding of personality processes to the amelioration of emotional difficulties in living. To this end, the series provides a scholarly integration of theoretical formulations, empirical data, and practical recommendations.

Six major aspects of studying and learning about human personality can be designated: personality theory, personality structure and dynamics, personality development, personality assessment, personality change, and personality adjustment. In exploring these aspects of personality, the books in the series discuss a number of distinct but related subject areas: the nature and implications of various theories of personality; personality characteristics that account for consistencies and variations in human behavior; the emergence of personality processes in children and adolescents; the use of interviewing and testing procedures to evaluate individual differences in personality; efforts to modify personality styles through psychotherapy, counseling, behavior, therapy, and other methods of influence; and patterns of abnormal personality functioning that impair individual competence.

IRVING B. WEINER

Fairleigh Dickinson University
Rutherford, New Jersey

Preface

The intent of this book is to provide a critical review of research and theory on juvenile delinquency, primarily from the psychological perspective. It is, of course, impossible to discuss delinquency without introducing sociological theory and research, but the emphasis here is clearly on the delinquent, his origin, and his treatment as described in psychological terms.

A reading of this volume should make it clear that juvenile delinquency is a complex phenomenon of relatively recent recognition as historical time goes, and that juvenile delinquents are by no means a psychologically homogeneous group. We hope that the reader will also recognize that delinquency is not really so different from child and adolescent deviance as defined in other ways and carrying other labels in other social systems. The parallels could be high-lighted by the reader's occasional consultation with the editor's volume (with John Werry and collaborators) *Psychopathological Disorders of Childhood*, third·edition (Wiley, 1986).

What may not be quite so obvious is that we have more knowledge about delinquency than we are currently putting to use. We can identify subgroups of delinquents who are different from one another in important ways. We do have an understanding of factors in society as a whole, and family settings in particular, that are related to delinquency, and that, at least in the case of families, can be modified. There are also some characteristics of individual delinquents that are important. Some delinquents who exhibit deviant social behavior and cognitive and moral functioning also seem amenable to change for the better.

We are also beginning to get an inkling about the operation of biological factors that may predispose youth to behavior that becomes defined as delinquent. These factors may also be remediable by newer, biologically based interventions in the same way that Attention Deficit Disorder (formerly hyperactivity) is ameliorated by medication in the majority of children. Further genetic research may provide clues as to the prevention of some or all of these adverse biological factors.

Despite the general pessimism surrounding rehabilitation, there are both institutional and community-based treatments that do work, albeit imperfectly. We can predict future delinquency and future crime, at least under some circumstances, at a much better than chance level.

Not least important is that we now recognize many of the methodological and conceptual errors of the past, and have developed, and no doubt will continue to develop, improved methods of research. There is, concomitantly, more hope for the development of theories which will permit more direct tests of the hypotheses that derive from them than has been true of theories of delinquency in the past.

It is the hope of the editor and all the contributors that readers of this book will have a better scientific understanding of juvenile delinquency than they had at the outset. If so, our efforts will have been rewarded.

HERBERT C. QUAY

Miami, Florida
March 1987

Contents

CHAPTER 1

An Historical
and Theoretical Introduction

ARNOLD BINDER

University of California, Irvine

Behavior that occurs in a social context may be roughly divided into three categories on the basis of general acceptability. First, there is behavior that is fully appropriate by the standards of the given culture or at least acceptable in the given setting. Second, there is behavior that is peculiar or unusual in the setting but not of a degree that creates disturbance. And finally, there is behavior that is so deviant that it arouses such reactions as fear, disgust, rage, or need for revenge. Intermediate between the behavior and the reaction to it may be loss of property, defacement of or damage to property, threatened violence, or actual injury.

Cultures have differed and continue to differ widely in levels of tolerance for various types of idiosyncratic behavior, in the laws and similar regulations that provide the guidelines for the boundaries of unacceptably deviant behavior, and in the formal structures and procedures for social reaction to unacceptable behavior. To illustrate, in our culture mildly drunk behavior on the part of an adult or mildly mischievous behavior by an adolescent may produce grimaces, rolls of the eyes, and some such comment as "He's loaded," or "Boys will be boys." But we have laws against "disturbing the peace" and "malicious mischief" that allow invocation of one of society's formal control mechanisms if the behavior goes beyond tolerated bounds. The system invoked may be the criminal or juvenile justice system if the behavior is proscribed in penal codes, or the mental health system if the behavior is of the type listed in the *Diagnostic and Statistical Manual of Mental Disorders:DSM-III* (American Psychiatric Association, 1980). Then, depending upon the specific behavior and the proclivities of the particular system, the individual may be designated a delinquent, a child in need of supervision, a criminal, an over-anxious adolescent, a schizophrenic, or whatever else seems appropriate. Corrective measures usually accompany the diagnosis.

The reaction to a given idiosyncratic or deviant behavior is not only a function of the general culture but varies within a culture according to immediate

1

personal and environmental conditions. A boy in Wisconsin, for example, derives great pleasure from letting air out of the automobile tires in his neighborhood. The people in that neighborhood may, on the one hand, be in a euphoric mood because of a major industrial development in the area and react to the behavior as an adolescent prank, a minor nuisance worthy of no more than a scolding call to his parents. On the other hand, the community may be tense because of a local or regional crisis, and may react by calling the police and having the boy arrested. The community response may take on an interactive complexity if the boy comes from a racial or religious group different from that of the immediate community, or if the father of the boy is a known criminal, and so on. It is important to note, therefore, that depending upon the composition or mood of the immediate community, the same boy behaving in an identical way may be tolerated as unusual or eventually officially designated as a juvenile delinquent.

The principal reason for reaction by one of society's systems is to control or change the behavior in question. The goals of control and change are evident when a very anxious patient is given psychotherapy, when a juvenile delinquent is sent to a foster home, or when a convicted drunken driver is required to complete a course of instruction in automobile safety. But why are certain actions taken to control or change a given behavior in preference to various other alternatives?

The link between behavior and the mode of controlling or changing that behavior is an understanding of why the behavior occurred. That understanding is an explanation for the behavior, or in more formal terms, a theory that accounts for the behavior. The understanding, explanation, or theory has embedded in it the means for changing the behavior. The process of moving from explanation or theory to specific corrective action is deductive reasoning.

Theories and Social Actions

With respect to juvenile delinquency, there are theories held by the general public, theories held by the people in authority who make and enforce the laws, and theories held by social scientists. A theory held by a given person—whether that person is a citizen, politician, law enforcer, or scientist—reflects the general social belief system of that individual as well as the behavior being explained. Thus, "conservative" people tend to explain delinquency as the result of an overly tolerant society that shows a breakdown of discipline, and to advocate measures emphasizing strict limit-setting, structure, and control. "Liberal" people, on the other hand, are much more likely to explain delinquency as proceeding from poor social and environmental conditions such as discrimination and poverty, and to advocate prevention or rehabilitation by methods that correct the effects of those deficiencies.

While social scientists may or may not be interested in the uses of their theories in practical decision making, their theories nevertheless often influence the actions of policy makers and the general public. To illustrate, one sociological theory emphasizes that delinquent behavior is an outcome of the great discrepancy in our culture between the goals of fame and success, on the one hand, and the opportunities available for impoverished youngsters to achieve those goals, on the other hand (Cloward & Ohlin, 1960). Television, radio, and movies intensify the frustration by highlighting the various aspects of the "good life." Using that (simplified) theoretical structure, one can deduce that reduction of delinquency will occur if one narrows the gap between the aspects of the good life portrayed and the opportunities for achieving them. And, to be sure, when individuals with that theoretical leaning instituted a program for delinquency prevention in various communities, they emphasized the creation of employment opportunities for youths, provision of vocational guidance, the training of youths in job-related skills, and other efforts aimed at making it possible for youths to earn the money necessary to purchase commodities (see the description of the Mobilization for Youth program in Grosser, 1969; see also Chapter 10).

As another illustration, some psychiatrists explain delinquency on the basis of inadequacies in parent-child relationships during the earlier years of life. Attempts to correct the problem, then, consist of psychotherapeutic sessions in which the patient speaks freely about life's experiences, with the expectation that many of the emotions that originally accompanied the experiences would be transferred to the relationship with the therapist and then resolved (e.g., Friedlander, 1947; see also Chapter 11). And since the dominant theories among psychologists who work in juvenile justice are behavioral, one finds concepts like contingency management, coping skills, shaping, anger management, and cognitive restructuring widely used in modern psychological approaches to the treatment of young offenders (Binder and Binder, 1983, in press; see Chapters 9, 10, and 11).

In contrast to those theories, many popular explanations of delinquency blame moral or religious weakness, inadequate expression in athletic and similar recreational activities, and even inadequate transcendental emanations for juvenile delinquency. Recommended remediation, then, consists, respectively, of indoctrination in moral and religious values, development of available recreational programs, and the wider use of Transcendental Meditation.

An Overview of Formal Theories and Their Bases

The principal disciplines that have contributed to empirical research and theorizing in the field of juvenile delinquency are psychiatry, psychology, and sociology. Within the United States, the domination of the field by sociology is so great that it is not much of an exaggeration to state that the field of scientific study of delinquency is a subdiscipline of sociology. In the United Kingdom and in much of continental Europe, on the other hand, psychological and psychiatric approaches have had and continue to have significant theoretical and practical impact. In her survey of the state of knowledge regarding delinquency and criminality in 1959, Wootton (p. 319) stated, "In this country [that is, the United Kingdom] it has so happened that psychiatrists and psychologists managed to establish themselves well and early in the study of social pathology" in order to explain the "lopsided concentration upon individual rather than upon social factors."

The point made by Wootton on the "lopsided concentration" upon such individual factors as personality and character by psychologists and psychiatrists in the United Kingdom is an important one. The effect of professional bias on the form a particular theory of delinquency is the organizational counterpart of the individual bias discussed previously in differentiating "conservative" and "liberal" preferences for explanatory systems. Both factors are so influential that one occasionally feels that the disposition of the theorist has more impact on theoretical form than the behavior being explained. In the construction of a scientific theory, the influence exercises itself in two ways. First, the individual theorist chooses the domain of observation, which may range from the interrelationships among members of a street gang to the results of psychological testing. Second, there is an enormous amount of slack between actual data and the constructs derived in the inferential process, allowing strong influence of biases derived from the theorist's personal proclivities and earlier learning experiences, and from immediate social forces.

When theorizing is entirely an academic enterprise that is self-correcting over a period of time by a counter-balancing of different biases, the fact of professional or personal biases is not a serious problem. But where a given theory determines, directly or indirectly, a practical program that involves a great many young (and not so young) lives and an enormous amount of social resources, the facts and factors upon which that theory is based may be critical indeed.

The principal point is that theories do not come from facts and observations, but from people who process the facts and observations through their own filtering systems. These filtering systems highlight certain factors, suppress others, and distort still others. Thus, while psychiatrists tend to use explanatory constructs that are based on intrapsychic conditions derived from earlier life experiences, sociologists tend to use constructs that explain human behavior on the basis of such constructs as social disorganization and social control.

To illustrate the process, we turn to polar opposites of theories that purport to explain delinquency. Hans Eysenck is a psychologist who has worked with individual patients in clinical settings, using concepts and procedures derived from traditional laboratory psychology. In his theory of delinquency and criminality (Eysenck, 1964), he argued that conscience and law-abiding behavior are learned by people in the same manner that dogs learn to salivate in response to a tone previously associated with meat. In fact, he has stated without equivocation "Conscience is indeed a conditioned reflex!" (p.110). The Pavlovian conditioning occurs when parents apply punishment in the form of shouting, slapping, and so forth whenever a child engages in such unacceptable behavior as beating up sister or urinating on the stairway. Misbehavior then becomes associated with anxiety and that anxiety is reduced by the avoidance of bad, and later illegal, behavior. In the case of a delinquent or criminal, that learning does not occur fully, so there is insufficient conscience-induced anxiety to counteract such temptations as theft and assaultive behavior (see Chapter 7 with regard to this general position).

Taylor, Walton, and Young (1973), on the other hand, are sociologists who consider themselves "new" or "radical" criminologists. Their theories are strongly influenced by their Marxist perspective. To them, what others call deviant is normal within a broader perspective of human diversity. It is the controlling repressive reaction of society to the different behaviors that criminalizes individual expression and generates an atmosphere of segregation and imprisonment. They argue that the behavior labeled delinquent or criminal by society represents a consciously chosen decision to maintain personal integrity in the domain of frustration imposed by the inequalities of power, wealth and authority in industrialized society.

Clearly these markedly different theories have dramatically different implications for the treatment of offenders as well as for the methods of primary prevention (see Chapter 13). Taylor, Walton and Young (1973) would certainly not spend much time modifying an individual's psyche, when they "know" that the real oppressor is society and its structures. And it is not likely Eysenck (1964) would advocate a major change in society to untangle a twisted conscience.

A BIT OF HISTORY

Antiquity to the Nineteenth Century

Children misbehave, sometimes outrageously, and there is every reason to believe that children have misbehaved, sometimes outrageously, throughout history. But, as discussed in the preceding section, cultures have differed in their tolerances for various types of misbehavior, their explanatory systems for understanding the idiosyncrasies of the young, and their modes of controlling unacceptable manifestations of youthful behavior. Those differences over cultures are functions of the dominant social and political values (as is the case with individuals), religious beliefs, forms of social organization, available methods of control, and the interactions of these and other cultural characteristics. For very old civilizations, our primary source of information regarding attitudes toward juvenile offenders and methods of control consists of sets of statements in codes that reflect prohibitions and remedies.

One of the oldest known legal codes is the Code of Hammurabi, dating from 2270 B.C. It represents the law of Babylonians on matters ranging over rental and leasing arrangements, husband-wife relationships and obligations, the uses of witnesses and contracts, mutual obligations of adopting parents and adopted children, and the requirements of various trade agreements.

It also has an extensive listing of the punishments warranted for violations of various personal and property rights. The following examples are from Kocourek and Wigmore, (1915, pp. 327–442):

8

If a man steal an ox, or sheep, or ass, or pig, or boat from a temple or palace, he shall pay thirty-fold; if it be from a freeman, he shall pay tenfold. If the thief has nothing with which to pay, he shall be put to death.

21

If a man make breach into a house [break into the house], one shall kill him in front of the breach [kill him on the spot], and bury him in it.

22

If a man carried on highway robbery and be captured, he shall be put to death.

196

If a man destroy the eye of another man, one shall destroy his eye.

201

If he knock out the teeth of a freedman, he shall pay one-third mina of silver.

260

If a man steal a watering-bucket or a plow, he shall pay three shekels of silver.

These and other statements of punishment for what are criminal acts in our culture use the masculine form in referring to the potential offender. The words "woman" and "female" are used in the code (as in "If a man strike a free-born woman, and produce a miscarriage . . . " and in references to a "female tavern-keeper") as is the genderless "one," so there is uncertainty as to whether the masculine form is used to encompass both sexes or whether only males are included in the prohibitions. But more important for our purposes, there is no indication of these implications for youths. Having a Western bias of the twentieth century, one might hastily conclude that children (or boys alone), as we know them, could not possibly be included when the word "man" is used. But, as we shall see, earlier cultures had markedly different perspectives on children. Regarding youths as adults only if above the age of 17 (for most purposes) is an arbitrary construction of our society, reflecting its general attitudes toward children and its various complexities.

Even the item stating, "If a son strike his father, one shall cut off his hands" carries ambiguity in its implications for children since there is no indication of how old the son must be to warrant the punishment.

The Old Testament (Mosaic Code) of course lists many types of unacceptable behavior, often with accompanying punishments for the behavior specified.

Thou shalt not kill. (Exodus 20:13)

Thou shalt not steal. (Exodus 20:15)

He that smiteth a man, so that he die, shall be surely put to death. (Exodus 21:12)

And he that curseth his father, or his mother, shall surely be put to death. (Exodus 21:17)

Again, there are no specifications to determine age-related applicability of punishments. However, there are numerous guides for the proper behavior of children throughout the Bible, and such admonitions as "Even a child is known by his doings, whether his work be pure and whether it be right" (Proverbs 21:11). And while the words of guidance throughout Proverbs are kindly (e.g., "Enter not into the path of the wicked, and go not in the way of evil men" 4:14), the tone of vengeance reflecting "eye for eye, tooth for tooth" is prevalent in other chapters. Deuteronomy emphasizes that wrathful perspective in (21:18–21):

If a man have a stubborn and rebellious son, which will not obey the voice of his father, or the voice of his mother, and that, when they have chastened him, will not hearken unto them: Then shall his father and his mother lay hold on him, and bring him unto the elders of his city, This our son is stubborn and rebellious, he will not obey our voice. . . .

And all the men of his city shall stone him with stones, that he die; so that thou put evil away from among you . . .

Ludwig (1950, p. 523) has argued that, in the Mosaic Code, "The severity of these penalties [for young offenders] was probably mitigated in practice and later by explicit provision of the Talmud." He has pointed out, for example, that a first offense of disobedience led to no more than warning and flogging.

Moreover, as particularly emphasized by Goldin (1952), the early Hebrew jurists put so many restrictions on the process of establishing guilt that execution of punishment was nearly impossible. He stated (p. 167):

. . . the Talmudic authorities, in keeping with their great work of reform and innovation, surrounded the interpretation of the Biblical text with so many technicalities, that in some instances it would seem to border on the ridiculous . . . under the Talmudic dispensation of justice an occurrence of the case of the stubborn and rebellious son was either impossible or at best very rare and remote.

The ancient Hebrews apparently developed a tripartite division of childhood. In it, infancy lasted from birth to six years of age; prepuberty started at seven and ended at 12 for females, 13 for males; and pre-adulthood started at puberty and lasted until majority was reached at 20. While there was no clear specification in the Talmud of the age at which personal responsibility for criminal actions began, it seems likely, according to Ludwig (1950), that liability for corporal punishment started at puberty and for capital punishment at majority.

Roman law developed extensively between the first codification in about 450 B.C. and the restating and reforming under the reign, ending in 565 A.D., of the Emperor Justinian. The codification of 450 B.C., called the XII Tables, has been variously referred to as the "fountain-head of the Roman Law" (Diamond, 1951, p. 76) and as a set of laws that "continued to be held in great reverence" (Buckland, 1963, p. 2). The code as originally constructed did not survive, but numerous references to its parts in later legal and popular writings have made limited reconstruction possible. One reconstructed version may be found in Kocourek and Wigmore, (1915).

While there is no evidence of differential considerations for youths in the XII Tables (see Kocourek and Wigmore, 1915), developments over subsequent years led to allowance for irresponsibility due to age in criminal matters. According to Buckland (1963, p. 158), *intellectus* came to be "material in respect of liability for wrongdoing" (criminal responsibility), and an *infans* (that is, one incapable of speaking) necessarily lacked *intellectus*. A child's incapacity to make intelligent decisions was considered substantially like that of an insane person.

By the time of the Justinian *Corpus Juris*, the terminus of infancy, and the presumed accompanying absence of responsibility for criminal acts, was fixed at seven. Puberty, eventually established at 14 for boys and 12 for girls after earlier preference for determination on the basis of the biological condition, became the age of full criminal responsibility, as well as the transition point when guardianship ended and marriage was allowed.

If there is no responsibility before age seven and full responsibility after puberty, what about the transition period? Ludwig (1950, p. 525) stated:

> Between infancy and puberty, criminal responsibility was made to depend on a combination of three factors: chronological age and its proximity to either infancy or puberty; nature of the offense; and mental capacity of the offender. Those near infancy (*proximi infantiae*), Justinian thought the same as infants. But one close to puberty (*proximi pubertati*) should be dealt with as responsible.

It was thought that being close to puberty meant that the youngster had criminal intent, knowing that the behavior was wrong.

The English tradition of law started with the Laws of Aethelberht, a Kentish king. This codification was apparently motivated by the conversion of Aethelberht to Christianity by Augustine in 597 A.D. For each of the offenses listed in the code, punishment was fixed in terms of the payment of damages, referred to as "bot." Even in the case of murder, we find, "If a man slay another, let him make 'bot' with a half 'lead-geld' of c. shillings" (Kocourek and Wigmore, 1915, pp. 512–518). There were no exceptions for children. Indeed, Ludwig (1950, p. 525) argued that for the entire Anglo-Saxon era:

> Reference to such [minority] responsibility among the Anglo-Saxons is fragmentary. Evidence extant points to a severe system which pushed criminal liability through group responsibility back to the cradle . . . Criminal responsibility began before seven.

Although there are traces of Roman influence on the laws dating back to Aethelberht (597 A.D.), generally speaking the Anglo-Saxon codes were not guided by the developing Roman law because the Angles, Saxons, and Jutes (in more limited numbers) who conquered England came from parts of northern Europe where there was little impact by Roman culture (see Diamond, 1951 and Various European Authors, 1968, for further discussion). Consequently, one does not find in the codes the sophisticated differentiations of Roman law for criminal responsibility by age. But there were sporadic statements of exemptions for children (Sanders, 1970, p. 3); in the Laws of Ine we have:

> 7. If any one steal, so that his wife and children know it not, let him pay LX shillings as "wite" [punishment]. But if he steal with the knowledge of all his household, let them all go into slavery [reflecting the group responsibility referred to above]. A *boy of X years* may be privy to a theft . . . (italics added).

And in the Laws of Aethelstan, there is:

> 1. First: that no thief be spared who may be taken "handhaebliende," [i.e., with the goods in his hand] *above XII years,* and above eight pence. And if any one so do, let him pay for the thief according to his "wer," . . . and let it not be the more settled for the thief, or that he clear himself thereby. But if he will defend himself, or flees away, then let him not be spared (italics added).

Finally, as Ludwig (1950) has pointed out, death penalties were indeed carried out against the young at the time of King Aethelstan. The king (p. 526):

> . . . sent word to the Archbishop that "it seemed to him too cruel that so young a man should be killed, and besides for so little, as he has learned has somewhere been done." It was then ordered that " . . . no younger person should be slain than sixteen years, except he should make resistance or flee, and would not surrender himself . . . "

There were other codifications during the Anglo-Saxon period of English law, but the overall picture remains as sketched above. The 300 years following the Norman conquest (1066) saw the establishment of the firm roots that later made English law a unique system in the balancing of individual and state rights. The grand jury was systematized in criminal procedure for determining the likelihood of guilt, the jury trial came into widespread use in criminal cases, and the requirement of "due process of law" prior to imposition of punishment in criminal matters was firmly established (see Mott, 1973; Plucknett, 1940). And to complete the picture, during this era, English law began showing influences of Roman, and its closely related canon law. Pollock wrote (1909, p. 120):

> From Stephen's reign [1135–1154] onwards, the proofs that Roman and canon law are being studied in England became more frequent. The letters of . . . John of Salisbury, the foremost scholar of the age are full of allusions to both laws.

An interesting exception for children occurs in the writings of the thirteenth century jurist Henry de Bracton, who was much influenced by Roman law. Bracton wrote of outlawry, the process of dealing with a wrongdoer who "has taken to flight" as follows: "A minor, however, one who is under twelve years of age, cannot be outlawed or put outside the law because until he reaches that age he is not under any law . . . " (Woodbine, 1968, p. 353).

The laws that evolved in England over subsequent centuries were summarized in mid-eighteenth century by Blackstone (1884, originally published 1765). One can see both Anglo-Saxon and Roman/canon influences in the following overview of Blackstone (p. 288):

> . . . by the law, as it now stands, and has stood at least ever since the time of Edward the Third, the capacity of doing ill, or contracting guilt, is not so much measured by years and days, as by the strength of the delinquent's understanding and judgment. For one lad of eleven years old may have as much cunning as another of fourteen; and in these cases our maxim is, that *"malitia supplet aetatem"*. Under seven years of age indeed an infant cannot be guilty of felony; for then a felonious discretion is almost an impossibility in nature: but at eight years old he may be guilty of felony. Also, under fourteen, though an infant shall be *prima facie* adjudged to be *doli incapax;* yet, if it appear to the court and jury that he was *doli capax,* and could discern between good and evil, he may be convicted and suffer death. Thus a girl of thirteen has been burnt for killing her mistress: and one boy of ten, and another of nine years old, who had killed their companions, have been sentenced to death, and he of ten years actually hanged; because it appeared upon their trials, that the one hid himself, and the other hid the body . . .

In addition to those developments in English criminal law, there are features of its civil law that are important to highlight because of precedents created for more recent law that applied only to juveniles. The court of equity (or chancery court) assumed jurisdiction in such matters as violations of contracts, conflicts regarding inheritance and guardianship, foreclosure of mortgages, and the operations of trusts and charities. Cogan (1970) traced the early development of chancery actions that involved children. He presents the following illustration (p. 149):

> In *White v. White,* between 1399 and 1413, a widow petitioned the king's chancellor, Thomas de Arundel, Archbishop of Canterbury. She asserted that her late husband willed her the profit of certain lands and the guardianship of their daughter during the daughter's nonage. One Thomas White, the petition asserted, had taken both the profits of the lands and the daughter. The widow prayed for their restoration.

Among the so-called "prerogatives" of the king was ultimate responsibility for the care and custody of people, such as "idiots" and "lunatics," who could not care for themselves. That responsibility was expanded to encompass the poor as another class of people who could not care for themselves, and then to the charities that ministered to the needs of the poor. Forms *pater patriae* and then *parens patriae* came into use to describe the protective role of the king (as carried out by his chancellor). Thus, Blackstone (1884, Vol. 1, p. 246) stated, "The king, as *parens patriae,* has the general superintendance of all *charities;* which he exercises by the keeper of his conscience, the chancellor."

Since the incapacities of nonage were equated to those of idiots and imbeciles as early as Anglo-Saxon days, one would expect the notion of the protective father, or *pater patriae,* to extend to children. And that did indeed occur in a case report of about 1700, which concerned the status of an inheritance when a condition of the will was not followed, though for good cause (*Falkland v. Bertie,* as discussed in Cogan, 1970).

In the decades following *Falkland v. Bertie*, chancery accepted a broader and broader array of cases concerned with various aspects of guardianship. But a most significant expansion beyond that occurred in 1756 when the court acted in response to a petition from a natural father (*Butler v. Freeman*), acknowledging that the action was not through guardianship but on the basis that the court "has a general right delegated by the Crown, as *pater patriae*, to interfere in particular cases, for the benefit of such who are incapable to protect themselves" (as quoted in Cogan, 1970, p. 178).

By the early part of the nineteenth century, further expansion had proceeded so far that Cogan (1970, p. 180) pointed out, "The expression [*parens patriae*] now not only signified the special care the court could give to infants who were properly before it but also implied the court could properly bring infants before it to give them special care."

The Nineteenth Century

Under common law at the outset of the nineteenth century, a child under seven was presumed not to have the mental elements necessary for a finding of criminal guilt; a child between seven and 14 was presumed to be *doli incapax* (not capable of a guilty mind), but the presumption was rebuttable; and a child above 14 had full criminal responsibility. In other words, children under seven were exempted from criminal prosecution, those between seven and 14 were exempted unless prosecution established knowledge of wrongfulness of the behavior in question, and the seven to 14 year olds with such "guilty minds" as well as all children above 14 could be convicted and punished as adults. In the words of the *Report of the Committee on Children and Young Persons,* 1960 (p. 21):

> Punishment was either fixed by law or graded by judicial practice according to the nature of the offense. Here little attention was paid to the age of the offender; the principle of equality before the law meant that children were hanged, transported or imprisoned on the rules and principles applicable to adults.

Following the American Revolution, the common law of England became law in the United States by incorporation in state constitutions, by so-called "reception" statutes, and by idiosyncratic approaches such as in Massachusetts where (Nelson, 1975, p. 8):

> reception was authorized by a clause in the Constitution of 1780 providing for the continuing effectiveness of all laws that had theretofore "been adopted, used, and approved" in the Commonwealth. Although that clause did not talk specifically of receiving English law, the Massachusetts courts, unable to determine precisely which laws were in effect in 1780, construed the clause as authorizing reception of the entire common law and statute law of England at the time of the Revolution, "except such parts as were judged inapplicable" to the commonwealth's "new state and condition."

On the other hand, the Delaware constitution, 1776, stated, "The common law of England as well as so much of the statute law as has been heretofore adopted in practice in this State, shall remain in force," except where there was conflict with the various granted "rights and privileges." And the state of New York passed a reception statute in 1786 that declared as law in New York, English common law and English statutes that had been effective in the colony up to April 19, 1775. The New York Constitution of 1821 stated that the common law would continue to be law while English statute law was not mentioned (several years later an act specifically announced that British statutes were inapplicable in the state). (For a fuller discussion and the source of the preceding quotes, see Friedman, 1973, p. 96.)

Such was the state of affairs at the start of the century, the nineteenth, that was to bring many profound social changes in both England and the United States. And those changes produced radically different methods of defining and dealing with young offenders. A summary of motivating forces for England is provided in the *Report of the Committee on Children and Young Persons,* (1960, p. 22):

The common law system [for handling youths] was, in its way, logical and coherent, but in the earlier years of the nineteenth century it was seen to be in need
of substantial reform. The harshness of the penal code and the changing social
conditions that followed the Industrial Revolution combined to produce, in the
first half of the nineteenth century, a sharp increase in the number of young
offenders, large numbers of whom were sentenced to imprisonment or trans-
portation.

A similar summary is provided for the United States by Binder (1979, p.
627):

If one were to characterize the nineteenth century in broad political-social terms,
one would use such expressions as rapid industrialization, intense urbanization,
massive immigration, and precipitous development of capitalism. Industrialization necessitated detachment of one or more persons from the family for long
periods and created class frictions, immigration brought culture conflict, urbanization produced exacerbation of conditions that favored learning and modeling
criminal behavior, and capitalism created class differences based purely on material wealth and elevated hopes of achieving that wealth. And all the preceding
consequences are assumed to have more or less direct effects on an increase in
delinquency or in society's sensitivity to (and willingness to react to) delinquent
behavior.

The problems created by industrialization, urbanization, and immigration
motivated attempts toward solution in the context of a society that showed
growing humanitarianism, concern for the underprivileged, and the begin-
nings of scientific medicine. In addition, the nineteenth century saw a mod-
eration in earlier harsh attitudes toward the disciplining of children, the development of attitudes of unlimited possibilities for redirecting children, and
the extension of notions of childhood to include youngsters between puberty
and majority. The concept of adolescence, with its accompanying notions of
continuing moral vulnerability, emotional turmoil, and plasticity became
prominent (see, e.g., Wishy, 1968; Ariès, 1962; and Hall, 1904).

As a result of the interaction among these nineteenth century forces, a number of significant changes occurred in the realm of juvenile delinquency during
the century. A few highlights: 1825—first facility for separate detention of
youngsters opened (New York House of Refuge); 1833—the use of the state
penitentiary for offenders under 18 was markedly restricted in Illinois;
1848—first state-sponsored reformatory for children opened in Massachusetts; 1869—provision made for presence in court of a state agent whenever
there was consideration of commitment of a child to a state reformatory (Massachusetts); 1870—trials of children under 16 began to be conducted separately
from criminal trials in Suffolk County (Boston); 1878—mayor of Boston was
authorized to appoint a probation officer with investigative and supervisorial
powers; 1898—Rhode Island segregated children under 16 awaiting trial and
provided for separate arraignment, trial, and record-keeping for children.

Along with that developing pattern of specialized facilities for child custody and treatment, including separate court processing and protective court services for children, another trend was much in evidence—the great expansion of the state's power to disrupt family relations and place children who had not committed criminal acts in secure institutions. Developments in Philadelphia which led to a seminal court case illustrate the process.

The Philadelphia House of Refuge was established in 1826. The act establishing the House (*Ex parte Crouse*, 4 Wharton at 10, 1838):

> declared that the managers should, "at their discretion, receive into the said House of Refuge, such children who shall be taken up or committed as vagrants, or upon any criminal charge, or duly convicted of criminal offences, as may be in the judgment of the Court of Oyer and Terminer, or of the Court of Quarter Sessions of the peace of the county, or of the Mayor's Court of the City of Philadelphia, or of any alderman or justice of the peace, or of the managers of the Alms-house and house of employment, be deemed proper objects."

A supplement to the above act passed in 1835 made it lawful for the managers of the House of Refuge (*Ex parte Crouse*, 4 Wharton at 10, 1838) "to receive into their care and guardianship, infants, males under the age of twenty-one years, and females under the age of eighteen years" who have been committed on "due proof" by an alderman or justice of the peace in either of the following cases: (1) "by reason of incorrigible or vicious conduct [the child] has rendered his or her control beyond the power of . . . parent, guardian or next friend" and it is "manifestly requisite that from regard for the future welfare of [the child], he or she should be placed under the guardianship of the managers of the House of Refuge," and (2) "in consequence of vagrancy or of incorrigible or vicious conduct" where because of "moral depravity" the parent or guardian "is incapable or unwilling to exercise . . . proper care and discipline."

Notice the marked contrast between, on the one hand, the inherited common law that exempted younger children and made older children subject to the same criminal law (and its accompanying procedural protections) and, on the other hand, a law that made it possible for an alderman or justice of the peace to send a youngster (to age 21) to an institution for incorrigibility or viciousness on "due proof."

The mother of a youngster by the name of Mary Ann Crouse complained to a justice of the peace that her daughter was vicious and uncontrollable, and he, in turn, committed Mary Ann to the Philadelphia House of Refuge. The girl's father objected to the action (the history of the disagreement between Mr. and Mrs. Crouse remains unclear) and sought the girl's release on the grounds that commitment to an institution without a jury trial was unconstitutional.

In a decision that had lasting significance, the Pennsylvania Supreme Court ruled, on appeal of the constitutional challenge (*Ex parte Crouse*, 4 Wharton at 11, 1838): that the object of the institutionalization was "training its inmates to industry," "imbuing their minds with principles of morality and religion," and "separating them from the corrupting influence of improper associates." Those ends were to be achieved on the part of the guardianship responsibility of the community, or *parens patriae*, when the natural parents were incapable of doing so. There is no "abridgement of indefeasible rights by confinement of the persons"; indeed, "The infant has been snatched from a course which must have ended in a confirmed depravity; and, not only is the restraint of her person lawful, but it would be an act of extreme cruelty to release her from it."

While the genuine concern for children inherent in humanitarianism was very likely a major force that led to state intervention in family matters on such grounds as incorrigibility, vicious conduct, and parental incapability of "proper care and discipline," other factors make the leap from purely criminal prosecution more understandable. Rendleman (1979), for example, has pointed out that the process of state placement in a House of Refuge was a straightforward extension of state placement of children in almshouses or poorhouses and of separating poor children from their families in the apprenticeship system. Fox (1970), on the other hand, has emphasized the great concern for controlling future delinquency and criminality in the state expansion of control over youths.

In accounting for the *Crouse* decision, Schlossman (1977, p. 10) stressed the importance of an affirmation of the constitutionality of placement in a House of Refuge on the basis of the developing idea of public education:

> A few years before the [*Crouse*] decision the city of Philadelphia, after a difficult political struggle, had placed its schools on a sound financial basis. Leaders of the public school movement—many of whom, it is important to note, also served as managers of the reformatory—looked forward to a period of unexampled growth. At this critical juncture an adverse judicial opinion on the constitutionality of government-financed reformatories would surely have been unwelcome; it would inevitably have tarnished the reformers' larger educational mission and the benevolent assumptions which underlay it.

There was only one major court decision that objected to state interference in the lives of noncriminal children on the basis of *parens patriae*. In *People ex rel. O'Connell v. Turner,* the Illinois Supreme Court ordered the release of a boy sent to a reform school for ungovernability without constitutional safeguards. The decision stated (51 Ill at 228, 1870):

> Even criminals can not be convicted and imprisoned without due process of law—without a regular trial, according to the courts of common law . . . Why should children, only guilty of misfortune, be deprived of liberty without "due process of law"?

Though the attitude shown in *O'Connell* and even aspects of its specific wording anticipated a key decision of the U.S. Supreme Court that came almost 100 years later, the *O'Connell* decision was "rationalized away in decisions that followed it over a short period of time, and ignored thereafter. The decision was not in tune with the times" (Binder, 1984, p. 358).

The developments of the nineteenth century in juvenile processing in courts, modes of care and treatment, definitions of behavior that could activate system actions, and legal requirements for decisions to incarcerate children, led, in 1899, to the Illinois Juvenile Court Act that consolidated those developments. That court and the juvenile court movement that swept the country in the twentieth century had certain main features, at least idealistically: Rehabilitation, not punishment, was the primary goal of the system and court proceedings were informal and designated as "hearings" rather than "trials," to highlight both the attempt to help children and the new diagnostic and prevention purposes of the court. Youths who committed criminal acts, youths who behaved in such inappropriate ways as to be designated uncontrollable, malicious, vagrant, or truant, and neglected and dependent children, all became subject to court adjudication. Detention facilities separate from those of adults were created for children awaiting court hearings, and the probation officer became a key player in the juvenile court drama, both as provider of reports for the judge's diagnostic evaluations in the hearings and as supervisor of offenders preferably placed back in their homes, rather than in institutions.

A word would seem in order regarding the position of Platt (1977) in opposition to the usual arguments that the juvenile court movement represented a triumph of humanitarianism. The latter perspective may be illustrated by the following statement in the *Gault* decision (*In re Gault,* 387 U.S. at 15, 1967):

> The early reformers were appalled by adult procedures and penalties and by the fact that children could be given long prison sentences and mixed in jails with hardened criminals. . . . The child—essentially good, as they saw it—was to be made "to feel that he was the object of [the state's] care and solicitude," not that he was under arrest or on trial.

Platt (1977), on the other hand, argued as follows in regard to the forces that led to modifications in juvenile justice (the "child-saving movement"):

> The conventional liberal view of the origins of the juvenile court is typified by the argument of the Presidential Commission that the child savers made an enlightened effort to alleviate the miseries of urban life and juvenile delinquency caused by an unregulated capitalist economy (p. xiv).

> This book destroys the myth that the child-saving movement was successful in humanizing the criminal justice system, rescuing children from jails and prisons, and developing dignified judicial and penal institutions for children (p. xvii).

The child-saving movement was not a humanistic enterprise on behalf of the working class against the established order. On the contrary, its impetus came primarily from the middle and upper classes who were instrumental in devising new forms of social control to protect their power and privilege (p. xx).

While Platt's book seems to have had a good deal of influence on thinking and writing about delinquency, serious objections to the work and its influence have been raised by Schlossman (1977) and by Binder (1979). Being influenced by those criticisms, especially the latter, the work of Platt is considered by this writer to be a mode of interpretation of history based flagrantly on ideology rather than as a trend-setter for historical reevaluation.

The Twentieth Century

Following the Illinois Act of 1899, the juvenile system model spread through-out the United States early in the twentieth century. It was assumed that the benign, protective, rehabilitative method of operation made the fundamental rights of criminal trials unnecessary under the new juvenile court law. The first major court ruling on that assumption came in 1905 when the Supreme Court of Pennsylvania upheld the constitutionality of that state's juvenile court act.

And so the pattern went in state after state—*parens patriae* provided the basis for the denial of fundamental rights to children. While there were objections to the pattern in the literature (see, for example Tappan, 1946), and adjustments in the states of California and New York (see Brantingham, 1979, and Binder, 1979), it was not until the years 1966–1967 that the U.S. Supreme Court decided that fundamental rights were necessary in juvenile court. In *Kent v. United States* (383 U.S. 541, 1966), the Court stated that due process was necessary in a waiver hearing that determined if a youngster's case was to be transferred to adult criminal court. And in *In re Gault* (387 U.S. at 27, 28 1967) it ruled on the adjudicatory hearing:

> The fact of the matter is that, however euphemistic the title, a "receiving home" or an "industrial school" for juveniles is an institution of confinement in which the child is incarcerated for a greater or lesser time . . . In view of this, it would be extraordinary if our constitution did not require the procedural regularity and the care implied in the phrase "due process." Under our Constitution, the condition of being a boy does not justify a kangaroo court.

Reasons why it took about two-thirds of a century for the U.S. Supreme Court to decide that *parens patriae* was not an acceptable substitute for due process in hearings that led to the institutionalizing of children have been provided by Binder (1984), who showed that nine of the 10 guarantees of the Bill of Rights were only made applicable in state criminal trials (through the Fourteenth Amendment) between 1962 and 1969, and one could not expect a special concern for rights in juvenile hearings before similar rights were established for adults. He argued that the incorporation (of provisions of the Bill of Rights through the due process clause of the Fourteenth Amendment) process was part of a more general pattern of concern for human welfare in what is called the "Positive State" dating "from the 1930s when the federal government recognized the well-being of the American public as its affirmative responsibility" (p. 362).

But not all due process rights have been granted to children. Thus, the right to a jury trial was denied in *McKeiver v. Pennsylvania* (403 U.S. 528, 1971) and there remains a process whereby a child may be subjected to the conditions of probation without a court hearing (see discussion of the relevant constitutional issues in Binder & Binder, 1982). The Court has clearly accepted a balancing between fundamental rights and the gains from informal juvenile processing.

And that is pretty much the state of juvenile law in the United States in the final decades of the twentieth century. As Binder (1984) argued, it does not seem that there will be major changes despite concomitant radical changes in attitudes regarding the "Positive State."

A BIT OF PSYCHOLOGICAL THEORY

As we noted earlier in the chapter, there are numerous theories that provide the explanations for the phenomenon of juvenile delinquency. There are also numerous ways of classifying these theories in attempting to achieve a certain orderliness in presentation. Thus, one can expect to find almost as many classifying schemes as there are texts and treatises dealing with such matters. In the following presentation there is one more way; probably neither logically nor aesthetically superior to many of the other schemes, only more in accord with the personal biases of the writer. As an incidental comment, as with other schemes, placement in one class rather than in another is at times arbitrary since several theories overlap the defining characteristics of two (or more) categories.

Psychological theories are of course primarily based on the individual characteristics of people. In theories of this type, it should be pointed out, the influence of social, biological, cultural, and environmental factors are not ignored; rather the effects of the factors are summarized in the form of constructs that are anchored in individuals.

The Early Years

As early as the turn of the nineteenth century, psychiatrists like Pinel, Esquirol, and Morel were describing pyromania and kleptomania in terms of distorted personality constellations. In 1835, Pritchard described the phenomenon he called "moral insanity" which matches in many ways what became "psychopathic personality" much later (see Chapters 5 and 7).

A major treatise on forensic psychiatry was written by Ray in 1838, in which he described the psychology of the offender in terms of the processes whereby aberrations such as mental disease, mania and idiocy "produce criminal acts." The vista was markedly expanded 25 years later when Maudsley (1863, 1867, 1870) began publishing his thoughts on the causes of crime. In his various works, he maintained a hereditary bias in his analyses of crime and delinquency while recognizing limited influence from "external factors and circumstances." Among the factors Maudsley mentioned as leading to crime were: overwork and overexertion, frustration, illegitimacy, teasing and irritation, and coercion.

In accord with the powerful evolutionary climate of his era, Cesare Lombroso (1876) viewed criminals as "atavistic" or primitive forms of human beings. The criminal type was identifiable by such physical anomalies as large ears, a long lower jaw, an asymmetrical cranium, low sensitivity to pain, and retarded psychological features. These views were tempered in subsequent editions of Lombroso's treatise where a wide range of environmental factors entered his schema.

The Lombroso tradition of biological determinism appeared on the American scene in the works of the anthropologist Hooton (1939) and the psychiatrist Sheldon (1949). Both revived the Lombrosan theory that criminals are biologically inferior: Hooton concentrated on such physical traits as shape of the cranium as "stigmata of degeneracy," while Sheldon differentiated criminals from noncriminals on the basis of body type (see Chapter 6 for further discussion).

As the juvenile justice system developed in the twentieth century and young offenders were more often considered independently of criminal offenders, separate treatises devoted to juvenile delinquents became prevalent. Thus, the book *The Individual Delinquent*, by the psychiatrist William Healy, appeared in 1915. The book is broadly eclectic with few theoretical positions, but its theme is shown in the following quotation (p. 24): "The dynamic center of the whole problem of delinquency . . . will ever be the individual offender."

There were studies during the nineteenth century that evaluated the amount of mental deficiency ("feeblemindedness") among the inmates of prisons and other correctional institutions. Later, Goddard (1914, 1915) argued that almost 50 percent of prison and reformatory inmates were feebleminded.

Healy and Bronner (1926) evaluated the Stanford-Binet intelligence quotients of repeat offenders and concluded that between 14 and 15 percent of the offenders were feebleminded. They noted, however (p. 208), "that for large series of repeated offenders, about 70 percent appear and continue to appear quite normal mentally." As will be discussed in Chapter 4, the best estimate is that delinquents, on average, score lower than the general population on intelligence tests by only about eight IQ points.

The developing influence of Freud and psychoanalysis beginning at the turn of the century, with its emphasis on the concepts id, demanding immediate pleasure; and superego, the counter-force representing social control, would naturally be extended to the problems of delinquency. While Freud himself (see Strachey, 1962–1964) did not pay much attention to delinquency or criminality, he did write on theoretical and practical differences between neurotics and criminals as early as 1906.

Alexander and Staub in 1931 described criminality as a form of neurosis with a compulsive need to alleviate guilt stemming from incestuous wishes, but it was Friedlander (1947) who was the first to apply the full weight of psychoanalytic theory to juvenile delinquency. She stressed that the delinquent operates, like the infant, under the pleasure principle and can neither endure frustration nor postpone gratification. A poorly formed and ineffective superego, stemming from inadequate handling in infancy, cannot overcome the pleasure-seeking forces of the moment, and the result is truancy, sexual offenses, theft, and other delinquent acts. Friedlander's emphasis is so strongly on early character formation in family relationships (primarily with the mother before the age of seven) that she considered only of secondary importance such environmental factors as peer influences, school experiences, neighborhood conditions, and unemployment.

Zilboorg was a psychoanalyst who did not accept the explanation of law-breaking behavior on the basis of impoverished superego development. Rather, he argued (1954, p. 144), "One of the most valuable things which modern psychiatry has discovered is the presence of a conscience in every criminal, no matter how brutal the crime; the presence of a sense of guilt in every criminal, no matter how carefree and callous he may appear; and the sense of community interests, a group cohesiveness, no matter how anti-social he may appear." A sort of compromise position was reached by Johnson (1949, 1959) who referred to "superego lacunae" in adolescent delinquents. These are gaps in the superego that represent areas in which parents unconsciously encourage criminal activity—in other areas the superego may be adequately developed for conformity with social norms.

That there is potentiality for long-range damage to personality and character stemming from early maternal separation is an obvious deduction within psychoanalytic theory. But writers like Goldfarb (1943) and Spitz (1945, 1946) elevated the relationship to a central role in producing permanent emotional damage. Bowlby (1946) used their perspective in explaining delinquency, expressing it as " . . . prolonged separation of a child from his mother (or mother-substitute) during the first five years of life stands foremost among the causes of delinquent character development and persistent misbehavior" (p. 41). He described the personality resulting from maternal deprivation as an "affectionless character," which he equated with psychopathic character. As will be demonstrated in Chapter 6, many psychologists have sought explanations in terms of characteristics such as impulsiveness, limited future time perspective, or losing control.

Theories Based on Classical Conditioning

In classical conditioning, there are two types of stimulus: An "unconditioned stimulus" produces an automatic, innate, reflexive response; and a "conditioned stimulus" produces that response (or, technically, one very much like it) only after being associated with the unconditioned stimulus.

One type of classical conditioning is that of avoidance, withdrawal or escape; the withdrawal of a dog's paw when an electric shock is applied to it is one example. In this case, the unconditioned stimulus if, of course, the electric shock. If a tone is sounded just before the shock is applied to the paw, and this process is repeated, the tone alone will produce the withdrawal of the paw as it has become a conditioned stimulus for an avoidance response.

Eysenck (1964, 1970, 1977), as presented in preliminary form earlier, used the model of avoidance conditioning to account for reactions that are frequently encompassed by the construct "conscience." With enough repetitions of association of "bad" behavior with punishment, the bad behavior becomes the conditioned stimulus for pain, fear, anxiety, or similar suffering. Since thought precedes such voluntary behavior, the thought of undesirable behavior itself produces the suffering, and the actual behavior is aborted. Finally, by the process called "generalization," thoughts and acts similar to the conditioned stimuli become conditioned in the avoidance chain. Thus, for example, the directly punished behaviors of "beating up one's sister," and "beating up one's friend" lead to desisting from all assaultive behavior. The child thereby acquires an "inner supervisor" or "inner policeman" (or conscience) to act in place of innumerable specific repetitions on the part of the representatives of society.

People differ in the rate at which conditioned associations are established. One factor making for such differences is the readiness of the nervous system to respond (excitability) and thereby form new associations. Another is an inhibitory factor—like fatigue—that acts increasingly in opposition to the buildup of strength of response as conditioning continues. If a rest period follows a stretch of classical conditioning, this inhibition decreases rapidly, and one gets the apparently anomalous result that the response to a conditioned stimulus is stronger after a rest (during which no practice occurs) than immediately prior to the rest. The differences between people's conditioning rates are assumed to result from differences both in excitability of the nervous system and in inhibitory reaction.

Delinquents, then, according to Eysenck (1964, 1976, 1977), are individuals who are resistant to social learning because of low excitability and high inhibitory reaction in the process of classical conditioning. He has argued, for example, that there is a relationship between the difficulty of establishing a tone as the conditioned stimulus for an eyeblink (for which the unconditioned stimulus is a puff of air) and the likelihood of a failure in learning society's behavioral prohibitions. He has found, moreover, a relationship between degree of introversion and ease of conditioning and between extroversion and difficulty of conditioning. It is, therefore, a simple link to postulate that introverts tend to be law-abiding, conforming people, while delinquents or criminals tend to be extroverted.

Eysenck (1964, 1976, 1977) has linked his theory relating delinquency to a failure in classical conditioning to his theory of personality containing the major dimensions, introversion-extroversion, and stability-neuroticism. Introverts tend to be quiet, have well-ordered lives, be planners, and like solitude, while extroverts are sociable, impulsive and aggressive, and like excitement. Introverts, according to Eysenck, have high cortical excitability and so condition easily; extroverts do not condition easily and so are more likely to commit delinquent acts for the reasons given above. Neuroticism, in the theory, exaggerates existing behavioral tendencies. Thus, neurotic leanings magnify the control of introverts and the impulsiveness leading to delinquency of extroverts.

Most recently, Eysenck has added another personality dimension to his schema—that of "psychoticism" (see Eysenck & Eysenck, 1976). This dimension was derived by factor analysis procedures with defining items indicating the following personality features: "solitary, troublesome, cruel, lacking in feeling, lacking in empathy, hostile to others, sensation-seeking, and liking odd and unusual things" (p. 202). Psychoticism is, unfortunately, not fitted smoothly into the broad avoidance conditioning theory of Eysenck; rather it is appended, as in the hypothesis (p. 120): "criminals and other people indulging in antisocial activities would be characterized by high P [psychoticism] scores in a significant number of cases. . . . " Further discussion of this position and similar theories may be found in Chapter 7.

Theories Based on Operant Conditioning

The expression "instrumental conditioning" is also used to designate this theory and its accompanying method of changing behavior. Since the prime mover in its development was considered to be Skinner, operant conditioning has in the past been referred to as the Skinnerian method or approach.

There are several differences between classical conditioning, upon which the theory of Eysenck is based, and operant conditioning. In classical conditioning, response occurs automatically and invariably when the unconditioned stimulus is presented. Because such behavior is so completely controlled by the stimulus, it is called "respondent." Operant behavior, on the other hand, is not under such direct stimulus control, but occurs naturally and freely in daily activities. Withdrawal of one's hand when a flame is applied is respondent behavior, while talking, pedaling a bicycle, and playing with a doll are operants.

In the process of classical conditioning, a response is linked to a conditioned stimulus that normally does not elicit it. Since the response must occur reflexively to the unconditioned stimulus, the range of responses subject to classical conditioning is necessarily quite limited—mostly of a simple, physiological type. But the range of responses potentially conditionable includes all behavioral interactions with the environment. That is where operant conditioning comes into the picture.

The central principle in operant conditioning is that any behavior that leads to a pleasurable or desirable outcome will be more likely to be repeated in a similar environmental context. If a child, for example, gets attention from his mother only when he cries, the likelihood of crying behavior in the home around his mother will increase. Processes and associated stimuli that follow a behavior and lead to increases in the probability of its occurrence are referred to as reinforcers. In the above example, the apparent desirable outcome was the removal of a lonely, detached feeling and the mother's attention was the reinforcer for crying. Other common reinforcers for children are food, money, social approval, toys, clothes, affection, social status, and symbols like prizes and medals.

Three important processes in operant theory are generalization, discrimination, and extinction. Generalization is the process of makng a response to stimuli like (but different from) the stimuli that were previously reinforced, while discrimination involves learning to respond to the stimuli that lead to reinforcement but not to other, similar, stimuli. A child shows generalization in smiling at women of the general age and shape of mommy, but eventually learns to discriminate by the fact that mommy provides reinforcers and other women usually do not. Differential reinforcement is the key to discrimination. Finally, extinction is when behavior stops occurring because of non-reinforcement; as when a baby stops crying after a long process of producing no positive results. Further discussion of operant theory may be found in Chapter 8.

Jeffery (1965) has used many of the concepts of operant conditioning in discussing criminal behavior within the structure of modern learning theory. More explicitly embedded in the language and theory of operant conditioning is the work of Burgess and Akers (1966) in reworking Sutherland's formal statements (the literature in the area is extensive, a review of relevant studies prior to the work of Burgess and Akers and a summary of differential association theory may be found, respectively, in Sutherland and Cressey, 1960; and Cressey, 1960).They, however, referred to the process as "modern behavior theory" rather than operant conditioning.

The concept of a "conditioned reinforcer" is important in the formulations of Burgess and Akers. It is similar to the conditioned stimulus in classical conditioning in the sense that it acquires the controlling properties of another phenomenon by being paired with it. In the case of the conditioned reinforcer, when a primary or unconditioned reinforcer like candy is repeatedly associated with another stimulus, that other stimulus will eventually take on reinforcing properties. These conditioned reinforcers, like a warm caress from mother who had previously been associated with dispensing such goodies as food and dry diapers, can then be used to strengthen other responses.

A vast amount of research has shown that the scheduling of reinforcement is as important as the quality and amount of reinforcement in channeling behavior. One may, on the one hand, reinforce a given behavior every time it occurs, every second time it occurs, or only after it has occurred at some specific number more than twice. These are "fixed ratio" schedules. One may, on the other hand, reinforce only after the behavior has been going on for a specified interval of time (two minutes, five minutes, or whatever). These are "fixed interval" schedules. "Variable ratio" and "variable interval" schedules are operative when the number of behavior occurrences or interval durations, respectively, vary from reinforcement application to reinforcement application.

One important finding is that behavior that is reinforced infrequently will be more resistant to extinction (once all reinforcement is removed) than behavior learned under continuing reinforcement—this is called the partial reinforcement extinction effect. And, as Burgess and Akers emphasize, social reinforcers are generally intermittent and so social behavior is resistant to extinction.

Power in influencing a child is a function of the number of reinforcers one controls. Early in life, the parents have a virtual monopoly on reinforcers, and so are the sources of great influence, while later in life some or much of the power shifts to teachers, peers, and so forth. By being the source of many positive reinforcers, an individual becomes a conditioned reinforcer in his own right. It has been shown that this leads the child to choose that individual as a model for imitating or following behavior (see also Chapters 5 and 9).

The primary thrust of Burgess and Akers's work was expressing Sutherland's statements of differential association theory in terms of operant conditioning. Thus, Sutherland's Statement 6 (1960), perhaps his central statement has become, "Criminal behavior is a function of norms which are discriminative for criminal behavior, the learning of which takes place when such behavior is more highly reinforced than noncriminal behavior" (pp. 143, 144). Similarly, Statement 2 has become, "Criminal behavior is learned both in nonsocial situations that are reinforcing or discriminative and through that social interaction in which the behavior of others persons is reinforcing or discriminative for criminal behavior" (p. 139).

It is worth pointing out that in the above formulation, delinquent and criminal behavior is learned in exactly the same way as conforming behavior, while in Eysenck's theory delinquent and criminal behavior results from a certain absence of learning stemming from weak conditionability. To highlight this difference, we have from Burgess and Akers (1966, p. 129) "criminal behavior is learned by the same processes and involves the same mechanisms as conforming behavior," and from Eysenck (1964, p. 267), "It would seem to follow quite logically that the absence of conscience in criminal and psychopathic persons may be due to the fact that they form conditioned responses very poorly, if at all, and even when these responses are formed, they extinguish rapidly."

Theories based on operant conditioning have led to a plethora of attempts to change the behavior of delinquent children. Treatment research using methods derived from operant theory are discussed in Chapters 9, 10, and 11. The reasoning is simple enough: If a certain pattern of reinforcement has led to a class of unacceptable behaviors, one can change reinforcement conditions and produce extinction of that class while producing acceptable behaviors as substitutes. One of the first interventions of that type was in the work of Schwitzgebel (1964) and Schwitzgebel and Kolb (1964) in which rewards were used to shape the behavior of adolescent delinquents in desired directions. Other examples of the use of operant conditioning follow: Tharp and Wetzel (1969) and Patterson, Reid, Jones, & Conger (1975) used an educational approach to guide people central in the lives of delinquents and potential delinquents in the proper use of reinforcement; and Stuart (1971) used contracts and accompanying reinforcement control within the families of young offenders.

Psychodynamic Theory

The psychodynamic perspective in delinquency is summarized in the following quotations from Abrahamsen (1960):

> Every element that prevents children from developing in a healthy way both physically and emotionally tends to bring about a pattern of emotional disturbances which is always at the root of antisocial or criminal behavior. Such behavior, when found in youngsters, is called juvenile delinquency (p. 56).

> The psychopathology of the juvenile delinquent and of the emotionally disturbed nondelinquent is manifold because each youngster goes through the same psychological development, although each one experiences it differently. Both may be said to be fixated at one or more stages of their development (p. 74).

The theories discussed above in the psychoanalytic tradition are of course examples of psychodynamic theory. In these theories, as well as in the quotes from Abrahamsen, one finds emphases on pathology, emotional disturbance, and inadequate psychological development. Perhaps the central reason for these emphases (beyond the general Freudian and neo-Freudian orientations of the theorists) is the fact that their observations have for the most part taken place in clinics where the most deviant of youngsters are likely to be referred.

Feldman (1969) has provided both a summary and a set of damaging criticisms of the psychoanalytic approach to crime and delinquency. Basic notions are that human behavior is motivated, that there are latent meanings to all actions and these meanings remain unconscious, and that an understanding of behavior, delinquent or otherwise, requires analysis of the particular process of socialization of the individual. To some, or perhaps most theorists, delinquency or criminality ''is undertaken as a means of maintaining psychic balance or as an effort to rectify a psychic balance which has been disrupted'' (Feldman, 1969, p. 436). The psychic balance refers to equilibrium among personal impulses and needs, environmental obstacles preventing satisfaction, and internalized social standards (conscience or superego). Diversity within this group of theorists consists of accounting for the mechanisms by which delinquent behavior "fulfills the function of helping retain psychic balance" (p. 437).

Other psychoanalysts argue that delinquency and criminality are forms of neurosis. A delinquent is a neurotic in the same fundamental sense as all other neurotics, differing only in that the delinquent expresses the illness in overt acts rather than by forming symptoms (see also Chapter 5). Still other psychoanalytic theorists maintain the view of the delinquent as an antisocial character who has been poorly socialized, operating under the pleasure principle of immediate gratification of needs. "Because the internalization of social norms is, for the antisocial character, in a weakened state, he has no strong internal guides to evaluate his actions" (Feldman, 1969, pp. 437, 438).

Another psychodynamic interpretation of delinquency is in terms of substitute sources of gratification for needs not satisfied in the family. When an individual is frustrated in the family setting, he or she may turn to the delinquent gang or to other groups with criminal orientations for acceptance and recognition. The delinquent "is an emotionally frustrated and perturbed individual who unconsciously seeks in his actions a resolution to his problems in the form of compensatory satisfactions which have been denied him in his familial relationships" (Feldman, 1969, p. 458). According to Feldman, the goal is attainment of psychic balance.

Finally, there is a group of psychodynamic theorists who contend that delinquency occurs in social settings where individual social and economic success are highly prized but where opportunities are limited. This interpretation has marked similarities to one in sociology developed from Durkheim's concept of "anomie" (see e.g., Merton, 1957). The gap between expectation and opportunity, according to the psychoanalysts, has the greatest psychological impact on those individuals "who are least equipped psychically to undertake the unrewarding pursuit of success" (Feldman, 1969, p. 440)—the passive, the compliant, and the dependent. These individuals repress these characteristics and act with exaggerated aggressiveness in the process of reaction formation. The result is eventually criminal behavior which simultaneously denies weaknesses and brings material rewards.

Feldman (1969) has raised three main objections to the psychodynamic approaches he has summarized. First, there is no way that the vast array of criminal behaviors can be allocated to a given type of personality. Thus, white-collar criminals surely operate under the reality, rather than the pleasure, principle, and a successful delinquent or criminal can hardly be accused of neurotic self-punishment. Second, the evidence "to date strongly suggests that the distribution of normal, pathological, and general personality traits among criminals is in approximately the same proportion as that found for the rest of the noncriminal population'' (p. 441; see also Chapter 6). And third, delinquents are not born but must learn their ideas and techniques in complex social interactions. In that process, the personality of a given delinquent is surely modified—it is not reasonable, for example, to expect that a youngster's personality that is formed in gentle family interactions will remain unchanged when he becomes and remains a member of a violent gang. Thus, it might be said that delinquency determines personality as much as personality determines delinquency. Yet, psychoanalysts widely maintain that personality is fixed in the early years of life (but see also Chapter 12 relative to the persistence of aggressive behavior).

In concluding this section on psychodynamic theory, we turn to the work of Stott as an example that is both comprehensive and contemporary. Stott published the second edition of his book *Delinquency and Human Nature* in 1980. While based on a study of 102 youths (15 to 18 years of age) who had been committed by courts to "approved schools" in England in the 1940s, the latest treatment represents Stott's theoretical perspective of the late 1970s. His overall perspective is based on the work of Bowlby (see particularly 1946) and his main thesis is "delinquent breakdown is an escape from an emotional situation which, for the particular individual with the various conditionings of his background, becomes at least temporarily unbearable" (Stott, 1980, p. 10).

He posits two "psychic needs" of the growing child. The first is a need for self-realization, which means being effective in coping with reality and being valued by other members of one's group. The second is a need for care, affection, and devotion from an adult. Denial of either of these needs leads to discomfort and frantic efforts to resolve the frustration. If those efforts fail, anxiety results which, if severe enough, leads to an "emergency reaction system." And the result is delinquent behavior that is aimed toward certain ends, the main ones being: (1) "avoidance excitement . . . the lad threw himself into a round of diversions and escapades as a means of keeping at bay what was to him an anxiety too poignant to be faced" (p. 352); (2) "spite, retaliation and resentment against the parents. . . . He may run away from home and indulge in an orgy of breaking in, or steal and smash up a car . . . " (p. 356); (3) "delinquent-attention . . . They attempted to solve this state of emotional uncertainty by testing the parents' loyalty to the uttermost, and the most drastic means of reassurance that occurred to them was to test it by resorting to crime" (p. 356); (4) "wish to secure removal from home" (p. 356)—in addition to the obvious, this included refusal to spend leaves from the approved school at home and the committing of infractions to prolong the commitment; (5) "inferiority-compensation—this reaction predominantly took the form of a pose of bravado . . . " (p. 357).

Stott has argued, in accord with his overall viewpoint, that diminished operating intelligence or mental effectiveness among delinquents results from their emotional disturbance rather than from deficient endowment. This assertion as to cause and effect remains, however, unique and, in a certain sense, the reverse of most expert opinion (see Hogan & Quay, 1984, and Chapter 4).

CONCLUSION

The concept of juvenile delinquency is anchored in legal terms that have been articulated over centuries of development of Anglo-American law. But explanations of delinquent behavior are in the terms and perspectives of such disciplines as sociology, psychology, and psychiatry. The array of behaviors to be explained thus show vast multiplicity and complexity from those perspectives, and the resulting theories are of course markedly divergent.

The divergent theories, in turn, lead to disciplinary-based differences in the approaches to preventing and treating delinquency. These are so great, in fact, that there often seems to be more of the beholder than of the young offender in the diverse recommendations for dealing with delinquents.

REFERENCES

Abrahamsen, D. (1960). *The psychology of crime*. New York: Columbia University Press.

Alexander, F., & Staub, H. (1931). *The criminal, the judge and the public*. London: Allen & Unwin.

American Psychiatric Association. (1980). *Diagnostic and statistical manual of mental disorders*. (3rd ed.). Washington, DC: Author.

Anson, Sir W. B. (1970). *The law and custom of the constitution part II. The crown* (Originally published 1892.). Oxford: The Clarendon Press.

Ariès, P. (1962). *Centuries of childhood: A social history of family life* (Robert Baldick, Trans.). New York: Vintage.

Binder, A. (1979). The juvenile justice system. Where pretense and reality clash. *American Behavioral Scientist, 22*, 621–652.

Binder, A. (1984). The juvenile court, the U.S. Constitution, and when the twain meet. *Journal of Criminal Justice, 12*, 355–366.

Binder, A., & Binder, V. L. (1982). Juvenile diversion and the Constitution. *Journal of Criminal Justice, 10*, 1–24.

Binder, A., & Binder, V. L. (1983). Juvenile diversion. *The Counseling Psychologist, 11*, 69–77.

Binder, A., & Binder, V. L. (in press). Behavioral treatment methods in the juvenile justice network. In R. A. Feldman & A. R. Stiffman (Eds.), *Advances in adolescent mental health*. Greenwich, CT:JAI Press.

Blackstone, Sir W. (1884). *Commentaries on the laws of England* (Vol. 2, Books III & IV). (3rd ed.). Chicago: Callaghan and Co.

Bowlby, J. (1946). *Forty-four juvenile thieves*. London: Bailliere, Tindall and Cox.

Brantingham, P. J. (1979). Juvenile justice reform in California and New York in the early 1960s. In F. L. Faust & P. J. Brantingham (Eds.), *Juvenile justice philosophy: readings, cases and comments* (2nd ed.). (pp. 259–268). St. Paul, MN: West Publishing.

Buckland, W. W. (1963). *A textbook of Roman law from Augustus to Justinian* (3rd ed.). rev. by P. Stein. Cambridge: Cambridge University Press.

Burgess, R., & Akers, R. (1966). A differential association-reinforcement theory of criminal behavior. *Social Problems, 14,* 128–147.

Cloward, R. A., & Ohlin, L. E. (1960). *Delinquency and opportunity.* New York: Free Press.

Cogan, N. H. (1970). Juvenile law, before and after the entrance of "parens patriae." *South Carolina Law Review, 22,* 147–181.

Cressey, D. R. (1960). The theory of differential association: An introduction. *Social Problems, 8,* 2–5.

Diamond, A. S. (1951). *The evolution of law and order.* London: Watts & Co.

Eysenck, H. J. (1964). *Crime and personality.* New York: Houghton Mifflin.

Eysenck, H. J. (1970). *Crime and personality.* (rev. ed.) London: Paladin.

Eysenck, H. J. (1976). The biology of morality. In T. Lickona (Ed.), *Moral development and behavior* (pp. 108–123). New York: Holt, Rinehart and Winston.

Eysenck, H. J. (1977). *Crime and personality* (3rd ed.) London: Routledge and Kegan Paul.

Eysenck, H. J., & Eysenck, S. B. G. (1976). *Psychoticism as a dimension of personality.* London: Hodder and Stoughton.

Feldman, D. (1969). Psychoanalysis and crime. In D. R. Cressey and D. A. Ward (Eds.), *Delinquency, crime and social process* (pp. 433–442). New York: Harper and Row.

Fox, S. J. (1970). Juvenile justice reform: An historical perspective. *Stanford Law Review, 22,* 1187–1939.

Friedlander, K. (1947). *The psycho-analytical approach to juvenile delinquency.* New York: International Universities Press.

Friedman, L. M. (1973). *A history of American law.* New York: Simon and Schuster (Touchstone).

Goddard, H. H. (1914). *Feeble-mindedness; Its causes and consequences.* New York: Macmillan.

Goddard, H. H. (1915). *The criminal imbecile: An analysis of three remarkable murder cases.* New York: Macmillan.

Goldfarb, W. (1943). Infant rearing and problem behavior. *American Journal of Orthopsychiatry, 13,* 249–265.

Goldin, H. E. (1952). *Hebrew criminal law and procedure.* New York: Twayne Publishers.

Grosser, C. (1969). *Helping youth. A study of six community organization programs.* Washington, DC: U. S. Government Printing Office.

Hale, Sir M. (1971). *The history of the common law of England.* (Edited by C. M. Gray from third edition published in 1739.) Chicago: University of Chicago Press.

Hall, G. S. (1904). *Adolescence: Its psychology and its relations to physiology, anthropology, sociology, sex, crime, religion and education.* (2 Vols.). New York: Appleton.

Healy, W. (1915). *The individual delinquent. A text-book of diagnosis and prognosis for all concerned in understanding offenders.* Boston: Little, Brown and Co.

Healy, W., & Bronner, A. (1926). *Delinquents and criminals: Their making and unmaking.* New York: Macmillan.

Hirschi, T., & Hindelang, M. J. (1977). Intelligence and delinquency. *American Sociological Review, 42,* 571–587.

Hogan, A. E., & Quay, H. C. (1984). Cognition in child and adolescent behavior disorders. In B. B. Lahey & A. C. Kazdin (Eds.), *Advances in clinical child psychology,* (Vol. 7, pp. 1–34). New York: Plenum.

Hooton, E. A. (1939). *Crime and the man.* Cambridge, MA: Harvard University Press.

Jeffery, C. R. (1965). Criminal behavior and learning theory. *The Journal of Criminal Law, Criminology and Police Science, 56,* 294–300.

Johnson, A. M. (1949). Sanctions for superego lacunae of adolescents. In K. R. Eissler (Ed.), *Searchlights on delinquency* (pp. 225–245). New York: International Universities Press.

Johnson, A. M. (1959). Juvenile delinquency. In S. Arieti (Ed.), *American handbook of psychiatry* (pp. 840–856). New York: Basic Books.

Kocourek, A., & Wigmore, J. H. (1915). *Sources of ancient and primitive law.* Vol. 1 of *Evaluation of law: select readings on the origin and development of legal institutions.* Boston: Little, Brown.

Lombroso, C. (1876). *L'uomo delinquente.* Turin, Italy: Bocca.

Ludwig, F. L. (1950). Rationale of responsibility for young offenders. *Nebraska Law Review, 29,* 521–539.

Maudsley, H. (1863). Homicidal insanity. *Journal of Mental Science, 9,* 327.

Maudsley, H. (1867). *The physiology and pathology of the mind.* London: Macmillan & Co.

Maudsley, H. (1870). *Body and mind.* London: Macmillan & Co.

Merrill, Maud A. (1947). *Problems of child delinquency.* Boston: Houghton Mifflin.

Merton, R. K. (1957). *Social theory and social structure.* Glencoe, IL: Free Press.

Morris, E. K. (1978). A brief review of legal deviance: References in behavior analysis and delinquency. In D. Marholin II (Ed.), *Child behavior therapy (pp. 214–238). New York: Gardner Press.*

Mott, R. L. (1973). *Due process of law.* New York: De Capo Press.

Nelson, W. E. (1975). *Americanization of the common law. The impact of legal change on Massachusetts society, 1760–1830.* Cambridge, MA: Harvard University Press.

Patterson, G. R., Reid, J. B., Jones, R. R., & Conger, R. E. (1975). *A social learning approach to family intervention.* (Vol. 1), *Families with aggressive children.* Eugene, OR: Castalia.

Platt, A. J. (1977). *The child savers. The invention of delinquency.* (2nd ed.). Chicago: University of Chicago Press.

Plucknett, T. F. T. (1940). *A concise history of the common law* (3rd ed.). London: Butterworth.

Pollock, Sir F. (1909). The history of English law (Vol. 1, 2nd ed.). Cambridge: The University Press.

Pritchard, J. C. (1837). *A treatise on insanity and other disorders affecting the mind.* Philadelphia: Haswell, Barrington, and Haswell.

Ray, J. (1838). *A treatise on the medical jurisprudence of insanity.* Boston: Charles C. Little and James Brown.

Rendleman, D. R. (1979). Parens patriae: From chancery to the juvenile court. In F. L. Faust & P. J. Brantingham (Eds.), *Juvenile justice philosophy: Readings, cases and comments* (2nd ed., pp. 58–96). St. Paul, MN: West Publishing.

Report of the committee on children and young persons (1960). London: Her Majesty's Stationery Office.

Sanders, W. B., (Ed.). (1970). *Juvenile offenders for a thousand years. Selected readings from Anglo-Saxon times to 1900.* Chapel Hill, NC: University of North Carolina Press.

Schlossman, S. L. (1977). *Love and the American delinquent.* Chicago: The University of Chicago Press.

Schwitzgebel, R. (1964). *Streetcorner research.* Cambridge, MA: Harvard University Press.

Schwitzgebel, R., & Kolb, D. A. (1964). Inducing behavior change in adolescent delinquents. *Behavior Research and Therapy, 1,* 297–304.

Seebohm, F. (1911). *Tribal custom in Anglo-Saxon law.* London: Longmans, Green.

Sheldon, W. H. (1949). *Varieties of delinquent youth: An introduction to constitutional psychiatry.* New York: Harper and Row.

Spitz, R. A. (1945). Hospitalism: An inquiry into the genesis of psychiatric conditions in early childhood. *Psychoanalytic study of the child* (Vol. 1), (pp. 53–74) London: Imago.

Spitz, R. A. (1946). Hospitalism: A follow-up report on investigation described in Volume 1, 1945. *Psychoanalytic study of the child* (Vol. 2), (pp. 113–117) London: Imago.

Stott, D. H. (1980). *Delinquency and human nature.* Baltimore, MD: University Park Press.

Strachey, J. (Ed.). (1962–1964). *The standard edition of the complete psychological works of Sigmund Freud.* (Vol. 2, 1962, pp. 13–24; Vol. 4, 1964, p. 342) London: Hogarth.

Stuart, R. B. (1971). Behavioral contracting within the families of delinquents. *Journal of Behavior Therapy and Experimental Psychiatry, 2,* 1–11.

Sutherland, E. H., & Cressey, D. R. (1960). *Principles of criminology* (6th ed.). Chicago: J. B. Lippincott Co.

Tappan, P. W. (1946). Treatment without trial. *Social Forces, 24,* 306–311.

Taylor, I., Walton, P., & Young, J. (1973). *The new criminology: For a social theory of deviance.* London: Routledge and Kegan Paul.

Tharp, R. G., & Wetzel, R. J. (1969). *Behavior modification in the natural environment.* New York: Academic Press.

Various European Authors (1968). *A general survey of events, sources, persons and movements in continental legal history.* New York: Augustus M. Kelley. (First published 1912, Boston: Little Brown).

Warren, M. Q. (1970). The case for differential treatment of delinquents. In H. L. Voss (Ed.), *Society, delinquency, and delinquent behavior* (pp. 419–430). Boston: Little Brown.

Wishy, B. W. (1968). *The child and the republic. The dawn of modern American child nurture.* Philadelphia: University of Pennsylvania Press.

Woodbine, G. E. (Ed.). (1968). *Bracton on the laws and customs of England*, translated by S. E. Thorne. Cambridge, MA: Belknap Press of Harvard University Press.

Wootton, B. (1959). *Social science and social pathology.* New York: Macmillan.

Zilboorg, G. (1954). *The psychology of the criminal act and punishment.* London: Tavistock.

CHAPTER 2

Epidemiology

DAVID P. FARRINGTON

Institute of Criminology
University of Cambridge

DEFINITION AND MEASUREMENT

This chapter reviews the relation between delinquency and the three major demographic factors of age, gender (sex), and ethnicity (race). Other major demographic factors of social class and area of residence are reviewed in Chapter 3 and these have also been discussed elsewhere by the present author (Farrington, 1986c). Conclusions about the epidemiology of delinquency depend crucially on the definition and measurement of delinquency and on the choice of epidemiological indicators such as prevalence and incidence. These issues will be discussed in this section.

Definition of Delinquency

The emphasis here is on acts prohibited by the criminal law. Delinquency is a heterogeneous concept, including behaviors as diverse as theft, burglary, robbery, vandalism, violence against persons, drug use, and various kinds of heterosexual and homosexual acts. In North America the category of delinquency has traditionally included not only these acts (which would be prohibited for adults) but also status offenses such as drinking alcohol and violating curfew. In England, the juvenile court has had both civil and criminal jurisdiction since its inception, and the term delinquency is usually restricted to acts such as theft and burglary which are dealt with under its criminal jurisdiction. Behavior dealt with under its civil jurisdiction, such as being a truant or beyond parental control, is not usually considered delinquent. The tendency in North America to eliminate status offenses from the category of delinquency (National Council on Crime and Delinquency, 1975) should result in more comparability between England and North America in the definition of delinquency.

This chapter is concerned primarily with criminal offenses such as theft and burglary. It is not concerned with status offenses or with minor motoring infractions. The inclusion of status and traffic offenses would make the category of delinquency well-nigh universal and would make it virtually impossible to carry out meaningful comparisons between delinquents and nondelinquents. For example, Shannon (1981) reported that the prevalence of recorded police contacts among males continuously resident in Racine, Wisconsin, was 84 percent for a cohort born in 1942 and 82 percent for a cohort both in 1949. These figures included contacts for status and traffic offenses and for investigation of suspected delinquency. The inclusion of unrecorded offenses (obtained, for example, using a self-report questionnaire) would undoubtedly push these figures close to 100 percent.

There are many problems in using legal definitions of delinquency. For example, the boundary between legal and illegal behavior may be poorly defined and subjective, as when school bullying gradually escalates into criminal violence. Legal categories may be so wide that they include acts which are behaviorally quite different, as when robbery includes armed bank robberies carried out by gangs of masked men and thefts of small amounts of money perpetrated by one schoolchild on another. Also, legal definitions rely on the concept of intent, which is difficult to measure reliably and validly, rather than on the behavioral criteria preferred by social scientists (see also Farrington, 1984). The main advantage of legal definitions is that, because they have been adopted by most delinquency researchers, their use makes it possible to compare and summarize results obtained in different projects.

An important question is the extent to which different types of delinquency offenses have anything in common other than being prohibited by the criminal law (presumably because they are believed to be harmful to society in some way). It is notable that persons who commit one type of offense tend also to commit other types, and that delinquency tends to be versatile rather than specialized (Klein, 1984). Farrington (1986a) developed an index of specialization, concluding that even when specialization was present to a statistically significant degree, there was a relatively low amount of it superimposed on a high amount of versatility. Hence, it is not unreasonable to use a general concept of delinquency and to assume that all persons can be ordered on a single dimension of delinquent activity.

This chapter is concerned not only with the epidemiology of delinquency in general but also with the epidemiology of specific types of delinquent acts, where information on this is available. It is particularly concerned with the most serious crimes. These are termed index offenses in the United States, and consist of murder, forcible rape, robbery, aggravated assault, burglary, theft, motor vehicle theft, and arson. In England, the most serious crimes are termed indictable offenses, and they include not only the aforementioned acts but also vandalism, receiving stolen property, fraud, and sex offenses other than forcible rape.

Legal categories have age boundaries that vary over time and place. In England, the minimum age for juvenile delinquency is the tenth birthday, and the maximum age is just before the seventeenth birthday. In most American states, the maximum age is just before the eighteenth birthday, while the minimum age can be as low as seven. In Canada, the recent Young Offenders Act should result in a minimum age of 12 and a maximum age of just before the eighteenth birthday in all provinces. Of course, in behavioral terms, there are no sharp cutoff points at particular ages, and acts such as stealing can occur before age seven (Achenbach & Edelbrock, 1981). This chapter is primarily concerned with delinquent acts occurring before age 18. Because of limitations of space, reviews here will be limited to the United States and England (including Wales).

Some definitional problems are raised by the fact that delinquency tends to be committed by groups rather than by individuals acting alone (Farrington, 1986c; Zimring, 1981). This raises the question of whether the individual is the most appropriate unit for analysis. However, juvenile groups probably have such a changeable composition that it would not be possible to study the prevalence or incidence of their offending. To the extent that offenses are committed in groups, self-report or official measures based on offenders will overestimate the number of offenses committed (since one offense committed by three offenders will be counted as three offenses). For example, if blacks committed the same number of offenses as whites but had more offenders involved in each offense on average, it would be concluded that offending was more prevalent among blacks. Future research should attempt to adjust for the size of delinquent groups, which has rarely been done in the past.

Epidemiology

Delinquency is quite common. In the American national survey by Williams and Gold (1972) of over 800 juveniles aged 13 to 16, 88 percent confessed to committing at least one chargeable offense in the three years prior to their interview. In 1983, 30 percent of all persons arrested in the United States for index offenses were under age 18 (Federal Bureau of Investigation, 1984). Similarly, in England in 1984, 30 percent of all persons found guilty or cautioned for indictable offenses were under age 17 (Home Office, 1985b).

These figures demonstrate not only the commonness of juvenile delinquency but also some of the problems which arise in discussing its epidemiology. In the public health literature, epidemiology refers to the study of the distribution of a disease over a population and how this distribution varies with population characteristics such as age, gender, and ethnicity. The two key concepts in epidemiology are prevalence and incidence. As Gordon (1976) pointed out, prevalence refers to the number of persons possessing the disease, while incidence refers to the number of occurrences (or contractions) of the disease. Translating this to the delinquency context, prevalence refers to the number of persons committing delinquent acts, while incidence refers to the number of delinquent acts committed *per offender.*

Following the terminology of Wilson and Herrnstein (1985, p. 30), the overall delinquency rate in a population in some specified time period is the product of the prevalence and the incidence:

$$\underset{\text{(Delinquency rate)}}{\frac{\text{No. delinquent acts}}{\text{Population}}} = \underset{\text{(Prevalence)}}{\frac{\text{No. delinquents}}{\text{Population}}} \times \underset{\text{(Incidence)}}{\frac{\text{No. delinquent acts}}{\text{No. delinquents}}}$$

An increase in the delinquency rate could reflect either an increase in the proportion of persons committing delinquent acts (prevalence) or in increase in the rate at which delinquent persons commit delinquent acts (incidence), or both. Similarly, if the delinquency rate of males is greater than that of females, this could mean either that a higher proportion of males than females commit offenses, or that the average male offender commits more offenses than the average female offender (or both).

For theoretical and policy purposes, it is important to separate the overall delinquency rate into prevalence and incidence. Taking the black:white ratio as an example, it is not inconceivable that a higher proportion of blacks than whites commit offenses, but that the average black offender is similar in incidence to the average white offender. Theories of the relation between ethnicity and delinquency might therefore have to explain why more blacks became offenders in the first place rather than why black offenders committed more offenses. As a policy example, the peak age of offending in the teenage years seems to reflect a peak in prevalence rather than in incidence (Farrington, 1986a). If this is true, the average teenage male offender coming before the courts is not committing offenses at a higher rate than the average 30-year-old male offender coming before the courts. Hence, special rehabilitative or incapacitative treatment aimed at the average teenage offender would not necessarily reduce the total number of crimes committed more effectively than equally successful treatment aimed at the average 30-year-old offender.

Official statistics of arrests or convictions typically provide information only about the overall delinquency rate and not about prevalence or incidence. For example, in England in 1984, there were eight males and 1.7 females per 100 population aged 14 to 16 convicted or cautioned for indictable offenses (Home Office, 1985b). It is impossible to know whether this gender ratio of nearly five to one means that five times as many males as females were officially processed or that the average male delinquent committed five times as many offenses as the average female delinquent. Since the short time period (one year) covered by these figures means that few delinquents have more than one conviction or caution, the overall ratio probably reflects a prevalence ratio rather than an incidence ratio. (In this chapter, ratios will be presented using the numerator only, and a denominator of one will be assumed.)

Self-reports of offending often provide no information about either prevalence or incidence. It is common for researchers to present average self-report scores, which may be based on the number of different acts admitted by each person. Where respondents are questioned about incidence, it is rare for exact numbers of acts to be recorded. The categories may be imprecise (e.g., "frequently" or "sometimes") or wide-ranging (e.g., three or more acts). Total self-report scores may also include seriousness or frequency weightings. However, some of the more recent surveys (e.g., Elliott, Huizinga, & Ageton, 1985) do provide information which makes it possible to calculate prevalence and incidence estimates.

In general, prevalence ratios will be lower than incidence ratios or delinquency rate ratios, because of the maximum possible prevalence of 100 percent. For example, in the longitudinal survey of 10,000 Philadelphia boys by Wolfgang, Figlio, and Sellin (1972), 29 percent of the whites were arrested as juveniles, giving a maximum possible black:white ratio of 3.4 (100:29). The actual ethnicity ratio was 1.7 (50:29). In this type of case, percentage differences may be more meaningful than percentage ratios. Imagine that a survey at one time found that 50 percent of males and 10 percent of females committed offenses, while a second survey some years later found that the corresponding figures were 80 percent of males and 40 percent of females. Taking the usual ratio measure, it might be concluded that the difference between males and females had decreased (from a ratio of five to a ratio of two). However, using percentage differences, 40 percent more males than females committed offenses at both times, so it might be concluded that males continued to be more delinquent than females to the same degree. For ease of comparison, the more usual ratio measures will be quoted in this chapter.

Both prevalence and incidence measures as defined above are crucially dependent on the time dimension. Obviously, the prevalence of offending at any given age will be less than the cumulative prevalence of offending during all the juvenile years (up to the eighteenth birthday, for example). Also, the definition of incidence as the rate of offending by those currently active as offenders draws attention to the need to establish when delinquency careers begin, how long they last, and when they end. The equation quoted above could be modified as follows to take account of the lengths of delinquency careers:

No. of delinquent acts committed by a cohort
up to the eighteenth birthday =

No. of delinquents in the cohort	Average rate of committing delinquent acts by each delinquent when active	Average length of active delinquency careers
(Prevalence)	$\times$ (Incidence)	$\times$ (Career Length)

In other words, a full description of the epidemiology of delinquency requires information about prevalence, incidence, and delinquency career length. Each of these factors might be differently related to characteristics such as age, gender, and ethnicity.

Information about prevalence, incidence, and career length can best be obtained in longitudinal research projects (Farrington, Ohlin, & Wilson, 1986). Similarly, relations with age which hold independently of gender and ethnicity, and relations with gender and ethnicity which hold independently of age, can best be established in longitudinal surveys. Hence, special attention will be paid to longitudinal projects in this chapter. The most relevant surveys involve community samples of at least several hundred persons. Clearly, the prevalence of delinquency cannot be established in studies which compare delinquent and control groups, and prevalence estimates obtained in small samples will have very large confidence limits. It is unfortunate that most of the published literature consists of cross-sectional studies of small samples.

The Measurement of Delinquency

As already indicated, delinquency is commonly measured using either official records or self-reports. Some other measurement methods—victim reports, informant reports, and direct observation—will be discussed at the end of this section. All methods are biased to some extent, and the most important issue is whether a correlation between delinquency and age, gender, or ethnicity reflects variation in delinquent behavior or in biasing factors. For example, if males were more willing to admit their delinquencies than females, this would create a measured association between gender and self-reported delinquency even if there were no real association between gender and delinquent behavior.

Historically, the most common method of measuring delinquency has been to use official records of arrests or convictions collected by the police and other criminal justice agencies. These records have many well-known problems (e.g., Farrington, 1979). In particular, the majority of delinquent acts are undetected, and hence do not result in a police record of an offender. From the point of view of drawing conclusions about the epidemiology of delinquency, this would not be so important if offenders who were officially recorded were a random sample of all offenders. However, it seems likely that the probability of an offense leading to an official record may depend on age, gender, or ethnicity. The major difficulty is that official records of crime reflect the behavior both of offenders and of official agencies, and these are hard to separate.

Official records are kept for the benefit of agency personnel rather than for researchers, and they are often kept inefficiently or unsystematically. It may be particularly difficult to obtain systematic coverage of a national sample of American juveniles, because of the lack of a central record-keeping system. The Attorney General's Task Force on Violent Crime (1981) recommended that the Federal Bureau of Investigation should store criminal history information of juveniles convicted of serious crimes in state courts, but this proposal has not yet been implemented. Arrest records include the largest proportion of offenders known to the police, but of course some arrested juveniles may be innocent. Conviction records in the United States are much less complete, and the types of recorded offenses may be misleading because of plea bargaining. In England, most arrests lead to an officially recorded conviction or caution, so that these records are the best official indicators of delinquency.

The most important alternative method of measuring delinquency is to use a self-report survey in which respondents are asked to say whether they have committed specified acts during a specified period such as the last year. Like official records, these surveys have many well-known problems. In particular, the most delinquent juveniles may be missing from the sample interviewed, because they are in the most transient living arrangements, incarcerated, the most difficult to find, the most uncooperative, or the most likely to be truants or dropouts (eliminating them from school surveys). Some juveniles may be unable to remember their delinquencies or may be prone to exaggerate or conceal them. The more trivial acts (such as stealing small amounts of money from home) tend to be overrepresented in self-report surveys, partly because these surveys are designed for the general population rather than for highly delinquent samples. In many cases, acts admitted in such surveys would probably never have led to any official record even if they had come to the notice of the police. Hence, self-report surveys may exaggerate the prevalence of delinquency. (See also Chapter 3.)

The advantages and disadvantages of official records and self-reports are to some extent complementary. In general, official records include the worst offenders and the worst offenses, while self-reports include more of the normal range of delinquent activity. Self-reports have the advantage of including undetected offenses, but the disadvantages of concealment and forgetting. The key issue is whether the same results are obtained with both methods. For example, if official records and self-reports both show that more males than females commit offenses, then it is likely that this result applies to delinquent behavior and that it is not entirely produced by biases in measurement.

Unfortunately, the earliest self-report surveys produced results which appeared to be at variance with those obtained using official records. For example, in their American national survey, Williams and Gold (1972) concluded that relations between delinquency and age, gender, and ethnicity were much weaker in self-reports than in official records. These kinds of results led many sociologists to argue that official processing for delinquency was biased against blacks, males, and young people. However, in more recent years the apparent discrepancies between official records and self-reports have largely been resolved. For example, Reiss (1975) pointed out that part of the discrepancy was that self-reports reflected prevalence and official records reflected delinquency rates. Hindelang, Hirschi, and Weis (1981) showed that male:female ratios in self-reports were consistent with those obtained in official records when analyses were restricted to comparably serious offenses. Also, Elliott and Ageton (1980) demonstrated that black:white ratios in self-reports were consistent with those obtained in official records when account was taken of the incidence of offending by offenders. Provided that like is compared with like, there may be little fundamental discrepancy between conclusions derived by the two methods, at least in regard to relations with age, gender, and ethnicity.

The major problem is the extent to which official records and self-reports are both valid measures of delinquency. In most cases, validity has been studied by comparing the two methods with each other, although sometimes they have been compared with another external criterion such as teacher ratings (e.g., Elliott & Voss, 1974). Generally, studies have found that juveniles who have been arrested or convicted have a high likelihood of admitting their offenses in a survey (Hindelang et al., 1981). For example, in their longitudinal survey of 400 London boys, West and Farrington (1977) showed that only 6 percent of convicted youths denied being convicted, and only 2 percent of unconvicted youths claimed to have been convicted. Furthermore, among unconvicted youths, large numbers of admitted offenses predicted future convictions (Farrington, 1973).

The most worrisome result in the literature is the demonstration by Hindelang et al. (1981) in surveys of Seattle youth that their self-report instrument was differentially valid by ethnicity. The percentage of officially recorded offenses which were not reported was 10 percent for white males, 15 percent for white females, 33 percent for black males, and 27 percent for black females. They concluded that valid black:white differences in official delinquency would not be duplicated in self-reports because of the tendency of black male official delinquents to underreport. In agreement with this, Huizinga and Elliott (1984) found in their national survey that black males underreported arrests more than white males (39 percent versus 16 percent). Also, Hackler and Lautt (1969) in another Seattle survey showed that correlations between self-reported delinquency scores and police and court records were lower for blacks than for whites.

Underreporting by black males has not always been discovered, however. Hirschi (1969), in his survey of over 2000 California boys, reported that similar percentages of blacks and whites with an official record (40 percent versus 39 percent) admitted that they had been picked up by the police. Also, Rojek (1983) in Arizona found that the degree of concordance between official records and self-reports was less for those with more severe records, but that it was not related to ethnicity independently of this. It may be that black males tend to underreport because they tend to have more extensive official records and because persons with more extensive records tend to underreport (perhaps because of forgetting or confusion).

Comparisons between self-reports and official records show that the two methods agree much better in identifying the offenders than in providing an index of the number of offenses. For example, in the survey of London males by Farrington (1983), 11 percent admitted burglary between ages 15 and 18, and 7 percent were convicted of burglary between these ages. However, the number of admitted burglaries was 10 times the number leading to convictions. Hence, it might be expected that self-reports and official records would agree better in regard to prevalence than in regard to incidence.

In addition to official records and self-reports, offending can be measured by victim reports, by informant reports, or by direct observation. Hindelang (1981) analyzed information collected in the American National Crime Survey, in which more than 130,000 people in 65,000 households were interviewed in each six-month period. Victims of crimes were asked to report the age, gender, and ethnicity of the offender, if possible. Hindelang used the data from personal crimes (rape, robbery, assault, and theft from the person) to calculate offending rates for different population subgroups. He estimated that, for juveniles aged 12 to 17, there were 2.1 of these offenses committed per year per 100 white females, 8.6 per 100 black females, 8.0 per 100 black males, and 43.2 per 100 black males. These figures suggest that offending is related to gender and ethnicity, but it is impossible to determine from victim reports how many different offenders were responsible for these offenses, and hence to separate these figures into the prevalence and incidence of offending.

In many ways, the most interesting examples of informant reports are the studies of detached workers associating with gangs in the 1960s. Short, Tennyson, and Howard (1963) showed that, in comparison with police records, their detached workers had no significant tendency to underreport or overreport. Their informant reports of different acts were all positively intercorrelated, reflecting the predominantly versatile nature of delinquency. Miller (1967) distinguished carefully between prevalence and incidence, showing, for example, that the male:female ratio for the prevalence of stealing by gang members was less than the male:female ratio for incidence. The survey by Gold (1966) was another interesting use of informant reports. He asked youths to report on the delinquencies of other youths which they had witnessed, and used these reports as an external criterion for the validity of the other youths' self-reports. He classified 72 percent of the self-reporting youths as truth-tellers, 17 percent as concealers, and the remaining 11 percent as questionables. This again suggested that the self-reports were reasonably valid. (See also Chapter 3.)

Direct observation has rarely been used to measure offending. However, Buckle and Farrington (1984) systematically observed shoplifting by a random sample of shoppers entering a department store. They found that males were twice as likely to steal as females, and that the oldest persons (those estimated to be over 55) were the most likely to steal. This chapter will concentrate on the most usual measurement methods of official records and self-reports.

DELINQUENCY AND AGE

The relation between delinquency and age has been investigated using national criminal statistics, surveys of official records, and self-report surveys. In each of these, the relation has been studied cross-sectionally and longitudinally. Information has been obtained about prevalence during a limited time period such as one year, about cumulative prevalence up to age 18, and about incidence. The emphasis here, as far as possible, is on relations with age which hold independently of gender and ethnicity. Other issues which will be discussed in this section are changes over time in the relation between delinquency and age, and possible explanations of this relation.

National Criminal Statistics

In England in 1984, the rate of findings of guilt or cautions of males for indictable offenses increased from 1.3 per 100 at age 10 to a peak at 8.6 at age 15, and then started decreasing, being 5.7 at age 20 (Home Office, 1985b). For females, the rate increased from 0.2 per 100 at age 10 to a peak of 1.9 at age 14, and then started decreasing, being 0.8 at age 20. The distribution of types of offenses changed with age. For males, offenses of theft or receiving decreased from 68 percent of all offenses at ages 10 to 13 to 59 percent at ages 14 to 16 and 46 percent at ages 17 to 20. In contrast, burglary stayed tolerably constant (at 22, 24, and 21 percent respectively), while violence increased (from 3 to 8 to 12 percent), and so did fraud (at 1, 1, and 4 percent). For females, theft or receiving decreased from 90 percent at ages 10 to 13 to 82 percent at ages 14 to 16 and 70 percent at ages 17 to 20. Burglary stayed tolerably constant (at 4, 5, and 5 percent respectively), violence increased (at 3, 9 and 7 percent), and so did fraud (at 1, 2, and 10 percent).

In the United States in 1983, the rate of arrests of males for index offenses increased from 4.2 per 100 at ages 13 to 14 to a peak of 7.7 at age 17, and then started decreasing, being 3.5 at age 24 (Federal Bureau of Investigation, 1984). For females, the rate increased from 1.2 per 100 at ages 13 to 14 to a peak of 1.6 at age 16, and then started decreasing, being 0.8 at age 24. The peak ages for violent offenses were somewhat higher than for nonviolent ones, especially for females. For males, the peak ages were 18 for violent offenses and 17 for nonviolent ones. For females, the peak ages were 20 for violent offenses and 16 for nonviolent ones. For males, the index offenses with the highest peak age (20) were murder, forcible rape, and aggravated assault, while arson had the lowest peak age (15). For females, murder had the highest peak age (23), and burglary, motor vehicle theft, and arson the lowest (15).

The above figures are cross-sectional estimates of delinquency rates. They provide no information about the relation between age and prevalence or incidence. It is sometimes possible, however, to derive cumulative prevalence estimates from a single year's national figures. Farrington (1981) added up the number of first convictions of 10-year-olds, 11-year-olds, 12-year-olds (and so on) in England in 1977 to calculate the cumulative prevalence of convictions by the seventeenth birthday for nontraffic offenses as 11.7 percent for males and 2.1 percent for females. The figures increased to 21.8 and 4.7 percent by the twenty-first birthday, and 43.6 and 14.7 percent over the lifetime.

Surveys of Official Records

The most famous American survey based on official records is the retrospective longitudinal survey of 10,000 Philadelphia males born in 1945, by Wolfgang et al. (1972). They showed that, for arrests of blacks for index offenses, the delinquency rate increased to a peak at age 16 and then decreased. For whites, the corresponding peak age for index offenses was 15. While 35 percent of the cohort were arrested for nontraffic offenses up to the eighteenth birthday, the cumulative prevalence of arrest for index offenses was only 12.7 percent. The peak age of arrest for a first index offense was 15.

In a reanalysis of their data, Barnett and Lofaso (1985) studied the arrest rate, and could find no evidence of termination of delinquency careers. In other words, all the gaps between the last arrest and the eighteenth birthday were explicable as intervals between offenses in a continuing offending career. If no offending careers terminate before age 18, it follows that the juvenile delinquency career length is inversely proportional to the age of onset. In agreement with this, Hamparian, Schuster, Dinitz, and Conrad (1978), in a retrospective longitudinal survey of violent juveniles in Columbus, Ohio, showed that the number of arrests after the age of onset increased linearly with the time available up to the eighteenth birthday.

In his London longitudinal survey, Farrington (1983) reported that the prevalence of convictions (the number of different males convicted) increased to a peak at age 17 and then declined. The prevalence of first convictions showed two peaks, at ages 14 and 17. The cumulative prevalence of convictions was 21 percent up to the seventeenth birthday and 34 percent up to the twenty-fifth birthday. The incidence of convictions, or the number of convictions per convicted youth, did not vary systematically between ages 10 and 20. However, the youths first convicted at the earliest ages (10 to 12) had a higher incidence of convictions during every age range than those first convicted later. The prevalence of convictions for most types of offenses peaked either at ages 14 to 16 or at ages 17 to 20. For example, 6.1 percent of the youths were convicted of burglary between ages 14 and 16, and 6.2 percent between ages 17 and 20. Shoplifting tended to peak early, at 14 to 16, and assault and vandalism later, at 17 to 20.

Somewhat similar results were obtained by the Home Office (1985a) in a follow-up of the conviction records of a national sample of children born in 1953. The cumulative prevalence of convictions of males was 13 percent up to the seventeenth birthday and 31 percent up to the twenty-eighth birthday. The peak age for the prevalence of first convictions was at 17, although there was a secondary peak at 14. The cumulative prevalence of convictions of females was 1.9 percent up to the seventeenth birthday and 6.3 percent up to the twenty-eighth, and their peak age for first convictions was also at 17.

Self-Report Surveys

The most important American self-report survey is the prospective longitudinal project of Elliott, Ageton, Huizinga, Knowles, and Canter (1983). They followed up a nationally representative sample of over 1700 juveniles aged 11 to 17 in 1976, interviewing them every year for five years until they were aged 15 to 21 in 1980, and asking them about offenses committed in the previous year. Unfortunately, their figures for the prevalence of offending seem to be subject to a great deal of sampling variability. Also, the percentage who had committed at least one index offense declined steadily over time, from 21 percent in 1976 to 12 percent in 1980.

Restricting the analysis to ages with at least three estimates from different cohorts and averaging these estimates, the peak age for the prevalence of index offenses was 15 to 17 (with 18 percent of the sample committing at least one index offense at each of these ages). There was no clear trend in the incidence of index offenses, which varied between five and 10 per index offender at all ages. Elliott and Huizinga (1984) presented further results obtained in this survey for types of offenses. The prevalence of felony assault and felony theft peaked at 17, robbery peaked at 15, minor theft at 16, and minor assault and vandalism at 14. Interestingly, the use of marijuana and other illicit drugs did not peak until age 20.

Gold and Reimer (1975) provided age-specific delinquency data from the national American self-report surveys they carried out in 1967 and 1972. Unfortunately, this consisted only of aggregate delinquency rates, covered only the ages 13 to 16, and was based on rather small numbers (between 59 and 132 at each age in each year). However, there was a clear increase in delinquency from 13 to 16 for males and females. This increase was also seen for individual index offenses such as burglary and vehicle theft (for the males; too few of these acts were admitted by the females). The increase with age was most dramatic for the use of marijuana and other drugs (in 1972 only).

Farrington (1983) published changes in self-reported offending with age in his London longitudinal survey. In general, the prevalence of most offenses peaked between 15 and 18. During these years, 62 percent of these youths were involved in fights, 21 percent damaged property, 11 percent committed burglary, 15 percent stole vehicles, 16 percent shoplifted, and 32 percent used illegal drugs. However, the number of offenses per offender did not change systematically with age.

Changes Over Time

It is not easy to disentangle effects attributable to age from other effects in cross-sectional and longitudinal surveys. In cross-sectional official statistics, persons of one age are compared with different persons of other ages in the same year. However, persons of one age may differ from those of other ages in factors other than age. For example, although the English criminal statistics provide no information about ethnicity, it seems likely that there would be a higher proportion of blacks among 15-year-olds than among 60-year-olds in 1984 (because of immigration patterns over time). Hence, differences in crime rates with age may reflect differences in cohort composition.

In a longitudinal survey, the same persons are studied at different ages, and so each person acts as his or her own control. However, changes with age are then confounded with changes over the historical period. For example, in the London longitudinal survey, the prevalence of drug use increased from less than 1 percent up to age 14 to 32 percent at age 15 to 18 (West & Farrington, 1977). This increase may reflect the period rather than aging, since the youths were 14 in 1967 and 18 in 1971 on average, and this period coincided with a considerable increase in drug use.

Over the last 50 years in England, the recorded crime rate has increased, and the cross-sectional age-crime curve has become more skewed and more sharply peaked in the teenage years, for males and females (Farrington, 1986a). Age-crime curves can also be derived longitudinally from the national criminal statistics. For example, the follow-up of persons born in 1960 would involve studying crime rates of 10-year-olds in 1970, 11-year-olds in 1971, 12-year-olds in 1972, and so on. These longitudinal curves also become more skewed and sharply peaked over time, with later birth cohorts (Farrington, 1986a). In other words, over time, the distinctive contribution of teenagers to the overall crime problem has markedly increased.

Age, cohort, and period effects can be disentangled if multiple cohorts are followed up through different time periods. Using the English Criminal Statistics, Farrington (1986a) plotted the delinquency rates of males of each age from 10 to 15 during the period of 1961–1983. He demonstrated that, for each birth cohort and in each year, the delinquency rate increased from age 10 to age 15. Hence, even though delinquency rates in general were increasing, the relation between delinquency and age held independently of cohort and period.

Explaining the Relation

Studies based on official records and self-reports agree in showing that the prevalence of delinquency increases to a peak somewhere between 15 and 17 and then decreases, for both males and females and for the most common types of offenses such as theft and burglary. It is far less certain that the incidence of delinquency changes during these years. Little is known about how lengths of offending careers vary with age, other than that most careers which begin in the juvenile years are probably still continuing at the eighteenth birthday.

Many explanations have been proposed for the aggregate age-crime curve, based on individual or environmental factors that change with age. If the age-crime curve primarily reflects prevalence, researchers should concentrate on explaining the onset and termination of delinquency careers rather than the incidence of offending. Hirschi and Gottfredson (1983) argued that the relation between age and crime was invariant, or in other words that it held independently of and could not be explained by reference to other variables. However, this seems unlikely.

There may be biological factors that influence some offenses at some ages. For example, delinquency has been linked to testosterone levels in males, which increase during adolescence and early adulthood and decline thereafter. However, the age-testosterone curve does not have the same sharp peak in the teenage years as the age-crime curve (Gove, 1985; Hirschi & Gottfredson, 1985). Physical factors may be important in some crimes. For example, the ability to climb buildings and hence to commit burglaries may peak in the teenage years. Some offenses, such as car theft, depend on skills and knowledge acquired during the years from childhood to adulthood. As skills and knowledge increase, so too will delinquency.

Explanations that link the age-crime curve to changes in the social environment are more popular and probably more important than those stressing changes only in individual factors. From birth, children are under the influence of their parents, who generally discourage offending. It is interesting that the best predictor of the onset of delinquency is poor parental control (Loeber & Dishion, 1983). However, during their teenage years, juveniles gradually break away from the control of their parents and become influenced by their peers, who may encourage delinquency in many cases. Elliott et al. (1985) found that the most important correlate of delinquency in their national longitudinal survey was having delinquent friends, and this factor also proved to be an important predictor in the London longitudinal survey (Farrington, 1986b).

After age 20, offending declines as peer influence gives way to family influence, except that now the family influence originates in spouses rather than in parents. Spontaneous comments by the youths in the London survey indicated that they saw withdrawal from the delinquent peer group as an important factor in ceasing to offend (West & Farrington, 1977). Also, West (1982) discovered that marriage led to a decrease in offending, provided that a young man married a nondelinquent woman. If he married a delinquent woman, his offending seemed to get worse.

Trasler (1979) outlined a variant of this theory which placed the emphasis on reinforcement contingencies in the environment. Parents tended to reward conformity and punish offending, and these external controls in many cases led to internal controls (a strong conscience) in the child. However, during the teenage years, offending tended to be reinforced by excitement and peer approval, and so it become more likely. In adulthood, people tended to desist from offending as adult reinforcers (employment, income, spouses, and children) became available. A similar explanation was proposed by Wilson and

Herrnstein (1985), who also emphasized people's increasing ability with age to delay gratification and to take account of the possible future consequences of their actions.

Greenberg (1979, 1983) advocated the importance of economic factors in explaining the relation between delinquency and age. He argued that juveniles desired to participate in social activities but that, because they were excluded from the labor market or limited to part-time, poorly paid jobs by child labor laws, they had insufficient funds from legitimate sources to finance these activities. They therefore committed crimes in order to meet their perceived needs. Furthermore, the absence from home of working parents meant that juveniles were often not subject to informal social control. When they became adults, employment, leaving school, military enlistment, and marriage eliminated major sources of criminogenic frustration and at the same time supplied informal social control. Hence, as Greenberg (1985) argued, a substantial part of the relation between delinquency and age could be explained by changing social influences. More careful research is needed to establish the extent to which the relation between age and the prevalence or incidence of offending holds independently of other factors.

DELINQUENCY AND GENDER

As in the case of age, the relation between delinquency and gender has been investigated using national criminal statistics, surveys of official records, and self-report surveys, and results obtained in each will be reviewed here. Conventionally, the relation has been summarized using the male:female ratio, and most information is available about prevalence, especially cumulative prevalence. Research on the relation between delinquency and gender has been summarized in two extensive reviews of the prevalence literature (Gordon, 1976; Visher & Roth, 1986) and in a detailed comparison of self-reports and official records (Hindelang et al., 1981). The emphasis here, as far as possible, is on relations with gender which hold independently of age and ethnicity. As before, changes over time and possible explanations will be discussed later.

National Criminal Statistics

In England in 1984, the male:female ratio for findings of guilt or cautions for indictable offenses was 5.5 over all ages (Home Office, 1985b). It was 5.2 at the minimum age of 10, declined to a low point of 3.4 at age 13, then increased to its maximum value of 7.5 at age 18, and finally decreased steadily to its lowest value of 2.5 at age 60 or over. For juveniles aged 14 to 16, the ratio was highest for burglary (22.6), damaging property (13.5), and robbery (8.0), close to the average value (of 5.0) for violence (4.8), and lowest for theft and receiving (2.6) and fraud (2.5).

In the United States in 1983, the male:female ratio for arrests for index offenses increased from 3.7 at ages 13 to 14 to a peak of 5.2 at age 18, and then decreased steadily to its lowest value of 2.3 at ages 60 to 64 (Federal Bureau of Investigation, 1984). For juveniles aged 16, the ratio was highest for burglary (15.8), robbery (14.6), murder (10.2), and vehicle theft (8.8), close to the average value (of 4.6) for aggravated assault (5.6) and arson (5.2), and lowest for theft (2.7). The American official statistics are therefore quite similar to the English ones.

These ratios are of course of delinquency rates, not of prevalence or incidence. The figures published by Farrington (1981) show that the male:female ratio for the cumulative prevalence of convictions, based on official statistics, was highest at the seventeenth birthday (5.6). It then steadily declined, being 4.7 at the twenty-first birthday and 3.0 for the lifetime prevalence. This decline reflected the proportionally greater prevalence of first convictions of females after the twenty-first birthday than before it. Whereas 21.8 percent of males had a first conviction after the twenty-first birthday, this was true for 10.1 percent of females, giving a male:female ratio of only 2.2. In general, official statistics show that the gender ratio is greatest in the juvenile years and subsequently declines.

Surveys of Official Records

Not content with following up one large cohort of Philadelphia males (10,000 born in 1945), Wolfgang and his colleagues then followed up an even larger cohort of Philadelphia males (13,000) and females (14,000) born in 1958. Up to the eighteenth birthday, 32.8 percent of the males and 14.1 percent of the females in the second cohort had a police record for a nontraffic offense (Tracy, Wolfgang, & Figlio, 1985). The gender ratio for the cumulative prevalence of delinquency was therefore 2.3. The average male offender had 3.5 recorded delinquencies, in comparison with 2.0 for the average female offender, giving a gender ratio for incidence of 1.8. The authors provide information about different offenses only for the overall delinquency rate (crimes per 1000 cohort members). The gender ratio was 4.2 for all delinquencies, 8.8 for index offenses, and 14 for violent index offenses. It was highest for vehicle theft (37), burglary (34), robbery (33), homicide (14), and aggravated assault (10), and lowest for theft (3.5).

According to Visher and Roth (1986), 22.7 percent of the Philadelphia white males and 9.2 percent of the white females had a police record for nontraffic offenses, giving a gender ratio of 2.5 for whites. The corresponding figures for blacks were 41.8 and 18.5 percent, respectively, giving a similar gender ratio of 2.3. For index offenses only, 17.9 percent of all the males and 4.0 percent of all the females had a police record, giving a cumulative prevalence gender ratio of 4.5. The corresponding ratio for whites was 4.9 (8.9 versus 1.8 percent), and for blacks was 4.3 (26.0 versus 6.0 percent). Hence, the gender ratio held independently of ethnicity.

Shannon (1981) followed up three birth cohorts of children (over 4000 in total) born in Racine, Wisconsin, in 1942, 1949, and 1955. Up to 1974, the percentage of males with police records for felonies or major misdemeanors (including burglaries and robberies) was 25.8 for the 1942 cohort, 28.4 for the 1949 cohort, and 32.3 for 1955 cohort. The corresponding female percentages were 4.4, 9.7, and 13.2, giving gender ratios for cumulative prevalence of 5.9, 2.9, and 2.4, respectively. Up to the eighteenth birthday, the average number of felonies or major misdemeanors per male cohort member was 0.31, 0.55, and 1.00 in the three cohorts. The corresponding female averages were 0.02, 0.07, and 0.17, giving gender ratios for delinquency rates of 15.5, 7.9 and 5.9, respectively.

In his national English longitudinal survey of over 5000 children born in one week of 1946, Wadsworth (1979) reported that 12.9 percent of the males and 2.2 percent of the females were convicted or cautioned for indictable offenses up to age 20. This gives a gender ratio for cumulative prevalence of 5.9. In the Home Office (1985a) follow-up of national samples born in 1953, 1958, and 1963, the percentage of males convicted of nontraffic offenses up to the seventeenth birthday was 13.4, 13.9, and 12.2, respectively for the three cohorts. The corresponding percentages for females were 1.9, 2.1, and 2.3, respectively, giving gender ratios of 7.1, 6.6, and 5.3. Finally, in her follow-up of over 2300 London children born in 1959–1960, Ouston (1984) found that 29 percent of the males and 6 percent of the females were convicted or cautioned for any offense up to ages 17 to 18. The cumulative prevalence gender ratio in this study was therefore 4.8.

Self-Report Surveys

In the national American longitudinal survey of Elliott et al. (1983), 29 percent of the males admitted at least one index offense at ages 11 to 17 in 1976, in comparison with 11 percent of the females. The gender ratio for prevalence was therefore 2.6. This ratio was 3.1 in 1977 (at ages 12 to 18), 3.0 in 1978 (at ages 13 to 19), 3.1 in 1979 (at ages 14 to 20), and 2.6 in 1980 (at ages 15 to 21). In 1976, the average male index offender committed 5.6 index offenses, whereas the average female index offender committed 2.9 index offenses. The gender ratio for incidence was therefore 1.9. This ratio was 3.4 in 1977, 2.8 in 1978, 1.0 in 1979, and 1.4 in 1980. The prevalence ratio was therefore more consistent than the incidence ratio.

The most frequently admitted index offense in the Elliott et al. survey was gang fights. However, it may be that many of these fights would not have been regarded as index offenses if they had come to the notice of the police. The same is true of sexual assaults (the actual wording of the item being "had, or tried to have, sexual relations with someone against their will", see Elliott et al., 1983, p. 13), and strong-arming students, teachers, and others. The least doubtful of their index offenses were aggravated assault, burglary, vehicle theft, and theft of an item worth more than fifty dollars.

Over the five surveys, the average percentage admitting aggravated assault was 7.2 for males and 2.4 for females, giving a prevalence gender ratio of 3.0. The corresponding ratio was 4.2 for burglary, 2.7 for vehicle theft, and 5.5 for theft of over fifty dollars. The corresponding incidence ratios were 1.2 for aggravated assault, 1.7 for burglary, 5.8 for vehicle theft, and 0.5 for theft of over fifty dollars. Therefore, it seemed that the very small number of females who admitted theft of over fifty dollars committed relatively large numbers of acts, although all these figures are based on small numbers of index offenders.

Better estimates of the prevalence of self-reported offending by male and female juveniles have been obtained in the "Monitoring the Future" project. In this survey, a nationally representative sample of about 3000 American high school students was interviewed each year from 1975 to 1983 and asked about their delinquency in the previous 12 months (McGarrell & Flanagan, 1985, Table 3.48). Taking the average over all nine years, 10.3 percent of males and 2.0 percent of females admitted theft of an item worth over fifty dollars, for a gender ratio of 5.2. Shoplifting was admitted on average by 36.7 percent of males and 24.2 percent of females, for a gender ratio of 1.5. Vehicle theft was admitted on average by 6.2 and 2.4 percent respectively, for a gender ratio of 2.6. Robbery using a weapon was admitted on average by 4.4 and 0.9 percent, for a gender ratio of 4.9. As usual, the most serious offenses tended to have the highest ratios, and vice versa. For example, 84.8 percent of males and 89.8 percent of females on average admitted that they had argued or had a fight with either of their parents in the previous year, for a low gender ratio of 0.9.

In their Seattle survey of some 1600 juveniles, Hindelang et al. (1981) provided gender ratios for the cumulative prevalence of different acts (the percentage who had ever committed them), separately for blacks and whites. For the most serious offenses, the gender ratios for whites were higher than those for blacks. For vehicle theft, the ratios were 9.7 for whites and 4.4 for blacks. For theft of over fifty dollars, they were 3.8 and 1.5 respectively. For robbery using a weapon, they were 3.7 and 2.4. For beating someone up so badly that they needed a doctor, they were 3.3 and 1.7. For carrying a weapon for use in a fight, they were 12.0 and 1.5. The smallest difference was for burglary (3.4 for whites and 3.0 for blacks).

In a survey of a nationally representative sample of 750 English juveniles aged 14 to 15, Riley and Shaw (1985) found that 49 percent of the males and 39 percent of the females admitted at least one delinquent act in the previous year. The gender ratio for prevalence was therefore only 1.3. Unfortunately, most of the acts admitted were rather trivial, and it is possible that the most serious offenders were among the 29 percent who were nonrespondents. It is not possible to calculate exact incidence rates, but similar percentages of male and female offenders admitted to five or more delinquent acts (42 percent of male and 44 percent of female offenders). Therefore, the incidence of offending may be similar for English males and females. In regard to the individual acts, the gender ratio was relatively high for the more clearly delinquent acts such as carrying a weapon intending to use it (2.8) and shoplifting (2.1). More females than males admitted the more trivial acts such as stealing from their family (a gender ratio of 0.9) and writing or spraying paint on buildings (0.6).

Changes Over Time

For delinquency rates in the English criminal statistics, the male:female ratio has declined in the last half-century. Taking the rate of 16-year-olds as an example, in 1938 there were 12.2 males for every female found guilty of an indictable offense (per 100 population). This ratio had decreased to 8.3 in 1951, and it was 8.0 in 1961, by which time the figures included official cautions as well as findings of guilt. By 1971, the ratio had dropped to 6.8, and according to the latest 1984 figures it is now 6.2. The same phenomenon is seen in the Home Office (1985a) follow-up of three cohorts quoted earlier. For the cumulative prevalence of convictions up to the seventeenth birthday, the gender ratio declined from 7.1 for the 1953 birth cohort to 5.3 for the 1963 cohort.

Steffensmeier and Steffensmeier (1980) have documented similar changes in the United States. For index offenses (excluding the male offense of forcible rape), the male:female ratio for arrests of juveniles between ages 10 to 17 declined from 6.8 in 1965 to 4.2 in 1977. Interestingly, however, the absolute difference between the male and female delinquency rates widened from 3.1 to 3.4 arrests per 100 population, so it was not true to say that females were catching up males during this period. Similarly, in the Shannon (1981) longitudinal survey quoted earlier, the gender ratio for the cumulative prevalence of police contacts up to the eighteenth birthday (for felonies or major misdemeanors) declined from 5.9 for the 1942 birth cohort to 2.4 for the 1955 cohort. Smith and Visher (1980), in a quantitative analysis of 44 studies of varying methodological adequacy carried out between 1946 and 1979, also found that the strength of the reported relationship between delinquency and gender decreased over time.

Similar trends were not seen in the "Monitoring the Future" self-report survey. For theft of over fifty dollars, the gender ratio was 10.7 in 1975, 4.6 in 1977, 4.0 in 1979, 4.0 in 1981, and 4.6 in 1983 (McGarrell & Flanagan, 1985). For vehicle theft, the ratio was 2.8 in 1975, 3.1 in 1977, 2.3 in 1979, 2.5 in 1981, and 2.6 in 1983. It seems likely that any changes over this short period were small in comparison to the statistical fluctuation of the gender ratio from year to year. In turn, this means that a sample size of even 3000 per year (possibly the largest known self-reported delinquency survey) may be too small for some purposes.

Explaining the Relation

In general, the prevalence, cumulative prevalence, and incidence of commission of serious offenses are considerably greater for males than for females.

This is true at all ages, for whites and blacks separately, and for all serious offenses, although the precise gender ratio varies in different conditions from about 1.5 to about 7. Over the last half-century, the gender ratio has declined. Various theories have been proposed to explain these results.

Gender differences in delinquency have been linked to gender differences in aggressiveness which, it has been argued, have a biological foundation. Maccoby and Jacklin (1974) pointed out that the gender differences in aggressiveness are found very early in life, before any differential reinforcement of aggression in boys and girls is observed. Furthermore, they argued that males were more aggressive than females in all human societies for which evidence was available, that similar gender differences in aggressiveness were found in subhuman primates as in humans, and that aggression was related to levels of sex hormones such as testosterone. Wilson and Herrnstein (1985) concluded that there was a statistical association between the menstrual cycle and female offending, again suggesting the influence of hormonal factors. Also, because males are generally stronger than females, males will be better able to commit offenses which require physical strength.

Not all offenses are linked to aggression or physical strength, of course. Another possible explanation for the relation between delinquency and gender is that boys and girls are socialized differently by their parents. As pointed out earlier, the best predictor of male delinquency is poor parental supervision (Loeber & Dishion, 1983). Generally, girls are supervised more closely by their parents than boys, and girls stay at home more. Hence, if they behave in a socially deviant fashion, their parents are more likely to notice this and react to it. Adults are generally more tolerant of incipient delinquency in boys than in girls, and encourage boys to be tough and to take risks. Therefore, assuming that the strength of the conscience depends on the reinforcement of appropriate behavior and the punishment of socially disapproved acts, it follows that girls will develop a stronger conscience and will be less likely to commit delinquent acts than boys.

The gender ratio can also be explained by reference to sex roles, social habits, and opportunities. Boys are more likely than girls to spend time hanging around on the street at night, especially in groups, and therefore are more likely to commit acts such as burglary and violence, which may often arise in this social situation. Girls are more likely than boys to spend time shopping, and so it is not surprising that shoplifting is the most common female offense. Boys have more interest in cars and weapons and more knowledge about how to use them, and so are more likely to commit car thefts and robberies. Later on in life, women have more opportunity to commit minor frauds because they are more likely to be collecting welfare benefits, and men are more likely to have the opportunity to steal from employers.

It has been suggested that the decreasing gender ratio over time is linked in some way to the increasing emancipation of women. As the social habits and employment patterns of females become more similar to those traditionally associated with males, it might be expected that the offending patterns of males and females would converge. To the extent that this theory is plausible, it is likely to apply to adults more than to juveniles. For example, Box and Hale (1984), in an analysis of English crime rates over a 30-year period, concluded that the female contribution to thefts from employers was significantly correlated over time with the female employment rate.

In general, the correlates of male and female delinquency are similar (e.g., Riley & Shaw, 1985). Hence, it seems likely that traditional theories of male delinquency can be used to explain female delinquency and the gender ratio.

DELINQUENCY AND ETHNICITY

Most research on ethnicity has compared blacks and whites in the United States. Unfortunately, annual English or American criminal statistics do not include offending rates per 100 population broken down by ethnicity. Given that such rates are the most reliable source of data about changes over time, there is little solid knowledge about trends in the black:white ratio. Information about this ratio has been obtained in surveys of official records and in self-report surveys. As in the case of gender, research on the black:white ratio has been summarized in two extensive reviews of the prevalence literature by Gordon (1976) and Visher and Roth (1986), and in a detailed comparison of self-reports and official records by Hindelang et al. (1981). As before, possible interpretations of the results will be discussed later.

Surveys of Official Records

In the first Philadelphia longitudinal survey of 10,000 males, Wolfgang et al. (1972) found that 50.2 percent of the blacks and 28.7 percent of the whites had police records for nontraffic offenses by their eighteenth birthday. This produced a black:white cumulative prevalence ratio of 1.7. The delinquency rate ratio was higher. For index arrests per 1000 boys per year, the black:white ratio decreased slightly from 4.5 at age 10 to 3.8 at age 17. Clearly, the black:white ratio held independently of age.

In the second Philadelphia longitudinal survey of 13,000 males, 41.8 percent of black males and 22.7 percent of white males had police records for nontraffic offenses by their eighteenth birthday, yielding a black:white cumulative prevalence ratio of 1.8. For the 14,000 females in the second survey, 18.5 percent of the blacks and 9.2 percent of the whites were arrested, yielding a black:white ratio of 2.0 (Visher & Roth, 1986). For index offenses only, the black:white ratios were higher; 2.9 for males and 3.3 for females. It seems from these figures that the black:white ratio also holds independently of gender.

In their longitudinal survey of 2600 California juveniles from age 14 to age 18, Elliott and Voss (1974) obtained recorded police contacts for each person. They published the average number of contacts per sample member, or the delinquency rate, rather than prevalence and incidence (as defined here). The average number of nontraffic offenses was lowest for Asians of Japanese or Chinese origin (0.46) and whites (0.54), and highest for Mexicans (0.72) and blacks (0.85). The black:white ratio was therefore 1.6. These figures were not given separately for males and females; for comparison, the male:female ratio was much higher, at 3.4. The average number of serious offenses (felonies) per sample member was also lowest for Asians (0.05) and whites (0.11), and highest for Mexicans (0.17) and blacks (0.37). The black:white ratio for serious offenses was therefore 3.4. (This was also lower than the corresponding male:female ratio of 8.7.)

In their Seattle survey of 1600 juveniles, Hindelang et al. (1981) estimated that 47 percent of black males and 28 percent of white males in the population had an official juvenile police or court record for offending. The same was true for 26 percent of black females and 9 percent of white females. Thus, the black:white cumulative prevalence ratio was 1.7 for males and 2.9 for females. These population estimates probably have large confidence limits, since they are based on relatively small samples. From their Tables 8.8–8.11, it is possible to estimate the incidence of offending, or the average number of recorded offenses per offender. The present estimate is conservative, because four or more offenses were counted as four. The incidence was 2.1 for black males, 1.8 for white males, 1.8 for black females, and 1.4 for white females. Therefore, the black:white ratio for incidence was 1.2 for males and 1.3 for females.

The most reliable English figures on delinquency and ethnicity are probably those obtained by Ouston (1984) in her longitudinal survey of 2300 London juveniles. She defined ethnicity according to the birthplace of the parents. Up to ages 17 to 18, 39 percent of males of West Indian origin were convicted or cautioned, in comparison with 28 percent of males of British origin and 21 percent of males of Cypriot origin. Making the reasonable assumption that the vast majority of those with West Indian parents were black and that the vast majority of those with British parents were white yields a black:white cumulative prevalence ratio for males of 1.4. The corresponding figures for females were 12.5 percent of West Indians, 5.1 percent of British, 1.1 percent of Cypriots, and a black:white ratio of 2.5.

There were very few Asians (originating in India, Pakistan, or Bangladesh) in Ouston's sample. However, two projects in Bradford, a city with a large Asian population, showed that Asians had an unusually low delinquency rate. Using locally available police and court statistics, Batta, McCulloch, and Smith (1975) calculated that the annual Asian recorded juvenile offending rate was only 1.7 per 100 population, in comparison with the rate for other (mostly white) juveniles of 4.3. The Asian rate was less than half the "other" rate for the major offenses of burglary, theft, receiving, and vehicle theft. Using later records, Mawby, McCulloch, and Batta (1979) calculated the annual rate of findings of guilt or cautions per 100 juveniles as 3.2 for Asians and 6.3 for others (again mostly whites). These figures indicate white:Asian delinquency rate ratios of 2.5 and 2.0, respectively.

Self-Report Surveys

In the national American longitudinal survey of Elliott et al. (1983), 29 percent of the blacks admitted at least one index offense at ages 11 to 17 in 1976, in comparison with 19 percent of the whites. The black:white ratio for prevalence was therefore 1.5. Comparable figures were also given for Hispanics (24 percent) but, as they comprised only 4 percent of the sample, they will not be discussed further. The black:white prevalence ratio was 1.3 in 1977, 1.1 in 1978, 1.5 in 1979, and 1.1 in 1980. In 1976, the average black index offender committed 5.2 index offenses, in comparison with 4.8 for the average white index offender, yielding a black:white ratio for incidence of 1.1. This ratio was 1.0 in 1977, 0.8 in 1978, 1.0 in 1979, and 0.9 in 1980. Clearly there was no tendency for blacks to be higher than whites in incidence, and only a slight tendency in prevalence.

Over the five surveys, the average percentage admitting aggravated assault was 7.0 for blacks and 4.8 for whites, giving a black:white prevalence ratio of 1.5. The corresponding ratio for burglary was 0.9, for vehicle theft was 0.7, and for theft of over fifty dollars was 0.9. The corresponding incidence ratios were 1.5 for aggravated assault, 2.4 for burglary, 0.3 for vehicle theft, and 0.9 for theft of over fifty dollars. Unfortunately, some of these figures (especially those for vehicle theft) were based on very small numbers of offenders and offenses.

Larger numbers were involved in the "Monitoring the Future" project, based on nationally representative samples of American high school students interviewed each year. Consistently, about 400 of the 3000 respondents were black. On average over all years of the project 6.1 percent of blacks and 5.8 percent of whites admitted theft of an item worth over fifty dollars, giving a black:white prevalence ratio of 1.1 (McGarrell & Flanagan, 1985). Vehicle theft was admitted on average by 4.6 percent of blacks and 4.1 percent of whites, for a ratio of 1.1. Shoplifting was admitted by 29.1 and 29.4 percent, respectively, for a ratio of 1.0. Robbery using a weapon was admitted by 3.8 and 2.2 percent respectively, for a ratio of 1.7. Clearly, ethnicity ratios in this research were much lower than gender ratios.

In their California survey, Elliott and Voss (1974) published self-reported delinquency rates which could be compared with official rates for the same people. The average number of serious self-reported offenses per sample member over a six-year period was 2.2 for whites, 2.5 for Mexicans, 2.7 for blacks, and 2.1 for Asians. The black:white ratio in self-reports was therefore 1.2, in comparison with the official ratio of 3.4. Not surprisingly, therefore, blacks had the most official police contacts per 100 self-reported offenses, 12.9, in comparison with 6.1 for Mexicans, 3.7 for whites, and 2.3 for Asians. The comparable figures for males and females were 5.5 and 1.2 respectively.

Hindelang et al. (1981), in their Seattle survey, provided black:white ratios for the cumulative prevalence of different acts (the percentage who had ever committed them) separately for males and females. In most cases, these ratios were greater for females. For vehicle theft, the ratios were 0.8 for males and 1.7 for females. For theft of over fifty dollars, they were 1.1 and 2.7, respectively. For robbery using a weapon, they were 1.9 and 3.0. For beating someone up so badly that they needed a doctor, they were 1.5 and 2.9. For carrying a weapon for use in a fight, they were 1.4 and 10.9. However, for burglary, the ratios were very close, being 0.8 for males and 0.9 for females.

Explaining the Relation

Especially for females and especially for serious offenses, the prevalence of official delinquency is greater for blacks than for whites. However, the differences between blacks and whites are not as great as differences over gender or age. There is not a great deal of difference between blacks and whites in official incidence rates or in self-reported prevalence or incidence. Also, there are some indications that certain ethnic groups (Asians in England and in the United States) have lower delinquency rates than whites.

The first question is why official records and self-reports produce somewhat discrepant conclusions about the relation between delinquency and ethnicity. Williams and Gold (1972) suggested that blacks and whites were treated differently by the police and the courts, and there is some evidence in favor of the hypothesis of ethnic bias in official processing. In the first Philadelphia cohort study, Thornberry (1973) found that, even after allowing for important factors such as the seriousness of the offense and the prior juvenile record, black males were more likely to be taken to court and given institutional sentences than whites. Similarly, in London, Landau (1981) showed that black offenders were more likely to be taken to court than whites, again after controlling for prior record and offense type.

The major alternative hypothesis, as indicated earlier, centers on the differential validity of the self-report technique. Hindelang et al. (1981) demonstrated that the most delinquent blacks were the most likely to under-report their recorded offenses. Another possibility is that the most delinquent blacks are particularly likely to be underrepresented in samples interviewed, because they are differentially institutionalized or uncooperative, or because of difficulties in locating them. The explanation proposed by Elliott and Ageton (1980), namely that earlier self-report questionnaires were too insensitive to detect ethnic differences which occurred more in the incidence and seriousness of offending than in prevalence, now seems less likely. The black:white incidence ratios in the survey by Elliott et al. (1983), which was designed to be more sensitive, hover around 1.0.

Available research does not establish conclusively whether the prevalence of delinquent behavior is higher among blacks than among whites. However, the fact that more blacks than whites were identified as offenders in victim reports (Hindelang, 1981) suggests that the prevalence or incidence of offending probably is greater for blacks, and hence that self-reports of offending probably are less valid for blacks. Future research needs to discover ways of overcoming problems of differential validity.

Various theories have been proposed to explain black-white differences in delinquency. Most of these suggest that ethnicity is not an important causal factor, but that blacks and whites differ on known precursors of delinquency such as low family income, poor parental child-rearing behavior, and low intelligence (Farrington, 1986b). It has been argued that, in general, blacks are more deprived economically than whites and that, partly because of the high proportion of black single-parent, female-headed households, there is less parental control and supervision in black families (Wilson & Herrnstein, 1985). Gordon (1976) suggested that black-white differences in the prevalence of offending reflected black-white differences in intelligence. In testing these and other theories, it is important to determine whether observed ethnic differences in offending hold independently of these known precursors. For example, Ouston (1984) showed that her black-white differences in official delinquency did not hold independently of differences in social class or school attainment.

Finally, research on delinquency and ethnicity has paid too little attention to ethnic groups other than whites and blacks. Results obtained with Asians in the United States and in England suggest that minorities can sometimes be less delinquent than the majority white population, and it is important to establish why this is so. The low delinquency rate of Japanese Americans has often been attributed to their close-knit family system, characterized by strong parental controls (e.g., Voss, 1966), and a similar explanation was proposed by Batta et al. (1975) and Mawby et al. (1979) for the low delinquency rate of Asians in England. Therefore, parental child-rearing techniques could be as important in explaining low delinquency rates as high ones.

CONCLUSIONS

The prevalence of serious delinquency varies markedly with age and gender. It increases to a peak at ages 15 to 17, and then decreases among both males and females. Both prevalence and incidence are higher for males than for females, although the male:female ratio often varies between 1.7 and 7 in different comparisons. Gender is related to delinquency independently of age and ethnicity. In contrast, black:white prevalence ratios are markedly greater than 1 only with official measures of delinquency and not with self-reports, and ethnicity is less strongly related to delinquency than is age or gender. The relations between delinquency and age, gender, and ethnicity can be explained by reference to variations in social influences and social reinforcements.

Considering that age, gender, and ethnicity are among the most basic and commonly recorded of all factors, it is surprising how little is known about their relation to delinquency. Future research should make an effort to break overall delinquency rates down into measures of prevalence, incidence, and delinquency career length. Future self-report research should be based on larger samples, in order to derive better estimates of the prevalence and incidence of the more serious offenses, and special efforts should be made to interview the worst offenders. Self-report and official record studies should include measures of the size of offending groups, so that offender estimates can be linked up better with offending estimates. Also, more efforts should be made to establish whether the relations between delinquency and age, gender, and ethnicity hold independently of other precursors such as low family income, low intelligence, and especially parental child-reading techniques, in prospective longitudinal surveys. A program of research along these lines would greatly increase knowledge about the epidemiology, and ultimately the causes, of delinquency.

REFERENCES

Achenbach, T. M., & Edelbrock, C. S. (1981). Behavior problems and competencies reported by parents of normal and disturbed children aged 4 through 16. *Monographs of the Society for Research in Child Development, 46* (1, Serial No. 188).

Attorney General's Task Force on Violent Crime. (1981). *Final Report*. Washington, DC: U. S. Department of Justice.

Barnett, A., & Lofaso, A. (1985). Selective incapacitation and the Philadelphia cohort data. *Journal of Quantitative Criminology, 1*, 3–36.

Batta, I. D., McCulloch, J. W., & Smith, N. J. (1975). A study of juvenile delinquency amongst Asians and half-Asians. *British Journal of Criminology, 15*, 32–42.

Box, S., & Hale, C. (1984). Liberation/emancipation, economic marginalization, or less chivalry:The relevance of three theoretical arguments to female crime patterns in England and Wales, 1951–1980. *Criminology, 22*, 473–497.

Buckle, A., & Farrington, D. P. (1984). An observational study of shoplifting. *British Journal of Criminology, 24*, 63–73.

Elliott, D. S., & Ageton, S. S. (1980). Reconciling race and class differences in self-reported and official estimates of delinquency. *American Sociological Review, 45*, 95–110.

Elliott, D. S., Ageton, S. S., Huizinga, D., Knowles, B. A., & Canter, R. J. (1983). *The prevalence and incidence of delinquent behavior: 1976–1980*. Boulder, CO: Behavioral Research Institute.

Elliott, D. S., & Huizinga, D. (1984). *The relationship between delinquent behavior and ADM problems*. Boulder, CO: Behavioral Research Institute.

Elliott, D. S., Huizinga, D., & Ageton, S. S. (1985). *Explaining delinquency and drug use*. Beverly Hills, CA: Sage.

Elliott, D. S., & Voss, H. L. (1974). *Delinquency and dropout*. Lexington, MA: Heath.

Farrington, D. P. (1973). Self-reports of deviant behavior: Predictive and stable? *Journal of Criminal Law and Criminology, 64*, 99–110.

Farrington, D. P. (1979). Longitudinal research on crime and delinquency. In N. Morris & M. Tonry (Eds.), *Crime and justice* (Vol. 1, pp. 289–348). Chicago: University of Chicago Press.

Farrington, D. P. (1981). The prevalence of convictions. *British Journal of Criminology, 21,* 123–135.

Farrington, D. P. (1983). Offending from 10 to 25 years of age. In K. T. Van Dusen & S. A. Mednick (Eds.), *Prospective studies of crime and delinquency* (pp. 17–37). Boston: Kluwer-Nijhoff.

Farrington, D. P. (1984). Measuring the natural history of delinquency and crime. In R.A. Glow (Ed.), *Advances in the behavioral measurement of children* (Vol. 1, pp. 217–263). Greenwich, CT: JAI Press.

Farrington, D. P. (1986a). Age and crime. In M. Tonry & N. Morris (Eds.), *Crime and Justice* (Vol. 7, pp. 29–90). Chicago: University of Chicago Press.

Farrington, D. P. (1986b). Stepping stones to adult criminal careers. In D. Olweus, J. Block, & M. R. Yarrow (Eds.), *Development of antisocial and prosocial behavior* (pp. 359–384). New York: Academic Press.

Farrington, D. P. (1986c). The sociocultural context of childhood disorders. In H. C. Quay & J. S. Werry (Eds.), *Psychopathological disorders of childhood* (3rd ed., pp. 391–422). New York: Wiley.

Farrington, D. P., Ohlin, L. E., & Wilson, J. Q. (1986). *Understanding and controlling crime: Toward a new research strategy.* New York: Springer-Verlag.

Federal Bureau of Investigation. (1984). *Uniform crime reports, 1983.* Washington, DC: U.S. Government Printing Office.

Gold, M. (1966). Undetected delinquent behavior. *Journal of Research in Crime and Delinquency, 3,* 27–46.

Gold, M., & Reimer, D. J. (1975). Changing patterns of delinquent behavior among Americans 13 through 16 years old: 1967–72. *Crime and Delinquency Literature, 7,* 483–517.

Gordon, R. A. (1976). Prevalence: The rare datum in delinquency measurement and its implications for the theory of delinquency. In M. W. Klein (Ed.), *The juvenile justice system* (pp. 201–284). Beverly Hills, CA: Sage.

Gove, W. R. (1985). The effect of age and gender on deviant behavior: A biopsychosocial perspective. In A. S. Rossi (Ed.), *Gender and the life course* (pp. 115–144). Hawthorne, NY: Aldine.

Greenberg, D. F. (1979). Delinquency and the age structure of society. In S. Messinger & E. Bittner (Eds.), *Criminology review yearbook* (pp. 586–620). Beverly Hills, CA: Sage.

Greenberg, D. F. (1983). Age and crime. In S. H. Kadish (Ed.), *Encyclopedia of crime and justice* (pp. 30–35). New York: Macmillan.

Greenberg, D. F. (1985). Age, crime, and social explanation. *American Journal of Sociology, 91,* 1–21.

Hackler, J. C., & Lautt, M. (1969). Systematic bias in measuring self-reported delinquency. *Canadian Review of Sociology and Anthropology, 6,* 92–106.

Hamparian, D. M., Schuster, R., Dinitz, S., & Conrad, J. P. (1978). *The violent few.* Lexington, MA: Heath.

Hindelang, M. J. (1981). Variations in sex-race-age-specific incidence rates of offending. *American Sociological Review, 46,* 461–474.

Hindelang, M. J., Hirschi, T., & Weis, J. G. (1981). *Measuring delinquency.* Beverly Hills, CA: Sage.

Hirschi, T. (1969). *Causes of Delinquency.* Berkeley, CA: University of California Press.

Hirschi, T., & Gottfredson, M. (1983). Age and the explanation of crime. *American Journal of Sociology, 89,* 552–584.

Hirschi, T., & Gottfredson, M. (1985). All wise after the fact learning theory, again: Reply to Baldwin. *American Journal of Sociology, 90,* 1330–1333.

Home Office. (1985a). *Criminal careers of those born in 1953, 1958, and 1963.* London: Home Office.

Home Office. (1985b). *Criminal statistics, England and Wales, 1984.* London: Her Majesty's Stationery Office.

Huizinga, D., & Elliott, D. S. (1984). *Self-reported measures of delinquency and crime: Methodological issues and comparative findings.* Boulder, CO: Behavioral Research Institute.

Klein, M. W. (1984). Offense specialization and versatility among juveniles. *British Journal of Criminology, 24,* 185–194.

Landau, S. (1981). Juveniles and the police. *British Journal of Criminology, 21,* 27–46.

Loeber, R., & Dishion, T. (1983). Early predictors of male delinquency: A review. *Psychological Bulletin, 94,* 68–99.

Maccoby, E. E., & Jacklin, C. N. (1974). *The psychology of sex differences.* Stanford, CA: Stanford University Press.

Mawby, R. I., McCulloch, J. W., & Batta, I. D. (1979). Crime amongst Asian juveniles in Bradford. *International Journal of the Sociology of Law, 7,* 297–306.

McGarrell, E. F., & Flanagan, T. J. (Eds.) (1985) *Sourcebook of criminal justice statistics, 1984.* Washington, DC: U.S. Department of Justice.

Miller, W. B. (1967). Theft behavior in city gangs. In M. W. Klein (Ed.), *Juvenile gangs in context* (pp. 25–37). Englewood Cliffs, NJ: Prentice-Hall.

National Council on Crime and Delinquency. (1975). Jurisdiction over status offenses should be removed from the juvenile court: A policy statement. *Crime and Delinquency, 21,* 97–99.

Ouston, J. (1984). Delinquency, family background, and educational attainment. *British Journal of Criminology, 24,* 2–26.

Reiss, A. J. (1975). Inappropriate theories and inadequate methods as policy plagues: Self-reported delinquency and the law. In N. J. Demerath, O. Larson, & K. F. Schuessler (Eds.), *Social policy and sociology* (pp. 211–222). New York: Academic Press.

Riley, D., & Shaw, M. (1985). *Parental supervision and juvenile delinquency.* London: Her Majesty's Stationery Office.

Rojek, D. G. (1983). Social status and delinquency: Do self-reports and official records match? In G. P. Waldo (Ed.), *Measurement issues in criminal justice* (pp. 71–88). Beverly Hills, CA: Sage.

Shannon, L. W. (1981). *Assessing the relationship of adult criminal careers to juvenile careers*. Washington, DC: National Institute of Juvenile Justice and Delinquency Prevention.

Short, J. F., Tennyson, R., & Howard, K. I. (1963). Behavior dimensions of gang delinquency. *American Sociological Review, 28,* 411–428.

Smith, D. A., & Visher, C. A. (1980). Sex and involvement in deviance/crime: A quantitative review of the empirical literature. *American Sociological Review, 45,* 691–701.

Steffensmeier, D. J., & Steffensmeier, R. H. (1980). Trends in female delinquency. *Criminology, 18,* 62–85.

Thornberry, T. P. (1973). Race, socioeconomic status, and sentencing in the juvenile justice system. *Journal of Criminal Law and Criminology, 64,* 90–98.

Tracy, P. E., Wolfgang, M. E., & Figlio, R. M. (1985). *Delinquency in two birth cohorts*. Washington, DC: National Institute of Juvenile Justice and Delinquency Prevention.

Trasler, G. B. (1979). Delinquency, recidivism, and desistance. *British Journal of Criminology, 19,* 314–322.

Visher, C. A., & Roth, J. A. (1986). Participation in criminal careers. In A. Blumstein, J. Cohen, J. A. Roth, & C. A. Visher (Eds.), *Criminal careers and "career criminals"* (Vol. 1, pp. 211–291). Washington, DC: National Academy Press.

Voss, H. L. (1966). Socioeconomic status and reported delinquent behavior. *Social Problems, 13,* 314–324.

Wadsworth, M. (1979). *Roots of delinquency*. London: Martin Robertson.

West, D. J. (1982). *Delinquency: Its roots, careers, and prospects*. London: Heinemann.

West, D. J., & Farrington, D. P. (1977). *The delinquent way of life*. London: Heinemann.

Williams, J. R., & Gold, M. (1972). From delinquent behavior to official delinquency. *Social Problems, 20,* 209–229.

Wilson, J. Q., & Herrnstein, R. J. (1985). *Crime and human nature*. New York: Simon & Schuster.

Wolfgang, M. E., Figlio, R. M., & Sellin, T. (1972). *Delinquency in a birth cohort*. Chicago: University of Chicago Press.

Zimring, F. E. (1981). Kids, groups, and crime: Some implications of a well-known secret. *Journal of Criminal Law and Criminology, 72,* 867–885.

CHAPTER 3

Social Ecology

MARTIN GOLD

Institute for Social Research
The University of Michigan

The social ecology of delinquency is the study of the geographic distribution of delinquency. The ecological studies that Clifford R. Shaw and Henry D. McKay began in the 1920s created a watershed regarding scientific and popular beliefs about the causes of delinquency and crime. Their findings effectively replaced genetic, often outspoken racist explanations with social ones, and significantly qualified sociocultural explanations as well. Shaw and McKay's work generated 60 years of active research which, while slackening in recent years, still goes on.

This chapter begins with a description of the sociocultural context in which Shaw and McKay began their studies. This section will bring to the fore the political motive that directed the questions Shaw and McKay asked, the methods they used, the implications for the theory that they drew from their findings, and the practical use to which they, Shaw particularly, put the beliefs created by their research. Then the original research will be described in some detail. It proved to be so seminal, in one way or another anticipating so many of the methodological and theoretical issues that were addressed by subsequent research, that the original studies can serve as a framework to organize this discussion of the whole body of literature. The next topic will be whether this research has advanced or hindered the understanding of why some individuals are more delinquent than others. The question of whether the ecological phenomenon the research purports to reveal is real or a figment based on a fundamental misinterpretation of the data will be raised. Finally, an evaluation of the contribution of the ecological research to our understanding of delinquency will be offered, including a consideration of whether this line of research is worth pursuing and what directions, if any, it might now usefully take.

SOCIOCULTURAL CONTEXT*

In the 1920s a political battle was raging over immigration policy. It centered on whether or not to open the gates again to huge waves of immigrants or to continue to restrict the tide. The main battle was being fought in the scientific literature, with geneticists, anthropologists, psychiatrists, and psychologists deployed on both sides. Clifford R. Shaw and Henry D. McKay entered the fray as sociologists at the University of Chicago.

Shaw began to locate the residences of delinquent boys in 1924, while he was a graduate student working under the supervision of Ernest W. Burgess (Bulmer, 1984). McKay took over most of this chore in 1927, when he joined Shaw's staff at the Illinois Institute of Juvenile Research (IJR). The task was enormous. In the first series of data alone, which covered only 1900 through 1906, there were 8056 court referrals and 3224 incarcerated boys to locate; later series included thousands of police arrests as well. Facilitating the job was the fact that the raw data had become more accessible. By 1924 the first juvenile court in the world had already been in existence for over 20 years in Chicago (Cook County), and the IJR had been organizing the court's files.

Shaw and McKay's was not the first study of the geographic distribution of crime. However, there were four significant factors that made Shaw and McKay's work different from other such studies: (1) it identified the residences of the (juvenile) offenders rather than the site of their crimes; (2) it was grounded in theory; (3) it had a longitudinal dimension; and (4) it had critical implications for the controversy over immigration.

Chicago was one of the centers of controversy. Thirty percent of its population in 1920 was foreign born (U.S. Census, 1922). Its population had quintupled between 1880 and 1920 and had consequently experienced in great force the change in the composition of the American population that began at around 1880. Whereas prior immigrants had come largely from England, northwestern Europe, and the Scandinavian countries, immigrants after 1880 came overwhelmingly from southern and eastern Europe. Meanwhile, migration from the southern United States had increased the black population of Chicago sixteen-fold from 1880 to 1920. The city's ethnic mix proved volatile, and a serious race riot broke out in 1919. Conditions in the United States had changed in a way that made immigrants from anywhere less welcome than they had been. The country was filling up, relatively speaking. By 1910, the nation no longer had a frontier, and recurring periods of high unemployment were becoming common.

In 1924, the Imperial Wizard of the Ku Klux Klan enunciated the KKK's beliefs regarding the new immigrants from both Europe and the American South: "The Negro is not a menace to Americanism in the sense that the Jew

*Major sources for this section are Bulmer (1984), Bursik (1984a), Carey (1975), Faris (1967), Hauser (1985), Short (1969), Slosson (1930), and Snodgrass (1976).

or the Roman Catholic is a menace. He is not actually hostile to it. He is simply racially incapable of understanding, sharing in or contributing to Americanism." (Quoted in Slosson, 1930, p. 309.)

At the national level, President Coolidge in 1923 observed that, "American institutions rest solely on good citizenship. They were created by people who had a background of self-government." (Quoted in Garis, 1927, pp. 169–170.) It was understood that the new immigrants did not have such a background. In 1924, the Congress passed and President Coolidge signed the most restrictive immigration law in American history.

The nation's leaders had drawn the impetus for restricting immigration from the sentiments of the already established children of immigrants, but they drew their rationale from the findings of scientists. The scientific bases were twofold, cultural and genetic; and under the influence of Lamarkian genetics, these two bases were commonly thought to be mutually supporting. The cultural argument was derived from Durkheim's sociology, which emphasized the consensual foundations necessary to social institutions and the inimical effects of normative dissension—anomie—on social order. For example, the nation's most famous sociologist, E.A. Ross, of the University of Wisconsin, who had been president of the American Sociological Society, in 1922 published an article in a popular magazine under the title, "The Menace of the Open Door," in which he wrote:

> As a result of the growing heterogeneity society can scarcely make up its mind any more save on matters of such elemental appeal as fire protection, sanctity of property, good roads and public improvements. The "interests", politicians, and the foreign nationalistic organizations play one element off against another so that we are not getting on as we should.
>
> Long ago Americans formed the habit of expecting their country to lead the world in popular progress but we have had the mortification of seeing people after people pass ahead of us in such matters as education, status of women, sanitation, law enforcement, vice supervision, public morals, etc. In infant saving thirteen peoples are ahead of us. Such stalling and fumbling is the inevitable result of the cross purposes and confusion of ideas that result from excessive heterogeneity. (Quoted in Garis, 1927, p. 219.)

Belief in the genetic basis of important differences among national and religious groups—typically referred to as "races"—also played an important role in the controversy over immigration policy. The genetic causes for delinquency had been presaged by America's leading expert on adolescence and founder of the Child Study Association, G. Stanley Hall, who wrote "The causation of crime . . . is a problem comparable with the origin of sin and evil. First, of course, comes heredity . . . " (but Hall continued, " . . . bad external conditions, bad homes, unhealthful infancy and childhood, overcrowded slums with their promiscuity and squalor, which are always near the border of lawlessness, . . . perhaps are the chief cause of crime.'') (1904, p. 406).

Fueling the genetic position were the results of the U.S. Army's intelligence testing during World War I. An article in the *Journal of Heredity* in 1922 concluded:

> The general trend of these draft figures is clear, unescapable, and incontrovert-ible. It shows in a most striking way that the average of american immigrants during the last quarter of a century is below that of the native-born white pop-ulation; and that the average of the countries which are sending over most of the immigrants, is even lower still. The last average is, indeed, so deplorably low that it is a fair and serious question whether the United States can eugenically afford to admit any more such average immigrants. (Quoted in Garis, 1927, p. 232.)

Snyderman and Herrnstein (1983) pointed out that mental testers were divided on the issue, arguing over the representativeness of draftees, the validity of the tests, and environmental versus hereditary causes.

There was a strong liberal opposition to restrictive immigration. Liberals protested that national and ethnic groups were in no sense "races" whose differences genetics might explain. Franz Boas made this point in an article entitled "The Question of Racial Purity" (1924), in the popular magazine *The American Mercury.* Abraham Flexner, who had authored the report that placed empirical science at the core of medical education and was himself the son of immigrants, recounted the contributions of immigrants to American sciences and culture in an article in the *Literary Digest* (Flexner, 1928).

Members of the University of Chicago faculty, particularly the sociologists, were active in local and national efforts to ameliorate ethnic problems. Ernest W. Burgess was the sociology department's liaison with the IJR, which despite its name was primarily devoted to casework for needy children and families in Chicago. Because of their mutual association with IJR, Burgess had the most direct influence first on Shaw and later on McKay as well.

The involvement of University of Chicago sociologists in social welfare was typical of sociologists at that time. For the Chicago School, however, the interest was subordinate to and atypically directed by their commitment to sociology as a science. The founder of the sociology department at the University of Chicago, Albion W. Small, constantly balanced the tension between social service and social science (Carey, 1975). Park, generally acknowledged to be the intellectual leader of the department in the 1920s, openly disparaged mere "do-gooders" (Faris, 1967).

Almost certainly Shaw and McKay's careers were changed by their coming under the influence of these men. It seems highly unlikely that they would have produced the voluminous empirical findings that they did had they not become graduate students in the University of Chicago department of sociology when they did.

ECOLOGICAL STUDIES OF SHAW AND MCKAY

The following account of Shaw and McKay's work is based largely on their 1942 book, *Juvenile Delinquency and Urban Areas,* revised in 1969, with data from Chicago and its suburbs through 1966 added by McKay. This volume presents the most wide ranging of their data, both in terms of time and space. It includes their most sophisticated methods and their ultimate interpretations of their findings.

Ecological and Social Psychological Theory

One of the major questions which Shaw and McKay put to themselves was:

> To what extent are the observed differences in the rates of delinquents between children of foreign and native parentage due to a differential geographic distribution of these two groups in the city? (1969, p. 4.)

and one of their most significant findings was that:

> No racial, national, or nativity group exhibits a uniform, characteristic rate of delinquents in all parts of Chicago. Within the same type of social area, the foreign born and the natives, recent immigrant nationalities, and older immigrants produce very similar rates of delinquents. (1969, p. 160)

> While it is apparent from these data that the foreign born and the Negroes are concentrated in the areas of high rates of delinquents, the meaning of this association is not easily determined. One might be led to assume that the relatively large number of boys brought into court is due to the presence of certain racial or national groups were it not for the fact that the population composition of many of these neighborhoods has changed completely, without appreciable change in their rank as to rates of delinquents. Clearly, one must beware of attaching causal significance to race or nativity. For, in the present social and economic system, it is the Negroes and the foreign born, or at least the newest immigrants, who have least access to the necessities of life and who are therefore least prepared for the competitive struggle. It is they who are forced to live in the worst slum areas and who are least able to organize against the effects of such living. (1969, p. 154–155.)

Later, looking back over the whole series of ecological studies from the vantage point of the 1960s, McKay observed:

> The most persistent finding in this examination of rates of delinquents among areas in Chicago has been the absence of significant changes in the production of delinquents in most city areas relative to other city areas. . . . [O]ne European ethnic group after another moved into areas of first settlement, which were for the most part inner city areas, where their children became delinquent in large numbers. As these groups became assimilated and moved out of the inner city

areas, their descendants disappeared from the group which took over the areas which had been vacated. (1969, p. 374.)

Probably the most interesting finding in this study is the evidence that rates of delinquents went up sharply in certain areas which were newly occupied by Negro populations, while at the same time the rates went sharply down in communities also occupied very largely by Negroes. (1969, p. 386.)

These facts, more than any other revealed by Shaw and McKay's painstaking collection of masses of time-series data covering over fifty years of dramatic demographic change in urban populations, established the superiority of social over genetic explanations of delinquency and crime. Furthermore, they suggested that while the conditions of immigration, as they were at the time, did indeed generate delinquency, this effect was not inevitable; these conditions, being social, were amenable to social control and could be ameliorated. Therefore, immigration was not necessarily detrimental to the nation. By 1950, in a volume urging liberalization of American immigration policy, Bernard could write without fear of contradiction, that "A study of delinquency in certain districts of Chicago shows that the delinquency rate remains high for specific areas even though the ethnic groups inhabiting these areas are constantly changing. Here the causative factors would appear to be environmental rather than cultural." (1950, pp. 124–125.)

The ecological study of delinquency was important theoretically as well as practically. Because the research yielded findings with a consistency over time and place unprecedented in social science, it gave strong support to the theory from which it sprang. This was ecological theory, taken from the biological sciences by Park and Burgess (1925) to explain the growth of cities. The general dynamic principle is that living organisms come to occupy certain niches in a spatial and temporal environment through processes of competition and co-operation. In these processes, each organism is guided by the evolutionary goal of maximizing reproduction of its kind. According to this principle, a city develops size, form, and internal structure as its individual human inhabitants compete and cooperate, each to maximize its chances of survival. The competition is not equal, and niches in the ecosystem are not equally benign. Consequently, disadvantaged individuals must locate in less suitable territories within the range. Applied specifically to the growth of American cities in the nineteenth and twentieth centuries, disadvantage was a matter of control over economic resources. Most new immigrants and blacks were disadvantaged in this respect and therefore were "forced to live in the worst slum areas and are . . . least able to organize against the effects of such living" (Shaw and McKay, 1969, p. 186).

Shaw and McKay depicted the ecological struggle in more social terms than Park and Burgess did. Whereas the latter emphasized physical survival and creature comforts—"biotic" goals—, Shaw and Mckay saw social values—prestige and status— as the prizes.

[I]t is assumed that the differentiation of areas and segregation of population within the city have resulted in wide variation of opportunities in the struggle for position within our social order. The groups in the areas of lowest economic status find themselves at a disadvantage in the struggle to achieve the goals idealized in our civilization. These differences are translated into conduct through the general struggle for those economic symbols which signify a desirable position in the larger social order. . . . Since, in our culture, status is determined largely in economic terms, the differences between contrasted areas in terms of economic status become the most important differences. (1969, pp. 186–187.)

Socioeconomic segregation was, according to Shaw and McKay, the ecological condition basically responsible for differences in rates of delinquency among areas. Concentrations of economically disadvantaged people is criminogenic for two reasons, selection and adaptation. First, the poor are powerless to resist the encroachments of those who, on account of socioeconomic disadvantage, sociocultural maladaptation, mental illness, alcoholism, or for whatever reasons, are more prone to behave in illegal and unconventional ways. Poor areas thus become criminal sinks. Similarly, their residents cannot resist invasion by those simply culturally different from themselves. Poor areas thus become extraordinarily subject to the "cross purposes and confusion of ideas that result from excessive heterogeneity."

In sum, selection processes create the criminogenic *social disorganization* that disables the community from controlling the behavior of its residents, including its youth. Second, a dense population of the poor leads to *criminogenic social organization,* that is to a community with a strong tradition of crime and an informal social structure to enact the tradition. This results because such an area harbors the conditions conducive to the development of a criminal culture; individuals in close communication who share a common problem amenable to a criminal solution.

The problem is of course obtaining the amenities, if not the necessities, of life in the absence of legitimate means to do so. The cultural solution is to tolerate if not to encourage illegitimate means, at least on the part of some, with some benefit for the whole. Shaw and McKay explicitly recognized that, even in the most highly delinquent areas, most of the residents, young and old, were more law-abiding than not. Their point was that segregation of the economically disadvantaged creates sociocultural conditions relatively more conducive to delinquency and crime. Poor areas are relatively disorganized and what social organization takes root there is relatively supportive of illegitimate activity.

Snodgrass (1976) has criticized Shaw and McKay for attributing high rates of delinquency solely to factors internal to areas. It should be pointed out, however, that their ecological theory recognizes that wider socioeconomic and political forces are responsible for the social disorganization and criminal tradition of high delinquency areas. Competition for the most desirable space is a basic process by which populations are sorted. This competition involves people and institutions throughout the whole urban range and beyond. Shaw and McKay were well aware that the decisions that made one area more desirable than another—decisions concerning road building and repair; residential, commercial, and industrial development; red-lining for racial segregation; garbage collection; and so on—were made elsewhere. If Shaw's remedial efforts through the Chicago Area Project did not typically confront real estate developers, industrialists, big merchants, City Hall, and the State House, it was not out of theoretical neglect of their influence. Rather, Shaw employed internal community organization as the strategy of choice because he believed that it would be more successful than political confrontation. It is likely that Shaw's own rural Indiana upbringing had impressed upon him the power of community to exercise sufficient social control to keep delinquency within reasonable bounds and moreover to enrich people's lives. The Chicago Area Project can be viewed as an attempt to nurture in urban soil the type of community that grows naturally in rural areas and small towns. Shaw tried to co-opt residents as well as influential people outside the areas toward this end. The theory of community provided the solution to the problem revealed by the ecological theory.

Shaw and McKay's social psychology of delinquency—their explanation for why individuals' delinquency varies—is not as well articulated as their ecological explanation; their explanation for why delinquency rates vary among urban areas. The first link in the causal chain is clear enough: Socioeconomic segregation breeds social disorganization and a relatively strong criminal tradition in poor areas. How Shaw and McKay supposed the individual youth were affected by these conditions seems more obscure.

The matter is addressed most explicitly and systematically in Chapter VII of *Juvenile Delinquency and Urban Areas* (1969, pp. 170-189). The concentration of criminal traditions in poor areas means that individuals living there stand a greater chance of being exposed to criminal norms and have easier access to informal associations with practicing delinquents and criminals. Here Shaw and McKay invoked E.H. Sutherland's theory of differential associations (Sutherland, 1939). Why some youth are more affected than others is not so clear. One can imagine that there is variation in the strength and practice of the criminal tradition even within a high delinquency area, so that individuals living by chance in one section are more or less exposed than individuals living in another. Normal processes of socialization would then generate variation among individuals. One can also imagine that, exposure being equal, some youth are more susceptible to delinquency than others; for instance, some may be more deprived than others living on the same block; or the families of some may be less able to exert countervailing social control. And it has been argued (Kobrin, 1951) that there is actually little variation among individuals in high delinquency areas; almost every boy at least acquires a police record and those that do not simply have not been caught.

Social disorganization affects individual youth most directly through their families. The selection of families into poor areas and the conditions of their lives there render families ineffective agencies of socialization. The backgrounds of immigrants have not equipped them with skills and motives suitable to parenting in urban areas of the New World. Moreover, disorganized native families sink into poor areas because they can afford no other. Many parents are inappropriate role models, and they also have little control over rewards and punishments. Thus, many families in poor areas cannot effectively perform one of the primary functions of family life—the social control of their children. They lose in the competition with the influence of the prevalent criminal tradition, even when it is not part of their own adaptation. (See also Chapter 8.)

Social disorganization also deprives weak families of the communal social support that they need most. Migration often breaks up the extended family. Cultural heterogeneity in poor areas breeds dissension among neighbors about standards of proper behavior and suspicion that alienates one family from another. The eagerness of residents to move out as soon as they can further saps their motivation to get to know and to help one another. The formal social agencies that might assist in the socialization process—the schools, churches, and welfare agencies—are staffed and controlled by outsiders and often do not really understand the problems of residents; residents often regard them as part of the problem rather than of the solution.

In short, many youth in poor areas are out of conventional control. They neither internalize conventional values nor become adequately responsive to legitimate external controls. Consequently, prompted by their own struggle for a place in the social order or simply by adolescent passions, and bonding together with peers who share these concerns, resident youth are exceptionally prone to delinquency. Shaw and McKay's social psychological explanations for the ecological differentiation of delinquency rates is compatible with any of the major theories of delinquency that take account of environment. These include psychoanalytic theories of ego control as formulated by Aichhorn (1935) and Erikson (1963); learning theory as employed by Bandura and Walters (1959); and the cognitive theory of moral development of Kohlberg (1981). (See Chapter 6.)

Methods

The bulk of Shaw and McKay's data were taken from the records of law enforcement agencies in Cook County and elsewhere. These data, aggregated in several ways, documented the ecological phenomenon. Evidence for underlying causes came from records of other social agencies and the U.S. Census, and from about one hundred life stories told to Shaw by young offenders.

There are three levels of official delinquency records representing different degrees of penetration into the juvenile justice system—police contacts with alleged offenders, referrals of alleged offenders to juvenile court, and commitments of adjudicated delinquents to public residential institutions. Police records are the most inclusive, of course, but incarcerations generally identify

the most serious and frequent offenders. These data are aggregated geographically, according to the residence of the offender, and are expressed as rates
of offenders recorded at least once in a specific year or period of years per
100 males 10 through 16 years old counted in the pertinent geographic area
by the most recent diennial census.

Data on female delinquents were not included in most of the studies, without explanation. One can in retrospect construct several rationales. Shaw and
McKay were undoubtedly aware that male offenders accounted for the over-
whelming bulk of the official records; thus, females would merely be swamped
and their inclusion would make no difference in the findings. Furthermore,
Shaw and McKay did not assume that ecological theory applied to all delinquency. "It applies primarily," they wrote, "to those delinquent activities
which become embodied in groups and social organizations. For the most part,
these are offenses against property, which comprise a very large proportion
of all the cases of boys coming to the attention of the courts" (1969, p. 321).
They probably believed that the offenses of most female delinquents, with
whom they had little personal experience, were of a different nature. In any
case, when they examined parallel rates of male and female delinquency in
Cincinnati (which, curiously enough, given McKay's meticulous work habits,
was placed in Cuyahoga rather than Hamilton County, Ohio—see p. 250 of
the 1942 and p. 262 of the 1969 editions); and when McKay included female
delinquents in updated analyses for the 1969 edition of *Juvenile Delinquency
and Urban Areas,* female offenders were distributed similarly to the males,
despite the different nature of their offenses.

The three different kinds of official records were each aggregated into two
different kinds of geographic areas. The basic unit in Chicago was typically
a square mile area, of which there were 140. The second unit of aggregation
was the zone, an area between arcs drawn at one-and-one half or two-mile
intervals and concentric to the city's central business district (Chicago had five
zones). Delinquency rates were computed for each square mile area and for
each zone. Shaw and McKay considered the zones the most informative level
of aggregation for most of their purposes. "They show the variations in rates
more conceptually and idealistically than do the rates for smaller units. . . .
It is because the zone rates eliminate the fluctuations evident for smaller areas
and present the general tendencies that they are interesting and important"
(1969, pp. 67–68).

In addition to analyses performed with areas and zones, there are some
based on straight-line radials extending from some origin of urban growth out
to its current perimeter. The rates along a radial are those of the square mile
areas through which the radial passes. Radial analyses are particularly useful
for comparing delinquency rates in urban areas where expansion was significantly affected by natural or man-made features such as a river or a canal.
In such instances, the zonal pattern is disturbed and does not accurately reflect
the socioeconomic distribution of the population.

Data that shed light on causal conditions consisted of evidence for socioeconomic and ethnic segregation, such as median rent of residential units, percent of families on welfare, and percent of population foreign born or black; evidence for social disorganization, such as transiency; and evidence for the presence of a criminal tradition, such as adult crime rates. Collateral social problems were represented by figures on infant mortality and commitments to public mental institutions and tuberculosis sanitaria. These data were also aggregated by the same square mile areas and zones as were the delinquency rates.

The last set of data, the set gathered and used least systematically, were the life stories. They were collected almost entirely by Shaw, who was skilled at eliciting these accounts from offenders (Snodgrass, 1976). Three were published in their entirety, *The Jack-Roller; A Delinquent Boy's Own Story* (Shaw, 1930); *Natural History of a Delinquent Career* (Shaw, 1931); and *Brothers in Crime* (Shaw, McKay, and McDonald, 1938). Excerpts were offered as idiographic evidence for the social psychological theory.

The statistical analyses performed on the data strike one now as primitive. However, one should consider that almost all of it was done virtually by hand, on mechanical or electric desk calculators. Subsequent research, assisted by computers, has performed much more complicated analyses, many of them using statistics that were not even invented when Shaw and McKay had finished the bulk of their analyses, much less amenable to hand calculators given such massive data sets. These later, more sophisticated statistical techniques have added little of any worth to the original findings.

Shaw and McKay demonstrated the ecological phenomenon primarily by means of paired comparisons of the delinquency rates of adjacent zones. It is interesting that Shaw and McKay used sample statistics to assess the "statistical significance" of the differences between zones. Strictly speaking, statistical tests are superfluous to their work; for their data purportedly include the universe of all the phenomena they represent—delinquency, socioeconomic conditions, and so on. The rates are in this sense not estimates. They are the actual rates, albeit open to clerical errors. Thus, simple inspection of the declining order of the delinquency rates by zones and by radials as one scans from the inner city to outer city, repeated from time series to time series over the span of sixty years and in half a dozen cities, testifies sufficiently to an ecological distribution of something.

Crucial to their most significant finding was Shaw and McKay's use of correlations between time series of delinquency rates. These analyses documented consistency over time in the order of square mile areas. They also revealed relationships between delinquency rates and the social conditions of the areas. Testifying to the stability of relative rates, typical coefficients were .85 between rates of juvenile court referrals in 1900–1906 and 1917–1923, and .61 between 1900–1906 and 1927–1933 (1969, p. 70). Consistent with the causal hypotheses, but, as Shaw and McKay acknowledged, not conclusively confirming them, were such correlations as .89 between percentage of families on relief in an area in 1934 and the rates of boys referred to the juvenile court from 1927–

1933, and .47 between referral rates in 1917–1923 and percent of owner occupied homes in 1920 (1969, pp. 147–149).

In order to substantiate the hypothesis that social conditions rather than race or nativity were responsible for delinquency, Shaw and McKay calculated partial correlations. For example, they demonstrated a decline from a correlation of .76 to .26 between the percent of foreign born and black residents and the delinquency rates of areas when percent of families on relief was held constant. Shaw and McKay concluded, "That, on the whole, the proportion of foreign born and Negro population is higher in areas with high rates of delinquents there can be little doubt; but the facts furnish ample basis for the further conclusion that the boys brought into court are not delinquent *because* their parents are foreign born or Negro but rather because of other aspects of the total situation in which they live" [Italics in original] (1969, pp. 163–164).

This description of Shaw and McKay's handling of their data—McKay was responsible for almost all of the statistical work—does not do justice to the amount or the detail. Each of their books and briefer reports are packed with maps, graphs, and tables. The focus here is only on the evidence pertaining to their major findings, which themselves are replicated over and over with different measures of delinquency, at different times, in different places. Flipping pages, one might get the impression that Shaw and McKay were arid empiricists, but this would be seriously mistaken. The work was grounded in a broad theory to which interpretations of findings were regularly referred, and implications for a bitter contemporary political and scientific controversy were frequently drawn.

ECOLOGICAL THEORY AND RESEARCH AFTER SHAW AND MCKAY

This review of subsequent efforts is organized around the several forms of response evoked by Shaw and McKay's work. One reaction was to challenge the ecological findings on theoretical and methodological grounds. A second was simply to try to replicate the results. A third was to further the effort with theoretical and methodological refinements. Fourth, some researchers tried to demonstrate empirically that the underlying social psychological processes that Shaw and McKay inferred were indeed responsible for the geographical distribution of delinquency. And fifth, scholars questioned whether the ecological phenomenon had any of the social psychological significance that Shaw and McKay attributed to it; that is, whether the geographical distribution of delinquency had any implications for why individuals are more or less delinquent.

The Challenges

Jonassen's critique aimed directly at Shaw and McKay's crucial finding: " . . . certain conclusions of Shaw and McKay in regard to the comparative influence of nationality or ethnic background and 'inherent' community elements as factors in juvenile delinquency . . . do not seem to have been substantiated by later research'' (1949b, p. 608). What is more, some of the ''later research'' to which Jonassen referred was Shaw and McKay's own.

The timing of Jonassen's critique and its theoretical relevance should be made clear here. He wrote it 20 years after Shaw, Zorbaugh, McKay, and Cottrell first published the findings (1929) and seven years after *Juvenile Delinquency and Urban Areas* hammered it fast. The controversy over restrictive immigration had subsided, and a more liberal American policy was manifested in the Displaced Persons Act of 1948. The nurture-nature issue in science was well into an interactionist resolution. So Jonassen was not injecting himself into a hot political and scientific issue concerning immigration. Jonassen contended with Shaw and McKay over ecological theory and, it appears, picked inappropriate adversaries.

The argument was about the relative weight to be given in human ecological theory to impersonal, ''biotic'' forces versus to culture. Should the theory posit a human organism struggling rather blindly for physical survival and reproductive success, or should the theory rest on the assumption of a social creature who creates culture in concert with others of its kind and strives purposely to realize its cultural values? In an article that appeared only a few months before his critique of Shaw and McKay, Jonassen stated, ''The crux of the problem seems to center around the relative influence of 'biotic', strictly economic, 'natural', and 'sub-social' factors on the one hand, and socio-cultural elements on the other hand'' (1949a, p. 32). As noted earlier, Shaw and McKay had already moved a good way from the biological orientation of Park and emphasized the sociocultural nature of both the goals of ecological competition and the relative strengths of the competitors. If there was any disagreement between Jonassen and Shaw and McKay, it was about the malleability of immigrant culture under the impact of urban conditions in the New World. Shaw and McKay assumed that ecological adaptation fairly quickly substantially altered those immigrant cultures which were less suited to the new environment; Jonassen assumed that the original culture would continue over generations to direct an ethnic group's way of life. Perhaps this disagreement arose from their different perspectives on immigrant reality: Shaw and McKay observed Poles, Slavs, Italians, and such, whose major migration to Chicago dated back only to the 1880s; Jonassen had in his mind's eye his Norwegian forebears, who began arriving in New York in substantial numbers in the 1830s and whose immigration had virtually halted by 1870.

In the most telling of his points, Jonassen pointed out that an adequate test of whether ethnicity bore any relationship to delinquency would have to compare rates among different ethnic groups that resided in the same areas. Jonassen did just that for several areas of Chicago. Reproducing two of Shaw and McKay's tables, he asserted that they showed that northern and western European groups contributed less than their share of delinquents than did southern and eastern European groups living in the same areas; that is, the proportion of delinquents among the former was smaller than their proportion in the total population of each area, and of the latter, larger.

Jonassen also claimed that Shaw and McKay were not consistent in the weight they gave to the culture of origin, observing that they had noted the low delinquency rates of Asians even in the most deteriorated sections of the city. Shaw and McKay did admit that ethnic cultures matter, Jonassen maintained, evidently missing Shaw and McKay's qualification that maladaptive cultures change in a generation or two and are not permanent features of an ethnic group.

Jonassen apparently sensed that Shaw and McKay's work was not driven purely by intellectual curiosity. "It is difficult to account for such contradictions as are apparent," he wrote,

> except by hypothesizing the presence of hidden biases which seem to warp inferences from the data in certain directions. The thread of ecological determinism is discernible all through the warp and woof of the theoretical formulations. . . . Apparent also in the fabric of their reasoning are hints of ideological predilections induced by a reluctance, even under empirical temptations, to sin against the "professional ideology of the social pathologist" or of democracy by entertaining the possibility that all nativity, racial and nationality groups are not equal in their ability to resist the "disorganization" of juvenile delinquency. (1949b, p. 613.)

Jonassen concluded by asserting that "[W]hile it is rather improbable, it is still possible that the position held by Shaw and Mckay is valid and that it might be demonstrated by different data and methodology" (1949b, p. 613).

Shaw and McKay responded in the same issue of the *American Sociological Review* in which Jonassen's article appeared. They began by expressing their pleasure with the opportunity to comment on the questions Jonassen had raised—"good questions" they wrote, "with which we have grappled for years" (1949, p. 613). That arch phrase is a clue to the annoyance Shaw and McKay probably felt at Jonassen's aspersion on their intellectual integrity. They proceeded, moreover, to frame Jonassen's argument in a way that Jonassen did not intend:

> The real difficulty which we have encountered in responding to this criticism has been our inability to determine what Mr. Jonassen assumed the basic issues to be. His objection to our explanation of the behavior of immigrant groups in terms of adjustive and distributive processes suggests that to him this is the real issue. The alternatives, however, are not clear unless one accepts the notion of the innate superiority of some peoples over others. (1949, p. 614.)

It appears clear that Jonassen was not proposing an "innate" genetic alternative to a cultural hypothesis. Shaw and McKay referred to Jonassen's earlier article (1949a) on the mobility of Norwegians in New York City, in which Jonassen mentioned "personal" or "volitional" elements that he considered "non-cultural." There is no reason to believe, however, from the context of that article, that Jonassen was invoking genetic influences; the reference is clearly to cultural adaptability to the contemporary bioecological forces prominent in Park's social ecology. Apparently, the din of the old battle had not died away for Shaw and McKay.

Shaw and McKay went on to make three points. First, they agreed that culture differentiates immigrant groups at first. Some, like the Asian cultures, are generally resistant to delinquency. In any case, the first generation of native-born Americans among most European immigrant groups is not affected much by their parent's culture; for good or ill, they become quickly assimilated into the culture of the inner city. That is where their delinquency rises. Second, they described unpublished data which showed that: there were differences in the socioeconomic conditions of sections within areas; ethnic groups were segregated within areas along the lines of socioeconomic demarcation; the group with the highest delinquency rates lived in the poorest sections; and as conditions approached equality, ethnic differences declined. Thus, ecological principles accounted for ethnic variations in rates within the same areas. Third, they recalled their findings that members of the same ethnic group displayed different rates of delinquency, depending on where in the city they resided; and that the relative areal rates remained stable despite large changes in the ethnicity of their population. Finally, Shaw and McKay addressed the problem of the delinquency rates in the black population, which were higher than whites' wherever blacks were found. They pointed out that, within their higher range, blacks' rates show the same covariations with areal socioeconomic conditions. And they argued that:

> [W]hile the delinquency rates of black boys are higher than the rates for white boys . . . it cannot be said that they are higher than rates for white boys in comparable areas, since it is impossible to reproduce in white communities the circumstances under which Negro children live. Even if it were possible to parallel the low economic status and the inadequacy of institutions in the white community, it would not be possible to reproduce the effects of segregation and the barriers to upward mobility. These combine to create for the Negro child a type of social world in which the higher rates of delinquents are not unintelligible. (1949, p. 617.)

Finally, Shaw and McKay turned directly to the matter of their intellectual integrity:

> It has been charged that there are hints of ideological predilections and for preference of democracy in our studies. . . . It is possibly true . . . that we have felt some satisfaction over the fact that our data suggest rather consistently that if circumstances were comparable, the rate of delinquency among devalued groups would not be unlike the rate for favored groups. But these biases, if such there

be, do not affect the data or the remarkable strain of internal consistency which characterize these data. (1949, p. 617.)

Shaw and McKay might have made more of the faults in the data that Jonassen employed to make his points, but they only alluded to the complications introduced by the "possibility of changing ratios of children to adults, and similar variables" (1949, p. 616). Obviously, if one ethnic group includes a smaller proportion of 10-through–16-year old males when it resides in a better part of a city than when it resides in the slums—a very plausible situation (Freedman, 1973)—its contribution to delinquency rates relative to the total local population is apt to be lower. These are the data that Jonassen used, rather than rates based on the local populations of boys in the specific ethnic groups. But the data are originally Shaw and McKay's and are as flawed for their purposes, so it is understandable that they pulled that punch.

From the present vantage point, it seems fair to say that Jonassen's challenge is valid. Shaw and McKay had shown that social conditions in an urban area related to delinquency rates, regardless of the ethnicity of the population. But they had not shown that social conditions made all the difference and ethnic culture, none. While the correlations between ethnic composition and areal rates declined when socioeconomic conditions were partialled out, they did not disappear. Ethnic groups seem to carry different degrees of propensity for delinquency with them, at least over several generations, wherever they settle. This may be due to the more enduring features of their culture, to genetic factors, or, especially in the case of blacks, to inescapably bad conditions. Shaw and McKay's data could not identify which.

Robison's critique was even more fundamental. Whereas Jonassen challenged the most significant conclusion that Shaw and McKay drew from their ecological findings, Robison questioned the reality of the ecological phenomenon itself. In *Can Delinquency be Measured?* (1972), she asserted that official records of the juvenile justice system were systematically distorted in a way that generated the ecological distribution that Shaw and McKay found.

> It is the thesis of the present study that the customs of the diverse nationality and cultural groups, no matter where they live, greatly affect the proportions of juvenile delinquents in these different groups who will become known to the courts and to institutions for the care of delinquents. . . . [N]eighborhoods have varying population with regard to race, nationality, and associated customs, which affect the amount of delinquency registered, although the behavior of the children may remain the same. . . . Differing behavior on the part of parents and authorities confronted with a troublesome child may be as much a modifier of neighborhood rates as different proportions of troublesome children. (p. 4.)

Robison contended that a better measure of delinquency would have shown that offenders were much more numerous and quite evenly distributed among urban areas. Robison's measure included boys who appeared as delinquent in the files of private agencies, along with the official delinquents. In Robison's ecological study of New York City, the unofficial delinquents accounted for 11.3 percent of the total.

After attempting to tabulate the delinquency rates of "health areas" of New York, comparable to Shaw and McKay's square miles of Chicago, Robison concluded that the analytic problems were insurmountable. The data were too gross, the populations of the areas too unstable, and the matching of data from the census, the courts, and other agencies too rough to permit any valid conclusions. Furthermore, Robison asserted that it made no sense to compare the rates of concentric zones or along radials in New York City because socioeconomic conditions in New York were not distributed in that pattern.

Shaw and McKay responded to Robison in their 1942 work (1969) focusing on the critical issue of how delinquency should be measured. They did not believe that it was desirable to include cases from agency files among the count of delinquents because many of these boys were guilty merely of "problem behavior" and emotional disturbances in which the law enforcement system had no interest. There was no reason to believe, they said, that the more inclusive index is a better index of delinquency. Shaw and McKay conceded that an official count was not a total count, but only a sample or index to "officially proscribed activity," which is indeed what they were interested in. They argued, nevertheless, that it seemed to be a reliable and valid index.

> Where two or more series of official delinquents exhibit close geographical association and covariance, even though separated in time by 10, 20, or 30 years and regardless of changes in nativity or national composition of the population, it seems reasonable to consider any one of them as a probable index of the more inclusive universe—the total number of boys within an area engaging in officially proscribed activity. (1969, p. 44.)

In other words, the measure worked time and time again, so it must be valid, a position anticipating the most modern approach to scientific validity. Shaw and McKay believed that official data on delinquency were the best available, and whereas Robison concluded that no really adequate measure of delinquency was then available, Shaw and McKay believed that official data were good enough.

Shaw and McKay were not aware when they responded to Robison's challenge that Porterfield (1943) had already completed a study which was apparently the first to employ self-reports as the measure of "officially proscribed activity." However, it was not until 15 years later that self-report methods began to appear regularly in the literature on delinquency. They did so then because one study (Nye, Short & Olson, 1958) yielded a finding that seriously threatened Shaw and McKay's theory, casting doubt on their interpretation of their findings and on the object of almost all the ecological studies.

Replications

A flood of replications followed after Shaw et al.'s initial report in 1929. A "partial listing" of 22 reported between 1931 and 1940 was presented in *Juvenile Delinquency and Urban Areas* (1969, p. 12). Some simply documented the ecological phenomenon, others also replicated the correlative analyses that spoke to causal factors. Shaw and McKay stated modestly that, "In general, these studies support the findings reported in the authors' earlier publication, *Delinquency Areas*" (1969, p. 13). In fact, the consistency of the findings was startling.

The concentric zonal pattern characteristic of Chicago does not necessarily appear elsewhere. While Robison and other scholars have taken this fact to be an important disconfirmation of Shaw and McKay's theories specifically, and of ecological theory generally, this view is mistaken. Not all cities are supposed by ecological theory to deteriorate from their core outward. Natural and man-made features of the terrain generate different patterns, as Shaw and McKay themselves acknowledged in their occasional employment of radials whose origins are elsewhere than in Chicago's Loop. In old European cities, the typical pattern places the present or former palaces of the nobility at the center, with the homes of the wealthy and well-maintained public buildings, squares and parks nearby. The poor locate in undesirable districts away from the inner city, near the docks or slaughterhouses or factories, on swampy ground or on the floodplains of rivers. For example, in Wallis and Maliphant's report on delinquency areas of London (1967), the maps showing delinquency rates and indices of socioeconomic conditions did not reveal any borough or set of boroughs that could be taken as the problem-ridden inner city. Nevertheless, Wallis and Maliphant's correlations of delinquency rates with the socioeconomic conditions of London's boroughs matched the ubiquitous findings of Shaw and McKay's analyses of square mile areas.

Similarly, DeFleur (1967) located the residences of 192 juvenile offenders in Cordoba, Argentina, and showed that they fell into no regular geographic distribution. That is because Cordoba has an ecological structure patterned after old Spanish cities. The city had many *villa miserias*—slums—but these were scattered about the urban range. The most desirable residential areas were adjacent to the commercial and cultural center of the city, where the environment was hospitable and municipal services were superior. The Cordoban offenders came disproportionately from the slums. Again, however, a culturally determined exception emerged: Many juvenile offenders were located in the affluent sections as well. These were girls who lived as servants in the homes of the rich and were sometimes charged with theft from their employers.

Replication has encouraged strong confidence in Shaw and McKay's findings. There is thus far no known empirical contradiction of Shaw and McKay's facts. Wherever and whenever official rates of delinquents have been aggregated by geographic areas, they co-vary with the socioeconomic conditions of these areas.

Filling in and Refining*

A large number of studies have gone beyond simply replicating Shaw and McKay's studies. They have aimed to document the intervening processes that Shaw and McKay inferred but never showed empirically, and to refine their theory and methods. This literature will be reviewed selectively, roughly in an order suggested by the causal chain that, according to Shaw and McKay, leads from ecological conditions to the delinquent behavior of individual boys.

Ecological Selection

Shaw and McKay asserted that "the longer the immigrant group has been in the community, the farther out from the center is their median location point and the more dispersed or 'integrated' is their residential pattern." (1969, p. 123) Hauser (1960) confirmed this assertion by tracing the migration of ethnic groups within Chicago over the decades up to 1950. Especially important for this chapter, Hauser pointed out that the rules and conditions of the ecological competition were beginning to change. Couples were living together for a longer period prior to producing children, and after children had grown up and left home. Two-person families, young and old, were becoming more common and had their distinctive housing needs. Urban renewal was beginning to affect the distribution of the supply of housing, with enormous multiunit projects, public and private, being erected on razed blocks of the inner city. Consequently, young people of various ethnicity were repopulating the inner city while the more elderly of previous residents were enduring there. Hauser also anticipated the "gentrification" of the inner cities which has drawn more affluent people to the center.

Hauser focused particularly on the distinctive internal migration of the black population. Whereas other ethnic groups tend to scatter as they move outward, blacks moved in coagulated streams. This was due, of course, to racial discrimination. Up until the late 1940s, legal barriers contained and directed black migration, and when the legal barriers fell, long-standing racial antagonism remained to perform the same function.

Adding to the continuity of ecological studies outside of the United States, Osborn (1980) showed that transiency and place of residence is related to official and self-reported delinquency in London, using longitudinal data on boys who were found originally in a high delinquency area in their eighth year and then were followed through their twenty-fourth. The families of more delinquent boys, as indicated by either the boys' convictions in court or their own confessions to interviewers, changed addresses more frequently during this time than did the families of the less delinquent.

As to whether the families of more delinquent boys remained in or moved to another high, rather than low, delinquency area, Osborn's data are not

---

*This section has profited greatly from the writings of Bursik (1984a), Kobrin (1951), and Kornhouser (1978).

clear. On the one hand, the families of boys who had never been convicted of delinquency did not move out of London in greater proportion than those who were convicted. But in general the families that moved did not move very far: While over two-thirds of the total sample had moved between the boys' fourteenth and eighteenth years, about half stayed within the same high delinquency, poorer section of London, and only 15 percent moved outside of the city. Furthermore, it is not certain, given Wallis and Maliphant's findings on London proper, that the areas just outside of London had lower delinquency rates than did the areas within London to which more families moved. On the other hand, boys who moved out of London became less delinquent afterward, according to both official and self-report data. Osborn attributed this differential change in behavior to living conditions rather than selection because the behavior and attitudes at age 18 of those who moved outside of London did not distinguish them from those who remained in the city. Osborn implied that what Shaw and McKay called "criminal tradition" was weaker outside of London.

Scheuerman and Kobrin's study of large housing projects for the poor (1981) is an example of how Shaw and McKay's application of a theory of ecological selection can make intelligible the effects of certain events that had not occurred much in American cities when Shaw and McKay began their research.

Scheuerman and Kobrin described what they believed is the typical process of areal change attendant on the erection of housing projects. To begin with, social and economic factors place the projects in blighted areas, and even the largest projects do not eliminate all of the blight. Second, economies of scale require multiunit, high-rise designs that concentrate population even more densely than before. Third, policies governing eligibility for residence, together with people's preferences for where and with whom they want to live, exclude all but the poor from the projects. Fourth, completion of a project occasions a rapid influx of residents, mostly strangers to one another and to other residents of the neighborhood. Thus, conditions are in place for social disorganization and criminogenic adaptation. Scheuerman and Kobrin demonstrated that high delinquency areas in Los Angeles remain high after housing projects are built in them. They warned that large housing projects which increase socioeconomic segregation can also blight a desirable neighborhood and elevate its delinquency rate. In this ecological process, delinquency rates are not only an effect; they become a cause as a neighborhood's reputation for crime is created, and thus affect people's decisions about where to live.

Human ecological processes are governed by social rules, and the rules are sometimes changed in an attempt to ameliorate negative consequences such as high delinquency. Certain attempts are unsuccessful, however, not because the ecological principles are wrong but because the efforts do not deal with them. History creates new conditions but does not change the ecological principles that govern their effects.

Bursik (1984b) has revealed the effects of changes in the social context of ecological competition on the correlates of areal delinquency rates. His analyses of data collected by Shaw and McKay show that the correlates of rates are similar in the data from 1940, 1960, and 1970: High rates are associated with indexes of social disorganization and the proportion of blacks in each area. In the 1950 data, however, while social disorganization is related to delinquency rates, the proportion of blacks is not. This is because some of the areas with the smallest proportions of blacks had very high delinquency rates in that year.

Bursik attributed the change in the correlates of delinquency rates to a condition of a sudden and radical change in the rules governing ecological competition. In the 1940s, the U.S. Supreme Court struck down racial segregation in housing. Racially restrictive covenants could no longer be legally enforced. One consequence of the change was that blacks began to move into more desirable, previously white ethnic enclaves. Heitgerd and Bursik (1984) found that rapid growth in the proportion of blacks in an area is significantly related to rising delinquency rates not only in that area but also in predominantly white adjacent areas.

Suttles (1968) has described the effects of ecological selection on rising juvenile delinquency rates under these conditions in terms of the "defended community." The function of keeping alien ethnics out is performed partly by teenagers who rally to the area's defense under the banners of the delinquent "gangs" legendary to their area. Antagonistic bands of juveniles carry illegal weapons, engage in interethnic gang fights, and vandalize each other's private and public properties. The police and court intervene and delinquency rates rise in the cluster of areas so affected. This of course constitutes one effect of the criminogenic social disorganization of which Shaw and McKay wrote. That it is not accurately indexed by a change in the social or ethnic mix of some areas is due to the boundary definitions of the areas rather than a breakdown of the ecological principles; clearly the areas are affected by rapid changes in population and consequent disorganization. An apparent paradoxical twist in the dynamics generated by the particular changes in competitive conditions is that the most entrenched and presumably most organized of the ethnic enclaves experience the most rapid rise in delinquency rates (Heitgerd and Bursik, 1984). But this is understandable: The population there stays and fights; in less organized areas, it departs in relative peace.

Another change in social policy affecting ecological phenomena has been the marked reduction in immigration to the United States. The variable of proportion of foreign born in an area has a different, perhaps opposite meaning today than it did from 1900 to 1940 because it occupies a much lower range. Now a relatively small foreign-born population indicates as much as anything else a high proportion of blacks in an area. That is, when once relatively few foreign born reflected more cultural homogeneity, it now reflects cultural heterogeneity and ethnic hostility.

Not only are the processes of ecological selection redirected by changes in public policy, they are also affected by the culture of the ethnic groups involved. Moore, Vigil, and Garcia (1983) described how strong kinship ties among Chicanos in Los Angeles affect areal delinquency rates. Chicano boys belong to the gang in their family's home *barrio,* rather than to gangs in their own neighborhood. And when gangs draw their membership from a geographically dispersed ethnic group and the delinquency of their members is charged to members' home addresses, the effect is that delinquency rates are distributed more evenly among areas about the city. Under this condition, the socioeconomic and other characteristics of urban areas do not relate so well to their delinquency rates. Moore et al. noted that in 15 of the 31 Chicano gangs they observed, 25 percent or more of the known members lived outside the territorial base of their gang. The families of many of these boys had once lived in the gang's neighborhood, near relatives, but for some reason they had moved. Still their family life and juvenile street life centered around the original *barrio*. Moreover, Chicano juvenile gangs are modeled on the extended family, with age-graded subgroups and feelings of *carnalismo*—blood brotherhood—among the members. So boys who move away return to hang around even with merely fictive *carnals*. Moreover, nonresident members sometimes recruit new members for their distant gang from among new neighbors. Thus as Moore et al. pointed out, the premise upon which juvenile gangs give rise to high delinquency rates in the areas of their members' residence—"that gang members all live in the turf they defend . . . is a product of the settlement and assimilation patterns of European ethnics of the early 20th century" (1983, p. 182). Where other mores prevail, such as the Chicano attachment to the area which the extended family regards as its *barrio,* the residential addresses of boys will not necessarily reflect the conditions under which they commit delinquent behavior.

Ecological Adaptation: Social Disorganization and Criminal Traditions

The next link in the causal chain hypothesized by Shaw and McKay is the effect of socioeconomic segregation on community organization and culture. Shaw and McKay theorized that areas in which the poor are concentrated are characterized by social disorganization and cultural adaptation that at least tolerates delinquent and criminal activities if it does not actually encourage them. They did not test this link directly, but they did show that some of the presumed antecedents of social disorganization are most prevalent in the poorest areas. These include large changes in the size of populations in an area between diennial censuses, cultural heterogeneity as reflected in the populations of foreign born of diverse ethnic origins and of blacks in residence, and transiency as indexed by small proportions of owner-occupied dwellings. They also showed that adult crime rates are high among the poor, suggesting a criminal tradition. These of course, are not direct measures of the weakness of a area's social institutions, social conflict, and a toleration of crime. Shaw and McKay did not collect such data.

There are studies following in the Shaw and McKay tradition which have tested this causal link. Bordua (1958) presented data taken from interviews with residents of the Detroit metropolitan area that relate income to social isolation at the individual level of analysis. The lower the income of the respondents, the less interaction they reported with neighbors and the less they participated in local organizations. Low income people also scored significantly higher on the Srole Anomie Scale (Srole, 1956). One may infer from these data that these tendencies toward social disorganization are characteristic of urban areas where the poor are concentrated. This inference might be wrong, however, because Bordua's data were not specific to poor people living in low income areas. Those that live among other poor people may not feel so alienated and so isolated when they are jammed together in the inner city. We will return later to the problems of making inferences to one level of analysis from data analyzed at another level.

Hackler, Ho, and Urquhart-Ross (1974) avoided the problem of cross-level inferences by aggregating data on alienation by census tract. Median scores of tracts on the Srole scale correlated with socioeconomic status (occupation of primary breadwinners) at an impressive -.97 (n = 12 tracts); but there was virtually no correlation between socioeconomic status and social isolation. Apparently the residents of poor urban areas felt alienated from social institutions, but not necessarily from one another. One may conclude from the findings of Hackler et al. that social disorganization characterizes formal relationships but not informal relationships in poor areas.

Ethnographic accounts of life in the slums and ghettos support the image of residents in many poor areas being distrustful of formal institutions but engaging comfortably in informal relationships. Whyte's description of social interaction in a poor Italian neighborhood of Boston in *Street Corner Society* (1955) and Suttles's of *The Social Order of the Slum* (1968) in a Chicago area in transition are filled with accounts of neighborliness and stable friendly relations. These informal relations are highly selective to be sure, typically occurring within age, status, and ethnic groups if not within an extended family. Ties are usually dyadic or, at their widest, between families. What association people have with formal groups is largely due to informal or kinship ties to another member or two. There is almost no commitment to the neighborhood as such, and most people want to get out as soon as they can.

Shaw and McKay may have exaggerated the degree of social disorganization consequent upon concentrations of the poor. While associations among the poor are not of the sort that give them much collective influence over what happens to their neighborhoods, the poor are not usually socially isolated. It is a matter of relative social disorganization, and what is important about relative differences among areas for understanding delinquency rates is how they affect young people's behavior (or perhaps how they affect the justice system's reactions to young people's behavior).

Social Disorganization, Criminal Traditions, and Delinquency

The last link in the causal chain forges a connection between the critical characteristics of poor urban areas and their rates of delinquency. Readers will note, especially if they are psychologists, that there remains to be discussed the relationship between areal delinquency rates and the behavior of individual youngsters. This is by no means a simple relationship; it involves a complex of theoretical and methodological issues. The topic will therefore be addressed later. At that point, however, the discussion goes beyond the scope of social ecology, but not of Shaw and McKay's interests. As stated at the beginning of the chapter, the social ecology of delinquency is the study of the geographic distribution of delinquency. It is not concerned with why individuals have higher or lower rates of delinquency than others. The geographic distribution of delinquency, and particularly the characteristics of the geographically defined aggregates, may have implications for why individuals are more or less delinquent. Then again, they may not. As will be shown, one cannot make any certain inference that the characteristics more common to a highly delinquent aggregate are also the characteristics more likely to be found in a highly delinquent individual.

Shaw and McKay proposed some social psychological processes which are consistent with their ecological findings. Their formulation is not the only conceivable consistent one, however. And it is not clear how much they were concerned about explaining differences in delinquency among individuals. It is possible that their social psychological speculations were intended only to demonstrate that their ecological findings were plausible, that is, that these findings could emerge from ordinary psychological processes. It is for this reason that we regard the ultimate dependent variable of social ecological studies to be geographically based delinquency rates and their explanation to be the last link in the causal chain.

Kobrin (1951) has offered a theoretical analysis of the sociocultural conditions tending toward either social disorganization or a criminal tradition in urban areas. His analysis begins with Shaw and McKay's premise that even in the most delinquent areas, most of the adults are committed to conventional norms and are law-abiding, but that there exists alongside conventional morality a lively criminal tradition, enacted regularly by some residents and tolerated by most others, who can, in any case, do little to combat it. According to Kobrin, the nature of the relationship between conventional and criminal culture determines whether a high delinquency area will be of the disorganized or criminal type. In stable ethnic ghettos, conventional and criminal elements are fairly well integrated; illegal activities are organized into stable enterprises such as gambling, fencing stolen goods, "chopping" stolen cars, dealing drugs, and the like; and their staffs participate in the area's conventional institutions as well—in the legitimate businesses, social clubs, churches, political organizations, and so on. In areas undergoing rapid transition, conventional and criminal elements are isolated from one another. Crime in these slums is unorganized, consisting of mugging, petty theft, and such. Kobrin made clear that he regarded these types as ideal rather than concrete; actually most areas fall somewhere along a continuum between the most and least integrated types.

Differences in integration among high delinquency areas affect the nature of the delinquency that those areas generate. In more integrated areas, stable criminal enterprises provide a structure for the apprenticeship of youth. Delinquency is carried on more or less under the supervision of adults and consists of running numbers, theft, drug dealing, and other utilitarian acts. Delinquency is more expressive and violent in less integrated areas. There one expects to find gang fights, muggings, vandalism, and such. Thus Kobrin's analysis leads not only to a typology of delinquency areas but to a typology of delinquency as well.

Kobrin's analysis anticipated the theory of blocked opportunity developed by Cloward and Ohlin (1960). Both analyses are rooted in Merton's (1957) seminal article on "Social Structure and Anomie," although most of Kobrin's inspiration seems to have come from Shaw and McKay rather than from Merton.

It has turned out that there is no empirical support either for the typology of delinquency areas, or for the typology of delinquent acts. Research on individual delinquents has shown that they cannot be typed reliably by their offenses, but rather that heavily delinquent youth are quite eclectic in their illegal behavior (Gold and Petronio, 1980). (See also Chapters 3 and 5). The necessary research on types of delinquency areas has not yet been done; this idea awaits empirical testing.

Many more studies have been done on the potential of social disorganization than on criminal tradition to generate high delinquency areas. Unfortunately, the empirical research on disorganization got started on misleading theoretical grounds, which led to inappropriate handling of the data and to unnecessary theoretical controversy. The problem can probably be traced back to Lander's study of delinquency areas in Baltimore (1954).

Lander intended that his study's contribution to the ecological approach be primarily methodological. He noted that more sophisticated statistical techniques with which to deal with the many variables that Shaw and McKay measured had become available. Collecting the same kinds of areal data in Baltimore as Shaw and McKay had collected in Chicago, Lander submitted them to factor analyses in order to reduce them to a few meaningful, coherent indices. He also computed multiple regressions in order to assess the relative power of the correlated indices in predicting delinquency rates.

Lander found two factors. He interpreted one as a measure of economic conditions because the variables of dilapidation, crowding, and educational attainment were most heavily loaded on it. Two variables, home ownership and racial balance, defined the second factor, which Lander interpreted to reflect social disorganization and called, following Durkheim, "anomie." Lander inferred that the latter factor reflected anomie for the same reasons that Shaw and McKay took these variables to indicate social disorganization: They assumed that the smaller the proportion of owner-occupied homes, the less stable and committed the population; and the more even the racial balance, the more cultural conflict.

Lander's factorial and multiple regression analyses produced results which he mistakenly took to contradict Shaw and McKay's theory: Anomie accounted for variation in areal delinquency rates and, with anomie held constant, economic conditions did not. "The factor analysis indicates," Lander concluded, that the delinquency rate is fundamentally related only to the *anomie* and not specifically to the socio-economic conditions of an area. The delinquency rate in a stable community will be low in spite of its being characterized by bad housing, poverty and propinquity to the city center. On the other hand, one would expect a high delinquency rate in an area characterized by normlessness and social instability. (1954, p. 89.)

Actually, as Kornhauser has pointed out, these words " . . . for the most part could have been written by Shaw and McKay" (1978, p. 84). For Shaw and McKay posited social disorganization as an intervening variable in the causal chain; it is hypothesized to be a condition which socioeconomic segregation tends to produce and which in turn tends to produce delinquency. Lander's results were just what Shaw and McKay's theory predicted.

Lander's analyses have been criticized on technical grounds (e.g., Gordon, 1967; Rosen & Turner, 1967), but the specifics of these criticisms need not concern us here. (See Chilton, 1964, and Chilton & Dussich, 1974, for reviews.) Rectification of the technical errors has revealed that some but by no means all of the effect of socioeconomic conditions on delinquency rates is through the social disorganization they create. This finding does not contradict social ecological theory. Therefore, subsequent research on this causal link will be reviewed without regard to the controversy, stirred up by Lander's interpretation, about whether poor economic conditions *or* social disorganization is responsible for high delinquency rates.

Despite the unfortunate digression created by Lander's interpretation of his data, his and the other studies in this line made two major contributions. First, factor analysis has made the data more manageable and interpretable. The many variables from the census databank were reduced to two or three coherent and reliable indices. The process of data reduction has made clear that the census data can usefully be organized into several discrete dimensions of urban areas which can reasonably be interpreted to reflect socioeconomic status, ethnic heterogeneity, and social disorganization. This constitutes a marked advance over Shaw and McKay's computations on dozens of characteristics of mile square areas.

With the data so organized, the second contribution became feasible; that is, to submit the reduced set of variables to multivariate analyses. In this way, their relative relationships with and interactive effects on delinquency could be assessed. As discussed earlier, the function of social disorganization as an intervening variable has been verified. At the same time, impoverished conditions have some independent effect on delinquency rates. One wonders whether, following Shaw and McKay, introduction of measures of criminal traditions in urban areas would account for much of the remainder of the effects of poverty. Apparently this has not yet been done because the measures have not been available.

Discovery of interactions in the effects of community characteristics on delinquency rates provides empirical support for Shaw and McKay's belief that each community area is in some way unique. Each is the site for a different interplay of universal ecological processes. Community characteristics most commonly investigated in this line of research are socioeconomic status; ethnic heterogeneity, usually measured in terms of percent of population which is black; and stable "familism," as reflected by higher proportions of non-working women, larger families, and single detached homes. These are largely uncorrelated dimensions which emerge repeatedly from orthogonal factor analyses of tract or area census data and have figured prominently in what has come to be called "social area analysis" (see Shevky and Bell, 1955).

Three studies (Chilton & Dussich, 1974; Polk, 1967; Willie, 1967) have identified interactions among community variables that permit a coherent and plausible construction of their joint effects on delinquency rates. In Polk's study of Portland, Oregon, favorable socioeconomic conditions and a high degree of familism were characteristics of areas with low rates. Where there was little familism, however, relative affluence ameliorated but did not prevent high rates of delinquency. There is evidence here then for the intermediation of social organization—familism—between socioeconomic conditions and delinquency rates.

In Indianapolis, Chilton and Dussich also found that poor but highly familistic areas have delinquency rates not very different from more affluent areas. Moreover, those affluent areas which were not very familistic also had relatively low rates. These are the independent effects. When the presumably socially disorganizing element of ethnic heterogeneity—an even racial balance—was taken into account, however, Chilton and Dussich found that even familism did not prevent high delinquency rates in poor areas. In Washington, D.C., Willie again found that socioeconomic conditions and familism have independent effects on delinquency rates, and the effect of the latter is greater. When the two characteristics operate in common, the ethnic composition of an area makes little difference. In areas where one is high and the other low, however, ethnicity does make a difference; in heavily white areas, both familism and affluence accounted for variation in delinquency rates; in heavily black areas, only socioeconomic conditions were influential.

Social organization, as it develops in an urban area heavily settled by conventional families, mediates between poverty and high delinquency rates. This social organization can be disturbed, however, by racial balance. All the same, in a heavily black community, working women, multifamily housing units, and nonconventional families—the hallmarks of low familism—have little effect on delinquency rates, perhaps because these conditions are so common in poor black neighborhoods that adequate cultural adaptations have been made to socialize children effectively despite them.

Clearly, the three community characteristics typically considered in social area analysis in combination affect delinquency rates in ways different from their simple additive effects. If criminal tradition or any of the other community characteristics that Shaw and McKay speculated about were added to these analyses, one would probably find even more complex interactions. Thus, it seems advisable to keep in mind Shaw and McKay's recognition of the uniqueness of each community area within a city before interpreting differences in delinquency rates among them. The exceptions may be the proverbial ones that actually prove the fundamental ecological rules.

The inferences one may draw from demographic data about the relationship between social disorganization and delinquency rates receive more direct support from survey data. Recall that Hackler et al. (1974) found that residents of poorer areas displayed greater anomie on the Srole scale than did residents of more affluent areas. This study also found that the greater the average anomie scores in a neighborhood, the higher the delinquency rate ($r = .67$). Moreover, the greater the alienation of residents, the more of them said they would call the police if their cars were vandalized rather than intervening informally by reporting the vandals to their parents or speaking to the youth directly. Further, the residents' willingness to intervene only formally was related to higher delinquency rates. These relationships were especially strong in areas that bear other indicators of social organization—relative affluence and residential stability. Indeed, in areas marked by poverty and transiency, residents' alienation and willingness to intervene were virtually unrelated to their delinquency rates. This is not surprising, given data reviewed earlier. Since residents of poor areas tend to distrust formal institutions, they probably do not call the police when they witness actual delinquency; so when transiency weakens informal relationships as well, then nothing the residents actually do affects delinquency rates.

Maccoby, Johnson, and Church (1958) also confirmed the link between social disorganization and delinquency rates. They found that fewer residents of a higher delinquency tract knew any of their neighbors by name, reported that they would "do something" if they witnessed delinquent behavior, or did anything when they had actually witnessed delinquent behavior. Maccoby et al., in this one study that attempted to test Shaw and McKay's hypothesis about criminal traditions, found no differences between the high and low delinquency areas in residents' attitudes toward delinquency.

Other Mediators Between Socioeconomic Segregation and Delinquency Rates

Other conditions have also been proposed as responsible for high delinquency rates where the poor are concentrated. The concentration of any population, poor or otherwise, may be criminogenic. The idea is that crowding can be stressful and evoke aggressive, antisocial behavior. This has been confirmed among certain nonhuman species such as rats, but not among others, such as vervet monkeys (see Gillis, 1974). Among humans, reactions to crowding seem to depend upon the sociocultural context which gives meaning to crowded conditions. Crowding under some circumstances may reflect low status, but, under others, it may mean having obtained residence in a popular place. Apparently, crowding is stressful to humans to the degree that they perceive it as being out of their control (Baron & Rodin, 1978).

There are at least two aspects of crowding which are usefully distinguished in their relationships to delinquency rates. One is external, represented by such measures as number of people per square mile or proportion of multiple housing in a given amount of space; this is usually called "density." The other is internal and is measured in such terms as people per square foot of living space or people per room. Density is not necessarily correlated with crowding; one can find high density areas in which people live comfortably in large apartments, and one can also find sparsely populated commercial and industrial areas where a few people live in crowded flats. Where the poor are concentrated, however, both kinds of crowding usually occur, and it is informative to identify their separate effects on delinquency rates. It is also helpful to assess their effects on delinquency rates independent of the characteristics of the people who must live under crowded conditions.

The findings regarding density and crowding seem fairly consistent (see Moos, 1976, pp. 146–151, for a review of recent studies). In data for Honolulu, both density and crowding were positively related to delinquency rates, but the effect of crowding disappeared when density and socioeconomic characteristics of the residents were controlled. The effect of density remains, however, when crowding and socioeconomic status are controlled. Data on Chicago (Galle, Gove, & McPherson, 1972) was consistent with the interpretation that density has an effect but crowding does not. In the Netherlands, again the effect of density withstood controls on socioeconomic status and ethnic heterogeneity, while the effect of crowding did not. According to Moos, however, the authors of the Dutch study (Levy & Herzog, 1974) pointed out that few people are really crowded in the Netherlands.

If the findings regarding crowding among nonhumans and humans have any relevance to the ecology of delinquency rates, one would have supposed that crowded living quarters rather than a densely populated neighborhood would prove to be more important. Gillis (1974) has contributed findings that may specify why density influences rates more. Gillis took type of residence into account, classifying structures as multiple or single detached. The presence of multiple housing in census tracts of Edmonton, Canada, was related to density ($r = .47$), but not to crowding ($r = .00$). When density, crowding, and building type were regressed jointly on delinquency rates, type of residence accounted for 34 percent of the variance, and density and crowding accounted for none additional. Gillis has shown that the predictive power of multiple housing is not altogether due to its being occupied more by the poor, although it is the case that multiple housing sheltered a disproportionate number of families on welfare there. Path analysis demonstrated a substantial direct relationship between multiple housing and high delinquency rates as well as an indirect relationship through selection of families on welfare into multiunit dwellings. Once variation in rates due to type of residence and proportion of welfare families was removed, then variations among areal density, crowding, median income, or proportion of foreign born accounted for no more.

Why should multiple housing increase delinquency rates in an area? Gillis considered the possibility that some spatial arrangements are more conducive than others to delinquency and crime. He invoked Newman's (1972) idea of "defensible space," a concept proposed originally to explain why more crime occurs in certain places than in others, rather than why more offenders live in certain places. The idea may be useful nevertheless to explain the residential distribution of juvenile offenders because juveniles in America tend more than adults to commit crimes close to home.

According to Newman, the characteristics of multiple housing provide more opportunities for crime. For example, entries to dwellings are more hidden, elevators and stairwells provide secluded spots for muggings, and residents of multiple housing are less able to distinguish residents from strangers in the vicinity. Multiple housing may set the stage for delinquency, tending to raise the rates in areas where the poor are concentrated. Thus, building type and its correlate in population density can be considered another variable, along with social disorganization and criminal tradition, mediating between socioeconomic segregation and delinquency rates.

DELINQUENCY RATES AND INDIVIDUAL DELINQUENCY

It does not necessarily follow from the ecological finding that poorer urban areas have higher delinquency rates, that poor urban families have more delinquent children. It is not only that correlations of aggregated data are larger than correlations of individual data on the same variables (Robinson, 1950), thus exaggerating the relationship. Relationships found at an areal level may distort and may even be the reverse of relationships at the individual level. Hammond (1973) has framed this in terms of covariance: The slope of a regression line representing the relationship between median income among urban areas and their delinquency rates may be negative, while the slope of the regression of families' income on the delinquency of their children within any or all the areas may be positive. It is conceivable, for example, that certain extremely disorganized families are forced to live in urban slums despite their higher than average income which is consumed by incompetent, alcoholic, or mentally ill family members, and that these families will produce more delinquent children than the predominantly poor in the slums.

There are two concrete instances of such reversals in studies already reviewed here. In Quinney's data on Lexington, Kentucky (1964), the higher the proportion of blacks in an area, the higher the delinquency rate; but it was the whites' rates of delinquency that was higher ($r = .51$), not the blacks' ($r = .03$). And in Wallis and Maliphant's (1967) data on London, the higher the divorce rate in an area, the lower the delinquency rate ($r = -.42$), although the children of divorced parents were more likely to be delinquent.

Shaw and McKay were undoubtedly aware of the pitfalls in ecological inference to individual behavior. Nevertheless, they believed that the ecological distribution reflected the socioeconomic forces operating on individual boys.

McKay, in his interpretation of the ecological data brought up to date to 1960, reiterated the social psychological processes that he and Shaw believed to underlie delinquency rates and did not even mention the technical criticisms that had been made since 1942 (Shaw & McKay, 1969, pp. 380–388). McKay asserted that poorer boys are disadvantaged in "the struggle for a more favorable position in the social order;" the social institutions responsible for their control, particularly their families, are ill suited to the urban environment, weak, and ineffectual. With time, these social institutions adapt, but their adaptation includes something of a criminal tradition to which boys are attracted. Shaw and McKay acknowledged exceptions to these processes among individuals and areas. They would assert, however, that the basic ecological forces are strong and are rarely contravened by conditions that render ecological inferences invalid. Furthermore, innumerable studies employing data on individuals have shown that poor boys are disproportionately represented in the records of police, juvenile courts, and reformatories.

The ecological and individual data were so consistent, the theory so compelling, and the political and social implications so positive that they became, in Kuhn's sense of the term (1962), paradigmatic. For about 30 years, from the late 1930s to the late 1960s, the method, the expected findings, and the basic interpretations were the basis of the science of delinquency. Delinquency was measured using official data on arrests, adjudications, and commitments, aggregated or individual. It was correlated with indices of socioeconomic status or with its consequent conditions, such as broken homes and alienation, with the result that the lower the status and the more prevalent its consequences, the more delinquency was found. Socioeconomic conditions were held causally responsible. Programs for prevention and treatment were mounted primarily to ameliorate these conditions—by putting a floor under poverty, subsidizing housing for the poor, organizing poor communities, desegregating the poor, helping poor families, giving poor children an educational head start, redirecting the activities of gangs in the slums, and so on.

This paradigm began to break under the challenge of a nonparadigmatic measure, self-report. When adolescents have been asked about their own recent delinquent behavior in the course of a personal interview or by means of a self-administered questionnaire, and their confessions correlated with the socioeconomic status of their families or neighborhoods, the data have shown either no relationship, a scant negative relationship, or in some instances, a scant positive relationship. (Nye, Short, & Olson, 1958; Dentler & Monroe, 1961; Clark & Wenninger, 1962; Erickson & Empey, 1965; Gold, 1970; Empey & Lubeck, 1971; Gold & Reimer, 1975; and Junger-Tas, 1984; to cite only some. See Tittle, Villemaz, and Smith, 1978 for a more complete list up to the early 1970s.) Self-report measures reveal what Shaw and McKay and Robison and others suspected—that there is a great deal of delinquent behavior that is not detected or recorded in the official files of the juvenile justice system. And these data support Robison's contention that the official data distort the distribution of "officially proscribed activity" in theoretically important ways.

Furthermore, Johnstone (1978) has shown that juveniles living in the lower status areas of Chicago do not report the most delinquent behavior. His study differed most importantly from earlier studies of its kind in measuring delinquency with a self-administered questionnaire to a sample of 1124 14-to-18-year-olds residing in 221 census tracts in the city and surrounding suburbs. The results were that areal characteristics were not significantly correlated with delinquent behavior. Johnstone observed that " . . . it is revealing that areal models should be the least effective of the predictors, especially in a study of delinquency in Chicago, the pioneer locale of ecological insights on crime and delinquency" (p. 68).

Contrary to most studies employing self-report measures, in Johnstone's data the socioeconomic status of families was highly correlated with their children's delinquent behavior ($r = .90$). This was due to the high level of delinquency reported by lower class boys and girls living in more affluent neighborhoods. Poor children from poor areas were not the most delinquent. Johnstone concluded that "the situation of being a 'have not' in a community of 'haves' represents a context which can produce high levels of utilitarian delinquency as well as contranormative behavior (e.g. drug abuse, and truancy) which may be aimed primarily at middle class authority" (p. 69). Next most delinquent to the lower class children living in more affluent areas were the middle class children whose families resided in poor neighborhoods; their anomalous residence may be taken to indicate the disorganization of these families.

Johnstone's data do not lend themselves to ecological interpretation. Social disorganization, alienation, and criminal adaptation may be evoked to explain the findings, but not at the level of community. The links from socioeconomic segregation and community characteristics to the family, and thence to individual delinquency, are not demonstrated. The more proximal links from the family and the schools to individual delinquency may be intact, however.

As the self-report method has challenged the ecological paradigm, so the method has been challenged in turn. (See Chapters 2 and 10.) At this time, its reliability and validity have been largely accepted, but some scholars inject two important qualifications; that at least certain frequently used self-report measures typically fail to differentiate the most frequent offenders who are most likely to be apprehended, and that self-report does not measure very well the most serious delinquent behavior that leads to court records and incarceration (Reiss & Rhodes, 1961; Hindelang, Hirschi, & Weis, 1979; Elliott & Ageton, 1980).

For one thing, most self-report indices include as many if not more trivial, albeit illegal, items as serious ones. For example, petty shoplifting is added up with burglary, and a sharp punch at a classmate, with an injurious assault. Second, some methods of figuring an individual's delinquency score truncate the range of scores at the top. In my own method (Gold, 1970) for example, no more than three instances of any one of 17 delinquent behaviors are counted. This is to avoid giving undue weight to the data of the few who report selling drugs or shoplifting or beating up on others or whatever "hundreds of times." Such devices may indeed fail to differentiate the most highly delinquent youth. Third, frequently and seriously delinquent youth are relatively rare. Even with truncated scores they occupy a long, low tail on a highly skewed distribution. In order to detect social class differences between these youth and the rest of a representative sample of youth, either the sample or the difference has to be quite large. In most studies, the samples have not been large and apparently what socioeconomic difference there may be is not large, either.

Hindelang et al. (1979) have asserted that because of these methodological shortcomings, self-report findings do not provide solid grounds for asserting that poor children are no more delinquent than affluent children. Furthermore, their review of studies in which both self-report and official data were collected on the same individuals led Hindelang et al. to conclude that, "In sum, although illusions of discrepancy abound, we are hard pressed to locate persuasive evidence that self-report and official methods produce discrepant results" (p. 1009). They observed that self-reports and official records of police contacts and arrests, both weighted with trivial offenses, were consistent in showing no differences among social classes, and that self-report studies were inadequate for testing the validity of social class differences in the serious offenses that were reflected in court and institutional records. Hindelang et al. pointed out, however, that the self-report method could be refined so as to identify the frequent and serious offenders who would be adjudicated and incarcerated if apprehended.

Elliott and Ageton (1980) did collect and analyze self-report data in ways that minimize the methodological problems, and indeed found a social class difference. This difference centers around the greater proportion of lower class youth confessing to extremely frequent "predatory crimes against property." These are just the offenses that are most likely to lead youth to be caught by police and acquire official records. It is worth noting here that the social class differences found by Johnstone were also due to these kinds of offenses. Elliott and Ageton's findings are consistent with Johnstone's, although, having been collected on a national sample, their data are not so amenable to a social area analysis. The relatively few extremely delinquent lower class youth responsible for the social class differences found by Elliott and Ageton may have resided in more affluent neighborhoods.

Elliott and Ageton's study gives some reason to believe that the social class differences typically found in official delinquency data reflect a real difference in "officially proscribed activity," recorded or not, as Shaw and McKay asserted. It is consistent with Shaw and McKay's beliefs that only a few youth are responsible for the difference, while the majority of even the poorest youth behave, if not perfectly, then at least as well as the children of middle and upper class parents. However, the social class differences which have been demonstrated do not necessarily support the ecological theory, and John-stone's data seriously challenge it. That is, the data do confirm Shaw and McKay's general emphasis on the causal effects of social conditions, rather than of genetics, psychological abnormality, or irremediable cultural crimi-nogenesis. But it seems that the ecological chain of causality is too weak to be stretched usefully all the way from socioeconomic segregation in urban areas to the delinquent behavior of individual youth. While each link may be valid, their compounded probabilities may not add up to a reliable cause-effect relationship between the characteristics of areas and the delinquent behavior of the youth who live in them. The proximal causes of delinquency may lie in youngsters' experiences at home, in school, and with peers, experiences which are not substantially influenced by the more distal areal characteristics essen-tial to ecological theory.

If this is the case, then what is the explanation for the ubiquitous relation-ship between socioeconomic characteristics of urban areas and their official delinquency rates? What is the meaning of the facts demonstrated repeatedly by Shaw and McKay and their successors? We turn finally to an alternative interpretation compatible with the data at hand.

THE SOCIAL ECOLOGY OF JUVENILE JUSTICE

The facts to be explained are the ubiquitous relationships between the delin-quency rates of urban areas and the socioeconomic and social organizational characteristics of those areas. Now it seems that poor children living in poor urban areas may not be more delinquent than children living elsewhere. If they are at all, their delinquency is, according to self-report measures, only mar-ginally greater and cannot account for the sizeable relationships between rates and areal characteristics, even granting that aggregated correlations exaggerate relationships at the individual level. Moreover, the poor children who are re-sponsible for the social class difference in delinquent behavior apparently are not the ones that live in poor urban areas; rather, they seem to live in more affluent areas, and *that,* rather than areal characteristics, may be responsible for their misbehavior.

A plausible alternative explanation starts with a reinterpretation of delin-quency rates. Rather than taking them as reflecting the "officially proscribed activity" of youth, this explanation assumes that rates reflect the "proscribing activity of officials"—that is, the behavior of the juvenile justice system. It proposes that the differences in delinquency rates among urban areas are largely if not wholly due to the differential distribution, not of delinquency, but of formal reactions to delinquency.

This explanation is, of course, not original here. Recall that Robison, com-menting on Shaw and McKay's findings, wrote, "Differing behavior on the part of parents and authorities confronted with a troublesome child may be as much a modifier of neighborhood rates as different proportions of troublesome children.'' (1972, p. 4). Polk (1957), discussing his finding that the proportion of blacks and Chicanos in areas of San Diego are positively related to the areas' delinquency rates, acknowledged that:

> we cannot rule out the possibility that the observed relationship between ethnic status and delinquency in our study may be due to differential treatment by law enforcement officers. (p. 216.)

In his textbook entitled *Delinquent Behaviors,* Gibbons (1981) featured this explanation of the ecological findings:

> One interpretation is that they demonstrate the phenomenon of *differential law enforcement.* If this is the case, the correlates of delinquency rates are not the causes of law-breaking. Instead, they are indicators of the characteristics of persons against whom the courts and the police are biased. (pp. 155–156, italics in original.)

One need not invoke ethnic, racial, or class biases to explain differential law enforcement. Although this matter will be considered shortly, we would first like to point to the possible relationship between characteristics of urban areas and efficient, unbiased law enforcement.

Areal characteristics may be major determinants of selective apprehension of offenders. Obviously, offenders are more likely to be discovered at their delinquent activity the greater the surveillance is of the area in which that activity occurs. Furthermore, such surveillance need not be conducted by police. Actually, observation by ordinary citizens accounts for a greater number of incidents that eventuate in contact with police (Roncek, 1979; Davidson, 1981). Several characteristics of urban areas in which the poor are segregated affect the amount of surveillance. These areas are typically transversed by heavily trafficked arteries—major roadways, streets lined with retail stores and commercial establishments—which, at least during daylight hours, attract large numbers of potential observers. These areas are also more densely populated (recall that density is positively related to delinquency rates) which means more eyes per foot. It might be argued that the multiple nature of the residential structures that create more densely populated areas actually reduces effective surveillance; but despite the potential for crime of more secluded sites, Hagan, Gillis, and Chan (1978) have found a positive correlation (.26) between the presence of multiple housing in an area and the number of citizens' reports of crime originating there.

Not only are there more citizen observers in poor urban areas, there are also more police per mile. Police patrols are heavier in these areas. More police are reasonably allocated where there are more people, as is done in commercial districts during the day. And crime prevention also prescribes more patrols at night when the commercial streets are relatively deserted because then there are large stores of valuable goods whose owners are away. Thus Jacobs (1979) has reported that, nationwide, the commercial density of an area (as indexed by the number of drug and liquor stores per capita), is a significant correlate of the police strength devoted to it. Jacobs also found more police per capita in areas where the extremely rich live quite near the very poor.

Poorer urban areas, Shaw and McKay and others have shown, tend to be occupied by new migrants. Their greater proportion in the population has been taken as indicative of social disorganization and, therefore, as conducive to delinquency. Now Junger-Tas (1984) has shown that, in a large Belgian city, the presence of new migrants for some reason is related to greater police surveillance of the area. This may of course be due to the greater amount of crime and delinquency among migrants, or at least to the belief among police that this is so.

In sum, youth living in poorer urban areas are subject to greater surveillance. If they engage in officially proscribed activity, they are more likely to be seen by someone. Thus, even if they commit no more delinquency than youth living elsewhere, their behavior has greater potential for raising official delinquency rates.

To be seen in the act of delinquency is not necessarily to become an official delinquency statistic, however. A delinquent becomes "official" when a citizen or police report is formally recorded. The area in which a child lives affects these actions. Hagan et al. (1978) have shown that, in a suburb of one of Canada's largest cities, the more incidents reported to the police by citizens of an area, the more the police record offenders, regardless of the actual amount of (self-reported) delinquency in the area. Since complaints are more numerous where population is more dense, more offenders acquire police records in areas of higher density. Hackler et al. (1974) have shown that the lower the socioeconomic status of an area, the more residents say that they would report observed delinquents to the police rather than to their parents. These two Canadian studies indicate that living in a lower class, densely populated area increased delinquents' chances not only of being observed misbehaving but also of entering formal records.

Once youngsters have come to the attention of the police then they are subject to deeper and deeper penetration into the juvenile justice system. Alleged offenders may be released by the police with just a warning, put on informal probation, referred to another agency, or referred to the juvenile court. The court may refuse to accept a referral, perhaps dismissing it altogether or diverting it to another agency. If the court takes jurisdiction, then the alleged offender may be found not guilty and dismissed (a rare occurrence), or declared "delinquent" and become subject to dispositions ranging from a warning through incarceration. Delinquency rates are based on records made at all of these levels in the system. The deeper the point in the system, the closer the relationship between the delinquency rates and the socioeconomic characteristics of the urban areas from which the offenders come. For example, in Shaw and McKay's data on Chicago from about 1927, arrests of juveniles living in the furthest zones of the city amount to 33 percent of the arrests of those from the innermost zones, 18 percent of those referred to the court, and 12 percent of those committed to an institution (1969, p. 88).

This is not to assert that an alleged offender's place of residence is a foremost criteria for determining penetration into the justice system. Most important are the severity of the offense and the prior record of the offender (Terry, 1967; Thornberry, 1973; Junger-Tas, 1984). In some jurisdictions, socioeconomic and racial characteristics of offender matter not at all after the characteristics of the present offense is taken into account (Terry, 1967), while in others, they appear still to exert some influence (Thornberry, 1973). It is to be expected that local law enforcement agencies will differ in the degree to which they take into account various criteria. The question is whether the residence of the offender is taken more into account in those jurisdictions where there are greater areal differences in delinquency rates.

Apparently the only study that addresses this question directly is that of Hagan et al. (1978). In addition to collecting data on characteristics of the areas, self-reported delinquency of a sample of resident juveniles, and several official delinquency rates, the researchers had the six juvenile police officers rank the 72 urban areas in terms of how much delinquency they believed occurred there. These rankings were then adjusted for the number of juveniles living in each area. The researchers found that the officers' image of an area's delinquency rate was a key variable in determining the areal arrest rate. The self-reported delinquent behavior of residents bore no significant relationship to an area's reputation, although the delinquent behavior rate was negatively related to the area's socioeconomic status. The socioeconomic status of an area affected the area's reputation independent of self-reported delinquent behavior, and its effect was both direct and indirect. The indirect effect was mediated by population density and the rate of citizens' complaints to the police. Thus, there is evidence that police officers in at least one jurisdiction take the residence of juveniles into account in decisions affecting areal delinquency rates. It is not necessary to assume that these officers were expressing some ethnic or class biases in their assessments of the urban areas under their jurisdiction. They were undoubtedly aware of where their caseloads tended to come from, and they may have also been schooled in the literature on the social ecology of delinquency.

We do not want to appear to be Pollyannas by deemphasizing the possibility that racial, ethnic, and class biases are responsible for the differential distribution of juvenile justice. Such biases may be operating. They have been documented on the individual level in some jurisdictions. One may also speculate that the relationships between official delinquency rates and ethnic heterogeneity and between police strength and disparity of income among an area's residents are indicative of police deployment to protect the affluent and the established from the poor and the newly arrived. We mean only to point out that reason and systematic observation support the existence of what might be called "institutionalized arealism," a process by which efficient law enforcement in the service of a general consensus about the duties of the police can result in the differential distribution of delinquency rates where there are no actual differences in delinquent behavior.

The social process offered for consideration here is not unidirectional. The reputation of an area and the reactions of the juvenile justice system to it might affect the rate of delinquent behavior that occurs there. While neither Johnstone (1978) nor Hagan et al. (1978) found any areal differences in self-reported delinquent behavior (even though both used measures adequate to yield relationships with individuals' socioeconomic status), the interpretation of an official delinquency rate as wholly or in large part due to the behavior of the juvenile justice system rather than the behavior of juveniles is not inconsistent with the possible findings of areal differences in delinquent behavior. If it should be true that there is a small but real excess in extremely serious and frequent behavior among lower class youth, as Elliott and Ageton's (1980) data indicate, and if this adds up to more real delinquency in some poor urban areas, still the socioeconomic conditions of the areas may not be responsible in the way that ecological theory proposes. The behavior of the juvenile justice system may mediate the socioeconomic effect. This could happen in two related ways.

First, the reputation of an area for delinquency and crime may select the population that lives there. Families who can move and who care about such matters may leave areas with a bad reputation, while those that cannot or are indifferent remain. It is plausible that the latter kind of family raises more delinquent offspring. The reputation of an area which prompts families to move may not depend in the first instance on the area's real delinquency rate. Reputation may be built out of the gross amount of delinquency that occurs in the area. This amount may be large because of the number of youth who live in the area, while the area's per capita rate may be only moderate or even low. The amount of delinquency that occurs in an area may also depend on how attractive it is to youth from elsewhere who come to the area to commit crimes. A real delinquency rate may be inconsequential to residents or prospective residents whose concerns are for their safety, which is more a matter of crime per time and space than per capita juveniles. In other words, it is likely that an area's victimization rate, rather than its delinquency rate, determines its reputation for crime. This reputation, rather than socioeconomic characteristics, may in turn select an area's residents such that its youth are marginally more delinquent in fact as well as in the official records.

A second factor involves the proportion of youth who become involved with the juvenile justice system. Data reviewed here suggest that youth from poor urban areas are picked up by the police, referred to court, and incarcerated disproportionately to their actual delinquent behavior. Their involvement in the justice system may be responsible for the marginally greater delinquent behavior of lower class youth generally and perhaps for whatever higher rates of actual delinquency that may be found in poor urban areas. It seems that contact with the juvenile justice system promotes rather than deters further delinquency (Gold & Williams, 1969; Gold, 1970; West & Farrington,

1977; Miller and Gold, 1984). Youth who are apprehended by the police subsequently commit more, and more serious delinquent acts than comparable and equally delinquent youth who are not caught.

This is a plausible explanation for the small but disproportionate number of lower class youth at the extremes of delinquency. More frequent delinquents, especially those who commit crimes against persons, are more likely to be caught. Being poor adds to the likelihood of apprehension, whether the youth lives in a poor area or in a better one (Johnstone, 1978). Thus, apprehension may drive a small but disproportionate number of frequent, predatory lower class delinquents to the extreme of delinquent behavior where Elliott and Ageton have found them. Apprehension by the police does not apparently boost delinquent behavior a great deal; it seems to make a small but real difference. This iatrogenic effect may be enough to account for marginally greater delinquency among working class youth. And it may, along with the other possibilities raised here, including the statistical exaggeration of a small individual difference into a larger ecological one, account for the differential distribution of delinquency rates among urban areas.

SUMMARY

From the present perspective then, what have been the contributions of social ecology to our understanding of juvenile delinquency?

First, the findings of Shaw and McKay and others who took up and refined their theory and method have turned explanations about delinquency directly and constructively away from genetics, abnormality, and decadent culture to normal social processes.

Second, the success of what became for awhile the paradigmatic approach for generating replicable and interpretable findings about delinquency generated a vast amount of useful, rigorously collected, and detailed data.

Third, the theory and findings misled scientists and the public to focus too much on socioeconomic characteristics of urban areas and of families to explain delinquency. Theory, research, and practice have in this respect been hindered.

It now seems that the social ecological approach should be taken in at least two directions. First, further research ought to be done to determine if there are areal differences in actual delinquent behavior. Cities characterized by socioeconomic segregation should be studied and both self-report and official delinquency data collected on ample samples of youth living in areas differentiated by the characteristics Shaw and McKay identified. These studies might go beyond establishing whether the distribution of delinquent behavior matches the ecological pattern of official delinquency. They might also investigate more thoroughly than heretofore the social psychological processes of social disorganization and criminal traditions. Since measurement of delinquent behavior requires some sort of sample survey anyway, the opportunity will also be provided to measure the social psychological processes directly.

Second, the reinterpretation of delinquency rates as a measure of the behavior of the juvenile justice system opens the way to fresh research on the culture and social organization of law enforcement. Indeed, this research, while particular to the juvenile justice system, may contribute to our understanding of social institutions generally. These would be studies of how the purposes, regnant beliefs, composition, organization, and other characteristics of social institutions affect their responses to their environments. This interest was far from Shaw and McKay's minds when they studied the social ecology of juvenile delinquency. But their methods and findings may prove to be more relevant to this subject than to the delinquent behavior of youth.

REFERENCES

Aichhorn, A. (1935). *Wayward youth.* New York: Viking Press.

Bandura, A., & Walters, R. H. (1959). *Adolescent aggression.* New York: Ronald Press.

Baron, R. M., & Rodin, J. (1978). Personal control as a mediator of crowding. In A. Baum, J. E. Singer, & S. Valins, (Eds.), *The urban environment.* Hillsdale, NJ: Halsted Press, 145-190.

Bernard, W. S. (Ed.). (1950). *American immigration policy* New York: Harper & Bros.

Boas, F. (1924). The question of racial purity. *The American Mercury, 3,* 163-169.

Bordua, D. J. (1958). Juvenile delinquency and "anomie": An attempt at replication. *Social Problems, 6,* 230-238.

Bulmer, M. (1984). *The Chicago School of sociology.* Chicago: University of Chicago Press.

Bursik, R. J., Jr. (1984a, November). *Ecological theories of delinquency since Shaw and McKay.* Paper presented at the annual meeting of the American Society of Criminology, Cincinnati, OH.

Bursik, R. J., Jr. (1984b). Urban dynamics and ecological studies of delinquency. *Social Forces, 63,* 393-413.

Carey, J. T. (1975). *Sociology and public affairs: The Chicago School* Beverly Hills, California: Sage.

Chilton, R. (1964). Continuity in delinquency area research. *American Sociological Review, 29,* 71-83.

Chilton, R., & Dussich, J. P. J. (1974). Methodological issues in delinquency research. *Social Forces, 53,* 73-82.

Clark, J. P., & Wenninger, E. P. (1962). Socio-economic class and area as correlates of illegal behavior among juveniles. *American Sociological Review, 27,* 826-834.

Cloward, R. A., & Ohlin, L. E. (1960). *Delinquency and opportunity. A theory of delinquent gangs.* Glencoe, Ill: Free Press.

Davidson, R. N. (1981). *Crime and environment.* London: Croom Helm.

DeFleur, L. B. (1967). Ecological variables in the cross-cultural study of delinquency. *Social Forces, 45,* 556–570.

Dentler, R. A., & Monroe, L. J. (1961). Social correlates of early adolescent theft. *American Sociological Review, 26,* 733–743.

Elliott, D. S., & Ageton, S. S. (1980). Reconciling race and class differences in self-report and official estimates of delinquency. *American Sociological Review, 45,* 95–110.

Empey, L. T., & Lubeck, S. G. (1971). *The Silverlake experiment.* Chicago: Aldine.

Erikson, E. H. (1963). *Childhood and society* (2nd ed.). New York: W. W. Norton.

Erickson, M. L., & Empey L. T. (1965). Class position, peers, and delinquency. *Sociology and Social Research, 49,* 269–282.

Faris, R. E. L. (1967). *Chicago sociology, 1920–1923.* San Francisco: Chandler.

Flexner, A. (1928). A mixing instead of a melting pot. *Literary Digest, 94,* 32.

Freedman, J. L. (Ed.). (1973). The effects of population density on humans. In J. T. Fawcett (Ed.), *Psychological perspectives on populations.* New York: Basic Books.

Galle, O. R., Gove, W. R., & McPherson, J. M. (1972). Population density and pathology: What are the relations for man? *Science, 176,* 23–30.

Garis, R. L. (1927). *Immigration restriction.* New York: MacMillan.

Gibbons, D. C. (1981). *Delinquent behaviors* (3rd ed.). Englewood Cliffs, NJ: Prentice-Hall.

Gillis, A. R. (1974). Population density and social pathology: The case of building type, social allowance, and juvenile delinquency. *Social Forces, 53,* 306–314.

Gold, M. (1970). *Delinquent behavior in an American city.* Belmont, California: Brooks/Cole.

Gold, M., & Petronio, R. J. (1980). Delinquent behavior in adolescence. In J. Adelson (Ed.), *Handbook of adolescent psychology,* New York: Wiley, 495–525.

Gold, M., & Reimer, D. J. (1975). Changing patterns of delinquent behavior among Americans 13 through 16 years old: 1967–72. *Crime and Delinquency Literature, 7,* 483–517.

Gold, M., & Williams, J. R. (1969). The effect of getting caught. *Prospectus, 3,* 1–12.

Gordon, R. A. (1967). Issues in the ecological study of delinquency. *American Sociological Review, 32,* 927–1944.

Hackler, J. C., Ho, K. Y., & Urquhart-Ross, C. (1974). The willingness to intervene: Differing community characteristics. *Social Problems, 21,* 329–344.

Hagan, J., Gillis, A. P., & Chan, J. (1978). Explaining official delinquency. *Sociological Quarterly, 19,* 386–398.

Hall, G. S. (1904). *Adolescence.* New York: D. Appleton.

Hammond, J. L. (1973). Two sources of error in ecological analysis. *American Sociological Review, 38,* 764–777.

Hauser, P. E. (1985). *Personal communication.*

Heitgerd, J. L., & Bursik, R. J., Jr. (1984, November). *The defended community and patterns of delinquency.* Paper presented at the annual meeting of the American Society of Criminology, Cincinnati, OH.

Hindelang, M. J., Hirschi, T., & Weis, J. G. (1979). Correlates of delinquency: The illusion of the discrepancy between self-report and official measures. *American Sociological Review, 44,* 995–1014.

Jacobs, D. (1979). Inequality and police strength: Conflict theory and coercive control in metropolitan areas. *American Sociological Review, 44,* 913–925.

Johnstone, J. W. C. (1978). Social class, social areas, and delinquency. *Sociology and Social Research, 63,* 49–72.

Jonassen, C. T. (1949a). Cultural variables in the ecology of an ethnic group. *American Sociological Review, 14,* 32–41.

Jonassen, C. T. (1949b). A re-evaluation and critique of the logic and some methods of Shaw and McKay. *American Sociological Review, 14,* 608–614.

Junger-Tas, J., & Junger, M. (1984). *Juvenile delinquency: Backgrounds of delinquent behavior.* The Hague, Netherlands: Ministry of justice.

Kobrin, S. (1951). The conflict of values in delinquency areas. *American Sociological Review, 16,* 657–658.

Kohlberg, L. (1981). *Essays in moral development.* San Francisco: Harper & Row.

Kornhauser, R. R. (1978). *Social sources of delinquency,* Chicago: University of Chicago Press.

Kuhn, T. S. (1962). *The structure of scientific revolutions.* Chicago: University of Chicago Press.

Lander, B. (1954). *Towards an understanding of juvenile delinquency.* New York: Columbia University Press.

Levy, L., & Herzog, A. (1974). Effects of population density and crowding on health and social adaptation in the Netherlands. *Journal of Health and Social Behavior, 15,* 228–240.

Maccoby, E. E., Johnson, J. P., & Church, R. M. (1958). Community integration and the social control of juvenile delinquency. *Journal of Social Issues, 3,* 38–51.

Merton, R. K. (1957). Social structure and anomie. In Merton, R. K. (Ed.), *Social Theory and Social Structure (rev. ed.).* Glencoe, Ill: Free Press. (Original work published 1949)

Miller, M. O., & Gold, M. (1984). Iatrogenesis in the juvenile justice system. *Youth and Society, 16,* 83–111.

Moore, J., Vigil, D., & Garcia, R. (1983). Residence and territoriality in Chicago gangs. *Social Problems, 31,* 182–194.

Moos, Rudolf H. (1976). *The human context,* New York: Wiley, 146–151.

Newman, O. (1972). *Defensible space.* New York: MacMillan.

Nye, F. I., Short, J. F., & Olson, V. J. (1958). Socioeconomic status and delinquent behavior. *American Journal of Sociology, 63,* 381–389.

Osborn, S. G. (1980). Moving home, leaving London and delinquent trends. *British Journal of Criminology, 20,* 54–61.

Park, R. E., & Burgess, E. W. (1925). *The city.* Chicago: University of Chicago Press.

Polk, K. (1957). Juvenile delinquency and social areas. *Social Problems, 5,* 214–217.

Polk, K. (1967). Urban social areas and delinquency. *Social Problems, 14,* 320–325.

Porterfield, A. L. (1943). Delinquency and its outcome in court and college. *American Journal of Sociology, 49,* 199–208.

Quinney, R. (1964). Crime, delinquency and social areas. *Journal of Research in Crime and Delinquency, 1,* 149–154.

Reiss, A. J., Jr., & Rhodes, A. L. (1961). The distribution of juvenile delinquency in the social class structure. *American Sociological Review, 26,* 730–732.

Robinson, W. S. (1950). Ecological correlations and the behavior of individuals. *American Sociological Review, 15,* 351–357.

Robison, S. M. (1972). *Can delinquency be measured?* New York: Columbia University Press. (Original work published 1936)

Roncek, D. W. (1979). *Blocks, tracts, and crimes: Methodological issues in analyzing urban crime patterns.* Paper presented at the annual meeting of the Society for the Study of Social Problems, Boston.

Rosen, L., & Turner, S. H. (1967). An evaluation of the Lander approach to ecology of delinquency. *Social Problems, 15,* 189–200.

Scheuerman, L. A., & Kobrin, S. (1981, August). *High risk delinquency neighborhoods and public housing projects.* Paper presented at the annual meeting of the Society for the Study of Social Problems, Toronto.

Shaw, C. R. (1930). *The jack-roller: A delinquent boy's own story.* Chicago: University of Chicago Press.

Shaw, C. R. (1931). *The natural history of a delinquent career.* Chicago: University of Chicago Press.

Shaw, C. R. & McKay, H. D. (1949). Rejoinder. *American Sociological Review, 14,* 614–617.

Shaw, C. R. & McKay, H. D. (1969). *Juvenile delinquency and urban areas* (rev. ed.). Chicago: University of Chicago Press. (Original work published 1942).

Shaw, C. R., McKay, H. D., & McDonald, J. F. (1938). *Brothers in crime.* Chicago: University of Chicago Press.

Shaw, C. R., Zorbaugh, F., McKay, H. D., & Cottrell, L. (1929). *Delinquency areas.* Chicago: University of Chicago Press.

Shevky, E., & Bell, W. (1955). *Social area analysis.* Stanford, California: Stanford University Press.

Short, J. F., Jr. (1969). Introduction to the revised edition of Shaw, C. R., & McKay, H. D. *Juvenile delinquency and urban areas.* Chicago: University of Chicago Press, xxv–liv.

Slosson, P. W. (1930). *The great crusade and after: 1914–1928.* New York: MacMillan.

Snodgrass, J., (1976). Clifford R. Shaw ad Henry D. McKay: Chicago criminologists. *British Journal of Ciminology, 16,* 1–19.

Snyderman, M., & Hernnstein, R. J. (1983). Intelligence tests and the Immigration Act of 1924. *American Psychologist, 38,* 986–995.

Srole, L. (1956). Social integration and certain corrolaries: An exploratory study. *American Sociological Review, 21,* 709.

Sutherland, E. H. (1939). *Principles of criminology.* Chicago: J. B. Lippincott.

Suttles, G. (1968). *Social order of the slum.* Chicago: University of Chicago Press.

Terry, R. M. (1967). The screening of juvenile offenders. *Journal of Criminal Law, Criminology, and Police Science, 58,* 173–181.

Thornberry, T. P. (1973). Race, socioeconomic status and sentencing in the juvenile justice system. *Journal of Criminal Law and Criminology, 64,*90–98.

Tittle, C. R., Villemez, W. J., & Smith, D. A. (1978). The myth of social class and criminality: an empirical assessment of the empirical evidence. *American Sociological Review, 43,* 643–656.

U.S. Census of Population, 1920. (1922). Washington, D.C.: U.S. Government Printing Office.

Wallis, C. P., & Maliphant, R. (1967). Delinquent areas in the county of London: Ecological factors. *British Journal of Criminology, 7,* 250–284.

West, D. & Farrington, D. W. (1977). *The delinquent way of life.* London: Heinemann.

Whyte, W. F. (1955). *Street corner society.* Chicago: University of Chicago Press.

Willie, C. V. (1967). The relative contribution of family status and economic status to juvenile delinquency. *Social Problems, 14,* 326–335.

AUTHOR NOTES

I want to thank Dr. Robert J. Bursik, Jr., of the University of Oklahoma, and Dr. D. Wayne Osgood, of Boystown, Nebraska, for their helpful comments on earlier drafts of this chapter.

CHAPTER 4

Intelligence

HERBERT C. QUAY

University of Miami

The notion that low intelligence may be a causative factor in crime and delinquency has a long history dating back to the very early work of Lombroso, as discussed in Chapter 1. The actual testing of the intelligence of delinquents began in 1912, when Goddard utilized his own translation of the early Binet scales. Much of the earlier work, especially that of Goddard (1921), made a great deal of a supposed relationship between mental deficiency and delinquency as causative. Studies from 1920 to 1926 generally reported mean IQs of delinquents to be 15 to 20 points below that of the general population (Caplan, 1965).

Since 1912 there have been hundreds of studies of the IQs of delinquents. As the IQ tests themselves improved and as the problem was approached with greater methodological sophistication (see the following section), the differences between the IQs of delinquents and nondelinquents began to shrink. However, systematic reviews (e.g., Caplan, 1965; Hirschi & Hindelang, 1977) have concluded that samples of delinquents generally have mean IQs of about 92; eight points (and, depending upon the test, about one-half a standard deviation) lower than the general population.

METHODOLOGICAL PROBLEMS

While Chapter 14 presents a detailed discussion of research problems in delinquency, some particular difficulties associated with establishing a relationship between intelligence and delinquency need brief discussion here. As we have seen in earlier chapters, adjudicated delinquents come more often from circumstances of lower socioeconomic status (SES). It is well known that lower SES is negatively correlated with intelligence (see Sattler, 1982, p. 54), so that selection of subjects who, whether delinquent or otherwise, are also of lower SES, will result in lower average IQ scores for that group. Thus, if delinquents are compared to nondelinquents and there is no control for SES, the delinquents may be expected to have lower IQ scores. There are, however, studies in which SES has been controlled and the negative relationship between intelligence and delinquency remains (see e.g., Hirschi, 1969; West, 1973; Reiss & Rhodes, 1961). In reviewing these studies, Wilson and Herrnstein (1985, p. 157) concluded that " . . . the evidence suggests that in direct comparisons of IQ and social class, IQ is generally more predictive of offending than social class or cultural backgrounds. . . . "In their summary of the data, Hirschi and Hindelang (1977, p. 576) asserted that "all in all, it seems reasonable to conclude on the basis of currently available data that IQ is related to official delinquency and, that, in fact, it is as important in predicting official delinquency as social class or race. We know of no current research findings contrary to this conclusion."

A recent study in Denmark deserves mention here. Moffitt, Gabrielli, Mednick, and Schulsinger (1981) found correlations of −.27, between both Full Scale and Verbal IQs on the Wechsler Intelligence Scale for Children (WISC), and number of offenses in a cohort of 129 males. When the effects of SES were partialled out, the correlations remained the same. In a second sample, and very large (n = 4552) cohort, the simple correlation between global IQ (using a Danish test for screening army recruits) was −.19 while the partial was −.17 (both highly significant given the sample size). It is also of interest that in the smaller sample who were administered the WISC, those who had no offenses had mean Full Scale IQs of 113, Verbal IQs of 110, and Performance IQs of 115. Among those with two or more offenses, the means were 102, 98, and 107. While both groups scored above the U.S. norms, the two or more offense group scored 11 points lower than the nonoffenders on Full Scale IQ and 12 points lower on Verbal IQ.

Potentially confounding factors other than SES have also been invoked in questioning the apparent relationship. It has been suggested that official delinquents are those more likely to be of lower IQ because they were not clever enough not to be apprehended. Evidence against this position is provided by data showing that self-reported delinquency is also negatively related to IQ (e.g., West & Farrington, 1977). There remains, however, the *possibility* that those who have difficulty reading the questionnaire due to low IQ may be more inclined to respond in the affirmative to items about delinquent acts that they have difficulty comprehending.

It has also been suggested that institutionalized delinquents may score lower due both to the fact that lower IQ may have entered into the decision to institutionalize them in the first place, and due in turn to the depressing effect of the institutional environment on intellectual functioning. Delinquents tested just prior to court appearance may be under stress; a situation which *can* depress performance on IQ tests.

These methodological issues, as well as others, are discussed in detail in Caplan (1965) and Wilson and Herrnstein (1985). They are not, nor are they ever likely to be, completely resolved. However, none of them seems powerful enough to explain the consistently obtained eight-point difference. At this juncture it seems reasonable to conclude that the difference is real and not due to any of the possible methodological or confounding factors that have been noted in the literature.

How does this IQ difference arise and what does it mean? We may try to answer these two related questions in a number of different ways. First, we may look at the nature of IQ tests themselves. Most individually administered intelligence tests contain two major components, Verbal and Performance. These two components of the total IQ score, while substantially positively related to one another, are not perfectly correlated. Thus, we may ask whether the difference between delinquents and nondelinquents is more likely to occur in the Verbal or the Performance area, or equally in both.

It is also the case that both the Verbal and Performance scores are themselves generally made up of scores from five to six narrower-band subscales. Therefore, it is possible that delinquents may differ from nondelinquents in the *pattern* of their (high versus low) scores on these subtests. The pattern question is more complex than the Verbal versus Performance one, as will be discussed in more detail as follows.

We need also seek the meaning of the lower global IQ scores, Verbal-Performance differences, or profile differences, by attempting to determine how each may translate into a propensity toward delinquency. The eight-point global IQ difference is clearly not so large as to result in frank mental retardation with a resultant seriously diminished capacity to know "right from wrong," or in uncontrolled behavior due to a total insensitivity to the likelihood of apprehension and punishment. We must, therefore, look for more subtle explanations of the link between IQ and delinquency.

VERBAL VERSUS PERFORMANCE INTELLIGENCE

Wechsler (1944), who designed the first intelligence test (the Wechsler-Bellevue) to provide both Verbal IQ (VIQ) and Performance IQ (PIQ) scores as well as a global or Full Scale IQ (FSIQ) score, was the first to suggest that antisocial adolescents had higher PIQs than VIQs. Subsequently, in their large scale study of 500 delinquents and 500 nondelinquents (matched for SES, race, age, anthropomorphic measurement *and* Wechsler Full Scale IQ scores) Glueck and Glueck (1950) found that while the PIQs were about the same for the two groups, the VIQ was slightly less for the delinquents (88.56 versus 92; about one-fourth of a standard deviation). However, Caplan (1965, pp. 110–111) argued that this difference was due to an imperfect match for FSIQ. Later studies of the Wechsler-Bellevue found both confirmatory results (e.g., Franklin, 1945; Altus & Clark, 1949), and either unconfirmatory results or differences too small to be considered (Foster, 1959; Sloan & Cutts, 1945; Strother, 1944).

The Wechsler-Bellevue, however, was to designed to be administered to individuals below age 16, and is therefore not valid for use with younger samples. The Wechsler Intelligence Scale for Children (WISC) was published in

1949 and the Wechsler Intelligence Scale for Children-Revised (WISC-R) in 1974. Both tests were constructed to have means of 100 and standard deviations of 15. These tests have supplanted most of the tests developed earlier for use with both children and adolescents.

The WISC-R covers an age range from 6–0 to 16–11 and is made up of 12 subtests. The Verbal Scale is comprised of six subtests: Information, Similarities, Arithmetic, Vocabulary, Comprehension, and Digit Span. The Performance Scale also contains six subtests: Picture Completion, Picture Arrangement, Block Design, Object Assembly, Coding, and Mazes. The test was standardized on a representative sample of the U.S. population. The FSIQs, VIQs, and PIQs are highly reliable, while the individual subtests have adequate, but less satisfactory reliabilities (Sattler, 1982, pp. 146–147).

When comparing the performance of one group to that of another with respect to differences between VIQ and PIQ, it is necessary to know beforehand what differences are obtained in the general population, what differences may be obtained by chance, and what factors may be associated with obtained differences.

Studies of the performance of normals (the substandardization sample) of both the WISC and WISC-R have appeared which are of great value in interpreting VIQ versus PIQ discrepancies of various sizes in delinquent samples. Seashore (1951), using the WISC standardization sample, found that 52 percent of that sample had VIQ-PIQ differences of eight points or less. Among the other 48 percent, half (24 percent) had VIQ>PIQ by more than eight points, while half had PIQ>VIQ by more than eight points. Thus, in a sample of delinquents, more than 24 percent would need to have PIQ>VIQ by more than eight points for there to be any discrepancy from normals.

Kaufman (1976a) has reported on the frequency of PIQ-VIQ discrepancies of various magnitudes for the WISC-R standardization sample. To be significant at the .05 level, the difference between VIQ and PIQ must be 12 points; for the .01 level the difference must be 15 points. In the WISC-R samples, one-third of all subjects had 12-point discrepancies while one-fourth had 15-point discrepancy. The mean discrepancy score was 9.7 and a VIQ>PIQ pattern was as frequent as the PIQ>VIQ pattern.

In his treatise on the use of the WISC-R, Kaufman (1979, p. 25) stated, "I consider 12 points to be a difference worthy of explanation." Of particular interest here was Kaufman's (1976a) finding that children of parents whose occupations fell into an unskilled category showed more PIQ>VIQ differences, while children of professional parents showed more of the reverse pattern.

Additional data have been provided by Taylor, Ziegler, and Parterio (1984) who obtained WISC-R scores on a stratified sample of 555 children almost equally divided among whites, blacks, and Hispanics. They reported an overall mean discrepancy of 10.74; the Hispanic discrepancy of 13.72 was significantly ($p = .01$) Greater than that for blacks (8.91) and whites (9.63). The directions of the discrepancy were similar for whites and blacks, where 49.7

percent and 51.1 percent respectively had PIQ > VIQ, but was significantly different for Hispanics, where 74.4 percent had PIQ > VIQ. The FSIQs were 112.36 for whites, 100.33 for Hispanics, and 96.17 for blacks; means elevated somewhat above the standardization samples (as reported by Sattler, 1982) to be 102 for white children and 86 for blacks.

In their early review, Prentice and Kelly (1963) found consistent patterns of PIQ > VIQ in studies of delinquents; however, they cautioned that this pattern could not be used as diagnostic of delinquency. Research done since their review has generally supported their conclusion.

Camp (1966) looked at PIQ-VIQ discrepancies on the WISC in both delinquent boys and girls, comparing the results for each group to Seashore's (1951) data noted previously. The pattern for delinquent girls was not significantly different from the normal pattern. The distribution for the delinquent boys, however, was significantly different from the normal pattern. Among delinquent boys, 42 percent had VIQs within eight points of their PIQs, as compared to 52 percent of the standardization sample. Of the remaining 58 percent only 12 percent had VIQ > PIQ, while 46 percent had PIQ > VIQ. As noted above, the standardization sample had a 50-50 split of the direction of the difference.

Ollendick (1979) compared the pattern of PIQ-VIQ discrepancies in a group of male delinquents to the pattern for discrepancies for the group of children whose parents were unskilled laborers as described by Kaufman (1976b). Among these children, Kaufman (1976b) had reported that 8 percent VIQ > PIQ by 15 points or more, and 13 percent had PIQ > VIQ by 15 points or more. Ollendick's delinquent sample had a mean PIQ of 90.2 and a mean VIQ of 81.7. Nearly 21 percent had discrepancies of 15 points or more. *All* of these discrepancies were in the direction of PIQ > VIQ. Ollendick concluded that, compared to normals, delinquents were characterized by a greater frequency of PIQ > VIQ and the absence of VIQ > PIQ.

Hubble and Groff (1981) also compared the distribution PIQ-VIQ discrepancies in white male delinquents to Kaufman's (1976a) report of discrepancies in the WISC-R standardization sample. As was found in Ollendick's (1979) study, although the magnitude of the discrepancies did not differ significantly, the direction of the discrepancies was significantly different for delinquents. Significant Verbal elevations were observed for only 9 percent of the delinquents, whereas the rate in the normal group was 19 percent. Significant Performance elevations were observed for 43 percent of the delinquents, while the rate in the normal group was 24 percent.

Most recently Grace and Sweeney (1986) reported that in their sample of 20 white and black delinquents, 35 percent had a PIQ > VIQ by 12 points or more on the WISC-R. For a similar sized sample tested with the WAIS-R, 28 percent showed such a difference.

Hubble and Groff (1980) also examined differences in psychometric performance between two groups of delinquents, one subsequently incarcerated and one subsequently placed on probation. No information was given on the nature of offenses for either group or on parental occupations of the sample. While no differences were found between the groups on VIQ or verbal subtests (VIQ means: 87.2 and 90.0 for incarceration and probation groups, respectively), PIQ differences were observed. PIQ was significantly higher for the group later released (90.5 versus 97.4). Block Design, Object Assembly, and Coding subtest means were significantly different for the two groups. The authors concluded that differences in nonverbal, rather than verbal abilities differentiate these groups of delinquents and that the two groups must be studied independently with respect to nonverbal abilities.

Henning and Levy (1967) and Hays and Smith (1980) reported larger PIQ-VIQ discrepancies for white relative to black delinquents. This result, however, may be a function of the fact that in both studies the FSIQs were lower for blacks, a finding consistent with Kaufman's (1976a) report of fewer discrepancies in groups with lower mean IQs.

Taking a slightly different perspective on Performance-Verbal discrepancies, Wolff, Waber, Bauermeister, Cohen, and Ferber (1982) made the case that, as a group, low SES male delinquents suffer from a pervasive language deficit relative to low SES male nondelinquents. Across psychometric linguistic tasks, low SES delinquents consistently performed more poorly than low SES normals, while no differences were observed on nonlinguistic tasks, suggesting that a severe and specific learning disability may characterize many low SES male delinquents. The authors nevertheless argued against any necessary relationship between poor language abilities and delinquency.

Two studies have tried to predict particular aspects of delinquent behavior from the size of the PIQ-VIQ discrepancy. Fernald and Wisser (1967) found a correlation of .17 between PIQ-VIQ score and degree of acting out (based on judges' ratings of court offenses). However, Tarter, Hegedus, Winsten, and Alterman (1985) found no relationship between the VIQ-PIQ differential and a self-rating of violent behavior. Haynes and Bensch (1981, 1983) found PIQ-VIQ more often in recidivists than in nonrecidivists (70 percent versus 42 percent for males; 83 percent versus 58 percent for females), but no relationship between the size of the PIQ-VIQ difference and recidivism.

Two studies have examined PIQ-VIQ discrepancies in subgroups of delinquents. Hecht and Jurkovic (1978) and Hubble and Groff (1982) divided groups of delinquents into subtypes of psychopathic, neurotic, and subcultural (see Chapter 5). Hecht and Jurkovic found that only the psychopathic group showed the PIQ-VIQ discrepancy, with a mean PIQ = 101.2 and mean VIQ = 81.4. However, the relative number of subjects in each subtype who had a higher PIQ than VIQ was not significantly different. Hubble and Groff found that psychopatic and neurotic groups showed the PIQ > VIQ discrepancy at significant levels; mean PIQs were 97.3 and 103.1, and mean VIQs were 91.7 and 97.6 for psychopathic and neurotic subjects, respectively. Like Hecht and Jurkovic, Hubble and Groff found no difference in the proportion of delinquents in each subgroup with significant PIQ > VIQ discrepancies. While the results of the two studies differ somewhat, with the neurotic subgroup showing significant discrepancies in only one study and the magnitude of the mean discrepancy for psychopathic delinquents differing (roughly 20 versus 6.5 points), the results indicate the value of differentiating delinquents according to behavioral subtypes in looking at cognitive performance.

It is important to note that most of these studies have reported mean VIQs for delinquent samples that are below the population (and nondelinquent) value. Prentice and Kelly (1963) reported a mean VIQ of 87.9 for all of the delinquent samples they reviewed, noting however that many contained substantial proportions of individuals not represented in the standardization samples of the tests used. More recent studies have reported mean VIQs of 81.7 (Ollendick, 1979; for lower SES institutionalized subjects), 92.5 (Andrew, 1974; for probationers), 81.4, 86.10, 90.86 (Hecht & Jurkovic, 1978; institutionalized, means for three behavioral subgroups respectively), 87.2 and 90.0 (Hubble & Groff, 1980), and 92.5 (Hubble and Groff, 1981), 83.4 and 76.5 (Grace & Sweeney, 1986; for whites and blacks, respectively), and 89.7 and 83.6 (Hunter & Kelly, 1986; for white and black institutionalized samples). While these means range from about 19 to about eight points below population values, most are about 10 to 12 points below expectations. This difference approaches a full standard deviation and indicates a greater disadvantage in the verbal area than in global IQ.

PATTERNS OF SUBTEST PERFORMANCE

A more fine-grained analysis of performance on IQ tests involves the pattern of scores earned on the various subtests making up the VIQ, PIQ, and FSIQ scores. Since, as was noted previously, the subtests are not as reliable as the FSIQ, VIQ or PIQ scores, differences will occur due solely to this unreliability Furthermore, some subscales are less reliable than others so that all comparisons cannot be judged by a single standard. According to Sattler (1982, p. 567), subtests must generally differ from one another by four scaled-score points to be reliably different at the .05 level. Feingold (1984) has also addressed this problem and has urged caution in interpreting profiles.

Ollendick (1979) compared subtest scatter in a sample of delinquents to the scatter reported for the laborer standardization sample (Kaufman, 1976b). He found that mean ranges for the scale scores were not significantly different, nor were the frequencies of individual subtest scores that deviated from each subject's mean different for the two groups.

Two studies have examined subtest performance as a potential predictor of aggressive behavior in delinquents or criminals. Kunce, Ryan, and Eckelman (1976) reported that performance on the Similarities subtest of the WAIS discriminated between violent and nonviolent groups. Using a ratio of the Similarities score to the total of all the subtests, the violent criminals had a mean ratio substantially lower than that of nonviolent criminals. Hays, Solway, and Schreiner (1978) were unable to replicate this finding, however, in a comparison of juvenile murderers and status offenders tested with the WISC. In fact, while the difference was not significant, the murderers had a slightly higher mean Similarities ratio. Hays et al. also reported that another study had failed to replicate the Similarities ratio prediction of violent crimes using the WAIS and concluded that the Similarities ratio was not a valid index of violent criminal behavior.

Groff and Hubble (1981) used a categorization system for the WISC-R devised by Bannatyne (1974) to compare the performance of 193 male delinquents to the performance of a group of learning disabled (LD) children reported by Smith, Coleman, Dokecki, and Davis (1977). Categories in the system are Spatial, Conceptual, Sequential, and Acquired Knowledge. Smith et al. had concluded that LD children show a unique pattern, with Spatial skills elevated relative to all others. Groff and Hubble found a similar pattern (elevated Spatial skills) in the sample of delinquents and concluded that the pattern is not diagnostically useful.

As has been the case in studies of other types of behaviorally deviant children, profile analysis of subtest scores has not been revealing with respect to subaspects of the intellectual functioning of delinquents.

The results of these more recent studies lead to a number of conclusions: (1) that while the magnitude of VIQ-PIQ discrepancies may not always be significant, the direction of PIQ > VIQ is about universal; (2) in most samples, neither the magnitude nor the frequency of PIQ > VIQ is so large as to be diagnostic of delinquency in individual cases; (3) when delinquents are subdivided on the basis of behavioral characteristics (see Chapter 5), the more aggressive, psychopathic individuals are more likely to show the largest PIQ > VIQ (from six to 20 IQ points); (4) the mean VIQ differs from standardization sample values by 10 to 12 points.

It now seems clear that the frequently obtained eight-point discrepancy is due to the less adequate performance of delinquents on tests involving verbal skills, including word knowledge, verbally coded information, and verbal reasoning. In fact, on these sorts of tests, delinquents, especially the more aggressive, perform at levels close to one standard deviation below nondelinquents.

The Role of Intellectual Abilities in Delinquency

Based on the evidence that we and others have reviewed, it appears that a major proportion, perhaps two-thirds, of delinquents are deficient (when compared to the general population) in verbal abilities as these are measured by standardized intelligence tests, most often the WISC and WISC-R. How is this diminished verbal ability related to delinquency? As we noted earlier, there are a number of possibilities.

Hirschi and Hindelang (1977) argued that the mechanism lies in performance in and attitudes toward school, since "as of now, there is no evidence that IQ had a direct impact on delinquency" (p. 585). While they do not themselves develop their argument for the school performance-attitude relationship, they apparently believe that low IQ leads to poor school performance, which leads to a negative attitude toward school, which in turn leads to delinquency. While there is little doubt that most adjudicated delinquents are academically retarded and possess negative attitudes about school, the direction of effect has not been well established. In fact, some studies (e.g., McMichael, 1979; see also Chapter 12) have suggested that antisocial behavior *precedes* school failure (see also, Menard & Moore, 1984 for an argument that schools react differently to children of differing IQs).

Rutter and Giller (1984, p. 165) have made an important point in noting that lower IQ is associated with troublesome behavior in the early years; as young as age three in one study (Richman, Stevenson, & Graham, 1982). Thus, lower IQ would seem related to a more general disturbance of conduct rather than to legally defined delinquency per se. There is additional evidence for this association, especially with respect to Verbal IQ (e.g., Richman & Lindgren, 1981).

Wilson and Herrnstein (1985) have also pinpointed "the intellectual deficit of the average offender as primarily verbal" (p. 164) but noted, as did we earlier in this chapter, that since verbal tests and performance tests are substantially correlated, "no sharp line can be drawn between verbal and nonverbal intelligence" (p. 164). In their discussion of how intelligence affects crime, they suggested that "low intelligence will favor impulsive crimes with immediate rewards and high intelligence, the inverse" (p. 167). They have also noted that IQ may be related to the opportunity to commit crime with low IQ criminals unlikely to be able to embezzle, counterfeit, or commit an elaborate fraud. Recognizing the difficulty of applying this hypothesis to delinquents, especially younger ones, they have listed other IQ-related factors such as school failure, limited future time perspective, lower level of moral reasoning, (see Chapter 6) and shallowness of disapprobation for bad conduct.

As Rutter and Giller (1984, p. 168) have pointed out, there is no single explanation for the IQ-conduct disturbance association. They have suggested that the major link may lie in the temperamental features which predispose to both educational failure and antisocial behavior.

We suggest that lower intelligence is one of many factors which may put a child at a disadvantage with respect to success in interacting in a variety of situations which all children face in the process of development. In the early years lower IQ may make a child more vulnerable to poor parenting and, in fact, even interact with a predisposed parent to make poor parenting more likely (see Chapter 8). Such an interaction would be all the more likely were the IQ deficit to be accompanied by a fussy or difficult temperament, motor overactivity, and poor inhibitory control (see Chapter 5). The result of all these forces can be the early onset of troublesome behavior. The affected child is now at a double disadvantage when he does enter school; he has both less intellectual ability, particularly in the verbal sphere, to cope with academic tasks, and he has oppositional and aggressive behavior problems that are alienating to teachers and peers. As development proceeds, both are, in combination, likely to lead to school failure, the results of which, in turn, reinforce more conduct-disordered behavior. At the same time, those higher order cognitive functions (e.g., verbal self-regulation, social problem-solving, moral judgment discussed in Chapter 6) fail to develop adequately. This is likely due both to the limited intellectual capacity and to the mutually nonreinforcing social interactions that now characterize the child's relations with others. All of these factors, and others as well (e.g., deviant parental and peer models) interact to produce behavior which is legally proscribed.

At the conclusion of his 1965 review, Caplan called for a redefinition of the problem and for the use of new investigative techniques. In recommending the study of higher order cognitive functioning, he was clearly foresighted. We have suggested elsewhere (Hogan & Quay, 1984) and reiterate here that poor verbal skills are likely to underlie such higher order "personality-cognitive" functions as interpersonal problem solving, perspective taking, person-perception, and moral reasoning. These higher order cognitive abilities are discussed in detail in Chapter 6.

REFERENCES

Altus, W. D., & Clark H. J. (1949). Subtest variation on the Wechsler-Bellevue for two institutionalized behavior problem groups. *Journal of Consulting Psychology, 13,* 444–447.

Andrew, J. M. (1974). Delinquency. The Wechsler P > V sign, and the I-level system. *Journal of Clinical Psychology, 30,* 33–334.

Bannatyne, A. (1974). Diagnosis: A note on recategorization of the WISC scaled scores. *Journal of Learning Disabilities, 7,* 272–273.

Camp, B. W. (1966). WISC performance in acting-out and delinquent children with and without EEG abnormality. *Journal of Consulting Psychology, 30,* 350–353.

Caplan, N. S. (1965). Intellectual functioning. In H. C. Quay (Ed.), *Juvenile delinquency: Theory and research.* Princeton: van Nostrand.

Fiengold, A. (1984). The reliability of score difference on the WAIS, WISC-R and WAIS-R. *Journal of Clinical Psychology, 40,* 1060–1063.

Fernald, P. S., & Wisser, R. E. (1967). Using WISC Verbal-Performance discrepancies to predict degree of acting out. *Journal of Clinical Psychology, 23,* 92–93.

Foster, A. L. (1959). A note concerning the intelligence of delinquents. *Journal of Clinical Psychology, 15,* 78–79.

Franklin, J. C. (1945). Discriminative value and patterns of the Wechsler-Bellevue Scales in the examination of delinquent negro boys. *Educational and Psychological Measurement, 5,* 71–85.

Glueck, S., & Glueck, E. T. (1950). *Unraveling juvenile delinquency.* New York: Commonwealth Fund.

Goddard, H. H. (1921). *Juvenile delinquency.* New York: Dodd, Mead.

Grace, W. C., & Sweeney, M. E. (1986). Comparison of the P > V sign on the WISC-R and WAIS-R in delinquent males. *Journal of Clinical Psychology, 42,* 173–176.

Haynes, J. P., & Bensch, M. (1981). The P > V sign on the WISC-R and recidivism in delinquents. *Journal of Consulting and Clinical Psychology, 49,* 480–481.

Haynes, J. P., & Bensch, M. (1983). Female delinquent recidivism and the P > V sign on the WISC-R. *Journal of Clinical Psychology, 39,* 141–144.

Hays, J. R., & Smith, A. L. (1980). Comparison of the WISC-R and culture-fair intelligence tests for three ethnic groups of juvenile delinquents. *Psychological Reports, 46,* 931–934.

Hays, J. R., Solway, K. S., & Schreiner, D. (1978). Intellectual characteristics of juvenile murderers versus status offenders. *Psychological Reports, 43,* 80–82.

Hecht, I. H., & Jurkovic, G. J. (1978). The Performance-Verbal discrepancy in differentiated subgroups of delinquent adolescent boys. *Journal of Youth and Adolescence, 7,* 197–201.

Henning, J. J., & Levy, R. H. (1967). Verbal-Performance IQ differences of white and negro delinquents on the WISC and WAIS. *Journal of Clinical Psychology, 23,* 457–463.

Hirschi, T. (1969). *Causes of delinquency.* Berkeley, CA: University of California Press.

Hirschi, T., & Hindelang, M. J. (1977). Intelligence and delinquency: A revisionist review. *American Sociological Review, 42,* 571–587.

Hogan, A. E., & Quay, H. C. (1984). Cognition in child and adolescent behavior disorders. In B. B. Lahey & A. E. Kazdin (Eds.), *Advances in Clinical Child Psychology* (pp. 1–34). New York: Plenum Press.

Hubble, L. M., & Groff, M. (1980). WISC-R profiles of adjudicated delinquents later incarcerated or released on probation. *Psychological Reports, 47,* 482–482.

Hubble, L. M., & Groff, M. (1981). Magnitude and direction of WISC-R Verbal-Performance IQ discrepancies among adjudicated male delinquents. *Journal of Youth and Adolescence, 10,* 179–184.

Hubble, L. M., & Groff, M. (1982). WISC-R Verbal Performance IQ discrepancies among Quay-classified adolescent male delinquents. *Journal of Youth and Adolescence, 11,* 503–508.

Kaufman, A. S. (1976a). Verbal performance IQ discrepancies on the WISC-R. *Journal of Consulting and Clinical Psychology, 44,* 739–744.

Kaufman, A. S. (1976b). A new approach to the interpretation of test scatter on the WISC-R. *Journal of Learning Disabilities, 9,* 33–41.

Kaufman, A. S. (1979). *Intelligent testing with the WISC-R.* New York: Wiley.

Kunce, J. T., Ryan, J. J., & Eckelman, C. C. (1976). Violent behavior and differential WAIS characteristics. *Journal of Consulting and Clinical Psychology, 44,* 42–45.

McMichael, P. (1979). 'The hen or the egg' which comes first—antisocial emotional disorders or reading ability? *British Journal of Educational Psychology, 49,* 226–238.

Menard, S., & Moore, B. J. (1984). A structuralist critique of the IQ-delinquency hypothesis: Theory and evidence. *American Journal of Sociology, 89,* 1347–1378.

Moffitt, T. E., Gabrielli, W. F., Mednick, S. A., & Schulsinger, F. (1981). Socioeconomic status, IQ and delinquency. *Journal of Abnormal Psychology, 90,* 152–157.

Ollendick, T. H. (1979). Discrepancies between verbal and performance IQs and subtest scatter on the WISC-R for juvenile delinquents. *Psychological Reports, 45,* 563–568.

Prentice, N. M., & Kelly, F. J. (1963). Intelligence and delinquency: A reconsideration. *Journal of Social Psychology, 60,* 327–337.

Reiss, A. J., & Rhodes, A. C. (1961). The distribution of juvenile delinquency in the social class structure. *American Sociological Review, 26,* 720–732.

Richman, L. C., & Lindgren, S. D. (1981). Verbal mediation deficits: Relation to behavior and achievement in children. *Journal of Abnormal Psychology, 90,* 99–104.

Richman, N., Stevenson, J., & Graham, P. J. (1982). *Pre-school to school: A behavioural study.* London: Academic Press.

Rutter, M., & Giller, H. (1984). *Juvenile delinquency: Trends and perspectives.* New York: Guilford.

Sattler, J. M. (1982). *Assessment of children's intelligence and special abilities* (2nd ed.). Boston: Allyn & Bacon.

Seashore, H. G. (1951). Differences between the verbal and performance IQ on the WISC. *Journal of Consulting Psychology, 15,* 62–67.

Sloan, W., & Cutts, R. A. (1945). Test patterns for defective delinquents on the Wechsler-Bellevue test. *American Journal of Mental Deficiency, 50,* 95–97.

Smith, M. D., Coleman, J. M., Dokecki, P. R., & Davis, E. E. (1977). Intellectual characteristics of school labeled learning disabled children. *Journal of Learning Disabilities, 10,* 352–357.

Strother, C. R. (1944). The performance of psychopaths on the Wechsler-Bellevue test. *Proceedings of the Iowa Academy of Sciences, 51,* 397–400.

Tarter, R. E., Hegedus, A. M., Winsten, N. E., & Alterman, A. I. (1985). *Journal of Psychology, 119,* 125–128.

Taylor, R. L., Ziegler, E. W., & Parterio, I. (1984). An investigation of WISC-R Verbal-Performance difference as a function of ethnic status. *Psychology in the Schools, 21,* 437–441.

Wechsler, D. (1944). *The measurement of adult intelligence.* Baltimore: Williams & Wilkins.

Wechsler, D. (1949). *Manual for the Wechsler Intelligence Scale for Children.* New York: Psychological Corporation.

Wechsler, D. (1974). *Manual for the Wechsler Intelligence Scale for Children-Revised.* New York: Psychological Corporation.

West, D. J. (1973). *Who becomes delinquent.* London: Heinemann.

West, D. J. & Farrington, D. P. (1977). *The delinquent way of life.* London: Heinemann Educational.

Wilson, J. Q., & Herrnstein, R. J. (1985). *Crime and human nature.* New York: Simon & Schuster.

Wolff, P. H, Waber, D., Bauermeister, M., Cohen C., & Ferber, R. (1982). The neurophysiological status of adolescent delinquent boys. *Journal of Child Psychology and Psychiatry, 23,* 267–279.

CHAPTER 5

Patterns of Delinquent Behavior

HERBERT C. QUAY

University of Miami

As has been pointed out earlier in this book (see Chapter 1), juvenile delinquency is a legal construct. Thus, the label "delinquent" cannot automatically be considered to carry with it any information about the behavior of the individual beyond their having committed some act(s) which have violated the law. Put another way, since delinquency is not a psychological construct (such as is "extravert," "anxious personality," or "conduct disorder"), the label does *not* imply that those who carry it are behaviorally or psychologically homogeneous.

However, the assumption that all delinquents exhibit some common set of psychological characteristics has been the basis for most of the early research into the psychological characteristics of delinquents (see Quay, 1965) and, unfortunately, remains so (see Chapter 6). If, in fact, delinquent youth are behaviorally and psychologically heterogeneous, the search for single psychological variables that can reliably separate delinquents from nondelinquents is not an effective research strategy. Neither will the search for the causes of or cures for delinquency which proceed on this assumption be effective. Searching for *the* cause of or *the* cure for delinquency is much like searching for *the* cause of and *the* cure for fever. Clearly, fever is caused by many different infections and these different infections are susceptible to different interventions. As Gibbons (1970), p. 93) so aptly put it " . . . nearly all would agree that there must be something radically different about gang delinquents, sex offenders, petty 'hidden' offenders, juvenile arsonists, hyper-aggressive delinquents, and the other lawbreakers who are lumped together under the term 'delinquent.' It does not make much sense to collect such a diverse bunch of youths and to compare them with other 'nondelinquents,' in the search for etiological variables."

An alternative approach is to consider each delinquent as an individual who shares few, if any, psychological attributes with others who have committed delinquent acts. While there is little doubt that every delinquent (and every person, for that matter) is in some ways unique, adopting this idiographic point of view would make scientific inquiry next to impossible. The third alternative is to assume that among those who are legally delinquent there may be a reasonable number of identifiable subgroups who are homogeneous with respect to some relevant subset of behavioral and psychological characteristics. This is a much more attractive possibility since it avoids the erroneous assumption of overall homogeneity while focusing research on a manageable number of subgroups rather than on an endless number of individuals.

The potential utility of reliable separation of delinquents into behaviorally homogeneous subgroups is multifaceted. Were there, in fact, to be a reasonably small number of subgroups, attempts to find (differential) correlates, etiologies, treatments, and outcomes for delinquency could be more directed. Were these subgroups to be behaviorally and psychologically equivalent, or nearly so, to those subgroups found among other deviant, but not necessarily legally delinquent, youth, the findings of a vast literature on child and adolescent psychopathology could be brought to bear on the problem of delinquency. Furthermore, a common descriptive framework would facilitate communication and, hopefully, cooperation, among those various societal agencies who have all been assigned some responsibility for reducing and preventing delinquency. The juvenile justice system, the mental health system, and the educational system could more easily see that each is dealing with the same basic patterns of behavioral deviance with or without involvement in legally defined delinquency.

Both theory and empirical research concerning subtypes of delinquents and delinquent behavior (offenses) have reasonably long histories. Offense typologies, whether derived either empirically (e.g., Quay & Blumen, 1963) or theoretically (e.g., Gibbons, 1965) have not systematically been related to causes or consequences (see Klein, 1984, for a review), and will not be considered further.

The development of subgroups based on behavior and/or personality characteristics (the latter are usually less easily observed and assessed) have been much more often the focus of research. As we shall see, some of these subgroups have proven to be *differentially* relevant to correlates, causative factors, interventions, and outcomes. As interventions based on homogeneous subgrouping are discussed in Chapter 9, the focus here will be on the empirical development of subgroups and on the research which has related these subgroups to behavioral and biological correlates, and to both short- and longer-term outcome.

THE DEVELOPMENT OF DELINQUENT SUBGROUPS

Empirical research dates from the 1940s (Hewitt & Jenkins, 1946; Jenkins & Glickman, 1947). These early studies provided a foundation upon which later research, utilizing analytic methods not then available, has built to extend and refine subgroup identification and assessment.

Concomitant with empirical research utilizing multivariate statistical techniques, typologies of delinquents were also being developed which were theory-driven (see Reiss, 1952; Hunt & Hardt, 1965; Sullivan, Grant, & Grant, 1957; Warren, 1969). While these typologies have provided a basis for research, especially of differential treatment (see Chapter 9), they have not been systematically extended into other populations of behaviorally deviant youth, nor have their correlates been extensively studied. While a detailed discussion of the derivation of these clinical-theoretical typologies will not be attempted, we will, later in this chapter, provide a cross-walk between the major subtypes derived from theory and clinical observation and those arising out of multivariate statistical analysis.

A discussion of the nature of and requisites for a behavioral taxonomy or classification system is also beyond the scope of this chapter and the reader is referred to Blashfield (1984), Megargee and Bohn (1979) and Quay (1986a) for more detailed discussion. We do note, however, that if subtypes are to be useful they must be reliably observable, discriminable from one another, reasonably frequently found among delinquents, and related in different ways to variables relevant to causes, treatments, and consequences.

MULTIVARIATE STATISTICAL STUDIES

In the vast majority of instances, multivariate statistical inquiries have utilized similar analytic techniques with methodological variations occurring mainly in the nature of the data analyzed. The usual approach has been first to identify samples of delinquents, usually institutionalized or at least adjudicated, so as to rule the occasional or accidental delinquent out of the sample. Data are usually obtained about overt behavior, personality characteristics, attitudes, and values. Sources of this information have most frequently been ratings of behavior, social histories, and the responses of the delinquents themselves to self-report questionnaires.

The most frequently used statistical technique has been factor analysis. While there are many different factor analytic methods which differ in their mathematical assumptions and algorithms, they all utilize the obtained intercorrelations among all of the variables being studied. The aim of factor analysis is to explain (in the statistical sense of accounting for the variance of the matrix of obtained intercorrelations) the interrelationships among all the variables by the derivation of a more limited number of factors or underlying dimensions. The method makes it possible to determine the degree of relationship between each of the variables and each of the derived dimensions. It is these relationships (expressed as factor loadings) which give meaning to the underlying dimensions and allow their interpretation in psychological terms.

While both the nature of the data and the techniques of factor analysis have varied, the vast majority of factor analytic studies have identified three to four major underlying dimensions. Summarizing and reviewing this body of research would be much easier had the various studies all used the same labels to describe their obtained factors. Not only have different researchers used different labels, the same workers have used different labels for similar factors arising in different studies; a charge to which the author of this chapter must plead guilty. Thus, "matching" factors obtained in different studies must be based more on a conceptual analysis of the variables associated with the obtained factors than on the label assigned by the researcher.

The labels used in this chapter are those which we hope will best convey the meaning of the dimensions as found among the legally delinquent, but at the same time tie this body of research to a much larger number of similar type studies done with behaviorally deviant (but not necessarily delinquent) children and adolescents.

Undersocialized Aggression

This dimension, originally labeled "Unsocialized Aggressive" by Hewitt and Jenkins (1946) and Jenkins and Glickman (1947) is ubiquitous. It has also been labeled "Psychopathic" (e.g., Quay, 1964a, 1964b, 1966) and, in the naive hope to avoid pejorative connotations, "Behavior Category III" (Quay & Parsons, 1971). An illustrative list of characteristics associated with this pattern, taken from behavior ratings and case history analyses, is presented in Table 5.1. As can be seen, these characteristics involve overt aggression, negativism, and a lack of concern for others. Undersocialized Aggression has also emerged prominently in analyses of other groups of children and adolescents, including those hospitalized for behavior disorders, those in public school classes for the emotionally disturbed, and clients of mental health clinics (see Quay, 1986a for a detailed review).

It seems obvious that the youth whose behavior typifies this dimension is likely to be at odds with everyone in the environment, and most particularly with those who must interact with him on a daily basis to raise, educate, or otherwise control him. As we shall see in subsequent sections of this chapter,

TABLE 5.1.   Illustrative Characteristics of Undersocialized Aggression, Socialized Aggression, Attention Deficit, and Anxiety-Withdrawal-Dysphoria

Undersocialized	Socialized	Attention Deficit	Anxiety-Withdrawal-Dysphoria
Assaultive	Bad companions	Preoccupied	Hypersensitive
Disobedient	Group stealing	Short attention span	Shy
Destructive	Loyal to delinquent friends	Daydreams	Socially withdrawn
Untrustworthy	Truant	Sluggish	Anxious
Boisterous	Stays out late at night	Impulsive	Sad

this pattern is the most troublesome to society, seems least amenable to change, and has the most pessimistic prognosis for adult adjustment.

Socialized Aggression

A second pattern, also identified early on, similarly involves "externalizing" (Achenbach, 1966) deviant behavior, but involves behavior of a less overtly aggressive and less interpersonally alienated nature (see Table 5.1). In fact, good peer relations in the context of stealing, truancy, and likely drug use (see Loeber & Schmaling, 1985b) are at the core of this pattern (see Hewitt & Jenkins, 1946; Quay, 1964b, 1966; Peterson, Quay & Cameron, 1959). This pattern has also been identified in deviant, but not necessarily officially delinquent, groups (e.g., Brady, 1970; Loeber & Schmaling, 1985a; Quay, 1986a). This pattern has been variously labeled "Socialized Delinquent," "Subcultural Delinquent," "Stealers," and "Behavior Category IV."

This pattern seems clearly to reflect gang delinquency, the focus of so much concern in the 1950s and 1960s. It is tempting to assume that the characteristics it subsumes are a "natural" outgrowth of an inner-city environment which abounds in opportunities for delinquency and reinforces them when they occur. While this remains an assumption, it will be clear from following sections of this chapter (and from Chapter 6), that there is little, if any, reason to ascribe psychopathology to those youth manifesting this pattern. While Socialized Aggression may represent deviance when viewed from the perspective of the criminal justice system (or the schools), it may well represent an adjustive response to the environmental circumstances in which it is most likely to be found (see, e.g., Jenkins, 1955).

Attention Deficit

This dimension (see Table 5.1) was not identified in the earliest research (e.g., Hewitt & Jenkins, 1946) but emerged in later studies (Quay, 1964a, 1966) where it was labeled "Immaturity." It, too, has since been found in studies of nondelinquent but otherwise deviant children, where it has also received a variety of labels (again, see Quay, 1986a for a review). The present label of "Attention Deficit" reflects the centrality of problems in focusing and sustaining attention and in coming to grips with task demands. This pattern, previously labeled "Hyperactivity" in the literature on childhood psychopathology, has been the object of extensive research over the last 15 years (see Campbell & Werry, 1986, for a recent review).

The relationship of the characteristics subsumed by this dimension to delinquency are less obvious than those of Undersocialized or Socialized Aggression, and those manifesting them do not seem to fit the stereotype of the juvenile delinquent. As will be discussed later in this chapter, the cognitive and social-behavioral correlates of this pattern seem to make those representative of it susceptible to environmental influences (particularly interpersonal ones) that can and do, given the right circumstances, lead to official delinquency.

Anxiety-Withdrawal-Dysphoria

This cluster (see Table 5.1) was also identified in early work and was labeled "overinhibited" by Hewitt and Jenkins (1946). It has since emerged in the vast majority of studies of deviant children. The "internalizing" (Achenbach, 1966) nature of its principal elements stands in contrast to the previously described patterns. The common perception of a juvenile delinquent does not often encompass anxiety, social withdrawal, and dysphoria. Yet, as we shall see, all of the various approaches to the subcategorization of delinquents include this pattern. Considering that anxiety has a long-standing place in psychology as a motivator of behavior, it is not difficult to see how acts considered delinquent (e.g., chronic truancy from school and home, car theft) could be motivated by a felt need to escape or avoid situations giving rise to subjectively experienced distress.

PREVALENCE OF EMPIRICALLY DERIVED SUBGROUPS

Up to this point we have glossed over the differences between dimensions of behavior and subgroups of delinquents. What the multivariate studies have actually produced are dimensions or patterns of behavior or personality characteristics which are statistically interrelated. Each individual, delinquent or not, has a place on each of these dimensions and that place can be determined only by assessing the degree to which the individual manifests the characteristics subsumed by the dimensions. This assessment can, in fact, be done in various ways, including the use of behavior ratings, analyses of life histories, and self-report instruments. A frequently used battery employs all three techniques and sums the scores to obtain a categorical placement (Quay & Parsons, 1971; see also Chapter 6). Most recently, the original behavior rating scale utilized in the battery has been revised so that it now measures all four dimensions (Quay, 1983; Quay & Peterson, 1983).There are also other well-researched rating scales which measure these dimensions, although sometimes under different names (e.g., Achenbach & Edelbrock, 1983).

What data there are on the prevalence of the four subgroups comes from institutionalized samples. Cavior and Schmidt (1978) provided data on the relative frequency of the four subgroups among inmates in two different federal correctional institutions who had been classified according to the procedures provided in Quay and Parsons (1971). In a sample of 402 males in an "open" (no perimeter fence) institution where the population averaged 17.8 years, the Undersocialized Aggressive group comprised 14 percent, the Socialized Aggressive group 28 percent, the Attention Deficit group 30 percent, and the Anxious group 28 percent. In a sample of 488 somewhat older youths (mean age of 19.8) in a more secure institution, there were 33 percent Under-socialized, 29 percent Socialized, 16 percent Attention Deficit, and 22 percent Anxious (see Cavior & Schmidt, 1978, Table 1, page 136, where the labels are BC-3, BC-4, BC-1, and BC-2, respectively. The calculations of the percentages provided above are mine.)

As part of a survey of two state institutions in Florida, the writer classified a total of 281 males into one of the four subgroups also using the procedures outlined in Quay and Parsons (1971). In this sample, 28 percent were Under-socialized Aggressive, 29 percent were Socialized Aggressive, 25 percent were Attention Deficit, and 18 percent were Anxious.

As can be seen from these data, the two Aggressive subgroups combined account for between 42 and 62 percent of the institutional populations. It is perhaps surprising that the two subgroups where aggressive behavior is not a central feature account for 38 to 58 percent of the population. These figures clearly illustrate that overt aggression is quite frequently *not* the primary be-havior problem of legally delinquent youth—even those incarcerated in federal and state correctional institutions.

We will return to a more detailed consideration of these four patterns in terms of their validity and/or utility later in this chapter. We note here, how-ever, the considerable conceptual similarity between the Undersocialized, the Attention Deficit, and Anxious-Withdrawn-Dysphoric patterns to those di-mensions found in extensive multivariate statistical studies of adult offenders (see Quay, 1984). We turn now to a brief discussion of subgroups which have arisen out of clinical-theoretical approaches.

CLINICAL-THEORETICAL APPROACHES
TO DELINQUENT SUBTYPES

While, as already noted, there have been a number of taxonomies proposed, the only clinical-theoretical system that has been the focus of any considerable degree of empirical research and has served as a basis for intervention research (see Chapter 10) is the California I-level System. This approach was concep-tualized out of a theoretical position in regard to stages of personality devel-opment, and was subsequently elaborated upon by extensive clinical obser-vation of delinquents (see Sullivan, Grant, & Grant, 1957; Warren, 1969; Palmer, 1974). The approach is phenomenological in that it recognizes among delinquents three commonly occuring levels of interpersonal maturity that are based upon the manner in which the individual delinquent perceives the world and those within it. Within these three maturity levels the system recognizes nine mutually exclusive delinquent subtypes. The subtypes occurring at the most prevalent maturity levels (II, III, and IV) and their principal reaction patterns are set out in Table 5.2. Although nine subtypes are differentiated, according to data provided by Warren (1969) and Jesness and DeRisi (1971),

TABLE 5.2. Brief Description of the Nine Delinquent Subtypes of the California I-Level System (after Warren, 1969)

Maturity Level 2
  Asocial, Aggressive
    Responds with active demands and open hostility when frustrated
  Asocial, Passive
    Responds with whining, complaining, and withdrawal when frustrated
Maturity Level 3
  Immature Conformist
    Responds with immediate compliance to whomever seems to have the power at the moment
  Cultural Conformist
    Responds with conformity to a specific reference group of delinquent peers
  Manipulator
    Operates by attempting to undermine the power of authority figures and/or usurp the power role for himself
  Neurotic, Acting-out
    Responds to underlying guilt with attempts to "outrun" or avoid conscious anxiety and condemnation of self
  Neurotic, Anxious
    Responds with symptoms of emotional disturbance to conflict produced by feelings of inadequacy and guilt
  Situational Emotional Reaction
    Responds to immediate family or personal crisis by acting-out
  Cultural Identifier
    Responds to identification with a deviant value system by living out his delinquent beliefs

the two Neurotic subtypes, the Immature Conformist, the Cultural Conformist, and the Manipulator comprise about 85 percent of the delinquent population.

More recently, however, on the basis of present extensive research on differential treatment (see Chapter 9), Palmer has suggested considering only three "wider-band" subtypes: the "Passive Conformist," the "Power-Oriented" and the "Neurotic" as, according to Palmer (1974; p. 4), these groups account for 14, 21, and 53 percent (total of 88 percent), respectively, of large samples of delinquents with whom he has worked. According to Palmer, the Passive Conformist encompasses the original subtype of Immature Conformist, while the Power-Oriented group is made up of the Cultural Conformists and the Manipulators. The Neurotic group subsumes both the original neurotic subtypes: the Neurotic Acting-Out and the Neurotic-Anxious.

Reducing nine subtypes to three makes comparison with the four statistically derived patterns a much easier task. The descriptions provided by Palmer (1974, p. 12; see Table 5.3) suggest that the Undersocialized and Socialized-Aggressive group might be combined to form the Power-oriented group, the Anxious-Withdrawn-Dysphoric subgroup seems akin to the Neurotic group and that the Attention Deficit Subgroup may match the Passive Conformist subgroup.

TABLE 5.3. Brief Description of the Three Delinquent Subtypes Suggested by Palmer (1974)

Power-Oriented

Thinks of self as delinquent and tough
Will "go along" with the gang to achieve status and acceptance
Attempts to undermine authority
Does not wish to conform to peers or adults

Passive Conformist

Fears, and responds with compliance to peers and adults
Expects to be rejected
Sees self as lacking in social "know-how"

Neurotic

Chronic or intense depression
Feelings of failure, inadequacy and guilt
May deny own feelings and attack others

It must be recognized that equivalence of the subtypes in the different approaches can really only be determined empirically by comparing the classifications obtained on the same sample by the two approaches. There have been no successful attempts to do so that are known to us. We note here that while Palmer has greatly simplified a complex system, the blurring of the distinction between the Undersocialized and Socialized Aggressive subgroups obscures some very important differences relevant to both etiology, treatment, and prognosis to be discussed later in this chapter.

The most widely used clinically derived classification system, which, is, of course, not at all specific to delinquents, is the *Diagnostic and Statistical Manual of Mental Disorders, Third Edition* (DSM-III, American Psychiatric Association, 1980). This system, already under revision, contains many more categories which are applicable to children and adolescents than have been identified in multivariate statistical research, but it does have counterparts to the four patterns described earlier (for a review and critique, see Quay, 1986a, 1986c). The general comparability between some of the major disorders in this taxonomy and those subgroups described earlier highlights the commonality between patterns of behavior among delinquents and those found in children defined as deviant by the mental health and educational systems.

THE UTILITY OF THE FOUR PATTERNS

No matter how often they appear and no matter how reliably they may be identified, the utility of any set of proposed subgroups must be addressed in additional research. This research should seek to enhance and expand the psychological meaning of the dimensions or subgroups by relating them to other variables with which they might be expected to relate (or *not* relate as the case may be). This is a process of establishing construct validity.

While all four patterns are clearly related to official delinquency, the nature of their behavioral and psychological constituents suggests that different factors are likely to give rise to them; that is, the etiologies of the four dimensions are likely to be different. Furthermore, different sorts of programs for both prevention and treatment would seem to be required. Finally, outcome in terms of later adjustment would seem to be different. What follows is a discussion of research which has investigated the psychosocial and biological correlates and the outcome of the four patterns. Treatment considerations are discussed in Chapter 9.

Psychological Correlates

As the practical problems associated with comparing subgroups on some concurrently obtained measure or laboratory task are much less complex than those involved in research related to etiology or outcome, there has been considerably more research in this much broader area. It is also the case that much of the research to date has been concentrated on the Undersocialized Aggressive than on the other three patterns. This group, which is often labeled "Psychopathic", (as we have noted previously), clearly has been the cause for much concern. Since the focus of this volume and this chapter is on delinquency, we will begin by looking at the correlates of the patterns with variables related to delinquency and juvenile corrections.

FACTORS RELATED TO DELINQUENCY AND JUVENILE CORRECTIONS

Institutional Adjustment

Within juvenile correctional institutions the Undersocialized-Aggressive pattern has been found both concurrently related to disciplinary problems (Quay, Peterson, & Consalvi, 1960; Schuck, Dubek, Cymbalisty, & Green, 1972) and predictive of them (Quay & Levinson, 1967). In the latter study, a sample of consecutive admissions to a federal juvenile correctional institution was assigned, without the knowledge of the institution staff, to one of the four subtypes using the measurement system outlined in Quay & Parsons (1971). In addition to evidencing a wider variety of disciplinary problems during their stay in the institution, the Undersocialized-Aggressive group was significantly less successful in a program involving working outside the institution during the day. The success rate of the Undersocialized group in a "work-release" program was only 25 percent compared to a success rate of 75 percent for the Anxious group. The Socialized Aggressive and Attentional Deficit groups were close to the base rate for the work-release group as a whole (50 percent). It is clear in this instance that had the Undersocialized group been excluded from the program the overall success rate would have risen considerably.

Smyth and Ingram (1970) compared youthful offenders classified into one of the four patterns as regards judged reasons for appearing at institutional sick call. Sick call visits were classified by medical staff as being primarily medical, emotional, or malingering. Although complete staff ignorance of the subgroup memberships of subjects could not be maintained, the size of the population and their newness to the institution (which had just opened) reduced possible contamination to a minimum. No differences among the groups were found for purely medical visits. However, the Anxious group had significantly more emotional sick calls; they accounted for two-thirds of the visits judged to be emotional, although they constituted less than 25 percent of the group studied. In contrast, the Undersocialized Aggressive group accounted for 39 percent of the visits judged to be malingering, while constituting only 16 percent of the sample.

It is abundantly clear that the Undersocialized Aggressive group is the most troublesome in the institutional setting and is apparently least likely to respond to standard institutional programs.

Recidivism

The tendency for the Undersocialized Aggressive group to be more frequently institutionalized has been demonstrated by Mack (1969) and Quay, Peterson, and Consalvi (1960). In a similar vein, Devies (1975) found failure while on probation to be more common among this group. In a study of juveniles who were participating in a diversion project (see Chapter 10), Quay and Love (1977) found that measures of both Undersocialized Aggression and Anxiety-Withdrawal-Dysphoria entered into an equation that predicted rearrest.

Thus, while it is certain that Undersocialized-Aggressive behavior is related to recidivism, there is some evidence that higher levels of anxiety and withdrawal are predictive of additional delinquency, at least in a sample of those who have already committed some delinquent act. Parenthetically, there is also data indicating that membership in the adult counterpart of the Undersocialized Aggressive group is also predictive of criminal recidivism (Quay, 1984). Longer-term outcome of the four patterns will be discussed in a subsequent section.

INSTRUMENTAL LEARNING

Since it is generally agreed that social behavior is learned primarily as a result of the consequences of that behavior in social settings, some researchers have studied the relationships of one or more of the four patterns to various facets of learning and reinforcement. An early study was undertaken by Stewart

(1972) whose subjects were institutionalized delinquents who had been classified as Undersocialized, Socialized, or Anxious. His subjects were given a sentence-building, verbal-conditioning task preceded by a frustration condition (working on an insoluble puzzle), or by a neutral condition. The conditioning tasks required the subject to make up a sentence using one of three kinds of verbs: aggressive, dependent, and neutral. The use of aggressive and dependent verbs were socially reinforced by approval from the experimenter.

Under the frustration condition, the Anxious and Socialized groups increased, while the Undersocialized group decreased, the use of the reinforced verbs. When conditioning was preceded by the neutral condition, the Anxious and Socialized Aggressives did not significantly increase their use of reinforced verbs, but the Undersocialized group again significantly decreased its use of them. Stewart's most interesting findings were that the Anxious group increased in the use of dependency verbs and decreased in the use of aggressive verbs over trials, whereas the Socialized group increased in the use of aggressive verbs. In addition to measures of conditionability, Stewart also measured "frustration-induced behavior" (e.g., requests for help, complaining, fidgeting). The Anxious group gave the highest number of such behaviors, followed by the Socialized and Undersocialized groups, respectively.

Two additional studies have dealt with the issue of reinforcement responsiveness in much more complex experimental designs. Moses (1974) used no less than seven reward conditions, while Dietrich (1976) varied both task structure and reward conditions. Both of these studies demonstrated differential response tendencies among the various delinquent subgroups, but the relationships were not nearly so straightforward as had been predicted—nor were they easily interpretable without recourse to a host of additional explanatory theories and constructs.

Akamatsu and Farudi (1978) studied the imitative behavior of a Socialized and Attention Deficit (Immature) group. As predicted, the Socialized group was more likely to imitate peer models, while the Attention Deficit group was more likely to imitate staff models. This finding is, of course, in accord with the notion that members of the Socialized Aggressive subgroup are responsive to, and greatly influenced by, their peers.

Most recently, interest has centered on the inability of the Undersocialized Aggressive group to inhibit responding in order to avoid punishment. Newman, Widom, and Nathan (1985) studied institutionalized delinquents whom they classified as "Psychopathic," "Anxious," "Anxious and Psychopathic," or "Nonanxious and Nonpsychopathic." They found that the Psychopathic group was less able to inhibit responding, particularly when such inhibition involved not performing a response that was also associated with reward. Other researchers as well have suggested that Undersocialized Aggressive or Psychopathic syndromes may be related to an excess of sensitivity to reward (see Gorenstein & Newman, 1980; Quay, 1986b, 1986d). Since this hypothesis about basic reward processes in Undersocialized Aggression is consonant with a considerable amount of data (see Quay, 1986b), it is well worth pursuing.

SUSTAINED ATTENTION AND STIMULATION SEEKING

The notion that extreme Undersocialized Aggressive behavior (psychopathy) might reflect inordinate tendencies toward stimulus seeking was advanced by this writer in 1965 (see Quay, 1965, 1977). Orris (1969) was the first to test this hypothesis experimentally using institutionalized delinquents as subjects. He predicted that the Undersocialized Aggressive (Psychopathic) group would show poorer performance on a (vigilance) task requiring continuous attention than would either Socialized Aggressive or Anxious subjects. His hypothesis was confirmed.

A later and more complex inquiry was that by Skrzypek (1969). He compared Undersocialized (Psychopathic) and Anxious institutionalized delinquents with respect to their preference for novelty and complexity of stimuli under conditions of both perceptual arousal and perceptual isolation. Initially, the Undersocialized Aggressive group indicated greater preference for the complex and the novel; in contrast, the Anxious group preferred the less complex and the more mundane. He also found that the effect of a brief period of perceptual isolation was to increase preference for novelty and complexity in the Undersocialized group. The arousal experience served to increase the anxiety of the Anxious subjects and to decrease their preference for complexity. The results of this experiment served to further demonstrate differences in stimulation-seeking propensities between the Undersocialized and Anxious groups. Later studies with institutionalized, but not necessarily legally delinquent, younger children have generally confirmed these findings (DeMyer-Gapin, & Scott, 1977; Whitehill, DeMyer-Gapin, & Scott, 1976). It is likely, however, that these stimulation-seeking tendencies, also found in adult psychopaths, can be subsumed within the more general reward-seeking model described above.

PEER RELATIONS

As we have seen, poor interpersonal relationships are among the central characteristics of the Undersocialized Aggressive pattern, while the opposite appears to be true of the Socialized pattern. It is only very recently, however, that investigators have become concerned with specifying the nature of peer relations in greater detail. Panella and Henggeler (1986) studied the social interaction patterns of black, male adolescents, most of whom were legally delinquent, whom they classified as Undersocialized, Anxious-Withdrawn, or well-adjusted. Compared to the controls, the Undersocialized group were less socially appropriate and showed a lower degree of positive affect and social competence when interacting both with strangers and with friends of their own age group. These researchers concluded that Undersocialized Aggressive adolescents have difficulty exchanging the sensitive, responsive, and positive behaviors that are characteristic of friendship relations (see also Chapter 6 with respect to social cognition).

With respect to Socialized Aggression, empirical research on the personal characteristics of group-oriented delinquents is exceedingly sparse, and, as suggested earlier, is not revealing of serious psychopathology (e.g., Cartright, Howard, & Reuterman, 1980). Greater susceptibility to peer influence has been documented in the study by Akamatsu and Farudi (1978) discussed earlier.

INTELLIGENCE, COGNITIVE FACTORS, AND ACADEMIC PERFORMANCE

The relationship of these variables to delinquency in general and to the four patterns are discussed in Chapters 4 and 6.

BIOLOGICAL FACTORS

Because of the often early onset and extreme nature of the behavior of those in the Undersocialized Aggressive subgroup, as well as its relative refractoriness to interventions, the possibility of a biological substrate that might at least serve as a predispositional factor has attracted some attention. One area of inquiry has involved electrodermal (GSR) responding. The GSR is an autonomic nervous system measure of emotional reactivity. The hypothesis advanced is that some of the behavior of Undersocialized Aggressive youth might be explained by an emotional underreactivity that, in turn, might lead to both the inadequate acquisition of fear-related motivation and to stimulation seeking due to the unpleasant hedonic tone associated with chronically low levels of arousal.

Borkovec (1970) was the first to find evidence for reduced GSR responding in Undersocialized as compared with Socialized and Anxious institutionalized delinquents. Subsequently, Siddle, Nichol, and Foggitt (1973) reported lower GSR reactivity in what were apparently Undersocialized Aggressive adolescents. A similar relative lack of GSR responsiveness has been reported by Raine and Venables (1984), and Delameter and Lahey (1983). These studies, as well as a more recent study by Schmidt, Solanto, and Bridger (1985) that used younger children who were not legally delinquent but nevertheless highly aggressive, are all highly suggestive of diminished emotional responsiveness.

These results are also in accord with considerable data (see Hare, 1978 for a review) indicating that adult psychopaths are underresponsive electrodermally. It has also been suggested that lowered electrodermal responding is associated with poor behavioral inhibition (Fowles, 1980). Thus, it may be that that Undersocialized Aggressive subgroup may be both reward-driven and suffer some deficiency in inhibitory processes.

Electroencephalographic (EEG) recordings were taken in an early study with Undersocialized, Anxious, and Socialized Aggressive girls who were patients on an adolescent unit of a psychiatric hospital. The investigators, (Mueller and Shamsie, 1967), reported that the Socialized group had the more regular and normal tracings while those of the Undersocialized group were interpreted as reflecting lack of inhibition. These findings are, of course, in accord with the hypothesis that the Socialized Aggressive subtype does not suffer from psychopathology while basic mechanisms related to behavioral inhibition are involved in Undersocialized Aggression.

There is now beginning to appear work on biochemical factors in Undersocialized Aggression (both in children, adolescents, and adults) which is concentrated on neurotransmitter substances and their precursors and metabolites (e.g., Rogeness, Hernandez, Macedo, & Mitchell, 1982; Rogeness, Hernandez, Macedo, Amrung, and Hoppe, 1984; Brown, et al., 1982). While studies have not yet been reported using juveniles who are officially delinquent, taken as a whole the results to date suggest the possibility of some biochemical abnormalities underlying deficient inhibitory processes, reward-driven behavior, and extreme aggression. A brief review may be found in Quay (1986b).

OUTCOME

As noted in the discussion on recidivism earlier in this chapter, short-term outcome is demonstrably worse for the Undersocialized Aggressive group. (A discussion of the prediction of official delinquency from early behavior problems may be found in Chapter 12.) We turn our attention here to the prediction of adult outcome; an area in which data are very sparse. In her classic studies, Robins (1966, 1974) found that antisocial behavior in childhood was predictive of criminal behavior in adulthood. Unfortunately, her research did not make use of the Undersocialized versus Socialized distinction but it is likely that most of her subjects, by virtue of their having been clients at a Metropolitan guidance clinic in the 1930s, were of the Undersocialized subgroup.

There is, however, a study which is revealing with respect to differential outcome. Henn, Bardwell, & Jenkins (1980) used the case files of a state institution for delinquent boys to classify their subjects as Undersocialized Aggressive, Socialized Aggressive, and Undersocialized but Nonaggressive. While this latter category does not match well with any of the four subgroups, it is probably most closely akin to the Anxious-Withdrawn-Dysphoric. The adult criminal records of the subjects were obtained from official sources and included arrest, conviction, prison terms, and types of crimes. These investigators' initial analyses revealed that the groups were comparable as to age at admission to the training school, ethnicity, number of children in the home, and urban-rural residence. Analysis of the training school records found that the Socialized group had done better while incarcerated than the two Undersocialized groups combined. The Socialized subjects had spent less time in the institution, had been discharged at a younger age, and had had fewer returns to the institution. These findings are, of course, in accord with studies discussed earlier in this chapter with respect to short-term recidivism.

The data on adult criminality indicated that the likelihood of conviction on an adult charge was significantly greater for the two Undersocialized groups than for the Socialized group (62.7 percent for the Undersocialized Aggressives, 57.1 percent for the Undersocialized Nonaggressives, and 42.1 percent for the Socialized group) as was the likelihood of incarceration (52.9 percent versus 46.9 percent versus 33.6 percent) and of an arrest for a violent crime (31.4 percent versus 12.2 percent versus 16.8 percent). While additional such research is needed, this study suggests a better adult outcome for the Socialized Aggressive subgroup than for the Undersocialized Aggressive subgroup.

CONCLUSIONS

In the opinion of this writer, it is unfortunate that there has been so little recent research into the nature of the four major behavioral subgroups as compared to studies which have considered delinquents as behaviorally and psychologically homogeneous. In contrast to the essentially negative findings of these studies (see Chapter 6), those relatively few studies utilizing subgroup classification have usually produced promising results in helping to understand not only how the subgroups may differ from nondelinquents but in how the subgroups may differ among themselves. Utilization of the subgroup approach also permits delinquency researchers and theorists to draw upon findings of studies of other deviant, but not necessarily delinquent, children and adolescents. A delinquent act is, after all, a behavior, albeit one which *may* happen to have legal consequences if the circumstances in which it occurs cause it to be observed and sanctioned.

Given that there is clearly a subgroup among adjudicated delinquents whose principal observable behavior problems involve poor attention, impulsiveness, and lack of perseverance, we can draw on an extensive literature on children diagnosed as either Hyperactive or having Attention Deficit Disorder to help us fill out the very sketchy picture we have of this subgroup when we rely, as we did in this chapter, only on studies of adjudicated delinquents. This literature (see Campbell & Werry, 1986 for a very recent review) tells us that this subgroup is replete with associated problems in cognitive functioning, academic skills, and peer relationships which can obviously predispose individuals in it to behave in ways which can lead, and obviously do lead in some percentage of cases, to official delinquency. This literature also tells us that about 80 percent of children (and adolescents) who are carefully diagnosed as manifesting this pattern show behavioral improvement when treated with stimulant medication. Yet this treatment is rarely, if ever, tried with institutionalized delinquent youth who may very well fit the Attention Deficit pattern.

What we know from the literature in child psychopathology about the distress of Anxious-Withdrawn-Dysphoric children can also be brought to bear on the delinquency problem. This literature (see Quay & La Greca, 1986, for a recent review) tells us that anxiety, too, interferes with cognitive processes, impedes the development of satisfactory social relationships, and provides a strong motivator to avoid further fear and anxiety producing situations. These factors can also be easily seen to predispose to behavior which may be considered delinquent, for as we have seen earlier in this chapter, the Anxious subgroup, however it violates the delinquent stereotype, can comprise one-quarter of the population of institutionalized delinquents.

A great deal of what we know about Undersocialized Aggressive youth has, in fact, come from studies of the legally delinquent who, while they fit the stereotype, make up only about one-fourth of the population of institutionalized delinquents. This group is most likely to be in continuous difficulties, has difficulty in inhibiting behavior (see also Chapter 4 and 6 for a discussion of diminished ability in self-control, and in verbal mediation and delayed moral reasoning ability), and is more likely to be criminal in adult life. Recent research suggests that such individuals may well have, at least in severe cases, a biological predisposition toward reward-seeking, a diminished inhibitory capacity, and excessive aggression. Even were we to recognize *only* this group as separate from the undifferentiated mass of delinquents, it would clearly be worth the effort.

The Socialized Aggressive subgroup, which does not appear to differ from nondelinquents in any significant way except in its officially delinquent behavior, comprises close to one-third those institutionalized. It would seem profitable to recognize individuals in this group as essentially the product of a lifetime of experiences that have channeled their behavior into delinquent activities while leaving their cognitive abilities, interpersonal relationships, and social skills unimpaired. It also seems probably that the behavior of this subgroup *is* best explained by social learning theory (see Chapter 8) and that it is this subgroup whose behavior is most likely to be explained by sociological theorizing as well (see Chapter 1).

If we continue to seek the causes, consequences, and cures of undifferentiated official delinquency, we are doomed to failure. If we continue to seek to treat all delinquents as if they were behaviorally homogeneous, we will, as illustrated in Chapters 9, 10, and 11, either fail or enjoy only very modest success. Psychological (and sociological) researchers should also recognize that to study official delinquency will, to an ever-increasing degree, take them out of the mainstream of research on deviant behavior in childhood and adolescence. Finally, all of the social systems involved—mental health, educational, and criminal justice—need to recognize that they are all dealing with the same patterns of behavioral deviance rather than with youth who are different because of a particular label which happens to have been attached to them. When this recognition occurs, communication and cooperation cannot help but be improved.

REFERENCES

Achenbach, T. M. (1966). The classification of children's psychiatric symptoms: A factor analytic study. *Psychological Monographs, 80,* 1–37.

Achenbach, T. M., & Edelbrock, C. (1983). *Manual for the Child Behavior Checklist and Revised Child Behavior Profile.* Burlington, VT: Queens City Printers.

Akamatsu, T. J., & Farudi, P. A. (1978). Effects of model status and juvenile offender type on the imitation of self-reward criteria. *Journal of Consulting and Clinical Psychology, 46,* 187–188.

American Psychiatric Association (1980). *Diagnostic and statistical manual of mental disorder,* (3rd ed.). Washington, D.C.: Author.

Blashfield, R. K. (1984). *The classification of psychopathology. NeoKrapelinian and quantitative approaches.* New York: Plenum.

Borkovec, T. D. (1970). Autonomic reactivity to sensory stimulation in psychopathic, neurotic and normal delinquents. *Journal of Consulting and Clinical Psychology, 35,* 217–222.

Brady, R. C. (1970). Effects of success and failure on impulsivity and distractibility of three types of educationally handicapped children. (Doctoral dissertation, University of Southern California). *Dissertation Abstracts International, 31,* 2167A (University Microfilms No. 70–23148).

Brown, G. L., Ebert, M. H., Goyer, P. F., Jimerson, D. C., Klein, W. J., Bunney, W. E., & Goodwin, F. K. (1982). Aggression, suicide, and Serotonin: Relationships to CSF amine metabolites. *American Journal of Psychiatry, 139,* 741–746.

Campbell, S. B., & Werry, J. S. (1986). Attention deficit disorder. In H. C. Quay & J. S. Werry (Eds.), *Psychopathological disorders of childhood* (3rd ed.). New York: Wiley.

Cartright, D. S., Howard K. I., & Reuterman, N. A. (1980). Multivariate analysis of gang delinquency: IV. Personality factors in gangs and clubs. *Multivariate Behavioral Research, 15,* 3–22.

Cavior, H. E., & Schmidt, A. A. (1978). Test of the effectiveness of a differential treatment strategy at the Robert F. Kennedy Center. *Criminal Justice and Behavior, 5,* 131–139.

Delamater, A. M., & Lahey, B. B. (1983). Physiological correlates of conduct problems and anxiety of hyperactive and learning-disabled children. *Journal of Abnormal Child Psychology, 11,* 85–100.

DeMyer-Gapin, S., & Scott, T. J. (1977). Effects of stimulus novelty on stimulation seeking in antisocial and neurotic children. *Journal of Abnormal Psychology, 86,* 96–98.

Devies, R. K. (1975). The use of differential behavioral classification system of the juvenile offender to distinguish probation successes from probation failures. (Doctoral dissertation, Kent State University). *Dissertation Abstracts International, 36,* 5819A. (University Microfilms No. 75–4921).

Dietrich, C. (1976). Differential effects of task and reinforcement variables on the performance of three groups of behavior problem children. *Journal of Abnormal Child Psychology, 4,* 155–171.

Fowles, D. C. (1980). The Three Arousal Model: Implications of Gray's two-factor learning theory for heart rate, electrodermal activity, and psychopathy. *Psychophysiology, 17*, 87–104.

Gibbons, D. C. (1965). *Changing the lawbreaker.* Englewood Cliffs, NJ: Prentice-Hall.

Gibbons, D. C. (1970). *Delinquent behavior.* Englewood Cliffs, NJ: Prentice-Hall.

Gorenstein, E. E., & Newman, J. P. (1980). Disinhibitory psychopathology: A new perspective and model for research. *Psychological Review, 87*, 301–315.

Hare, R. D. (1978). Electrodermal and cardiac correlates of psychopathy. In R. D. Hare & D. Schalling (Eds.), *Psychopathic behavior: Approaches to research* (pp. 107–144).

Henn, F. A., Bardwell, R., & Jenkins, R. L. (1980). Juvenile delinquents revisited. *Archives of General Psychiatry, 37*, 1160–1163.

Hewitt, L. E., & Jenkins, R. L. (1946). Fundamental patterns of maladjustment, the dynamics of their origin. Springfield, IL: State of Illinois.

Hunt, D. E., & Hardt, R. H. (1965). Developmental stage, delinquency and differential treatment. *Journal of Research in Crime and Delinquency, 20*, 20–31.

Jenkins, R. L. (1955). Adaptive and maladaptive delinquency. *The Nervous Child, 2*, 9–11.

Jenkins, R. L., & Glickman, S. (1947). Patterns of personality organization among delinquents. *The Nervous Child, 6*, 329–339.

Jesness, C. F., & DeRisi, W. (1971). The Preston Typology Study. An experiment with differential treatment in an institution. *Journal of Research in Crime and Delinquency, 8*, 38–52.

Klein, M. W. (1984). Offense specialisation and versatility among juveniles. *British Journal of Criminology, 24*, 185–194.

Loeber, R., & Schmaling, K. B. (1985a). Empirical evidence for overt and covert patterns of antisocial conduct problems: A metaanalysis. *Journal of Abnormal Child Psychology, 13*, 337–352.

Loeber, R., & Schmaling, K. B. (1985b). The utility of differentiating between mixed and pure forms of antisocial child behavior. *Journal of Abnormal Child Psychology, 13*, 315–336.

Mack, J. L. (1969). Behavior ratings of recidivist and nonrecidivist delinquent males. *Psychological Reports, 25*, 260.

Megargee, E. I., & Bohn, M. (1979). *Classifying criminal offenders: A new system based on the MMPI.* Beverley Hills, CA: Sage.

Moses, J. A. (1974). Two choice discrimination learning of delinquent boys as a joint function of reinforcement contingency and delinquency subtype. (Doctoral dissertation, University of Colorado) *Dissertation Abstracts International, 35*, 1922B. (University Microfilms No. 74–22, 375).

Mueller, H. F., & Shamsie, S. J. (1967, June). Classification of behavior disorders in adolescents and EEG findings. Paper presented at the 17th annual meeting of the Canadian Psychiatric Association, Quebec City.

Newman, J. P., Widom, C. S., & Nathan, S. (1985). Passive avoidance in syndromes of disinhibition: Psychopathy and extraversion. *Journal of Personality and Social Psychology, 48*, 1316–1327.

Orris, J. B. (1969). Visual monitoring performance in three subgroups of male delinquents. *Journal of Abnormal Psychology, 74*, 227–229.

Palmer, T. (1974). The California Youth Authority Treatment Project. *Federal Probation, 38*, 3–14.

Panella, D., & Henggeler, S. W. (1986). The peer relations of conduct disorder, anxiety-withdrawal disorder, and well adjusted black adolescents. *Journal of Abnormal Child Psychology, 14*, 1–12.

Peterson, D. R., Quay, H. C., & Cameron, G. R. (1959). Personality and background factors in juvenile delinquency as inferred from questionnaire responses. *Journal of Consulting Psychology, 23*, 392–399.

Quay, H. C. (1964a). Personality dimensions in delinquent males as inferred from the factor analysis of behavior ratings. *Journal of Research in Crime and Delinquency, 1*, 33–37.

Quay, H. C. (1964b). Dimensions of personality in delinquent boys as inferred from the factor analysis of case history data. *Child Development, 35*, 479–484.

Quay, H. C. (1965). Psychopathic personality as pathological stimulation-seeking. *American Journal of Psychiatry, 122*, 180–183.

Quay, H. C. (1966). Personality patterns in preadolescent delinquent boy. *Educational and Psychological Measurements, 16*, 99–110.

Quay, H. C. (1977). The three faces of evaluation: What can be expected to work? *Criminal Justice and Behavior, 4*, 341–354.

Quay, H. C. (1983). A dimensional approach to children's behavior disorder: The Revised Behavior Problem Checklist. *School Psychology Review, 12*, 244–249.

Quay, H. C. (1984). *Managing adult inmates.* Washington, D.C.: American Correctional Association.

Quay, H. C. (1986a). Classification. In H. C. Quay & J. S. Werry (Eds.), *Psychopathological disorders of childhood* (3rd. ed. pp. 1–33). New York: Wiley.

Quay, H. C. (1986b). Conduct disorders. In H.C. Quay & J.S. Werry (Eds.), Psychopathological disorders of childhood (3rd. ed. pp. 35–71). New York: Wiley.

Quay, H. C. (1986c). A critical analysis of DSM III as a taxonomy of child and adolescent disorders. In T.R. Millon & G. Klerman (Eds.), *Contemporary issues in psychopathology* (pp. 151–166). New York: Guilford Press.

Quay, H. C. (1986d). The behavioral reward and inhibition systems in childhood behavior disorder. In L.M. Bloomingdale (Ed.), *Attention deficit disorder* 3. New York: Spectrum.

Quay, H. C., & Blumen, L. (1963). Dimensions of delinquent behavior. *Journal of Social Psychology, 61*, 273–277.

Quay, H. C., & La Greca, A. M. (1986). Disorders of anxiety, withdrawal, and dysphoria. In H. C. Quay & J. S. Werry (Eds.), *Psychopathological disorders of childhood* (3rd ed.). New York: Wiley.

Quay, H. C., & Levinson, R. B. (1967). *The prediction of the institutional adjustment of four subgroups of delinquent boys.* Report to Bureau of Prisons, U.S. Department of Justice. Unpublished paper.

Quay, H. C., & Love, C. T. (1977). The effect of a juvenile diversion program on rearrests. *Criminal Justice and Behavior, 4*, 377–396.

Quay, H. C. & Parsons, L. B. (1971). *The differential classification of the juvenile offender* (2nd ed.). Washington, D. C.: U.S. Bureau of Prisons.

Quay, H. C., & Peterson, D. R. (1983). *Interim Manual for the Revised Behavior Prob-*

lem Checklist. Available from the senior author, Box 248074, University of Miami, Coral Gables, FL 33124.

Quay, H. C., Peterson, D. R., & Consalvi, C. (1960). The interpretation of three personality factors in juvenile delinquency. *Journal of Consulting Psychology, 24,* 555.

Raine, A., & Venables, P. H. (1984). Electrodermal nonresponding, antisocial behavior, and schizoid tendencies in adolescents. *Psychophysiology, 21,* 424–433.

Reiss, A. J. (1952). Social correlates of psychological types of delinquency. *American Sociological Review, 27,* 710–718.

Robins, C. N. (1966). *Deviant children grown up.* Baltimore: Williams & Wilkins.

Robins. C. N. (1974). *The Vietnam drug user returns.* Special Action Office Monograph, Series A, No. 2. Washington, D.C.: Government Printing Office.

Rogeness, G. A., Hernandez, J. M., Macedo, C. A., Amrung, S. A., & Hoppe, S. K. (1984). *Dopamine-beta-hydroxlase and conduct disorder in emotionally disturbed boys.* Unpublished manuscript, University of Texas Health Science Center, Department of Psychiatry, San Antonio.

Rogeness, G. A., Hernandez, J. M., Macedo, C. A., & Mitchell, E. L. (1982). Biochemical differences in children with conduct disorder socialized and undersocialized. *American Journal of Psychiatry, 139,* 307–311.

Schmidt, K., Solanto, M. V., & Bridger, W. H. (1985). Electrodermal activity of undersocialized aggressive children: A pilot study. *Journal of Child Psychology and Psychiatry, 26,* 653–660.

Schuck, S., Dubeck, J. A., Cymbalisty, B. Y., & Green, C. (1972). Delinquency, personality tests and relationships to measures of guilt and adjustment. *Psychological Reports, 31,* 219–226.

Siddle, D. A. T., Nicol, A. R., & Foggitt, R. H. (1973). Habituation and over-extinction of the GSR component of the orienting response in anti-social adolescents. *British Journal of Social and Clinical Psychology, 12,* 303–308.

Skrzypek, G. J. (1969). Effect of perceptual isolation and arousal on anxiety, complexity preference, and novelty preference in psychopathic and neurotic delinquents. *Journal of Abnormal psychology, 74,* 321–329.

Smyth, R. A., & Ingram, G. (1970). Relationship between type of offender and for seeking medical care in a correctional setting. *Nursing Research, 9,* 456–458.

Stewart, D. J. (1972). Effects of social reinforcement on dependency and aggressive responses of psychopathic, neurotic and subcultural delinquents. *Journal of Abnormal Psychology, 79,* 76–83.

Sullivan, C., Grant, M. Q., & Grant, J. D. (1957). The development of interpersonal maturity: Applications to delinquency. *Psychiatry, 23,* 73–385.

Warren, M. Q. (1969). The case for differential treatment of delinquents. *Annals of the American Academy of Political Science, 381,* 47–59.

Whitehill, M., DeMyer-Gapin, S., & Scott, T. J. (1976). Stimulation-seeking in antisocial preadolescent children. *Journal of Abnormal Psychology, 85,* 101–104.

CHAPTER 6

Personality

JACK ARBUTHNOT and DONALD A. GORDON

Ohio University

GREGORY J. JURKOVIC

Georgia State University

Research on personality and delinquency since Quay's review of 20 years ago (1965a) has in some ways demonstrated aspects of the growing maturity of this field, but in other ways has shown remarkably little change. In the latter regard, we are still looking at univariate paper-and-pencil predictors of a univariate definition of delinquency. Not only does this approach shed little light on the problems of youthful antisocial behavior, what light is shed is often inconsistent and weak rather than providing the beacon we need.

However, most delinquency researchers have not made use of Quay's earlier (1965a) well-founded recommendation to consider behavioral subtypes as the basis for research. This is in spite of the increasing consensus as to the major behavioral subtypes and the utility of subtypes discussed in Chapter 5.

Where the field shows a growing maturity is (1) in a shift toward a greater emphasis on developmental aspects of the sociocognitive functioning of antisocial youth, as well as (2) consideration of the influences of various social systems (e.g., the family) on the etiology of antisocial behavior. Both of these factors add to the development of theory, as well as providing suggestions for treatment.

Some persistent problems continue to hamper empirical progress. Among these are definitional difficulties. For the most part, as noted, in Chapters 1 and 5, we continue to define delinquency in legal rather than psychological terms. Part of the reason for this is, no doubt, the resultant clarity in knowing who fits the definition and who doesn't. This apparent clarity may not reflect reality, for we find that with few exceptions samples consist of those who not only have failed at conventional life but also at delinquency. As noted in Chapter 2, we have ample indication that the official delinquent population overlaps very little with the self-reported delinquent population, and we have good self-report scales. The few researchers who have studied both official and self-reported delinquents have found different results. Yet few of us make use of samples obtained by means other than court or institutional records.

In addition, the field suffers from the lack of a clear understanding of what is meant by "personality" and how it should be assessed. Some still study intrapsychic phenomena of vague properties, the existence and variation of which must be inferred in a subjective manner from indirect responses to a questionnaire or other stimuli. Should one rely on the subject's responses or seek out the views of others who have contact with him or her? Should assessment occur only under one set of perhaps artificial circumstances, rather than spanning a time sampling over different situations? Presumably personality traits or characteristics are relatively enduring qualities of an individual, but they must reflect to some degree that individual's interpretation of situations. Personality can have meaning only if it can explain behavior by accounting for an appreciable amount of the variance.

In the review which follows, we have attempted to find as much of the literature as possible which has been published since Quay's (1965a) review. No doubt some important studies were missed, and many had to be eliminated because of design problems so serious as to leave the results uninterpretable, or because they made no new contribution to the field. Some unpublished studies are reported, but usually only if cited in other published sources. Studies have been included if they dealt with juveniles legally defined or self-reported as delinquents, nominated as "delinquent" or, in some cases, thought to be at "high risk" for delinquency ("pre-delinquents"). We have left the definition of "personality" to the discretion of the researchers. As a result, the review includes both the more traditional personality constructs, as well as person variables of a more cognitive (but not intellectual in the IQ sense—see Chapter 4) nature, such as sociomoral reasoning, interpersonal problem solving, role taking, and empathy. In accord with the conclusions reached in Chapter 4, we view such sociocognitive variables as a significant and promising direction for the field.

MULTIVARIATE PERSONALITY INVENTORIES AND DELINQUENCY

The empirical research in this area is perhaps some of the oldest and most extensive in the psychological literature. In one of the first reviews of personality correlates of crime and delinquency, Schuessler and Cressey (1950) reported the use of 29 tests in 113 studies. Waldo and Dinitz (1967) later cited the same number of tests in their review of 94 investigations, and Tennenbaum (1977) found that researchers had used 52 tests in 44 different studies conducted since Waldo and Dinitz's report. In total, 101 different tests have been employed across all the studies cited in these reviews (Tennenbaum, 1977). Another trend that emerged in Tennenbaum's findings is that projective tests have been used more sparingly in recent years as objective and performance tests have gained in popularity.

Investigators in this area have concerned themselves with a wide array of questions, although the one that has predominated is whether offenders differ from nonoffenders. Is there an ubiquitous "criminal or delinquent personality?" It is now generally assumed (see Chapter 5) that this line of investigation, which has historically yielded inconsistent and inconclusive results, has obscured significant differences within offender and nonoffender samples. Delinquents are not an homogeneous group. Moreover, many of the stable group effects that have been shown, for example, on the Psychopathic Deviate (Pd) and Socialization (So) Scales of the Minnesota Multiphasic Personality Inventory (MMPI) and the California Psychological Inventory (CPI), respectively, can be attributed to methodological artifact. The Pd and So Scales were empirically derived from offender and psychopathic samples; it is thus neither surprising nor enlightening that offenders have differed from their law-abiding counterparts on these measures in subsequent research (Scheussler, 1954; Schuessler & Cressey, 1950; Tennenbaum, 1977; Waldo & Dinitz, 1967). While these measures may be used as "delinquency scales," assessing aspects of delinquency itself, they offer little explanation of delinquent conduct (Schuessler, 1954).

Numerous methodological and attendant conceptual shortcomings of research on personality correlates of delinquency have been discussed by Waldo and Dinitz (1967), Schuessler and Cressey (1950), Schuessler (1954), Tennenbaum (1977), Gearing (1979), Reppucci and Clingempeel (1978), and Lauffer, Skoot, and Day (1982). These include problems in sampling and subject variability, demand characteristics, trait model assumptions (e.g., cross-situational consistency in personality functioning), methods of profile interpretation, and various types of validation (protocol, construct, and external).

In an attempt to circumvent problems of this nature, researchers concerned with personality and delinquency have more recently explored behavioral dimensions within delinquent groups, (See Chapter 5), have conducted increasingly sophisticated investigations of personality variables that are predictive of delinquent behavior (See Chapter 12), and have sought to better validate the personality instruments used. A representative sampling of research along these lines will be discussed next with an emphasis on self-report personality inventories that have received the most attention in recent years: the CPI, MMPI, Jesness Inventory (JI), Eysenck Personality Inventory (EPI), and the Personal Opinion Survey (POS).

MMPI

The MMPI continues to be one of the most popular instruments. As Tennenbaum (1977) noted, certain scales of the MMPI, especially the Psychopathic Deviate (Pd) Scale, have enjoyed the most use by researchers, although the relation of code types and combined scale scores to delinquency is receiving greater attention.

A number of investigations have focused on the psychometric properties of the MMPI with delinquent samples. Gendreau, Grant, Leipciger, and Collins (1979), for example, called for more current delinquent norms, which they provided on a Canadian sample (see Lanyon, 1968). Earlier, Ono, Kataoka, and Shindo (1969) collected normative data on a Japanese group of delinquents (see also Abe, 1969). Their results raised questions about the appropriateness of the F scale as a measure of response validity for delinquent subjects, as scores on this scale covaried directly with degree of delinquency. High F may, in fact, reflect a clinically significant code type among delinquent respondents (see Gregory, 1977). More normative research of this kind is needed using samples in the United States.

Other investigators have examined the construct and predictive validity of the MMPI with delinquents. In an interesting study, Hawk and Peterson (1974) provided evidence suggesting that Pd scale scores reflect deviancy from social norms generally rather than psychopathic deviancy per se. Attempts to predict delinquent conduct and recidivism among identified adolescent offenders on the basis of the MMPI have produced equivocal results. For example, neither Smith and Lanyon (1968) nor Gendreau, Grant, Leipciger, and Collins (1979) were able to predict recidivism. Nor has the MMPI consistently differentiated recidivists from nonrecidivists (See, e.g., Mack, 1969). Follman, Dickinson, Corbin, Burg, and Cech (1972) also failed to find significant correlations between two delinquency prediction scales and the MMPI. There are indications, however, that a multivariate approach, in which MMPI scores are combined with other data (family and school), can enhance prediction (Briggs, Wirt, & Johnson, 1961). See also Rempel's (1958) earlier review of findings in this area.

A number of studies have also shown significant differences between different delinquent groups on the MMPI, for example, youths petitioned for certification as adults versus youths with similar arrest records not petitioned (Solway, Hays, Schreiner, & Cansler, 1980), and socialized delinquents versus unsocialized aggressive delinquents versus runaways (Schinohara & Jenkins, 1967; Tsubouchi & Jenkins, 1969). Although differences between social and solitary delinquents had been reported in earlier research (e.g., Randolph, Richardson, & Johnson, 1961), Hindelang (1973) failed to replicate this finding when using self-reported rather than official delinquents and when controlling for type of offense. Huesmann, Lefkowitz, and Eron (1978) discovered that the sum of T scores for scales F, Pd, and Hypomania (Ma) was a valid measure of aggression in a general sample of 19-year-olds, and also discriminated delinquents from general populations of males and females, even controlling for intelligence and social status. In an actuarial approach to describing delinquency, Gregory (1977) reported seven MMPI code types, further pointing to the heterogeneity of personality functioning within groups of delinquents.

CPI

As Laufer et al.'s (1982) review and extensive bibliography reflect, the CPI is being used increasingly by researchers interested in personality and delinquency. Like the Pd scale of the MMPI, the So scale of the CPI has been central in research in this area, although interest in the other original and more recent experimental scales (e.g., the Empathy Scale, Hogan, 1969) has increased over time.

Many of the early studies using the CPI simply compared undifferentiated groups of delinquents, predelinquents, and nondelinquents. In one of the better investigations along those lines, Hindelang (1972) found that self-reported delinquency related, as expected, to scores on the Pd scale of the MMPI, and the So, self-control (Sc), and responsibility (Re) scales of the CPI. Similar findings emerged in Mizushima and DeVos's (1967) study of Japanese delinquents and nondelinquents. The discriminatory effectiveness of the So and Re scales, in particular, has received support from other studies as well (e.g., Dinitz, Reckless, & Kay, 1958; Dinitz, Scarpitti, & Reckless, 1962; Peterson, Quay, & Anderson, 1959; Reckless, Dinitz, & Kay, 1957). Dinitz et al. (1962) originally discovered expected differences on the So scale for groups of boys nominated by their teachers as likely to become delinquent or not. A four-year follow-up, indeed, verified the teachers' expectations, and the boys' scores on the So scale remained stable.

There are also indications that the CPI can distinguish types of criminals among adolescents as well as adults. Stein, Gough, and Sarbin (1966), for example, empirically derived and validated a typology based on the So scale responses of delinquent and nondelinquent boys. Other researchers (e.g., Kendall, Deardorff, & Finch, 1977; Hogan, Mankin, Conway, & Fox, 1970) have demonstrated the value of considering scores on both the So and Empathy Scales of the CPI in differentiating groups of offenders (e.g., first from repeat offenders).

The JI

The JI (Jesness, 1972) was designed for assessment purposes with juvenile offenders as well as to provide personality data on nondelinquent adolescents. In conjunction with other data, the JI also can be used to classify delinquent youths according to level of interpersonal maturity (See Chapter 5), and more recently has been cross-checked for validity and reliability by investigators in this and other countries.

Although Jesness (1972) reported adequate reliability for the JI, test-retest data found in other investigations with Australian male delinquents (Putnins, 1980) and American male delinquents and nondelinquents (Shark & Handal, 1977) raised questions about its stability. In his criticism of the Shark and Handal study, Jesness (1977) questioned their methodology; however, he did concur that caution should be exercised, particularly when using the test with younger children. Based on a comparative study of English and American delinquents, Fisher (1967) also pointed to the problem of the international exchangeability of the JI and other psychological tests. His results suggested that cultural differences in test-taking attitude (for example, a pronounced acquiescent response set in English boys), represent a confounding factor.

Questions about reliability notwithstanding, there is considerable evidence supporting the concurrent, convergent, and predictive validity of the JI. A number of studies (Baker & Spielberg, 1970; Cowden, Peterson & Pacht, 1969; Graham, 1981; Martin, 1981; Saunders & Davies, 1976; Vallance & Forrest, 1971; Yiannakis, 1976) have found the JI to discriminate between predelinquent or delinquent and nondelinquent groups, and with few exceptions (Martin & Clarke, 1969; Biggs, Bender, & Foreman, 1983), between various delinquent groups. The Asocial Index failed to distinguish delinquents and nondelinquents in Shark and Handel's (1977) investigation; however, the definition of delinquency they used was questionable (see Jesness, 1977).

Evidence for the convergent validity of the JI has been presented by Smith (1974), who found expected correlations between the JI and the EPI. The Asocial Index score has also been shown to be predictive of institutional adjustment of delinquents (Woychick, 1970) and future delinquency (Graham, 1981). The JI proved less successful, however, in predicting the future behavior of young adult soldiers incarcerated for AWOL offenses in Fraas and Price's (1972) study. In sum, the JI promises to represent a valuable addition to the delinquency researcher's armamentarium, and deserves further scrutiny.

The EPI

Based on his model of personality and criminality, Eysenck (1977) developed the adult and junior forms of EPI (Eysenck & Eysenck, 1975). Each form contains the following scales: Neuroticism (N), Extroversion (E), Psychoticism (P), Lie (L), and the experimental scale for Criminal Propensity (C). It is assumed that for different reasons, high scores on the N, E, and P scales are associated with criminality. For example, Eysenck (1977) has hypothesized that high scorers on the E scale are less conditionable than low scorers, and thus are more likely to violate social norms. Criminals with a high N score are also assumed to engage in more antisocial activity than those with low scorers on N; the anxiety associated with neuroticism, acting as a drive, amplifies habitual antisocial behavior. (See also Chapter 5.) Eysenck also speculated that the high P scorer is predisposed to social isolation and insensitivity to others, traits that provide a weak barrier against delinquent and criminal activity.

Numerous studies have tested the validity of Eysenck's assumptions, using the EPI with both official and self-reported delinquents (see, e.g., Cochrane, 1974; Feldman, 1977; Passingham, 1972; Rushton & Chrisjohn, 1981). In general, while the results with officially recognized groups of offenders have been mixed, the data from diverse samples of self-reported delinquents have supported the relation of high E and P to antisocial behavior. High N, however, has not been significantly associated with misbehavior in adolescent samples. As Rushton and Chrisjohn (1981) observed, neuroticism may assume a less salient role in the early development of antisocial behavior than in the later stages when the habit is more fully formed and, consequently, affected to a greater extent by anxiety.

In addition to tests of the concurrent validity of the EPI, studies have examined the convergent and predictive validity of Eysenck's measure. Shuck, Dubeck, Cymbalisty, and Green (1972), for example, found expected correlations between various scales of the EPI, the POS (see Quay & Parsons, 1971), and the Mosher Guilt Inventory. Other researchers (e.g., Eysenck & Eysenck, 1974; Putnins, 1982) have checked the validity of the EPI in predicting antisocial behavior. Only the E scale was associated with future delinquency in the Eysenck and Eysenck (1971) study, whereas Putnins found the P and C scales to be predictive.

Experimental (e.g., Stein, 1976), cluster (McEwan, 1983), and discriminant (Forrest, 1977) analyses of the EPI have raised important questions about Eysenck's model, further suggesting that the EPI has mixed support at this point. Nevertheless, unlike most of the other measures considered in this section, the EPI rests on a rich theoretical base that has substantial heuristic value.

The POS

The POS was developed as a result of factor analytic inquiry into the patterns of delinquent behavior discussed in Chapter 5. This 100-item, true-false questionnaire yields scores on three dimensions: psychopathic delinquency, neurotic delinquency, and socialized delinquency. Although the POS can be used alone to assess a youngster's standing on these dimensions, it can also be combined with scores from the other instruments (Quay & Parsons, 1971).

In general, research has shown the POS to be a reliable and valid measure (see Quay & Parsons, 1971). An impressive body of data has also supported the use of the battery in differentially classifying delinquents. As noted in Chapter 5, meaningful differences among groups of juvenile offenders, differentiated according to this scheme, have emerged on a variety of psychological and physiological variables.

As noted earlier, research on personality and delinquency from a psychometric perspective has improved over the years; however, a number of pitfalls still remain. A major one inheres in the psychometric approach. Its basis in trait-derived methods create the impression that responses to personality questionnaires represent enduring and cross-situationally consistent characteristics. The role of environmental variables, particularly as they interact with personality, deserves more attention (see Repucci & Clingempeel, 1978). Added emphasis also needs to be placed on the strengths and adaptive qualities of the juvenile offender's personality functioning. An unfortunate byproduct of the trait-derived approach is that the focus tends to be on pathology (Repucci & Clingempeel, 1978).

UNIVARIATE PERSONALITY CONSTRUCTS

Time Orientation

It is sometimes assumed that delinquents are highly present-oriented, since the behavior of some appears to be nonreflective, impulsive expressions of a desire for immediate gratification with apparently little consideration of future consequences (see, e.g., Wilson & Herrnstein, 1985). The literature on this dimension, however, is not entirely clear, suggesting that this conceptualization may be oversimplified.

Studies reviewed by Quay (1965a), as well as subsequent research (e.g., Stein, Sarbin, & Kulik, 1968), suggested shorter future orientations for delinquents. Mischel (1961) and Mischel and Gilligan (1964) found delinquents to prefer immediate rewards over delayed gratification. However, Rosenquist and Megargee (1969) found this relationship to be inconsistent, varying over groups. While Siegman (1966) found faster "internal clocks" for delinquents, in an earlier study (1961), he found no such relationship.

Landau (1975) attempted to resolve inconsistencies by controlling for institutionalization as well as delinquency status, noting that most studies have failed to separate the effects of these two variables. He found that both factors have limiting effects on future time perspective, and that a narrowing in the range of future time perspective is observed as institutional release approaches for both delinquents and nondelinquents (soldiers). Landau (1976) later observed that few studies examine perspectives on present and past as well as future time. Given the disruptive effects of institutionalization, this would seem to be a serious omission. For example, Magargee, Cooper-Price, Frohworth, & Levine (1970) found that youthful prison inmates were more oriented toward the future and past than to the present, with affective reactions being positive toward the future, but negative toward the past and present. Landau (1976) examined the effects of institutionalization on four groups of older (17 to 21), low SES and low education delinquents and nondelinquents, both institutionalized (prison inmates and soldiers) and noninstitutionalized (probationers and vocational students). Controlling for age, SES, and social desirability, most of the study's eight hypotheses were confirmed (five fully, two partially): All groups placed greater emphasis on the future and less on the past, but the remainder of the results indicated distinct effects on various aspects of time orientation for both institutionalization and delinquency. For delinquents, institutionalization produced an early increased salience of the present, an effect noted later for the soldiers. This was accompanied for delinquents by a drastically reduced orientation to the future, a phenomenon attenuated by approaching release. However, the salience of the present was not found to be greater for delinquents than for nondelinquents—a result attributed to the greater impact of institutionalization than delinquency on this issue.

Regarding affective reactions, delinquency status was accompanied by negative feelings about the past and positive feelings about the future, while institutionalization was associated with negative evaluations of the present. It is of interest to note, then, that delinquents have shorter future perspectives (Landau, 1976), but also have highly positive views of their future. This "wishful thinking" phenomenon may also reflect the oversimplified nature of earlier conceptions of delinquency and time perspectives, in that delinquents may have quite unrealistic assessments of the likelihoods of both positive (overestimated) and negative (underestimated) future events and consequences of their present behavioral choices.

Finally, studies of different groups of delinquents and of the effects of individual demographic differences show generally weak and mixed results. Roberts, Erickson, Riddle, and Bacon (1974) examined various aspects of time orientation just prior to institutional release, and then compared those who within one year had (1) no contact or (2) some contact with the courts, or who had (3) been reinstitutionalized (with no differences in age, IQ, ethnicity, or institutional history). While the no-contact group scored as more future-oriented on the future events test, no differences were observed on a measure of future time perspective. And, while rating scales by the experimenter (a psychologist) showed predicted group differences, those completed by supervisors and principals did not.

Within institutionalized delinquent samples, few demographic differences are found in time orientation. Sex differences have received little attention, but Davids and Falkof (1975) found no differences. Neither do race differences emerge, although Davids and Falkof found larger variances for blacks, and Cross and Tracy (1971) observed greater future perspectives with increasing interpersonal maturity for blacks (but not whites). Perhaps consistent with this latter finding, Davids and Falkof noted significantly greater future orientations with increasing age. Finally, Davids and Falkof noted a significantly lower future orientation over a 15-year period (1959–1974) within one institution in a cross-sectional study—a finding of uncertain meaning, but one which introduces a need for caution in comparing studies of time orientation across generations.

In sum, time orientation appears not to differ in a simple and consistent fashion for delinquents and nondelinquents. What differences do exist appear to reflect differing histories of institutionalization, maturity, and realism in anticipating future events.

Impulsivity and Inability to Delay Gratification

Impulsivity and the inability to delay gratification no doubt have some degree of conceptual overlap with time orientation. For example, Shapiro (1965) has suggested that impulsivity is associated with a lack of "abiding, long-range personal plans or ambitions, not to mention more abstract aims, purposes, or values." Lavik (1969) found that disturbances in future time perspectives of delinquents were associated with inability to delay gratification. Indeed, numerous studies seem to indicate the greater impulsivity of delinquents, including research employing self-report measures (Marohn, Offer, & Ostrov, 1971), projective tests (the Rorschach: Curtiss, Feczko, & Marohn, 1979), and psychomotor tasks (spiral maze: Gibson, 1964; Porteus Maze: Docter & Winder, 1954; Eisen, 1956; Porteus, 1959).

Empirical research is not unanimous in support for the impulsivity phenomenon, however. For example. Saunders, Reppucci, and Sarata (1973) conducted two studies which challenged the association between delinquency and impulsivity, and, moreover, questioned the validity of the scales employed to measure impulsivity. Their first study compared scores on two commonly used self-report measures (the Barratt Impulsivity Scale, 1959; and the Hirschfield Scale, 1965), as well as one psychomotor test (the Matching Familiar Figures Test, MFFT; (Kagan, 1966). The participants were adolescent males from a minimum security camp, a maximum security reformatory, and a high school, all of comparable age, social class, and ethnicity. Neither delinquent sample was found to be more impulsive than the students; in fact, on the Hirschfield Scale, the students scored as significantly more impulsive. Moreover, while the two self-report measures correlated modestly ($r = .45$), neither was appreciably correlated with the MFFT.

Their second study compared institutionalized youth who, during their first incarceration, either did or did not have a record of running away (presumably a behavioral reflection of impulsivity). This study also used the Barratt Scale and the MFFT, and added the Arrow-Dot Test (see Dombrose & Slobin, 1958, for a description of this scale). Again, no differences were found on any of the three measures which differentiated runners from nonrunners. And, while the two psychomotor measures correlated very modestly ($r = .36$), neither correlated with the Barrett.

O'Keefe (1975) has challenged the validity of another psychomotor test commonly employed as an indicator of impulsivity—the Porteus Maze. His samples included institutionalized delinquent boys, as well as nondelinquent boys in an institution for neglected and dependent children. The boys in each setting were assigned to a high-impulsive or low-impulsive group based on ratings by teachers, social workers, group leaders, and counselors. Contrary to expectations, those rated low on impulsivity appeared to obtain higher (though not significantly so) Q scores. Q scores (for "qualitative") presumably measure impulsivity of responding; TQ scores (for "test quotient") presumably measure nonverbal foresight and planning ability. Furthermore, comparisons of delinquent and nondelinquent boys showed the *latter* to obtain significantly higher Q scores. Finally, a comparison of extreme groups also found higher Q scores for the low impulsive group. O'Keefe suggested that previous studies by Porteus (and others) may have found differences not because of some characteristics of delinquents, per se, but because of other variables associated with institutionalization. In this light, O'Keefe suggested that high Q scores are characteristic of dependent and neglected children in general, and not of delinquent children in particular. He further suggested that it may be erroneous to interpret the lifting of a pencil from the paper during the psychomotor task as indicative of impulsivity; an equally compelling interpretation is that it reflects inhibition of responses to permit surveying of the overall task and planning of future action, even though it is against the rules.

Several studies have compared subgroups of delinquents on both impulsivity and ability to delay gratification. On the former, Erickson and Roberts (1966) found incarcerated male delinquents whose institutional behavior was disruptive to have higher Q (but not TQ) scores than those rated as more conforming, a result replicated for different samples 12 months later. Roberts, Erickson, Riddle and Bacon (1974), in a comparison of recidivist versus non-recidivist institutionalized male delinquents, found the recidivists to have lower TQ and higher Q scores, which they interpreted as reflecting poorer foresight and planning, as well as greater impulsivity. In a one-year follow-up study, Roberts et al. found the recidivist group to have the highest "impulsivity" (Q) scores, while the non-contact group had the lowest. No differences were found for TQ. In addition, experimenter ratings (but not teacher or supervisor ratings) showed the no-contact group to be superior on motivation, foresight, planning, maturity, ability to delay gratification, success after discharge, and success within one year. In a related study, Roberts and Erickson (1968) administered the Porteus Maze Test and both a verbal and behavioral measure of ability to delay gratification to newly institutionalized male delinquents. Significant differences were found between both verbal and behavioral delayers and nondelayers: Nondelayers scored lower on TQ and higher on Q (the latter result parallels that obtained for nonrecidivists versus recidivists). In addition, better adjustment to the institution was related to both ability to delay gratification and to Q scores.

In sum, there appears to be a good deal of inconsistency in the impulsivity literature, with studies showing both nondelinquents and delinquents to have higher impulsivity scores on psychomotor tests, as well as studies showing no differences. While the literature as a whole suggests more consistency than inconsistency for greater impulsivity in delinquents, recidivists, and misbehaving incarcerated youth, there are some serious assessment problems. The results of both O'Keefe's (1975) and Saunders, et al.'s (1973) research pointed to inconsistency in the ability of psychomotor tests, in particular, to distinguish delinquent and nondelinquent samples, and raised serious questions about the convergent validity of the various types of tests which allegedly measure impulsivity. O'Keefe, in fact, raised the issue of whether high or low Q scores on the Porteus Maze Test should be interpreted as indicative of impulsivity. It would appear that research in this area requires the development of more criterion-based measures before we can have confidence in the delinquency-impulsivity relationship—and certainly before we develop and assess interventions based on this presumed relationship.

Sensation Seeking

Zuckerman (Zuckerman, Bone, Neary, Mangelsdorff, & Brustman, 1972) has described the personality trait of "sensation seeking" as "related to an uninhibited, nonconforming, impulsive, dominant type of extraversion, but not particularly related to the socialization type of extraversion" (p. 319). Following Quay's (1965b) earlier hypothesis with regard to psychopathic personality, Farley and Sewell (1976) posited the delinquent as having an exaggerated need for stimulation, a need which is at least to some extent attributable to a physiologically based arousal deficit. This deficit is thought to be in part inherited, and to interact with environmental opportunities for stimulation. In this view, the delinquent is seen as having a higher-than-normal optimal level of stimulation; how this greater need for stimulation is met is largely dependent upon various aspects of the social environment. Presumably, an environment characterized by a deficit of stimulating and socially acceptable experiences will channel high stimulus seekers into antisocial behaviors if those behaviors can meet the individual's needs.

Some support has been found for this model. Farley and Farley (1972) studied behavioral differences between institutionalized delinquent girls assessed as high or low stimulation-seekers on Zuckerman's (Zuckerman, Kolin, Price, & Zoob, 1964) Sensation Seeking Scale (SSS). Incarcerated high scorers showed significantly greater incidences of escape attempts and of being punished for disobedience. Farley and Sewell (1976) examined differences in SSS scores for male and female black delinquents and nondelinquents. A significant, though modest, difference was observed between delinquent and nondelinquent youth, and the means for both groups were lower than those reported for comparably aged whites (although the samples were not matched in SES). Karoly (1975) provided data from institutionalized delinquent ("incorrigible") and nondelinquent girls of approximately equivalent SES, and of the same age range as Farley and Sewell's sample. Racial differences were found, independent of delinquency status (with whites scoring significantly higher for both groups). Differences by delinquency status were very small and favored the nondelinquent group.

In sum, differences on the sensation-seeking dimension between unselected delinquents and nondelinquents lack consistency and are modest when observed. Other studies already discussed in Chapter 5 have consistently related psychopathic subgroups to stimulus seeking and have utilized behavioral measures of sensation seeking rather than relying on self-report paper-and-pencil tests. These studies have also illustrated the value of subgrouping the heterogeneous population of "delinquents."

Locus of Control

Rotter (1966) has suggested that individuals can be ordered along a dimension in terms of how one percieves the causes or origins of their behavioral outcomes. Those who perceive events as largely caused by luck, fate, chance, or powerful others are characterized as "externals," whereas those who perceive personal control over their life events are characterized as "internals." The literature on locus of control has been reviewed elsewhere (see, e.g., Phares, 1976).

It has been suggested that delinquents should score as significantly more external in locus of control, reflecting perceptions that the forces which shape their lives, and/or block legitimate achievement, are largely beyond their own personal control. However, the evidence is not particularly consistent. For example, two studies (Beck & Ollendick, 1976; Duke & Fenhagen, 1975, black females), using Nowicki and Strickland's (1973) Locus of Control scale, as well as studies using Rotter's scale (Parrott & Strongman, 1984) and Bialer's (1961) Children's I-E scale (Kumchy & Sawyer, 1980), both reported delinquent samples to be significantly more external than matched nondelinquents. In contrast, other studies using Rotter's scale report no differences (Farley & Sewell, 1976, blacks; Valliant, Asu, & Howitt, 1983, Caucasians and Native Americans analyzed separately). Parrott and Strongman, as well as Kumchy and Sawyer, used the Intellectual-Achievement Responsibility Scale (Crandall, Katovsky, and Crandall, 1965) and found delinquents to make more external attributions in academic settings for negative-outcome situations. Finally, Cross and Tracy (1971) found black delinquents to be more external than whites, for externality to increase with increasing Interpersonal Maturity scores (See Chapter 5) for blacks, but for internality to increase with increasing scores for whites.

In sum, the results for the locus of control construct provide little understanding of delinquent-nondelinquent differences. Effects appear to be inconsistent—perhaps a result of the multidimensionality of the scale, subcultural differences, or a reflection of real social environmental differences in locus of control. When included in multivariate analyses (e.g., Valliant et al., 1983), the I-E dimension contributed nothing to overall predictions relative to other personality dimensions.

Self Concept

Self concept has played a role in various explanatory models of delinquency over the past three decades, beginning with the sociological theories discussed in Chapter 3. We shall review (1) the cross-sectional studies and (2) studies which test various explanatory models.

Cross-Sectional Studies

Much of the literature on the self concepts of delinquents has utilized for assessment the Tennessee Self Concept Scale (TSCS; Fitts, 1965). Fitts and Hamner (1969) have reviewed some 60 studies (many unpublished) on this multi-dimensional scale, eight of which pertain to delinquent or behavior-disordered youth, which show them to score lower on various TSCS scales than nondelinquent samples (which were often matched on various demographic indices). Two of the studies were with non-American samples (Korea and Mexico), suggesting consistency across cultures. Subsequent research with the TSCS confirms the earlier findings (Eyo-Isidore, 1981; Lund & Salary, 1980).

Research with other standard or *ad hoc* scales has produced less consistent results. For example, Dietz (1969), using a semantic differential format, compared self concepts of institutionalized delinquent males with nondelinquent high school males, and found no differences in the self evaluations of the two groups. Similarly mixed, weak, or nonsignificant results are not uncommon (e.g., Hughes & Dodder, 1980; Long, Ziller, & Bauber, 1970; Teichman, 1971; Thompson, 1974). Research providing generally consistent results with various scales other than the TSCS include Burke, Zilberg, Amini, Salasnek, and Forkin (1978), Dorn (1968), and Jensen (1972).

Among the more consistent findings which emerge from the cross-sectional studies comparing delinquents with nondelinquents are, with respect to delinquents: a negative self concept, with little liking, valuing, or respect of the self; an uncertain and unclear picture of the self; an external locus of control and evaluation (see preceding section, however); a confusing and contradictory self concept; difficulty in coping with external pressures, frustration, and stress due to a lack of personality integration or inner strength; considerable tension, dissonance, and discomfort; and a pervasive discrepancy between the self-view and beliefs about how they are seen by their parents or teachers (with the latter generally being more negative). This last finding suggests that delinquents may develop self concepts in a different frame of reference than nondelinquents. The fact that high self concepts of delinquents appear to be related to ego defensiveness suggests unrealistic self views and unresponsiveness to the feedback of parents—a further indication of inadequate or incomplete socialization, at least among some behavioral subgroups (see Chapter 5).

It should be noted, however, that nearly all of the studies reported were conducted with male participants, and few report the use of mixed races or analyses by race. That demographics may be important moderators is suggested by Armstrong's (1980) data showing that aggressiveness in males was most successfully predicted by low self concept combined with high masculine sex-role identity, and Atkins's (1974) study, using the Coopersmith (1967) inventory, which showed delinquent-nondelinquent differences in self esteem only for higher SES youth.

The cross-sectional studies comparing subgroups of delinquents are few in number, and appear to indicate lower self concepts for recidivists versus first-time offenders (three studies reviewed in Fitts and Hamner, 1969). It is not clear, however, whether this reflects characteristics of the recidivist or of institutionalization. Both Dorn (1968) and Fitts and Hamner (1969) reported inconsistent findings on the effects of institutionalization versus noninstitutional treatment, as well as on the effects of length of institutionalization (e.g., repeated or lengthy incarceration may indicate more serious offenders, or may—because of the oppressive nature of institutions—produce lowered self concepts). Culbertson (1975), however, reported a clear decline as a function of duration of incarceration.

Models and Mechanisms

Among the more straightforward explanations of the relationship between low self concept and delinquency is that it reflects a labelling phenomenon. Jensen (1972) found that the use of the official label of "delinquent" produces adverse effects on self concept, and that this effect is particularly pronounced for middle-to-upper SES white youth, an effect consistent with Atkins' (1974) data reported previously. Ageton and Elliott (1974) found a significant relationship between amount of police contact and delinquency orientations, especially for whites. Bliss (1977) argued that lower self concept scores accompany increasingly deviant labels (institutionalized delinquents versus delinquents on probation versus nondelinquents)—a result found by several others (see, e.g., Dorn, 1968, and Fitts and Hamner, 1969). However, there is no evidence in these studies of the direction of causality. While labelling is felt by most practitioners to be a serious concern, its effects are difficult to establish clearly without time-lagged or experimental designs.

Reckless and Dinitz (1972) proposed that self esteem acts as an insulator against forces which have been thought by some to lead to delinquency. Their initial study (Reckless, Dinitz, and Murray, 1956) compared sixth-grade boys in a high delinquency area who had been nominated by teachers as "good" or "bad" ("headed for trouble with the law"), with the former having better self concepts. In follow-up studies, the "bad" boys had more frequent police contacts (39 percent versus 4 percent), leading the authors to conclude that self concept is a good predictor of (and good self concept an insulator of) delinquency. However, several critiques have been made of Reckless and Dinitz's work (e.g., Orcutt, 1970; Tangri & Schwartz, 1967). Among the problems commonly cited are the following: (1) the "good" boys appear to have come from stable homes with the external pressures caused by association with delinquents—it is therefore "ludicrous" to speak of insulations against forces they didn't experience; (2) the "forces" are sometimes the same as the "insulators" since the definition of self concept includes such items as delinquent/nondelinquent companions and stable/unstable home background; (3) potential awareness of delinquent activities by the nominating teachers; and (4) other methodological deficiencies, including differential treatment of the two groups and contamination of interviewers.

The most predominant interpretation of the self-concept/delinquency relationship is the "esteem enhancement" model (Kaplan, 1975, 1980; Wells, 1978). This model assumes that low self-esteem acts as a "drive mechanism" which propels individuals toward behavior choices that would lead to an increased regard for the self. Delinquency is seen as an adaptive or defensive response to self-devaluation (see, e.g., Gold and Mann, 1972; Gold, 1978; Kaplan, 1975, 1980; and Chapter 3). Should conventional behavioral choices fail to provide sufficient opportunities for creating positive self-regard, unconventional (deviant, delinquent) choices will likely follow in the resulting weakened attachment to (and perhaps hostility toward) conventional values and activities. This model is interactive, in that self-derogation is but one of several factors necessary for delinquency (e.g., it is a necessary but not a sufficient condition), and that other social situational variables affect both the availability and utility of specific behavioral choices.

The research which purports to support the model is inadequate, however. The model, being developmental, would presumably predict low self-concepts for "predelinquents" or those early in their career, as well as for those who are unsuccessful (e.g., incompetent at delinquency and/or are apprehended). It would predict increased self-regard for those who, over their career, are successful. Thus, most of the studies which appear to support a self-enhancement model (several reviewed in Fitts and Hamner, 1969; Gold, 1978; Kaplan, 1975) are limited to apprehended delinquents and are cross-sectional in nature. Among the longitudinal studies, Rosenberg and Rosenberg (1978), using cross-lagged correlations, concluded that self-esteem was a more potent causal determinant and contributes more to delinquency than vice versa. The amounts of variance involved were small, however, and other potential causal factors reflecting social experiences and evaluations were not considered. Brynner, O'Malley, and Bachman (1981), studying the same data but adding later waves in the study panel, using multivariate analyses, and including additional controls (social life, educational attainment, and SES), reported both a negative correlation between self-esteem and delinquency and a positive effect of delinquency on self-esteem. Kaplan (1980) has summarized a series of his own studies and concluded that negative social experiences are related to lowered self-esteem, that self-derogation is associated with subsequent delinquency, and that such behavior is related to increased self-esteem among self-derogating youth.

While the longitudinal studies are far stronger than those of a cross-sectional nature, Wells and Rankin (1983), using path analysis, reported that when the effects of prior causal factors (grades, social rejection, and family relationships) were partialled out, there was no substantial effect of self-esteem on subsequent delinquency—even when various types of delinquency were analyzed, or when separate analyses were done for high and low SES. (When separate analyses were calculated by race, however, a stronger effect of delinquency on subsequent self-esteem was found for blacks.) In spite of this, Wells and Rankin did not reject the model. They recommended use of a less global conception of self-esteem, and consideration of possible critical periods.

In addition to the recommendations of Wells and Rankin, it also seems that this body of research suffers from failure to incorporate individual differences in the respondents' cognitive reactions to negative social experiences and evaluations. Since not all who suffer these do self-derogate, and not all (not even many) self-derogators choose deviancy or delinquency as an ameliorative activity, the role of factors affecting the decision-making process requires investigation. Researchers would do well to explore the individual's decision-making processes. For example, youth with varying values, attitudes, and sociomoral reasoning abilities should be expected to respond differently, not only in their causal schemas for the events they experience, but also in their behavioral choices and how they interpret the outcomes of these choices.

In sum, research on self concept and delinquency needs to deal with several problems to enhance progress. Among these are: (1) We lack a clear conception of what self-concept is and is not; with the exception of the multidimensional TSCS, there appears to be little agreement on how to define or measure self-concept. (2) Greater attention needs to be paid to the developmental histories of positive and negative self-concepts, in general, as well as for different aspects of self-concept; they no doubt have different etiologies, and may have vastly different implications for causing delinquent behavior. (3) It is unlikely that the subtypes discussed in Chapter 5 function personologically (or in other respects) in a similar fashion; studies distinguishing (but including) subtypes might help clarify the cause-and-effect relationship between self-concept and delinquency. Finally, (4) greater attention needs to be paid to other individual differences variables which no doubt mediate the effect of low self-concept on behavior; these may include cognitive factors (such as IQ, cognitive style, sociomoral reasoning stage), or other personological variables (such as locus of control and impulsivity).

SOCIOCOGNITIVE CONSTRUCTS

We turn now to a discussion of variables that are generally considered as reflecting higher order cognitive function as much as, if not more so, than personality characteristics. This discussion essentially begins where the discussion of intelligence in Chapter 4 left off.

Morality and Moral Reasoning

Of all the assumptions regarding the beliefs of researchers, professionals, and lay persons involved in the study or treatment of delinquency, probably the safest is that we all believe that the behavior of delinquents and nondelinquents (as well as ourselves) is related in some fashion to knowledge of what is "right" and "wrong," affective reactions to conventional morality, and/or how one constructs a moral worldview. In fact, Quay (1965a) observed that the earliest assumptions about the nature of the personality characteristics which distinguish delinquents and nondelinquents was that they had to do with morality or righteousness. This section will evaluate the empirical literature which addresses the relationship of each of these three aspects of morality to delinquent or immoral behavior.

Moral Knowledge

The classic studies by Hartshorne and May (1928; Hartshorne, May, & Maller, 1929; Hartshorne, May, & Shuttleworth, 1930) found little relationship between simple knowledge of moral rules or conventions and specific moral behaviors. Neither has there emerged since that time a body of research which demonstrates such a consistency. The reasons now appear to be obvious—we should not expect mere knowledge of "right from wrong" to predict behavioral choices without also considering the actor's attitudes about particular moral rules, how the actor interprets the moral demands pressing upon the ethical-behavioral event, a variety of situational factors, and other personal qualities that moderate the relationships among all of these variables.

Moral Attitudes

The study of the relationship of moral attitudes and behavior enjoys certain advantages over the moral knowledge approach, largely in terms of the ability to consider the individual's affective reactions to the moral rules of which one has knowledge. It does suffer, however, from many of the problems inherent in the study of the relationship of attitudes and behavior. While it is beyond the scope of this chapter to explore this issue, it can be noted that attitudes are often poor predictors of behavior except when: (1) other influences on both are minimized; (2) the attitudes correspond very closely with the behavior under study; and (3) the actors are aware of their attitudes. Furthermore, attitudes and behavior often have a reciprocal nature, meaning that each, in part, helps shape the other. In that sense, we often form our moral attitudes *after* we see what we have done, thereby justifying our behavior (see, e.g., Ajzen & Fishbein, 1978; Myers, 1983).

While the simplest model is that delinquents are "immoral" (i.e., subscribe to "deviant" moral codes) while nondelinquents have adopted conventionally moral attitudes, alternate models have been proposed. For example, Matza (1964) suggested that delinquents essentially hold conventional moral values, and that nondelinquents also share some of the deviant or subterranean values from which delinquency arises. The difference in behavior then derives from various situational or sociological pressures. Heather's (1979) data from lower and middle SES delinquents and nondelinquents seemed to indicate equivalent value structures (conventional and subterranean/deviant). However, self-reported delinquency was lower for those with dominant conventional systems (and/or absent deviant attitudes). In addition, some delinquents had clearly dominant deviant attitudes, and the commission of delinquent acts appeared to be a function of the relative strengths of the dominant value systems. Hindelang's (1974) study showed that act-committers were more approving of the act than noncommitters, and the former were likely to believe that their friends were either equally or less approving (as opposed to more approving) of the act. (While Hindelang's findings appear to contradict Matza's hypothesis, there is a question of which had temporal priority—attitudes or behaviors.) Stein,

Sarbin & Chu (1967) reported highly reliable differences on such moral values of "snitching" and aggression, while Goldberg and Guilford (1972) reported mixed results, with differences on three of six factors (Delinquent, Alienated, and Sociopathic values, but not on Academic, Acting Out, or Masculine (reversed)).

Affective reactions to transgression may also be indicative of moral attitudes. It is not unusual to hear that delinquents lack a "conscience" and experience no guilt over their behavior—an apparent indicator of the absence of positive moral attitudes. Ruma and Mosher (1967) reported a significant correlation between the guilt scale and moral judgments of delinquents, but in the absence of a nondelinquent comparison group, we do not know if the level of guilt was less, equivalent to, or greater than that experienced by "normals." Persons (1970) reported normative data on the Mosher Guilt Scale (1966) from reformatory inmates and college students. While scores correlated modestly with MMPI subscales associated with inhibition, and negatively with those associated with acting-out, the two samples did not differ significantly on any of the guilt subscales (Sexual, Moral, Hostility, and Total). Thus, while Persons claimed support for construct validity, the scales lacked discriminant validity for delinquents and nondelinquents—a serious problem for a construct that presumably inhibits violation of moral standards.

Perhaps a more direct assessment of post-transgression reactions would prove more useful than indirect assessments of such intrapsychic constructs as "guilt." For example, Sagi and Eisikovits (1981), in Israel, found delinquents (relative to both lower- and middle-class nondelinquents) to score lower on a behavioral measure or resistance to temptation, as well as on moral stage, confession, and post-transgression affect.

In sum, it appears that at least some clear differences exist between delinquents' and nondelinquents' attitudes about the acceptability of various offenses, as well as in affective reactions to offenses. While for some this may reflect a deviant or subterranean subculture, this certainly cannot account for most middle-class and a major portion of lower-class delinquents. These differences need exploring in relation to the subgroups discussed in Chapter 5. Perhaps a clearer understanding of the differences observed will be found in individual cognitive variations in the ability to conceptualize the underlying structural bases of conventional moral value systems.

Moral Reasoning

Jurkovic (1980) observed that most theories of delinquency have focused on the *content* of the offender's moral worldview (i.e., their knowledge of and attitudes and beliefs about moral rules and roles—the first two approaches discussed above). The cognitive-developmental approach, in contrast, is concerned with the structure of one's moral orientation (i.e., the logical process employed, and the degree of differentiation and integration of perspectives and thought).

In the cognitive-developmental model, the focus is on one's reasoning about moral or ethical "oughts" in various situations or dilemmas which one faces. This reasoning is assessed by asking respondents about what one *should* do in a given situation, rather than what one *would* do. One can observe in the responses to questions of moral "oughts" a series of qualitatively distinct modes of thought which form a developmental sequence of stages (see Table 6.1). Each stage, as a structured whole, is characterized by a hierarchically more abstract and complex mode of reasoning. Progress through the stages is a constructive process, rather than one of passive learning, and is a result of the individual's interaction with the larger social environment. For example, a substantial literature suggests that dysfunctional families contribute in large part to high risk of delinquency (see Chapter 8). Such highly power-assertive, disharmonious home situations largely preclude role-taking and decision-making opportunities, and are characterized by high levels of conflict, dominance, hostility, lack of warmth, and disciplinary styles which are authoritarian and lacking in the inductive techniques which would foster the child's understanding of how a transgression has resulted in harm or hurt for others (see, e.g., Jurkovic & Prentice, 1974). This would preclude advance from preconventional stages of moral reasoning (characterized by physicalistic, egocentric concerns, pragmatic exchanges, and instrumental motives) to conventional stages (reasoning based on mutual interpersonal expectations, prosocial intentions, maintenance of the social system for its own sake, motives as duties and respect).

In fact, several cross-sectional and correlational studies of parenting styles and moral reasoning development have shown higher moral reasoning in children whose parents utilize higher moral reasoning, who encourage participation and spend more time in collective problem solving, who use induction versus power assertion in discipline, give and receive more support, and use less love-withdrawal (Holstein, 1972, 1976; Olejnik, 1980; Peterson, Hey, & Peterson, 1979). In intervention studies with families, significant increases in children's moral reasoning scores have been produced by counteracting these dysfunctional parenting styles through training parents in moral reasoning education techniques (Grimes, 1974) and training families in communication skills, conflict resolution, democratic approaches to problem solving, and the like (Bunzl, Coder, & Wirt, 1977; Stanley, 1978).

The potential role of the inadequate moral atmosphere of the dysfunctional family in contributing to delinquency is indicated by studies such as that by Hudgins and Prentice (1973), who found mothers of delinquents to have lower moral reasoning stage scores than mothers of nondelinquents. Further, Daum and Bieliauskas (1983), in a comparison of urban, adjudicated delinquent males from father-absent or father-present homes (there were no group differences in age, IQ, SES, birth order, family size, or aggressiveness of offense), found the former to score significantly lower on Kohlberg's Moral Judgment Interview (MJI; Kohlberg, Colby, Speicher-Dubin, and Lieberman, 1978). Delinquents from father-absent homes were limited to Stage 1 or 2, while those

TABLE 6.1 Kohlberg's Stages of Moral Development, with Perspectives on Law Issue

Level	Stage Characteristics of Reasoning	Law Issue
I. Preconventional. Social perspective is centered around self. Events are perceived in terms of physical dimensions or consequences. General lack of awareness of purpose of rules or conventions.	1 Heteronomous Morality. Equates right behavior with concrete rules backed by power and punishment. Concern with size and importance of damage and participants.	Laws are seen as simple labels. (Breaking laws would result in punishment).
	2 Individualism, Instrumental Purpose, and Exchange. Right behavior is that which serves one's own interests. Aware of other's needs, but not of rights. Fairness is strict, rigid. Reciprocal agreements are very pragmatic.	Laws are seen as intentions of lawmakers. (Breaking laws would result in loss to self.)
II. Conventional. Social perspective is centered on larger group or society. Concern for opinions of others and need for rules to regulate desired behavior. Member-of-society perspective.	3 Mutual Interpersonal Expectations, Relationships, and Interpersonal Conformity. Right behavior is the "good" that is approved by significant others. Concern for expectations of others, proper role behavior.	Laws relate to prosocial motives and conduct; diffuse normative expectations. (Breaking laws is selfish, deceitful, will make people think badly of you.)
	4 Social System and Conscience. Right behavior is meeting agreed upon obligations, following rules of society to preserve order, contributing to the good of society and its institutions.	Laws protect specific rights, practices, and institutions necessary for the social system. (Breaking laws undermines various rights; engenders disrespect for the law and can lead to social instability.)
III. Post-Conventional, or Principled. Social perspective is prior-to-society. Laws should be based on principles of justice. Human rights and respect for individual dignity are universal.	5 Social Concern or Utility; Individual Rights; Universal Ethical Principles. Right behavior is determined by universal ethics, principles of justice.	Laws protect fundamental human rights against infringement by others. (Breaking laws is generally unacceptable since they are made with common agreement; may be broken if they violate fundamental human rights.

Source: Arbuthnot, J., & Gordon, D. A. (1983). Moral reasoning development in correctional intervention. *The Journal of Correctional Education, 34,* 133–138.

from father-present homes were predominantly moving into Stage 3, with some remaining Stage 2 structures.

Finally, progress through moral reasoning stages is also dependent upon the acquisition of more general (i.e., Piagetian see Piaget & Inhelder, 1969) logical reasoning structures—a necessary but not sufficient condition for stage advancement (see, e.g., Arbuthnot, Sparling, Faust, & Kee, 1983; Colby, Kohlberg, Gibbs, and Lieberman, 1983; Walker, 1980). There is also indication that delinquents are characterized by lower Piagetian reasoning stages than matched nondelinquent samples (e.g., Arbuthnot & Martin-Benedict, 1986).

Delinquency, then, in the cognitive-developmental view, may be seen as associated with moral worldviews which are relatively immature in a developmental sense.

CROSS-SECTIONAL STUDIES OF MORAL REASONING AND DELINQUENCY. Since in the cognitive-developmental view morality resides in the reasoning which underlies a moral choice, one may encounter some difficulty in labelling a specific behavior as moral or immoral without consideration of reasoning (e.g., stealing a car for a joy-ride may be "immoral," while stealing the same car to transport an accident victim to a hospital may be morally justifiable). Therefore, moral reasoning should properly be seen as one of several potential influences on moral behavior. That it does play a significant role has been demonstrated in Blasi's (1980) review of over 30 studies showing moral reasoning maturity to be related to a variety of behaviors, including delinquency, honesty, altruism, conformity, classroom behaviors, resistance to temptation, honoring contracts, aggression, sexual activities, generosity, cheating, expression of guilt feelings, and political behaviors.

To date, some two dozen studies have been reported (many reviewed by Blasi, 1980, or Jennings, Kilkenny, and Kohlberg, 1983) which have compared delinquent and nondelinquent (or, in a few, "predelinquent" with nondelinquent) samples on maturity of moral reasoning. Of the studies using the MJI, 10 of 14 found lower scores for delinquents (Critchley, 1961, in Jennings, Kilkenny & Kohlberg, 1983; Fodor, 1972, 1973; Hawk & Peterson, 1974; Hickey, 1972; Hudgins & Prentice, 1973; Kohlberg, 1958; Kohlberg & Freundlich, 1977 (three studies) in Blasi, 1980).

One study reported mixed results (Jurkovic & Prentice, 1977), with psychopathic subtype delinquents (See Chapter 5) lower than nondelinquents, but no differences between the latter and Neurotic (Anxious-Withdrawn-Dysphoric) and Subcultural (Socialized Aggressive) delinquents. Three studies failed to find differences (Jurkovic & Prentice, 1974; Ruma, 1967; Ventis, 1976). Of the studies of predelinquents, all four found lower moral reasoning scores in comparison to normals (Bear & Richards, 1981; McColgan, Rest, & Pruitt, 1983; Sigman, Ungerer, & Russell, 1983; Wright, 1977). And Campagna and Harter (1975) found institutionalized "sociopaths" to score lower than normals. Of 19 studies using the MJI, then, only three failed to find significant differences.

In studies using production measures other than the MJI, Gibbs and his colleagues (Gavaghan, Arnold, & Gibbs, 1983; Gibbs, Widaman, & Colby, 1982; Gibbs & Widaman, 1979) have shown the Sociomoral Reflection Measure (SRM) to effectively discriminate delinquent and nondelinquent samples, even with age, SES, and IQ covaried. Arbuthnot and Martin-Benedict (1986), however, found no difference, and an objective version of the SRM failed to discriminate when age, SES, and IQ were covaried (Gibbs, et al., 1984).

Six studies report comparisons using Rest's (1979) objective measure, the Defining Issues Test (DIT). The DIT is a recognition (versus production) measure, of moderate correlation with the MJI, but useful for studying correlates of moral reasoning. Five studies have reported significant differences, three with delinquents versus nondelinquents (Hains & Miller, 1980; Hanson & Mullis, 1984; McColgan, 1975), one with antisocial predelinquents (McColgan, Rest, & Pruitt, 1983), and one with self-reported delinquency among college students (Renwick & Emler, 1984). One study (Hains & Ryan, 1983) reported mixed results, with differences only for older delinquents on some dimensions of social problem solving.

In sum, nearly all studies utilizing moral reasoning assessment devices with acceptable psychometric properties have shown delinquents to have lower moral reasoning maturity than their peers.

There is little clarity, however, for the question of whether or not delinquents are limited to preconventional stages (Stages 1 and 2), while their nondelinquent age-mates have progressed into Stage 3 or higher. It does appear to be the case (in nearly all studies that permit examination) that one finds greater proportions of delinquents or predelinquents at preconventional than at conventional stages, while the reverse is true for the nondelinquent controls. Many studies have reported average moral maturity scores (MMSs) that clearly indicate that dominant Stage 2 reasoning is typical for delinquent or predelinquent samples (Arbuthnot & Gordon, 1986; Arbuthnot & Martin-Benedict, 1986; Campagna & Harter, 1975; Critchley, 1961, in Jennings, Kilkenny, & Kohlberg, 1983; Fodor, 1972, 1973; Hudgins & Prentice, 1973; Jurkovic & Prentice, 1977; Kohlberg, 1958; Kohlberg & Freundlich, 1977; McColgan, Rest, & Pruitt, 1983; Ventis, 1976; Wright, 1977). However, a few of these studies found some delinquents as high as Stage 4, and many others have reported substantial numbers of delinquents at Stage 3 or higher or with appreciable numbers with minor Stage 3 reasoning (e.g., Bear & Richards, 1981; Gibbs, Widaman, & Colby, 1982; Hawk & Peterson, 1974; Hickey, 1972; Jurkovic & Prentice, 1974; Ruma, 1967). These patterns do not appear to be systematically related to age, social class, or severity of offenses. (It may be that these high stages, at least in part, reflect scoring error or systematic scoring differences). It is also possible that studies of institutionalized samples may have found artifactually lower moral reasoning scores due to the oppressive effects of institutionalization itself (see, e.g., Scharf, 1973), or to selection factors involved in the institutionalization process. However, in comparing studies which find average stage scores of 2(3) or lower versus 2/3 or higher, one finds 50 percent of the former group to be institutionalized samples, versus 67 percent of the latter, so this appears not to be a problem. Finally, most studies have not controlled for differences in verbal IQ, a variable likely to differ for many comparison groups (see Chapter 4). However, scoring procedures for the MJI and SRM largely minimize effects of differences in verbal IQ, and among more objective measures, the DIT also controls for such differences in the construction of items.

DELINQUENCY SUBTYPES AND MORAL REASONING.   Given the heterogeneity of the concept of delinquency, an examination of differential moral reasoning among delinquent subgroups would further clarify the role of basic cognitive functioning in antisocial behavior. Petronio (1980) compared first offenders with repeat offenders (within two years of initial placement on probation) among juveniles on probation for committing property offenses. The two groups did not differ on SES (low income), age (15 years), or IQ (X = 100). Contrary to expectations, the recidivists scored significantly *higher* in MMS (176 versus 207). While the author interpreted this outcome as partial support for Sykes and Matza's (1957) view that delinquents rationalize their misbehavior to avoid the condemnation of self and others, it is more parsimonious to suspect the validity of the scoring procedures, since (1) Petronio also claimed that the most frequent repeat offenders scored at Stage 5 (at age 15, this is highly unlikely), and (2) faking high, for whatever motive, is conceptually impossible.

Several studies have examined delinquents as behaviorally subgrouped (see Chapter 5). Jurkovic and Prentice (1977), who observed no differences between undifferentiated delinquents and nondelinquents, found that Psychopathic delinquents reasoned exclusively at Stages 1 and 2, while the average for each of the other groups approached Stage 3. Jurkovic (1980) also pointed out that the Psychopathic group functioned at the level of Piaget's (Piaget & Inhelder, 1969) concrete operations and showed little evidence of reflective perspective-taking, whereas the other groups "exhibited more age-appropriate formal operational and perspective-taking skills." Similar data were obtained by Campagna and Harter (1975), and Fodor (1973) with Psychopathic delinquents for both delinquent/nondelinquent group differences, as well as differences reflective of more primitive Piagetian reasoning on the part of the Psychopathic subgroup. Heyns, van Niekerk, and Le Roux (1981) also provided consistent data showing relationships between Inadequacy-Immaturity (see Chapter 5) and lack of principled morality as measured by Rest's DIT. Ventis (1976), on the other hand, who observed no differences between delinquents and nondelinquents, also found no differences between Psychopathic delinquents and matched nondelinquents. This suggests that there may have been something unique about his sample—13-to-16-year-old probationers, excluding repeated hard drug offenders—while all of the other studies used institutionalized offenders. Ventis's sample, then, may have been appreciably less seriously Psychopathic. In support of this, Gotthardt (1985; see Arbuthnot & Gordon, 1984) also found no differences between "predelinquents" classified as either aggressive or combined Anxiety-Withdrawal/Immature.

Implications of Moral Reasoning for Delinquency

In sum, the literature seems to be quite clear in indicating a general developmental delay in moral reasoning abilities on the part of delinquents in general, and Undersocialized Aggressive delinquents in particular. However, while delinquents are disproportionately found at the preconventional stages (1 and 2), many are found at higher stages. Whether these higher-stage delinquent reasoners differ from their lower-stage peers in some other relevant characteristics (e.g., type of offense, isolated nature of offense, impulsivity, etc.), is not yet known.

Delinquency should come as no surprise if a youth cannot take the perspectives of others and empathize with others' circumstances, if he or she cannot see the value of conforming to certain behavioral expectations or rules to ensure order and protect civility, if property has no meaning beyond possession, and if friendship (or even life) has no value beyond utility. More advanced sociomoral worldviews may be necessary for one to summon up eloquent moral justifications for right behavior, and to find the courage to act accordingly in the face of temptation, economic deprivation, and/or intense peer-group pressures. Given the robustness of the general findings, it seems appropriate for the field to move its resources in the direction of interventions. If higher stage (e.g., Stage 3, conventional) moral reasoning can provide the delinquent with a less conditional worldview, one in which standards or rules of a prosocial nature provide guides for desirable and approved behavior, then presumably delinquent behavior choices may abate. In the first study of both immediate and long-term behavioral outcomes of a moral reasoning development program with predelinquent, behavior-disordered adolescents (Arbuthnot & Gordon, 1986; see also Chapter 11), such changes were produced and maintained. The field now needs to assess the utility of this approach with more serious offenders, and to find the moderators of its success.

Related Constructs

Research on cognitive skills other than those directly involved in sociomoral reasoning has also shown significant development deficits to be characteristic of delinquents. These include problem solving, social skills (with cognitive components), and empathy and/or role taking.

Problem Solving and Social Skills

Freedman, Rosenthal, Donahoe, Schlundt, and McFall (1978) developed the Adolescent Problems Inventory, which was designed to identify strengths and weaknesses in the personal and interpersonal skills repertoires of adolescent boys. Institutionalized delinquent boys were found to score lower than either of two nondelinquent groups of teenage boys ("good citizens" and "leaders"). In addition, among institutionalized delinquent boys, those with more frequent behavior problems received lower scores on the API. Similar results have been obtained in other research, as well (e.g., Collingwood & Genthner, 1980; Roff, Sells, & Golden, 1972).

Empathy and Role Taking

A criticism often leveled at proponents of the moral reasoning model is that its focus is too narrowly cognitive; that is, it reflects but one of several dimensions of morality. Being able to generate higher order moral arguments and to evaluate values claims qualitatively may not lead to moral behavior in the absence of an emotional or affective concern for the plight (or rights) of others (as well as the moral courage to act on one's judgments and feelings). The literature, however, often fails to separate the affective from the more purely cognitive aspects of role-taking abilities. It is often argued, in fact, that the former is enabled by the capacity to take cognitively the point of view of the other, such that the persistence of egocentric thought would preclude affective caring.

Chandler (1973) has pointed out that a sizable body of literature links prosocial behavior to the development of age-appropriate role-taking and/or perspective-taking abilities, and that a variety of antisocial behaviors have been linked with the persistence of egocentric thought. Individuals characterized by developmental delays in these capacities " . . . have been shown to systematically misread societal expectations, to misinterpret the actions and intentions of others, and to act in ways which were judged to be callous and disrespectful of the rights of others" (p. 326). Chandler compared the social egocentrism of serious and chronic delinquent and nondelinquent youth. Marked and significant differences were observed, with almost no overlap between the distributions of the two samples (this study further demonstrated that the skill deficits of the delinquents can be ameliorated, and that improvements are associated with reductions in delinquent behavior—see Chapter 11).

Little and Kendall (1979) found substantial deficits in a sample of female delinquents, as well. Other studies, however, which have compared the relative deficits of delinquents and nondelinquents on both cognitive and affective role taking abilities, have found only the latter to be lacking (e.g., Rotenberg, 1974). Kaplan and Arbuthnot (1985) found no differences in cognitive role taking for 13-to-15-year-old male and female delinquents and a sample of nondelinquents matched on race, SES, and IQ, nor were significant differences observed for a self-report measure of affective empathy. However, significant differences did favor the nondelinquent group on a production measure of affective empathy.

Taken together, these few studies suggest that while cognitive role taking may play an enabling role in preventing delinquency, it appears not to be a sufficient factor by itself. Affective empathy—that is, not only seeing the situation from the other's perspective, but also caring at an emotional level about the other's plight—appears to play a significant role in moderating delinquent behaviors. Intervention programs designed to foster development of affective empathy would seem to be a much needed next step, a direction further suggested by the more general (nondelinquent) literature showing consistent effects of empathy as an inhibitor of aggression and other antisocial behaviors (e.g., Mehrabian & Epstein, 1972; Rotenberg, 1974).

DELINQUENT SUBTYPES

In this section we will briefly examine the literature which attempts to characterize personality differences between "official" subtypes of delinquents, including status offenders versus adjudicated delinquents, and recidivists and repeat offenders versus first or one-time offenders.

Status Offenders Versus Adjudicated Delinquents

Stott and Olezak's (1978) study served to dispel the notion that with increasing seriousness of offense type will be found a simple increase in the magnitude of personality disorder. Consistent with the earlier research of Burkhart (1975) and Thomas (1976), Stott and Olezak reported that status offenders receive scores indicative of *greater* personality disturbance on the JI, including Social Maladjustment, Value Orientation, and Manifest Aggression. No differences were found on the remaining subscales. In addition, Stott and Olezak reanalyzed some of Thomas's data, and found that status offenders were significantly *more* likely to recidivate than were samples of adjudicated delinquents who had committed misdemeanors or felonies. Tempering the potential importance of their data is the fact that Stott and Olezak did not report on the degree of seriousness of their delinquent samples' offenses, and their results may be somewhat limited in generalization by the fact that *all* participants in the research had been referred for psychiatric evaluations.

Multiple Offenders

As noted in earlier chapters, among the myriad difficulties encountered by delinquency researchers are problems of definition and categorization. This problem arises in distinguishing official and unofficial delinquents (i.e., those who offend, are apprehended, and are processed in the juvenile or adult justice systems, versus those who offend but are either not caught or are not officially processed). Similarly, many delinquents (whether official or unofficial) commit multiple offenses, but only a fraction of these multiple offenders are officially processed. Thus, when we examine the literature on multiple offenders, we are limited to the study of those few who are processed and convicted more than once ("recidivists") or to those who indicate by self-report that they have committed multiple offenses. Of course, even "nondelinquents" commit offenses—often multiply—which would result in prosecution if they were caught (see, e.g., Erickson & Empey, 1963; Hindelang, Hirschi, & Weis, 1981).

Several "personality" correlates of recidivism and multiple offenses have been identified (along with several nonpersonality variables), including: "aggressive acting out" (Mack, 1969a,b); conduct disorder (Ganzer & Sarason, 1973), Anxiety-Withdrawal (Quay & Love, 1977); social immaturity (Sealy & Banks, 1971); and hostility, social deviancy, and low motivation (Roe, Howell, & Payne, 1974). Kendall, Deardorff, and Finch (1977) found repeat offenders to score lower on the So scale of the CPI. Hindelang (1972) reported that the frequency of delinquent involvement was related to the Pd scale of the MMPI, as well as to the So, Sc, and Re scales of the CPI. Collingwood and Genthner (1980) found recidivists to be deficient in various cognitive and social skills, including attending, observing, listening, responding, defining alternate courses of action, logically selecting courses of action, defining goals, and defining steps to reach goals.

Hanson, Henggeler, Haefele, and Rodick (1984) conducted an ambitious multivariate study to identify the strongest predictors of repeated and serious arrests among juvenile offenders and their siblings. The study included demographic, individual, and family relationship variables, with participants including 74 father-present and 89 father-absent families of which approximately two-thirds had an adolescent son with an arrest record. The families were mostly of low SES, the majority were black, and were large (with average size in excess of six members). Among the individual predictor variables were the EPI, and Quay and Peterson's (1975) Behavior Problem Checklist (measuring the four empirically derived dimensions of psychopathology, as discussed in Chapter 5). Based on stepwise multiple regression analyses, the most powerful predictor of serious and repeated arrests was Socialized-Aggressive behavior (as rated by parents), especially so for father-absent homes.

Again, reflective of a strong systemic origin for multiple offenses, the Socialized-Aggressive dimension reflects an adaptive, collaborative involvement in a delinquent peer group that leads to support and acceptance. Conduct Disorder, on the other hand, is characterized by a confrontational, aggressive posture that is often alienating, and this proved to be a strong predictor of criminality only in father-present homes (which, perhaps, permit greater levels of parent-adolescent disagreement). It seems clear from both the univariate and multivariate research, then, that both identification and treatment of multiple offenders should be focused on systemic variables (both peer group and family), rather than on the individual alone.

VIOLENT JUVENILE OFFENDERS

Among juvenile offenses, those of a violent nature (e.g., assault, rape, homicide) appear to have a rather distinct etiology from crimes against property or nonviolent crimes against persons. Unlike nonviolent delinquency, violent offenses are disproportionately committed by males of low SES from ghettoes, and offenders are more often black, Latino, or Asian in ethnicity (e.g., Curtis, 1978; Gold & Reimer, 1975; Hamparian, Schuster, Dinitz, & Conrad, 1978; Miller, 1976; Smith, Alexander, Halatyn, & Roberts, 1980; Strasburg, 1978, 1984; Wolfgang, Figlio, & Sellin, 1972). In addition, unlike nonviolent offenses, violent juvenile crimes are committed more often when alone than in groups (Aultman, 1980). And, while it appears that violent youthful offenders have a more active delinquent history, there is little evidence that this history is particularly violent—the offenses, for many, being the result of momentary panic (see, e.g., Russell, 1973; Vinson, 1979).

Violent juvenile offenders do, however, have family histories which are atypical of the population as a whole, if not different from those of delinquents in general. For discussions of these variables, see Chapter 8.

Several studies have examined personality traits of violent offenders, finding such characteristics as social alienation and a need for immediate gratification (Vachss & Backal, 1979); poor ego strength, ego decomposition, or immature ego (Schoenfeld, 1971); depression (Anthony, 1968; Cocozza & Hartshorne, 1978); depressed anxiety (Kulik, Stein, & Sarbin, 1968); low self-esteem and strong feelings of rage (Strasburg, 1978); cognitive rigidity (Breskin & Burchill, 1971); behaviors based largely on emotions or feelings as opposed to cognitions (King, 1975); greater need for personal space (Boorhem & Flowers, 1977); and lack of impulse control, lack of empathy, exaggerated fearfulness, and failure to find fulfillment in steady, long-term adaptive social behavior (Sorrels, 1977, 1980).

Sorrels' studies focused on juveniles who had committed homicide, finding them almost always to be males from poor families, and from uniformly chaotic, usually brutal and violent families. In comparison with other types of delinquents, he did not find this group to be unusually disturbed as a whole—some were anxious or depressed, some were social isolates and overcontrolled, some were hostile and explosive, and some seemed quite healthy and well-adjusted.

Yates, Beutler, and Crago (1983) studied 339 incarcerated youthful offenders, dividing them into three groups: murderers, other offenders against persons, and offenders against property. In a comparison of common psychiatric diagnoses (neurotic, personality disorder, substance-abuse, adjustment disorder, conduct disorder, etc.) across the three groups, no significant difference was found. On other dimensions, person offenders differed little from murderers, while both groups combined were less likely than property offenders to have histories of severely impaired relationships or to have been labelled as emotionally disturbed or as learning disabled in school records. These results suggest strongly the need for appropriate comparison groups in studies of violent juvenile offenders, as well as for greater attention to be paid to personal and familial histories as opposed to paper-and-pencil or interview-based psychiatric categorizations.

CONCLUSIONS

Earlier reviews of the personality and delinquency literature have generally concluded that the data are inconclusive, at best, and that the combined results of several decades of research have failed to demonstrate systematic associations between personality variables and delinquent behavior (Quay, 1965a; Schuessler & Cressey, 1950; Tennenbaum, 1977; Waldo & Dinitz, 1967). With few exceptions, the research of the past 20 years reviewed here does little to change these conclusions.

Some of the multivariate scales are improvements in both psychometric properties and utility, most notably the factorially derived scales measuring the dimensions discussed in Chapter 5, and, to some extent, the JI and the CPI. The use of the MMPI, as well as lesser-known scales, would appear to add little, either theoretically or practically.

With the possible exception of self-concept, all of the univariate personality constructs (e.g., time orientation, impulsivity, sensation seeking, locus of control) have yielded results that are equivocal at best. When positive associations were found, they were for the most part quite modest, and often obfuscated by psychometric problems. Consistent and meaningful differences were noted, however, for those dimensions with a strong sociocognitive component: sociomoral reasoning, interpersonal problem solving, role taking, and empathy.

The strongest conclusion reached by Quay in 1965(a) (and echoed in Chapter 5) was the need for the field to move away from consideration of delinquents as a homogeneous population, and for research to focus on the causes and correlates of behavior associated with the relatively distinct subtypes of delinquents. The impact of the use of the empirically-derived dimensions has generally been positive, especially when it has been used with relatively serious offenders (versus "predelinquents," etc.), but it is remarkable that so few researchers have chosen to utilize subtypes in their research. The recommendation deserves to be reiterated here, although one might add that other classification schemas should be investigated, thereby perhaps generating a system of wider appeal to researchers and practitioners.

Several other conclusions seem warranted on the basis of the present review. First, a persistent problem has been noted with the psychometric aspects of personality assessment. Inconsistencies in outcomes can often be traced to differences in assessment procedures and/or in operational definitions of personality dimensions (e.g., impulsivity). It seems imperative that we develop and utilize tests or measures which are behavioral in nature, or at least are validated against behavioral criteria that clearly reflect the dimension under study.

Several researchers, most notably Reppucci and Clingempeel (1978) have suggested that a focus only on personality measures in our attempts to understand, identify, and/or treat delinquents is quite myopic—there is a strong need to consider interactions of person variables with those of an environmental nature. In addition, personality researchers have largely limited their research to pathological aspects of the person, excluding the more adaptive qualities and strengths of the juvenile offender. This leads us to several additional conclusions and recommendations. When selecting participants for delinquency research, whether predictive, epidemiological, or treatment oriented, we really ought to make use of multiple measures and types of assessments, both to reduce error as well as to obtain a broader picture of the dynamics of the individuals under study. (We are hampered to some extent in this direction by the fact that most scales are merely descriptive in nature, and do not suggest avenues for diversion or treatment).

A serious problem concerns the identification and selection of samples for study. Adjudicated—and especially institutionalized—delinquents are not representative of antisocial youth in general. Therefore, even consistent results obtained with such samples will be of potential use only in tertiary treatment and prevention for those segments of the antisocial adolescent population, and not for general selection of youth for primary or secondary prevention, or for the development and testing of general models of delinquency (see Chapter 12). We need to make use of other means of choosing samples—including self-report and nominations (behaviorally referenced) by others (e.g., parents, teachers, youth workers, etc.) who have frequent contact with the youth.

Related to the problems of selection of delinquents is the corollary problem of selection of controls. Who are the appropriate comparison groups? Is it sufficient to simply match delinquents with nondelinquents of similar socioeconomic and demographic backgrounds? Should we require matching with individuals from similar family structures and neighborhood environments? This is especially problematic in developmental or etiological studies. Reminiscent of Reppucci and Clingempeel's (1978) concerns, studies of the etiology of delinquency tend to focus on the differences between delinquents and "normals" without attempting to deal with the vast number of dimensions on which no differences are found. Similarly, there are no doubt many more normals who have the same traits, backgrounds, pressures, and so forth, as delinquents, who nonetheless do not transgress the law or become delinquents.

An additional avenue of research which may help us to understand why some but not all (or even many) individuals with given characteristics and/or backgrounds will "choose" to transgress or offend is to examine variables which directly impinge upon the process of choice itself. The strength and consistency, as well as theoretical clarity, of the more cognitively based constructs point to a potentially very fruitful new direction for researchers and practitioners in delinquency. Ample evidence seems to indicate that most delinquents suffer from some (or multiple) form(s) of developmental delay in sociocognitive functioning: sociomoral reasoning, empathy; role taking; and/or interpersonal problem solving. These are of even greater importance in light of indications that delinquents also appear to function at less complex levels of intellectual development (as noted in Chapter 4). These developmental delays are highly consistent with dysfunctional family and other early social environment characteristics, and may also reflect underlying maturational phenomena of a biological nature. Taken together, this area of research holds considerable promise for basic research in the etiology of delinquency, as well as for both individual and systemic intervention programs of a primary, secondary, and tertiary nature.

Finally, the bottom line in research and model building in any area with such important practical applications as antisocial behavior must be to lead us eventually to intervention programs that are demonstrably effective. Most of the univariate and multivariate personality constructs currently (and historically) under study do not suggest prevention or treatment programs, nor do they seem to have any clear implications for understanding the causes of delinquency. Some *may* have utility as moderator variables (although the cognitive dimensions would appear to have greater utility in this regard also), but even here, to be useful, such moderators must help us to understand the delinquent's decision to transgress. Short of primary prevention, it is at this decision point where we will have the greatest (and perhaps only) opportunity to affect the course of antisocial behavior.

REFERENCES

Abe, M. (1969). The Japanese MMPI and its delinquency scale. *Tohoku Psychologica Folia, 84*, 54–68.

Ageton, S. S., & Elliott, E. S. (1974). The effects of legal processing on delinquent orientations. *Social Problems, 22*, 87–100.

Ajzen, I., & Fishbein, M. (1978). Attitude-behavior relations: A theoretical analysis and review of empirical research. *Psychological Bulletin, 84*, 888–918.

Anthony, H. S. (1968). The association of violence and depression in a sample of young offenders. *British Journal of Criminology, 8*, 346–365.

Arbuthnot, J., & Gordon, D. A. (1984). *Remedial social development for high-risk youth in school.* Paper presented at the National Conference of the Association for Moral Education, Columbus, Ohio, November.

Arbuthnot, J., & Gordon, D. A. (1986). Behavioral and cognitive effects of a moral reasoning development intervention for high-risk behavior-disordered adolescents. *Journal of Consulting and Clinical Psychology, 54*, 208–216.

Arbuthnot, J., & Martin-Benedict, D. (1986). *The sociomoral and Piagetian reasoning abilities of delinquent and non-delinquent adolescents.* Paper presented at National Conference of the Association for Moral Education, Chicago, November.

Arbuthnot, J., Sparling, Y., Faust, D., & Kee, W. (1983). Logical and moral development in pre-adolescent children. *Psychological Reports, 52*, 209–210.

Armstrong, J. S. (1980). The relationship of sex-role identification, self-esteem, and aggression in delinquent males. *Dissertation Abstracts International, 40(B)*, 3900.

Atkins, J. W. (1974). Delinquency as a function of self-esteem. *Dissertation Abstracts International, 34(B)*, 4650.

Aultman, M. G. (1980). Group involvement in delinquent acts—a study of offense types and male-female participation. *Criminal Justice and Behavior, 7*, 185–192.

Baker, J. W., II, & Spielberg, M. J. (1970). A descriptive personality study of delinquency-prone adolescents. *Journal of Research in Crime and Delinquency, 7*, 11–23.

Barratt, E. (1959). Anxiety and impulsiveness related to psychomotor efficiency. *Perceptual and Motor Skills, 9*, 191–198.

Bear, G. G., & Richards, H. C. (1981). Moral reasoning and conduct problems in the classroom. *Journal of Educational Psychology, 73*, 644–670.

Beck, S. J., & Ollendick, T. H. (1976). Personal space, sex of experimenter, and locus of control in normal and delinquent adolescents. *Psychological Reports, 38*, 383–387.

Bialer, I. (1961). Conceptualization of success and failure in mentally retarded and normal children. *Journal of Personality, 29*, 303–320.

Biggs, S. J., Bender, M. P., & Foreman, J. (1983). Are there psychological differences between persistent solvent-abusing delinquents and delinquents who do not abuse solvents? *Journal of Adolescence, 6*, 71–86.

Blasi, A. (1980). Bridging moral cognition and moral action: A critical review of the literature. *Psychological Bulletin, 88*, 1–45.

Bliss, D. C. (1977). The effects of the juvenile justice system on self-concept. *Criminal Justice Abstracts, 10*, 297–298.

Boorhem, C. D., & Flowers, J. V. (1977). Personal space variations as a function of criminal. *Psychological Reports, 41*, 1115–1121.

Breskin, S., & Burchill, P. G. (1971). Nonverbal rigidity and severity of criminal offense in a group of juvenile delinquents. *Journal of Psychology, 78*, 265–267.

Briggs, P. S., Wirt, R. D., & Johnson, R. (1961). An application of prediction tables to the study of delinquency. *Journal of Consulting Psychology, 25*, 46–50.

Brynner, J., O'Malley, P., & Bachman, J. (1981). Self-esteem and delinquency revisited. *Journal of Youth and Adolescence, 10*, 407–441.

Bunzl, M., Coder, R., & Wirt, R. D. (1977). Enhancement of maturity of moral judgment by parent education. *Journal of Abnormal Child Psychology, 5*, 177–186.

Burke, E. L., Zilberg, N. J., Amini, F., Salasnek, S., & Forkin, D. (1978). Some empirical evidence for Erikson's concept of negative in delinquent drug abusers. *Comprehensive Psychiatry, 19*, 141–152.

Burkhart, K. A. (1975). *The child and the law: Helping the status offender.* New York: Public Affairs Committee.

Campagna, A., & Harter, S. (1975). Moral judgment in sociopathic and normal children. *Journal of Personality and Social Psychology, 31*, 199–205.

Chandler, M. (1973). Egocentrism and antisocial behavior: The assessment and training of social perspective-taking skills. *Developmental Psychology, 9*, 326–332.

Cochrane, R. (1974). Crime and personality: Theory and evidence. *Bulletin of the British Psychological Society, 27*, 19–22.

Cocozza, J. J., & Hartshorne, E. (1978). Research and evaluation on the Bronx (N.Y.) Court Related Unit: An interim report. Albany: New York State Department of Mental Hygiene, Bureau of Special Projects Research.

Colby, A., Kohlberg, L., Gibbs, J. C., & Lieberman, M. A. (1983). A longitudinal study of moral judgment. *Monographs of the Society for Research in Child Development, 48*, (1–2, Serial No. 200).

Collingwood, T. R., & Genthner, R. W. (1980). Skills training as treatment for juvenile delinquents. *Professional Psychology, 11*, 591–598.

Coopersmith, S. (1967). The *antecedents of self-esteem*. San Francisco: Freeman.

Cowden, J. E., Peterson, W. M., & Pacht, A. R. (1969). The MCI versus the Jesness Inventory as a screening and classification instrument at a juvenile correctional institution. *Journal of Clinical Psychology, 25*, 57–60.

Crandall, V. C., Katovsky, W., & Crandall, V. S. (1965). Children's beliefs in their own control of reinforcements in intellectual-academic situations. *Child Development, 36*, 91–109.

Cross, H., & Tracy, J. (1971). Personality factors in delinquent boys: Differences between blacks and whites. *Journal of Research in Crime and Delinquency, 8*, 10–22.

Critchley. (1961). In Jennings, W., Kilkenny, R., & Kohlberg, L. (1983). Moral-development theory and practice of youthful and adult offenders. In W. S. Laufer, J. M. Day (Eds.), *Personality theory, moral development, and criminal behavior.* (pp. 281–355). Lexington, MA: Lexington.

Culbertson, R. G. (1975). The effect of institutionalization on the delinquent inmate's self-concept. *Journal of Criminal Law and Criminology, 66*, 88–93.

Curtis, L. A. (1978). Violence and youth. *Research into violent behavior: Overview and sexual assaults.* Washington, D.C.: U.S. Congress, House Committee on Science and Technology.

Curtiss, G., Feczko, M. D., & Marohn, R. C. (1979). Rorschach differences in normal delinquent white male adolescents: A discriminant function analysis. *Journal of Youth & Adolescence, 8*, 379–392.

Daum, J. M., & Bieliauskas, V. J. (1983). Fathers' absence and moral development of male delinquents. *Psychological Reports, 53*, 223–228.

Davids, A., & Falkof, B. B. (1975). Juvenile delinquents then and now: Comparison of findings from 1959 and 1974. *Journal of Abnormal Psychology, 84*, 161–164.

Dietz, G. E. (1969). A comparison of delinquents with nondelinquents on self-concept, self-acceptance, and parental identification. *Journal of Genetic Psychology, 115*, 285–295.

Dinitz, S., Reckless, W. C., & Kay B. (1958). A self-gradient among potential delinquents. *Journal of Criminal Law, Criminology, and Police Science, 49*, 230–233.

Dinitz, S., Scarpitti, F. R., & Reckless, W. C. (1962). Delinquency vulnerability: A cross group and longitudinal analysis. *American Sociological Review, 27*, 515–517.

Docter, R. F., & Winder, C. L. (1954). Delinquent vs. nondelinquent performance on the Porteus Qualitative Maze Test. *Journal of Consulting Psychology, 18*, 71–73.

Dombrose, L., & Slobin, M. (1958). The IES test. *Perceptual Motor Skills, 8*, 347–389.

Dorn, D. S. (1968). Self-concept, alienation, and anxiety in a contraculture and subculture: A research report. *Journal of Criminal Law, Criminology, and Police Science, 59*, 531–535.

Duke, M. P., & Fenhagen, E. (1975). Self-parental alienation and locus of control in delinquent girls. *The Journal of Genetic Psychology, 127*, 103–107.

Eisen, V. (1956). *An evaluation of several psychological tests for differentiating female delinquents from female nondelinquents.* Unpublished doctoral dissertation, Fordham University, New York.

Erickson, E. (1963). *Childhood and society.* New York: Norton.

Erickson, M. L., & Empey, L. T. (1963). Court records, undetected delinquency, and decision making. *Journal of Criminal Law, Criminology, and Police Science, 54,* 456–469.

Erickson, R. V., & Roberts, A. H. (1966). A comparison of two groups of institutionalized delinquents on Porteus Maze. *Journal of Consulting Psychology, 30,* 567.

Eyo-Isidore, D. (1981). British delinquents and non-delinquents on seven domains of the self-concept. *Journal of Psychology, 109,* 137–145.

Eysenck, H. J. (1977). *Crime and personality.* (3rd ed.). London: Granada.

Eysenck, H. J., & Eysenck, S. B. G. (1975). *Manual of the Eysenck Personality Inventory.* San Diego: Educational and Industrial Testing Service.

Eysenck, S. B. G., & Eysenck, H. J. (1974). Personality and recidivism in Borstal boys. *British Journal of Criminology, 14,* 385–387.

Farley, F. H., & Farley, S. V. (1972). Stimulus-seeking motivation and delinquent behavior among institutionalized delinquent girls. *Journal of Consulting & Clinical Psychology, 39,* 94–97.

Farley, F. H., & Sewell, T. (1976). Test of an arousal theory of delinquency. *Criminal Justice & Behavior, 3,* 315–320.

Feldman, M. P. (1977). *Criminal behavior: A psychological analysis.* London: Wiley.

Fisher, R. M. (1967). Acquiscent response set, the Jesness Inventory and implications for the use of "foreign" psychological tests. *British Journal of Social and Clinical Psychology, 6,* 1–10.

Fitts, W. H. (1965). *Tennessee Self-Concept Scale manual.* Nashville, TN: Counselor Recordings and Tests.

Fitts, W., & Hammer, W. (1969). *The self-concept and delinquency.* Nashville: Counselor Recordings and Tests.

Fodor, E. M. (1972). Delinquency and susceptibility of social influence among adolescents as a function of moral development. *Journal of Social Psychology, 86,* 257–260.

Fodor, E. M. (1973). Moral development and parent behavior antecedents in adolescent psychopaths. *Journal of Genetic Psychology, 122,* 37–43.

Follman, J., Dickinson, J., Corbin, L., Burg, E., & Cech, E. (1972). Delinquency prediction scales and personality inventories. *Child Study Journal, 2,* 99–103.

Forrest, R. (1977). Personality and delinquency: A multivariate examination of Eysenck's theory with Scottish delinquent and non-delinquent boys. *Social Behavior and Personality, 5,* 157–167.

Fraas, L. A., & Price, R. L. (1972). The Jesness Inventory as a predictor of AWOL recidivism. *Psychological Reports, 31,* 741–742.

Freedman, B. J., Rosenthal, L., Donahoe, C. P., Schlundt, D. G., & McFall, R. M. (1978). A social-behavioral analysis of skill deficits in delinquent and non-delinquent adolescent boys. *Journal of Consulting and Clinical Psychology, 46,* 1448–1462.

Ganzer, V. J., & Sarason, I. G. (1973). Variables associated with recidivism among juvenile delinquents. *Journal of Consulting & Clinical Psychology, 40*, 1–5.

Gavaghan, M.P., Arnold, K. D., & Gibbs, J. C. (1983). Moral judgment in delinquents and nondelinquents: Recognition vs. production measures. *The Journal of Psychology, 114*, 267–274.

Gearing, M. L., II. (1979). The MMPI as a primary differentiator and predictor of behavior in prison: A methodological critique and review of the recent literature. *Psychological Bulletin, 86*, 926–963.

Gendreau, P., Grant, B. A., Leipciger, M., & Collins, S. (1979). Norms and recidivism rates for the MMPI and selected experimental scales on a Canadian delinquent sample. *Canadian Journal of Behavioural Science, 11*, 21–31.

Gibbs, J. C., Arnold, K. D., Morgan, R. L., Schwartz, E. S., Gavaghan, M. P., & Tappan, M. B. (1984). Construction and validation of a multiple-choice measure of moral reasoning. *Child Development, 55*, 527–536.

Gibbs, J. C., & Widaman, K. F. (1979). *Social intelligence: Measuring the development of sociomoral reflection.* Englewood Cliffs, NJ: Prentice-Hall.

Gibbs, J. C., Widaman, K. F., & Colby, A. (1982). Construction and validation of a simplified, group administerable equivalent to the Moral Judgment Interview. *Child Development 53*, 895–910.

Gibson, H. B. (1964). The spiral maze: The psychomotor test with implications for the study of delinquency. *British Journal of Psychology, 55*, 219–225.

Gold, M. (1978). Scholastic experiences, self-esteem, and delinquent behavior: A theory for alternative schools. *Crime & Delinquency, 24*, 290–308.

Gold, M., & Mann, D. (1972). Delinquency as defense. *American Journal of Orthopsychiatry, 42*, 463–479.

Gold, M., & Reimer, D. J. (1975). Changing patterns of delinquent behavior among American 13 through 16 year olds—1967–1922. *Crime and Delinquency, 7*, 483–517.

Goldberg, L., & Guilford, J. S. (1972). *Delinquent values: It's fun to break the rules.* The preceedings from the 80th Annual Convention of the American Psychological Association, Honolulu, Hawaii.

Gotthardt, J. (1985). *Behavioral and cognitive effects of moral reasoning, combined, and social skills interventions with aggressive and nonaggressive behaviorally disordered adolescents.* Unpublished doctoral dissertation, Ohio University, Athens.

Graham, S. A. (1981). Predictive and concurrent validity of the Jesness Inventory Asocial Index: When does a delinquent become delinquent? *Journal of Consulting and Clinical Psychology, 49*, 740–742.

Gregory, R. J. (1977). The actuarial description of delinquency: Seven MMPI code types. *Dissertation Abstracts International, 33*, 5017.

Grimes, P. (1974). *Teaching moral reasoning to 11-year-olds and their mothers: A means of promoting moral growth.* Unpublished doctoral dissertation, Boston University, Boston.

Hains, A., & Miller, D. (1980). Moral and cognitive development in delinquent & nondelinquent children and adolescents. *Journal of Genetic Psychology, 137*, 21–35.

Hains, A. A., & Ryan, E. B. (1983). The development of social cognitive processes among juvenile delinquents and nondelinquent peers. *Child Development, 54*, 1536–1544.

Hamparian, D. M., Schuster, R., Dinitz, S., & Conrad, J. P. (1978). *The violent few: A study of dangerous juvenile offenders.* Lexington, MA: D. C. Heath.

Henson, C. L., Henggeler, S. W., Haefele, W. F., & Rodick, J. D. (1984). Demographic, individual, and family relationship correlates of serious and repeated crime among adolescents and their siblings. *Journal of Consulting & Clinical Psychology, 52*, 528–538.

Hanson, R. A, & Mullis, R. L. (1984). Moral reasoning in offender and non-offender youth. *The Journal of Genetic Psychology, 144*, 295–296.

Hartshorne, H., & May, M. A. (1928). *Studies in the nature of character.* New York: Macmillan.

Hartshorne, H., May, M. A., & Maller, J. B. (1929). *Studies in the nature of character: Vol. II. Studies in self-control.* New York: Macmillan.

Hartshorne, H., May, M. A., & Shuttleworth, F. K. (1930). *Studies in the nature of character: Vol. III. Studies in the organization of character.* New York: Macmillan.

Hawk, S. S., & Peterson, R. A. (1974). Do MMPI psychopathic deviancy scores reflect psychopathic deviancy or just deviancy? *Journal of Personality Assessment, 38*, 362–368.

Heather, N. (1979). The structure of delinquent values: A repertory grid investigation. *British Journal of Social and Clinical Psychology, 18*, 263–275.

Heyns, P. M., van Niekerk, H. G., & Le Roux, J. A. (1981). Moral judgment and behavioral dimensions of juvenile delinquency. *International Journal for the Advancement of Counselling, 4*, 139–151.

Hickey, J. (1972). *The effects of guided moral discussion upon youthful offenders' level of moral judgment.* (Doctoral dissertation, Boston University, School of Education). *Dissertation Abstracts International, 33*, 1551A (University Microfilms No. 75-25, 438).

Hindelang, M. J. (1972). The relationship of self-reported delinquency to scales of the CPI and MMPI. *Journal of Criminal Law, Criminology, & Police Science, 63*, 75–81.

Hindelang, M. J. (1973). Variations in personality attributes of social and solitary self-reported delinquents. *Journal of Consulting and Clinical Psychology, 40*, 452–454.

Hindelang, M. J. (1974). Moral evaluations of illegal behavior. *Social Problems, 21*, 370–385.

Hindelang, M. J., Hirschi, T., & Weis, J. G. (1981). *Measuring delinquency.* Beverly Hills, CA: Sage.

Hirschfield, P. (1965). Response set in impulsive children. *Journal of Genetic Psychology, 107*, 117–126.

Hogan, R. (1969). Development of an empathy scale. *Journal of Consulting and Clinical Psychology, 35*, 307–316.

Hogan, R., Mankin, D., Conway, J., & Fox, S. (1970). Personality correlates of undergraduate marijuana use. *Journal of Consulting and Clinical Psychology, 35*, 58–63.

Holstein, C. (1972). The relation of children's moral judgment level to that of their parents and to communication patterns in the family. In R. C. & M. S. Smart (Eds.), *Readings in child development and relationships.* (p. 484–494.) New York: Macmillan.

Holstein, C. (1976). Irreversible, stepwise sequence in the development of moral judgment: a longitudinal study of males and females. *Child Development, 47,* 51–61.

Hudgins, W., & Prentice, N. (1973). Moral judgment in delinquent and non-delinquent adolescents and their mothers. *Journal of Abnormal Psychology, 82,* 145–152.

Huesmann, L. R., Lefkowitz, M. M., & Eron, L. D. (1978). Sum of MMPI scales F, 4, and 9 as a measure of aggression. *Journal of Consulting and Clinical Psychology, 46,* 1071–1078.

Hughes, S. P., & Dodder, R. A. (1980). Delinquency and dimensions of self. *Psychology, 77,* 15–22.

Jennings, W., Kilkenny, R., & Kohlberg, L. (1983). Moral-development theory and practice of youthful and adult offenders. In W. S. Laufer, J. M. Day (Eds.), *Personality theory, moral development, and criminal behavior.* (p. 281–355). Lexington, MA: Lexington.

Jensen, G. F. (1972). Delinquency and adolescent self-conceptions: A study of the personal relevance of infraction. *Social Problems, 20,* 84–103.

Jesness, C. F. (1972). *The Jesness Inventory* (rev. ed.). Palo Alto, CA: Consulting Psychologists Press.

Jesness, C. F. (1977). When is a delinquent a delinquent? A reply to Shark and Handal. *Journal of Consulting and Clinical Psychology, 45,* 696–697.

Jurkovic, G. J. (1980). The juvenile delinquent as a moral philosopher: A structural-developmental perspective. *Psychological Bulletin, 88,* 709–727.

Jurkovic, G., & Prentice, N. M. (1974). Dimensions of moral interaction and moral judgment in delinquent and nondelinquent families. *Journal of Consulting & Clinical Psychology, 42,* 256–262.

Jurkovic, G., & Prentice, N. (1977). Relation of moral and cognitive development to dimensions of juvenile delinquency. *Journal of Abnormal Psychology, 86,* 414–420.

Kagan, J. (1966). Developmental studies in reflection on analysis. In A. Kidd & J. Rivoire (Eds.), *Perceptual development in children.* New York: International Universities Press.

Kaplan, H. B. (1975). *Self-attitudes and deviant behavior.* Pacific Palisades: Goodyear Press.

Kaplan, H. B. (1980). *Deviant behavior in defense of self.* New York: Academic Press.

Kaplan, P., & Arbuthnot, J. (1985). Affective empathy and cognitive role-taking in delinquent and non-delinquent youth. *Adolescence, 20,* 323–333.

Karoly, P. (1975). Comparison of "psychological styles" in delinquent and nondelinquent females. *Psychological Reports, 36,* 567–570.

Kelley, F., & Baer, D. (1971). Physical challenge as a treatment for delinquency. *Crime and Delinquency, 17,* 437–445.

Kendall, P. C., Deardorff, P. A., & Finch, A. J. (1977). Empathy and socialization in first and repeat juvenile offenders and normals. *Journal of Abnormal Child Psychology, 5,* 93–97.

King, C. (1975). The ego and the integration of violence in homicidal youth. *American Journal of Orthopsychiatry, 45,* 134–146.

Kohlberg, L. (1958). *The development of modes or moral thinking and choice in the years ten to sixteen.* Unpublished doctoral dissertation. University of Chicago.

Kohlberg, L., Colby, A., Speicher-Dublin, B., & Lieberman, M. (1978). *Standard form scoring manual.* Cambridge, MA: Moral Education Research Foundation.

Kohlberg, L., & Freundlich, D. (1973). Moral reasoning and delinquency. Unpublished paper, Harvard University of Human Development, Cambridge, Mass.

Kulik, J. A., Stein, K. B., & Sarbin, T. R. (1968). Dimensions and patterns of adolescent antisocial behavior. *Journal of Consulting and Clinical Psychology, 32,* 375–382.

Kumchy, C. I. G., & Sawyer, L. A. (1980). Locus of control in a delinquent adolescent population. *Psychological Reports, 46,* 1307–1310.

Landau, S. F. (1975). Future time perspective of delinquents and nondelinquents. *Criminal Justice and Behavior, 2,* 22–36.

Landau, S. F. (1976). Delinquency, institutionalization, and time orientation. *Journal of Consulting & Clinical Psychology, 44(5),* 745–759.

Lanyon, R. I. (1968). *A handbook of MMPI group profiles.* Minneapolis: University of Minnesota Press.

Laufer, W. S., Skoog, D. K., & Day, J. M. (1982). Personality and criminality: A review of the California Psychological Inventory. *Journal of Clinical Psychology, 38,* 562–573.

Lavik, N. J. (1969). Future time perspective and adolescent behavior disorders. *Acta Psychiatrica Scandinavia, 45,* 153–171.

Little, V. L., & Kendall, P. C. (1979). Cognitive-behavioral interventions with delinquents: Problem-solving, role-taking, and self-control. In P. Kendall & S. Hollon (Eds.), *Cognitive-behavioral interventions: Theory, research, and procedures.* New York: Academic Press.

Long, B. H., Ziller, R. C., & Bauber, J. (1970). Self-other orientations of institutionalized behavior-problem adolescents. *Journal of Consulting and Clinical Psychology, 34,* 43–47.

Lund, N. L., & Salary, H. M. (1980). Measured self-concept in adjudicated juvenile offenders. *Adolescence, 15,* 65–74.

Mack, J. L. (1969a). Behavior ratings of recidivist and nonrecidivist delinquent males. *Psychological Reports, 25,* 260.

Mack, J. L. (1969b). The MMPI and recidivism. *Journal of Abnormal Psychology, 74,* 612–614.

Marohn, R. C., Offer, D., & Ostrov, E. (1971). Juvenile delinquents view their impulsivity. *American Journal of Psychiatry, 128(4),* 418–423.

Martin, R. D. (1981). Cross-validation of the Jesness Inventory with delinquents and nondelinquents. *Journal of Consulting and Clinical Psychology, 49,* 10–14.

Martin, R. D., & Clarke, R. V. G. (1969). The personality of approved school boy absconders. *British Journal of Criminology, 9,* 366–375.

Matza, D. (1964). *Delinquency and drift.* New York: Wiley.

McColgan, E. (1975). *Social cognition in delinquents, predelinquents and nondelinquents*. Unpublished doctoral dissertation, University of Minnesota.

McColgan, E. B., Rest, J. B., & Pruitt, D. B. (1983). Moral judgment and antisocial behavior in early adolescence. *Journal of Applied Developmental Psychology, 4*, 189–199.

McEwan, A. W. (1983). Eysenck's theory of criminality and the personality types and offences of young delinquents. *Personality and Individual Differences, 4*, 201–204.

Megargee, E. I., Cooper-Price, A., Frohworth, R., & Levine, R. (1970). Time orientation of youthful prison inmates. *Journal of Counseling Psychology, 17*, 8–14.

Mehrabian, A., & Epstein, H. (1972). A measure of emotional empathy. *Journal of Personality, 40*, 525–543.

Miller, W. B. (1976). *Violence by youth gangs and youth groups in major American cities: Final report*. Cambridge: Harvard University Law School.

Mischel, W. (1961). Preference for delayed reinforcement and social responsibility. *Journal of Abnormal and Social Psychology, 62*, 1–7.

Mischel, W., & Gilligan, C. (1964). Delay of gratification, motivation for the prohibited gratification, and responses to temptations. *Journal of Abnormal and Social Psychology, 69*, 411–417.

Mizushima, K., & DeVos, G. (1967). An application of the California Psychological Inventory in a study of Japanese delinquency. *Journal of Social Psychology, 71*, 45–51.

Mosher, D. L. (1966). The development of multitrait-multimethod matrix analysis of three measures of three aspects of guilt. *Journal of Consulting Psychology, 30*, 25–29.

Myers, D. G. (1983). *Social psychology*. New York: McGraw-Hill.

Nowicki, S., & Strickland, B. L. (1973). A locus of control scale for children. *Journal of Consulting and Clinical Psychology, 401*, 148–154.

O'Keefe, E. J. (1975). Porteus Maze Q score as a measure of impulsivity. *Perceptual & Motor Skills, 41*, 675–678.

Olejnik, A. (1980). Adults' moral reasoning with children. *Child Development, 51*, 1285–1288.

Ono, N., Kataoka, G., & Shindo, H. (1969). A basic research for MMPI-profile interpretation: Normative data for the juvenile sample. *Japanese Journal of Criminal Psychology, 6*, 60–66.

Orcutt, J. (1970). Self-concept and insulation against delinquency: Some critical notes. *Sociological quarterly, 11*, 381–390.

Parrott, C. A., & Strongman, K. I. (1984). Locus of control and delinquency. *Adolescence, 19*, 459–471.

Passingham, R. E. (1972). Crime and personality: A review of Eysenck's theory. In V. D. Nebylitsyn & J. A. Gray (Eds.), *Biological bases of individual behavior* (pp. 342–371). New York: Academic Press.

Persons, R. (1970). The Mosher Guilt Scale: Theoretical formulation, research review, and normative data. *Journal of Projective Techniques & Personality Assessment, 34*, 266–270.

Peterson, D. R., Quay, H. C., & Anderson, A. C. (1959). Extending the construct validity of a socialized scale. *Journal of consulting Psychology, 23*, 182.

Peterson, G. B., Hey, R. N., & Peterson, L. R. (1979). Intersection of family development and moral stage frameworks: Implications for theory and research. *Journal of Marriage and the Family*, May, 229–235.

Petronio, R. J. (1980). The moral maturity of repeater delinquents. *Youth & Society, 12*, 51–59.

Piaget, J., & Inhelder, B. (1969). *The psychology of the child*. New York: Basic.

Phares, E. J. (1976). *Locus of control in personality*. Morristown, NJ: General Learning Press.

Porteus, S. D. (1959). *The Maze Test and clinical psychology*. Palo Alto, CA: Pacific Books.

Putnins, A. (1980). Reliability of the Jesness Inventory. *Applied Psychological Measurement, 4*, 127–129.

Putnins, A. C. (1982). The Eysenck Personality Questionnaires and delinquency prediction. *Personality and Individual Differences, 3,* 339–340.

Quay, H. C. (1965a). Personality and delinquency. In H. C. Quay (Ed.), *Juvenile delinquency: Research and theory* (pp. 139–169). Princeton, NJ: Van Nostrand.

Quay, H. C. (1965b). Psychopathic personality as pathological stimulation-seeking. *American Journal of Psychiatry, 122*, 180–183.

Quay, H. C., & Anderson (1959).

Quay, H. C., & Love, C. T. (1977). The effects of a juvenile diversion program on rearrest. *Criminal Justice and Behavior, 4*, 377–396.

Quay, H., C., & Parsons, L. (1971). *The differential behavioral classification of the juvenile offender*. Washington, D.C.: U.S. Bureau of Prisons.

Quay, H. C., & Peterson, D. R. (1975). *Manual for the Behavior Problem Checklist*. Unpublished manuscript.

Randolph, N. H., Richardson, H., & Johnson, R. C. (1961). Comparison of social and solitary male delinquents. *Journal of Consulting Psychology, 25*, 293–295.

Reckless, W., & Dinitz, S. (1972). *The prevention of juvenile delinquency: An experiment*. Columbus, Ohio: Ohio State University Press.

Reckless, W. C., Dinitz, S., & Kay, B. (1957). The self component in potential delinquency and potential non-delinquency. *American Sociological Review, 22*, 566–570.

Reckless, W. C., Dinitz, S., & Murray, E. (1956). Self-concept as an insulator against delinquency. *American Sociological Review, 21*, 744–746.

Rempel, P. P. (1958). The use of multivariate statistical analysis of Minnesota Multiphasic Personality Inventory scores in the classification of delinquent and non-delinquent high school boys. *Journal of Consulting Psychology, 22*, 17–23.

Renwick, S., & Emler, N. (1984). Moral reasoning and delinquent behavior among students. *British Journal of Social Psychology, 23*, 281–283.

Reppucci, N. D., & Clingempeel, W. G. (1978). Methodological issues in research with correctional populations. *Journal of Counseling and Clinical Psychology, 46*, 727–746.

Rest, J. R. (1979). *Development in judging moral issues*. Minneapolis: University of Minnesota Press.

Roberts, A. H., & Erickson, R. V. (1968). Delay of gratification, Porteus Maze Test performance, and behavioral adjustment in a delinquent group. *Journal of Abnormal Psychology, 73*, 449–453.

Roberts, A. H., Erickson, R. V., Riddle, M., & Bacon, J. G. (1974). Demographic variables, base rates, and personality characteristics associated with recidivism in male delinquents. *Journal of Consulting and Clinical Psychology, 42*, 833–841.

Roe, A. V., Howell, R. J., & Payne, I. R. (1974). Comparison of prison inmates with and without juvenile records. *Psychological Reports, 34*, 1315–1319.

Roff, M., Sells, B., & Golden, M. M. (1972). *Social adjustment and personality development in children*. Minneapolis: University of Minnesota Press.

Rosenberg, F., & Rosenberg, M. (1978). Self-esteem and delinquency. *Journal of Youth and Adolescence, 7*, 279–291.

Rosenquist, C. M., & Megargee, E. I. (1969). *Delinquency in three cultures*. Austin: University of Texas Press.

Rotenberg, M. (1974). Conceptual and methodological notes on affective and cognitive role-taking (sympathy and empathy): An illustrative experiment with delinquent boys. *Journal of Genetic Psychology, 125*, 177–185.

Rotter, J. B. (1966). Generalized expectancies for internal vs. external control of reinforcement. *Psychological Monograms, 80*, (Whole No. 609).

Ruma, E. H. (1967). *Conscience development in delinquents and nondelinquents: The relationship between moral judgment, guilt, and behavior*. Doctoral dissertation, Ohio State University, Columbus, Ohio. *Dissertation Abstracts International, 28*, 2631B (University Microfilms No. 67–16,331).

Ruma, E. H., & Mosher, D. L. (1967). Relationship between moral judgment and guilt in delinquent boys. *Journal of Abnormal Psychology, 72*, 122–127.

Rushton, J. P., & Chrisjohn, R. D. (1981). Extraversion, neuroticism, psychoticism, and self-reported delinquency: Evidence from eight separate samples. *Personality and Individual Differences, 2*, 11–20.

Russell, D. H. (1973b). Who are assaultive juveniles—a study of 100 cases *Journal of Forensic Sciences, 18*, 385–397.

Sagi, A., & Eisikovits, Z. (1981). Juvenile delinquency and moral development. *Criminal Justice and Behavior, 8*, 79–93.

Saunders, G. R., & Davies, M. B. (1976). The validity of the Jesness Inventory with British delinquents. *British Journal of Social and Clinical Psychology, 15*, 33–39.

Saunders, J. T., Reppucci, N. D., & Sarata, B. P. V. (1973). An examination of impulsivity as a trait characterizing delinquent youth. *American Journal of Orthopsychiatry, 43*, 789–795.

Scharf, P. (1973). *Moral atmosphere and intervention in the prison: The creation of a participation community in prison*. Unpublished doctoral dissertation, Harvard University.

Schoenfeld, C. G. (1971). A psychoanalytic theory of juvenile delinquency. *Crime and Delinquency, 17*, 469–480.

Schuessler, K. (1954). A review of analyzing and predicting juvenile delinquency with the MMPI. *American Journal of Sociology*, 321–322.

Schuessler, K. F., & Cressey, D. B. (1950). Personality characteristics of criminals. *American Journal of Sociology*, 476–484.

Sealy, A. P., & Banks, C. (1971). Social maturity, training, experience, and recidivism amongst British borstal boys. *British Journal of Criminology, 11*, 245–264.

Shapiro, D. (1965). *Neurotic styles*. New York: Basic Books.

Shark, M. L., & Handal, P. J. (1977). Reliability and validity of the Jesness Inventory: A caution. *Journal of Consulting and Clinical Psychology, 45*, 692–695.

Shinohara, M., & Jenkins, R. L. (1967). MMPI study of three types of delinquents. *Journal of Clinical Psychology, 23*, 156–163.

Shuck, S. Z., Dubeck, J. A., Cymbalisty, B. Y., & Green, C. (1972). Delinquency, personality tests, and relationships to measures of guilt and adjustment. *Psychological Reports, 31*, 219–226.

Siegman, A. W. (1961). The relationship between future time perspective, time estimation, and impulse control in a group of young offenders and in a control group. *Journal of Consulting Psychology, 30*, 320–328.

Siegman, A. W. (1966). Effects of auditory stimulation and intelligence on time estimation in delinquents and non-delinquents. *Journal of Consulting Psychology, 30*, 320–328.

Sigman, M., Ungerer, J., & Russell, A. (1983). Moral judgment in relation to behavioral and cognitive disorders in adolescents. *Journal of Abnormal Child Psychology, 11*, 503–512.

Smith, C. P., Alexander, P. S. Halatyn, T. V., & Roberts, C. F. (1980). *A national assessment of serious juvenile crime and the juvenile justice system: Final report*. Sacramento, CA: American Justice Institute.

Smith, D. E. (1974). Relationships between the Eysenck and Jesness Personality Inventories. *British Journal of Criminology, 14*, 376–384.

Smith, J., & Lanyon, R. I. (1968). Prediction of juvenile probation violators. *Journal of Consulting and Clinical Psychology, 32*, 54–58.

Solway, K. S., Hays, J. R., Schreiner, D., & Cansler, D. (1980). Clinical study of youths petitioned for certification as adults. *Psychological Reports, 46*, 1067–1073.

Sorrels, J. M. (1977). Kids who kill. *Crime and Delinquency, 23*, 312–320.

Sorrels, J. M. (1980). What can be done about juvenile homicide? *Crime and Delinquency, 26*, 152–161.

Stanley, S. (1978). Family education to enhance the moral atmosphere of the family and the moral development of adolescents. *Journal of Counseling Psychology, 25*, 110–118.

Stein, J. R. (1976). Effects of feedback on performance of introverted and extraverted delinquents and nondelinquents. *Criminal Justice and Behavior, 3*, 371–378.

Stein, K. B., Gough, H. G., & Sarbin, T. R. (1966). The dimensionality of the CPI scale and an empirically derived typology among delinquent and nondelinquent boys. *Multivariate Behavioral Research, 1*, 197–208.

Stein, K. B., Sarbin, T. R., & Chu, C. L. (1967). Adolescent morality: Its differentiated structure and relation to delinquent conduct. *Multivariate Behavioral Research, 2,* 199–210.

Stein, K. B., Sarbin, T. R., & Kulik, J. A. (1968). Future time perspective and its relation to the socialization process and the delinquent role. *Journal of Consulting and Clinical Psychology, 32,* 257–264.

Stott, M. W., & Olezak, P. V. (1978). Relating personality characteristics to juvenile offense categories: Differences between status offenders and juvenile delinquents. *Journal of Clinical Psychology, 34,* 80–84.

Strasburg, P. A. (1978). *Violent delinquents: A report to the Ford Foundation from the Vera Institute of Justice.* New York: Monarch.

Strasburg, P. A. (1984). Recent national trends in serious juvenile crime, In R. A. Mathias, P. DeMuro, & R. S. Allinson (Eds.), *Violent juvenile offenders: An anthology.* San Francisco: National Council on Crime and Delinquency.

Sykes, G. M., & Matza, D. (1957). Techniques of neutralization: A theory of delinquency. *American Sociological Review, 22,* 664–620.

Tangri, S., & Schwartz, M. (1967). Delinquency and the self-concept variable. *Journal of Criminal Law, Criminology, and Police Science, 58,* 182–190.

Teichman, M. (1971). Ego defense, self-concept, and images of self ascribed to parents by delinquent boys. *Perceptual and Motor Skills, 32,* 819–823.

Tennenbaum, D. J. (1977). Personality and criminality: A summary and implications of the literature. *Journal of Criminal Justice, 5,* 225–235.

Thomas, C. W. (1976). Are status offenders really so different? *Crime and Delinquency, 22,* 438–460.

Thompson, B. (1974). Self-concepts among secondary school pupils. *Educational research, 17(1),* 41–47.

Tsubouchi, K., & Jenkins, R. C. (1969). Three types of delinquents: Their performance on MMPI and PCR. *Journal of Clinical Psychology, 25,* 353–358.

Vachss, A. H., & Bakal, Y. (1979). *Life-style violent juvenile—The secure treatment approach.* Lexington, MA: Heath Lexington Books.

Vallance, R. C., & Forrest, A. R. (1971). A study of the Jesness Personality Inventory with Scottish children. *British Journal of Educational Psychology, 41,* 338–344.

Valliant, P. M., Asu, M. E., & Howitt, R. (1983). Cognitive styles of Caucasion and native Indian juvenile offenders. *Psychological Reports, 52,* 87–92.

Ventis, W. L. (1976). *Moral development in delinquent and non-delinquent males and its enhancement.* Paper presented to the Southeastern Psychological Association.

Vinson, T. (1979). Juvenile aggression. *Australian Journal of Forensic Sciences, 11,* 139–152.

Waldo, G. P., & Dinitz, S. (1967). Personality attributes of the criminal: An analysis of research studies, 1950–1965. *Journal of Research in Crime and Delinquency, 4,* 185–202.

Walker, L. J. (1980). Cognitive and perspective-taking prerequisites for moral development. *Child Development, 51,* 131–139.

Wells, L. E. (1978). Theories of deviance and the self-concept. *Social Psychology Quarterly, 41,* 189–204.

Wells, L. E., & Rankin, J. H. (1983). Self-concept as a mediating factor in delinquency. *Social Psychology Quarterly, 46*, 11–22.

Wilson, J. Q., & Herrnstein, R. J. (1985). *Crime and human nature.* New York: Simon & Schuster.

Wolfgang, M., Figlio, R., & Sellin, T. (1972). *Delinquency in a birth cohort.* Chicago: University of Chicago Press.

Woychick, T. (1970). Asociability Index scores' relationship to adjustment of youthful offenders. *Correctional Psychologist, 4*, 68–72.

Wright, I. (1977). Moral reasoning and conduct of selected elementary school students. *Journal of Moral Education, 1*, 199–205.

Yates, A., Beutler, L. E., & Crago, M. (1983). Characteristics of young violent offenders. *Journal of Psychiatry & Law, 11*, 137–149.

Yiannakis, A. (1976). Delinquent tendencies and participation in an organized sports program. *Research Quarterly, 47*, 845–849.

Zuckerman, M., Bone, R. N., Neary, R., Mangelsdorff, D., & Brustman, B. (1972). What is the sensation seeker? *Journal of Consulting & Clinical Psychology, 39*, 308–321.

Zuckerman, M., Kolin, A., Price, L., & Zoob, I. (1964). Development of a sensation seeking scale. *Journal of Consulting Psychology, 28*, 477–482.

CHAPTER 7

Biogenetic Factors

GORDON TRASLER

University of Southampton, England

The term "biogenetic" may be unfamiliar to many. It relates to temperamental, cognitive, and reactive characteristics that are thought to be genetically transmitted, and are governed to some degree by the physiological systems (in the brain and the autonomic nervous system, for example), that have an effect on behavior, and (in particular) are thought to have the potential to promote or to restrain various kinds of delinquent and criminal behavior.

This chapter is divided into four main sections. The first is concerned with evidence which has been put forward in support of the belief that genetic inheritance plays some part in the development and persistence of delinquency. The second is concerned with those biological and psychophysiological mechanisms that might constitute the links between inheritance and delinquent behavior. The third briefly examines some examples of crime which seem to be the direct result of persisting or induced abnormalities of physiological functioning. Finally, we attempt an evaluation of the role and validity of biological models of delinquency and criminality.

Biological theories are currently rather unpopular among criminologists, and have been so for perhaps two decades. There are several reasons for this. Biological studies, and in particular the search for evidence that criminals were atavistic degenerates—"throwbacks" to more primitive times and the product of generations of morally and physically inferior people—were influential in the earliest years of criminology (see Chapter 1). For that reason, biological and genetic studies appear old-fashioned and crude by association, as it were. In many people's minds, they also have overtones of positivism and the supposed unmodifiablity of constitutional characteristics which many people find negative and unattractive. The sociological study of deviance, which dominated Western criminology in the 1960s and early 1970s, seemed less pessimistic, eschewing the mechanistic positivism of the period immediately following the end of the World War II. Even the notion of "just deserts," which now greatly influences thinking in criminology and penology, does at least accord to the offender freedom of choice and decision, and so, control of his or her own life.

It is arguable that this conception of the essential, pessimistic logic of genetic and biological studies of delinquency and crime is to a substantial degree mistaken. The belief that biological and sociological approaches to the study of crime are locked in competition, so that support for one approach entails the rejection of the other, is still held by criminologists. Yet this attitude is surely based on a misconception of the relations between these ways of looking at delinquency and crime. Social behavior is manifestly the outcome of a long and highly complex sequence of interactions between the individual as a motivated, sentient, adaptive organism and his physical and social environment (see Chapter 8). The pattern of the early years of life is reflected in sensitivity or unresponsiveness to certain stimuli, such as the threat of punishment or the anticipation of reward, the establishment of affectional attachments, and the development of the belief that one is in command of events—or conversely, that one is the prisoner of forces which he or she is powerless to control.

We shall examine, in this chapter, several theoretical approaches to the explanation of delinquent conduct which may broadly be said to be "biological," since the explanations they offer are partly based upon contemporary knowledge of various characteristics of the human organism which may mediate those processes that result in conformity and compliance, or inability or unwillingness to assimilate the rules, customs, and mores which govern social behavior. There are problems of definition, since the data that we shall consider have been gathered by several types of research. They include twin studies and cross-fostering studies, which are intended to establish whether characteristics relevant to delinquency are in fact transmitted biologically from one generation to the next; attempts to establish differences between delinquents and others that might be significant—for example, low autonomic nervous system reactivity, difficulties in forming conditioned responses of various kinds, or slow rates of electrodermal recovery; and studies which attempt to identify connections between abnormal chromosome complements and a tendency to become involved in delinquency and crime—especially persistent and violent crime.

GENETIC STUDIES OF DELINQUENCY AND CRIME

The nature of the genetic contribution to concordance for delinquency is not well understood. There is a temptation to think in terms of a fixed physical attribute, such as eye color, which remains constant throughout life, regardless of the impact of differing environments. Another analogy is phenylketonuria, in which a genetically transmitted characteristic interacts with diet to result in poisoning, with disastrous effects upon the developing individual. If it is the case, as we shall attempt to demonstrate, that an increased likelihood of being involved in criminal activities attaches to the inheritance of an autonomic nervous system that is ill-adapted to learning through punishment, then one would expect this characteristic to have its effect in each of the very large number of interactions with parents, siblings, teachers, age-peers, and others which constitute a major part of the process of growing up and socialization in our culture. The effects upon the developing individual will be pervasive and incremental, and not (as with eye-color) fixed and unchanging almost from the moment of conception. There are closer analogies with physical strength, sensory acuity, and intelligence, where a genetically-transmitted talent becomes the basis, in favorable conditions, of high levels of performance.

As Bodmer (1973) has pointed out, the social scientist must resort to highly complex statistical methods to study behavioral phenomena in natural conditions, while his colleagues in the biological sciences can employ experimental procedures to control for environmental variations. Breeding is also subject to control by the biological experimenter. Additionally, psychologists normally deal with patterns of heredity that are partially controlled by many genes of small effect—a much more difficult task than studying the operation of a single gene, or a small number of genes which exert a large degree of influence upon behavior. Bodmer has noted that in one extreme case—that of a hypothetical population of persons with identical genetic endowment (clones)—all of the variability between persons would be attributable to variations in their early social and physical environments. At the other extreme, if every individual in the population were to be brought up in social and physical circumstances identical to those experienced by every other member of the population, such individual differences as might exist would be wholly attributable to genetic differences. These extreme cases are, of course, not present in reality, but they do draw attention to the fact that estimates of heritability are *wholly* specific to particular populations in particular environmental circumstances, and that (contrary to the impression given by advocates of the view that the disposition to commit offenses is largely controlled by hereditary factors) attempts to assess the contribution of nonenvironmental influences upon delinquency can gain no support at all from those research designs which derive from classical studies in behavior genetics. To quote Bodmer (1973), "As the population and its environment changes, so does the heritability." He points out that "The potential for genetic differences between individuals is staggering, even within a family. The numbers of genetically different types of sperm and egg which any one individual could in principle produce is many millionfold more than the numbers of humans who have ever lived. This extraordinary genetic uniqueness of the individual must apply to all his attributes . . . "(pp. 315–316). Bodmer's comments should encourage caution in the interpretation of empirical observations derived from twin studies and other strategies for the assessment of genetic influences upon phenotypes specified in terms of observable behaviors; what seem to be simple comparisons turn out to be, on further scrutiny, peculiarly difficult inferences from available data. One might venture the comment that social scientists often think in excessively simple terms about the respective influences of genetic and environmental factors in controlling delinquent behavior.

Twin Studies

The belief that some genetically transmitted characteristic might be implicated in criminality and juvenile delinquency has a long history. For many years it rested on conjecture and deductive reasoning rather than empirical study, for the lack of an appropriate research technique. It is therefore not surprising that when the significance of comparisons between monozygotic (MZ) and dizygotic (DZ) twins had been grasped, the twin study method should have been applied in attempts to quantify the role of inheritance. The first such study to attract attention from criminologists was Lange's (1928) work in Bavarian prisons. Lange found thirty-seven individuals who were twins (the "probands"), thirteen of whom seemed to be MZ twins, and seventeen of whom seemed to be DZ twins. Ten of the thirteen MZ twins of the individuals in prison had also served prison sentences, while among the DZ twins only two had been imprisoned. These figures appeared to be impressive evidence for the importance of genetic inheritance in criminality (or at least in criminality sufficiently serious to warrant a prison sentence) and they are still quoted today in support of the belief that there is a strong hereditary component in criminality. Lange was hampered by the absence of reliable tests of zygosity, by the selective nature of his research samples, and by the lack of understanding, in his day, of the strengths and weaknesses of the twin study method as a means of assessing the relative importance of inheritance and interaction with the physical and social environment in determining patterns of social behavior.

There followed a series of studies, some (such as Christiansen's, published in 1968) involving large samples of twin pairs, and others analyzing small samples but presenting apparently impressive evidence of genetic transmission of the propensity to break the law. A review of later twin studies reveals two matters of great interest. The first is that the more precise the methods employed, the less pronounced are the differences between MZ and DZ twin pairs, with respect to the criterion (variously being sentenced to imprisonment, acquiring a criminal record, or becoming "known to the police"). Secondly, the differences between MZ and DZ twin pairs are greater in the case of adult, recidivist offenders, and least in the case of juvenile delinquents. Dalgaard and Kringlen (1976) have offered a useful resume of published researches, but see also Forde (1978) for a critique of their arguments. It is worth spending a little time to consider why these conditions should apply.

It was customary, in the decade immediately following World War II, to make an apparently sharp distinction between the minority of delinquent youngsters and the much greater number of "nondelinquent" adolescents. We now know, however, from self-report studies of delinquency, that most adolescent males in the urban areas occasionally commit delinquencies that could land them in court, and possibly in custody (see Chapter 2). The distinction between "delinquents" and "nondelinquents" seems to be a matter of degree of the frequency and seriousness of the individual's criminal activities, and luck in avoiding being caught. Adolescent delinquents destined for an adult criminal career are to some extent identifiable (West & Farrington, 1973, 1977; see also Chapter 12) but it is also the case that many adult offenders have no record of crime as juveniles (Langan & Greenfeld, 1983), a fact that has largely escaped the attention of criminologists. The relations between adolescent offending and adult recidivism are much more complicated than we had previously assumed.

Other problems concerned the methodology of twin studies. Dalgaard and Kringlen (1976) and Christiansen (1977a, 1977c) have referred to several sources of error in investigations of this kind. There are problems of sampling. For example, studies which rely upon probands from particular segments of the criminal justice system, such as admissions to prison, are especially vulnerable to sampling artifacts. We have already noted the problem of accurately distinguishing between MZ and DZ twins, a difficulty that has been overcome by the development of methods of blood and serum testing. These authors also have noted that the social and physical environments of MZ twins tend to be more similar than those of DZ twins, and there is some evidence that members of MZ twin pairs are, for some reason, more likely to be imprisoned for crime than DZ twins or individuals who are not twins.

Some of these problems can be compensated for by studying all of the twin pairs in a given population, rather than relying on a sample or making use of probands, and by employing modern tests for zygosity. These conditions are met by Christiansen's (1977b, 1977c) study of 444 pairs of twins born in Denmark between 1870 and 1910 who survived to the age of fifteen years, and by Dalgaard and Kringlen's (1976) investigation of all surviving male twin pairs born in Norway between 1921 and 1930. Christiansen found pairwise concordance rates of 33.3 percent in MZ twins, compared with 10.9 percent in DZ twins; Dalgaard and Kringlen found corresponding rates of 25.8 percent and 14.9 percent. These findings are in striking contrast to those of earlier studies. Lange's figures were 76.9 percent for MZ twins, and 11.8 percent for DZ twins, and the fairly extensive study by Rosanoff, Handy, and Plesset (1934) in the United States yielded concordance rates of 67.6 percent and 17.9 percent respectively. Dalgaard and Kringlen examined their data further in order to identify twin pairs (both MZ and DZ) who were brought up together in a close relationship, being treated and dressed alike. They reported that "in such a comparison the difference in concordance almost completely disappears. These findings support the view that hereditary factors are of no significant importance in the etiology of common crime" (1976, p. 231). Christiansen also argued that "a greater frequency of concordance among MZ than among DZ pairs only means that similar hereditary factors and/or similar prenatal, natal, or postnatal environmental conditions result in greater likelihood of similarity in social behavior than disparate hereditary factors and/or disparate environmental conditions" (p. 95).

Apart from Rowe's (1985) research, most twin studies have dealt with adult offenders, or a mixture of adults and juveniles. An exception is the research of Rosanoff, Handy, and Rosanoff (1934), whose samples included a group of 46 male juvenile pairs, of whom 29 were identified as MZ and 17 as DZ. Pairwise concordance rates for both groups were high, at 100 percent for the MZ pairs and 71 percent for the DZ pairs (compared with figures of 76 percent and 22 percent for adult male MZ and DZ pairs). The fact that rates for both identical and fraternal twins were very high (with DZ juveniles almost comparable with MZ adults), taken together with the observation that many adolescent offenders cease to commit delinquencies when they reach adulthood (an observation to which we have already referred), suggests that social (or subcultural) influences must play a major part in prompting their offenses, for if this were not the case, one would expect a much greater difference between concordance rates for MZ and DZ twins. It may be thought that the comparatively early study by Rosanoff and his colleagues lends support to some of the conjectures of Dalgaard and Kringlen (1976) about the contribution of social bonds to measures of concordance. There is a meticulously careful discussion of the twin studies to which we have referred in Christiansen (1977a). The basic lesson to be drawn from twin studies seems to be that the inter-generational mechanism which predisposes some MZ twin pairs to high concordance for officially-recorded delinquency is probably mediated both by genetic transmission and by social processes of bonding and interdependence: there is no known way in which the respective influences of inherited characteristics and learned social patterns can be disentangled. In particular, the logic involved in making *general* estimates of the variance to be assigned to genetic, as contrasted with environmental, influence is invalid, since the proportions of variance quoted relate to a specific set of genetic/environmental conditions. Attempts to calculate estimates of the contribution of genetic factors to behavior have only limited validity in very narrowly defined circumstances. They are not, and cannot be, situation-independent estimates (see Jencks, 1980, for a useful discussion of the limitations of the twin study method in assessing the relative contribution of heredity and environmental influences in the causation of human behavior).

Adoption and Cross-Fostering Studies

A second source of support for the influence of genetically transmitted characteristics is a group of studies of adopted and fostered children, carried out mainly in Denmark because of the unmatched accuracy of demographic records in that country, together with some more restricted studies in the United States of America. In principle, such studies offer valuable opportunities for distinguishing between the effects of genetic and social influences upon the developing child. Adoptions and foster-family arrangements are commonly made within a few days or weeks of birth, so that the child rarely has contact with, or knowledge of, his biological parents. In practice the characteristics of the surrogate family are seldom wholly independent of those of the child's biological family, if only because casework practice often involves an attempt to place the child with a family that resembles his own parents in certain respects, such as social and economic status. It is arguable, also, that most children who have been removed from their own parents to be cared for by substitute parents, even at a very early age, have suffered some degree of trauma, which may itself issue in delinquent behavior later in their lives (Trasler, 1960). Nevertheless, careful analysis of the relations between criminality in the biological parents, the adoptive parents, and the child offers useful opportunities for identifying the existence, if not the extent, of biological (nonsocial) influences of parents upon children reared by substitute parents. These opportunities have been skillfully exploited by Hutchings and Mednick (1977) and Mednick, Gabrielli and Hutchings (1982) (reported by Pollock, Mednick and Gabrielli (1983 as an "unpublished manuscript"). Their research seemed to demonstrate that criminality in biological parents of children adopted early in their lives was a more reliable predictor of adolescent or adult criminality than the presence or absence of criminal convictions in the adoptive or fosterparents. This area of research is a methodological minefield, because of the complex and unexplicit policies of adoption and fostering agencies. Agencies usually refrain from placing children in families where the parents have criminal records, but of course they may be convicted for the first time after the child has been placed. Rather different criteria may be applied in adoption with relatives. It follows that very careful examination of the circumstances in which the decision to place the child was taken is necessary to determine the extent of such selection effects, as these may contaminate the comparisons being attempted. These reservations apart, Mednick and his colleagues have made a moderately convincing case for the argument that biological characteristics, transmitted genetically, are influential in determining whether or not a young person will become an offender, and have built a strong case for the contention that the potential to become a persistent (that is, recidivist) offender is to a major extent determined by the individual's biological inheritance (Pollock, Mednick and Gabrielli, 1983).

There are undoubtedly other, putatively "biological" factors which exert some influence on the likelihood that an individual born of a particular set of parents will acquire a criminal record, including schizophrenia and psychopathy (Schulsinger, 1977). Data apparently connecting somatotype with susceptibility to delinquency have proved too vague and general to be helpful (Glueck & Glueck, 1950). Existing knowledge is, therefore, patchy. Although much juvenile delinquency can be plausibly explained in terms of the immediate pressures impinging upon the underprivileged or otherwise unsuccessful individual in a highly competitive society (see Chapters 1 and 2), the evidence of the existence of genetically transmitted vulnerability or susceptibility to particular kinds of depredation against the property, or (more rarely) the persons of other people seems persuasive. It is much more difficult to establish what form such a characteristic could have, and how it could be transmitted from one generation to the next.

Sex Chromosome Abnormalities

Since the 1960s, there has been considerable interest in certain abnormal sex chromosome complements that may be associated with a high risk for delinquency, and especially violent behavior. The first studies were carried out in hospitals and other institutions with highly selected populations, and were initially received rather uncritically by the medical profession (most were published in clinical journals) and presented in dramatic form in the popular press. (For a useful historical account, a bibliography, and a good summary of the findings of the first decade of research in this field and its legal implications, see Shah, (1970). The nature of these abnormalities, their supposed origins, and the techniques used to detect them are clearly explained by Forssmann and Hambert (1967). Most of the published studies have been concerned with the possession of an extra X chromosome (47,XXY or Klinefelter's Syndrome) or a supernumerary Y chromosome (47,XYY). Mosaicism (mixed chromosome complement) has not as yet been given much attention as a possible correlate of delinquency. Virtually all of the published research relates to males.

The 47,XXY Complement

The presence of more than one X chromosome can be readily discerned by staining for sex-chromatin, and it is estimated that the prevalence of such males in the general population is of the order of two per thousand; the corresponding figure for males in institutions for the mentally handicapped is about 10 per thousand. Casey, Segall, Street & Blank (1966) found that 2.2 percent of male patients in two British state hospitals for subnormal patient with violent, aggressive, or criminal tendencies were sex-chromatin positive. Of the total count of 21, 12 had the XXY complement, seven showed the XXYY configuration, and two were presumed to have XXY/XY mosaicism. Court Brown (1962) contended that an apparently high proportion of positive males in institutions for the mentally defective had histories of antisocial acts, but gave no details of his sample. Neither did he indicate the frequency of histories of antisocial behavior among patients with normal chromosome patterns. Hunter (1966), in an extensive survey of subnormal patients in England, reported that sex-chromatin positive patients included an abnormally high proportion of men with antisocial behavior abnormalities (64.7 percent compared with the figure of 19.5 percent for all male patients) and especially of aggressive offences (45.5 percent against 17 percent). Several other studies of subnormal populations have yielded similar findings (Forssmann & Hambert, 1967). But while the association between behavior disorders and the possession of one or more supernumerary X chromosomes seems to have been convincingly established in subnormal populations, it is not clear whether the association holds for those of normal intelligence. It is perhaps significant that Wegmann & Smith (1963) found only two sex-chromatin positive individuals among 1232 boys and young men in three state institutions for delinquents—a lower incidence than in the general population.

The 47,XYY Complement

The task of identifying individuals in this category was initially a much more laborious and expensive business, as it was necessary to prepare cultures. For that reason, reliable estimates of the prevalence of this form of abnormality in normal populations could not be made. It was believed that XYY males must be less common than XXY males; Slater (1967) suggested that the frequency might be of the order of one per 2000—one for every four males with the Klinefelter pattern. The identification of nine men with the XYY complement (together with an XXYY individual and an XY/XYY mosiac) in a group of 315 patients in a secure hospital for dangerous (mainly criminal) subnormals was therefore particularly striking (Jacobs, Brunton, Melville, Brittain, & McClemont, 1965). Careful studies of these men (Price, Strong, Whatmore, & McClemont, 1966; Price & Whatmore, 1967a, 1967b), comparing them against the rest of the population from which they were drawn, revealed differences of considerable criminological interest. Their criminal records were no worse than those of the controls, and included relatively few crimes of violence against the person. But their criminal careers had started earlier; the average age at which they were first convicted was 13 years, compared with a mean of about 18 years for patients with normal chromosome patterns. They did not differ from the rest of the hospital population in measured intelligence, but they demonstrated an absence of genuine remorse or guilt, a limited capacity for affection and an inability to establish normal interpersonal relationships—a description that suggests psychopathy (see Chapter 5).

As it was known that XYY men tend to be abnormally tall, some investigators sought to minimize the cost of laboratory testing by concentrating their attention on individuals of greater than average height. For example, Casey, Blank, Street, Segall, McDougall, McGrath, & Skinner (1966) followed this strategy in searching several populations for XYY men. They found 18 XYY individuals among 124 males, six feet or more in height, detained in hospitals or prisons because of antisocial behavior. On the other hand they could find no instance of this pattern among 30 equally tall, noncriminal patients in a psychiatric hospital, or in a similar group of "normal" men.

The development of a new technique for identifying the number of Y chromosomes in human cells (Pearson, Bobrow, & Vosa, 1970) permits cheap and simple surveys of large populations, but it is thought that there may be difficulties in recognizing small Y chromosomes (Shah, 1970, Appendix C-4).

A more recent study by Witkin et al. (1976) is more satisfactory than its predecessors because it is based upon an entire population rather than institutionalized subgroups, but it still relies upon the believed association between supernumerary Y chromosomes and unusual tallness, and the observation that 47, XXY males also tend to be tall (Close, Goonetilleke, Jacobs, & Price, 1968). As in any such investigation, there was some loss of individuals through death, migration, or refusal to cooperate, but the investigators managed to secure data from about 90 percent of the target population (all males of 184 cm or more in height, born in the city of Copenhagen in the four-year period 1944–1947). There proved to be 12 XYY men and 16 XXYs, together with 13 XYs with other chromosomal anomalies. The XYY males had "little or no recorded evidence of violent behavior," (p. 93) but according to the researchers they did have a higher rate of criminal convictions than other men of comparable height, intelligence, and social class. Mednick and his colleagues reported data concerning the EEG characteristics of their XYY subjects, apparently indicating "remarkably slow alpha and excessive theta activity" (p. 94) and slow electrodermal recovery but they found no evidence to support the popular belief that XYY males were prone to violent crime (Mednick & Volavka, 1980).

Chromosomal anomalies may take the form of damage to particular chromosomes or abnormalities of size or separation. The phenotypic (behavioral) implications of these anomalies are presently rather obscure, although a meticulous, controlled study of young offenders by Kahn, Reed, Bates, Coates, and Everitt (1976) yielded some indication that individuals with abnormally long Y chromosomes tend to have more extensive criminal records than other youths of similar backgrounds.

It would appear that the belief that young males with supernumerary Y chromosomes are especially prone to violence is without foundation. The 47,XYY complement is probably as rare among convicted offenders as it is in the population at large, though those XYY males that are committed to penal establishments or secure hospitals generally have rather more extensive histories of nonviolent delinquencies and crimes than men of similar age and background. The 47,XXY pattern (Klinefelter's syndrome) is more common among institutionalized delinquents, as it is in the general population. Individuals of XYY and XXY configuration (and possibly those with mosaic complements) who do become delinquent seem to start their criminal careers earlier than other young male offenders. The suggestion that the possessors of supernumerary Y chromosomes are prone to crime because of their "extra maleness" (e.g., Slater, 1967) is not supported by the evidence: Forssmann and Hambert's (1967) conjecture that there is an association between sex chromosome abnormalities and minimal brain damage has not as yet secured experimental support.

SUMMARY

We have reviewed in three categories which has been presented in support of the notion that the disposition to behave in a delinquent or criminal fashion is partly a function of the biological inheritance if the individual offender. Two of these areas of research—twin studies and investigations of people who have been placed in foster homes or adopted during the first few weeks or months of life—have yielded results which are not inconsistent with such an interpretation. The third possibility, that certain forms of delinquency may be the expression of genetic abnormalities, is so far without empirical support, and can be discounted for the time being. Tentatively adopting the proposition that some biological characteristic may be implicated in delinquency, it is reasonable again to ask what kind of characteristic this might be. As Shah and Roth (1974) have pointed out, "*Genotype* refers to the totality of factors that make up the genetic complement of an organism. *Phenotype* refers to the totality of that which can be observed, physically or chemically, about the organism. It is axiomatic that the phenotype cannot be inherited. Rather, it develops as a function of interactions between the genotype and the environment. Environmental influences must be considered in the broadest sense to include all events following conception that produce changes in the organism" (p. 105; emphasis in the original).

BEHAVIORAL INHIBITION

Most delinquent and criminal acts take the form of acquisitive, violent, or sexually aggressive behavior which may reasonably be attributed to basic and universal human motives. They are distinguished from noncriminal actions by the fact that they are forbidden by the criminal law, and usually, though not invariably, but the *mores* of the society in which they occur. Although some crimes demand special techniques or skills (for example, the forgery of documents) most do not. It is for this reason that psychologists who have tried to construct adequate accounts of the origins of delinquency have generally sought to explain why some individuals fail to inhibit those forbidden behaviors which most people have learned to avoid. This is not to say that criminal skills and delinquent habits may not be strengthened by their consequences—they probably are in many cases—but upbringing and control by competent parents ensures that children seldom experience such reinforcing events. In attempting to understand complex sequences of behavior, psychologists generally look for appropriate models or analogies to the well-understood phenomena of the laboratory. The most familiar of such models—operant conditioning—does not seem to fit a process which does not involve the reinforcement of operants, but results in the inhibition of existing, strong operants. The closest parallel seems to be what Mowrer (1950, 1960) called "passive avoidance conditioning" (also known as "aversive inhibitory conditioning"), and this model has accordingly been adopted by several writers (for example, Eysenck, 1964; Fowles, 1980; Hare, 1965; Mednick, 1977; Trasler, 1962). Mowrer's analysis rests upon the familiar assumption that the process of learning to inhibit behavior that is regarded with strong disapproval takes place initially during the early years of childhood. Adult morality and conforming behavior represent an extension of such basic values to meet the different, and possibly more complex, conditions of the adult world. The elements of Mowrer's analysis are as follows: The child spontaneously behaves in ways that are characterized by his parents as inappropriately aggressive, untruthful or predatory. His conduct earns a rebuke or punishment, in the form of an expression of disapproval, that evokes dismay and anxiety in the child, as he is still greatly dependent upon parental support in a potentially threatening world. After this sequence of misbehavior and punishment has been repeated several times, the impulse to break the prohibition results in revival of the "unpleasant state of arousal" (that is, the anxiety or fear which followed punishment for previous transgressions), with the consequence that the child breaks off this sequence of behavior. The discontinuing of the response is immediately followed by anxiety reduction, which reinforces the tendency to inhibit the previously punished behavior. Mowrer's model assigns important roles to the individual's responsiveness to external stimuli (and especially to aversive stimuli), his capacity to establish links between his actions and events temporally connected with them (associative conditioning) and also, some would argue, the rate at which his autonomic nervous system returns to its tonic (basal) or resting level. It requires that for early training to be effective, the individual must be able to recognize signals of impending punishment (that is to say, events which have previously been followed by aversive experiences) and to make the connection between response-produced signals and the outcome.

A substantial body of research has sought to discover why psychopaths (see Chapter 5), in particular, and other kinds of delinquents, fail to acquire inhibitory responses during the process of early social training, and offend repeatedly against laws and other social rules. Investigators have paid attention to the several elements of Mowrer's model in so far as they are reflected in autonomic nervous system (ANS) characteristics. Some researchers have compared institutionalized delinquents with "nondelinquent" controls (that is, people without formal criminal records, though self-report studies furnish good reasons to be cautious about this comparison); others compare persistent delinquents with controls; and still others, psychopaths with nonpsychopathic offenders and noncriminal controls. Each of these strategies has drawbacks, and the wide range of experimental subjects with regard to such characteristics as age, length and type of criminal record, ethnicity, and socioeconomic status, presents great difficulties to anyone who wishes to review the current state of knowledge of the psychophysiological correlates of delinquency and criminality. The least unsatisfactory of possible designs—prospective studies of cohorts of individuals, with the object of discovering those preexisting characteristics which discriminate the future delinquent or the future criminal from those members of the cohort who do not, in fact, acquire criminal records—are costly and necessarily take a long time to complete. The few studies of this kind to be completed have yielded extremely valuable information about the early phases of criminal careers.

PSYCHOPATHY

Studies of psychopaths have a very particular relevance in this field. Psychopathic individuals are identified as people who seem to take no heed of *any* social rules, including the criminal law, widely recognised moral precepts, and the less dramatic, but nevertheless very important conventions of loyalty, truthfulness, and concern for others that govern the everyday transactions between men and women in contemporary society. Characteristics of psychopathy are discussed in more detail in Chapter 5.

The diagnosis of psychopathy usually turns on the existence of behavior patterns that cannot be accounted for by the lack of *opportunity* to acquire normal inhibitory responses (see Hare & Cox, 1978; and Chapter 5), and may therefore contribute to our understanding of those learning processes, and the psychological and physiological systems that support them, which are involved in the social development of the ordinary, adequately socialized individual (see Siddle & Trasler, 1981; Trasler, 1978).

Our knowledge of the psychophysiological correlates of psychopathy is more secure than most insights into the origins of delinquency and criminality. In particular, a series of experimental studies of psychopaths directed by Robert Hare of the University of British Columbia, and other research by Daisy Schalling and her colleagues at the Karolinska Institute in Stockholm, have yielded convincing evidence of ANS abnormalities of psychopaths which, while not present to the same degree in nonpsychopathic, persistent offenders, nevertheless offer some clues about possible defects in ANS functioning in at least some individuals who have not responded to normally adequate opportunities to acquire appropriate inhibitory responses (see Hare & Schalling, 1978). For this reason we shall refer to some studies of psychopaths in the commentary which follows. However, as Quay (1983) has reminded us, "unsocialised or psychopathic criminals . . . probably constitute less than 25 percent of all offenders," (p. 340) and it seems likely that the corresponding proportion for adolescent delinquents is substantially smaller than this (see Chapter 5). It is important constantly to bear in mind the heterogeneity of most samples of young delinquents or adult offenders. In general, the most convincing evidence of differences between offenders and others comes from studies of highly selected samples. Psychopaths (or "sociopaths"), identified by the methods developed by Hare and his colleagues (Hare & Cox, 1978) form samples of this kind, being found within the recidivist population of a secure penitentiary according to criteria which effectively exclude individuals whose criminality might be explained by a preexisting condition of psychosis, neurosis, or subnormality. (This issue is discussed at length in Siddle & Trasler, 1981). There are things to be learned about the complex business of becoming socialized that are most clearly apparent in the characteristics of this extreme group of people.

AUTONOMIC NERVOUS SYSTEM (ANS)

The sections which follow consider the existing evidence (some of it, unfortunately, rather fragile) concerning ANS characteristics which appear to be relevant to the complex process of learning to inhibit behavior which has been followed by punishment. We shall present the findings of research within the framework of Mowrer's model of passive avoidance conditioning or, as we would prefer to call it, "aversive inhibitory conditioning."

Tonic Arousal

It is usual to make distinction between tonic arousal (resting level of arousal), and phasic arousal, or the magnitude of responses to stimuli. There is some evidence that psychopaths, in particular, have low levels of tonic arousal (Hare, 1968, 1970), the implication being that they will only respond adequately to strong stimuli. It is contended that conditioning procedures which are effective with normal subjects will not make a sufficient impact upon the "underaroused" ANS of the psychopath unless the intensity of the stimulus is raised, or further stimulation is provided in the form of background noise. A third possibility is to employ a pharmacological agent to manipulate the tonic level of arousal (see, for example, Schachter, 1971 and Schachter and Latané, 1964; but note also Hare's criticisms of this work, 1973; and the work of Chesno & Kilman, 1975). On the other hand, Quay (1965, 1977) has argued that the crucial ANS defects of the psychopath are best described as low reactivity and, perhaps less likely, rapid habituation, and that "sensation seeking" is an important characteristic of the psychopath (see also Zuckerman, 1978). The issues raised are of considerable technical and theoretical complexity, and (as is common in this field of research) it may well be that these writers are basing their analyses on differently composed but heterogeneous samples. It seems reasonable, for example, to suggest that either low levels of tonic arousal or rapid habituation will render the individual less responsive to the childhood training procedures upon which our culture depends for the transmission of its values and inhibitions. It might be noted, also, that other theories (such as Eysenck's) also entail the assumption that many individuals in a representative sample of offenders will exhibit "stimulus hunger"—in this case, because extraverts are said to be both resistant to conditioning (as we shall see shortly) and also understimulated.

Phasic Responses

What has been said concerning individual differences in tonic levels of arousal has implications about the magnitude of phasic responses and also what are generally termed "nonspecific" responses—that is, responses which have not been elicited by an external stimulus—since these characteristics of ANS functioning are apparently interrelated in a rather complex fashion. People who are said to be underaroused typically show a low level of tonic arousal, small (phasic) responses to stimuli, and low rates of nonspecific responding. It is presently difficult to arrive at a reliable assessment of the relations between low levels of phasic responding and delinquency, because experimental data are comparatively sparse and relate to a variety of experimental procedures using a range of aversive and appetitive unconditioned stimuli and widely varying task requirements of vigilance and resistance to boredom.

Responsiveness to Aversive Stimuli

Since the Mowrer model is based upon the notion that parents make use of aversive stimuli (punishment or overt disapproval) to restrain certain types of behavior in their children, there has been a great deal of interest in the following question: Are psychopaths, and (presumably to a lesser extent) other offenders, less responsive than the rest of us to aversive stimuli? Two studies by Hare, involving the use of a loud auditory stimulus (Hare, 1978), and the insertion of a hypodermic needle (Hare, 1972), seemed to indicate that psychopaths are less responsive to aversive stimuli than nonpsychopathic offenders and other citizens. (It is arguable that this is the wrong question to ask. The Mowrer model does not require low responsiveness to aversive stimuli, but hyporesponsiveness to *signaled* aversive stimuli.) Hare and Quinn (1971), and also Hare and Craigen (1974), provide evidence that psychopaths show smaller conditioned skin conductance responses in experiments using electric shock as the unconditioned stimulus than do nonpsychopathic controls.

Conditionability

There seems to be no doubt that some criminal or delinquent individuals have difficulty in forming conditioned responses in certain conditions. Mednick and Volavka (1980, p.123) concluded from their review of published data that, "The antisocial individual evidences relatively poor skin conductance conditioning. This finding is reliable and not contradicted. In discussions of this literature there has been a tendency to imply that the psychopath simply cannot learn an ANS conditioned response. Perhaps it would be more accurate to say that at equivalent levels of aversive stimulation (noise or electric shock) the antisocial individual evidences a deficit in ANS conditioning." It has been suggested that psychopaths may be unable to identify contingent relationships between stimuli, or at least that they are incapable of verbalising them and therefore of processing the information in a form in which they can be remembered. However, a study by Ziskind, Syndulko, and Maltzmann (1978), in which psychopathic subjects were informed before the experiment began about the relations between the unconditioned stimulus and the conditional stimulus, showed the same deficit in conditioning. Hare (1965a) and Lippert and Senter (1966) seem to have established that psychopaths exhibit virtually no increase in skin conductance in response to signals of impending aversive stimulation, although the actual onset of the aversive stimulus does elicit an apparently normal skin conductance response (SCR). This characteristic has not been found in nonpsychopathic offenders. However, Hare, and Craigen (1974) report that a group of psychopaths displayed significantly larger cardiac acceleration in anticipation of an unpleasant stimulus than did nonpsychopaths, a finding that is not easy to explain (Siddle & Trasler, 1981). Considerable controversy has resulted from these research findings.

Eysenck (1964) has offered an interpretation based on the thesis that people differ from one another with respect to their receptiveness to conditioning, arguing that offenders (including psychopaths and juvenile delinquents, and also, surprisingly, unmarried mothers can be discriminated from other people in the same categories of socioeconomic status, age, ethnicity and gender in terms of his three-dimension model of personality. With respect to the dimension of extraversion—introversion, he has argued that extraverted people are poor conditioners (that is, they form conditioned responses slowly and with difficulty) and that conditioned responses in extraverts are readily extinguished. Since, following Mowrer, he takes the view that socialization is mediated by conditioning, among poorly socialized individuals there will be a preponderance of extraverts, and that one might expect convicted offenders to have difficulty in acquiring conditioned responses (in, for example, ANS conditioning procedures). In relation to the dimension of neuroticism—stability (also described as emotionality), those neurotics who have developed delinquent, criminal, or antisocial habits will engage in these activities with greater frequency than extraverted, emotionally stable individuals, since neurotic anxiety is a drive which enhances the likelihood that a habit will issue in behavior. Individuals in the high-extraversion, high-neuroticism quadrant of the model might be expected to include a disproportionate number of antisocial and criminal people, and especially of "high rate" criminals.

Eysenck's position depends upon two assumptions: first, that there exists a stable characteristic of "conditionability"—that is to say, that (at least in principle) individuals differ from one another in their responsiveness to conditioning of all kinds (presumably involving both appetitive and aversive unconditioned stimuli, various response systems, and several sensory modalities; and that (since "conditionability" is claimed to be primarily a function of extraversion) convicted offenders will, as a class, be more extraverted than the population at large. (However, there is some ambiguity about this. Passingham (1972) draws attention to a comment by Eysenck in the *Psychological Bulletin* in 1965 that "correlations between different types of conditioning are relatively low, or may even be near zero," (p. 344) a remark which suggests doubts about the existence of a general factor of conditionability, or conceivably the effects of large measurement errors, which are of course characteristic of some indices of ANS activity.)

Surprisingly, in view of the popularity which Eysenck's theory of criminality has attained, at least in Britain, the only evidence he offers in support of the existence of a general factor of conditionability is a paper by Barr and McGonaghy (1972), using two response systems (the SCR and a measure of peripheral blood flow), involving both aversive and appetitive procedures, which yielded correlations varying between .14 and .31 across response systems, and correlations between aversive and appetitive modes of .43 and .01 (Eysenck, 1977, p. 209). Lovibond (1964) has pointed out that there are great technical difficulties in establishing the existence of a general factor of conditionability. It seems likely that thee are group factors which may or may not share some common variance. It will be argued later in this chapter that one such group factor (if such factors exist) must relate to aversive inhibitory conditioning.

As to the relations between extraversion and delinquency, Farrington, Biron, and LeBlanc (1982) list 14 studies which compared prisoners and institutionalised delinquents with control samples. In five of these the incarcerated group showed a higher mean extraversion score than the controls, in four, they had a lower mean E-score, and in the remaining five studies the findings were equivocal in relation to extraversion. Differences between samples were almost always slight; as the authors point out, "even when the delinquent group is significantly high on extraversion, this seems to be primarily a case of very small differences in very large samples" (p. 163; see also Chapter 6).

Electrodermal Recovery

Several investigators have reported differences between convicted offenders and others in one particular aspect of SCR conditioning; namely, the rapidity with which skin conductance returns to the normal level following a response (usually termed "electrodermal recovery" or EDRec). Siddle (1977), Hare (1978), and Mednick (1977a) have each provided summaries of the data that were available in the late 1970s. Hare (1978, Note 1) compared a group of primary psychopaths with a group of nonpsychopathic criminals. His psychopathic subjects showed slower EDRec to a novel tone (a change stimulus following a series of 16 identical tones), and also slower recovery to fast-onset, high-intensity tones of 120 dB. Levander, Schalling, Lidberg, Bartfai and Lidberg (1980), in a study of 25 male criminals, found a substantial correlation (0.47: p < .05) between mean EDRec and score on a Delinquency Scale, indicating that their more psychopathic subjects had characteristically slower recovery. Mednick (1974) reported results from a long-term study of "high-risk" subjects which seemed to show a relationship between criminality and slow EDRec, and Siddle, Mednick, Nicol and Foggitt (1976) reanalysed data from an earlier study of borstal inmates to show that those with histories indicating strongly antisocial tendencies exhibited slower EDRec than their less antisocial peers.

In a 10-year follow-up of prisoners in a maximum-security penitentiary, Hare (1978a) found that EDRec distinguished (though not very well) between recidivists and others. Finally, in perhaps the most tantalizing fragment of research, Loeb and Mednick (1977) reported data suggesting that slow EDRec in adolescents and young adults may be prognostic of future criminality. One can say, in brief, that although there have certainly been some negative findings, there is evidence for the existence of some kind of association between criminality and slow EDRec. In endeavoring to explain these observations, Mednick (Mednick et al, 1974) adopted the essentials of the Mowrer model of passive avoidance conditioning, taking as his point of departure "the possibility that the psychopath and the criminal have some defect in avoidance learning which interferes with their ability to learn to inhibit asocial responses" (p. 2). He went on to specify the conditions necessary for the acquisition and maintenance of an inhibitory response: a "censuring agent" (typically the family); an adequate fear response; the ability to experience fear in anticipation of an asocial act; and fast dissipation of fear which will quickly reinforce the inhibitory response. He then endeavored to identify the key variables in the Mowrer model with measurable features of the EDR. He argued that the EDR indexes the onset and offset of fear—that the amplitude of the EDR reflects the intensity of fear, and that the rapidity of EDRec reflects the rate of fear dissipation. He made the working assumption that the rate of fear dissipation determines the effectiveness with which the avoidant response is reinforced, suggesting that rapid EDRec indicates maximal reinforcement of the learned inhibition (by fear reduction). Thus the contemplation of a forbidden action triggers anticipatory fear which is peripherally indexed by an increase in skin conductance. The individual momentarily contemplates, but rejects, this course of action (that is, he inhibits the behavior). The inhibitory response is reinforced by the consequent reduction of fear, which is reflected in the EDRec.

Mednick's theory rests upon the assumption that for inhibition to be maintained, fear must be elicited whenever the individual finds himself in circumstances in which such acts would be feasible. He will not necessarily be conscious of the onset of fear, but it would be discernible as an electrodermal response. There is also an assumption that the conditioned fear response does not become attenuated as a function of time or number of trials. That is said to be the reason for the resistance to extinction which characterizes passive avoidance.

There is general, if not universal (Hodgson & Rachman, 1974; Mineka, 1979) agreement that it is necessary to subject the individual to an aversive stimulus (or to withhold an expected reward—Gray, 1975) in order that he may learn to inhibit behavior. However, the acquisition of a response and the subsequent performance of a response which has been firmly established are not the same thing, and there is some evidence in support of the contrary proposition—that the continued elicitation of fear is *not* a necessary condition for the maintenance of active avoidance (Rachman, 1976; see also Seligman and Johnson, 1967, p. 169).

What is known of the role of fear in the acquisition and maintenance of inhibitory responses in humans is even more sketchy. Experiments using the Lykken avoidance task (Lykken, 1957; Waid, 1976; Schmauk, 1970) show, with reasonable consistency, that subjects who have difficulty in learning the avoidance task (the "latent task") tend to produce skin conductance responses to the punishing stimulus of lower mean amplitude than subjects who learn the task readily.

Let us now turn our attention to EDRec as a psychophysiological measure. Although psychologists have used various characteristics of electrodermal activity as indices of central processes for many years, little attention was paid to EDRec until Edelberg's (1970) pioneer study. It had generally been assumed that the time taken to recover after emitting an electrodermal response was determined by the amplitude of the response. Edelberg's significant contribution was the demonstration that, in most circumstances, the rate of recovery is largely independent of the amplitude of the response (see Venables, 1974).

There is much less agreement about the significance of different rates of recovery. Edelberg was initially inclined to the view that fast recovery reflected "involvement in goal-oriented performance" (1972, p. 520) and that slow EDRec probably indicated a defensive reaction to an aversive stimulus. Venables (1974) offered the alternative proposal that EDRec reflected "openness-closedness to the environment," (p. 131) but this interpretation does not now seem tenable (Venables, Gartshore, & O'Riordan, 1980). Siddle (1977; Siddle & Trasler, 1981) has also suggested that speed of EDRec has to do with the degree of attention to events in the environment. This hypothesis gains some support from the observation of Levander and his colleagues, that the most clear-cut differences between individuals relate to the contrast between first and subsequent presentations of a stimulus; that is, in responses to novel and familiar stimuli (Levander, Schalling, Lidberg, & Lidberg, 1979).

Each of these interpretations presents a challenge to Mednick's proposal that (at least in the special circumstances of passive avoidance responding) the rate of EDRec reflects rate of dissipation of conditioned fear, but none of them has as yet attracted significant empirical support. What is much more damaging to Mednick's theory is the contention that EDRec is a function of immediately preceding electrodermal activity, rather than a feature of the response to the immediate stimulus (Bundy & Fitzgerald, 1975).

While this observation presents general problems concerning the independence of EDRec from other indices of electrodermal activity, it poses particular difficulties for the interpretation of research showing differences between psychopaths, other criminals, and so-called "normal" controls, since some writers contend that psychopaths and criminals show a lower rate of spontaneous ("nonspecific") activity than noncriminal individuals (Schalling, Lidberg, Levander and Dahlin, 1973; Hare, 1978b, and critical comment by Siddle, 1977). If this were so, it would follow that a psychopath is less likely than a nonpsychopath to have made a spontaneous electrodermal response immediately before an elicited response—a state of affairs which could in principle account for the slower EDRec which has been observed in studies of psychopaths and other offenders. Whether this is the explanation of the reported group differences has not been established; further research, taking account of prior spontaneous responding, is clearly required.

Until these questions have been resolved it would clearly be unwise to assume that EDRec is independent of other parameters of electrodermal activity. It is worth pointing out that Mednick's theory does not require such independence, although his own data, showing this variable, but not rise time or amplitude, distinguishes between deviants and others, seem to imply it. But it is necessary for Mednick to assume that rapidity of EDRec is a reliable attribute of persons—that an individual who exhibits slow recovery in one situation will do so in another, at least in conditions of aversive stimulation. There are three aspects to this question. The first concerns to degree of error which arises in the detection and recording of both the EDR and its recovery limb, a task which is complicated by the tendency of some subjects to produce spontaneous responses before the elicited response has decayed. The second aspect of the question concerns the stability of EDRec over successive trials and experimental sessions. Here we do have some data, but they are conflicting. Levander et al. (1980) found a high degree of within-subject consistency in a single experimental session. On the other hand, the same group of investigators reported a study in which 24 arrested men who were awaiting disposal by the courts were subjected to three testing sessions at weekly intervals, the last occasion being immediately before the court appearance. The authors reported that the between-session intercorrelations for each measure were small and non-significant both for EDRec to the initial stimulus of the series and for mean EDRec to the remaining 10 stimuli of the series, indicating a pronounced effect of situational variance or a low reliability. One must, of course, take account of the authors' intention to secure the maximum possible manipulation of extraneous stress—they were trying to see how much they could influence EDRec by this means—but these results are a sobering indication of the dangers of regarding EDRec, measured on a single occasion, as a reliable index of stable individual differences. A further study by Siddle and Heron (1976) underscores this. It was specifically addressed to the question of consistency over time. Using a test-retest interval of between three and six months, they found that although retest reliability estimates for most parameters of electrodermal activity were fairly high, those for EDRec were not. There is, of course, a great deal more to be said concerning the retest reliability of the several available measures of EDRec. A recent review by Venables and Christie (1980) is a useful source.

The third aspect of reliability which must be considered is the extent to which individuals exhibit consistency, in terms of characteristic rapidity or slowness of EDR, in different task or stimulus conditions. The results of investigations are reasonably consistent in showing that novel, unexpected, or aversive stimuli generally elicit responses with slow recovery, while repeated, nonaversive stimuli prompt rapid recovery (Edelberg, 1970, 1972, 1973; Lockhart, 1972; Hare, Frazelle, & Cox, reported in Hare, 1978b; Ohman, Fredrikson, & Hugdahl, 1978; Levander et al., 1979; Levander et al., 1980). Hare (1978b) has also reported experimental data which appear to show that the intensity and rise time of the stimulus may be important if the design does not include some element of novelty or "disparity." He found that it was necessary to use an extremely intense stimulus (120 dB) of rapid onset in order to differentiate criminals and noncriminals. Less intense stimulation, or stimulation by means of an intense tone of slow onset, yielded no differences in recovery half-times between the experimental and control groups.

It seems clear, then, that there is presently no justification for regarding the rate of EDRec as a situation-independent characteristic of individuals. It is necessary to specify much more exactly than has hitherto been the practice, the stimulus conditions for eliciting the electrodermal response. Until this is done the question of the reliability (stability) of recovery measures cannot be resolved. For the purpose of testing Mednick's hypothesis concerning the relations between rate of recovery and fear dissipation, it is obviously desirable that aversive rather than neutral stimuli be employed. Hare's data further indicate that high intensity and rapid onset are necessary conditions.

There is one respect in which virtually all of the studies which we have considered are inappropriate tests of Mednick's theory: they involve the direct elicitation of the electrodermal response by an unconditioned stimulus, in the form of a loud noise or an electric shock. However, the two-process theory of avoidance specified that the state of fear, the reduction of which reinforces the inhibitory response, is elicited by *conditioned* stimuli. As Mednick has put it, "after a sufficient quantity or quality of punishment, just the thought of the aggression" (or other delinquency) "should be enough to produce a bit of anticipatory fear. . . . If this fear response is large enough, the aggressive response will be successfully inhibited" (1977, p. 3). In Mowrer's terms, fear elicited by parental punishment (the unconditioned stimulus) becomes associated with response-correlated stimuli (the preliminary phases of the action sequence which provoked punishment) which now act as the conditioned stimulus, eliciting conditioned fear whenever the action sequence is begun. According to Gray (1975) there is no reason to expect close correspondence between the manner in which an individual responds to an unconditioned aversive stimulus, on the one hand, and to a conditioned stimulus which has acquired secondary aversive properties through association with punishment, on the other hand—and indeed, there are good theoretical grounds for expecting these responses to be different. If Gray is right, then the demonstration that delinquents differ from nondelinquents in EDRec time following response to a primary (unconditioned) stimulus can cast no light whatever on the validity of

Mednick's theoretical position. There seems to be only one instance in the literature in which a conditioning paradigm was used and that is the Hare and Quinn (1971) experiment, the skin-conductance records from which were subsequently rescored by Hare to provide EDRec data (Hare, 1978), but unfortunately no information is given concerning electrodermal responses to the conditioned stimulus. Although Hare did show that the difference in EDRec between psychopathic and control subjects was eliminated when the US was preceded by a CS ("signalled"), the significance of this finding is rather obscure.

The conclusions to be drawn from this review are fragmentary and largely cautionary. It now seems clear that Mednick's belief that measures of EDRec could be used directly to tap and calibrate the central mechanisms which mediate conscience, the capacity to acquire and maintain the inhibition of asocial behavior, was excessively optimistic. EDRec measures are less precise and much more situation-dependent than we realised in the exciting period following Edelberg's (1970) paper.

Against these rather gloomy reflections one has to set the fact that Mednick's belief in the existence of some relationship between what he calls "law-abidance" and the rapidity of EDRec to aversive stimuli has not been wholly undermined; there remain some stubborn data which are not easily explained away. There are hints, however, that EDRec is not, as Mednick first thought, directly tapping central processes and reflecting differential refractoriness to conscience acquisition; it now seems rather more likely that it indexes the attentional correlates of conscientious behavior, and the tendency of the individual to pay heed to certain kinds of cues in his immediate environment, and that these things are at least as much affected by prior learning as they are by "wired-in" characteristics of the ANS. It has, in the writer's view, been a consistent feature of psychophysiological progress that our studies of the input characteristics of men, women, and children have been at their most valuable in defining those stimuli, those messages from the external world, which are significant in bringing about enduring changes in behavior (Trasler, 1978). The research which has been stimulated by Mednick's work promises major gains of this kind once we have succeeded in digesting its implications.

CONCLUSIONS

In this section we will consider the general implications of the work which we discussed and attempt to identify the significance of studies of the biological, genetic, and psychophysiological correlates of delinquency and crime.

Certain research designs, notably cross-fostering analyses, and, to a lesser degree, studies of MZ and DZ twin pairs, are useful in an attempt to identify the presence of a biologically transmitted characteristic, but these need to be better planned, to make use of modern techniques for determining zygosity, and to define appropriate samples (or, greatly to be preferred) whole populations from which subjects may be drawn. Even quite sophisticated research designs cannot properly be used to establish the *extent* of the variance explained by genetic mechanisms, since this depends upon the variability of environmental conditions, including the interactions which the developing individual has with parents, other adults, and his age-peers, throughout childhood and adolescence. These seem impossible to measure, but all the evidence suggest they greatly affect the character of the developing individual in terms of behavioral repertoire, sensitivity to various kinds of stimuli, and ability to respond to contingent events, both external and internal. It is clear that the results of twin studies published over several decades cannot be treated as additive data, since they represent findings drawn from research of widely differing quality and design, conducted in disparate conditions. There is presently great vagueness as to the characteristics being transmitted genetically, and there is no reliable evidence implicating abnormal chromosome complements of damage of malformation with increased risk of crime in general, or violent crime in particular.

Attempts to demonstrate that delinquents (or, in more general terms, offenders) are poor learners, or are resistant to conditioning, have not been successful. However, a series of experimenters, starting with David Lykken (1957), have reported that some persistent offenders have difficulty in learning to inhibit behavior that is preceded by a signal of impending punishment. Several explanations for this deficit have been suggested: low levels of tonic and phasic arousal of the ANS; difficulties in recognizing contingent relations between aversive events and the individual's own conduct; boredom and lapses of attention; and rapid habituation. Since our culture relies to a very considerable extent upon aversive inhibitory conditioning as a means of socialization, difficulties in learning through punishment (which in practice usually means a rebuke) obviously presents problems. It is certainly not suggested that a substantial impairment of this kind is present in more than a minority of adolescent offenders (some of whom may be diagnosed as psychopathic). The results of invasive research using animal subjects gives some indication of the complex involvement of the limbic system in this particular form of conditioning which seems to explain the effects of certain drugs (such as alcohol and the so-called "minor tranquilizers") in temporarily blocking inhibitory responses, and also the effects of intracranial traumata and disease upon these learned responses.

A major recent development in the attempt to identify the relationship between certain parameters of ANS functioning has concentrated on individual differences in EDRec. Mednick, Volavka and their colleagues have proposed that slow EDRec is characteristic of individuals who have particular difficulties in acquiring conditioned inhibitory responses, and they and other scholars have put forward some interesting data in support of this contention. However, there are difficulties about the legitimacy of the theoretical model the reliability of the measures used in this research which may or may not prove to be fatal. Because of contemporary interest in this work and the absence of critical commentary elsewhere, it has been examined in some detail in this chapter.

THE STATUS OF "BIOLOGICAL" OR "BIOSOCIAL" THEORY

There has been much misunderstanding of the potential contribution of the biological sciences in explaining aspects of delinquency and crime. Some enthusiasts for biologically based theories appear to be confident that research of this kind, indicating correlations between ANS functions, hormone levels, unusual patterns of EEG activity, and idiosyncratic responses to experimental procedures, will in due course yield a biology of crime and delinquency which explains, and suggests ways of responding to, the actions of the offender—without the need to take account of the social contexts in which crime occurs and where some part of the disposition to break the law is formed. It is significant, in this regard, that Mednick, the late Karl Otto Christiansen, and others who have been influential in reintroducing some of the concepts and procedures of the biological sciences into criminology have been careful to describe their activities as progress toward an understanding of biosocial bases of crime. They thus acknowledge that they are not seeking to build a science that is in competition with the sociology of delinquency, deviance, and crime, but to explore the impact of the social environment upon the characteristics of individuals—characteristics which are mediated by the complexities of human personality and its structural underpinning.

There is a natural, but unfortunate, tendency to regard the biological and psychophysiological correlates of delinquency as causes, or at least phenomena much closer to the real causes of delinquency than the desires, fears, loyalties, and accumulated experiences of individuals. The insecure nature of this assumption has been pointed out by several writers—Quay (1965, 1977), Rotenberg (1978), Siddle (1977) and Zuckerman (1978) among them. To take a simple example, hyporesponsivity (attenuated phasic ANS responses) to stimuli in the experimental laboratory may mean that the subject is the unfortunate possessor of an insensitive ANS, and is therefore incapable of responding; alternatively he may be bored, depressed, or otherwise inattentive (Siddle & Trasler, 1981). Further investigation of the psychophysiological data is needed to determine which is the better explanation. Studies of EDRec, in particular those carried out by Schalling and her colleagues, suggest that situational features of the experiment—where and how it is conducted, the subject's understanding of its purpose, and his current state of anxiousness or calmness, may greatly affect the outcome of the experiment.

Two principles of some importance—both familiar, perhaps, but still deserving of emphasis—emerge from a review of biological or biosocial contributions to the study of delinquency and crime. The first is that theories exist for a purpose; they are framed in terms of limited or specific aspects of what may be highly complex phenomena; they are intended to identify the relations between this subset of observations; they are useful for particular purposes. They should be seen not as statements of fundamental truths, but as tentative, provisional characterizations of events. (The reader will recognize this as an adaptation of George Kelly's (1955) principle of "constructive alternativism.") Second, biological models are used in several different ways, and it is important to identify which of these is intended. They sometimes emerge, initially, as analogies. For example, Mowrer's (1950) two-factor theory was based on the observation that the process of acquiring behavioral inhibitions and "internalized" moral controls bore some resemblance to "passive avoidance conditioning" in the animal laboratory. Since this fairly simple experimental paradigm was well understood, Mowrer and others attempted to see whether the similarities between these processes suggested problems to explore, in relation (for example) to interstimulus intervals, the intensity of the unconditioned stimulus, and resistance to extinction. The immediate analogy held—if you treat a human infant as you would train a laboratory rat, effective avoidance can be achieved. Other psychologists, such as Bandura (1965) and Walters & Parke (1964), extended the model to take account of the capacity of human children to distinguish between objects and situations, to verbalize and to understand rules, and to learn through modeling and vicarious reinforcement. At about the same time, and in a very different area of psychology, McCleary (1966) analyzed apparently contradictory findings of the effects of hippocampal lesions on inhibitory responses, and Douglas (1967) added the observation that active and passive avoidance, long believed to be simply two manifestations of a single process, were in fact mediated by different neurophysiological systems. These studies paved the way for Gray's masterly two-process theory of learning, and further developments in the theory of aversive inhibitory conditioning contributed by Fowles (1980) and others. Thus in this intriguing story an analogy from the animal laboratory developed into a model of inhibitory conditioning in humans, leading in turn to an interest in paradoxical effects of lesions of the septohippocampal system on avoidance learning, and finally to the development of a neuropsychological theory of considerable potential.

It may be that the Mednick-Volavka research will follow a similar course, beginning with the Mowrer-Miller notion of avoidance conditioning, noting the role of anxiety reduction in the model, and making the rather daring connection with EDRec. Perhaps when we know more about phasic changes in skin conductance, nonspecific responses, and rates of recovery, the present difficulties will be resolved. Meanwhile, it has to be said that cross-fertilization between "biological" concerns of genetics, psychophysiology, and neuropsychology on the one hand, and experimental and naturalistic observations of social behavior, on the other, has already opened up new and exciting lines of research in the study of delinquency.

REFERENCES

Bandura, A. (1965). Vicarious processes: a case of no-trial learning. *Advances in Experimental Social Psychology. 2,* 3–55.

Barr, R. F., & McConaghy, N. (1972). A general factor of conditionability: A study of galvanic skin responses and penile responses. *Behavior Research & Therapy, 10,* 215–227.

Bodmer, W. (1973). Genetics and intelligence: The race argument. *Times Literary Supplement.* Reprinted in A. H. Halsey (Ed.), Heredity and environment. London: Methuen (p. 312–322).

Bundy, R. S., & Fitzgerald, H. E. (1975). Stimulus specificity of electrodermal recovery time: An examination and reinterpretation of the evidence. *Psychophysiology, 12,* 506–511.

Casey, M. D., Blank, C. E., Street, D. R. K., Segall, L. J., McDougall, J. H., McGrath, P. J., & Skinner, J. L. (1966). YY chromosomes and antisocial behaviour. *Lancet, 2,* 859–860.

Casey, M. D., Segall, L. J., Street, D. R. K., & Blank, C. E. (1966). Sex chromosome abnormalities in two state hospitals for patients requiring special security. *Nature, 209,* 641–642.

Chesno, F. A., & Kilmann, P. R. (1975). Effects of stimulation intensity on sociopathic avoidance learning. *Journal of Abnormal Psychology, 84,* 144–150.

Christiansen, K. O. (1968). Recidivism among collaborators. In M. Wolfgang (Ed.), *Crime and culture: Essays in honour of Thorsten Sellin.* New York: Wiley.

Christiansen, K. O. (1977a). A review of studies of criminality among twins. In S. A. Mednick & K. O. Christiansen (Eds.), *Biosocial bases of criminal behavior* (pp. 45–88). New York: Gardner Press.

Christiansen, K. O. (1977b). A preliminary study of criminality among twins. In S. A. Mednick & K. O. Christiansen (Eds.), *Biosocial bases of criminal behavior,* (pp. 89–108). New York: Gardner Press.

Christiansen, K. O. (1977c). Seriousness of criminality and concordance among Danish twins. In R. Hood (Ed.), *Crime, criminology and public policy* (pp. 63–77). London: Heinemann.

Close, H. G., Goonetilleke, A. S. R., Jacobs, P. A., & Price, W. H. (1968). The incidence of sex chromosomal anomalies in mentally subnormal males. *Cytogenetics, 7,* 277–285.

Court Brown, W. M. (1962). Sex chromosomes and the law. *Lancet, 2,* 508.

Dalgaard, O. S., & Kringlen, E. (1976). A Norwegian twin study of criminality. *British Journal of Criminology, 16,* 213–232.

Douglas, R. J. (1967). The hippocampus and behavior. *Psychological Bulletin, 67,* 416–442.

Edelberg, R., (1970) The information content of the recovery limb of the electrodermal response. *Psychophysiology, 6,* 527–539.

Edelberg, R. (1972). Electrodermal recovery rate, goal-orientation and aversion. *Psychophysiology, 9,* 512–520.

Edelberg, R. (1973). Mechanisms of electrodermal adaptations for locomotion, manipulation, or defense. *Progress in Physiological Psychology, 5,* 155–209.

Eysenck, H. J. (1962). Conditioning and personality. *British Journal of Psychology, 53,* 299–305.

Eysenck, H. J. (1964). *Crime and personality.* London: Routledge & Kegan Paul.

Eysenck, H. J. (1965). Extraversion and the acquisition of the eyeblink and GSR conditioned responses. *Psychological Bulletin, 63,* 258–270.

Eysenck, H. J. (1977). *Crime and personality* (3rd ed.). London: Routledge & Kegan Paul.

Farrington, D. P., Biron, L., & LeBlanc, M. (1982). Personality and delinquency in London and Montreal. In J. Gunn & D. P. Farrington (Eds.), *Abnormal offenders, delinquency and the criminal justice system,* (pp. 153–201). New York: Wiley.

Forde, R. A. (1978). Twin studies, inheritance and criminality. *British Journal of Criminology, 18,* 71–74.

Forssmann, H., & Hambert, G. (1967). Chromosomes and antisocial behavior. *Excerpta criminologica, 7,* 113–117.

Fowles, D. C. (1980). The three arousal model: implications of Gray's two-factor learning theory for heart rate, electrodermal activity and psychopathy. *Psychophysiology, 17,* 87–104.

Fox, R., & Lippert, W. W. (1963). Spontaneous GSR and anxiety level in sociopathic delinquents. *Journal of Consulting Psychology, 27,* 386.

Glueck, S., & Glueck, E. (1950). *Unraveling juvenile delinquency.* New York: Commonwealth Fund.

Gray, J. A. (1975). *Elements of a two-process theory of learning.* New York: Academic Press.

Hare, R. D. (1965a). Temporal gradient of fear arousal in psychopaths. *Journal of Abnormal Psychology, 70,* 442–445.

Hare, R. D. (1965b). Acquisition and generalization of a conditioned-fear response in psychopathic and non-psychopathic criminals. *Journal of Psychology, 59,* 367–370.

Hare, R. D. (1968). Psychopathy, autonomic functioning, and the orienting response. *Journal of Abnormal Psychology Monograph Supplement, 73,* 1–24.

Hare, R. D. (1970). *Psychopathy: Theory and research.* New York: Wiley.

Hare, R. D. (1972). Psychopathy and sensitivity to adrenaline. *Journal of Abnormal Psychology, 79,* 138–147.

Hare, R. D. (1973). The origins of confusion. *Journal of Abnormal Psychology, 82,* 535–536.

Hare, R. D. (1975). Psychopathy. In P. H. Venables & M. J. Christie (Eds.), *Research in psychophysiology* (pp. 325–348). Chichester: Wiley.

Hare, R. D. (1975b). Psychophysiological studies of psychopathy. In D. C. Fowles (Ed.), *Clinical applications of psychophysiology* (pp. 77–105). New York: Columbia University Press.

Hare, R. D. (1978a). Psychopathy and crime. In L. Otten (Ed.), *Colloquium on the correlates of crime and the determinants of criminal behavior.* Rosslyn, VA: Mitre.

Hare, R. D. (1978b). Electrodermal and cardiovascular correlates of psychopathy. In R. D. Hare & D. Schalling (Eds.), *Psychopathic behaviour: Approaches to research* (pp. 1–21). Chichester: Wiley.

Hare, R. D., & Cox, D. N. (1978). Clinical and empirical conceptions of psychopathy, and the selection of subjects for research. In R. D. Hare & D. Schalling (Eds.), *Psychopathic behaviour: Approaches to research* (pp. 1–21). Chichester: Wiley.

Hare, R., D., & Craigen, D. (1974). Psychopathy and physiological activity in a mixed-motive game situation. *Psychophysiology, 11,* 197–206.

Hare, R. D., Frazelle, J., & Cox, D. N. (1978). Psychopathy and physiological responses to threat of an aversive stimulus. *Psychophysiology, 15,* 165–172.

Hare, R. D., & Quinn, M. J. (1971). Psychopathy and autonomic conditioning. *Journal of Abnormal Psychology, 77,* 223–235.

Hare, R. D., & Schalling, D. (1978) *Psychopathic behaviour: Approaches to research.* New York: Wiley.

Hodgson, R., & Rachman, S. (1974). Desynchrony in measures of fear. *Behaviour Research and Therapy, 12,* 319–326.

Hunter, H. (1966). YY chromosomes and Klinefelter's syndrome. *Lancet, 1,* 984.

Hutchings, B., & Mednick, S. A. (1977). Criminality in adoptees and their adoptive and biological parents. In S. A. Mednick & K. O. Christiansen (Eds.). *Biosocial bases of criminal behavior* (pp. 127–141). New York: Gardner.

Jacobs, P. A., Brunton, M., Melville, M. M., Brittain, R. P., & McClemont, W. F. (1965). Aggressive behaviour, mental sub-normality, and the XYY male. *Nature, 208,* 1351–1352.

Jencks, C. (1980). Heredity, environment and public policy reconsidered. *American Sociological Review, 45,* 723–736.

Kahn, J., Reed, F. S., Bates, M., Coates, T., & Everitt, B. (1976). A survey of Y chromosome variants and personality in 436 borstal lads and 254 controls. *British Journal of Criminology, 16,* 233–244.

Kelly, G. A. (1955). *The psychology of personal constructs.* New York: Norton.

Langan, P. A., & Greenfeld, L. A. (1983). *Career patterns in crime* (special report of the Bureau of Justice Statistics). Washington, D.C.: U.S. Department of Justice.

Lange, J. (1928). *Crime as destiny* (English translation published in 1931). London: George Allen & Unwin.

Levander, S. E., Schalling, D., Lidberg, L., & Lidberg, Y. (1979). *Electrodermal recovery time, stress and psychopathy.* Report from the Laboratory for Clinical Stress Research (No. 59). Karolinska Institute, Stockholm.

Levander, S. E., Schalling, D. S., Lidberg, L., Bartfai, A., & Lidberg, Y. (1980). Skin conductance recovery time and personality in a group of criminals. *Psychophysiology, 17,* 105–111.

Lippert, W. W., & Senter, R. J. (1966). Electrodermal responses in the sociopath. *Psychonomic Science, 4,* 25–26.

Lockhart, R. A. (1972). Interrelation between amplitude, latency, rise time and the Edelberg recovery measure of the galvanic skin response. *Psychophysiology, 9,* 437–442.

Loeb, J., & Mednick, S. A. (1977). A prospective study of predictors of criminality: 3. Electrodermal response patterns. In S. A. Mednick & K. O. Christiansen (Eds.), *Biosocial bases of criminal behavior,* (pp. 245–254). New York: Gardner.

Lovibond, S. H. (1964). Personality and conditioning. In B. A. Maher (Ed.), *Progress in experimental personality research, 1,* 115–168.

Lykken, D. T. (1957). A study of anxiety in the sociopathic personality. *Journal of Abnormal and Social Psychology, 55,* 6–10.

McCleary, R. A. (1966). Response-modulating functions of the limbic system: Initiation and suppression. In F. Stellar & J. M. Sprague (Eds.), *Progress in Physiological Psychology* (Vol. 1, pp. 209–272). New York: Academic Press.

Mednick, S. A. (1974). Electrodermal recovery and psychopathology. In S. A. Mednick, F. Schulsinger, J. Higgins & B. Bell (Eds.), *Genetics, environment and psychopathology.* Oxford: North-Holland.

Mednick, S. A. (1977). A bio-social theory of the learning of law-abiding behavior. In S. A. Mednick & K. O. Christiansen (Eds.), *Biosocial bases of criminal behavior* (pp. 1–8). New York: Gardner.

Mednick, S. A. (1977). Some considerations in the interpretation of the Danish adoption studies. In S. A. Mednick & K. O. Christiansen (Eds.), *Biosocial bases of criminal behavior* (pp. 159–164). New York: Gardner.

Mednick, S. A., Gabrielli, W. F., & Hutchings, B. (1982). Genetic influences in criminal behavior. Unpublished manuscript. Los Angeles: University of Southern California (quoted in Pollock, Mednick & Gabrielli, 1983).

Mednick, S. A., Schulsinger, F., Higgins, J., & Bell, B. (1974). *Genetics, environment and psychopathology.* Amsterdam: North-Holland.

Mednick, S. A., & Volavka, J. (1980). Biology and crime. In N. Morris & M. Tonry (Eds.), *Crime and justice* (Vol. 2, pp. 85–158). Chicago: Chicago University Press.

Mineka, S. (1979). The role of fear in theories of avoidance learning, flooding, and extinction. *Psychological Bulletin, 86,* 985–1010.

Mowrer, O. H. (1950). *Learning theory and personality dynamics.* New York: Ronald.

Mowrer, O. H. (1960). *Learning theory and behavior.* New York: Wiley.

Ohman, A., Fredrikson, M., & Hugdahl, K. (1978). Orienting and defensive responding in the electrodermal system: Palmar-dorsal differences and recovery rate during conditioning to potentially phobic stimuli. *Psychophysiology, 15,* 93–101.

Passingham, R. E. (1972). Crime and personality: A review of Eysenck's theory. In V. D. Nebylitsin & J. A. Gray (Eds.), *Biological bases of individual behavior* (pp. 342–371). New York: Academic Press.

Pearson, P. L., Bobrow, M., & Vosa, T. G. (1970). Technique for identifying Y chromosomes in human interphase nuclei. *Nature, 226,* 78–80.

Pollock, V., Mednick, S. A., & Gabrielli, W. F. (1983). Crime causation: Biological theories. In S. H. Kadish (Ed.), *Encyclopaedia of crime and justice,* (Vol. 1, pp. 308–316). New York: Free Press and Macmillan.

Price, W. H., Strong, J. A., Whatmore, P. B., & McClemont, W. F. (1966). Criminal patients with XYY sex chromosome complement. *Lancet, 1,* 565–566.

Price, W. H., & Whatmore, P. B. (1967a). Criminal behaviour and the XYY male. *Nature, 213,* 815.

Price, W. H., & Whatmore, P. B. (1967b). Behaviour disorders and the pattern of crime among XYY males identified at a maximum security hospital. *British Medical Journal, 1,* 533.

Quay, H. C. (1965). Psychopathic personality as pathological stimulation seeking. *American Journal of Psychiatry, 122,* 180–183.

Quay, H. C. (1977). Psychopathic behavior: Reflections on its nature, origins and treatment. In I. C. Uzgiris & F. Weizmann (Eds.), *The structuring of experience* (pp. 371–383). New York: Plenum.

Quay, H. C. (1983). Crime causation: Psychological theories. In S. H. Kadish (Ed.), *Encyclopaedia of crime and justice,* (Vol. 1, pp. 330–342). New York: Free Press and Macmillan.

Rachman, S. (1976). The passing of the two-stage theory of fear and avoidance: Fresh possibilities. *Behaviour Research & Therapy, 14,* 125–131.

Rosanoff, A. J., Handy, L. M., & Plesset, I. R. (1934). Criminality and delinquency in twins. *Journal of Criminal Law & Criminology, 24,* 923–934.

Rotenberg, M. (1978). Psychopathy and differential insensitivity. In R. D. Hare & D. Schalling (Eds.), *Psychopathic behaviour: Approaches to research* (pp. 187–196). New York: Wiley.

Rowe, D. C. (1985). Sibling interaction and self-reported delinquent behavior: A study of 265 twin pairs. *Criminology, 23,* 223–240.

Schachter, S. (1971). *Emotion, obesity and crime.* New York: Academic Press.

Schachter, S., & Latané, B. (1964). Crime, cognition and the autonomic nervous system. In M. R. Jones (Ed.), *Nebraska symposium on motivation* (pp. 221–275). Lincoln: University of Nebraska.

Schalling, D., Lidberg, L., Levander, S. E., & Dahlin, Y. (1973). Spontaneous autonomic activity as related to psychopathy. *Biological Psychology, 1,* 83–97.

Schmauk, F. J. (1970). Punishment, arousal and avoidance learning in sociopaths. *Journal of Abnormal Psychology, 76,* 325–335.

Schulsinger, F. (1977). Psychopathy: Heredity and environment. In S. A. Mednick & K. O. Christiansen (Eds.), *Biosocial bases of criminal behavior* (pp. 109–126). New York: Gardner Press.

Seligman, M. E. P., & Johnson, J. C. (1973). A cognitive theory of avoidance learning. In F. J. McGuigan & D. B. Lumsden (Eds.), *Contemporary approaches to conditioning and learning* (pp. 69–110). Washington, D.C.: Winston.

Shah, S. A. (1970). *Report on the XYY chromosomal abnormality.* Washington, D.C.: National Institute for Mental Health.

Shah, S. A., & Roth, L. H. (1974). Biological and psychophysiological factors in criminality. In D. Glaser (Ed.), *Handbook of criminology* (pp. 101–173). Chicago: Rand McNally.

Siddle, D. A. T. (1977). Electrodermal activity and psychopathy. In S. A. Mednick & K. O. Christiansen (Eds.), *Biosocial bases of criminal behavior* (pp. 199–211). New York: Gardner.

Siddle, D. A. T., & Heron, P. A. (1976). Reliability of electrodermal habituation measures under two conditions of stimulus intensity. *Journal of Research in Personality, 10,* 195–200.

Siddle, D. A. T., Mednick, S. A., Nicol, A. R., & Foggitt, R. H. (1976). Skin conductance recovery in antisocial adolescents. *British Journal of Social and Clinical Psychology, 15,* 425-428.

Siddle, D. A. T., & Trasler, G. B. (1981). The psychophysiology of psychopathic behaviour. In M. J. Christie & P. G. Mellett (Eds.), *Foundations of psychosomatics* (pp. 283-304). Chichester: Wiley.

Slater, E. (1967). Genetics of criminals. *World Med.* 44-45.

Stott, D. H. (1982). *Delinquency: The problem and its prevention.* New York: Spectrum.

Trasler, G. B. (1960). *In place of parents.* London: Routledge & Kegan Paul.

Trasler, G. B. (1962). *The explanation of criminality.* London: Routledge & Kegan Paul.

Trasler, G. B. (1973). Criminal behaviour. In H. J. Eysenck (Ed.), *Handbook of abnormal psychology* (2nd ed., pp. 67-96). London: Pitman Medical.

Trasler, G. B. (1978). Relations between psychopathy and persistent criminality: Methodological and theoretical issues. In R. D. Hare & D. Schalling (Eds.), *Psychopathic behaviour: Approaches to research* (pp. 273-298). Chichester: Wiley.

Venables, P. H. (1974). The recovery limb of the skin conductance response in "high risk" research. In S. A. Mednick, F. Schulsinger, J. Higgins & B. Bell (Eds.), *Genetics, environment and psychopathology.* (pp. 117-133). Oxford: North-Holland.

Venables, P. H. & Christie, M. J. (1980). Electrodermal activity. In P. H. Venables & I. Martin (Eds.), *Techniques in psychophysiology* (pp. 3-67). New York: Wiley.

Venables, P. H., & Fletcher, R. P. (1980). The status of skin conductance recovery time: an examination of the Bundy effect. (as yet unpublished).

Venables, P. H., Gartshore, S. A., & O'Riordan, P. W. (1980). The function of skin conductance response recovery and rise time. *Biological Psychology, 10,* 1-6.

Wadsworth, M. E. J. (1976). Delinquency, pulse rates and early emotional deprivation. *British Journal of Criminology, 16,* 245-256.

Waid, W. M. (1976). Skin conductance to both signalized and unsignalized noxious stimulation predicts level of socialization. *Journal of Personality and Social Psychology, 34,* 923-929.

Walters, R. H., & Parke, R. D. (1964). Influence of response consequences to a social model on resistance to deviation. *Journal of Experimental Child Psychology, 1,* 269-280.

Wegmann, T. G., & Smith, D. W. (1963). Incidence of Klinefelter's syndrome among juvenile delinquents and felons. *Lancet, 1,* 274.

West, D. J., & Farrington, D. P. (1973). *Who becomes delinquent?* London: Heinemann.

West, D. J., & Farrington, D. P. (1977). The delinquent way of life. London: Heinemann.

Witkin, H. A., Mednick, S. A., Schulsinger, F., Bakkestrom, E., Christiansen, K. O., Goodenough, D. R., Hirschhorn, K., Lundsteen, C., Owen, D. R., Philip, J., Rubin, D. B. & Stocking, M. (1976). Criminality, aggression and intelligence among XYY and XXY men. *Science, 193,* 547.

Ziskind, E., Syndulko, K., & Maltzmann, I. (1978). Aversive conditioning in the sociopath. *Pavlovian Journal, 13,* 199–205.

Zuckerman, M. (1978). Sensation seeking and psychopathy. In R. D. Hare & D. Schalling (Eds.), *Psychopathic behaviour: Approaches to research* (pp. 165–185). New York: Wiley.

CHAPTER 8

Family Interaction
and Delinquent Behavior

JAMES SNYDER and GERALD PATTERSON

Witchita State University
Oregon Social Learning Center

Investigation of the role of the family in the development of delinquent behavior is carried out in three steps. Initially, delinquent behavior must be adequately operationalized and described. Second, the potential contribution of family characteristics and interactional patterns to delinquency must be identified by use of cross-sectional and longitudinal designs. Because cross-sectional and longitudinal designs are correlational in nature, they do not permit an unambiguous delineation of the causative status of family variables in the development of delinquent behavior. Therefore, a third research strategy is required. Those family variables shown by correlational studies to be associated with or to antedate delinquent behavior must be manipulated in order convincingly to demonstrate their causal status. Using high-risk samples, preventative interventions that effectively alter those family variables identified as critical to the development of delinquent behavior need to be designed and implemented. The causal status of these family variables would be unambiguously demonstrated if children from families targeted by these interventions engaged in fewer delinquent behaviors than those from families who were not targeted for intervention (see Chapter 13).

This chapter, reflecting the current state of research on family variables and delinquent behavior, will focus primarily on the second step in this investigatory process. However, some basic descriptive issues which have critical implications for understanding this research will be briefly reviewed. At the end of the chapter, the implications of the research will be reviewed in terms of manipulative designs.

DESCRIPTIVE ISSUES

The Measurement of Delinquent Behavior

As described in Chapters 2 and 3, the two primary approaches to measuring delinquent behavior are official arrests/convictions and self-reports. Although each of these approaches is subject to bias, the biases are somewhat different. Official records appear to reflect more serious and persistent offending, while self-reports reflect less serious delinquent behavior. The two approaches are not independent and appear to be complementary. Family studies using official records to study delinquent behavior are probably focusing on those individuals who are persistently delinquent and who engage in more serious antisocial acts. Those studies using self reported delinquency may be focusing on individuals who engage in less persistent criminal activity (Rutter & Giller, 1984). This may result in some variation in those family variables found to be associated with delinquent behavior.

The Homogeneity of Delinquent Individuals

As we saw in Chapter 5, individuals who engage in delinquent behavior do not represent a psychologically or behaviorally homogeneous group. Distinctions have been made on the basis of both the frequency and types of delinquent activity. The frequency of official arrests/convictions has been used to classify delinquents into recidivists (at least two offenses) and nonrecidivists (one offense only). Between 15 and 35 percent of all males are arrested before the age of 18, but the majority are arrested only once. Recidivists make up 5 to 10 percent of this officially delinquent population, but account for half or more of all juvenile crime (Farrington, 1979; Wolfgang, Figlio & Sellin, 1972). Recidivists appear to be different from nonrecidivists. They are younger at the age of their first arrest, engage in more serious types of criminal acts, and are more likely to continue their criminal activity into adulthood (Farrington, 1981; Hamperian, Shuster, Dimitz, & Conrad, 1979; McCord, 1979). Thus, the recidivist-nonrecidivist distinction has important practical and theoretical implications. Practically, the delineation of those family variables associated with recidivist delinquency provides the potential for a focused, economical means of preventing a large percentage of crime. Theoretically, different developmental paths and variables may characterize recidivists and nonrecidivists.

As noted in earlier chapters, distinctions between delinquents have also been made on the basis of the type of antisocial or criminal behavior in which they engage. These distinctions include property versus person offenses (e.g., McCord, 1979), status versus nonstatus offenses (e.g., Elliott & Huizinga, 1983), covert (stealing, firesetting) versus overt (fighting) antisocial acts (e.g., Patterson, 1982a), and aggressive (unsocialized) versus delinquent (socialized) antisocial behavior (see Chapter 5). The distinctions according to frequency and type of delinquent behavior are not totally independent. Chronic, recidivist delinquents appear to be versatile; they engage in both overt (aggressive, person-oriented) and covert (delinquent, property-directed) types of antisocial behavior (Rojeck & Erickson, 1982: Loeber & Schmaling, 1985a).

Such systematic variation (and covariation) in the onset, persistence, and topography of antisocial and delinquent behavior may be associated with somewhat discrete familial characteristics and interaction patterns (Loeber & Schmaling, 1985b; Hetherington & Martin, 1979). Thus, in addition to focusing on variables which differentiate the families of delinquent and nondelinquent children, we will examine the degree to which family variables are differentially associated with subtypes of delinquency based on the frequency and type of antisocial behavior.

DELINQUENT BEHAVIOR AS A FAILURE IN SOCIALIZATION

Research suggests that antisocial behavior does not occur, *de novo,* at the time of the first delinquent act, arrest, or conviction. Rather, it is the end-product of inadequate socialization whose roots can be observed in childhood. Antisocial and aggressive behavior, especially in its extreme forms, is quite stable over time. Children who engage in high-frequency fighting, stealing, and lying, and who do so in many settings, are also found to engage in antisocial behavior as adolescents and adults (Loeber, 1982; Loeber & Dishon, 1983; Olweus, 1979). For example, correlations (corrected for attenuation) between two measures of aggressive behavior separated in time range from about .75 when the time interval is one year to about .40 when the time interval is 21 years (Olweus, 1979). Although not all antisocial children become antisocial or delinquent adolescents, very few seriously delinquent adolescents were not also antisocial as children. Training in antisocial, aggressive behavior begins early.

A frequent, though not necessary, concomitant to antisocial behavior is a failure to acquire adequate social, work, and academic skills. Children who lack social skills, who are disliked and rejected by peers (Pulkkinen, 1983; Roff, Sells, & Golden, 1972; West & Farrington, 1977), who do poorly in school, and who are rated as lazy and troublesome by teachers (Farrington, 1979; Mitchell & Rosa, 1981; Wolfgang et al., 1972; Wadsworth, 1979) are more likely to self report high rates of delinquent behavior, to be arrested and convicted, and to engage in a variety of other antisocial acts (licit and illicit drug use, sexual promiscuity, etc.) as adolescents. Longitudinal studies suggest that deficits in social, academic, and work skills are antedated by behavior problems like noncompliance, distractability and aggression. But these deficits appear to further amplify the deviancy training process by obviating involvement and interaction with normative socialization agents and agencies (Elliott, Huizinga & Ageton, 1982; Wilson & Herrnstein, 1985).

Disruption in the socialization can be thought to occur in two stages. This two stage process is shown in Figure 8.1. The first stage occurs during childhood and primarily occurs in the home setting. Inept family socialization practices like poor discipline result in high frequencies of relatively trivial antisocial behaviors by the child, like noncompliance, fighting, temper tantrums, petty theft, and lying. These inept practices any also result in poor interpersonal and work skills. Given that the child is antisocial and lacks skills, he is likely to move into the second stage of antisocial training. He is placed at risk for rejection by peers and adults, and for academic and work failure (Hartup, 1983; Putallaz & Gottman, 1981; Patterson, 1976, 1982a). The child's coercive and clumsy style "puts people off." This reduces the child's opportunities to develop skilled behavior. The rejected child is also likely to associate with other unskilled, coercive children, thereby increasing his opportunities to acquire, perform, and hone antisocial behavior. This association appears to be the result of an active peer selection process in which children gravitate toward peers with similar behavioral (as well as age, sexual, and racial) characteristics (Hartup, 1983; Kandel, 1978).

As the child continues to develop in a family environment with poor socialization practices and to associate with deviant peers, his performance of antisocial behavior becomes increasingly frequent, varied, serious, and successful. Although much of the second stage training takes place outside of the home, the family continues to be important. Via supervision and ongoing disciplinary practices, parents can influence the peers with whom the child interacts and the activities in which he engages (Patterson & Dishon, in press; Snyder, Dishon, & Patterson, in press). During both stages, parent-child and peer-child influences are reciprocal. The antisocial child is a product and an architect of his environment.

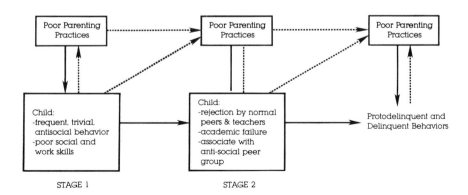

Figure 8.1. Family contributions to delinquent behavior: a proposed developmental sequence.

FAMILY INTERACTION AND DELINQUENT BEHAVIOR

The family interaction patterns and characteristics found to be associated with delinquent behavior have been operationalized and labeled in diverse ways. To simplify presentation, the data will be organized around five themes: discipline; positive parenting; monitoring; conflict and problem solving; and sociodemographic characteristics. For clarity, each of these themes will be considered separately. The interrelationships and multivariate nature of these variables will then be summarized.

Discipline

Discipline is a complex construct that refers to methods used by family members to discourage behavioral excesses or antisocial behavior in children. While effective methods of discipline vary with age and characteristics of the child, they generally consist of: (1) the accurate definition and labelling of certain behaviors as excessive or antisocial; (2) the consistent tracking of those behaviors over time and across settings; and (3) the consistent and contingent use of effective but not harsh methods to inhibit those behaviors.

Poor and erratic disciplinary practices contribute to the development of delinquent behavior in both a direct and an indirect fashion. Parents may contribute directly to the development of antisocial behavior by failing adequately and consistently to label, track, and consequate its performance, and by modeling and reinforcing aggressive antisocial modes of problem solving and relating to other family members. Both in terms of opportunities and consequences, the family provides the training ground for the child to become skilled in the use of coercive modes of dealing with other people. The resulting high-frequency performance of antisocial, aggressive behavior contributes to delinquency indirectly by increasing the likelihood of rejection by normal peers and association with aggressive, antisocial peers.

Several longitudinal studies provide evidence supporting the predictive association between poor parental disciplinary practices during childhood and the incidence of later delinquent behavior. Discipline described as lax or neglectful, as erratic or inconsistent (Glick, 1972; Olweus, 1980; Pulkkinen, 1983; West & Farrington, 1973), and as overly harsh or punitive (Simcha-Fagan, Langer, Gersten, & Eisenberg, 1975; McCord, 1978, 1979; Olweus, 1980; Pulkkinen, 1983; West & Farrington, 1973) are predictive of adolescent delinquency and aggression. This predictive relationship has been found for both self-report and official indices of delinquency (e.g., West Farrington, 1973). The relationship has been found for both crimes against persons (Simcha-Fagan et al., 1975; McCord, 1978), and against property (Pulkkinen 1983). The disciplinary practices of recidivists are worse than those of one-time offenders which, in turn, are worse than those of nonoffenders. The more frequent and probably more serious the offending, the worse are the disciplinary practices (Pulkkinen, 1983; West & Farrington, 1973). Good disciplinary practices may be delinquency preventative in otherwise disrupted environments (McCord, 1978).

As well as playing a role in the development of antisocial behavior prior to delinquency, there are numerous studies which show a concurrent association of poor parental discipline and delinquent behavior. These studies include both "known group" comparisons of the families of delinquents and nondelinquents, and cross sectional studies of broad samples of families with adolescent children. Laxness in defining and tracking antisocial behavior (Patterson, 1980; Schaefer, 1965; Stanfield, 1966), a general lack of control (Hanson, Henggeler, Haefile, & Rodick, 1984), a lack of consistency and contingency in discouraging antisocial behavior (Glueck & Glueck, 1968; Patterson, 1980; Patterson, Dishon, & Bank, 1984; Stanfield, 1966), and the use of harsh physical punishment and threats (Glueck & Glueck, 1968; Gold, 1970; Kraus, 1977; Nye, 1958; Loeber, Weisman & Reid, 1983) have all been associated with delinquent behavior measured both by self-report (e.g., Stanfield, 1966) and by official records (e.g., Hanson et al., 1984). In those studies which differentiated recidivists and nonrecidivists (Gold, 1970; Hanson et al., 1984; Loeber & Schmaling, 1985a), the effectiveness of parental discipline was negatively associated with the frequency of crime. Family disciplinary practices influence delinquent behavior (Stanfield, 1966) and fighting (Patterson, Dishon, & Bank, 1984) over and above the influence of peers.

The strength of the relationship between discipline and antisocial behavior can be estimated by looking at a sample of longitudinal and cross-sectional studies (see Table 8.1). The various measures of discipline in these studies account for 1 to 40 percent of the variance in child antisocial behavior. Discipline is modestly but significantly related to official delinquency, aggression, stealing, and drug use.

A more thorough understanding of how inept discipline fosters aggressive, antisocial behavior can be achieved by reviewing studies which have compared families intensively with aggressive, antisocial children with those with nonaggressive children. Two somewhat separate disciplinary styles have been found to characterize families with antisocial children: enmeshed and lax. In the enmeshed style, parents are overinclusive in defining behaviors as problematic (Holleran, Littman, Freund, & Schmaling, 1982; Schmaling & Patterson, 1984). These parents don't ignore even very trivial excessive behaviors. They issue more and poorer commands (Lobitz & Johnson, 1976; Forehand, King, Pied, & Yoder, 1975), use verbal threats, disapproval, and cajoling more frequently (Patterson, 1982a; Snyder, 1977), but fail to consistently and effectively back up these verbal reprimands with nonviolent, nonphysical punishment (Patterson, 1981; 1982a). They inadvertently provide more positive consequences for deviant child behavior (Snyder, 1977). This ineffective though frequent use of punishment often sets up a coercive pattern of family interaction which elicits, maintains, and exacerbates the aggressive behavior of all family members (Deur & Parke, 1970; Sawin & Parke, 1979). In this coercive interaction, when one family member behaves aversively, others respond in

TABLE 8.1   The Amount of Variance in Antisocial Behavior Accounted for by Discipline in Sample Studies

Longitudinal Studies	Discipline Measure	Antisocial Measure	Variance Accounted For
McCord (1979)	Parent aggression	Property crimes (official)	1%
	Parent aggression	Person crimes (official)	4%
West & Farring-ton (1973)	Cruel, neglecting attitude and strict or erratic discipline	Official delinquency	4%[a]
Olweus (1980)	Maternal negativism	Aggression against peers	5–12%[b]
	Maternal permissiveness of aggression	Aggression against peers	10–12%[b]
Elder et al. (1983)	Father hostile	temper tantrums	11%
	Mother hostile	temper tantrums	8%

Cross Sectional Studies	Discipline Measure	Antisocial Measure	Variance Accounted for
Patterson (in press)	Parent disicpline	Fighting, aggression	8–20%[c]
	Parent discipline	Stealing	6–38%[c]
Dishon & Loe-ber (1983)	Parent discipline	Alcohol use	8%
Stanfield (1966)	Paternal discipline	Official delinquency	4%[a]

[a]Variance is estimated on a Phi coefficient calculated from Chi^2.
[b]Based on two separate samples.
[c]Depends upon the age of the target child.

kind and an aversive interchange ensues and escalates until one family member gives in. Because continuation and escalation of the aversive behavior successfully terminates the other member's aversive behavior (is negatively reinforced) some of the time, each family member is likely to use highly aversive means of interacting with family members and with peers on future occasions. Highly aggressive children teach their parents to use high intensity, harsh disciplinary tactics, and the parents teach their child to persist in and to escalate their aversive behavior in the face of sibling, peer, and parental punishment of that behavior (Patterson, 1976; 1979).

The association of antisocial behavior with harsh and frequent punishment appears paradoxical. The paradox is resolved by distinguishing between the frequency and severity of punishment and its consistent and contingent use. Enmeshed parents can't punish each instance of misbehavior. Consequently a large number of the child's misbehaviors go unpunished, and, as the child responds with counter-coercive measures, often result in negative (and sometimes positive) reinforcement. The resulting intermittent punishment schedule and rich negative and positive reinforcement schedules do not suppress aggressive, antisocial behavior.

In the lax disciplinary style, parents are underinclusive in defining child behavior as excessive or antisocial (Reid & Patterson, 1976). For example, because parents didn't see their child steal or fight, or because they can't prove their child is lying, they feel unsure about whether it really occurred. If it occurred, they feel they can't do much about it. As a result, very few antisocial behaviors are punished. These parents, especially fathers, use punishment very infrequently, and when punishment is used, it has minimal deterrent effect (Patterson, 1980). In both lax and enmeshed discipline styles, punishment is not used consistently, contingently, and effectively to discourage the aggressive, antisocial behavior of the child.

In summary, the data strongly suggest that ineffective disciplinary practices characterize the families of delinquents both prior to the time children engage in delinquent behavior, and during and after the time when they begin engaging in that behavior.

Positive Parenting

Positive parenting refers to interactions between the parent and the child which foster interpersonal, academic, and work skills, and which encourage the development of normative values and standards of behavior. In part, positive parenting consists of an accurate labeling and tracking of desired behaviors, providing consistent and contingent positive feedback to the child when performing those desired behaviors, and allowing the child freedom of choice within the child's capacity. Positive skills and normative values are also fostered when the parents demonstrate and communicates interest in the child in a positive, noncritical fashion, when the parents communicate support and caring to the child, and when the parents and child share mutually pleasurable leisure activities. The interest, communication, and shared activities provide the child with parental models of skilled behavior and foster the "reinforcement power" of the child and parents for each other.

During stage one, early child development, the family is integrally involved in the development of positive skills and normative values. These skills and values have an effect on delinquency by influencing the child's acceptance by normal peers, association with skilled peers, and the likelihood of school success. Peers and teachers, in turn, provide continued opportunities, models, and reinforcement for skilled behaviors and normative values. The importance of these skills and values in the development of delinquency have been demonstrated frequently. Delinquents are less interpersonally skilled (Freedman, Rosenthal, Donahue, Schlundt, & McFall, 1978), fail to identify with and value normative socialization agents like the family and the school (Elliott, Huizinga, & Ageton, 1982), and have poorer academic and work skills (Dishon, Loeber, Stouthamer-Loeber, & Patterson, 1984) than their nondelinquent counterparts. The relationship between skills deficits and antisocial behavior is reciprocal. Conduct problems during childhood interfere with the development of skills and may lead to rejection by normative socialization agents.

This lack of skills reduces further socialization opportunities and fosters association with deviant peers which, in turn, promotes continued antisocial behavior.

Several longitudinal studies have demonstrated the predictive relationship between positive parenting practices during childhood and the incidence of later delinquent behavior. Parental coldness and rejection (Simcha-Fagan et al., 1975), a lack of involvement with the child (Wadsworth, 1979), a lack of affection for the child (McCord, 1978, 1979), parental passivity and neglect (West & Farrington, 1973), and a lack of shared leisure time (West & Farrington, 1977) are predictive of delinquent behavior. Products of poor positive parenting, including a lack of family cohesion (Glick, 1972), a lack of bonding with the family, and a communication of normlessness (it is permissible to use deviant means to obtain one's ends) (Elliott & Voss, 1974; Elliott et al., 1982) have also been shown to be predictive of delinquency. These relationships have been found in studies using both self report (Elliott et al., 1982) and official (McCord, 1978; West & Farrington, 1977; Simcha-Fagan et al., 1975) measures of delinquent activity. Pulkkinen (1983) found that a lack of child-centeredness and positive parenting was related to recidivism as well as to one-time delinquency. The lack of positive parenting has been associated with crimes against persons and against property, and with status as well as nonstatus offenses (McCord, 1978; Simcha-Fagan et al., 1975).

The data concerning the impact of positive parenting on delinquent behavior obtained in cross-sectional studies are consonant with those from longitudinal studies. Relative to the parents of nondelinquents, the parents of delinquents are found to be less supportive and affectionate (Hanson et al., 1984; Patterson, 1980; Glueck & Glueck, 1968), more rejecting and negativistic (Nye, 1958; Olweus, 1980), and spend less time with their children (Canter, 1982; Glueck & Glueck, 1968). Delinquent children are, in turn, less accepting of their parents' values and standards, and report using their parents as models less frequently than do nondelinquents (Canter, 1982; Gold, 1963). Wilson (1974), in studying a homogeneous, high risk group, found no relationship between home atmosphere, affection, and delinquent behavior. The homogeneity of the sample in this study may have precluded sufficient variation in positive parenting to adequately assess its effect on delinquent behavior. In cross-sectional studies, the lack of positive parenting is shown to be associated with delinquent behavior measured by self-report and official records (Canter, 1982; Gold, 1963), with various types of delinquency (Canter, 1982), and with recitivism (Gold, 1963; Hanson et al., 1984).

How much variance in antisocial behavior is accounted for by positive parenting practices? Using the sample of longitudinal and cross-sectional studies shown in Table 8.2, positive parenting has been found to account for 1 to 28 percent of the variance in official delinquency, aggression, stealing and self control. This is a modest but significant relationship.

The child development literature provides a clearer picture of the manner in which positive parenting fosters the development of competence and nor-

TABLE 8.2   The Amount of Variance in Antisocial Behavior Accounted for by Positive Parenting in Sample Studies

Longitudinal Studies	Positive Parenting Measure	Antisocial Measure	Variance Accounted for
McCord (1979)	Parental affection	Property crimes (official)	3%
	Parental affection	Person crimes (official)	9%
West & Farrington (1973)	Parental interest in child	Official delinquency	1%[a]
	Child leisure time with family	Official delinquency	2%[a]
	Parental job aspiration for child	Official delinquency	4%[a]
Pulkkinen (1983)	Child-centered guidance	Self-control	14–28%[b]

Cross Sectional Studies	Positive Parenting Measure	Antisocial Measure	Variance Accounted for
Patterson (in press)	Positive parenting	Fighting, aggression	10–20%[c]
	Positive parenting	Stealing	1–26%[c]
Hanson et al. (1984)	Mother supportive statements	Official delinquency	13%
	Mother-son affect	Official delinquency	10%

[a]Variance estimated on a Phi coefficient calculated from Chi^2.
[b]Based on two independent measures of self-control.
[c]Depends upon the age of the target child.

mative values. Parents who communicate clear expectations and standards of mature behavior, and who track and encourage that behavior enhance the child's social and academic competence (Baumrind, 1967, 1971). Parents who talk with their children regularly, who show interest in their school activities (Pulkkinen, 1983), who use reasoning and provide an explanation for desired behavior (Elder, 1980; Hoffman, 1970), and who are caring (Block, 1971) foster self control, the acquisition of normative values, social competence, and achievement motivation in their children. The relationship between positive parenting and child behavior is, of course, reciprocal. Children who engage in high rates of antisocial behavior and who are unskilled are likely to be rejected by their parents, who in turn reduce the frequency of reinforcers and expressions of affection to the child (Patterson, 1982b).

In summary, the data suggest that a failure by parents to foster a child's skills, to model and encourage normative values, and to provide a caring environment, places a child at risk for delinquency. This inadequate parenting is also evident at the time when the child is engaging in delinquent activities.

Monitoring

Monitoring or supervision is a construct which refers to parents' awareness of their child's peer associates, free time activities, and physical whereabouts when outside the home. Effective monitoring requires clear communication of a set of rules about when the child should be home from school, weekday and weekend curfews, persons with whom the child may not associate, and places that are off limits to the child. As well as setting rules, the parents must occasionally "check up" or track compliance with those rules, and take effective disciplinary action when the rules are violated. Monitoring also consists of parental awareness of the child's school attendance and performance, a sensitivity to drug use, and a supervision of the TV programs and movies consumed by the child.

The amount of time children spend in direct contact with their parents or other adults decreases with the child's age (Stouthamer-Loeber, Patterson, & Loeber, 1983). Monitoring is thereby likely to play an increasingly central role in the development of antisocial and delinquent behavior as the child moves into preadolescence and adolescence. Monitoring has both direct and indirect effects on the probability of delinquent behavior. In a direct fashion, good parental monitoring makes it likely that the parent will attend to antisocial and delinquent behaviors and take appropriate remedial action. Indirectly, effective parental monitoring can limit the child's access to negative peer associates and negative activities, and can foster involvement with positive peers and activities, and with the school (Snyder et al., in press; Patterson & Dishon, in press). This indirect effect may be particularly potent given the central role of peers in the development of delinquent behavior (Elliott et al., 1982) and drug use (Kandel, Kessler, & Margules, 1978).

Monitoring begins to play a central role in the frequency of antisocial behavior when the child is nine or ten years of age. Ineffective monitoring during this period has been associated with fighting, lying, and stealing in the home setting (Strouthamer-Loeber et al., 1983), and with parent-reported stealing and firesetting outside the home (Patterson, 1980; Reid & Patterson, 1976). It is also related to teacher and peer reports of dishonesty, bullying, property damage and truanting in the school setting (Snyder et al., in press; Wilson, 1980). Monitoring appears to be important in discouraging early delinquent behaviors.

The importance of effective monitoring in discouraging delinquent behavior receives substantive support from longitudinal studies. Direct measures of parental monitoring are consistently found to be predictive of delinquent behavior (Glick, 1972; McCord, 1978, 1979; Pulkkinen, 1983; West & Farrington, 1973). Indirect indices of supervision, like the amount of leisure time spent outside the home, alcohol and tobacco use (West & Farrington, 1977), a lack of parental concern or involvement in how their child is doing in school (Wadsworth, 1979), and association with deviant peers (Elliott et al., 1982), have also been found to be predictive of delinquent behavior. This predictive relationship is found for crimes against persons and property (McCord, 1978, 1979). The degree to which parents do a poor job of monitoring their children discriminates between one time and recidivist offenders (Pulkkinen, 1983; Wilson, 1980) and between those who engage in more versus less serious crimes (Wadsworth, 1979). Monitoring is predictive of both self-reported and official delinquency (West & Farrington, 1973; Wilson, 1980). Poor monitoring is associated with children beginning delinquency early (McCord, 1978). It appears to be particularly important in preventing delinquent behavior in children who are raised in disadvantaged, delinquency-prone environments (McCord, 1978; Wilson, 1980). Supervision adds to the power of the predictive relationship between association with delinquent peers and delinquent behavior (Snyder et al., in press; Patterson & Dishon, in press).

In concurrent studies of monitoring and delinquency, the parents of delinquents relative to those of nondelinquents are found to have poorer monitoring skills. Both direct (Hirschi, 1969; Dishon & Loeber, 1983; Patterson & Dishon, in press; Stouthammer-Loeber et al., 1983; Wilson, 1974) and indirect measures of parental monitoring like number of evenings spent outside of the home (Nye, 1958) and the degree of influence of peers (Gold, 1963) are associated with delinquent behavior. Only one of the studies reviewed (which focused on trivial antisocial acts) failed to find an association between monitoring and delinquency (Richards, Berk, & Forster, 1979). Cross-sectional studies also find that monitoring is associated with the variety and frequency of antisocial acts (Dishon & Loeber, 1983; Gold, 1963; Hirschi, 1969; Loeber & Schmaling, 1985b; Wilson, 1980). Similar to longitudinal studies, cross sectional studies find that monitoring is a particularly important element in preventing delinquency in children raised in disadvantaged environments (Wilson, 1974).

The strength of the relationship between monitoring and antisocial behavior can be estimated from sample studies presented in Table 8.3. The amount of variance in antisocial behavior accounted for by monitoring ranges from 1 to 46 percent. Monitoring consistently accounts for a moderate portion of antisocial behavior whether measured by official or self reported delinquency, association with antisocial peers, and peer estimates of antisocial behavior.

In summary, parental monitoring influences the frequency and variety of antisocial behaviors of young children both in the home and the school setting. Parental monitoring becomes even more important as the child enters and proceeds through adolescence. During this time, good supervision fosters appropriate parental reaction to antisocial and delinquent behaviors, and indirectly minimizes the adolescents' contact with delinquency-promoting circumstances, activities, and peers.

Problem Solving and Conflict

Family members are consistently confronted with problems, irritants, and stressors in their transactions with other family members and with people and agencies outside of the family. These problems or stressors may be major crises like unemployment or divorce, or may be minor daily "hassles" like argu-

TABLE 8.3   The Amount of Variance in Antisocial Behavior Accounted for by Parental Monitoring in Sample Studies

Longitudinal Studies	Monitoring Measure	Antisocial Measure	Variance Accounted for
McCord (1979)	Parental supervision	Property crimes (official)	15%
	Parental supervision	Person crimes (official)	7%
West & Farrington (1973)	Parental vigalence	Official delinquency	13%[a]

Cross Sectional Studies	Monitoring Measure	Antisocial Measure	Variance Accounted for
Wilson (1980)	Parental supervision	Self-reported misbehavior	13%[a]
	Parental supervision	Official delinquency	4%[a]
Snyder et al. (1984)	Monitoring	Association with deviant peers	27–34%[b]
Stouthamer-Loeber et al. (1983)	Monitoring	Self-reported delinquency	14–42%[b]
	Monitoring	Official delinquency	15–46%[b]
	Monitoring	Peer-reported antisocial behavior	10–12%[b]

[a]Variance is estimated from Phi calculated from Chi^2.
[b]Depends upon the age of the target child.

ments or the vagaries of coworkers. Successfully coping with these stressors requires that family members acquire and use problem-solving skills and coping strategies.

The failure to acquire and use adequate problem-solving strategies and coping skills may facilitate the development of antisocial behavior in children and adolescents in several ways. First, high levels of stress resulting from unresolved problems are known to disrupt highly skilled behaviors. The irritability and distraction resulting from stress may disrupt effective parenting skills like good discipline, monitoring, and positive parenting. Second, the family is the primary context in which a child observes and practices problem solving skills. Opportunities, models, and feedback concerning effective problem solving in the family context provides the child with the skills needed for adequate interpersonal, school, and work adjustment when he or she leaves the home setting. Finally, stress and irritability within the family setting may be frequent and intense when family members have poor problem-solving skills, resulting in conflict, arguments, and physical fighting. This section will focus on stress, conflict, and problem solving as it is observed in the family context. The impact of extrafamilial sources of stress on family functioning and interaction will be discussed in the next section.

Several longitudinal studies have found that parent-parent and parent-child conflict are predictive of delinquent behavior. McCord (1978, 1979) found that parental conflict antedated delinquent behavior even when controlling for the socioeconomic status of the families being studied. West and Farrington (1973) similarly found parental conflict to predict delinquency in the child, measured by self-report and official records. Simcha-Fagan et al. (1975) reported that children reared in families characterized by excessive quarreling, conflict, and unhappy marriages were at greater risk for future delinquency. High levels of family conflict may be more strongly associated with crimes against persons than with crime against property (McCord, 1978; Simcha-Fagan et al., 1975). Familial conflict is predictive of recidivism as well as of one-time offenses (McCord, 1978).

These findings are replicated in cross-sectional studies. Conflict is greater in the homes of delinquents than of nondelinquents (Hanson et al., 1984; Hetherington, Stouwie, & Ridberg, 1971; Nye, 1958; Richards et al., 1979). Low intimacy in communication, a lack of give and take in problem solving, and spending little time in problem talk is more descriptive of the parent-child relationships of delinquents than of nondelinquents. This is true whether using self-report or official records of delinquency (Hanson et al., 1984; Hirschi, 1969; Richards et al., 1979), and is descriptive of one-time and recidivist offenders (Hirschi, 1969; Gold, 1963). Several studies have focused on delineating the specific differences in the problem solving of delinquent versus nondelinquent families. Problem solving in delinquent families is characterized by more anger, more defensiveness, more blaming, less friendly talk, less acceptance of responsibility, less problem specification, and less solution evaluation (Alexander, 1973; Prinz, Foster, Kent, & O'Leary, 1979; Robin & Weiss, 1980; Stuart, 1969). Both the parents and the children in antisocial families expect that the other party will argue and make accusations prior to the actual problem solving interchange (Alkire, Goldstein, Rodnick, & Judd, 1971).

The style of familial problem solving may influence the type of delinquent behavior performed by the child. In families with "neurotic" delinquents, the mother is dominant and the locus of conflict is between the parents. In families with a "socialized aggressive" delinquent, the father is dominant and the locus of conflict is between the father and the son. In families with a "conduct disordered" delinquent, the father and mother are both active and the locus of conflict is between the parents and the child (Hetherington et al., 1971).

The amount of variance in child antisocial behavior accounted for by family conflict and problem solving measures can by estimated by assessing the sample studies presented in Table 8.4. The variance accounted for ranges from 1 to 18 percent. Thus, the association between problem-solving/conflict and antisocial behavior is quite modest and somewhat sketchy. However, it appears that those families whose members are highly irritable and have inadequate problem-solving and coping skills to deal with stress are more likely to produce or already have a delinquent child. As mentioned at the beginning of this section, there are several possible mechanisms that could mediate this association, but there are insufficient data at this time to conclusively support any.

TABLE 8.4   The Amount of Variance in Antisocial Behavior Accounted for by Family Conflict and Problem Solving in Sample Studies

Longitudinal Studies	Problem Solving, Conflict Measure	Antisocial Measure	Variance Accounted for
McCord (1979)	Parent conflict	Property offenses (official)	1%
	Parent conflict	Person offenses (official)	4%
West & Farrington (1973)	Parent conflict	Official delinquency	3%[a]
West & Farrington (1977)	Parent-child conflict	Official delinquency	4%[a]
Elder et al. (1983)	Discipline conflicts	Temper tantrums	18%
	Discipline conflicts	Difficult child	8%
Cross-Sectional Studies	Problem Solving, Conflict Measure	Antisocial Measure	Variance Accounted for
Patterson (in press)	Problem solving	Fighting, aggression	1–14%[b]
	Problem solving	Stealing	0–2%[b]
Hanson et al. (1984)	Mother-child problem solving	Official delinquency	12%

[a]Variance is estimated from Phi calculated from Chi^2.
[b]Depends upon the age of the target child.

Family Sociodemographic Characteristics

As described in Chapter 3, there are a number of noninteractional, sociodemographic characteristics of families that are frequently associated with antisocial and delinquent behavior. These include socioeconomic status, broken homes (parental absence), parent criminality, and family size.

As we have seen earlier in this volume, there is some evidence that delinquent behavior is more likely and more frequent in adolescents from low socioeconomic backgrounds. The evidence indicates a modest association (Braithwaite, 1981), especially for official (Wadsworth, 1979, for example) but also self reported delinquency (Elliot & Ageton, 1980). This social class differential is most apparent when comparing extreme ends of the socioeconomic scale. It appears to be most important when predicting serious delinquent acts (Rutter & Giller, 1984).

Given this association, what does this mean? The key issue is whether low socioeconomic status per se, or the association between low socioeconomic status and some other variable(s) like parenting practices, are causative of delinquency. Generally, the correlation between social class and delinquency diminishes or disappears when other family variables are taken into account. Farrington (1979), for example, found no association between social class and delinquency when parental monitoring was taken into account. Not all families of low socioeconomic status produce delinquent children; some other factors must therefore be operating. Family management variables like monitoring and discipline which predict one-time delinquency and recidivism do so across social class (McCord, 1979; Robins, 1978; West & Farrington, 1973) and in homogeneous, disadvantaged populations (Wilson, 1974, 1980).

This suggests that the association of social class and delinquency is mediated, in part, by the quality of the parenting or family interaction. Inadequate parenting may be one facet of a general inadequacy indicated by low socioeconomic status, or it may be a product of the disruption of parenting skills that are the result of such stressors as unemployment, lack of social supports, and the lack of material resources (Patterson, 1982a). Elder, Liker and Cross (1983), for example, found that antisocial child behavior was associated with increasing parental irritability and arbitrary discipline which, in turn, were increased following job loss. In day-to-day interactions with their children, the rates at which mothers issue commands and behave irritably, and inappropriately consequate both problem and desired child behavior have been shown to covary with maternal reports of stress levels (Snyder & Patterson, 1984). Mothers who are under high levels of stress are also more likely to see neutral child behavior as aversive (Middlebook & Forehand, 1984). Extrafamilial stressors have been found to have a disruptive effect on monitoring (Patterson & Bank, 1985).

Another commonly cited demographic correlate of delinquency is broken homes or parental (father) absence. While broken homes have been associated with an increasing likelihood of delinquent behavior (Gibson, 1969; Rutter, 1971), it is also increased in unbroken but discordant and conflict-ridden home settings (see the previous section on problem solving and conflict, and Power, Ash, Schoenberg, & Sorey, 1974). It may be that conflict and discord rather than parent absence or divorce is the critical variable (Rutter, 1971). Discord and conflict disrupt discipline and positive parenting (Hetherington, Cox & Cox, 1979), and are associated with child antisocial behavior (Emery & O'Leary, 1982; Porter & O'Leary, 1982). Consequently, it may contribute to early (stage one) training in antisocial behavior and disrupt the development of social and academic skills. Conflict and discord have also been shown to disrupt parental monitoring of children and adolescents (Wilson, 1974, 1980; Wilson & Herbert, 1978), and may consequently facilitate the child's access to delinquent peers and settings. When parenting skills are taken into account, the association between broken homes and delinquency diminishes dramatically (McCord, 1978).

Many characteristics of parents have also been associated with delinquent behavior, but one of the more striking is parent criminality (Farrington, Grundy, & West, 1975; Johnson, 1979; Robins, West, & Herjanic, 1975; West & Farrington, 1973). This association is strongest when the parent is a recidivist and when the parent's crime record extends into the child-rearing period (Osborn & West, 1979; Robins et al., 1975). Delinquency is also associated with a host of other indicators of poor parental adjustment, such as excessive drinking, unemployment, and abnormal personality patterns.

The explanation of the association between parent criminality and delinquency is not clear. It may involve some genetic mechanism such as a propensity to aggression or a reduced responsiveness to reinforcement and punishment (see Chapter 5) that characterizes both the parent and the child. There may be a greater surveillance of criminal families (West & Farrington, 1973) although the association holds for self-reported delinquency after controlling for convictions (Farrington, 1979). It is not likely to involve direct parental involvement of the child in conjoint criminal activity because the association is still apparent in those cases where the parent ceased criminal activity before the child was born (West, 1982). Finally, it may be that the criminal parent models general antisocial behavior or fails to use effective parenting skills with the child. Wilson (1980), for example, has found that parents with criminal records do a worse job in monitoring their children than parents without criminal records.

In summary, the manner in which noninteractional characteristics of the family are associated with delinquency is not clear. At least part of their effects seem to be mediated by family interaction, although direct social effects and genetic mechanisms may also play a part. In so far as these characteristics are mediated by a disruption in parenting practices, there is likely to be a facilitation of antisocial child behaviors and a disruption in social skills development. These early childhood outcomes, along with poor parental monitoring and living in an environment with easy access to delinquency-prone peers, settings, and activities, may provide the training ground in which delinquent behavior is shaped, modeled, practiced, and reinforced.

The Multivariate Nature of the Association of Parenting Practices and Delinquent Behavior

Up to this point, the discussion concerning the association of family variables and delinquent behavior has focused on one family variable at a time. One may legitimately ask how these variables are related. Do they carry redundant information, or is a multivariate combination of these family variables a better predictor of delinquent behavior than any one variable alone? How much variance in delinquency can we account for? How accurately can we predict which persons will engage in (serious and frequent) delinquent behavior and which will not? (see also Chapter 12.)

The family variables discussed are not totally redundant. Correlations between family variables range from .14 (monitoring with problem solving) to .73 (discipline with positive parenting) (Patterson, in press). Monitoring and discipline have been shown to be best described as separate measures of those constructs (Patterson & Bank, 1985).

The multivariate combination of several family variables is a better prediction of antisocial or delinquent behavior than single family variables alone. In reviewing predictors of delinquency, Loeber and Dishon (1983; see also Chapter 9) found that single family variables improved prediction over chance on the order of 20 percent, while the use of multiple family variables improved prediction by 50 to 80 percent over chance levels. Using parent criminality, poor parenting practices, low income, and large family size as risk factors, West and Farrington (1977) found that the probability of delinquency was about 25 percent for those adolescents with one risk factor, but was 70 percent for those with three risk factors.

The amount of variance in antisocial and delinquent behavior that can be accounted for by multivariate combinations of family variables alone, or of family variables in conjunction with nonfamily variables, is shown in Table 8.5. Several tentative conclusions can be drawn from these data. First, several family variables are predictive or concurrently associated with child antisocial behavior and delinquency. Although these variables are not totally independent, each carries some unique predictive value. The more parenting practices that are disrupted and the more seriously they are disrupted, the greater the likelihood, severity, and frequency of delinquency and antisocial behavior. Approximately 10 to 20 percent more variance is accounted for by multivariate combinations of family variables than any one family variable alone.

Second, the family is not the sole determinant of delinquent and antisocial behavior. The behavioral characteristics and skills acquired in the family setting which the child uses in interactions in other settings, and the types of peers with whom the child associates, also affect the development of antisocial behavior. Those studies which simultaneously focus on family and nonfamily (especially peer) variables tend to account for the largest amount of variance. In these studies, family variables contribute uniquely to delinquent behavior even when nonfamily variables are taken into account.

Third, child, peer, and parental influences are reciprocal and interactive. Delinquency and antisocial behavior are the result of several multidimensional processes which overlap in time.

SUMMARY: CURRENT KNOWLEDGE AND LIMITATIONS

The data consistently suggest that parenting practices and family interaction are associated with the development of antisocial and delinquent behavior. These findings are consistent in studies using cross sectional and longitudinal designs, and are consistently replicated using different modes of measuring the various parenting and family interactional constructs. The same variables are implicated whether delinquency is defined using self-report measures or official arrests and convictions.

The impact of family and parenting variables on the frequency of delinquent behavior is relatively clear. Parents of recidivist offenders, both during childhood and concurrent with the actual delinquent behavior, are less skilled in discouraging antisocial behavior and in encouraging skilled behavior than the parents of one-time offenders (Dishon & Loeber, 1983; Gold, 1970; Hanson et al., 1984; Hirschi, 1969; Loeber & Schmaling, 1985a; McCord, 1978;

TABLE 8.5 The Amount of Variance in Antisocial Behavior Accounted for by Family Variables Alone or in Combination with Nonfamily Variables in Sample Studies

Longitudinal Studies	Predictor Variables	Criterion Variable	Variance Accounted for
McCord (1979)	Family social status + Parent characteristics + Child rearing practice	Property Crimes (Official)	38%
		Person Crimes (Official)	36%
		Total Crimes (Official)	38%
McCord (1977)	Parental conflict + Supervision + Parental aggression + Parent affect	Official delinquency	15%
Olweus (1980)	Mother negativism + Mother permissive of aggression + Parental use of power assertion + Child temperament	Aggression	21–34%[a]
Elder et al (1983)	Father irritable + Early child behavior problems + Income loss + Father arbitrary discipline	Child temper tantrums	26%
		Child difficult	39%

234

Cross-Sectional Studies	Predictor Variables			Criterion Variable	Variance Accounted for
Patterson & Dishon (1984)	Child social skill	+ Child academic skill	+ Parental monitoring + Association with deviant peers	Delinquent behavior (official & Self-report)	53%
Patterson, Dishon, & Bank (1984)	Discipline	+ Negative family interaction	+ Poor peer relations	Fighting	34%
Dishon & Loeber (1983)	Parental monitoring	+ Mother alcohol use	+ Association with deviant peers	Alcohol use Marijuana use	14% 25%
Hanson et al. (1984)	Early child behavior problems	+ Age at first arrest	+ Mother-son problem solving	Official delinquency	45%[b]
	Early child behavior problems	+ Parent child affect	+ Mother-son problem solving	Official delinquency	35%[b]

[a]Based on two different samples.
[b]Official delinquency weighted for seriousness and presence versus absence of delinquency.

235

Pulkkinen, 1983; West & Farrington, 1973). The same parenting dimensions appear to be important, but the breakdown is greater in recidivist families, which provide more opportunities, shaping, and practice for frequent and serious antisocial behavior inside and outside the home. The more parenting practices that are disrupted, and the more seriously they are disrupted, the earlier the delinquent behavior occurs, the more likely it is to be serious, and the more likely it is to be repeated.

The differential association of family variables with distinguishable types of antisocial and delinquent behavior is less clear. There are a limited number of studies which have attempted such a differentiation, and those studies have not categorized delinquent behavior according to type in equivalent ways. However, some very tentative conclusions can be made if the types utilized in these studies are distributed into one of two rough categories: overt antisocial behavior (aggression/assault, aggressive conduct disorders, person-oriented crimes); and covert antisocial behavior (lying/stealing, nonaggressive conduct disorders, property-oriented crimes). Relative to covert behavior, children who engage in overt antisocial behavior come from families that are more punitive, harsh, and restrictive (Farrington, 1978; Hetherington et al., 1971; Loeber et al., 1983; Patterson, 1980; Simcha-Fagan et al., 1975). There also may be more intrafamily conflict and aggression (McCord, 1978; 1979; Simcha-Fagan et al., 1975), more parental rejection of the child (Hewitt & Jenkins, 1946; Lewis, 1954), and more frequent and friendly parent-child interaction (Patterson, 1980) in the homes of overt antisocial children. Relative to overt, children who engage in covert antisocial behavior come from homes characterized by lax and permissive discipline (Farrington, 1978; Hetherington, et al., 1971; Hewitt & Jenkins, 1946; Lewis, 1954; Patterson, 1980), and greater distance and less involvement between the parents and the child (Hewitt & Jenkins, 1946; Lewis, 1954; Patterson, 1980). Poor monitoring appears to be a critical element in the development of both overt and covert antisocial behavior (McCord, 1978; 1979; Stouthamer-Loeber et al., 1983).

Inept parenting contributes to the shaping and performance of antisocial behavior and to deficits in social and academic skills during childhood. However, families do not play an exclusive role. Peers are also important. Given that a child receives early training in antisocial behavior in the family context and fails to acquire basic skills in the home setting, the child is at risk for delinquency. This risk is further increased by associating with antisocial peers which, along with poor parental monitoring, provides the advanced training, opportunities, and reinforcement for accomplished antisocial and delinquent behavior.

There are many "traditional" family characteristics, like poverty and broken homes, that serve as marker variables for delinquency. The association of these characteristics with delinquent behavior appears to be mediated, at least in part, by parenting practices. These marker variables may be one general indicator of the poor skills of the parents, or may be indicators of stressors impinging on the family which disrupt effective parenting practices.

There are many unanswered questions. These questions focus on both the internal and external validity of the existing data sources. In terms of external validity, to whom can we generalize these findings? The data reviewed focus almost exclusively on the development of delinquent behavior in males. It may be that a different set of (family) variables are associated with the development of delinquent behavior in females. While many investigators have focused on at-risk groups, it is unclear how representative these samples are of the general delinquent population. While a few studies have focused on inner-city, minority, extremely poor samples, this is the exception rather than the rule. Which, if any, family variables are more or less important in the development of delinquent behavior in these inner-city, minority, poor samples is not clear.

It is becoming increasingly clear, however, that distinctions between delinquents are important. Attempts to identify family variables that differentially characterize one-time versus recidivist offenders and/or overt versus covert versatile delinquents may enhance our understanding of the development of antisocial behavior, and promote the development of preventative and clinical programs suited to the particular type of antisocial behavior displayed.

Another limitation is a lack of understanding of the processes by which family interactional and parenting variables, stressors impinging on the family, and peer associates influence the development of delinquent behavior. Parents, peers, and other socialization agents do not have a unidirectional effect on the developing child; the effect is reciprocal. The child is both a victim and an architect of his own environment. In terms of the development of antisocial behavior, these processes can be conceptualized as a series of positive feedback loops; inept parenting fosters antisocial child behavior and skills deficits, which child characteristics in turn make parenting more difficult, and so on. Similarly, child antisocial behavior and skills deficits lead to peer rejection, which in turn leads to further antisocial behavior and increasing skills deficits. In this positive feedback process, the problem is exacerbated over time. Research using process rather than static models are needed to address these questions.

In terms of internal validity, neither longitudinal nor cross-sectional designs unambiguously establish the causal nature of family and parenting variables in the development of delinquent behavior. The association of parenting and family variables with delinquency may simply reflect their prior association with some third (causative) variable. Several such possible variables exist. Inept parenting and delinquency may both be the result of residing in high stress, poor, high crime environments. While the effects of these types of environments appear to be mediated via parenting and family interactional variables, this can be more clearly established in experimental or manipulative designs.

Another possibility is that genetic rather than environmental (family) variables are important. In this case, the inept family management practices of the parents and the antisocial behavior of the child are expressions of a genetically shared predisposition which, under stress, is evident in the parents and the child. While it is unlikely that the mechanism is purely genetic, there are insufficient data to rule out the influence of such a mechanism. It is also possible that some child characteristic, like insensitivity to reinforcement and punishment or difficult temperament, may disrupt parenting practices and thus serve as the impetus for the development of antisocial child behavior. The question here is largely one of the direction of the effect. Rather than the parents (exclusively) influencing the child, the child may influence the parent with the association between poor parenting and delinquency both being a result of child characteristics. However, it seems quite likely that the effect is bidirectional as suggested by the process notion discussed above.

The lack of clear causal status for parenting or family variables in the development of delinquency leads to the third step alluded to at the beginning of the chapter. Those family and parenting variables found to be associated with delinquency must be manipulated to convincingly demonstrate their causal status. This could be done by selecting an at risk group of families, randomly assigning them to an intervention powerful enough to significantly alter family or parenting variables of interest, and to a control group. If family variables play a causative role in the development of delinquency, children in the intervention group, during their subsequent child and adolescent development, should engage in fewer and less serious delinquent acts than those from the control group. Thus, a clear understanding of the role of the family in the development of delinquent behavior lead us to and should involve effective preventative and clinical intervention strategies.

REFERENCES

Alexander, J. F. (1973). Defensive and supportive communication in normal and deviant families. *Journal of Consulting and Clinical Psychology, 40,* 223–231.

Alkire, A. A., Goldstein, M. J., Rodnick, E. H., & Judd, L. L. (1971). Social influence and counter-influence within families of four types of disturbed adolescents. *Journal of Abnormal Psychology, 77,* 32–41.

Baumrind, D. (1967). Child care practices anteceding three patterns of preschool behavior. *Genetic Psychology Monographs, 75,* 43–88.

Baumrind, D. (1971). Current patterns of parental authority. *Developmental Psychology Monographs, 4,* (1, Pt. 2).

Block, J. (1971). *Lives through time.* Berkley, CA: Bancroft Books.

Braithwaite, J. (1981). The myth of social class and criminality reconsidered. *American Sociological Review, 46,* 36–57.

Canter, R. J. (1982). Family correlates of male and female delinquency. *Criminology, 20,* 149–160.

Deur, J. L., & Parke, P. D. (1970). The effects of inconsistent punishment on aggression in children. *Developmental Psychology, 2,* 403–411.

Dishon, T., & Loeber, R. (1983). *Male adolescent marijuana and alcohol use: The role of parents and peers revisited.* Unpublished manuscript, Oregon Social Learning Center, Eugene, OR.

Dishon, T., Loeber, R., Stouthamer-Loeber, M., & Patterson, G. J. (1984). Skill deficits and male adolescent delinquency. *Journal of Abnormal Child Psychology, 12,* 137–154.

Elder, G. (1980). *Family structure and socialization.* Arno Series, Dissertation in Sociology.

Elder, G. H., Liker, J. K., & Cross, C. E. (1983). Parent-child behavior in the Great Depression: Life course and intergenerational influences. In P. Baltes & O. Brim (Eds.), *Life span development and behavior* (Vol. 6, pp. 307–322). New York: Academic Press.

Elliott, D. S., & Ageton, S. S. (1980). Reconciling race and class differences in self reported and official estimates of delinquency. *Sociological Review, 45,* 95–110.

Elliott, D. S., & Voss, H. L. (1974). *Delinquency and dropout.* Lexington, MA: D. C. Heath.

Elliott, D. S., & Huizinga, D. (1983). Social class and delinquent behavior in a national youth panel. *Criminology, 21,* 149–177.

Elliott, D. S., Huizinga, D., & Ageton, S. S. (1982). *Explaining delinquency and drug use: The national youth survey project.* Report No. 21, Behavioral Research Institute: Boulder, CO.

Emery, R. E., & O'Leary, K. D. (1982). Children's perception of marital discord and behavior problems of boys and girls. *Journal of Abnormal Child Psychology, 10,* 11–24.

Farrington, D. P. (1978). The family backgrounds of aggressive youths. In L. A. Hersov, M. Berger, & D. Shaffer (Eds.), *Aggression and antisocial behavior in childhood and adolescence* (pp. 73–93). Oxford: Pergamon Press.

Farrington, D. P. (1979). Longitudinal research on crime and delinquency. In N. Morris & M. Tonry (Eds.), *Criminal justice: An annual review of the research* (Vol. 1, pp. 289–348). Chicago: University of Chicago Press.

Farrington, D. P. (1981). *Delinquency from 10 to 25.* Paper presented at the Society for Life History Research, Monterey, California.

Farrington, D. P., Grundy, G., & West, D. J. (1975). The familial transmission of criminality. *Medicine, Science, and the Law, 15,* 177–186.

Forehand, R., King, H., Pied, S., & Yoder, P. (1975). Mother-child interactions: Comparisons of noncompliant clinic group and non-clinic group. *Behavior Research and Therapy, 13,* 79–84.

Freedman, B. J., Rosenthal, L., Donahue, L. P., Schlundt, D. G., & McFall, R. M. (1978). A social-behavioral analysis of skill deficits in delinquent and nondelinquent adolescents. *Journal of Consulting and Clinical Psychology, 46,* 1448–1462.

Gibson, H. B. (1969). Early delinquency in relation to broken homes. *Journal of Child Psychology, 10,* 195–204.

Glueck, S., & Glueck, E. (1968). *Delinquents and non-delinquents in perspective.* Cambridge: Harvard University Press.

Glick, S. J. (1972). Identification of predelinquents among children with school behavior problems as a basis for multiservice program. In S. Glueck & E. Glueck (Eds.), *Identification of predelinquents.* (pp. 84–90) New York: Intercontinental Medical Books.

Gold, M. (1963). *Status forces in delinquent boys.* Ann Arbor: University of Michigan Press.

Gold, M. (1970). *Delinquent behavior in an American city.* Belmont, CA: Brooks/Cole.

Hamperian, D. M., Schuster, R., Dinitz, S., & Conrad, J. P. (1979). *The violent few.* Lexington, MA: Heath.

Hanson, C. L., Henggeler, S., Haefile, W., & Rodick, J. (1984). Demographic, individual and family relationship correlates of serious and repeated crime among delinquents and their siblings. *Journal of Consulting and Clinical Psychology, 52,* 528-538.

Hartup, W. W. (1983). Peer relations. In P. H. Mussen (Ed.), *Handbook of child psychology* (Vol. 4, pp. 103-196). New York: John Wiley & Sons.

Hirschi, T. (1969). *Causes of delinquency.* Berkley, CA: University of California Press.

Hetherington, E. M., Cox, M., & Cox, R. (1979). Family interaction and the social, emotional and cognitive development of children following divorce. In V. Vaughan & T. Brazelton (Eds.), *The family: Setting priorities.* (pp. 89-117). New York: Science and Medicine.

Hetherington, E. M., & Martin, B. (1979). Family interaction. In H. C. Quay & J. S. Werry (Eds.), *Psychopathological disorders of childhood. (2nd ed., pp. 247-302) New York: Wiley.*

Hetherington, E. M., Stouwie, R., & Ridberg, E. H. (1971). Patterns of family interaction and child rearing related to three dimensions of juvenile delinquency. *Journal of Abnormal Psychology, 77,* 160-176.

Hewitt, L. E. & Jenkins, R. L. (1946). *Fundamental patterns of maladjustment: The dynamics of their origin.* Springfield, Illinois: Green.

Hoffman, M. C. (1970). Moral development. In P. Mussen (Ed.), *Carmichael's manual of child psychology* (Vol. 2, pp. 261-359). New York: Wiley.

Holleran, P. A., Littman, D. C., Freund, R. D., & Schmaling, K. B. (1982). A signal detection approach to social perception: Identification of positive and negative behavior by parents of normal and problem children. *Journal of Abnormal Child Psychology, 10,* 547-558.

Johnson, R. E. (1979). *Juvenile delinquency and its origins.* Cambridge: Cambridge University Press.

Kandel, D. B. (1978). Homopily, selection and socialization in adolescent friendships. *American Journal of Sociology, 84,* 427-436.

Kandel, D. B., Kessler, R. C., & Margulies, R. Z. (1978). Antecedents of adolescent initiation into stages of drug use: A developmental analysis. In D. B. Kandel (Ed.), *Longitudinal research on drug use: Empirical findings and methodological issues.* (pp. 73-99) Washington D.C.: Hemisphere Publishing Company.

Kraus, J. (1977). Causes of delinquency as perceived by juveniles. *International Journal of Offender Therapy and Comparative Criminology, 21,* 79-86.

Lewis, A. (1954). *Deprived children.* London: Oxford University Press.

Lobitz, G. K., & Johnson, S. M. (1976). Normal versus deviant children: A multimethod comparison. *Journal of Abnormal Child Psychology, 3,* 353-373.

Loeber, R. (1982). The stability of antisocial and delinquent child behavior: A review. *Child Development, 53,* 1431-1446.

Loeber, R., & Dishon, T. (1983). Early predictions of male delinquency: A review. *Psychological Bulletin, 93,* 68–99.

Loeber, R., & Schmaling, K. B. (1985a). Emprirical evidence for overt and covert patterns of antisocial conduct problems: A meta-analysis. *Journal of Abnormal Child Psychology, 13,* 337–353.

Loeber, R., & Schmaling, K. B. (1985b). The utility of differentiating between mixed and pure forms of antisocial child behavior. *Journal of Abnormal Child Psychology, 13,* 315–335.

Loeber, R., Weisman, W., & Reid, J. B. (1983). Family interaction of assaultive adolescents, stealers and non-delinquents. *Journal of Abnormal Child Psychology, 11,* 1–14.

McCord J. (1978). *A longitudinal study of the link between broken homes and criminality.* Paper presented at the National Council on Family Relations.

McCord, J. (1979). Some child rearing antecedents of criminal behavior in adult men. *Journal of Personality and Social Psychology, 9,* 1477–1486.

Middlebrook, J. L., & Forehand, R. (November, 1984). *The effects of the interaction of child behavior with situational variables on parental perception of deviance.* Paper presented at the 18th Annual Convention of the Association for the Advancement of Behavior Therapy, Philadelpnia.

Mitchell, S., & Rosa, P. (1981). Boyhood behavior problems as precursors of criminality: A fifteen year follow-up study. *Journal of Child Psychology and Psychiatry, 22,* 19–33.

Nye, F. I. (1958). *Family relationships and delinquent behavior.* New York: Wiley.

Olweus, D. (1979). Stability of aggressive reaction patterns in males: A review. *Psychological Bulletin, 86,* 852–857.

Olweus, D. (1980). Familial and temperamental determinants of aggressive behavior in adolescents: A causal analysis. *Developmental Psychology, 14,* 644–660.

Osborn, S. G., & West, D. G. (1979). Conviction records of fathers and sons compared. *British Journal of Criminology, 19,* 120–133.

Patterson, G. R. (1976). The aggressive child: Victim and architect of a coercive system. In L. A. Hamerlynck, J. C. Handy, & E. J. Mash (Eds.), *Behavior modification and families: Theory and research* (Vol. 1, p. 267–316) New York: Brunner/Mazel.

Patterson, G. R. (1979). A performance theory for coercive family interaction. In R. Cairns (Ed.), *The analysis of social interaction: Methods, issues and illustrations.* (pp. 119–162.). Hillsdale, NJ: Erlbaum.

Patterson, G. R. (1980). Some speculations and data relating to children who steal. In T. Hirschi & M. Gottfredson (Eds.), *Theory and fact in contemporary criminology.* (pp. 204–234). Beverly Hills, CA: Sage Publications.

Patterson. G. R. (1981). Mothers: The unacknowledged victims. *Monographs of the Society for Research in Child Development, 46,* (Whole No. 5).

Patterson, G. R. (1982a). *Coercive family process.* Eugene, OR: Castilia.

Patterson, G. R. (1982b). The unattached mother: A process analysis. In W. Hartup & Z. Rubin (Eds.), *Social relationships: Their role in children's development.* (pp. 260–283). Harwichport, MA: Harwichport Conference.

Patterson, G. R. (in press). The contribution of siblings to training for fighting: A microsocial analysis. In D. Olweus, J. Block, & M. Radke-Yarrow (Eds.), *Devel-*

opment of antisocial and prosocial behavior: Research, theories and issues. New York: Academic Press.

Patterson, G. R., & Bank, L. (1985). When is a nomological network a construct? In D. Peterson & D. Fishman (Eds.), *Assessment for decisions: psychology in action.*

Patterson, G. R., & Dishon, T. J. (in press). Contributions of families and peers to delinquency. *Criminology.*

Patterson, G. R., Dishon, T. J., & Bank, L. (1984). Family interaction: A process model of deviance training. *Aggressive Behavior, 10,* 253-267.

Porter, B., & O'Leary K. D. (1982). Marital discord and childhood behavior problems. *Journal of Abnormal Child Psychology, 8,* 287-296.

Power, M. J., Ash, P. M., Schoenberg, G. E., & Sorey, E. C. (1974). Delinquency and the family. *British Journal of Social work, 4,* 13-38.

Prinz, R. J., Foster, S., Kent, R. N., & O'Leary, K. D. (1979). Multivariate assessment of conflict in distressed and non-distressed mother-adolescent dyads. *Journal of Applied Behavior Analysis, 12,* 691-700.

Pulkkinen, L. (1983). Finland: The search for alternatives to aggression. In A. P. Goldstein & M. H. Segal (Eds.), *Aggression in a global perspective.* (pp. 104-144). New York: Pergamon.

Putallaz, M. & Gottman, J. M. (1981). Social skills and group acceptance. In S. R. Asher & J. M. Gottman (Eds.), *The development of children's friendships.* (pp. 116-149) New York: Cambridge University Press.

Reid, J. B., & Patterson, G. R. (1976). The modifications of aggression and stealing behavior of boys in the home setting. In A. Bandura & E. Rikes (Eds.), *Behavior modification: Experimental analyses of aggression and delinquency.* (pp. 123-146). Hillsdale, New Jersey: Lawrence Erlbaum.

Richards, P., Berk, R. A., & Forster, B. (1979). *Crime as play: Delinquency in a middle class suburb.* Cambridge, MA: Ballinger.

Robin, A. L., & Weiss, J. G. (1980). Criterion related validity of behavioral and self report measures of problem solving communication skills in distressed and non-distressed parent-adolescent dyads. *Behavioral Assessment, 2,* 339-352.

Robins, L. N. (1978). Sturdy childhood predictors of adult antisocial behavior. *Psychological Medicine, 8,* 611-622.

Robins, L., West, P. A., & Herjanic, B. L. (1975). Arrests and delinquency in two generations: A study of black urban families and their children. *Journal of Child Psychology and Psychiatry, 76,* 125-140.

Roff, M., Sells, S. B., & Golden, M. M. (1972). *Sexual adjustment and personality development in children.* Minneapolis: University of Minnesota Press.

Rojeck, D. G., & Erickson, M. L. (1982). Delinquent careers: A test of the career escalation model. *Criminology, 20,* 5-28.

Rutter, M. (1971). Parent-child separation: Psychological effects on the children. *Journal of Child Psychology and Psychiatry, 12,* 233-260.

Rutter, M., & Giller, H. (1984). *Juvenile delinquency: Trends and perspectives.* New York: Guilford Press.

Sawin, D. B., & Parke, R. D. (1979). The effects of interagent inconsistent discipline on children's aggressive behavior. *Journal of Experimental Child Psychology, 28,* 528-535.

Schaefer, E. S. (1965). Children's reports of parental behavior: An inventory. *Child Development, 36,* 413–424.

Schmaling, K. B., & Patterson, G. R. (1984). *Maternal classifications of deviant and prosocial child behavior and reactions to the child in the home.* Unpublished manuscript, Oregon Social Learning Center, Eugene, OR.

Simcha-Fagan, O., Langer, T. S., Gersten, J. C., & Eisenberg, J. G. (1975). *Violent and antisocial behavior: A longitudinal study of urban youth.* Unpublished report, Office of Child Development.

Snyder, J. J. (1977). Reinforcement analysis of problem and nonproblem families. *Journal of Abnormal Psychology, 86,* 528–535.

Snyder, J. J., Dishon, T., & Patterson, G. R. (in press). Determinants and consequences of associating with deviant peers. *Journal of Early Adolescence.*

Snyder, J. J., & Patterson, G. R. (1984). *Determinants of child compliance to parental commands.* Unpublished manuscript, Oregon Social Learning Center, Eugene, OR.

Stanfield, R. E. (1966). The interaction of family variables and gang variables in the aetiology of delinquency. *Social Problems, 13,* 411–417.

Stouthamer-Loeber, M., Patterson, G. R., & Loeber, R. (1983). *Parental monitoring and antisocial behavior in boys.* Unpublished manuscript, Oregon Social Learning Center, Eugene, OR.

Stuart, R. B. (November, 1969). *Assessment and change in the communication patterns of juvenile delinquents and their parents.* Paper presented at the annual convention of the Association for the Advancement of Behavior Therapy, Washington, D. C.

Wadsworth, M. E. J. (1979). *Roots of delinquency: Infancy, adolescence and crime.* Oxford, England: Robertson.

West, D. J. (1982). *Delinquency: It's roots, careers and prospects.* London, Heinemann.

West, D. J. & Farrington, D. P. (1973). *Who becomes delinquent.* London: Heinemann Educational Books.

West, D. J., & Farrington, D. P. (1977). *The delinquent way of life.* London: Heinemann Educational Books.

Wilson, H. (1974). Parenting in poverty. *British Journal of Social Work, 4,* 241–254.

Wilson, H. (1980). Parental supervision: A neglected aspect of delinquency. *British Journal of Criminology, 20,* 203–235.

Wilson, H., & Herbert, G. W. (1978). *Parents and children in the inner city.* London: Routledge & Kegan Paul.

Wilson, J. Q., & Herrnstein, R. J. (1985). *Crime and human nature.* New York: Simon & Schuster.

Wolfgang, M. R., Figlio, R. M., & Sellin, T. (1972). *Delinquency in a birth cohort.* Chicago: University of Chicago Press.

CHAPTER 9

Institutional Treatment

HERBERT C. QUAY

University of Miami

Despite the emphasis on decriminalization of status offenses (see Chapter 1) and the movement toward deinstitutionalization of all juvenile offenders (see Chapter 10) which begin in the 1960s, the commitment of juveniles to local and state-operated institutions remains a major court-ordered disposition.

As of June, 1985, there were 24,340 males and 2786 females in state institutions and training schools (American Correctional Association, 1986). There were, of course, many more who had come and gone during the previous 12 months; three times as many would be a conservative estimate. Furthermore, these figures do not include adjudicated juveniles in privately operated facilities where they may have been housed in lieu of being sent to a state institution. In fact, Sherraden and Doons (1984) reported that the rate of institutionalization of delinquents rose from 1960 to 1970 and has risen steadily since 1850.

Given the current emphasis on community placement and other alternative interventions (see Chapter 10), it is not unreasonable to assume that most of these juvenile offenders had been failures in less restrictive programs, had had lengthy arrest and court appearance records, and/or had been found guilty of those (mostly violent) offenses which made them unacceptable to community facilities (see Regnery, 1985).

Clearly these "hard-core" repeat offenders whose behavior poses more of a threat than that of many less seriously involved youth are a particularly difficult problem for institutions whose mission it is to "rehabilitate" juvenile delinquents. The difficulties facing these institutions are exacerbated by a number of forces operating on them which include an increasingly punitive philosophy arising out of the conclusion that "nothing works," and diminishing resources arising as a result of the adoption of this punitive philosophy by both politicians and correctional administrators.

Thus, over the last 10 years, institutions have been forced to deal with an increasingly difficult population with diminished resources and with mixed messages from those in position of power as to whether the goal is rehabilitation or punishment. It is, no doubt, the combination of these forces that has come to restrict seriously research on the effects of institutional treatment.

After a period of considerable research activity in the 1960s and early 1970s, the publication of large-sample controlled studies has diminished almost to the vanishing point. Later in this chapter we will be describing studies that were carried out more than a decade ago but still represent the best examples of research into the efficacy of institutional treatment for juvenile delinquents.

DOES ANYTHING WORK?

The effectiveness of correctional treatment, both institutional and community, adult and juvenile, has been hotly debated since the appearance of the influential reviews by Martinson (1974) and Lipton, Martinson, and Wilks (1975), and the follow-up into adulthood of clients of a major early delinquency prevention program by McCord (1978). Martinson's (1974, p. 25) conclusion that "with few and isolated exceptions, the rehabilitative efforts that have been reported so far have had no appreciable effect on recidivism" ushered in an area of pessimism and punitiveness on the part of many correctional administrators and politicians.

The dissenting voices were not nearly so loud or so convincing. With respect to juveniles, Palmer, (1975, 1978, 1983) a major figure in the differential classification and treatment movement (see Chapter 5 and the following), questioned both Martinson's methods of analysis and his conclusions. He and others (e.g., Palmer, 1984; Romig, 1978; Ross & Gendreau, 1980) argued that rehabilitation was effective given certain treatments for certain types of offenders in certain settings (the differential treatment view). While many other reviewers have addressed various aspects of the issue (e.g., studies using behavior modification; see Davidson & Seidman, 1974; Johnson, 1977; Emery & Manholin, 1977), it is only recently that Garrett (1984, 1985) has analyzed the voluminous research literature in a more sophisticated way, pointing out that the various earlier methods of review did not provide a measure of *how much* change was associated with treatment. Her technique, meta-analysis (see Glass, McGaw, & Smith, 1981; Bangert-Drowns, 1986, and Chapter 10), provided a measure of how much change has taken place—the effect size. We will return to the effectiveness question and to her review later in this chapter.

WHAT CAN BE EXPECTED TO WORK?

While the debate raged with respect to the effectiveness of correctional treatment, this writer (Quay, 1977) was prompted to take a careful look at a widely cited study of the use of group counseling with adult offenders (Kassebaum, Ward, & Wilner, 1971) which had reported no effect on recidivism. This study was a model of experimental design, having used random assignment of subjects to treatment and control conditions, and had been reported in much greater detail than is usual for intervention studies. What was striking was the serious lack of what we termed "program integrity." The treatment, group counseling, was discussed in general terms and its facets were not delineated in ways that lent themselves to implementation. The majority of those responsible for carrying out the treatment were not convinced that it would affect recidivism (the major dependent variable of the study), and the group leaders (*not* professional counselors) were poorly trained. The treatment was clearly not well implemented (see Quay, 1977). Yet, this study had been cited as a failure of treatment without any consideration of the myriad factors serving to dilute any possible effects.

The assessment of the strength and integrity of the treatment is crucial if one is to know what, if anything, took place; the concept has been further discussed by Sechrest, West, Phillips, Redner, and Yeaton (1979, Scheirer & Rezmovic (1983), and Salend (1984) (see also Chapter 14). It remains unfortunate that the reporting of intervention research, while almost always providing necessary details about the outcome measures and the experimental design, most often provides little or no data on program integrity.

WHAT IS INSTITUTIONAL TREATMENT?

The ideal conception of institutional *treatment* (as contrasted with deterrence, incapacitation, and punishment as reasons for institutionalization) is that the institution provides a milieu that is therapeutic in its totality. Supposedly, everything that occurs within the institution has a therapeutic purpose. However, the nature of this therapeutic milieu is most often developed out of beliefs rather than on the basis of empirical data about its efficacy. Institutional programs may also set out to provide many different sorts of formalized interventions—Guided Group Interaction, Transactional Analysis, Behavior Modification, individual psychotherapy, Reality Therapy, and social skills training are common examples. Institutional programs may also include academic education, vocational training, recreation, and other "nonpsychological" interventions. Thus, there is no such thing as a standard and universal "institutional treatment"; the concept itself has to be further specified if the question of effectiveness is to be answered.

It is also important to recognize that most formal psychologically based interventions were originally developed for use with a generally willing clientele. The problem with implementing such interventions in correctional institutions was aptly put by a prominent correctional administrator who once pointed out that corrections is society's only behavior-change agency that doesn't have *any* volunteers among its clients.

It is also the case that what is supposed to occur according to the prescription for the intervention (see also the previous discussion relative to program integrity) is not always what is actually taking place. More than 20 years ago, Buehler, Patterson, and Furniss (1966) documented how staff reinforced behavior of clients which was contrary to the institution's stated goals. More recently, Sanson-Fisher and Jenkins (1978) have reported on the small amount of staff behavior that involved the creation of therapeutic opportunities for inmates to learn and exhibit appropriate behavior. Along the same lines, Johnson (1981) has provided data demonstrating how staff moved away from assigned tasks to those more immediate and less demanding.

There is continuing concern with respect to the problems in implementing institutional treatment. Colyar (1983) has listed 10 "laws" of residential treatment, pointing out many of the things that can go wrong, while Uranish (1983–1984) has highlighted the potential negative role of program administration. (See also Miller & Ohlin, 1985, Ch. 2). Striking differences in how two published reports describe the *same* intervention have been provided by Mayers (1980) and Tremblay (1984). The differences between program plans and objectives and the realities of program implementation present serious problems both for carrying out and evaluating institutional interventions. Advocates of all treatment approaches should evidence the same degree of concern for the measurement of the treatment itself as has been evidenced by some behaviorists (see, e.g., Wodarski, Feldman, & Pedi, 1974; Peterson, Homer, & Wonderlich, 1982; Billingsley, White, & Munson, 1980).

EXPERIMENTS IN INSTITUTIONAL TREATMENT

Before further discussion of the effectiveness issue and various ramifications flowing from it, we will discuss in detail five major program and research efforts in institutional treatment. These projects involve differing theoretical approaches, treatment modalities, settings, and a variety of outcome measures, even though some measure of recidivism (defined in one way or another, see Chapter 14) was used in all of them. A reading of this section should give the reader both a feel for institutional intervention at its higher levels of complexity and an appreciation of the complexity of the research undertaking.* As we noted earlier in this chapter the "classic" studies were all completed in the 1970s.

The Preston Typology Study

This study (Jesness, 1971) was the first to use the California I-level classification system (see Chapter 5) as a basis for the application of differing treatment strategies to different subgroups in a residential setting. The study took place in a large (900-bed) institution for male delinquents, ages 16 to 20, operated by the California Youth Authority. The institution served the more serious cases; 45 percent had had a previous commitment to another California institution.

Subjects were assigned randomly either to the experimental or control groups. The 518 control boys were assigned to living units on the basis of the

---

*These studies have been previously discussed in Quay (1986).

institution's preexisting criteria, which did not involve personality classification. The 655 experimental subjects were assigned to a living unit based on their delinquent subtype.

Considerable effort was devoted to staff training of both management personnel, group supervisors, and youth counselors and was centered on the characteristics and treatment of the particular subtype that was the responsibility of each treatment team. There was also an attempt to match the personality, interests, and working style of staff to the treatment needs of the various subtypes.

Different programs were developed for each of the six experimental units based on the apparent needs of the different subtypes. Program elements included staff style and behavior, staff expectations and goals, individual versus group counseling, degree of limits and structure, and academic programming. Program monitoring was accomplished by means of questionnaires administered to both staff and inmates with supplemental ratings by experts.

Results were reported both in terms of in-program and post-program criteria. According to Jesness, "Data on the immediate impact of the experimental program on the institution indicated fairly consistently that the introduction of the I-level system tended to decrease unit management problems. During the operational phase of the study, significantly fewer reports of serious rule infractions and peer problems were reported in the experimental units" (Jesness, 1971, p. 44–45, 47). One cannot, of course, rule out differential staff responses to the inmates' behavior as opposed to actual changes in the behavior itself when accounting for these results. Additional in-program data with regard to changes on psychometric instruments were also reported with the Manipulators showing greater changes in self-report measures and the Cultural Eventual Conformists and Neurotic Acting-Out groups showing greater improvement in behavioral criteria.

Post-program effects were measured by parole violations at both 15 months and 24 months after release. An overall comparison of the experimental and control cases revealed no differences in parole violations. Fifty-four percent of both groups had violated on or before 15 months, while 64 percent of both groups had violated on or before 24 months. Neither were there any differences in outcome between any of the subtypes either in the experimental or control groups.

The results of this study were clearly disappointing in terms of effects on post-program rates of law violations. However, the decrease in conflict within the institution and the increase in staff professionalism and morale reported, while not related to a reduction in recidivism, could clearly have had longer-term effects for subsequent treatment in the host institution. An overall evaluation of this pioneering study must also take into account its influence in encouraging other research studies in the use of rationally derived differential treatment strategies for delinquents subclassified according to psychological and behavioral characteristics as already described in Chapter 5.

The California Community Treatment Project (CTP)

This effort, a landmark in the treatment of delinquent youth, was begun in 1961 and was established to avoid the need for institutional placement for certain kinds of delinquents. A review of the entire program has been provided by Palmer (1974).

While the emphasis of this project had been on nonresidential treatment, in 1969, based on the earlier recognition that "the difficulties and delinquent orientation of 25 to 35 percent were hardly being influenced by the intensive CTP program" (Palmer, 1974, p. 7), a residential component was added to serve some youths in the initial stages of their career in the California Youth Authority.

The initial step in selecting clientele for the residential component involved a staff decision as to whether institutionalization should be the initial step (followed by community treatment), or whether direct placement should be made to the community component for a given case. After this decision was made, assignment to the two conditions was then made randomly. The same staff, it should be noted, served both the community and the residential components.

The method of case assignment provided for four groups: (1) those deemed in need of initial institutional placement and who were placed in a facility; (2) those deemed in need of initial institutionalization who were placed directly in the community program; (3) those seen as not needing institutional experience but who received it; and (4) those seen as amenable to direct placement in a community who were so placed. Thus, the research design permitted the comparison of judged amenables versus nonamenables in the two treatment conditions. Furthermore, the design also allowed comparisons among youths of the differing subtypes of the California I-level system.

The residential facility normally housed about 25 youths at one time. It was staffed by carefully selected "youth counselors" and "group supervisors" (Palmer, 1974, p. 9) and was continually accessible to all other personnel in the project. Program features (see also Palmer & Werner, 1972) included three to four visits per week by the parole agent, individualized counseling averaging 2.6 hours per week by the parole agent, group counseling for about one hour per week, school attendance for 87 percent of the youths, athletics, arts and crafts, and out-of-dorm activities such as musical events and other cultural activities.

The major outcome measure was rearrest during the first 18 months on parole. Results for the initial 106 cases indicated that of those judged as needing initial residential placement and actually receiving it, 58 percent were rearrested; of those judged in need but not receiving needed residential placement, 94 percent were rearrested. The mean number of offenses for the two groups was .96 versus 1.56; for each month on parole the mean rates were .066 versus .140. According to Palmer (1974) these differences were significant when background variables such as age, IQ, socioeconomic status, race, delinquent sub-type, and levels of parole risk were controlled.

Among the group judged amenable to direct community placement, there were few substantial differences between those first institutionalized and those placed appropriately. Overall, looking at those appropriately placed against those inappropriately placed, the mean rate of offending per month was .067 for the former and .107 for the latter; a difference Palmer reported as signif-icant.

With regard to the results, Palmer concluded, "The various findings which have bene presented here seem to suggest the obvious: delinquent behavior can probably be reduced in connection with community and residential pro-grams *alike* by means of careful diagnosis and subsequent placement of in-dividuals into appropriate rather than inappropriate or less-than-optimal set-tings and programs" (Palmer, 1974, p. 10).

The size of the samples upon which the results were obtained clearly did not suffice for much in the way of analyses of the performance of nine dif-ferent delinquent subtypes. Palmer (1974) suggested, however, that the initial residential placement in the special facility was helpful in the case of Neurotic youths with aggressive tendencies, whereas it did not seem to be helpful in the case of the Power Oriented subtype (see Chapter 5).

These results, which can be considered preliminary, suggest strongly that initial residential placement is helpful for those deemed, on the basis of clinical judgment, as needing it. The results also suggest that the determination of those who should receive institutional placement might be made on the basis of a classification system with a very limited number of categories.

The Close-Holton Study

This study (Jesness, 1975) compared the effects of Behavior Modification and Transactional Analysis on a variety of outcome criteria. The setting for the experiment was two newly opened institutions, the O. H. Close School and the Karl Holton School of the California Youth Authority, each housing about 400 youths in 50-bed living units.

Experimental subjects, approximately 400 at each of the two schools, were between 15 and 17 and were assigned randomly to either of the two experi-mental programs. The median age was 16.6; 33 percent had had a prior com-mitment to the Youth Authority; 56 percent were white, 28 percent black, 13 percent Mexican-American, and 2 percent other. At admission, each youth was classified into one of the nine delinquent subtypes of the California I-level system.

To implement the treatment modalities, training in both techniques was car-ried out both prior to the implementation of the research design and contin-uously throughout the experiment. All eight living units and all classrooms in the Holton School operated under a token economy and a parole-contingent point system. Behaviors targeted were classified as convenience, academic, and critical deficiencies. The latter were those seen as most likely to affect the probability of parole success, and 27 percent of a boy's points toward parole had to be earned in this category.

In the Close School each boy was given a primer on Transactional Analysis when he was admitted. After residence assignment, a counselor conducted a life-script interview that ended with the negotiation of a mutually agreeable verbal treatment contract. In addition to twice-weekly small-group therapy sessions, the principles of transactional analysis were utilized in management, in classrooms, and in large group community meetings. Program detail may be found in Jesness and DeRisi (1973) and Jesness (1975).

Boys at the Close School averaged a 30-week stay and participated in an average of 40 Transactional-Analysis-group sessions. Boys at Holton stayed 35 weeks on the average and negotiated an average of 19 written contracts related to critical behavior deficiencies.

As to the extent to which the "ideals" of the two programs were actually implemented, Jesness noted: "Counselors at Close were expected to conduct at least two Transactional Analysis sessions with their clients each week. In addition to the academic contracting, Holton counselors were expected to negotiate at least one behavioral contingency contract each week with their clients. Staff at Close fulfilled two-thirds of their expected quota, Holton staff one-half of theirs" (Jesness, 1975, p. 764). This study is unusual in that it provided a quantified estimate as to the actual degree of implementation of the treatment program.

A variety of outcome measures were obtained upon completion of the program, including opinion scales, achievement tests, a personality inventory, staff ratings of behavior, and a measure of ego development. Particular attention was given to a measure of "positive regard" as an index of the overall quality of the relationship between the boy and the staff, as perceived by the boy upon leaving the program. In addition, reconviction data were obtained for follow-up periods of 6, 12, 18, and 24 months.

The outcome variables were analyzed with respect to the effects of each program separately, differences between the two programs, and the interaction of the programs with comparisons of the various delinquent subtypes. Here these results can only be summarized. Boys in both programs made academic gains beyond those projected. The contingency management program (Holton), contrary to expectation, enjoyed an advantage with higher maturity subjects, while the Close classrooms were more effective with lower maturity subjects.

Boys in both programs obtained more favorable scores on the personality inventory, with the Transactional Analysis subjects more frequently improving to a greater extent. There were also some differential effects of the two programs on the delinquent subtypes, with the Manipulators seeming to benefit most from the Transactional Analysis experience.

On the staff ratings of behavior, there were some differences between the programs and some differential effects; the Behavior Modification program apparently enjoying the greatest success with the Acting-Out Neurotics, while the Transactional Analysis program produced the greatest changes in the Cultural Conformists. Overall, behavior ratings were slightly, but significantly, more affected by the Behavior Modification program. Positive regard was generally higher for the transactional analysis program with about 65 percent of Close subjects indicating high positive regard as contrasted with only about 45 percent at Holton.

The parole follow-up data was not revealing of any differences between the programs at any of the parole exposure periods. By 24 months, slightly more than 47 percent of boys at each institution had violated parole and had been returned to an institution. However, the rates of parole violation at one year for both schools were lower than they had been at the two institutions in the two years prior to the implementation of the experiment. Rates of violation for both Close and Holton were also lower than for two other California institutions serving boys of approximately the same age. With respect to differential effects on the nine delinquent subtypes, the only significant finding was that the Transactional Analysis program was more successful in reducing subsequent violations among the Manipulators.

A final analysis of outcome used the measure of positive regard. When high and low positive regard groups were compared, those in the higher regard group generally showed more improvement; a finding that was true in regard to parole outcome as well as to the behavior rating and self-report measures. In fact, positive regard accounted for as much of a variance of the outcome measures as did the two treatments; about 15 percent in each case.

The Close-Holton Study is the most elaborate evaluation of specific treatment modalities in an institutional setting undertaken to date. The conclusions that can be drawn are that neither treatment was implemented to preset standards, that neither was superior to the other overall, that both were superior to no specified treatment in reducing parole violations at 12 months, that self-report measures were more positively affected by the Transactional Analysis approach while rated behavior was more affected by Behavior Modification, that different subtypes of the California I-level system were differentially affected to some degree, and that the boys' positive regard for their experiences was a significant factor in all outcome variables.

For a postscript on this program in terms of current concerns in correctional philosophy, the interested reader should see Jesness (1980).

The Robert F. Kennedy Youth Center (KYC) Study

This study, analyzing the differential treatment of delinquent males with an average age of 17, used a classification method that arose out of multivariate statistical research as discussed in Chapter 5.

An attempt was made to conceptualize differential psychological interventions for inmates classified into one of the four groups, and to implement these methods by means of living units composed of homogeneous groups (Gerard,

1970). For the Undersocialized Aggressive cases, Behavior Modification was used; for the Anxious Withdrawn group, a program of both individual and group counseling was implemented; and for the Socialized Delinquent group, the treatment method was Reality Therapy. There was considerable difficulty in conceptualizing and implementing a treatment approach for the Immaturity (Attention Deficit) cases; however, an intervention based on the principles of Transactional Analysis was finally implemented well into the study period.

In addition to the subtype-specific treatments, the entire institution had an overriding token economy and used an innovative decentralized approach to the organization of a correctional institution (see Levinson & Gerard, 1973). In addition, academic and vocational education, recreation, religious programs, and self-enlightenment programs were available to all inmates. The setting of the program was a newly constructed, architecturally innovative, open institution with a generally treatment-oriented and experimentally minded staff.

While it was possible to specify the nature of the formal subtype-specific treatments reasonably well, and attempts were made by institution management to monitor them, this study illustrated all too well the problem of distinguishing possible effects of treatment from the effects of the setting itself, including the institution-wide token economy, the innovative management organization, and the physical plant.

Although a variety of measures of in-program performance have been reported, including academic skill-gains, reduced disciplinary problems and positive behavior changes (see Thomas, 1974; Johnson, 1977), the formal evaluation rested on recidivism, defined as a return to any state or federal prison for at least 60 days over a three-year period following release.

The experimental design as reported by Cavior and Schmidt (1978) involved a comparison of the four subgroups ($n = 281$) of experimentals with four similar subgroups who were incarcerated in a more typical institution ($n = 405$). Unfortunately, it was not possible to randomly assign youths to the two institutions from a pool of eligibles. Because of its openness and lack of security, KYC was not assigned cases whose histories included physical violence; the control institution cases were also of a higher mean age (19.8 versus 17.8). However, on a basis of an actuarial prediction formula, the KYC sample was predicted, *a priori,* to do worse on parole.

Results indicated that the KYC group did not do significantly better on parole than did the control cases either before or after being equated for *a priori* risk. There were suggestive differences with regard to the effect of both institutions on certain subgroups; for example, the KYC success rate for the undersocialized (Psychopathic) group was 65.5 percent compared to 56.0 percent for the control institution. However, none of the differences between the subgroups were statistically significant. By the end of the three-year follow-up, 58 percent of both experimental and control groups had been in prison for at least 60 days sometime during that period, despite exposure to both traditional and highly innovative correctional programs.

Achievement Place

In this treatment model a trained child-care couple, called teaching-parents, live in a home with a small group (generally about six) of young people, ages 10 to 16, who have usually had repeated contacts with juvenile authorities. The range of intelligence has been from dull to superior, but most have been labeled by the schools as slow learners. Thirty percent have been in special educational programs and more than half have failed one or more grades. Most have been truant, and about two-thirds have been suspended prior to entering treatment. A wide variety of diagnostic labels have been used by professionals, to describe their psychopathology (Wolf, et al., 1976).

The program is based on the principles of Behavior Modification and involves "teaching, self-government, motivational, relationship-development and advocacy procedures" (Braukmann, Kirigin, & Wolf, 1976). When children enter an Achievement Place, they are introduced to a point system and given a point card on which their behavior and the number of points they earn and lose is recorded. Initially, points are exchanged for privileges every day-subsequently, exchanges are made on a weekly basis. As soon as possible, an attempt is made to phase out the point system, and the child goes on a merit system in which no points are given or taken away and all privileges are free. The merit system is the last step to be attained prior to leaving the group home. Points reinforce a variety of behaviors, including performance in the public school that the children continue to attend. A more complete description of the program may be found in Phillips, Phillips, Fixsen, and Wolf (1973) and in Wolf et al. (1976).

The teaching parents are trained over a one-year period by means of workshops, supervised practicum experiences, and consultations. The teaching parents are also provided with feedback from schools and community agencies with which they are in continuous contact, as well as from parents and the children themselves.

A variety of in-program effects have been carefully documented in a series of published studies. Positive effects have been recorded for social behaviors, cleanliness, punctuality, school work, conversational skills, and conflict negotiation. (See Kifer, Lewis, Green, & Phillips, 1974; Minkin et al., 1976; Phillips, 1968; Phillips, Phillips, Fixsen, & Wolf, 1971.)

Post-program evaluation has involved comparing treated cases in terms of pre- and post-program rates of offenses and comparing Achievement Place cases with similar cases treated in other group homes. Braukmann et al. (1976) reported that the 28 cases in the original Achievement Place had averaged 3.4 offenses per year prior to treatment. The average during the treatment year dropped to .9 offenses per case. Sixteen comparison cases had averaged 3.4 offenses prior to treatment but increased to an average of 7.3 while in treatment. A similar drop in in-program offenses occurred for 45 cases treated in five later replications of the original Achievement Place.

In terms of institutionalization, either during the program or within one year following, the rates were 14 percent for the original setting, 31 percent for the three comparison homes, and 18 percent for the later replications. Finally, offenses occurring during the year following treatment were compared. The original Achievement Place cases and the comparison cases were no different; each averaged about two offenses per child. The later replication seemed to be doing slightly better, averaging just over one offense per case.

The post-program offense rates were clearly disappointing and Braukmann et al. (1976) have suggested that both after-care and longer periods of treatment might be helpful. Hoefler and Bornstein (1975) have pointed out that, while Achievement Place has been genuinely successful in changing in-program behavior, more attention needed to be given to generalization and maintenance and to a more precise analysis of the influence of multiple factors in producing in-program change.

Further evidence for in-program but not post-program success has been provided by Kirigin, Braukmann, Atwater, and Wolf (1982) who compared 13 Achievement Place homes with nine comparison group homes; 102 boys and 38 girls were in the experimental group while 22 boys and 30 girls were in the comparison homes. The number of cases involved in recorded offenses was obtained for three time periods: one year pre-treatment, during treatment, and one year post-treatment. For boys there were no differences in pre-treatment involvement (94 percent versus 91 percent), a significant reduction during treatment, (56 percent versus 86 percent), but no differences post-treatment (57 percent versus 73 percent). For girls the pattern was the same: no pre-treatment differences (95 percent versus 73 percent), significant in-treatment differences (41 percent versus 85 percent), and no post-treatment differences (27 percent versus 47 percent). There were similar findings for number of offenses per case; significant differences in favor of the experimental group during, but not following, treatment.

From the original site, the program, now referred to as the Teaching Family Model (TFM), expanded into a large network of group homes. Weinrott, Jones, and Howard (1982) conducted an extensive and complex longitudinal summative evaluation of 26 TFM and 25 comparison group home programs and have provided an effectiveness analysis. They concluded that the TFM houses outperformed the comparison programs in cost-effectiveness only on measures of educational progress; there were no differences in reduced deviant behavior, occupational status or social/personality adjustment. However, as Weinrott, et al. (1982; p. 146) pointed out, "although the average youth (or program) outcome did not favor the TFM over the comparison group (or vice versa), the beneficial pre-to-post changes for youth in both groups may mean that the TFM and comparison treatment programs were equally effective." they also noted that not all youth benefited equally from the TFM programs, but attributed the differences primarily to differences in quality of the programs and demographic characteristics of the youth served.

Finally, in a rather sobering conclusion to their work, Weinrott et al. (1982) noted, "One thing is abundantly clear. Community based residential treatment of the type described herein is very, very expensive in light of the following results: First, only 45 percent of youths in both samples completed all phases of their programs. The remaining 55 percent failed to function adequately (13 percent), ran away and never returned (10 percent), were removed by the court for serious and repeated offenses (9 percent), or left for reasons unrelated to progress in treatment (23 percent). Second, there were very few differences between program completers and dropouts on outcome measures obtained during the second and third years following discharge'' (p. 197) (see also Chapter 10).

While there is now good evidence for positive in-program changes, the problem of generalization and maintenance (not unique to the TFM model) remains unsolved.

A true appreciation of the complexity of the five projects reviewed above can only be obtained by reading the many original reports which have described the various program elements as well as the research designs. One cannot help but be impressed by the immensity of the undertakings which, in all instances except Achievement Place, demanded the conceptualization and implementation of from two to six different treatment programs. Overall, however, the results of these major studies, at least in terms of the reduction of later arrests, were disappointing. We turn now to a more detailed analysis of the effectiveness of institutional treatment.

AN OVERVIEW OF TREATMENT EFFECTIVENESS

As we noted earlier in this chapter, there has been no dearth of reviews on the effectiveness of correctional treatment broadly defined. However, as most recently noted by Garrett (1984, 1985) there are problems associated with many of these reviews, including inadequate descriptions of the selection and/or exclusion criteria and sampling procedures for choosing which studies to review, lack of data as to the characteristics of the subjects, inadequate descriptions of outcome criteria, and the use of an arbitrary Alpha level (usually .05) as the criterion of success. Almost all reviews have had problems in assessing the effectiveness of different elements of the treatment (see also the discussion later in this chapter on component analysis), and in taking into consideration the possible interaction effects of offender, treatment, and setting characteristics. Finally, many of the reviews offered conclusions that went well beyond the data, including Martinson (1974) and Romig (1978) and reviews by the same authors sometimes offered different conclusions (see Garrett, 1984, p. 38 on Martinson, 1974; versus Lipton, Martinson, & Wilks, 1975).

Garrett's Meta-Analysis

Concurring with those who have argued that the effectiveness issue was unresolved (e.g., Sechrest, White, & Brown, 1979; Palmer, 1978), Garrett (1984,

1985) undertook an analysis designed to alleviate as many of the problems associated with the prior reviews as possible. Using the technique of meta-analysis mentioned earlier in this chapter, Garrett analyzed 111 studies that: (1) were completed between 1960 and 1983; (2) were located in an institution or community residential setting; (3) utilized adjudicated delinquents aged 21 or younger as subjects; and (4) included some form of control procedure. As we have noted earlier, there has been a considerable decline over the last 10 years in research on the effectiveness of institutional treatment. The decline is attested to by the fact that Garrett's review included 45 studies published in the five-year period 1975–1979, but only 10 in the four-year period 1980–1983.

To correct the problems noted in previous reviews, a large number of characteristics of each study were noted and coded, including: (1) control procedures, including a rating of internal validity (e.g., control and treatment groups not comparable at the start); (2) number of threats to internal validity; (3) number of treatments; (4) number of comparisons (e.g., older versus younger subjects); (5) number of outcome measures; (6) age of subjects; (7) sex of subjects; (8) ethnicity of subjects; (9) SES; (10) modal offense type (e.g., person versus property); (11) corrections history; (12) setting for treatment; (13) setting for controls; (14) treatment modalities used; (15) the dominant treatment; (16) employment of a typology for classifying subjects; (17) presence or absence of a post-release parole period; (18) a rating of intensity of treatment; (19) duration of treatment; (20) degree of detail of treatment description; and (21) cost effectiveness.

Effect sizes (ES) (the mean of the treatment group minus the mean of the control group divided by the standard deviation of the controls) were calculated for treatments in terms of recidivism, measures of institutional, psychological, community, and vocational adjustment, and academic improvement.

Overall, Garrett analyzed 225 treatment versus control comparisons and calculated 433 separate ESs. There were a total of 8076 experimentals and 4979 controls involved, of whom about 75 percent were males with an average age of about 16 years. Ninety of the studies had been carried out in institutions while 21 took place in a community residential setting. Thirteen different categories of dominant treatment were identified and seven different outcome categories utilized.

Obviously, the number of variables coded and the diversity within some codes (e.g., treatments and outcomes) required combining some categories for the mean ES to be based on enough studies (and cases) to be meaningful. Four superordinate treatment categories were created. In the psychodynamic category were studies of individual, group, and family counseling or therapy. A behavioral category encompassed contingency management, cognitive-behavioral treatment, Guided Group Interaction/Positive Peer Culture (GGI/PPC), and milieu therapy. The life skills category included drug/alcohol, academic, vocational, and outdoor experience approaches. In the "other" category were such treatments as music therapy, megavitamin treatment, small living unit size, and undifferentiated "skills." We note here that while the specific treatments were generally logically grouped, the inclusion of GGI/PPC and milieu therapy with contingency management and cognitive-behavioral intervention, whose procedures are highly specific, seems an unfortunate choice.

The results of this monumental and meticulous analysis cannot be described here in the rich detail in which they are found in Garrett (1984, 1985). Even the highlights, however, are informative. According to Garrett (1985, p. 293), "The overall average ES for all studies was +.37. This means that, across all treatments, settings, offender types, and outcome measures, the treated group performed, on the average, at a level of +.37 standard deviations above the level of the untreated group, the group that received only the regular institutional program. In other words, youths will, on the average, perform at the 64th percentile on the outcome measure relative to the juvenile who does not receive the treatment over and above the regular institutional program. The average subject, not receiving treatment (or receiving only the regular treatment) performs at the 50th percentile."

Effectiveness and Experimental Rigor

Since it is "conventional wisdom" that rigor of the experimental design enhances the confidence that can be placed in the results, a comparison of the average ES for the 58 more rigorous versus the 53 less rigorous studies was undertaken. The average ES was .24 for the former and .65 for the latter; a sizable difference. Thus, more rigorous controls *did* produce diminished effects (59th percentile versus 64th percentile for all studies) but positive effects nonetheless. Even the most rigorous procedure, random assignment, produced an ES of .23 in the 41 studies in which it was used. At the other extreme, the pre-post no-control produced an ES of 1.15 in the 27 studies in which it was used.

Comparative Effectiveness of Treatment Categories

When all studies were considered without regard for rigor, average ESs of .17 (57th percentile) for psychodynamic, .63 (74th percentile) for behavioral, .31 for life skills, and .30 for "other," were obtained. When only the more rigorous studies are included, average ESs dropped to .17, .30, .32, and .27, respectively.

When specific treatments were considered, many of the resulting ESs were based on very small numbers of studies. In light of our previous comment about the components of the superordinate behavioral category, it is of interest to note that, overall, contingency management (26 studies) and cognitive-behavioral approaches (17 studies) produced ES's of .86 and .56 while the values of GGI/PPC (8 studies) and milieu (5 studies) were .24 and .31. For the more rigorous studies only, the ES were .23, .44, −.30, and −.24 for the four treatments, although sample sizes were considerably reduced. Thus, the inclusion of GGI/PPC and milieu therapy in the behavioral category clearly dilutes the measured effectiveness of contingency management and cognitive behavioral interventions. It is also of interest that, overall, family therapy resulted in an ES of .81 as compared to .14 for individual and .17 for group therapies.

Effect on Different Outcome Measures

The results described so far relate to all outcome measures taken together. While there are many problems with recidivism, including how to define it (see Chapter 14), it is the effect of treatment on recidivism which has been at the core of the "what works" debate. Overall, the analysis of recidivism measures produced an average ES of .13 (55th percentile). The ES for the more rigorous studies was .10; for the less rigorous .29.

However, other measures of behavior change are also important, not only because of the problems with recidivism as an outcome, but in their own right. For example, in and of itself, better institutional adjustment results in less conflict, violence, and likelihood of injury, both physical and physiological, to clients and staff alike.

Since "adjustment" measures tend to be more "reactive," that is, subject to change by factors not related to the treatment, we will consider ESs for them derived only from the more rigorous studies. For the more rigorous studies only, the average ES for institutional adjustment was .27; for psychological adjustment, .45; for community adjustment, .72; for academic improvement, .42; and for vocational adjustment, .06. Among all the outcome measures across all studies and across both more and less rigorous breakdowns, only vocational adjustment shows essentially no treatment effects.

Outcome Measures by Treatments

Considering all the studies, without regard to rigor, recidivism was not reduced by psychodynamic interventions (ES $= -.01$) while being only modestly influenced by behavioral (.18), life skills (.28), and other (.33) interventions. Separating out the specific behavioral interventions revealed an ES of .25 for contingency management (10 studies), .24 for cognitive-behavioral (two studies), $-.07$ for GGI/PPC (two studies), and .79 for milieu therapy (two studies). Even given the surprising ES for milieu therapy, the data here further argue against the inclusion of GGI/PPC and milieu therapy in the behavioral category. Again, family therapy (.28) is more effective than group ($-.03$) or individual (.07). However, only group therapy was used in more than one study where recidivism was an outcome measure.

When only the rigorous studies are considered neither the grouped psychodynamic ($-.01$) nor behavioral ($-.08$) interventions were effective, while life skills (.30) and other (.33) interventions were. Unfortunately, the relatively small number of rigorous studies precluded analysis of the effect of individual treatments on recidivism. Following our procedure of considering only the more rigorous studies in evaluating other outcome measures, we find that institutional adjustment was more influenced by behavioral (.33), followed by psychodynamic (.30), and least by life skills ($-.80$). Psychological adjustment was clearly most affected by life skills (1.31) than by behavioral (.58) and psychodynamic (.48) interventions. Community adjustment was most influenced by "other" (1.02) then by psychodynamic (.91) and life skills (.38). There were no rigorous studies of behavioral treatments using community adjustment as an outcome measure. Academic skills were most affected by behavioral interventions (.61) and least by life skills (.42) and psychodynamic (.34) approaches.

Effect Size and Individual Differences

As was noted earlier in this chapter, critics of the "nothing works" conclusion argued that individual and subgroup differences interacted with settings, treatments, and outcome. In fact, the studies discussed in detail in the preceding section provided some data in support of that position, as does Chapter 5. At this level of analysis, however, Garrett found too few studies reporting the necessary data to examine the effects of individual treatments, so that the behavioral category may well have had its effectiveness diluted by the apparently mistaken inclusion of GGI/PPC.

While only 16 of the studies were with females, the overall ES was .58 (72nd percentile) for females versus .35 (64th percentile) for males. Among the rigorous studies the ES was .54 versus .22. There was a clear effect for age with ESs of .69 for those under 15, .35 for those 15 to 17, and .19 for those over 17. While Garrett found few studies reporting results separately by ethnicity, those that did found no difference by race. Not enough data on comparative SESs were analyzed to make differences interpretable.

While there was, again, little data on differential results of person versus property offenders, the few studies of person offenders provided an average ES of .35 as against .18 for 27 studies of property offenders. Given the likely unreliability of the raw data (offenses of both types not recorded for both groups), the true difference in ES could be even greater than the obtained difference due to a systematic bias in the raw data (likelihood of property offenses not attributed to those classified as person offenders). No differences in effect sizes were found between the nine studies which did (ES = .34) and did not ES = .37) use an offender typology. There was apparently inadequate data to assess different effects for different subtypes, however.

It is obvious that Garrett has made a major contribution toward answering the effectiveness question. Not only has she demonstrated an overall positive effect, but she has teased out the differential effects of differing interventions on differing outcome criteria. She has demonstrated that some interventions do work, and that in certain instances these interventions quite well. She has provided an unmistakably clear message that certain interventions, especially contingency management, cognitive-behavioral therapy, family therapy, and some of the life-skill interventions, warrant extensive further research.

Her results also indicate that those who are younger and less likely to be deeply enmeshed in a delinquent lifestyle are better bets for successful institutional intervention; results which run counter to the do-everything-else first philosophy of intervention.

However, it is important to keep in mind that what produced these positive effects were treatment programs that were formalized and structured enough to be evaluated. Under current conditions, it is not unlikely that much of what may be labeled "institutional treatment" is not treatment at all, but simply confinement with only the vaguest of rehabilitative intent.

The influence of Garrett's meta-analysis will likely first impact the researcher and scholar, then the better-informed correctional administrators, and, eventually, it is hoped, the policymakers. Let us hope that the 10 years post-Garrett will see a return to the more rehabilitative and humane ideal which was so severely damaged in the 10 years post-Martinson.

COMPONENT ANALYSIS: ORDER OUT OF CHAOS?

As we have seen, what may constitute institutional treatment may be very, very broadly defined. Thus, it is clearly necessary to delve more deeply into the question raised earlier in this chapter as to what *is* institutional treatment. In fact, we need to examine this question in even more detail than simply specifying a predominant treatment modality. What is needed is some sort of analysis to tell us what *specific* aspects of an intervention lead to what specific consequences.

Extracting components from a total institutional program is obviously no easy matter, and the components themselves have been described with greater or lesser specificity as witnessed by Jesness's (1975) identification of "positive regard" versus physical proximity (Solnick, Braukmann, Bedlington, Kirigin, & Wolf, 1981); both staff characteristics related to positive client outcome.

Given the difficulty of defining and measuring what might be important components and the problems associated with determining their effects independent of (or in interaction with) other components, it is little wonder that research is sparse. It should also not be surprising that most of what has been accomplished has been within a behavior modification context, since this approach has been historically concerned with the precise measurement of behavior.

In an early paper, Willner et al. (1977) argued that staff should be trained in behavior that not only is effective in changing clients but is preferred by clients themselves, citing Jesness's (1975) results as to the influence of positive regard as partial justification. In their research, they identified offering to help, "getting to the point," giving reasons why a behavior is important, providing descriptions of alternative behaviors, positive feedback, smiling, and positive motivational incentives as client-preferred behavior that new staff could be trained to perform. They also cited other work by their research group indicating that these preferred behaviors lead to positive client change.

As noted above, later research by Solnick, et al. (1981) identified staff's talking to and physical proximity to clients as factors in positive behavior change.

Spence and Lee (1985) found that boys' positive perceptions of staff were correlated with observed degrees of staff's asking for information and the use of praise by staff. However, these investigators did not attempt to study the direct effect of staff behavior on client performance.

Research into component analysis requires painstaking definition, careful observation and control of a host of other variables, thus making it difficult and expensive. If we are ever to know "what works" in any definitive way, such analyses seem absolutely necessary.

REFERENCES

American Correctional Association. (1986). *Juvenile and adult correctional departments, institutions, agencies, and paroling authorities.* College Park, MD: Authors.

Bangert-Drowns, R. L. (1986). Review of developments in meta-analytic method. *Psychological Bulletin, 99,* 388–399.

Billingsley, F., White D. R., & Munson, R. (1980). Procedural reliability: A rationale and example. *Behavioral Assessment, 2,* 229–241.

Braukmann, C. J., Kirigin, K. A., & Wolf, M. W. (1976). *Achievement Place: The researcher's prospective.* Paper presented at the meeting of the American Psychological Association, Washington, DC.

Beuhler, R. E., Patterson, G. R., & Furniss, J. M. (1966). The reinforcement of behavior in institutional settings. *Behavior Research and Therapy, 4,* 157–167.

Cavior, H. E., & Schmidt, A. A. (1978). Test of the effectiveness of a differential treatment strategy at the Robert F. Kennedy Center. *Criminal Justice and Behavior, 5* 131–139.

Colyar, D. E. (1983). Ten laws of residential treatment: What can go wrong when you're not looking. *Child Care Quarterly, 12,* 136–143.

Davidson, W. S., II, & Seidman, E. (1974). Studies of behavior modification and juvenile delinquency: A review, methodological critique, and social perspective. *Psychological Bulletin, 81,* 998–1011.

Emery, R. E., & Manholin, P., II. (1977). An applied behavior analysis of delinquency: The irrelevancy of relevant behavior. *American Psychologist, 32,* 860–873.

Garrett, C. J. (1984). *Meta-analysis of the effects of institutional and community residential treatment on adjudicated delinquents.* Unpublished doctoral dissertation, University of Colorado.

Garrett, C. J. (1985). Effects of residential treatment on adjudicated delinquents: A meta-analysis. *Journal of Research and Crime and Delinquency, 22,* 287–308.

Gerard, R. E. (1970). Institutional innovations in juvenile corrections *Federal Probation, 36,* 37–44.

Glass, G. V., McGaw, B., & Smith, M. L. (1981). *Meta-analysis in social research.* Beverly Hills, CA: Sage.

Hoefler, S. A., & Bornstein, P. H. (1975). Achievement Place: An evaluative review. *Criminal Justice and Behavior, 2,* 146–168.

Jesness, C. F. (1971). The Preston Typology Study. An experiment with differential treatment in an institution. *Journal of Research in Crime and Delinquency, 8,* 38–52.

Jesness, C. F. (1975). Comparative effectiveness of behavior modification and trans-actional analysis programs for delinquents. *Journal of Consulting and Clinical Psychology, 43,* 758–779.

Jesness, C. F. (1980). Was the Close-Holton project a "Bummer"? In R. R. Ross & P. Gendreau (Eds.), *Effective correctional treatment* (pp. 361–366). Toronto: Butterworths.

Jesness, C. F., & DeRisi, W. (1973). Some variations in techniques of contingency management in a school for delinquents. In J. S. Stumphauzer (Ed.), *Behavior therapy with delinquents.* Springfield, IL: Charles C. Thomas.

Johnson, V. S. (1977). An environment for treating youthful offenders: The Robert F. Kennedy Youth Center. *Offender Rehabilitation, 2,* 159–171.

Johnson, V. S. (1981). Staff drift: A problem in program integrity. *Criminal Justice and Behavior, 8,* 223–231.

Kassebaum, G., Ward, D., & Wilner, D. (1971). *Prison treatment and parole survival: An empirical assessment.* New York: Wiley.

Kifer, R. E., Lewis, M. A., Green, D. R., & Phillips, E. C. (1974). Training predelinquent youths and their parents to negotiate conflict situations. *Journal of Applied Behavior Analysis, 7,* 357–364.

Kirigin, K. A., Braukmann, C. J., Atwater, J. D., & Wolf, M. M. (1982). An evaluation of teaching-family (Achievement Place) group houses for juvenile offenders. *Journal of Applied Behavior Analysis, 15,* 1–16.

Levinson, R. B., & Gerard, R. E. (1973). Functional units: A different correctional approach. *Federal Probation, 39,* 8–16.

Lipton, D., Martinson, R., & Wilks, J. (1975). *The effectiveness of correctional treatment: A survey of treatment evaluation studies.* New York: Praeger.

Martinson, R. (1974). What works? Questions and answers about prison reform. *Public Interest, 35,* 22–24.

Mayers, M. D. (1980). *The hard-core delinquent.* Farnborough, Houts: Saxon House.

McCord, J. (1978). A thirty-year follow-up of treatment effects. *American psychologist, 33,* 284–289.

Miller, A. D., & Ohlin, L. E. (1985). *Delinquency and community: Creating opportunities and controls.* Beverly Hills, CA: Sage.

Minkin, N., Braukmann, C. J., Minkin, B. L., Timbers, G. D., Timbers, B. I., Fixsen, D. L., Phillips, E. L., & Wolf, M. M. (1976). The social validation and training of conversation skills. *Journal of Applied Behavior Analysis, 9,* 126–139.

Palmer, T. (1974). The Youth Authority's community treatment project. *Federal Probation, 38,* 3–14.

Palmer, T. (1975). "Martinson revisited." *Journal of Research in Crime and Delinquency, 12,* 133–152.

Palmer, T. (1978). *Correctional intervention and research: Current and future prospects.* Lexington, MA: Lexington Books.

Palmer, T. (1983). The effectiveness issue today: An overview. *Federal Probation, 47,* 3–10.

Palmer, T. (1984). Treatment and the role of classification: A review of basics. *Crime and Delinquency, 30,* 245–267.

Palmer, T., & Werner, E. (1972). *California Community Treatment Project, Research Report #12. The Phase III Experiment: Progress to date.* Sacramento: California Youth Authority.

Peterson, L., Homer, A. L., & Wonderlich, S. A. (1982). The integrity of independent variables in behavior analysis. *Journal of Applied Behavior Analysis, 15,* 477–492.

Phillips, E. L. (1968). Achievement Place: Token reinforcement procedures in a home-style rehabilitation setting for "pre-delinquent" boys. *Journal of Applied Behavior Analysis, 1,* 213–223.

Phillips, E. L., Phillips, E. A., Fixsen, D. L., & Wolf, M. M. (1971). Achievement Place: Modification of the behaviors of predelinquent boys within a token economy. *Journal of Applied Behavior Analysis, 4,* 45–59.

Phillips, E. L., Phillips, E. A., Fixsen, D. L., & Wolf, M. (1973). Achievement Place: Behavior shaping works for delinquents. *Psychology Today, 7,* 75–79.

Quay, H. C. (1977). The three faces of evaluation: What can be expected to work? *Criminal Justice and Behavior, 4,* 341–354.

Quay, H. C. (1986). Institutional treatment. In H. C. Quay & J. S. Werry (Eds.), *Psychopathological disorders of childhood* (3rd ed.) (pp. 558–582). New York: Wiley.

Regnery, A. S. (1985). From the administrator. *NIJ Reports,* November, p. 8. Washington, D.C.: National Institute of Justice/NCJRS.

Romig, D. A. (1978). *Justice for our children.* Lexington, MA: D.C. Heath.

Ross, R. R., & Gendreau, P. (1980). *Effective correctional treatment.* Toronto: Butterworths.

Salend, S. J. (1984). Therapy outcome research: Threats to treatment integrity. *Behavior Modification, 8,* 211–222.

Sanson-Fisher, B., & Jenkins, H. J. (1978). Intervention patterns between inmates and staff in a maximum security institution for delinquents. *Behavior Therapy, 9,* 703–716.

Scheirer, M. A., & Rezmovic, E. L. (1983). Measuring the degree of program implementation: A methodological review. *Evaluation Review, 7,* 599–633.

Sechrest, L., West, S. G., Phillips, M. A., Redner, R., & Yeaton, W. (1979). Some neglected problems in evaluation research: Strength and integrity of treatments. In L. Sechrest, S. G. West, M. A. Phillips, R. Redner, & W. Yeaton (Eds.), *Evaluation: Studies Review Annual,* Vol. 4. Beverly Hills, CA: Sage.

Sechrest, L. B., White, S. O., & Brown, E. D. (Eds.), (1979). *The rehabilitation of criminal offenders: Problems and prospects.* Washington, D.C.: National Academy of Science.

Sherraden, M. W., & Doons, S. W. (1984). Institutions and juvenile delinquency in historical perspective. *Children and Youth Services Review, 6,* 155–172.

Solnick, J. V., Braukmann, C. J., Bedlington, M. M., Kirigin, K. A., & Wolf, M. M.

(1981). The relationship between parent-youth interaction and delinquency in group homes. *Journal of Abnormal Child Psychology, 9,* 107–119.

Spence, S. H., & Lee, P. (1985). Observation and social validation of staff behaviors in a residential care setting. *Behavioral Psychotherapy, 13,* 43–58.

Thomas, P. R. (1974). *Effects of contingent-noncontingent structural environments on selected behaviors of Federal youth offenders.* Unpublished doctoral dissertation, West Virginia University.

Tremblay, R. E. (1984). Treatment of hard-core delinquents in residential establishments: The Ardsdale case. *British Journal of Criminology, 24,* 384–393.

Uranich, W. B. (1983–1984). Administration as an opposing force to rehabilitation: A case in point. *Juvenile and Family Court Journal, Winter,* 11–20.

Weinrott, M. R., Jones, R. R., & Howard, J. R. (1982). Cost-effectiveness of teaching family programs for delinquents: Results of a national evaluation. *Evaluation Review, 6,* 173–201.

Willner, A. G., Braukmann, C. J., Kirigin, K. A., Fixsen, D. L., Phillips, E. L., & Wolf, M. M. (1977). The training and validation of youth-pictured social behaviors of child-care personnel. *Journal of Applied Behavior Analysis, 10,* 219–230.

Wodarski, J. S., Feldman, R. A., & Pedi, S. J. (1974). Objective measurement of the independent variable: A neglected methodological aspect in community-based behavioral research. *Journal of Abnormal Child Psychology, 2,* 239–244.

Wolf, M. M., Phillips, E. L., Fixsen, D. L., Braukmann, C. J., Kirigin, K. A., Willner, A. G., & Schumaker, J. (1976). Achievement Place: The teaching family model: *Child Care Quarterly, 5,* 92–103.

CHAPTER 10

Community-Based Interventions

RAND GOTTSCHALK, WILLIAM S. DAVIDSON II, LEAH K. GENSHEIMER,
and JEFFREY P. MAYER

Michigan State University

As was indicated in Chapter 1, approaches to delinquency have been characterized by a struggle between a desire to help wayward children and the need to protect society from their wrongdoing (see also Krisberg & Austin, 1978; Empey, 1981). Similar debates have been held over the role of the juvenile justice system as a concerned surrogate parent versus its function as a criminal court of law. In addition, as discussed in Chapter 9, there is an overriding concern with the efficacy of interventions with delinquents.

The issue of juvenile delinquency has remained prominent in American society. In annual surveys conducted from 1972 through 1984, United States citizens were asked, "Is there more crime in this area than there was a year ago, or less?" In each year save one, the most common response was "more crime," indicating the belief that crime has been an ever increasing phenomena in this society (Gallup, 1982). Over the last decade, crime and lawlessness have been consistently mentioned as the first, second, or third issues about which people are most concerned (Roper, 1985).

Reported index crimes appeared to level off somewhat over the same period. There was an increase in all arrests of 31 percent. During this interval, arrests for violent crimes increased 37 percent (Federal Bureau of Investigation, 1981).

Although survey results and official records suffer from methodological difficulties which make direct interpretation a tricky undertaking (Kushler & Davidson, 1981), a strong case can be made that crime remains at the forefront of the American scene. Of particular concern has been the proportion of the crime problem which involves juvenile offenders. Juveniles comprise over one-fifth of all arrests (Federal Bureau of Investigation, 1984). It has been argued that youthful antisocial behavior is likely to produce antisocial behavior in adulthood, and hence interventions hold at least the theoretical promise of preventing adult criminal activity (Fareta, 1981; Robins, 1981). Further, juveniles are viewed as the group most amenable to intervention because of their age.

This chapter will present a meta-analysis of the research literature on community-based interventions with juvenile offenders. Prior to presenting the actual meta-analysis, the treatment efficacy question will be placed in its historical and theoretical context. Next, the specifics of the meta-analysis methods used will be described drawing heavily on the work of Hunter, Schmidt, and Jackson (1982) and Glass, McGaw, and Smith (1981). This will be followed by a description of the results of the meta-analysis. Finally, the implications of the results of the meta-analysis for community based interventions with juvenile offenders will be drawn.

HISTORICAL CONTEXT

As already noted in Chapter 1, the advent of official forms of juvenile delinquency dates back to the late 1800s. The beginning of the juvenile court is often cited as the beginning of community-based treatment for juveniles. Juvenile courts were to treat juvenile offenders as would a concerned surrogate parent. Further, whenever possible, juveniles were to be treated in "homelike" settings (Krisberg & Austin, 1978).

Created with all the fervor of a progressive social movement at the turn of the century, the handling of juvenile offenders proceeded with little controversy or attention until the middle 1960s. Interventions with juveniles then came under attack on three fronts: treatment efficacy, legal issues, and criticisms of intervention assumptions (Blakely & Davidson, 1981).

A series of systematic investigations and reviews appeared which criticized the effectiveness of treatment approaches to juvenile delinquents. Such reviews consistently concluded that traditional treatment approaches were not effective (Grey & Dermody, 1972; Kahn, 1965; Levitt, 1971; Lipton, Martinson, & Wilkes, 1975; Romig, 1978; see also Chapter 9).

The juvenile justice system was further criticized for failing to follow through on its "deal" with juvenile offenders under the *parens patriae* doctrine. Under this legal doctrine, juveniles had exchanged their legal rights to due process protection for the parent-like treatment of the court. Given both the inhumane conditions and ineffective treatments that juveniles were subjected to, the United States Supreme Court held in the case of Gault (1967) that procedural informality was no longer justified. In its majority opinion, the Supreme Court stated that regardless of the good intentions of procedural informality and parent-like treatment, "the condition of being a boy does not justify a kangaroo court" (see Chapter 1).

Finally, it was argued that intervention approaches had overly relied on assumptions that the causes of delinquency were best understood by studying the individual offenders. One conclusion from this assumption was that delinquency was primarily a lower-class phenomenon. However, several self-report studies of youths' involvement in various illegal behaviors indicated that such behaviors were widespread, and consequently raised the possibility that unlawful acts were unrelated to social standing (Erickson, 1973; Williams & Gold, 1972). Thus, it was argued that studying apprehended or institutionalized youth would tell us considerably more about the decision processes of juvenile justice system officials than it would about the causes of antisocial behavior (see Chapter 3).

It was against this background that support for community-based treatment was born. Community-based interventions received support from two rather divergent streams of theory and research. One major influence was the focus on individual differences. Essentially, this group's specific theoretical position emphasized the physiological and psychological differences between delinquent and nondelinquent youth. It was argued that individuals who possess certain physiological or psychological characteristics tend to become delinquent.

Within the area of juvenile delinquency, the classic paradigm was laid out by the Gluecks (1951). Their classic study compared 500 institutionalized delinquent subjects with 500 noninstitutionalized "normal" youth. From the large number of statistically significant differences which were observed, prediction schemes were developed to identify delinquents. Subsequent group comparison studies consistently reported differences between delinquents and nondelinquents (e.g., Andrew, 1981; Waldo & Dinitz, 1967; Smith and Ausnew, 1974; Prentice, 1972; Alexander & Parsons, 1973; Broder, Dunivant, Smith, & Sutton 1981; Gaffney & McFall, 1981; Stuart, 1971; Mednick & Christiansen, 1977; Spivack & Schure, 1982; see also Chapters 5, 6, & 12). Most attempts at community-based treatment drew heavily on one or more of these sets of theoretical propositions. It was argued that if individual differences could be reliably identified, then early identification of delinquents and preventive treatment in community settings is desirable and likely to produce the most positive effects.

The second prominent stream of theory and research used to explain delinquency and guide community-based intervention efforts focused on environmental variables. If the source of delinquent behavior is found in the natural environment, then treatment in far-away institutional settings makes little conceptual sense. As detailed in Chapter 3, cultures, social structures, social opportunities, social control mechanisms, and social institutions have all been cited as causally related to delinquency.

Observing that some societies were remarkably lacking in evidence of aggression led to propositions that cultural factors were the source of antisocial behavior. Viniaminov reported no cases of murder in the over 20 years he spent living among the Aleutian people (Pelto & Pelto, 1976). In contrast, it has been suggested that the social conflict inherent in complex materialistic societies such as the United States fosters crime due to anomie (Cloward & Ohlin, 1960; Mertin, 1957). In a related way, social control theory specified the processes through which many theoretical variables actually affect delinquent behavior. The theory suggested that a variety of conditions lead to the situation where the youth's ties to the conventional order are weakened (Hirshi, 1969; Elliot, Ageton, & Canter, 1979; Elliot & Voss, 1974; Polk & Schaefer, 1972).

A final position suggested that delinquency can only be understood in the context of both the behavior of individuals and the societal response to that behavior. Often termed "social labeling theory," such interactionist positions argued that society defined deviants. In essence, this position stated that environmental labeling, in response to a perceived deviant act, makes "deviants" deviant (e.g., Becker, 1963; Glaser, 1975; Matza, 1969). If labeling was a critical process in explaining delinquency, intervention in the community would minimize the negative labeling processes inherent in institutional treatment.

STATUS OF COMMUNITY-BASED INTERVENTIONS: THE NEED FOR META-ANALYSIS

By the middle 1970s, reviews of the efficacy of community-based interventions with juvenile delinquents began to appear. Scientific reviews of the research literature have been generally negative (Bailey, 1966; Grey & Dermody, 1972; Levitt, 1971; Lipton et al., 1975; Romig, 1978). These reviews have consistently pointed out the need for increased methodological rigor (see also Chapter 14).

This chapter will address the question of the efficacy of community-based treatment of juvenile offenders using the methods of meta-analysis proposed by Hunter et al. (1982) and Glass et al. (1981). As noted in Chapter 9, meta-analysis was developed in response to the perceived need to bring specificity, standardization, and replicability to the process of literature reviews. Typically, reviewers summarized a body of research literature by either their overall impression or vote counting. Vote counting, a less sophisticated form of cumulating results across studies, involves assessing how many of the group of studies reviewed demonstrated a significantly positive, significantly negative or no effect. Such reviews were often concluded by statements like "of the____studies reviewed,____percent demonstrated the hypothesized relationship." In the raging debates which often followed such reviews, particularly in such areas as the efficacy of psychotherapy, disagreements have often arisen over the method of the review, particularly arguments concerning the replicability of the study selection process (Smith, Glass, & Miller, 1980).

A further issue frequently involved in discussions of meta-analysis focuses on the conversion of results from different studies to a common metric. A serious problem with narrative and vote-counting reviews is the difficulty in replicating conclusions due to differences in outcome variables, research designs, and statistical standards across studies. Once the outcome variables have been converted to a standard metric, as in meta-analytic procedures, an examination of the relationship, if any, among outcomes and other study characteristics becomes possible. This allows the reviewer to address a series of interesting questions. For example, what is the strength of the evidence for the efficacy of community-based interventions with juvenile delinquents? What is the size of the effect which is observed? How strong is the relationship among various interventions and desired outcomes? Are there any particular characteristics of the interventions which appear to lead to more positive or more negative outcomes? Finally, are there particular methodological characteristics of research which are related to the size of the observed effects?

Aspects of the Meta-Analysis

Conceptual Domains and Sampling Strategy

This meta-analysis covers the published and unpublished literature from 1967 through 1983. These years included follow-ups of studies dating back to 1953. Three criteria were used to select studies. First, only outcome studies were included. A study had to measure dependent variables which showed generalization across time, behavior, and/or setting. For example, studies reporting only results of behavior within the treatment setting were excluded and considered process studies. Second, only studies which included officially labeled delinquents were included. The study had to involve youth referred by juvenile or family court officials or the police for official delinquency. This resulted in the exclusion of studies involving troubled youth, maladjusted youth antisocial youth, underachieving children, and adjustment reactions of adolescents. Given that the above labels may vary from locale to locale, we felt that including only officially defined delinquents would specify the population of interest much more precisely than would otherwise be possible. Third, the treatment had to take place either in the youth's own home or in a facility located in a community (as opposed to institutional) setting.

Two examples of the types of programs included should help the reader understand the type of program included in the meta-analysis. First, a variety of nonresidential programs were included, such as the police-based diversion program described by Davidson et al. (1977). This program involved having trained undergraduate college students work one-on-one with juvenile offenders using behavioral contracting and child advocacy intervention modalities, and was four and a half months in duration. Eight hours of intervention were provided per week in the youth's natural environment. Second, community-based residential programs, such as the teaching family model employed at Achievement Place already described in Chapter 9, were included. As noted, the Achievement Place program involved youth living in a group home of six to eight staffed by a teaching parent couple. A residential token economy tied to a variety of in-house and community behaviors constituted the intervention.

The meta-analysis was based on studies obtained from a computer search of *Psychological Abstracts* and a mail campaign to prominent authors in the area of juvenile treatment and delinquency. The computerized literature search used the following sequential key words: "juvenile delinquents," "treatment," "intervention," and "outcome studies."

Coding Methods for the Meta-Analysis

The aforementioned literature search produced 643 studies. Of these 643, 163 involved outcome studies with juvenile delinquents. These 163 studies were read for potential inclusion in the review.

One major point of clarification concerning coding should be emphasized. When we referred to a certain number of "studies," previously, this term was meant to signify one article or paper. Throughout the remainder of this chapter, the word "study" will be used in a manner consistent with meta-analytic practice. That is, "study" will refer to a single experimental or research design. An article or paper could contain multiple designs, each coded as a "study" for the purposes of meta-analysis. The articles and papers contained 90 studies (in a meta-analytic sense) used in the data analysis to follow.

The circumstances under which a given article or paper was separated into multiple "studies" should be emphasized. This meta-analysis takes a "treatment orientation" by separating an article into multiple designs when discrete treatments were used. For example, an article reporting the results of two different treatment modalities versus a control group, would be coded as two designs in the meta-analysis (e.g., treatment one versus control and treatment two versus control). We felt that this approach would best represent and depict the results of various treatment modalities employed in community settings. In general, the goal of the coding procedure was to capture important characteristics of the study (including treatment and subjects) and to specify a standard metric for outcome results.

STUDY CHARACTERISTICS. Table 10.1 presents a summary of the information coded for each study. These variables include coding of the study publication format and date, characteristics of the subjects, components of the intervention, characteristics of the investigator, and methodological characteristics of the study. Coding of these variables allowed for a broad description of the literature, and an assessment of the relationship among these variables and study outcomes.

EFFECT SIZE (ES) CALCULATION. Two different streams of work involving meta-analysis can be discerned. The more well-known work and procedure is that of Glass et al. (1981). This procedures was originally applied to the study of the effects of psychotherapy. Essentially, Glass et al. (1981) recommended coding all possible study characteristics that might be of importance and correlating these characteristics with an estimate of effect size.

The work of Hunter et al. (1982) comes from industrial organizational psychology. This area has faced numerous legal challenges to the issue of employment testing on the basis that the results of the tests underpredict the performance of minorities on the job. Hunter et al. (1982) developed their

TABLE 10.1.   Information Collected for Each Study

Study Form and Date

1. Source of study—coded book, journal, or other
2. Publication date

Subject Dimensions

1. Adjudicated—coded yes/no
2. Percent male
3. Average age

Relationhsip to Juvenile Justice System

1. Intervention inside system—coded yes/no
2. Intervention included diversion—coded yes/no

Intervention Components

1. Duration—the average length of the intervention in weeks
2. Intensity—the average number of hours of intervention
3. Primary type of intervention—coded once per study for: behavioral, educational/ vocational, individual psychotherapy, casework/probation, and other nonspecific
4. Types of intervention present—coded multiple times per study for: group therapy, modeling/role playing, token economies, academic, positive reinforcement, behavioral contracting, service brokerage, probation, vocational, intensive casework, advocacy, psychodynamic therapy, client centered therapy, transactional analysis, cognitive therapy, and reality therapy

Characteristics of Investigator

1. Discipline of authors
2. Intervener influence over treatment process—coded none, to some extent, to a great extent
3. Investigator influence over treatment process—coded none, to some extent, to a great extent

Methodological Characteristics

1. Implementation measurement—coded presence/absence of assessment of intervention integrity
2. Evidence of unplanned variability in intervention—presence/absence of evidence of lack of compliance or other problems in treatment integrity
3. Data collectors blind to experimental conditions and/or hypotheses—coded yes/no
4. Description of control group—coded no treatment, treatment as usual, subjects as own control (pre/post)

methodology to assess the impact of various statistical artifacts on the obtained validity of tests. Essentially, Hunter et al. (1982) recommended *first* statistically assessing the extent to which the variance in an observed relationship is due to various statistical artifacts (including sampling error). If more than 75 percent of the variance is due to statistical artifacts, it is reasoned that it is likely that the remaining portion of the variance is due to artifacts that cannot be assessed or corrected for (including typographical errors). If less than 75 percent of the variance is accounted for by statistical artifacts, then analyses of possible moderator variables proceeds.

As noted in Chapter 9, the heart of meta-analytic methods is the calculation of the ES. The ES is used to transform results of different statistical procedures into a common metric. The two approaches described above do not differ in their recommendations concerning the calculation of ES. Our research used four potential ES indices for each of several types of outcome variables. First, we assigned an overall effectiveness rating to each study. Second, a rating was assigned to the study based on the overall conclusion drawn by the study's author regarding the effectiveness of the treatment. Third, a specific rating of effectiveness was assigned to each dependent variable within each study based on our conclusions concerning the treatment effect on each dependent variable studied. These first three ratings of treatment efficacy were made on a three point scale of positive effect, no effect, and negative effect. These three indices represent alternative versions of "ballot box" or "voting methods" of literature review (Jackson, 1980).

Finally, standardized ESs were calculated for each reported pre/post change and experimental/control difference for each dependent variable within each study. In general, the ES was calculated by subtracting the control group or pre-mean from the experimental group or post-mean and dividing by the control group or pre-standard deviation, producing an ES in standard deviation units.

Table 10.2 summarizes the information coded for each dependent variable within each study. Types of dependent variables coded included recidivism, self-report delinquency, program behaviors, vocational behavior, academic performance, other social behavior, school or work attendance, attitudinal variables, self-esteem, ratings of global adjustment, and other cognitive variables.

RELIABILITY OF CODING PROCEDURE.   An estimate of inter-rater reliability was obtained by having two of the four authors code eight different studies. All possible pairs of the four authors were compared to one another. Across all variables included in the meta-analysis, the percentage of exact agreement was 86 percent. This was deemed acceptably high.

Results of the Meta-Analysis

Descriptive Findings

Table 10.3 provides a description of the variables included and is analogous to the demographics of the sample. The table has been divided into sections describing the publication form, subject dimensions, relationship to the juvenile justice system, components of the intervention, investigator characteristics, and methodological characteristics.

TABLE 10.2.   Calculation of Effect Size

For each of the following types of dependent variables, ratings were made for each study when sufficient data were present.

1. *Recidivism*—outcomes including arrests, court charges, or other indicants of official involvement in the juvenile justice system for illegal behavior. Up to three recidivism outcomes were coded per study.
2. *Self reported delinquency*—this outcome included self reports of illegal acts.
3. *Program behavior*—outcomes including assessments of within program behavior such as subsequent diagnoses, rates of release, violations of probation, rates of rule compliance, etc. Up to two program behavior outcomes were coded per study.
4. *Vocational behavior*—this outcome included all assessments of job or employment related performance.
5. *Academic behavior*—outcomes including assessments of academic performance such as achievement test, grades, etc. Up to two academic behavior outcomes were coded per study.
6. *Other social behavior*—outcomes including assessments of other interpersonal performances. Up to two social behavior outcomes were coded per study.
7. *School/work attendance in school or a job*—up to two attendance outcomes were coded per study.
8. *Self concept*—this outcome included assessments of esteem and self-concept.
9. *Other attitudinal*—this outcome included assessments of other attitudes.
10. *Other cognitive*—this outcome included assessments of othe cognitive variables.
11. *Ratings of global adjustment*—this outcome included ratings or reports of nonspecific adjustment not covered under the above variable categories.

Variables coded for each dependent variable:

1. *Method of data collection*—coded as behavioral observation, archival, self-report, paper and pencil, interview, rating by someone other than subject.
2. *Reliability assessment*—type of reliability reported, if any.
3. *Magnitude of reliability assessment.*
4. *Research design for specific dependent variable*—coded using the Campbell and Stanley (1966) numbering scheme.
5. *Length of follow-up period*—coded in weeks.
6. *Number of subjects involved in pre/post comparisons.*
7. *Effect size for pre/post comparison.*
8. *Effectiveness rating of pre/post change for specific dependent variable*—coded negative, zero, or positive.
9. *Number of experimental subjects involved in experimental/control comparisons.*
10. *Number of control subjects for experimental/control comparisons.*
11. *Effect size for experimental/control comparison.*
12. *Effectiveness rating of experimental/control difference for specific dependent variable*—coded negative, zero, or positive.

Seventy-three percent of the studies appeared originally in journals. The category "other" represents unpublished technical reports obtained as a result of the mail requests to well-known authors in the area. Most of the studies have been published since 1975. Again, it should be noted that the unit of analysis is the design rather than the study. The body of literature summarized by this review, in general, represents journal articles published after 1975.

TABLE 10.3. Description of Studies

Study Form and Date

1. Publication form:

	No. of studies	% of studies
Book	3	3%
Journal	65	73%
Other	22	24%

2. Publication date:

1967—1	1974—6	1979—4
1968—3	1975—9	1980—9
1971—1	1976—9	1981—18
1972—4	1977—10	1982—4
1973-6	1978—5	1983—1

Subject Dimensions

1. Percentage of studies involving youth who had been adjudicated	74%
2. Average percentage male in studies	76%
3. Median percentage male in studies	85%
4. Average size	14.6
5. Median age	14.5

Relationship to Juvenile Justice System

1. Intervention took place within system	38%
2. Intervention included diversion	52%

Intervention Components

1. Average weeks intervention duration	22.3
2. Median weeks intervention duration	14.9
3. Average hours intervention duration	41.8
4. Median hours intervention duration	15.1
5. Primary intervention type:	
Behavioral	28%
Educational/vocational	9%
Individual psychotherapy	6%
Group psychotherapy	18%
Case work/probation	13%
Nonspecific	27%
6. Percent of studies using:	
Service brokerage	29%
Academic	29%
Group therapy	28%
Positive reinforcement	27%
Vocational	24%
Modeling/role playing	22%
Advocacy	21%
Behavioral contracting	19%
Token economy	16%
Intensive casework	16%
Probation	11%
Client centered therapy	6%

(cont.)

TABLE 10.3. *(continued)*

Intervention Components

Psychodynamic therapy	4%
Cognitive therapy	2%
Transactional analysis	1%

Investigator Characterisics

1. Percent of authors who are psychologists	46%
2. Service deliverer influence:	
Great extent of influence	46%
Some influence	48%
No influence	6%
3. Experimenter influence:	
Great extent of influence	34%
Some influence	20%
No influence	46%

Methodological Characteristics

1. Percent of studies measuring implementations	33%
2. Evidence of unplanned treatment variation	21%
3. Percent of studies including blind data collectors	11%
4. Control group type:	
No treatment	34%
No control group	6%
Treatment as usual	44%
Subjects as own controls	12%
Other	3%
5. Percent of studies including random assignment to treatment	38%
6. Percent of studies including random assignment to intervener designs), or not control group	0%
5. Assignment of subjects to treatment—coded random, matching, or nonrandom	
6. Assignemtn of interveners to participants—coded as random, matching, or nonrandom	

Seventy-four percent of the studies involved youths who had been formally adjudicated through the system. The average sample in this study was composed of 76 percent males of an average age of 14.6. This would seem typical of the delinquent population. Thirty-eight percent of the interventions were delivered by representatives of the court system. Fifty-two percent of the interventions included some form of diversion.

The average intervention lasted roughly 22 weeks and involved 42 hours of contact between the intervener and the youths. The median figures are somewhat different and probably reflect the typical intervention better than do the averages. The median intervention lasted roughly 15 weeks and involved 15 hours of contact with the youths. A picture of not particularly intense interventions seemed to emerge. The primary intervention was mostly behavioral or nonspecific in nature. It is difficult to determine what the typical intervention involved in the way of service to the youth. However, it is safe to say that most interventions involved more than one type of program component. The most popular types of interventions were some type of service brokerage, academic support or counseling, group therapy, and/or positive reinforcement.

The majority of authors were psychologists. The next largest percentage was the "can't tell" category, followed by authors who were in the criminal justice field. No other grouping of authors represented more than 10 percent of the sample.

In all but 6 percent of the studies, the service deliverers had either some or a great deal of influence in designing the intervention. This indicates that this literature is dominated by studies using change agents central to the setting in which the intervention took place rather than by bringing in "outsiders" to deliver the treatment. Additionally, in the majority of the studies the investigator played a role in designing and implementing the intervention. However, the difference in these rates of involvement indicates that for the most part, investigators and service deliverers were not the same people.

Methodologically, these studies appear to have a number of problems. Few studies measured the implementation of the treatment (see Chapters 9 and 14), included data collectors blind to the experimental hypotheses, or used random assignment to treatment, and no studies included random assignment of the service deliverer. In addition, over 20 percent of the studies reported some kind of unplanned variation in the treatment. Finally, 50 percent of the studies included no control group, or had a treatment-as-usual control group, making it more difficult to estimate the true strength of the intervention.

Effectiveness Results

Table 10.4 shows the "ballot box" effectiveness ratings for each of the dependent variables. The results of both our ratings and those of the studies' authors suggest that most interventions have either a positive effect or no effect. Ratings of negative effect are rare. This pattern is true also for ratings averaged across all dependent variables (Calculated Overall Effectiveness). The pattern of positive results holds for most of the variables, with the exception of Self-Report Delinquency and Attendance.

The data in Table 10.5 lead to very different conclusions. Each of the columns in Table 10.5 requires some explanation. First, in order to produce reasonable numbers of studies for the various dependent variables, the calculated ES was averaged across a number of dependent variables. The overall ES is a combination of all ESs within a study averaged across the number of outcome variables. Recidivism was left as a single outcome variable. Behavioral outcomes are a combination of in-program behavior, academic performance, social behavior, and attendance. Attitudinal outcomes are a combination of cognitive measures, ratings of global adjustment, self-esteem, and attitude

TABLE 10.4.   Rated Effectiveness

Variable	Positive Effect	No Effect	Negative Effect
Overall Rating of Effectiveness			
Our rating	42(47%)	42(47%)	6(7%)
Author's rating	50(56%)	39(43%)	1(1%)
Recidivism			
Pre/Post vote	10(67%)	0	5(33%)
E/C vote	31(74%)	1(2%)	10(24%)
Self-Report Delinquency			
Pre/Post vote	0	17(94%)	1(6%)
E/C vote	2(10%)	18(85%)	1(5%)
Program Behavior			
Pre/Post vote	Insufficient number (N = 0)		
E/C vote	Insufficient number (N = 0)		
Academic Performance			
Pre/Post vote	3(75%)	0	1(25%)
E/C vote	Insufficient number (N = 0)		
Social Behavior			
Pre/Post vote	11(85%)	0	2(15%)
E/C vote	5(83%)	0	1(17%)
Attitude Measures			
Pre/Post vote	10(100%)	0	0
E/C vote	Insufficient number (N = 1)		
Attendance			
Pre/Post vote	3(43%)	0	4(57%)
E/C vote	9(69%)	0	4(31%)
Calculated Overall Effectiveness			
Pre/Post vote	31(66%)	10(21%)	6(13%)
E/C vote	41(54%)	25(33%)	10(13%)

measures. Column A is the number of studies or designs for each dependent variable. Column B is the total number of subjects across all studies. Column C is the mean ES averaged across each study. Column D is the average ES weighted by sample size such that those studies with more subjects are given more weight in the computation (Hunter et al., 1982). Column E is the variance of the ES corrected for sampling error. Column F is the percentage of the obtained variance that is due to sampling error. As discussed above, when

TABLE 10.5. Calculated Effect Size

Variable	A[a]	B[b]	C[c]	D[d]	E[e]	F[f]	G[g]
			Calculated Overall Effectiveness				
Pre/Post	35	3795	.927	.297	.420	8%	−0.96 to 1.56
E/C	66	11317	.365	.232	.077	23%	−0.31 to 0.77
			Recidivism				
Pre/Post	14	2514	.649	−.081	.323	7%	−1.56 to 1.19
E/C	61	11463	.325	.218	.080	21%	−0.34 to 0.77
			Behavioral Outcomes				
Pre/Post	19	1414	1.03	.697	.408	12%	−0.06 to 1.95
E/C	16	662	.398	.111	.154	39%	−0.66 to 0.88
			Attitudinal Outcomes				
Pre/Post	16	823	.515	.495	.052	61%	+0.05 to 0.94
E/C	10	253	.928	.588	.494	25%	−0.79 to 1.97

[a]Number of studies reporting relationship; [b]Total number of subjects across all studies reporting relationship; [c]Unweighted mean effect size; [d]Weighted mean effect size; [e]Variance across studies corrected for sampling error; [f]Percent of observed variance due to sampling error; [g]95% confidence interval of weighted effect size.

the variance due to sampling error is greater than 75 percent, then all variance is considered to be due to artifactual sources rather than to real differences among studies. If the variance due to all artifactual sources is less than 75 percent, then it is suggested that moderator variables exist. Finally, Column G presents the 95 percent confidence interval around each ES. It should be noted that in Table 10.5 the number of subjects overall and the number of subjects for Experimental/Control comparisons on recidivism differs in a counter-intuitive way. This is due to different methods of weighting. The number of subjects on Calculated Overall Effectiveness represents the total number of subjects across all studies averaged within study across dependent variables. The number of subjects on the other dependent variables represents the total number of subjects within each study added together within study and across study.

One way to summarize Table 10.5 would be to suggest that we are unable to reject the null hypothesis of no treatment effect. With the exception of pre/post attitudinal outcomes, all of the confidence intervals include zero. Additionally, the amount of variance due to sampling error does not reach substantial proportions with the exception of attitudinal outcomes. In all cases except the attitudinal outcomes, the pre/post effect sizes are greater than the experimental/control effect sizes. Given the selection, maturational, and historical artifacts likely to be operating in pre/post comparisons, particularly in adolescent populations, extreme caution is necessary. Since sampling error did not account for a large proportion of variance a search for moderator variables was carried out.

Moderator Variables

Table 10.6 presents the results of analyses which examined the relationship of study characteristics with rated effectiveness and calculated ES. Column A presents the correlation between calculated ES for the overall experimental/control comparison and the specific study characteristic. A dash represents that it was inappropriate to compute the correlation since the variable was categorical. A designation of "ns" indicates that no significant relationship was observed. Numerical entries represent significant correlations. Due to the exploratory nature of these analyses, a p < .10 criterion was used. Column B presents the same correlations for rated effectiveness. The ratings made by the coders of the study were used as the criteria since they were highly correlated with the authors' ratings. Finally, Column C presents relationships which were examined with categorical data. Included are the percentages of positive effect ratings for those studies falling in each category.

A number of interesting relationships are apparent. First, the date the study was published was negatively related to the ES and the rating of effectiveness. Older studies tended to have more positive effect sizes. There are a number of possible explanations for this finding. It could be that more recent studies were carried out more carefully than older studies. However, this assumes that studies which are better methodologically will obtain lower effect sizes. This is not necessarily the case (but see Chapter 9). Results to be discussed later suggest that there is a small positive correlation between ES and use of random assignment to treatment. A second explanation would posit that older studies used more intensive interventions than later studies. However, there is no support for this in the data. A third explanation which cannot be ruled out might be that older studies were published less often with negative results than newer studies. However, it should be noted that we did analyze unpublished studies that would not be expected to be subject to this same bias.

TABLE 10.6. Study Characteristics and Their Relationship to Outcome

	A[a]	B[b]	C[c]
Study Form and Date			
1. Source of study	—	—	42%
2. Publication date	−.22*	−.27	—
Subject Dimensions			
1. Adjudicated	—	—	28%*
2. Percent male	.32*	ns	—
3. Average age	ns	ns	—

TABLE 10.6   *(continued)*

	A[a]	B[b]	C[c]
Relationship to Juvenile Justice System			
Effectiveness rate when intervention:	—	—	40%
1. Inside system			
2. Included diversion	—	—	40%
Intervention Components			
1. Duration in weeks	ns	ns	—
2. Hours of treatment	.35*	ns	—
3. Primary intervention effectiveness rate:			
Behavioral (N=25)	—	—	64%*
Group psychotherapy (N=12)	—	—	50%*
Casework/probation (N=12)	—	—	33%*
Educational/Vocational (N=8)	—	—	50%*
Individual psychotherapy (N=5)	—	—	20%*
Other nonspecific (N=24)	—	—	38%*
4. Effectiveness rates for interventions including:			
Service brokerage (N=26)	—	—	27%
Academic (N=26)	—	—	31%
Group therapy (N=25)	—	—	28%
Positive reinforcement (N=24)	—	—	65%
Vocational (N=22)	—	—	32%
Modeling/role playing (N=20)	—	—	45%
Advocacy (N=19)	—	—	32%
Behavioral contracting (N=17)	—	—	53%
Token economy (N=14)	—	—	57%
Intensive casework (N=14)	—	—	36%
Probation (N=10)	—	—	60%
Client centered therapy (N=5)	—	—	80%
Psychodynamic therapy (N=4)	—	—	50%
Cognitive therapy (N=2)	—	—	0%
Transactional analysis (N=1)	—	—	100%
Characteristics of Investigator			
1. Intervener influence over treatment process	.25*	.37	52%*
2. Investigator influence over treatment process	.51*	.41	72%*
Methodological Characteristics			
1. Implemented measure	ns	−.19	10%*
2. Unplanned variability in intervention	ns	ns	7%
3. Data collectors blind to experimental hypothesis	ns	ns	40%
4. Type of control group:			
No treatment	—	—	42%
No control group	—	—	40%
Treatment as usual	—	—	45%
Subjects as own controls	—	—	66%
5. Random assignment to treatment	.16*	ns	44%

*p < .10

[a]Correlation between calculated overall experimental/control effect size and study characteristic; [b]Correlation between rated effectiveness and study characteristic; [c]Percentage of positive effects for variable falling into category.

Subject dimensions did relate to the outcome of the study. Nonadjudicated youth were more likely to be successful than adjudicated youth. This relates to the effectiveness of diversion programs. Additionally, the more the sample was composed of males, the more likely a higher ES.

Relationship to the juvenile justice system did not appear to be a viable moderator. However, a few intervention components were related to outcome. The number of hours of treatment was significantly related to the ES, indicating that the more treatment that was provided, the greater the effect. In addition, the primary intervention type was related to the effectiveness of the program such that those interventions involving behavioral, educational/vocational, and group psychotherapy interventions were more likely to be effective.

Intervener and investigator influence over the treatment process were both significantly related to ES, rated effectiveness, and rate of effectiveness. However, of the two, the investigators influence appears to be slightly more important as indicated by the size of the correlations and difference in effectiveness rates. This difference in correlation does not approach statistical significance, and thus no interpretation will be made of it.

Finally, in terms of methodological characteristics, the use of an implementation measure was significantly negatively related to rated effectiveness. The low success rate combined with this negative correlation could indicate that a measure of implementation is used by authors as an excuse when the treatment does not work. In other words, if the treatment does not produce the expected positive findings, then the author looks to see if the treatment was truly implemented as planned. If everything goes well, on the other hand, there is no need for the authors to monitor the implementation. Somewhat surprisingly, random assignment to treatment was positively related to the mean ES. In light of the findings of this review, it could be that studies involving random assignment to treatment were conducted with either higher quality interventions or had less variability within the control group (thus producing a larger effect size) than studies that did not randomly assign subjects to treatment. Given the low effect sizes reported in this review, it may be that one needs a thorough study in order to detect the rather small effects of these interventions.

Discussion and Implications

We have reported the results of a meta-analysis to assess the size of treatment effects with juvenile delinquents in community settings. This method, putting the results from different studies into a common metric, provides more definitive evidence concerning the effects of treatment than either any one study alone or than a traditional literature review. Obviously, analyzing 90 studies involving over 11,000 subjects, allowed a much more powerful look at the issue of treatment effectiveness than any one single study could possibly do.

It was found that treatments in community settings did not have a large effect on outcomes; findings parallel to those conclusions drawn in earlier reviews (Grey & Dermody, 1972; Kahn, 1965; Levitt, 1971; Lipton et al., 1975; Romig, 1978). In that light, it should be noted that vote-counting indices tended to show more positive treatment effects than did the calculation of ESs. At least two different explanations are possible. First, study authors are usually invested in the outcome of the treatment and would tend to emphasize the positive effects of the treatment (however small) rather than the finding of no effect. Emphasizing a finding of no effect can lead to accusations of accepting the null hypothesis, a dubious practice at best.

Second, most literature in this area does not report (or calculate) standardized ESs used with traditional experimental designs such as omega squared and eta squared (Davidson & Seidman, 1974). Without the calculation of the amount of variance in the dependent variable due to the treatment, one can be misled by a finding of statistical significance into accepting that there is a large treatment effect. The methods employed here demanded that ES be considered.

We found that almost all of the confidence intervals included zero for the calculated ES, indicating that the null hypothesis of no effect for treatment could not be ruled out. However, this finding should be considered with a number of cautions. First, stating that the treatments had no effect is accepting the null hypothesis with all the dangers inherent in that position. Second, although most of the confidence intervals did include zero, most of the weighted ES and all of the unweighted ESs were positive in direction. Similar findings have led others to conclude positive effects in the context of treatment generally (e.g., Smith et al., 1980; see also Chapter 9). Third, the meta-analysis covered all studies regardless of any judgment concerning quality. Such inclusion might have led to the addition of variance making the confidence intervals for the ESs larger than might have been the case. Finally, treatments tended to be of short duration both in terms of intensity and length. It may be that most interventions simply were not powerful enough (see Chapter 14).

This last explanation seems to be supported somewhat by the data as shown by the positive correlation between ES and length of treatment. In addition, we found some evidence of experimenter effects in the positive correlation among the amount of intervener and service deliverer influence and ES. There was also some evidence that unplanned treatment variation as assessed by measurement of the treatment implementation was used by authors to account for lack of significant or strong treatment effects rather than as an accurate reflection of treatment integrity.

These findings suggest some circumstances under which community interventions with delinquents may have positive effects. If a strong treatment is used and care is taken *during* the treatment to ensure that the treatment is actually being implemented as designed, then more positive effects may emerge, as has been suggested before (e.g., Romig, 1978).

Finally, this study was hindered by the lack of complete reporting of results that is the plague of all meta-analytic investigations. In many studies, the information reported concerning treatment effects, intervention components, and subject characteristics was very sketchy. Past research reports cannot be made more complete in these respects. However, in order that future quantitative literature reviews may have a more complete database to draw on, it is imperative that future research reports be more detailed in their descriptions than past research.

REFERENCES

Alexander, J. F., & Parsons, B. V. (1973). Short-term behavioral intervention with delinquent families: Impact on family process and recidivism. *Journal of Abnormal Psychology, 81,* 219–225.

Andrew, J. M. (1981). Delinquency: Correlating variables. *Journal of Child Clinical Psychology, 10,* 136–140.

Bailey, W. (1966). Correctional outcome: An evaluation of 100 reports. *Journal of Criminal Law, Criminology, and Police Science, 57,* 153–160.

Becker, H. S. (1963). *The outsiders.* Clencoe, IL: The Free Press.

Blakely, C., & Davidson, W. S., (1981). Prevention of aggression. In A. Goldstein, E. Carr, W. S. Davidson, & P. Wehr (Eds.), *In response to aggression.* (pp. 249–270) New York: Pergamon Press.

Broder, P. K., Dunivant, N., Smith, E. C., & Sutton, L. P. (1981). Further observations on the link between learning disabilities and juvenile delinquency. *Journal of Educational Psychology, 73,* 838–850.

Cloward, R., & Ohlin, L. (1960). *Delinquency and opportunity.* Clencoe, IL: The Free Press.

Davidson, W. S., & Seidman, E. (1974). Studies of behavior modification and juvenile delinquency. *Psychological Bulletin, 81,* 998–1011.

Elliot, D. S., Ageton, S. S., & Canter, R. J. (1979). An integrated theoretical perspective on delinquent behavior. *Journal of Research in Crime and Delinquency, 16,* 3–27.

Elliot, D. S., & Voss, H. L. (1974). *Delinquency and dropout.* Lexington, MA: Lexington Press.

Empey, L. T. (1981). *American Delinquency: Its meaning and construction.* Homewood, IL: Dorsey Press.

Erickson, M. L. (1973). Group violations, socioeconomic status, and official delinquency. *Social Forces, 52,* 41–52.

Fareta, G. A. (1981). A profile of aggression from adolescence to adulthood. *American Journal of Orthopsychiatry, 51,*439–453.

Federal Bureau of Investigation. (1981). *Uniform Crime Reports.* Washington, DC: U.S. Government Printing Office.

Federal Bureau of Investigation. (1984). *Uniform Crime Reports.* Washington, DC: U.S. Government Printing Office.

Gaffney, L. R., & McFall, R. M. (1981). A comparison of the social skills in delinquent and nondelinquent adolescent girls using behavioral role-playing inventory. *Journal of Consulting and Clinical Psychology, 49,* 959–967.

Gallup, G. H. (1982). *The Gallup report: Report No. 200.* Princeton, New Jersey.

Glaser, D. (1975). *Strategic criminal justice planning.* Washington, DC: U.S. Government Printing Office.

Glass, G. V., McGaw, G., & Smith, M. L. (1981). *Meta-analysis in social research.* Beverly Hills, CA: Sage.

Glueck, S., & Glueck, E. (1951). *Unraveling juvenile delinquency.* Cambridge, MA: Harvard University Press.

Grey, A. L., & Dermody, H. E. (1972). Report of casework failure. *Social Casework, 16,* 207–212.

Hirchi, T. (1969). *Causes of delinquency.* London: University of California Press.

Hunter, J., Schmidt, F., & Jackson, G. (1982). *Meta-analysis: Cumulating research findings across studies.* Beverly Hills, CA: Sage.

Jackson, G. B. (1980). Methods for integrative reviews. *Review of Educational Research, 50,* 438–460.

Kahn, A. J. (1965). A case of premature claims. *Crime and Delinquency, 11,* 217–228.

Krisberg, B., & Austin, J. (1978). *The children of Ishmael.* Pale Alto, CA: Mayfield Press.

Kushler, M., & Davidson, W. S. (1981). Community and organizational level change. In A. Goldstein, E. Carr, W. Davidson, & P. Wehr (Eds.), *In response to aggression.* (Pp. 346–401). New York: Pergamon.

Levitt, E. L. (1971). Research on psychotherapy with children. In A. Bergin & S. Garfield (Eds.), *Handbook of psychotherapy and behavior change.* (Pp. 474–494). New York: Wiley.

Lipton, D., Martinson, R., & Wilks, J. (1975). *The effectiveness of correctional treatment.* New York: Praeger.

Matza, D. (1969). *Becoming deviant.* Englewood Cliffs, NJ: Prentice-Hall.

Mednick, S., & Christiansen, S. O. (1977). *Biosocial basis of criminal behavior.* New York: Gardner Press.

Merton, R. K. (1957). *Social theory and social structure.* New York: The Free Press.

Pelto, G. H., & Pelto, P. J. (1976). *The human adventure.* New York: Macmillan.

Polk K., & Schaefer, W. K. (1972). *Schools and delinquency.* Englewood Cliffs, NJ: Prentice-Hall.

Prentice, N. M. (1972). The influence of live and symbolic modeling on promoting moral judgements of adolescent delinquents. *Journal of Abnormal Psychology 80,* 157–161.

Robins, L. N. (1981). Epidemiological approaches to natural history research. *Journal of the American Academy of Child Psychiatry, 20,* 566–580.

Romig, D. A. (1978). Diversion from the juvenile justice system. In D. A. Romig (Ed.), *Justice for our children.* (pp. 117–123). Lexington, MA: Lexington Books.

Roper Organization. (1985). Opinion roundup. *Public Opinion, 5,* 12.

Smith, M. L., Glass, G. V, & Miller, T. I. (1980). *The benefits of psychotherapy.* Baltimore: Johns Hopkins University Press.

Smith, P. M., & Ausnew, H. R. (1974). Socialization as related to delinquency classification. *Psychological Reports, 34,* 677-678.

Spivack, G., & Shure, M. B. (1982). The cognition of social adjustment. In B. B. Lahey and A. E. Kazdin (Eds.)., *Advances in child clinical psychology.* (pp. 139-164) New York: Plenum.

Stuart, R. B. (1971). Behavioral contracting within the families of delinquents. *Journal of Behavior Therapy and Experimental Psychology, 2,* 1-11.

Waldo, G. P., & Dinitz, S. (1967). Personality attributes of the criminal: An analysis of research studies 1950-1965. *Journal of Research in crime and Delinquency, 4,* 185-202.

Williams, J. R., & Gold, M. (1972). From delinquent behavior to official delinquency. *Social Problems, 20,* 209-229.

PAPERS REVIEWED IN THE META-ANALYSIS

Alexander, J. F., & Parsons, B. V. (1973). Short term behavioral intervention with delinquent families. *Journal of Abnormal Psychology, 81,* 219-225.

Alexander, R. N., Corbett, T. F., & Smigel, J. (1976). The effects of individual and group consequences on school attendance and curfew violations with predelinquent adolescents. *Journal of Applied Behavioral Analysis, 9,* 221-226.

Barkwell, L. J. (1976). Differential treatment of juveniles on probation: An evaluative study. *Canadian Journal of Criminology and Corrections, 18,* 363-378.

Baron, R., & Feeney, F. (1973a). *Preventing delinquency through diversion: The Sacramento County Probation Department 601 Diversion Project.* Report to the Sacramento County Probation Department.

Baron, R., & Feeney, F. (1973b). *The Sacramento County Probation Department 601 Diversion Project: A first year report.* Report to the Sacramento County Probation Department.

Braukmann, C. J., Fixsen, D. L., Phillips, E. L., & Wolf, M. M (1974). An analysis of a selection interview training package for predelinquents at Acheivement Place. *Criminal Justice and Behavior, 1,* 30-42.

Collingwood, T. R., & Genthner, R. W. (1980). Skills therapy as a treatment for juvenile delinquents. *Professional Psychology, 11,* 591-598.

Collingwood, T. R., Williams, H., & Douds, A. (1976). An HRD approach to police diversion for juvenile offenders. *Personnel and Guidance Journal, 54,* 435-437.

Cotton, M., & Fein, D. (1976). Effectiveness of a community-based treatment program in modifying aggressiveness of delinquent behavior. *Corrective and Social Psychiatry and Journal of Behavior Technology, Methods and Therapy, 22,* 35-38.

Csapo, M., & Agg, B. (1976). Educational rehabilitation of delinquents in a community setting. *Canadian Journal of Criminology and Corrections, 18,* 42-48.

Davidson, W. S., Koch, J. R., Lewis, R. G., & Wresinski, M. D. (1981). *Evaluation strategies in criminal justice.* New York: Pergamon Press.

Davidson, W. S., & Robinson, M. R. (1975). Community psychology and behavior modification. *Corrective and Social Psychiatry, 21,* 1-12.

Davidson, W. S., Seidman, E., Rappaport, J., Berck, P. L., Rapp, N. A., Rhodes, W., & Herring, J. (1977). Diversion programs for juvenile offenders. *Social Work Research and Abstracts, 13,* 40-49.

Davidson, W. S., & Wolfred, T. R. (1977). Evaluation of a community-based behavior modification program for prevention of delinquency: The failure of success. *Community Mental Health Journal, 13,* 296-306.

Douds, A. F., & Collingwood, T. R. (1978). Management by objectives: A successful application. *Child Welfare, 57,* 181-185.

Dunford, F. W., Osgood, D. W., & Weichselbaum, H. F. (1981). *National evaluation of diversion projects.* Washington, D.C.: The National Institute of Juvenile Justice and Delinquency Prevention.

Eitzen, D. S. (1974). Impact of behavior modification techniques on locus of control of delinquent boys. *Psychological Reports, 35,* 1317-1318.

Eitzen, D. S. (1975). The effects of behavior modification on the attitudes of delinquents. *Behavior Research and Therapy, 13,* 295-299.

Eitzen, D. S. (1976). The self-concept of delinquents in a behavior modification treatment program. *Journal of Social Psychology, 90,* 203-206.

Eller, B. F., & Stone, J. (1979). Corrective procedures for academic failure and school truancy with a delinquent adolescent male. *Corrective and Social Psychiatry and Journal of Behavior Technology, 25,* 21-24.

Elliot, D. S., & Blanchard, F. (1975). *An impact study of two diversion projects.* Paper presented at the American Psychological Association, Chicago.

Elliot, D. S., & Knowles, B. A. (1978). *Social development and employment: An evaluation of the Oakland Youth Work Experience Program.* Paper presented at the Conference on Employment Statistics and Youth, UCLA.

Fryrear, J. L., Nuell, L. R., & Ridley, S. D. (1974). Photographic self-concept enhancement of male juvenile delinquents. *Journal of Counseling and Clinical Psychology, 42,* 915.

Garber, J., Tapp, J. T., Dundan, M., Tulkin, S. R., & Jens, K. (1976). A psychoeducational therapy program for delinquent boys: An evaluation report. *Journal of Drug Education, 6,* 331-342.

Gilbert, G. R. (1977). Alternative routes: A diversion project in the juvenile justice system. *Evaluation Quarterly, 1,* 301-318.

Haapanen, R., & Rudisill, D. (1980). *The evaluation of youth service bureaus.* Final report to Law Enforcement Assistance Administration.

Handler, E. (1975). Residential treatment programs for juvenile delinquents. *Social Work, 20,* 217-222.

Higgins, P. S. (1978). Evaluation and case study of a school-based delinquency prevention program: The Minnesota youth advocate program. *Evaluation Quarterly, 2,* 215-235.

Jackson, P. (1983). Some effects of parole supervision on recidivism. *British Journal of Criminology, 23,* 17-34.

Kahn, M. W., Lewis, J., & Galvez, E. (1974). An evaluation study of a group therapy procedure with reservation adolescent indians. *Psychotherapy: Theory, Research and Practice, 11,* 239-242.

Kifer, R. E., Lewis, M. A., Green, D. R., & Phillips, E. L. (1974). Training predelinquent youths and their parents to negotiate conflict situations. *Journal of Applied Behavior Analysis, 7,* 357–364.

Kirgin, K. A., Braukmann, C. J., Atwater, J. D., & Wolf, M. M. (1982). An evaluation of teaching-family (Achievement Place) group homes for juvenile offenders. *Journal of Applied Behavior Analysis, 15,* 1–16.

Klein, N., Alexander, J., & Parsons, B. (1977). Impact of family systems intervention on recidivism and sibling delinquency: A model of primary prevention and program evaluation. *Journal of Consulting and Clinical Psychology, 45,* 469–474.

Lee, R., & Haynes, N. M. (1978). Counseling juvenile offenders: An experimental evaluation of Project Crest. *Community Mental Health Journal, 14,* 267–271.

Lipsey, M. W., Cordray, D. S., & Berger, D. E. (1981). Evaluation of a juvenile diversion program: Using multiple lines of evidence. *Evaluation Review, 5,* 283–306.

O'Dell, B. N. (1974). Accelerating entry into the opportunity structure: A sociologically-based treatment for delinquent youth. *Sociology and Social Research, 58,* 312–317.

Palmer, T., Bohnstedt, M., & Lewis, R. (1978). The evaluation of juvenile diversion projects: Final report. *Report to the Law Enforcement Assistance Administration.*

Palmer, T. B. (1972). *The group home project: Differential placement of delinquents in group homes.* California Youth Authority.

Parsons, B. V., & Alexander, J. F. (1973). Short-term family intervention. *Journal of Consulting and Clinical Psychology, 41,* 195–201.

Piercy, F., & Lee, R. (1976). Effects of a dual treatment approach on the rehabilitation of habitual juvenile delinquents. *Rehabilitation Counseling Bulletin, 19,* 482–491.

Quay, H. C., & Love, C. (1977). The effect of a juvenile diversion program on rearrests. *Criminal Justice and Behavior, 4,* 377–396.

Reid, J. B., & Patterson, G. R. (1976). The modification of aggression and stealing behavior of boys in the home setting. In E. Ribes-Inesta & A. Bandura (Eds.), *Analysis of delinquency and aggression.* (pp. 165–173) Hillsdale, NJ: Erlbaum.

Roundtree, G. A., Parker, J. B., & Jones, A. (1979). Behavioral management in the resocialization of a group of adjudicated delinquents. *Corrective and Social Psychiatry and Journal of Behavior Technology, Methods, and Therapy, 25,* 15–17.

Savery, L. J., & Whitaker, J. M. (1982). Juvenile diversion: An experimental analysis of effectiveness. *Evaluation Review, 6,* 753–774.

Schwitzgebel, R., & Baer, D. (1967). Intensive supervision by parole officers as a factor in recidivism reduction of male delinquents. *The Journal of Psychology, 67,* 75–82.

Shore, M., & Massimo, J. (1973). After ten years: A follow-up study of comprehensive vocationally oriented psychotherapy. *American Journal of Orthopsychiatry, 43,* 128–132.

Spence, S. H., & Marzillier, J. S. (1979). Social skills training with adolescent male offenders: I. Short term effects. *Behavior Research and Therapy, 17,* 7–16.

Spence, S. H., & Marzillier, J. S. (1981). Social skills training with adolescent male offenders: II. Short term, long term and generalized effects. *Behavior Research and Therapy, 19,* 349–368.

Spergel, I. A., Reamer, F. G., & Lynch, J. P. (1981). Deinstitutionalization of status offenders: Individual outcome and system effects. *Journal of Research in Crime and Delinquency, 6,* 4–33.

Venezia, P. (1972). Unofficial probation: An evaluation of its effectiveness. *Journal of Research in Crime and Delinquency, 9,* 149–170.

Viano, E. C. (1975). Growing up in an affluent society: Delinquency and recidivism in suburban America. *Journal of Criminal Justice, 3,* 223–235.

Weathers, L., & Liberman, R. P. (1975). Contingency contracting with families of delinquent adolescents. *Behavior Therapy, 6,* 353–366.

Weinrott, M. R., Jones, R. R., & Howard, J. R. (1982). Cost-effectiveness of teaching family programs for delinquents. *Evaluation Review, 6,* 173–201.

Werner, J. S., Minkin, N., Minkin, B. L., Fixsen, D. L., Phillips, E. L., & Wolf, M. M. (1975). Intervention package: An analysis to prepare juvenile delinquents for encounters with police officers. *Criminal Justice and Behavior, 2,* 55–85.

Willner, A. G., Braukmann, C. J., Kirgin, K. A., & Wolf, M. M. (1977). Achievement Place: A community treatment model for youths in trouble. In D. Marholin (Ed.), *Child behavior therapy.* (pp. 239–273) New York: Gardner Press.

Wunderlich, R. A., Lozes, J., & Lewis, J. (1974). Recidivism rates of group therapy participants and other adolescents processed by a juvenile court. *Psychotherapy: Theory, Research, and Practice, 11,* 243–245.

CHAPTER 11

Individual, Group, and Family Interventions

DONALD A. GORDON and JACK ARBUTHNOT

Ohio University

In coping with the problem of juvenile delinquency, society struggles between protecting and rehabilitating children and adolescents and protecting society as the victim of juvenile crime. These disparate goals have been the focus of much debate within the juvenile justice system. As already discussed in Chapters 9 and 10, central to this debate is the efficacy of various interventions (rehabilitative efforts) to treat and prevent delinquency, and public concern lends an urgency to finding answers as to the most effective approach to take. As was also pointed out in Chapter 10, the bulk of literature reviews of various rehabilitative programs for juvenile offenders have had a decidedly negative tenor. It is against this backdrop of pessimism that this chapter is written. In the authors' views, the pessimism is justified, but not on the basis of negative outcomes of treatment studies. It is the ability of the collective rehabilitative and scientific community to evaluate treatment approaches that engenders our pessimism.

The scope of this chapter is the portrayal and evaluation of psychologically based interventions that focus on the juvenile delinquent individually, in groups with other delinquents, or in the delinquent's family. Excluded are interventions that are primarily vocational and educational in nature. Several criteria were applied in selecting studies to evaluate. Studies had to be well designed so that obvious extraneous factors could be controlled (such as maturation). Random assignment of delinquents to treatment and control groups was preferred. Studies with comparison groups matched on important variables were also included. The target population had to be delinquents, or children labelled as predelinquents because of antisocial and disruptive behavior. The outcome measures had to be related to delinquency, such as truancy or rearrests, rather than personality changes. Exceptions to these criteria were occasionally made when a study was noteworthy either because of the clarity of the intervention applied or its basis in theory related to delinquency causation.

INDIVIDUAL APPROACHES

The most frequently used specific treatment approach for delinquents, both in institutions and in community settings, has been individual counseling or therapy. A one-on-one relationship between a juvenile and a caseworker, social worker, psychologist, or psychiatrist has been seen as the mainstay of rehabilitative attempts to change delinquents' behavior to fit conventional norms. Several historical trends and practical considerations are responsible for the continued predominance of the individual-oriented approach.

One view of delinquency (see Chapter 6) is that it is caused by defects in the personality of the delinquent, and that delinquency could best be understood by studying individual differences between delinquents and normal children. Helping professionals, particularly mental health personnel, were the most appropriate people to diagnose and remediate personality disorders. Their training has been heavily influenced by the medical model, with its attendant exclusive focus on the individual. For example, most of the practicum or intervention training for mental health (social work, psychiatry, clinical psychology) professionals is with individuals rather than with groups or systems. This defect or medical model view of juvenile delinquency is consistent with society's view of the delinquent as being deviant, rather than seeing the disruptive adolescent as the product of a particular social system that is dysfunctional. In the medical model, conceptual simplicity is usually preferred over complexity.

Most settings where treatment is delivered favor an individual focus. Community outpatient services such as mental health clinics can more easily schedule appointments and bill for individuals who come to their facility than they can go to the neighborhoods, homes, and schools of delinquents. Staff efficiency and safety are also frequently voiced objections to outreach efforts. In addition, juvenile courts can refer or coerce individuals into treatment more readily than can significant others (family, peers, teachers). Finally, in institutional settings, often located far from the juvenile's community, individual treatment may be the only supplement to the institutional milieu (see Chapter 10). It is also the case that individual treatment may be *the* treatment studied with institutional programs.

Casework

Casework involves not only regular individual counseling sessions, often aimed at establishing a supportive relationship and exploring the causes of the delinquent behavior, but also networking with other agencies. When casework as the primary intervention has been investigated with appropriate comparison groups, literature reviews have been conclusively negative (i.e., Fischer, 1973; Romig, 1978). One of the most well-known delinquency prevention projects, the Cambridge-Somerville Youth Study, compared the police records for 325 predelinquent boys receiving moderately intensive casework to a matched control group, and found no differences in subsequent rearrest rates or seriousness of offenses (Powers & Witmer, 1951). In a later project, predelinquent girls attending a vocational high school were randomly assigned to casework and group therapy versus no treatment, and did not differ four years later on any school or juvenile court measures (Meyer, Borgatta, & Jones, 1965). The Chicago Youth Development Project (Gold & Mattick, 1974) utilized an intensive but variable casework approach with 970 inner-city delinquent boys. A comparison group of 571 in a different inner-city area served as the controls. There were no differences between the two groups in recidivism, dropouts, or unemployment.

In the better-designed studies of casework, serious problems prevent the unequivocal acceptance of the findings. The integrity and specificity (discussed in Chapters 10 and 14) of the interventions are not demonstrated to a degree that would allow replication. Also, the actual degree of contact the treated youth have with the intervention is usually not reported, so it cannot be determined whether an adequate amount of treatment (also unspecified) was delivered.

Traditional Individual Psychotherapy

When individual psychotherapy is used in institutional settings, it is often combined with other approaches (group therapy, token economies, vocational counseling), and few investigators have conducted random assignment studies. In one of the few exceptions in the literature, Adams (1961b) randomly assigned 164 institutionalized male delinquents to individual therapy or control conditions. The individual therapy was dynamic, insight-oriented, and based on a traditional psychodynamic approach. No differences were found in recidivism, as measured by parole revocation and suspension rates, between the treatment and control groups. Adams (1959) reported similar results for institutionalized delinquent girls, with combined individual and group therapy showing no difference in recidivism compared to individual therapy and no treatment (passage of time) control groups. However, when clinical staff diagnosed institutionalized youths as amenable to treatment or not, and group assignment was randomly determined, therapy outcome was affected (Adams, 1961a). Recidivism (parole revocation) was significantly lower for treated youths considered amenable compared to control youths also considered amenable to treatment. For those considered not amenable to treatment, recidivism did not differ significantly between those receiving therapy and the controls. Unfortunately, the criteria for diagnosing youths as amenable or not were not specified, nor were reliability estimates offered. Seriousness and frequency of offenses and age appear to have figured prominently in the diagnoses, meaning that the less involved were more amenable.

In another study of individual psychotherapy with institutionalized older male adolescents, 215 youths were randomly assigned to psychiatric treatment for two hours per week, or to no treatment, for eight months (Guttman, 1963). There were no group differences in institutional disruptive behavior, and the treated youths fared significantly *worse* than the controls on parole revocation 15 months following release. The same investigator repeated this procedure with younger boys (15 years versus 17.5 years for the previous sample). There were significantly greater disciplinary infractions while in the institution for the 62 boys randomly assigned to the treatment group in which the emphasis was fostering a positive, warm relationship between therapist and client. No differences in parole revocation rate occurred 15 months post-release between the treatment and control groups.

A moderately intensive intervention with younger adolescent delinquents (mean age was 14.5 years) in an institution compared 40 hours of insight-oriented psychotherapy to a passage-of-time control condition (Sowles & Gill, 1970). No significant differences occurred on any institutional behavior measures nor on recidivism 10 years after release. The treatment group did show a positive change in attitude test scores. That the addition of individual psychotherapy to institutional treatment has consistently failed to reduce recidivism or even to change institutional behavior may invite the conclusion that individual therapy is ineffective. It is possible, however, that these investigators are trying to detect effects on coarse outcome measures of a relatively weak and nonintrusive intervention (individual therapy) added to a heavily intrusive intervention (institutionalization) (see Chapter 10).

Individual Behavioral Therapy

Behavioral approaches differ from casework and individual psychotherapy with an insight focus in several ways, but are primarily characterized by a focus on changing specific overt behaviors that are usually related to delinquency. Examples of behaviors targeted are school attendance and grades, disruptive classroom behavior, appropriate social behavior in public, and recidivism and seriousness of offenses. The majority of the studies of individual-oriented behavioral therapy, in which appropriate control groups were constituted, involved school behavior, often in an institutional setting. These studies are more prevalent in the literature than reports of nonbehavioral methods, and their numbers simplify somewhat the task of drawing conclusions about factors associated with treatment success.

Behavioral interventions usually involve differential reinforcement of adaptive behaviors in the adolescent, and contingency contracting in which the adolescent agrees to participate in earning a variety of rewards. Increased test scores, improved school attendance and classroom participation, and decreased disruptiveness commonly result from such interventions (i.e., Tyler & Brown, 1968; Bednar, Zelhart, Greathouse, & Weinberg, 1970; Schwitzgebel, 1967). In these studies it is not uncommon for investigators to train nonprofessionals to use behavioral techniques. This is one advantage of behavioral over more traditional approaches. Fitzgerald (1974) trained a probation officer to individualize contingency contracts with his delinquent probationers in order to work off court-ordered fines. Clearly specified rewards (activities, time off probation sentence) produced increases in time worked. Fo and O'Donnell (1974) trained adults answering a newspaper ad to increase school attendance of 42 predelinquent and delinquent youth who were disruptive and truant. The students were randomly assigned to one of four conditions including a noncontingent positive relationship, social approval and material reward for school attendance, and a no-treatment control group. School attendance was doubled by the contingent conditions and unaffected by the noncontingent relationship condition. Grades, on the other hand, were unaffected by condition, nor were they targeted. An expansion of this approach, the "buddy system," failed to produce significant differences in the rate of youths who committed offenses outside of school (Fo & O'Donnell, 1975).

In a study representative of social learning interventions that target specific behaviors related to delinquency, Schlichter and Horan (1979) randomly assigned 27 disruptive youths with anger-control problems to (1) a stress-innoculation, coping skill, and self-instructional skill approach, versus (2) a relaxation training group, or (3) a no-treatment control group. The skill training condition, utilizing modeling and role playing, produced significantly fewer aggressive responses in a laboratory situation relative to the other two conditions, but did not produce other behavioral changes outside the laboratory. As in most of the studies of behavioral interventions, no follow-up data were reported.

Conclusions

The consistent findings of lack of treatment effects for individual psychotherapy and casework (see also Chapter 10), when contrasted with the few studies showing improvement following treatment, beg for explanation. When the treatment goals are global and vague (such as self-awareness) and when the treatment description is similarly nonspecific and extremely brief (such as providing a warm relationship with the therapist and helping the delinquent achieve insight into his/her behavior), reductions in subsequent delinquent behavior are rarely achieved. On the other hand, success in behavioral improvement is associated with specific behavioral treatment goals, a treatment plan specific to those goals, and goals that are not complex and that are potentially teachable to the client. It should not be surprising that the former approaches fail. (It is unfortunate that they are still the standard fare for the vast majority of delinquents, particularly in outpatient settings). Therapists who do not know where they are taking their clients cannot give them feedback as to their progress along the way. Neither therapists nor clients know how to judge when therapy should be terminated, since they don't know what success is. The number of individual therapy or casework sessions is generally unrelated to positive outcome, or occasionally is inversely related—longer treatment is associated with increased maladaptive behavior relative to controls (Berleman,

Seaburg, and Steinburn, 1972; McCord & McCord, 1959). Perhaps the delinquent makes negative attributions about him/herself when deviant behavior continues in spite of treatment, thereby counteracting any positive influences on the delinquent from a warm supportive therapeutic relationship.

Some conclusions regarding individual behavioral interventions with delinquent youth seem justifiable. Success at behavior change is accomplished when the target behaviors are discrete and within the behavioral repertoire of the youth and are consequated meaningfully and predictably by the change agents. Complex behaviors, such as communication skills and interpersonal problem solving, must be broken down into discrete components in order to be acquired in a relatively short period of time, with careful differential reinforcement and contingency contracting. These more general daily living skills are useful in decreasing acting out but are not generally taught in the studies reviewed (see section on group interventions). Very few of the studies demonstrating successful behavior change have shown reductions in recidivism, long-term maintenance of behavior changes, or generalization across different settings. Thus the individual behavioral approaches offer only limited promises and directions.

Some factors associated with positive outcomes are contingency contracting that involve youth in setting their own goals, practicing the new behavior in the problem setting, and evaluating and modifying goals. Social casework and individual psychotherapy are not characterized by such factors, but rather aim for global cognitive changes such as insight and a new understanding of the causes of behavior, against the backdrop of a warm, supportive relationship. Attempts to produce cognitive changes are not necessarily absent in a behavioral approach, but are seldom mentioned. Recent attention in the behavioral literature on clinical skills and the client-therapist relationship (see Patterson, 1985, and Chapter 10) has focused on a description of factors accompanying therapeutic interventions that many researchers have taken for granted, such as warmth, empathy, dealing with resistance, and educating clients on multiple determinants of behavior. Until these components, along with a good behavioral technology, are isolated and manipulated in sound experimental procedures, their relative contribution to successful therapy will remain unclear.

GROUP INTERVENTIONS

Providing treatment to groups rather than to individuals has been a major vehicle for mental health service delivery for institutionalized delinquents. Group treatment, particularly behavioral approaches, is also prevalent in schools. Outpatient groups at mental health centers are less commonly evaluated in the literature, perhaps because of the difficulty in maintaining continuity of treatment. Relative to investigation of individual therapy, however, group therapy has been studied more frequently and more rigorously. The greater efficiency in staff time, larger number of subjects, and greater integrity or homogeneity of treatment, may account for group treatment studies being more frequent than individual treatment studies. Also, the early research indicated that positive outcomes could be attributed to the group approach, in stark contrast to other rehabilitative efforts. Improvements in academic achievement, self-concept, and positive behavior were achieved with several nondirective therapy groups (Yonge & O'Connor, 1954; Caplan, 1957; Snyder & Sechrest, 1959; all cited in Romig, 1978) relative to matched or randomly assigned control groups. Unfortunately no follow-up data were reported, so it is not known if further delinquent behavior was affected.

In the 1960s and the early 1970s, discussion groups and psychoanalytic, client-centered, and didactic teaching groups were subjected to adequately controlled scrutiny. Romig (1978) reviewed 22 of these studies, the majority of which were conducted with captive juveniles in institutions. Most of the interventions involved 20 to 40 hours of group therapy over a four- to six-month period. Approximately half of these studies reported some positive changes for the treated groups, primarily in attitude and personality test score changes, and also fewer rule infractions, improved academic functioning, and fewer school dropouts. The other half of the studies showed no advantages for the treated groups over the control groups. Only three of the 22 studies (14 percent) demonstrated an effect on recidivism at follow-up, so there has been scant evidence, on the whole, for the efficacy of the more traditional forms of group therapy. The small sample sizes (modal $n = 40$ per comparison group) and the use of coarse and vague outcome measures for which reliability information was not provided, again prevents a confident test of the null hypothesis.

Of those studies showing an impact on post-institutional behavior or long-term maintenance of treatment effects, Truax and his colleagues have replicated the procedures and successes they had with girls with a sample of 40 delinquent boys (Truax, Wargo, & Silber, 1966; Truax, Wargo, & Volksdorf, 1970; cited in Romig, 1978). Therapists were trained in Truax's counseling model to exhibit high levels of empathy and warmth conditioned upon youths discussing personally relevant issues, and met with groups of 10 twice weekly for three months. Relative to a randomly assigned control group who did not receive group therapy, the treated subjects showed significant gains on some personality measures and reduced time of incarceration at follow-up a year later. In a carefully designed study involving prematching pairs of boys on several variables and random assignment to group therapy or a control group, Persons (1966) used role playing and differential verbal reinforcement to teach warm interpersonal relationship skills. Institutional behavior improved as well as personality test scores, and a nine-month post-release follow-up showed fewer parole violations, but no differences in the number of offenses, between the treated and untreated groups. Romig (1978) concluded from his review that failure to demonstrate treatment effects is the rule, and is associated with interventions lacking in specificity for the behaviors which the group intervention is targeting, and with lack of follow-up treatment to help youths transfer whatever they learned in group treatment to other settings. (See, however, Chapter 10.)

Beginning in the late 1960s, and moreso in the late 1970s and into the current decade, clinical investigators started increasing the specificity with which they approached delinquents. The emergence of the cognitive-behavioral model expanded both the scope and relevance of behaviors that researchers could attempt to measure reliably and change. The "pure" operant method of using reinforcement and punishment to alter discrete behaviors gave way to a social learning approach emphasizing interactional skills that could be taught via role playing and modeling, combined with differential reinforcement.

Cognitive-Behavioral Interventions

As discussed extensively in Chapters 5 and 6, among the few clear and simple conclusions that can be reached about delinquents is that they do not represent a homogeneous entity, in spite of the propensity of members of the justice system (and, not infrequently, social scientists) to treat them as such. Rather, like adults, delinquents commit different offenses for a variety of reasons—reasons which may be attributable to one or more of a large array of potential causes, including genetic or biological predispositions, neurological impairments, cognitive deficits, personality disorders, family dysfunctions, and socioeconomic impediments. And, as Little and Kendall (1979) have observed, even though behaviorally based classification systems for subtyping delinquents have been found to be both reliable and valid for some purposes (see Chapter 5), the utility of such grouping of offenders for treatment purposes has not yet been convincingly demonstrated (see Chapter 10). Little and Kendall (1979), among others, recommend, then, a "purposeful focus on *specific observable problems* that are found to be common among large numbers of those who are labeled 'delinquent'" (emphasis in original; p. 81). This section will review representative research from interventions with delinquent and behavior-disordered youth which have as their focus the development of (1) interpersonal problem solving abilities, (2) control over impulsivity, (3) role-taking abilities, and (4) sociomoral reasoning abilities.

Interpersonal Problem-Solving Skills

The research of Spivack and colleagues offers some insights into cognitive processes and maladjusted persons (delinquent, emotionally disturbed). Deficient interpersonal problem-solving skills were demonstrated by both prison inmates and maladjusted persons relative to nondeviant controls (Spivack, & Shure, 1974; Mahoney & Arnkoff, 1978), that is, a lower quantity of perceived solutions to problem situations was generated by the deviant subjects, and the anticipated outcomes to many solutions was judged to be unrealistic, compared to those of normal subjects (Mahoney, 1979). Thus, attempts to remediate these problem-solving deficits carry the potential for reducing delinquent behavior to the extent that the absence of good problem-solving skills play a causative role in delinquency.

Probably the most frequently cited work in this area is that of Sarason and Ganzer (Sarason, 1968; Sarason & Ganzer, 1969, 1973), who have provided direct training of social skills to institutionalized delinquents. While this program does not specifically emphasize cognitive abilities, there no doubt is a substantial cognitive problem-solving component to their training, the content of which is related to common social, educational, and vocational situations (e.g., how to take problems to a teacher or counselor, how to apply for a job, how to resist antisocial peer pressure, etc.). The emphasis of the training (16 one-hour sessions) was on both alternative and consequential thinking. Three groups were studied, each comprised of 64 randomly assigned institutionalized male first offenders. They included: (1) a modeling condition, including rehearsal and critiques; (2) a discussion condition, which excluded all references to role playing; and (3) an untreated control condition. Dependent variables included self-report measures of personal characteristics, self-concept, future goals, activity preferences, and locus of control, as well as counselor ratings of behaviors and adjustment, plus post-release follow-ups (with recidivism data gathered nearly three years after the treatments). All participants combined showed improvements on 10 of the 12 repeated dependent measures, including attitudes, self-concept, and overt behaviors. Intergroup comparisons revealed only two differences: (1) the modeling group showed a reduction in emotional reactivity; and (2) both treatment groups showed a shift toward a more internal locus of control. Behavior ratings by staff members revealed little significant change, although control subjects tended to show a greater proportion of negative than positive changes, while the reverse was true for the treatment groups. Classification of delinquents by subtypes (see Chapter 5) was associated with differential outcome. More importantly, however, for a three-year follow-up period the proportions of recidivists were significantly lower in the treatment conditions than either the control condition or the population as a whole.

Other researchers using similar training programs have achieved significant behavioral changes. Scopetta (1979), using role plays of problem solving first by staff members and then by institutionalized delinquents, produced a greater reduction in subsequent antisocial behavior than that found for a discussion-only treatment. Collingwood and Genthner (1980), training both offenders and their parents in interpersonal and problems-solving skills, produced both lower recidivism (24.3 percent versus 42.7 percent), as well as lower severity of offenses for those who did recidivate, as compared to an untreated control group. Unfortunately, it is not clear in this study which skills among the diverse skills taught accounted for the changes in behavior.

Not all such interventions produce strong or clear results, however. Thelen, Fry, Dollinger, & Paul (1976), for example, found improvements among group-home delinquents for group-home situations, but found no generalization when training shifted to school situations, and improvements were not maintained at follow-up. Spence and Marziller (1981), working only with youth showing clear skill deficits, compared a treatment group with both attention and no-treatment control groups, randomly assigned. The treatment consisted of six weeks of two hours per week of discussions, modeling, role plays, and homework on a variety of skills, ranging from maintaining eye contact and listening, to dealing with police, bullying, and teachers' criticisms. Some minor improvements were found for the treatment group (eye contact, fidgeting, etc.), but these decreased at a long-term follow-up. No differences were found across groups for court convictions six months after the treatment ended. It is unfortunate that since status offenders were treated with hard-core felony offenders, outcomes were not reported separately. Ollendick (1978) compared social skills and discussion treatments for a small sample of incarcerated delinquents matched on age, locus of control, and IQ. Training dealt with problems of relating to one another and to the staff. The social skills condition included not only discussion of alternatives, but also rehearsal, modeling, feedback, social reinforcement, and homework. The discussion treatment consisted solely of discussions of the same problems dealt with in the social skills condition. The social skills group demonstrated significantly greater improvement in eye contact, requests for new behavior, latency of responses, decreased aggression in role plays, decreased self-reported anxiety, and increased internal locus of control. However, acting-out behaviors showed only a nonsignificant trend for the social skills group at a two-week follow-up. No follow-up was reported so the effect on recidivism could not be assessed.

In sum, a strong point of this approach is the specificity of targeting for interventions those social or interpersonal problem-solving abilities which appear to be related either to antisocial behaviors or to negative consequences in interpersonal exchanges (which, of course, may lead to a variety of intervening phenomena, including negative labeling and self-fulfilling prophecies in school, family, and criminal justice settings). While the number of reported studies with delinquents in this area is as yet small, given the general success of this approach with other youthful populations (see, e.g., Kendall & Hollon, 1979; Urbain & Kendall, 1980), this would appear to be a very promising approach for both preventative and treatment programs (see also Chapter 10).

Reduction of Impulsivity

It has been generally thought that delinquents are characterized by a general impulsivity, a characteristic that presumably results in poor behavioral choices as a result of failure to consider either alternatives or consequences (although the literature on impulsivity and delinquency is not entirely clear; see Chapter 6). Camp and her colleagues (Camp, 1977, 1979; Camp & Bash, 1981; Camp, Blom, Herbert, & van Doornick, 1977; Camp, van Doornick, Zimet, & Dahlem, 1977) maintain that despite normal verbal IQs, young aggressive boys show verbal mediational deficiencies, more immature private speech than nonaggressives, and less adequate private speech for self-regulation in both cognitive and motor tasks. Camp's "Think Aloud" program is typical of those which attempt to instill in behavior-disordered youth a more reflective and less impulsive style. Such programs rely on modeling and rehearsal of cognitive strategies in a variety of problem situations. The strategies involve learning and saying aloud (and gradually fading) specific steps such as: (1) "What's my problem?" (2) "What's my plan?" (3) "Am I using my plan?" and (4) "How did I do?". While Camp et al. (1977) found no differences in teacher-rated aggression relative to randomly assigned controls (all groups improved), teachers did rate the treatment group as superior on prosocial behaviors. In addition, some cognitive measures (but not others) showed improvements. Furgurson (1980), using a program similar to Camp, as well as Kendall and Finch (1976, 1978, 1979), produced improved teacher ratings on impulsive behaviors in a sample of institutionalized emotionally disturbed aggressive boys. Williams and Akamatsu (1978), using Meichenbaum and Goodman's (1971) self-guidance procedure, trained delinquents on the children's form of the Matching Familiar Figures Test, and then tested them on the adult form. The self instruction procedure resulted in a less impulsive performance than did the attention control, which simply included verbal instructions from the experimenter. In addition, the improved performance generalized to the WISC-R picture arrangement test, but no group differences were found on delay of gratification.

In sum, this approach appears to be promising for delinquent youth characterized by impulsive styles which interfere with adequate decision making. The technology involved is highly developed, and appears to be effective over a wide range of populations (see e.g., Kazdin, 1982; Kendall & Hollon, 1979; Meichenbaum, 1977; Urbain & Kendall, 1980; see also Chapter 10).

Role Taking

Cognitive-developmental theorists have long maintained that young children lack the cognitive ability to take more than one perspective of an object or event at a time, and, as a result, are limited in their ability to make distortion-free judgments. With normal maturation and development, the ability to decenter is acquired, permitting qualitatively superior thought and more successful interpersonal relationships. However, should an individual experience developmental delay, a relative inability to take the perspectives of others would persist. Individuals so characterized have been shown " . . . to systematically misread societal expectations, to misinterpret the actions and intentions of others, and to act in ways which were judged to be callous and disrespectful of the rights of others" (Chandler, 1973, p. 326). And, as has been shown earlier in Chapter 6, such perspective-taking deficits have been found significantly more often among delinquent than nondelinquent samples.

In a frequently cited study, Chandler (1973) has demonstrated that (1) role-taking abilities can be enhanced through systematic developmental interventions, and (2) long-term recidivism is significantly and substantially lower for those experiencing such an intervention compared to matched controls. Chandler's intervention consisted of 10 weekly half-day sessions in which chronically delinquent boys developed, portrayed, acted out, videotaped, and critiqued skits involving events typically experienced by people their age. Skits were reenacted a sufficient number of times for each person to occupy each role. Those in the experimental group (versus matched placebo and nontreatment control groups) not only improved significantly on Chandler's measure of role-taking ability, but also demonstrated significant reductions in recidivism at an 18-month follow-up. This research has been partially replicated by Little (1980). In addition, numerous interventions with nondelinquent populations have significantly enhanced perspective-taking or role-taking abilities, and role taking appears to be a major component in most social skills training programs, both with delinquent and nondelinquent populations (see, e.g., Kendall & Hollon, 1979; Urbain & Kendall, 1980).

Theoretically, however, it is not entirely clear that enhanced interpersonal awareness or perspective-taking abilities by themselves will prove sufficient for preventing antisocial behavior. This may be more true of cognitive than of affective role-taking abilities; the former merely require the ability to see a situation from another's point of view, while the latter imply an ability to feel the emotions being experienced by the other person. In the absence of psychopathy (see Chapter 5), the latter is likely to have a more profound impact on behavior choices. For example, one can imagine a delinquent learning cognitive role-taking abilities, and then using this skill to plan and execute more effective crimes. Thus, role-taking abilities may perhaps best be viewed as necessary but not sufficient for delinquency prevention and treatment. What is needed, in addition (from a cognitive perspective, at least), is the development of less antisocial and more prosocial motives and sociomoral worldviews (see Chapter 6).

Sociomoral Reasoning

The nature of the stages of moral reasoning is thoroughly discussed in a variety of sources (e.g., Arbuthnot & Faust, 1981; Kohlberg, 1984; and in Chapter 6). It is also apparent from Chapter 6 that some delinquents, especially the more psychopathic, are generally characterized by lower stages of moral reasoning, usually reasoning at the preconventional level. Delinquency itself can be seen as more typical of the preconventional reasoner, since antisocial acts are by definition oriented toward meeting the immediate wants or needs of the actor, without the tempering influence of a broader, social-systemic perspective. However, recognizing that delinquent behavior is multidetermined, one can also see that having a Stage 3 or higher sociomoral worldview will not necessarily prevent illegal or antisocial behaviors. Similarly, being limited to a Stage 1 or 2 sociomoral worldview does not imply that one is condemned to illegal or antisocial behavior. Some delinquents are at Stages 3 and 4; most

Stage 1 and 2 reasoners are not delinquents. However, it does seem reasonable that if delinquents who reason at preconventional stages can, through developmental interventions, acquire Stage 3 reasoning abilities and perspectives, this more mature worldview can *enable* the amelioration of delinquent behaviors. In other words, while conventional reasoning structures, by themselves, may not be sufficient to prevent further delinquency (either for all delinquents, or across all domains for each delinquent), they may permit and facilitate more mature behavioral choices.

There is ample evidence that many individuals can experience an advance in moral reasoning stage as a result of structured interventions which typically use guided dilemma discussions (or related techniques, e.g., role playing) to arouse cognitive disequilibrium, combined with exposure to one-stage-higher ("+1") reasoning (see, e.g., Arbuthnot & Faust, 1981; Cochrane & Manley-Casimir, 1980; Lockwood, 1978). Weekly sessions lasting about 45 minutes over a period of 10 to 20 weeks will typically result in upward movement of one-quarter to one-half of a stage for one-quarter to one-half of the participants. Failure to experience upward movement may be due to a variety of factors, including qualities of the program (e.g., skills of the leader, appropriateness of the dilemmas, etc.), as well as qualities of the participants (e.g., lack of interest, lack of requisite cognitive abilities). There is evidence which suggests that delinquents are more often at lower Piagetian stages than matched nondelinquents (e.g., Martin, in Arbuthnot and Gordon (1984) found delinquents to be far less likely to demonstrate beginning formal operational thought than carefully matched nondelinquents). If this result is pervasive, it suggests that interventions with delinquents will have limited success, at least with a significant proportion of delinquents, in raising reasoning levels to Stage 3.

Numerous studies have demonstrated the efficacy of dilemma discussion and related techniques for raising the moral reasoning stage scores of delinquent and behavior-disordered youth, clearly showing that at least a significant proportion of these youth are not permanently arrested at lower cognitive-developmental levels (see, e.g., Arbuthnot & Gordon, 1986; Fleetwood & Parish, 1976; Gibbs, Arnold, Ahlborn & Cheesman, 1984; Hickey & Scharf, 1980; Rosenkoetter, Landman, & Mazak, 1980; Seguin-Tremblay & Kiely, 1979; Ventis, 1976). In addition, Jennings and Kohlberg (1983) have demonstrated similar effectiveness by using a broader approach; the democratic or just community within a juvenile detention facility. A few studies have reported little or no appreciable change in moral reasoning as a result of interventions with delinquent or behavior-disordered youth (Copeland & Parish, 1979; Schmidlin, in Gibbs, et al., 1984; Wright, 1977), but each of these suffers from problems related to the nature or duration of the intervention, or with the assessment of change.

Only one research program to date has examined not only changes in moral reasoning, but also attendant changes in relevant behavior. In Arbuthnot &

Gordon (1986), 35 male and 13 female students in grades 7 through 10 who had been nominated and rated by teachers as seriously behavior disordered were matched pair-wise on severity of ratings and then randomly assigned to a treatment or nontreatment condition. The former participated in a 16 to 20 week structured dilemma-discussion (one 45-minute session per week). Immediately post-test, analyses of covariance (with pretest scores as covariants) showed that the experimental (but not control) participants experienced significant improvements in moral reasoning stage, frequency of disciplinary referrals, police and court contacts, school tardiness, and grades in the social studies-humanities area. Nonsignificant differences were found for teacher ratings and absenteeism. Furthermore, correlational analyses showed changes in moral reasoning maturity scores to correlate significantly with changes in all outcome measures. Equally important, this study included a long-term follow-up (one year after termination of the intervention), providing data which have been conspicuously absent in the moral-reasoning development literature. The two groups continued to diverge: For the experimental group, moral reasoning, teacher ratings and absenteeism became significantly better after termination, while tardiness, disciplinary referrals, and grades retained the differences (favoring the experimental group) found at termination. Recorded police and court contacts were reduced to zero for both groups (a result which no doubt reflects the lack of sensitivity of this variable as an index of antisocial behavior in the community).

In sum, developmental interventions of a cognitive nature appear to be quite successful both internally (in terms of acquisition of cognitive skills) and externally (in terms of behavioral improvement). Both the work of Chandler and of Arbuthnot and his colleagues have shown links between broad perspective-taking (interpersonal and sociomoral, respectively) development programs and improved behavior and reduced recidivism. The cognitive-developmental approach is a highly promising one, then. Its effectiveness should be further enhanced with more careful selection of those youth showing the clearest developmental delays and who also have (or can acquire through other developmental efforts) the general (i.e., Piagetian) reasoning and perspective-taking abilities to benefit from the more specific sociomoral reasoning programs. In addition, the search for interactive approaches should continue, since most theorists agree that changes in reasoning skills alone may permit but will not necessarily lead to behavioral changes. In this regard, the development of prosocial motives and/or caring seem worthwhile goals. Further needs include a demonstration of the effectiveness of these programs with more serious and/or incarcerated offenders. Finally, the micro-individual approach representative of nearly all of the research described here should be extended to probational and community and alternate-sentencing programs, and the more macro-institutional approach utilized thus far only by Jennings and colleagues (Jennings & Kohlberg, 1983) should be explored further in juvenile detention settings, as well as in school systems and in the families of juvenile offenders.

FAMILY INTERVENTIONS

There has been a sharp increase in the number of articles written about family therapy, relative to other forms of therapy, over the past two decades. The growing popularity of treating delinquents via family interventions is due to several developments. Recognition of the inefficacy of other treatment approaches, coupled with expansion of training programs offering family interventions, has fueled this popularity. Also important is the contribution of systems theory in which delinquent acting-out is seen as caused by family tension and parental conflict (Haley, 1971). Social learning theory, with its emphasis upon the learning environment in the family, spurred studies of family predictors of delinquent behavior and of interventions to reduce antisocial and delinquent behaviors by changing parenting practices. Chapter 8 of this volume has already detailed many of the differences.

Interventions which target the family and these particular patterns often result in an immediate decrease in oppositional behavior, as Patterson's (i.e., 1974a, 1974b, 1985) extensive work clearly shows. Much of the family intervention research covered here also shows that long-term changes in deviant child behavior, such as fewer juvenile offenses and fewer out of home placements, follow interventions that attempt to change family behavior. We have also seen in Chapter 10 that family therapy carried out in the institutional setting seems to have promise. Although these lines of evidence do not prove that for most delinquents the family is the sole cause of their deviant behavior, the family can be seen as at least being a primary mediating variable. For instance, it is possible that other causative factors are affected by family interventions, such as declining influence by a deviant peer group as family cohesiveness increases. It may be that a number of family characteristics, such as clear communication, paternal involvement with children, maternal supervision, and consistent discipline, act as insulators against a child becoming delinquent.

Reviews of the literature on family therapy have proliferated, and some have focussed specifically on delinquency (i.e., Romig, 1978; Ulrici, 1983). Behavioral interventions involving families have been included in larger behavior modification reviews of delinquency interventions (Emery & Marholin, 1977; Braukmann, Fixsen, Phillips, & Wolf, 1975; Gross & Brigham, 1980). Wells and Dezen (1978) limited their review, on the other hand, to nonbehavioral family studies. They concluded that strong treatment effects were often reported in uncontrolled single group studies, but found no advantage of nonbehavioral family therapy (with a few exceptions) over alternative treatments when studies were adequately controlled. They called for a demonstration of efficacy of the systems approaches using single-case experimental designs, such as the use of multiple-baseline designs to detect treatment effects on frequently occurring observable behaviors (i.e., truancy, Dixon 1985).

Romig (1978) included behavioral family interventions in his review and found positive behavior change to be demonstrated in well-controlled studies (random assignment), but no strong evidence that family therapy affects recidivism. In a more recent and optimistic review of family interventions with delinquents, Ulrici (1983) covered studies missed by Romig and was less critical. She compared behavioral with systems-oriented interventions and concluded that behavioral interventions applied without consideration of family dynamics can change target behaviors but don't deter recidivism. In general she asserted that family interventions to be evaluated as to their success in reducing recidivism, must be compared to no-treatment and alternative-treatment comparison groups. On the basis of a few questionable studies, she also concluded that research that focused on family dynamics and did not utilize behavioral techniques was just as effective as combined behavioral-systems approaches.

In light of the consistent attempt by many reviewers to isolate the critical variables in family intervention research and the differing conclusions reached, the present review was organized to once again attempt to bring greater clarity to this promising yet hopelessly complex field. Studies in three areas will be presented including: (1) systems and nonbehavioral interventions; (2) behavioral parent training and family skills training; and (3) combined behavioral-systems approaches. Any attempt at categorization involves considerable subjective judgment that often reflects the reviewer's biases; the present three-category effort is no exception. The biggest hindrance to categorizing studies accurately is the appalling lack of detail in the description of the interventions. However, crude attempts are made, simply to help organize the information for the reader. The studies selected for mention, with a few noted exceptions, met three criteria: (1) an adequately controlled design (random assignment or carefully described control groups); (2) behavioral outcome measures directly related to delinquency, and (3) target populations of delinquents or children identified as clearly at risk for delinquency.

Systems and Nonbehavioral Family Therapy

Since Wells and Dezen's (1978) review, only five family therapy studies with a nonbehavioral focus have met the criteria. Four of these labeled their approach as systems-oriented (Beal & Duckro, 1977; Johnson, 1977; Stringfield, 1977; Michaels & Green, 1979) and one could not be clearly identified as behavioral (Druckman, 1979). Beal and Duckro (1977) offered families short-term (six to eight weeks) family therapy as an alternative to immediate filing of a complaint against an unruly child. After initial crisis intervention with the family, the authors describe the weekly or biweekly family sessions as derived primarily from the writings of Satir (1967), Jackson (1965), and Haley (1971). Therapists were juvenile court counselors presumably trained and supervised by the authors. Their training emphasized clear communication skills, and how to teach these skills to the family. Effectiveness was judged by comparing the number of complaints filed for a random sample of 44 families opting for this diversion (17 percent filed complaints) to 54 families randomly selected from status offender clients a year before the diversion program's inception (35 percent filed complaints). Half of the families treated were referred to mental health centers for continued services. With this mild population (potential first-time status offenders), it is not known whether the family intervention itself, the six to eight week delay while therapy was being conducted, or possible differential receptivity of court workers to complaints being filed, accounted for the differences in diversion rates. Stringfield (1977) used a more difficult population of male repeat offenders to evaluate the effectiveness of Satir's conjoint family therapy model on juvenile recidivism. Of 52 white, black, and Hispanic adolescents (mean age was 16 years) living in a peer milieu treatment, 20 were randomly assigned to family therapy, ranging from six to 20 sessions. All subjects received group therapy. One year after treatment and release, the rate of incarceration was 25 percent for the group receiving family therapy and 56 percent for the controls. No other data were reported (i.e., police and court contacts), nor was it possible to determine if the decision to reincarcerate was affected by knowledge of which families had cooperated with family therapy.

Another court-run study of family intervention services was reported by Johnson (1977), who used a family systems approach, described only as "ideas drawn principally from the work of Erikson, Haley, Minuchin, and Whittaker" (p. 30). Juveniles who were status offenders or committed misdemeanors (percentages not reported) were ordered into family treatment by a judge or probation officer according to criteria not specified (n = 190). A comparison group of 190 juveniles was constructed of those never receiving family therapy by matching on age, sex, ethnic background, socioeconomic level, and class of offense. The total number of offenses (petitions adjudicated) for the treatment and control groups was 360 and 364, respectively, prior to group assignments. Both groups were similar, in the number of petitions filed (recidivism), in a period encompassing treatment and one year after termination (90 versus 117). Two years following the inception of treatment, the treated subjects committed only three offenses versus 19 for the matched controls (recidivism rates of 1 percent versus 5 percent, respectively). The two-year follow-up differences were not significant, owing to the influence of powerful unknown factors that depressed recidivism for both groups below what is normally expected (around 50 to 60 percent).

In Druckman (1979), a small sample of female status offenders (mean age was 15 years) was offered family therapy for eight to 12 weeks after two weeks of parent education group meetings. No clear model for the family therapy was articulated, but the author described early involvement of the family in formulating treatment goals and a treatment plan, emphasis on communication skills, fair-fight training, and awareness of feelings. Training and supervision of the two B.A. level "family therapists" was not described. The comparison group consisted of dropouts from the family therapy. Only 22 percent of the families completed the voluntary program, indicating a substantial confounding of motivation between the groups. Scores on the Moos Family Environment Scales (Moos, 1974) did not differ in pre/post improvement. Recidivism of fully treated families was significantly higher than for the early dropout families (50 percent versus 33 percent).

Another study utilizing systems (based on Haley's and Minuchin's theories) family therapy with status offenders was reported by Michaels and Green (1979). Very little information regarding the selection process or the therapy program was provided, but some detail of the intensity of training and supervision (live) for children services workers makes this study unusual. The comparison group of 64 status offenders did not receive family intervention, compared to 75 cases accepted for outpatient family therapy. For a two-year period during and following treatment the treatment group had a 4 percent recidivism and out-of-home placement rate, compared to a 33 percent recidivism and 44 percent out-of-home placement rate for the controls. Since the intervention was performed by children's services workers who also made decisions about out-of-home placements, the criteria for further court action for the two groups were highly different and a source of confounding.

In sum, the use of a systems approach to families for delinquency treatment is consistent with the systems theory view of the causes of delinquency. The handful of studies of systems-based family interventions reviewed here were the best designed in the literature, but were so incomplete in terms of description of interventions, selection procedures, subject characteristics, intervenor characteristics, and independence of outcome assessment, that firm conclusions cannot be made about the efficacy of these approaches to reduce recidivism. There is cause for optimism since three of the five studies did reduce recidivism relative to a comparison group not receiving family treatment, but the experimental designs were contaminated.

Behavioral Parent Training and Skills Training Family Interventions

The most carefully described and designed studies involving changing children's behavior by intervening with the family are consistently behavioral (social learning) in their theoretical emphasis. The behaviors that are targeted for change are usually interactive and oppositional and thus, presumably, related to delinquency. The goal of such studies is typically to increase parental monitoring and control and the families' social skills (communication, contracting, problem solving). Parent training, as it is generally described, differs from family therapy in that the focus of most of the sessions is on teaching parents specific child management skills in a relatively structured, didactic fashion. In family therapy, the focus is on assessing the interrelationships among all family members' and the target child's behaviors, and overcoming family members' resistance to change. Skill training, if it occurs, comes later in the treatment and generally consumes a minor portion of the total contact time.

Stuart and his colleagues (Stuart, 1971; Stuart & Lott, 1972; Stuart, Jayaratne, & Tripodi, 1976) taught parents of delinquents and predelinquents to use behavioral contracts. Contracts were tailored to each family and stated both privileges and responsibilities for adolescents and their parents. Class attendance, but not recidivism, was improved in Stuart and Lott (1972). However, the likelihood of court contacts for both groups was very low given the pretreatment rate of 3 percent and 0 percent for experimental and control subjects. Treatment was of moderate duration (average family contact of nine hours and teacher contact of six hours). In a study with inadequate controls and with a much smaller sample (six families) who were taught contracting, Weathers and Liberman (1975) compared several behavioral outcome measures to those of 16 families who did not remain in treatment. They invested only 5.6 hours per family and found only one behavior, verbal abusiveness, to improve.

Csapo and Friesen (1981) studied 20 multiply offending delinquents, half of whom were assigned with their parents to a behavior management program. Ten delinquents were assigned to a control group, after being matched with treated subjects on sex, age, economic, and parental employment variables. Selection criteria for the treated group were not specified. The treatment was seven hours of group behavioral management training, followed by an unspecified number of weekly sessions with a graduate psychology student who functioned as an advisor in parental tailoring of contracts with the child, and differentially reinforced appropriate and problem behaviors. There were significant reductions in observed deviant behavior in the home from pre- to post-intervention for the treated group, and in problem behaviors reported in a behavior checklist. Parents in the treated group, relative to the controls, showed an increase in knowledge of behavior management procedures. Recidivism was not affected during the duration of treatment, as no offenses were committed by either group, and no follow-up data were available.

From this type of short-term, short-contact (five to 10 hours) parent-training approach with predelinquent and delinquent children, one cannot find much support for the view that serious delinquency can be avoided, particularly in deprived families. This conclusion was reached by McAuley (1982), who's review showed parent training to work best in modifying the behavior of children in stable, middle-class families, and with aggressive children.

G. R. Patterson and colleagues at the Oregon Social Learning Center have invested more time per family with a younger target group. They have systematically altered the parenting practices of parents of socially aggressive children in a series of well-described studies (i.e., Patterson & Reid, 1973; Patterson, Reid, Jones, & Conger, 1975; Patterson & Fleischman, 1979). Even the behaviors of nontargeted siblings improved and were maintained at a six-month follow-up (Arnold, Levine, & Patterson, 1975). In several studies employing control groups, relative to the pre/post designs of the studies just cited, the Oregon Social Learning Center group focused on lower to middle class predelinquent males who were conduct problems and usually socially aggressive. Wiltz and Patterson (1974) treated six families in the home and in a clinic who had nine- and ten-year-old aggressive boys. The parents received brief (30 minutes per week for five weeks) training in the use of behavioral techniques such as tracking and providing consequences for inappropriate behavior with time-out. Parents also collected data, charted the boys' progress, and used a programmed text. Relative to untreated control boys matched on age, socio-economic status, and baseline rates of deviant behavior, the treated boys showed significant reduction in deviant behavior, but only on those behaviors that were targeted during treatment. In a similar study with 27 lower-social-class, conduct-problem boys, Patterson (1974a) found deviant behavior rates after treatment to fall within the range of those behaviors for nonproblem children, and to have persisted at a one year follow-up. In Patterson, Chamberlain, and Reid (1982), behavioral parent training was done more intensively (17 hours) in the home and clinic with ten families of highly aggressive children by a sophisticated clinical staff. Compared to nine families of aggressive children randomly referred to community treatment, the social learning group showed greater improvement in deviant child behavior. Bernal, Klinnert, and Schultz (1980) were not able to maintain initial treatment superiority of a behavioral parent-training group over subjects randomly assigned to client-centered treatment, but the intervention was brief, time-limited (10 sessions), and was performed by graduate student therapists.

Very recently Patterson and colleagues have extended their procedures to older and more challenging subjects—multiply offending delinquents (Marlowe, Reid, Patterson, & Weinrott, 1986). Fifty-five boys (mean age was 14 years) from lower socioeconomic class families, and who had committed at least two offenses, were randomly assigned to either the social learning approach or to conventional (unspecified) treatment in the community. The experimental treatment consisted of training parents to set rules, monitor and discipline their children, and to work as a family to do contingency contracting. Family problems presumably not directly related to the youth's delinquency, such as parental depression or marital conflict, were also dealt with. Over 21 hours of therapist time per family and an additional 15 hours during the follow-up year were required. Results indicated that the experimental group committed significantly fewer offenses during the treatment year than the community group, although the difference was not significant at a one-year follow-up. The experimental delinquents also spent significantly fewer days in institutions during the treatment year and follow-up year, resulting in a savings in excess of $135,000 over a three-year period. Improvement in family interaction was associated with lowered frequency of offenses.

Several other approaches to family therapy have emphasized skills training, but were not as carefully developed, described, or evaluated as the extensive program at the Oregon Social Learning Center. Although there were design problems, the external validity, innovativeness and/or results deserve brief mention. An in-home family therapy program that focused on families where an out-of-home placement was imminent was established to provide an on-call crisis intervention to 80 families (Kinney, Madsen, Fleming, & Hoopala, 1976). The majority of the identified patients were adolescents who were status offenders from low-income families. Therapists were trained in parent-effectiveness skills, fair fight techniques, assertiveness, and behavior modification. The in-home treatment, which could occur daily up to a six-week period (mean treatment time unreported), began with defusing the situation and a behavioral definition of the problem. General problem resolution and communication skills were taught. Out-of-home placement (primarily foster care) was prevented for 97 percent of the at-risk clients at a three- to 16-month follow-up, at a substantial cost savings of over $2000 per client in projected foster care costs (no comparison group was presented).

Ostensen (1981) treated 28 adolescent middle-class runaways with communication and crisis-intervention-oriented family counseling, and compared treatment effectiveness to a nonparticipating matched control group. During a three- to twelve-month follow-up period, 25 percent of the treated adolescents versus 62 percent of the comparison group ran away. It is not known what selection factors influenced group assignment, or if the two follow-up periods were comparable. In a similar communication-oriented family treatment program, Maskin (1976) compared 30 first-time male status offenders in a work-oriented institutional program with 30 similar males (matched on age and academic achievement) who participated in an institutional program which emphasized parent-child communication through individual, group, and family counseling. No information on the treatment program, treatment intensity, treatment duration, reasons for differential assignment, length of follow-up period, skills of the intervenors, family cooperation, or attrition was provided. Significantly less recidivism (defined as two detentions or reinstitutionalization but not differentiated) occurred in the communication-oriented program. This study is mentioned as an example of the poor quality of outcome studies generally found in the delinquency treatment literature, but it still was more rigorous than two-thirds of the published studies on family interventions.

Behavioral-Systems Family Therapy

An approach which combines the systems focus on the entire family as the object of change with the behavioral skill training approach was developed by Alexander and colleagues specifically for treating juvenile offenders. In this approach, described in detail in a training manual (Alexander & Parsons, 1982), therapists assess behavioral sequences to determine interpersonal payoffs or functions, relabel those sequences so as to cause a change in attribution and perspective in the family, and then provide instruction appropriate to the skill deficits of the family (communication, problem solving, contingency contracting, limit setting, reinforcement, etc.). In a well-designed study comparing various treatment approaches, Alexander and Parsons (1973) randomly assigned 116 first-time status offenders to behavioral-systems family therapy, client-centered family therapy, psychodynamic-eclectic family therapy, and a probation-only control. Juveniles and their families, mostly middle-class Mormons, were treated in the community by clinical psychology graduate students for the behavioral systems approach. Their training and supervision was well described, a rarity in this literature. Families received approximately eight 90-minute sessions over a four-week period. Results indicated changes in family interactions (see also Parsons & Alexander, 1973), and in a six- to 18-month follow-up reductions occurred in recidivism (26 percent) only for the behavioral-systems families, compared to client-centered (47 percent), psychodynamic (73 percent), and no-treatment (48 percent) groups. The rates of participation in treatment for the comparison groups are not reported. Siblings of the referred delinquents were followed for two and one-half to three and one-half years after termination. Recidivism in the behavioral-systems group was significantly lower (20 percent) than for the other groups (40 percent to 63 percent) (Klein, Alexander, & Parsons, 1977). According to the authors, these results underscore the validity of changing a dysfunctional system that produces delinquency.

In an examination of therapist skills related to outcome, Alexander, Barton, Schiavo, and Parsons (1976), found positive relationship (see also Chapter 10) and structuring skills to improve outcome and to be associated with longer participation in therapy. Thus, the contribution of therapist variables, as well as the theoretical model upon which the intervention is based, was evaluated in one of the few prolific research programs in the therapy outcome literature.

This promising approach was recently replicated with a very different sample of delinquents in an economically depressed rural region. Gordon, Arbuthnot, Gustafson, and McGreen (1986), and Gordon, McGreen, and Arbuthnot (1984), compared delinquents whose families were treated with Alexander's behavioral-systems family therapy in the home to a comparison group of probation-only delinquents. Nonrandom assignment to the family therapy group (n = 27) was based on the actual or imminent removal of a disruptive adolescent from the home, with the comparison group (n = 28) being at lower risk for recidivism or out-of-home placement. The training and supervision of the graduate student therapists were longer in duration than in Alexander and Parsons (1973), and the intervention procedures were described in detail. Very little attrition occurred, with only one of 27 families dropping out of treatment very early, partly due to the fact that all sessions occurred in the home.

After a two to two-and-a-half year follow-up period, recidivism (court adjudications) for the treatment group was 11 percent versus 67 percent for the controls. Treated youths also showed a decrease in offense severity. These results represent an improvement over those of Alexander and Parsons (1973) in that the recidivism rate of the treated group was one-fifth that of the controls even with the longer follow-up period and higher risk of the treated group. These differences were attributed to time-unlimited and longer treatment (mean of 16 sessions), increased rapport related to being in the home, and focusing on parental resistance during much of the supervision of therapists. A cost-benefit analysis of the out-of-home placement costs for the two groups showed the cost of the treated group, including all costs of treatment, were less than for the probation control group (Gustafson, Gordon, & Arbuthnot, 1986). In addition, sibling court contacts for the family therapy group were lower than the control group.

Barton, Alexander, Waldron, Turner, and Warburton (1985) reported on three studies in which this same model (functional family therapy) was used in field settings, with less formally trained paraprofessionals. Undergraduates trained in the model saw 27 families in the home, and 26 percent of the referred multiple status offenders had repeat offenses during a 13-month follow-up. No comparison group was used. McPherson, McDonald, and Ryer (1983) used a model of family interventions that might best be described as behavioral-systems, based upon the theoretical assumptions the therapists made when treating families. Unfortunately the training and supervision of the therapists was not mentioned. In this study, 15 families of delinquents, mostly first offenders, were randomly assigned to family counseling, and 60 to a probation control group. Treatment consisted of 20 hours of parent and 10 hours of child counseling, with some parental sessions including the referred children. Seven months after assignment to treatment or control groups, the difference in recidivism rates of the two groups were not quite significant (40 percent versus 63 percent, respectively), while criminal referrals (arrests) were greater for the control group. These recidivism rates are quite high for such a short follow-up period, but the data indicate that the intervention slowed the rate.

The small number of studies using the relatively new behavioral-systems hybrid approach to family therapy are noteworthy in several respects. The rationale for the intervention model and the training and supervision of the intervenors was presented in a way that invites replication. Therapist variables and client characteristics were addressed in two studies, and measures of family change that were related to the behavioral-systems model were reported. The recidivism of status offenders and multiple offenders alike was reduced significantly relative to alternative family treatments or probation control groups, and these results were maintained over a two- to three-year follow-up period. The general results are similar to the Oregon Social Learning Center results with highly aggressive boys, in that independent replications of the effectiveness of a moderately well-articulated treatment model occurred in different sites with different populations. This similarity bodes well for the hope for further replications of these approaches, and with them the ability to identify the influence of moderator variables (therapist, client, and model characteristics) on treatment efficacy.

The two approaches that have most consistently produced and maintained treatment gains for predelinquents and delinquents, Patterson's version of behavioral parent training and behavioral-systems family, therapy may not differ enough to warrant separate labels. The theoretical orientation is different, and the written description of the procedures reflect the biases of the authors in their choice about what procedures to describe in what terms as being most salient. For example, when parental resistance was encountered by behavioral therapists, the therapists' attempts to overcome the resistance, if they were mentioned at all, were often described simply as the parents being "persuaded" to try the techniques.

The systems and nonbehavioral therapists spent much of their time in assessing and describing causes of resistance and methods for overcoming resistance in families. Since resistance is encountered more often in the poor, less educated, multiproblem families that characterize the majority of delinquents, the problem of how to get good behavioral technology and skills training to "take" becomes critical. Patterson and colleagues devote most of their clinical discussions to this issue, and Patterson (1985) has written about them (e.g., a reliable coding system for client resistance has been developed). He recommends as necessary for producing lasting behavior change in difficult-to-treat families, the following three components: (1) a child management technology; (2) good "soft" clinical skills for overcoming parental resistance; and (3) a therapist support system for motivation and brainstorming with regard to the most difficult families. Failures to replicate Patterson's successes (i.e., Fleishman, 1979; Bernal et al., 1980) lacked the latter two components.

Future Directions in Family Intervention Research

The volume of studies in the past decade that have focused on intervening in the family to combat delinquency and antisocial behavior have done little to advance our knowledge about the perplexing problem, already mentioned in Chapter 10, about what works under what conditions. The primary reasons are poor experimental design, grossly inadequate descriptions of and control over the interventions and the intervenors, inadequate description of the treated families or analysis of client variables, and insensitive, unreliable, and irrelevant measures of outcome. A more careful analysis of interventions needs to be planned prior to the inception of the study so that *post hoc* evaluations of heterogeneous treatments and populations, using whatever archival data are available, can be avoided (see also Chapter 14). Before systematic replications of effective interventions can yield information on moderator variables, the interventions must be operationalized. This includes describing the selection and training of the intervenors, coding the procedures used and the stylistic characteristics of the intervenors, and establishing discriminant validity for the intervention. The development of training manuals for therapists, much like those for the cognitive treatment of depression, is a necessary step toward standardization. Patterson and Alexander have made efforts in this direction. Treated families need to be described in terms of standard demographics such as family size, ages and sexes of children, SES, employment, marital status, and cultural variables; and these variables should be related to the variations in outcome. The number and percentage of sessions attended by each family member would yield "dosage" levels. Outcome measures, in addition to using more sensitive measures of the delinquents' behavior, should include changes in family behavior as this is assumed to be necessary for mediating changes in the delinquent's behavior. For example, several discriminators of delinquent from nondelinquent families can be measured reliably. These include: defensive versus supportive communication, talk time, frequency of interruptions (Alexander & Parsons, 1973); supervision and monitoring of children, support (reinforcement) to children, discipline clarity and consistency (Patterson, 1985); and cooperation versus resistance to therapists (Patterson, 1985).

Another variable, occasionally reported, that becomes increasingly important to policymakers and administrators who fund the interventions that have been reported here is cost. Several investigators have found the cost of family interventions to be less than the cost of the increased out-of-home placements that would have occurred in their absence (Marlowe et al., 1986; Gustafson et al., 1986; Barton et al., 1985). Comparing the relative costs of various treatment or nontreatment decisions to the benefits derived should lead to the proliferation of the most cost-effective interventions. For researchers, this event would reduce the quantity of programs that have never succeeded and increase the opportunity to focus on the multitude of variables moderating generally effective interventions.

CONCLUSIONS

The published reports of individual and group interventions for delinquents have provided a very noisy backdrop against which to discern definitive conclusions. The past 20 years of research have not moved the field substantially closer to discovering what kinds of interventions are effective to what degree with which kinds of delinquents. We have some clearer ideas about which approaches have consistently failed to prove their usefulness, and some clearer ideas about those approaches that generally are effective. As was discussed in Chapter 10, many reviewers have concluded that virtually nothing reduces recidivism reliably, but the studies upon which they based these conclusions, with few exceptions, do not meet commonly accepted standards of scientific rigor. The policymaker who accepts these conclusions as based on the scientific method can end up throwing the baby out with the bathwater (see Regnery, 1985).

Of the most rigorous studies presented here, we can take comfort in some consistent successes associated with certain approaches (i.e., group skills training, family interventions focusing on skills training). There have been few of these successful studies (in the family intervention area) that have been replicated by independent investigators, and we are limited in what we can attribute the successes to, and in our confidence in the reliability of the findings. To summarize what has been learned from the individual, group, and family approaches reviewed here, several common factors are associated with modest treatment success. These are: involvement of the investigator in the design, implementation, and evaluation of the intervention; ecological assessment of problem behaviors; specific behavioral goals related to the referral problem; evaluation of the client's progress and feedback to the client during the intervention; structured teaching of skills directly related to problem behavior; practice of skills in the problem setting with appropriate feedback; involvement of significant others in the juvenile's natural environment; ensuring an adequate dose of the treatment (more than 30 minutes per week).

As with institutional treatment, many of the better-designed studies have failed to reduce recidivism significantly. Perhaps this is because of a great divergence between the theory and practice of rehabilitation. Therapeutic interventions are primarily educational processes: A therapist tries, with varying degrees of directiveness, to lead the client through cognitive, affective, and behavioral changes that will make him/her less dysfunctional. The therapist should know what the cognitive, affective, and behavioral characteristics of the client are in natural, frequently occurring situations so that he or she can help the client set realistic goals. Subsequently the therapist should have a structured educational plan tailored to the abilities of the client, so that the client will know if the therapist is sticking to the plan. Finally, the therapist should have an objective method for evaluating whether the client is learning and generalizing what the therapist is trying to teach, so that the plan may be altered accordingly.

The great majority of interventions contain few of the aforementioned steps in the educational process. A medical analogy would be an attempt to treat a variety of symptoms with a drug containing known impurities and varying amounts of active ingredients that were occasionally effective in laboratory situations. These drugs would be dispensed by practitioners who had not received any standardized training in their administration, and practitioner effects would be known to exist but would be uncontrolled. The practitioners would not know the minimal dosage levels for the drugs, nor would they be able to consistently deliver a minimal dose. Finally, the practitioners would not have access to information on drug effects when the clients left their offices, and would not know when and for how long the effects might be detectable. It is no wonder that the majority of studies have not led to clear conclusions about what factors account for behavior change or the failure to achieve change.

The lack of specificity of treatment is compounded by the fact that the theoretical rationale for the intervention is generally not presented or developed. There should be a direct link between the theory of delinquency causation and the intervention (see also Chapter 13). This link is more likely to be present in the skills training approaches than in the broadly defined relationship, insight, or discussion group approaches. Examples of congruence between theory and intervention are the parenting deficit remediation interventions of G. R. Patterson, the family communication and problem solving interventions of J. Alexander, and role-taking and moral reasoning interventions of Chandler and Arbuthnot. Measures of the presumed intervening variables (child monitoring, family communication, role taking and moral reasoning) were included in these investigations.

A variety of factors are responsible for the uncertainty about treatment efficacy that continues despite the increased volume of studies. One major reason that one cannot confidently conclude that particular interventions do not produce meaningful behavior change is the insensitivity and unreliability of juvenile recidivism as the only outcome measure (see Hawkins, Cassidy, Light, & Miller, 1977; and Chapter 14). Police and court contacts represent low estimates of a delinquent's chargeable behavior (except perhaps status offenses). Lipsey's (1982) test-retest coefficients for several arrest-based measures of delinquency were in the .23 to .54 range. Self-report measures of delinquent behavior, though reactive, are better than arrest measures (Hindelang, Hirschi, & Weis, 1981), which vary according to police policy practices and detection accuracy. Lipsey (1985) argued that the likelihood of detecting a treatment effect using arrest-based measures is small. In reviewing 15 well-designed treatment studies meeting strict criteria, he found them to have only a 41 percent chance, on the average, of detecting a large treatment effect. The typically small sample sizes (less than 100) put a great demand on the sensitivity and reliability of the outcome measures to reflect a treatment effect.

Another factor contributing to the uncertainty over treatment effects is that the interventions are described so superficially that it is difficult even to categorize similar studies, much less identify the "active ingredients" of the interventions. Replication is thus impossible. In fact, even with specified interventions and close supervision and control over the treatment, independent replications, when occasionally attempted, are as likely as not to fail (i.e., Bernal et al., 1980; Fleischman, 1979). An additional problem plaguing cross-study comparisons is the lack of comparability of samples of delinquents. Pertinent data on subject characteristics are usually not available, and when they are, they are rarely evaluated for their effects on outcome measures. It may well be that among the mass of null results, some interventions were effective for some subgroups of delinquents but not for others, with the net effect being undetectable or negative (see also Chapters 10 and 11). Classifying delinquents by subtypes, which when occasionally done has produced differential results, has not been a practice of most researchers.

To remedy the multitude of deficiencies in evaluation studies, several coherent, well-designed programs of evaluation should be implemented. With adequate funding and control, a series of multisite, multiinvestigator treatment studies could be coordinated in such a way as to yield maximal comparability. Several treatment approaches that have yielded fruit could be tested at different sites with intervenors trained via standardized treatment manuals and common supervision procedures. The delivery of the intervention could be coded and checked for consistency and model fidelity, as well as for the clinical skills of the intervenors. Large samples of delinquents (to insure adequate power to detect treatment effects) could be randomly assigned to different treatment approaches, and the characteristics of the delinquents coded via commonly agreed-upon measures. Delivery systems for the treatment should be developed so that an adequate dose of the treatment is delivered at the lowest cost (i.e., home- and school-based interventions). Outcome measures that are reliable, sensitive to treatment effects, and that include positive measures such as school attendance, participation in community activities, employment length, and success, could be standardized. In this way, our knowledge of the interactive effects of treatment model, subject characteristics, and therapist characteristics would be advanced. Our subsequent efforts to rehabilitate delinquents would be far more efficient and successful, and this would in turn increase funds available for early identification and prevention approaches.

REFERENCES

Adams, S. (1959). *Effectiveness of the youth authority special treatment program: First interim report.* Research Report No. 5, California Youth Authority.

Adams, S. (1961a). *Effectiveness of interview therapy with older youth authority wards: An interim evaluation of the PICO project.* Research Report No. 20, California Youth Authority.

Adams, S. (1961b). *Assessment of the psychiatric treatment program: Third interim report.* Research Report No. 21, California Youth Authority.

Alexander, J. F., Barton, C., Schiavo, R. S., & Parsons, B. V. (1976). Systems behavioral intervention with families of delinquents: Therapist characteristics, family behavior, and outcome. *Journal of Consulting and Clinical Psychology, 44,* 656–664.

Alexander, J. F., & Parsons, B. V. (1973). Short-term behavioral intervention with delinquent families: Impact on family process and recidivism. *Journal of Abnormal Psychology, 81,* 219–225.

Alexander, J. F., & Parsons, B. V. (1982). *Functional family therapy.* Monterrey, CA: Brooks/Cole.

Arbuthnot, J., & Faust, D. (1981). *Teaching moral reasoning: Theory and practice.* New York: Harper and Row.

Arbuthnot, J., & Gordon, D. A. (1986). Behavioral and cognitive effects of a moral reasoning development intervention for high-risk behavior-disordered adolescents. *Journal of Consulting and Clinical Psychology, 54,* 208–216.

Arbuthnot, J., & Gordon, D. A. (1984, November). *The secondary school and youth services as moral agents: Remedial social development for high-risk youth in school and family contexts.* Specialized seminar presented at the annual conference of the Association for Moral Education, Columbus, OH.

Arnold, J., Levine, A., & Patterson, G. R. (1975). Changes in sibling behavior following family intervention. *Journal of Consulting and Clinical Psychology, 43,* 683–688.

Barton, C., Alexander, J. F., Waldron, H., Turner, C. W., & Warburton, J. (1985). Generalizing treatment effects of functional family therapy: Three replications. *American Journal of Family Therapy, 13,* 16–26.

Beal, D., & Duckro, P. (1977). Family counseling as an alternative to legal action for the juvenile status offender. *Journal of Marriage and Family Counseling, 3,* 77–81.

Bednar, R. L., Zelhart, P. F., Greathouse, L., & Weinberg, W. (1970). Operant conditioning principles in the treatment of learning and behavior problems with delinquent boys. *Journal of Counseling Psychology, 17,* 492–497.

Berleman, W. C., Seaberg, J. R., & Steinburn, T. (1972). Delinquency prevention of the Seattle Atlantic Street Center—A final evaluation. *Social Science Review, 46,* 323–346.

Bernal, M. E., Klinnert, M. D., & Schultz, L. A. (1980). Outcome evaluations of behavioral parent training and client centered parent counseling for children with conduct problems. *Journal of Applied Behavior Analysis, 13,* 677–691.

Braukman, C. J., Fixsen, D. L., Phillips, E. L., & Wolf, M. M. (1975). Behavioral approaches to treatment in the crime and delinquency field. *Criminology, 13,* 299–331.

Camp, B. W. (1977). Verbal mediation in young aggressive boys. *Journal of Abnormal Psychology, 86,* 145–153.

Camp, B. W., & Bash, M. B. (1981). *Think aloud: Increasing social and cognitive skills—A problem-solving program for children.* Champaign, IL: Research Press.

Camp, B. W., Blom, G. E., Herbert, F., & van Doornick, W. J. (1977). "Think Aloud": A program for developing self-control in young aggressive boys. *Journal of Abnormal Child psychology, 5,* 157–168.

Camp, B. W., van Doornick, W. J., Zimet, S. G., & Dahlem, N. W. (1977). Verbal abilities in young aggressive boys. *Journal of Educational Psychology, 69,* 129–135.

Caplan, S. (1957). The effects of group counseling on junior high school boys' concepts of themselves in school. *Journal of Counseling Psychology, 4,* 124–128.

Chandler, M. (1973). Egocentrism and antisocial behavior: The assessment and training of social perspective-taking skills. *Developmental Psychology, 9,* 326–332.

Cochrane, D. B., & Manley-Casimir, M. (1980). *Development of moral reasoning: Practical approaches.* New York: Praeger.

Collingwood, T. R., & Genthner, R. W. (1980). Skills training as treatment for juvenile delinquents. *Professional Psychology, 11,* 591–598.

Copeland, T. F., & Parish, T. S. (1979). Attempt to enhance moral judgments of offenders. *Psychological Reports, 45,* 831.

Csapo, M., & Friesen, J. (1981). Training parents of hard core delinquents as behavior managers of their children. *Canadian Journal of Criminology and Corrections, 18,* 42–48.

Dixon, S. (1985). *Strategic family therapy with truants: A multiple baseline study.* Unpublished doctoral dissertation, Georgia State University.

Druckman, J. M. (1979). A family-oriented policy and treatment program for female juvenile status offenders. *Journal of Marriage and the Family, 41,* 627–636.

Emery, R. E., & Marholin, D. (1977). An applied analysis of delinquency. *American Psychologist, 32,* 860–871.

Empey, L. T. (1982). *American delinquency: Its meaning and construction.* Homewood, ILL: Dorsey Press.

Fischer, J. (1973). Is casework effective? A review. *Social Work, 18,* 5–21.

Fitzgerald, T. J. (1974). Contingency contracting with juvenile offenders. *Criminology: An Interdisciplinary Journal, 12,* 241-248.

Fleetwood, R. S., & Parish, T. S. (1976). Relation between moral development test scores of juvenile delinquents and their inclusion in a moral dilemma discussion group. *Psychological Reports, 39,* 1075-1080.

Fleischman, M. J. (1979). Training and evaluation of aggressive children. Proposal submitted to NIMH Crime and Delinquency Section. Cited in Patterson (1985).

Fo, W., & O'Donnell, C. (1974). The buddy system: Relationship and contingency conditions in a community intervention program for youth with nonprofessionals as behavior change agents. *Journal of Consulting and Clinical Psychology, 42,* 163-168.

Fo, W., & O'Donnell, C. (1975). The buddy system: Effect of community intervention on delinquent offenses. *Behavior Therapy, 6,* 522-524.

Furgurson, L. K. (1980). Cited in Urbain, E. S., & Kendall, P. C. Review of social-cognitive problem-solving interventions with children. *Psychological Bulletin, 88,* 109-143.

Gibbs, J. C., Arnold, K. D., Ahlborn, H. H., & Cheesman, F. L. (1984). Facilitation of sociomoral reasoning in delinquents. *Journal of Consulting and Clinical Psychology, 52,* 37-45.

Gold, M., & Mattick, H. W. (1974). *Experiment in the Streets: The Chicago Youth Development Project.* Springfield, VA: National Technical Information Service.

Gordon, D. A., Arbuthnot, J., Gustafson, K., & McGreen, P. (1986). *Home-based family interventions with court-referred disadvantaged delinquents.* Unpublished manuscript.

Gordon, D. A., McGreen, P., & Arbuthnot, J. (June, 1984). *Short-term family therapy with court-referred delinquents.* Paper presented at Society for Psychotherapy Research, Smuggler's Notch, VT.

Gross, A. M., & Brigham, T. A. (1980). Behavior modification and the treatment of juvenile delinquency: A review and proposal for future research. *Corrective and Social Psychiatry, 26,* 98-108.

Gustafson, K., Gordon, D. A., & Arbuthnot , J. (1986). *A cost benefit analysis of in-home family therapy vs. probation in treating delinquents.* Unpublished manuscript.

Guttman, E. S. (1963). *Effects of short-term psychiatric treatment.* Research Report No. 36, California Youth Authority.

Haley, J. (1971). *Changing families: A family therapy reader.* New York: Grune and Stratton.

Hawkins, J. D., Cassidy, C. H., Light, N. B., & Miller, C. A. (1977). Interpreting official records as indicators of recidivism in evaluating delinquency prevention programs. *Criminology, 15,* 397-424.

Hickey, J., & Scharf, P. (1980). *Toward a just correctional system.* San Francisco: Jossey-Bass.

Hindelang, M. J, Hirschi, T., & Weiss, J. G. (1981). *Measuring delinquency.* Beverly Hills, CA: Sage.

Jackson, D. D. (1965). The study of the family: Family rules. *Family Process, 12,* 589–594.

Jennings, W. S., & Kohlberg, L. (1983). Effects of a just community program on the moral development of youthful offenders. *Journal of Moral Education, 12,* 33–50.

Johnson, T. (1977). The results of family therapy with juvenile offenders. *Juvenile Justice, 23,* 29–32.

Jurkovic, G. J., & Prentice, N. M. (1974). Dimensions of moral interaction and moral judgment in delinquent and nondelinquent families. *Journal of Consulting and Clinical Psychology, 42,* 256–262.

Kazdin, A. E. (1982). Current developments and research issues in cognitive-behavioral interventions. *School Psychology Review, 11,* 79–82.

Kendall, P. C., & Finch, A. J., Jr. (1976). A cognitive-behavioral treatment for impulsivity: A case study. *Journal of Consulting and Clinical Psychology, 44,* 852–857.

Kendall, P. C., & Finch, A. J., Jr. (1978). A cognitive-behavioral treatment for impulsivity: A group comparison study. *Journal of Consulting and Clinical Psychology, 46,* 110–118.

Kendall, P. C., & Finch, A. J., Jr. (1979). Developing non-impulsive behavior in children: Cognitive-behavioral strategies for self-control. In P. C. Kendall & S. D. Hollon (Eds.), *Cognitive-behavioral interventions: Theory, research, and procedures.* (pp. 37–79). New York: Academic Press.

Kendall, P. C., & Hollon, S. D. (1979). Cognitive-behavioral interventions: Overview and current status. In P. C. Kendall & S. D. Hollon (Eds.), *Cognitive-behavioral interventions: Theory, research, and procedures.* (pp. 1–9). New York: Academic Press.

Kinney, J. M., Madsen, B., Fleming, T., & Hoopala, D. (1976). Homebuilders: Keeping families together. *Journal of Consulting and Clinical Psychology, 45,* 667–673.

Klein, N. C., Alexander, J. F., & Parsons, B. V. (1977). Impact of family systems intervention on recidivism and sibling delinquency: A model of primary prevention and program evaluation. *Journal of Consulting and Clinical Psychology, 45,* 469–474.

Kohlberg, L. (1984). *Essays on moral development, volume II: The psychology of moral development, the nature and validity of moral stages.* San Francisco: Harper and Row.

Lipsey, M. W. (1982). *Measurement issues in the evaluation of the effects of juvenile delinquency programs.* Technical Report. Washington, D.C.: National Institute of Justice, Office of Research and Evaluation Methods.

Lipsey, M. W. (1985). *Malpractice in program evaluation? The case of delinquency prevention intervention.* Unpublished manuscript.

Little, V. L. (1980). Cited in E. S. Urbain & P. C. Kendall, Review of social cognitive problem-solving interventions with children. *Psychological Bulletin, 88,* 109–143.

Little, V. L., & Kendall, P. C. (1979). Cognitive-behavioral interventions with delinquents: Problem solving, role-taking and self-control. In P. C. Kendall & S. D. Hollon (Eds.), *Cognitive-behavioral interventions: Theory, research, and procedures.* (pp. 81–115). New York: Academic Press.

Lockwood, A. L. (1978). Effects of values classification and moral development curricula on school-age subjects: A critical review of recent research. *Review of Education Research, 48,* 329–364.

Mahoney, M. J. (1979). Cognitive issues in the treatment of delinquency. In J. S. Stumphauzer (Ed.), *Progress in behavior therapy with delinquents* (pp. 22–33) Springfield, IL: Charles C. Thomas.

Mahoney, M. J., & Arnkoff, D. B. (1978). In S. L. Garfield & A. E. Bergin (Eds.), *Handbook of psychotherapy and behavior change* (2nd ed., pp. 689–722). New York: Wiley.

Marlowe, H., Reid, J. B., Patterson, G. R., & Weinrott, M. (1986). *Treating adolescent multiple offenders: A comparison and follow up of parent training for families of chronic delinquents.* Unpublished manuscript.

Maskin, M. B. (1976). The differential impact of work-oriented vs. communication-oriented juvenile correction programs upon recidivism rates in delinquent males. *Journal of Clinical Psychology, 32,* 432–433.

McAuley, R. (1982). Training parents to modify conduct problems in their children. *Journal of Child Psychology and Psychiatry, 23,* 335–342.

McCord, W., & McCord, J. (1959). *Origins of crime: A new evaluation of the Cambridge-Somerville youth study.* New York: Columbia University Press.

McPherson, S. J., McDonald, L. E., & Ryer, C. W. (1983). Intensive counseling with families of juvenile offenders. *Juvenile and Family Court Journal, 34,* 27–33.

Meichenbaum, D. (1977). *Cognitive-behavior modification: An integrative approach.* New York: Plenum Press.

Meichenbaum, D. H., & Goodman, J. (1971). Training impulsive children to talk to themselves: A means of developing self-control. *Journal of Abnormal Psychology, 77,* 115–126.

Meyer, H. J., Borgatta, E. F., & Jones, W. C. (1965). *Girls at vocational high: An experiment in social work intervention.* New York: Sage.

Michaels, K. W., & Green, R. H. (1979). A child welfare agency project: Therapy for families of status offenders. *Child Welfare, 58,* 216–220.

Moos, R. (1974). *Family, work and group environment scales manual.* Palo Alto, CA: Consulting Psychologists Press.

Ollendick, T. H. (1978). *Social skills training for juvenile delinquents.* Unpublished manuscript, Indiana State University.

Ostensen, K. W. (1981). The runaway crisis: Is family therapy the answer? *American Journal of Family Therapy, 9,* 3–12.

Parsons, B. V., & Alexander, J. F. (1973). Short-term family intervention: A therapy outcome study. *Journal of Consulting and Clinical Psychology, 41,* 195–201.

Patterson, G. R. (1974a). Interventions for boys with conduct problems: Multiple settings, treatments and criteria. *Journal of Consulting and Clinical Psychology, 42,* 471–481.

Patterson, G. R. (1974b). Retraining of aggressive boys by their parents: Review of recent literature and follow up evaluations. In F. Lowy (Ed.), Symposium on the seriously disturbed preschool child. *Canadian Psychiatric Association Journal, 19,* 142–161.

Patterson, G. R. (1985). Beyond technology: The next stage in developing an empirical base for training. In L. L'Abate (Ed.), *Handbook of Family Psychology and Therapy* (Vol. 2, pp. 1344-1379). Homewood, ILL: Dorsey Professional Books.

Patterson, G. R., Chamberlain, P., & Reid, J. (1982). A comparative evaluation of a parent training program. *Behavior Therapy, 13,* 638-650.

Patterson, G. R., & Fleischman, M. J. (1979). Maintenance of treatment effects: Some considerations concerning family systems and follow-up data. *Behavioral Therapy, 10,* 168-185.

Patterson, G. R., & Reid, J. B. (1973). Intervention for families of aggression boys: A replication study. *Behavior Research and Therapy, 11,* 383-394.

Patterson, G. R., Reid, J. B., Jones, R. R., & Conger, R. E. (1975). *A social learning approach to family intervention* (Vol. 1). *Families with aggressive children.* Eugene, OR.: Castalia Publishing.

Persons, R. W. (1966). Psychological and behavioral change in delinquents following psychotherapy. *Journal of Clinical Psychology, 22,* 337-340.

Powers, E., & Witmer, H. (1951). *An experiment in the prevention of delinquency. The Cambridge-Somerville Youth Study.* New York: Columbia University Press.

Regney, A. S. (1985). Getting away with murder: Why the juvenile justice system needs an overhaul. *Policy Review, 34,* 1-4.

Romig, D. A. (1978). *Justice for our children.* Lexington, MA: Lexington Books.

Rosenkoetter, L., Landman, S., & Mazak, S. (1980). Use of moral discussion as an intervention with delinquents. *Psychological Reports, 16,* 91-94.

Sarason, I. G. (1968). Verbal learning, modeling, and juvenile delinquency. *American Psychologist, 23,* 254-266.

Sarason, I. G., & Ganzer, V. J. (1969). Developing appropriate social behaviors of juvenile delinquents. In J. Krumboltz & C. Thoresen (Eds.), *Behavior counseling cases and techniques* (pp. 178-193) New York: Holt, Rinehart and Winston.

Sarason, I. G., & Ganzer, V. J. (1973). Modeling and group discussion in the rehabilitation of juvenile delinquents. *Journal of Counseling Psychology, 20,* 442-449.

Satir, V. (1967). *Conjoint family therapy.* Palo Alto: Science and Behavior Books.

Schlichter, K. J., & Horan, J. J. (1979). *Effects of stress inoculation training on the anger management skills of institutionalized juvenile delinquents.* Paper presented at annual meeting of the American Educational Research Association, San Francisco, CA.

Schmidlin, S. S. (1984). In Gibbs, J. C., Arnold, K. D., Ahlborn, H. H., & Cheesman, F. L., Facilitation of sociomoral reasoning in delinquents. *Journal of Consulting and Clinical Psychology, 52,* 37-45.

Schwitzgebel, R. (1967). Short-term operant conditioning of adolescent offenders on socially relevant variables. *Journal of Abnormal Psychology, 72,* 134-142.

Scopetta, M. A. (1979). Cited in Little, V. L., & Kendall, D. C., Cognitive-behavioral interventions with delinquents: Problem solving, role-taking, and self-control. In P. C. Kendall & S. D. Hollon (Eds.), *Cognitive-behavioral interventions: Theory, research, and procedures.* (pp. 81-115). New York: Academic Press.

Seguin-Tremblay, G., & Kiely, M. (1979). Development du judgment moral chez l'adolescente en reeducation. *Canadian Journal of Behavioral Science, 11,* 32-44.

Snyder, R., & Sechrest, L. (1959). An experimental study of directive group therapy with defective delinquent boys. *American Journal of Mental Deficiency, 64,* 117–123.

Sowles, R. C., & Gill, J. H. (1970). Institutional and community adjustment of delinquents following counseling. *Journal of Consulting and Clinical Psychology, 34,* 398–402.

Spence, S. H., & Marziller, J. S. (1981). Social skills training with adolescent male offenders: II. Short term, long term and generalized effects. *Behavior Research and Therapy, 19,* 349–368.

Spivack, G., & Shure, M. B. (1974). *Social adjustment of young children: A cognitive approach to solving real-life problems.* San Francisco: Jossey-Bass.

Stringfield, N. (1977). The impact of family counseling in resocializing adolescent offenders within a positive peer treatment milieu. *Offender Rehabilitation, 1,* 349–360.

Stuart, R. B. (1971). Behavioral contracting with the families of delinquents. *Journal of Behavior Therapy and Experimental Psychiatry, 2,* 1–11.

Stuart, R. B., Jayaratne, S., & Tripodi, T. (1976). Changing adolescent deviant behavior through reprogramming the behavior of parents and teachers: An experimental evaluation. *Canadian Journal of Behavioral Science, 8,* 132–144.

Stuart, R. B., & Lott, L. A. (1972). Behavioral contracting with delinquents: A cautionary note. *Journal of Behavioral Therapy and Experimental Psychiatry, 3,* 161–169.

Thelen, M. H., Fry, R. A., Dollinger, S. J., & Paul, S. C. (1976). Use of videotaped models to improve the interpersonal adjustment of delinquents. *Journal of Consulting and Clinical Psychology, 44,* 492.

Truax, C. B., Wargo, D. G., & Silber, L. D. (1966). Effects of group psychotherapy with high adequate empathy and nonpossessive warmth upon female institutionalized delinquents. *Journal of Abnormal Psychology, 71,* 267–274.

Truax, C. B., Wargo, D. G., & Volksdorf, F. R. (1970). Antecedents to outcome in group counseling with institutionalized juvenile delinquents. *Journal of Abnormal Psychology, 76,* 235–242.

Tyler, V., & Brown, G. (1968). Token reinforcement of academic performance with institutionalized delinquent boys. *Journal of Educational Psychology, 59,* 164–168.

Ulrici, D. K. (1983). The effects of behavioral and family interventions on juvenile recidivism. *Family Therapy, 10,* 25–36.

Urbain, E. S., & Kendall, P. C. (1980). Review of social-cognitive problem-solving interventions with children. *Psychological Bulletin, 88,* 109–143.

Ventis, W. L. (1976). *Moral development in delinquent and non-delinquent males and its enhancement.* Paper presented to the Southeastern Psychological Association. Available from the author, College of William and Mary, Williamsburg, Virginia.

Weathers, L., & Lieberman, R. P. (1975). Contingency contracting with families of delinquent adolescents. *Behavior Therapy, 6,* 356–366.

Wells, R. A., & Dezen, A. E. (1978). The results of family therapy revisited: The non-behavioral methods. *Family Process, 17,* 251–274.

Williams, D. Y., Akamatsu, T. J. (1978). Cognitive self-guidance training with juvenile delinquents: Applicability and generalization. *Cognitive Therapy and Research, 2,* 285–288.

Wiltz, N. A., & Patterson, G. R. (1974). An evaluation of parent training procedures designed to alter inappropriate aggressive behavior of boys. *Behavior Therapy, 5,* 215–221.

Wright, I. (1977). Moral reasoning and conduct of selected elementary school students. *Journal of Moral Education, 7,* 199–205.

Yonge, K. A., & O'Conner, N. (1954). Measurable effects of group psychotherapy with defective delinquents. *British Journal of Psychiatry, 100,* 944–952.

CHAPTER 12

Prediction

ROLF LOEBER and MAGDA STOUTHAMER-LOEBER

Western Psychiatric Institute and Clinic
School of Medicine
University of Pittsburgh

Monahan (1981), in his summary of work on the prediction of violent behavior, wrote that the human race probably would not have survived as well as it has if humans had not attempted to predict how nature would affect them. Thus, we learned that as most lions bite and falling rocks crush, it is better to avoid both. Similarly, people have tried to predict which youngsters are likely to become delinquent and victimize others by causing physical harm or property loss.

There are a number of ways that predictive information on delinquency can be used. First, such information can help court officials, case workers, and parents in their decisions as to which individuals are most likely to become delinquents or become chronic offenders, and therefore may need more intensive intervention. Predictive information serves the second purpose of helping policy makers and investigators formulate which groups appear most at risk for a delinquent career, and should receive preventive services (see Chapter 13). Predictive information fulfills a third purpose in that it constitutes one of the ways to test the adequacy of theories about the development of delinquency.

THE PREDICTION OF THE BEHAVIOR OF INDIVIDUALS

Predictive data on future offending have been used in systematic ways in the field of parole and probation, and also in the setting of bail (Simon, 1971; Gottfredson & Gottfredson, 1984). Attempts to predict the dangerousness and violence-proneness of individuals have been less successful (Monahan, 1978; 1981). More recently the use of predictive data has been suggested for "selective incapacitation," that is, the identification of high-rate offenders and the application of longer sentences to them as a means of reducing the level of crime in the streets (Greenwood & Abrahamse, 1982). Another, less explored field is the identification by parents, teachers, or child guidance staff of youths at risk for delinquency (e.g., Loeber, Dishion, & Patterson, 1984; Spivack, 1983). The common thread in these approaches is that once high-risk individuals have been identified they can be offered some form of intervention in order to steer them away from anticipated unfavorable outcomes.

THE IDENTIFICATION OF RISK GROUPS

Increasingly, policymakers and investigators require the identification of groups of individuals at risk for delinquency. Usually, the goal is to achieve early identification of specific high-risk groups, such as violent or chronic offenders, with the aim of intensively studying the characteristics of these groups, or exposing them to a special intervention in order to reduce the likelihood of offending. Risk identification is defined here as "the ability to identify groups of individuals who, on the average, do not show the disorder or only show components of the disorder, [and] who have a statistically significant likelihood of showing the disorder in full form at a later time, in comparison with a non-risk group" (Bell & Pearl, 1982, p. 2; see also Chapter 13). Risk identification is increasingly linked to policy decisions either in mental health or in the administration of criminal justice, so that financial resources and program development can be concentrated on high-risk groups.

DEVELOPMENTAL THEORIES OF DELINQUENCY

As we have seen in Chapter 1 and 3, most theories dealing with the development of delinquency have been based on the analysis of cross-sectional data rather than longitudinal research findings. Moreover, these theories have often paid little attention to the question of how stable or changeable delinquent behavior is over time. The lack of attention to the continuity and predictability of criminal behavior over time is partly a result of the belief, expressed by Empey (1982), that "it could be . . . that delinquent behavior cannot be readily predicted because most young people are neither consistently good nor bad" (p. 289). Accordingly, juvenile conduct problems and delinquent acts appear to emerge *de novo* during adolescence in these theories rather than being an extension of behavior acquired earlier (Hirschi, 1969; Richards, Berk, & Forster, 1979). This notion can be contrasted with a multitude of research findings that preadolescent antisocial child behavior is among the most consistent forms of psychopathology over time, and that early conduct problems are predictive of later delinquency (Kohlberg, Ricks, & Snarey, 1984; Robins, 1966; Robins & Ratcliff, 1979). We will later review this evidence in detail.

Those who have held to the inherent unpredictability of delinquent behavior may have been led astray by the fact that the consistency of a pattern of behavior over time does not have to involve exactly the same specific acts. While it is easier to grasp that early theft could be related to later theft, it is less immediately obvious that early truancy may be related to later delinquent acts. In a different context, Kagan (1971) has spoken of *heterotypic continuity,* that is, the view that phenotypically different behaviors are linked over time in one theoretical conceptual framework. Emmerich (1964) distinguished between stability and continuity. Stability refers to the degree to which individuals retain their relative position on a characteristic over time, whereas continuity refers to whether the quality or meaning of the behavior remains the same over time. Within this conceptualization, continuity may mean that conduct problems and delinquent acts become more diversified over time, or that they increase in seriousness, or are replaced by less serious acts.

This waxing and waning of delinquency is one of the central points to be accounted for in developmental theories of delinquency prediction. As Farrington (1976) has succinctly expressed it, "potentially the most useful function of a criminological prediction study is to investigate the validity of competing theories about the causes of crime and delinquency" (p. 3; see also Chapter 2). In that sense, theories of delinquency need to specify which factors determine why some become delinquent over time, why others persist, and a third group desist in their delinquent activities, thus accounting for differences in individual crime rates (Blumstein, Farrington, & Moitra, 1985).

The possibility of predicting delinquency has elicited widely divergent reactions. Some have advocated early identification of children at risk for delinquency, and early preventive intervention (e.g., Chaiken & Chaiken, 1984). Others have warned that prophesies would be self-fulfilling, and would turn innocent children into criminals (Lemert, 1951; Tannenbaum, 1938). A third, mostly academic group, has advocated prediction of delinquency because it would help them to verify theories of delinquency.

The purpose of this chapter is to summarize existing longitudinal studies and address a number of central questions concerning prediction of delinquency:

1. What are the best predictors of delinquency in general, of serious delinquency, and of recidivism?
2. To what extent is it possible to predict specific forms of crime, such as violent, property, or drug offenses?
3. Is it possible to identify future chronic offenders at an early age?
4. Are there critical periods that foreshadow times when precursors of delinquency increase in predictive efficiency?
5. Which methodological factors tend to weaken predictive efficiency?
6. Is it possible to improve predictions by better predicting who will remain nondelinquent and who will cease early conduct problems?
7. How can predictive modeling of delinquency processes be done?
8. What are efficient screening methods to identify youths at risk for delinquency?

This chapter focuses on the documentation of predictors of juvenile and adult delinquency on the basis of information gathered during childhood and adolescence. In that sense it expands on former summaries of such predictors (Loeber & Dishion, 1983; Loeber & Stouthamer-Loeber, 1986). Most of the studies are based on assessments of children's behavior at home, school, or in clinics. Studies on the assessment of behavior in institutions are less common and are not included here. Predictors will be limited to overt behavioral manifestations. Self-reported personality and psychophysiological assessments will not be included. A distinction will be made between exponential predictors, that is, variables that are representative of the youth's behavior patterns, and circumstantial predictors (i.e., variables in the youth's environment) (Toby, 1961). Official delinquency based on police or court records, as well as self-reported delinquency, will both serve as outcome measures. Distinctions will be made between delinquency in general, serious delinquency, and recidivism. Special attention will be paid to the prediction of chronic offending; arbitrarily defined as at least four arrests or convictions.

PREDICTORS OF DELINQUENCY

The following review concerns predictors of delinquency that can be evaluated in two-by-two tables as shown in Figure 12.1. The object is to correctly identify future delinquents (valid positives) and future nondelinquents (valid negatives). At the same time, the aim is to minimize the number of individuals considered at risk who do not become delinquent (false positives), and to min-

	Delinquent	Nondelinquent	
Presence of Predictor	Valid Positives (a)	False Positives (b)	a + b
Absence of Predictor	False Negatives (d)	Valid Negatives (c)	d + c
	a + d	b + c	(total)

Figure 12.1. Elements of a two-by-two prediction table.

imize the number of others not identified as being at risk who later become delinquent (false negatives).

In order to compare different predictors across studies, we will use an index called Relative Improvement Over Chance (RIOC). RIOC is a measure of association between two categorical variables that summarizes valid positives and valid negatives. It also corrects for chance, and for maximum values whenever there is an discrepancy between selection ratio and base rate (see below). RIOC was preferred over other measures of association as it is largely independent of selection ratio and base rate (Loeber & Dishion, 1983; Loeber & Spyrou, 1986).

The formula for RIOC is:

$$\text{RIOC} - \frac{\text{Total correct} - \text{Chance correct}}{\text{Maximum Correct} - \text{Chance Correct}} \times 100$$

Using the parameters shown in Figure 12.1, this is computed in the following way:

$$\text{RIOC} = \frac{(a + c) - \dfrac{(a + d) \times (a + b)}{t} + \dfrac{(b + c) \times (d + c)}{t}}{\max (a + c) - \dfrac{(a + d) \times (a + b)}{t} + \dfrac{(b + c) \times (d + c)}{t}} \times 100$$

The adjustment for maximum correct is necessary because discrepancies between base rate (percent actually delinquent = $(a + d)/t$) and selection ratio (percent predicted to be delinquent = $(a + b)/t$) are quite common in delinquency prediction studies. The maximum correct refers to the maximum values for the valid positives (a) and valid negatives (c) that result from these discrepancies. For example, if the base rate is 10 percent and the selection ratio is 30 percent, then the maximum valid positives is 10 percent, and the maximum valid negatives is 70 percent, resulting in a maximum total correct of 80 percent. This implies that under this condition 20 percent of the subjects can never be correctly identified (see Loeber & Dishion, 1983 for details). For predictors that perform better than chance, RIOC has a theoretical range from 0 to 100. A negative value indicates as association at a level below chance. In studies where there were more than two categories per variable, the categories were dichotomized in such a way as to optimize the fit between base rate and selection ratio. RIOC was not calculated in cases where either base rate or selection ratio was very small (<5 percent) since estimates of RIOC can vary greatly at the extremes of the distribution. Confidence intervals for RIOC have been reported by Loeber and Spyrou (1986).

Before the data are presented, several points should be made. Even though some data on females and blacks will be presented, the majority of studies are concerned with while males. Therefore, our conclusions will mainly apply to this group. Furthermore, the predictor variables are often measured with few items and with little attention to retest or internal reliability. To a lesser extent this is also the case for the outcome variables. However, these measurement weaknesses are balanced against the relatively large sample sizes and the aggregation of evidence across studies. By summarizing many studies we will, of necessity, disregard some of the specific characteristics of each, such as the type of sample, type of respondent, the prediction interval, or the exact content of the behavior ratings. We may gain, however, a better understanding of the relationships between specific predictors of delinquency and later outcomes.

The material is organized in tables by principal categories of predictors, and by sex of the subjects. Within each table, entries are arranged by outcome, that is: delinquency in general, serious delinquency, and recidivism. Whereas delinquency in general includes status offenses in most studies, serious delinquency usually refers to those offenses contained in Part I of the FBI crime index, such as arson, robbery, rape, and manslaughter. Within each section of the tables, predictors referring to behavior in the home or more general behavior not bound to a specific locale are listed before predictors referring to behavior in the school. The tables show all the information contained in two-by-two prediction tables. This makes it possible for the reader to locate the number of valid positives, or subjects correctly predicted to fit the delinquency criterion; and the number of valid negatives, or subjects correctly predicted not to fit the delinquency criterion. The tables also show the number and percentages of prediction errors (Meehl & Rosen, 1955). The false positive error rate reported here is the proportion of those found to be nondelinquent who were initially thought to be at risk (calculated as $b/(b + c)$ in Figure 12.1), while the false negative errors are the proportion of later delinquents who were originally thought not to be at risk (calculated as $d/(a + d)$). In some studies, the false positive error rate has been calculated as $b/(a + b)$ (e.g., Wilson & Reichmuth, 1985), which is more relevant for the assessment of the sensitivity of a potential screening device. The raw data presented in the following tables will allow readers to compute this version of false positive error rate, as well as measures of sensitivity and specificity (Dunn, 1981). Although the formula for calculating RIOC does not differentially weigh false positive and false negative errors, the raw data presented here allows readers to apply different utility functions (Loeber & Dishion, 1983). The tables also show the base rate of the criterion and the selection ratio of the predictor, each expressed in percentages.

EXPONENTIAL PREDICTORS

We will first review the results pertaining to exponential predictors. This review expands on a prior summary of such predictors by Loeber and Dishion (1983).

Aggression

The studies listed in Table 12.1 refer to interpersonal aggression rather than to destructiveness of property. Aggression was consistently related to later delinquency. The median RIOC for predicting delinquency in boys was 45.3 percent (range = 16.4 − 51.4 percent), and 25.2 percent (range = 17.0 − 30.3 percent) for studies of both boys and girls. The median RIOC was marginally lower for studies predicting recidivism (38.3 percent with a range of 28.1 − 38.5 percent). (As will be discussed later, aggressiveness appears to play an important role in the development of chronic offending.) It should be noted that the studies in Table 12.1 used either teacher ratings, peer ratings, or self-reports as measures of aggression. Therefore, it is unclear how well early aggression in the home predicts later delinquency.

Table 12.1 shows that, on the average, the proportion of false negative errors was high, indicating that about half of the youths who eventually became delinquent were initially nonaggressive (see also Robins, in press). The high false negative rate is not unique to early aggression, but, as we will see, also applies to a number of other predictors. We will come back to the significance of this type of error.

Drug Use

We found only three studies in which drug use was linked to later delinquency (see Table 12.2). The median RIOC for general delinquency was 53.0 percent (range = 27.0 − 79.0 percent). Drug use also predicted continuing recidivism in a small group of boys who were already multiple offenders (RIOC = 41.6 percent; Osborn & West, 1980). Unlike other predictors that had been measured in late childhood, drug use was measured only in late adolescence. This is understandable since young children engage far less in drug use. Only in one study (Robins, Darvish, & Murphy, 1970), was a distinction made regarding type of drug. The use of soft drugs are almost normative for certain age groups and may be a less strong predictor of delinquency than the use of hard drugs.

A number of studies have shown that many chronic offenders are polydrug users, or drug and alcohol users (Petersilia, Greenwood, & Lavin, 1977; Tuchfield, Clayton, & Logan, 1982). We know little about how the emergence of substance use relates to the emergence of delinquency. Is substance use a precursor of delinquency, or is it the other way around? Data presented by Johnston, O'Malley, & Eveland (1978) indicated that delinquent involvement was higher among later drug users than among nonusers. Also, the same study showed that the more serious the prior delinquency, the more serious the later involvement with drugs. For further studies supporting Johnston et al.'s (1978) findings, the reader is referred to Loeber (1986), who also discussed evidence showing that delinquency can accelerate following sustained drug use.

TABLE 12.1. Aggression as Predictor of Later Delinquency

Study	Predictor	Valid Positives	False Positives n	False Positives %	Valid Negatives	False Negatives n	False Negatives %	N	% BR[a]	% SR[b]	Criterion	Prediction Interval	RIOC[c]
					Prediction: Male Delinquency in General								
Magnusson (1984)	Aggressiveness & motor activity (teacher rating)	35	25	6.0	395	92	72.4	538 Normal small town	23.6	11.2	Adult crime	13–(18–26)	45.3
Farrington (1979)	Involved in fights after drinking (self-report)	49	76	25.4	223	41	45.5	389 Normal/inner city	23.1	32.1	Conviction	18–21	49.3
Havighurst, Bowman, Liddle, Matthews, & Pierce (1962)	Aggressiveness (teacher & peer rating)	32	40	24.7	122	15	31.9	262 Normal/small town	22.5	34.4	Police contact	(12–13)–(18–19)	51.4
Mulligan, Douglas, Hammond & Tizard (1963)	Aggressiveness (teacher rating)	54	189	10.0	1700	120	69.0	2063 Normal	8.4	11.8	Conviction	13–15	21.5
West & Farrington (1973)	Aggressiveness (teacher rating)	23	59	18.3	264	45	66.1	391 Normal/inner city	17.4	21.0	One or more adjudicated offenses	(8–10)–17	16.4

Prediction: Male and Female Delinquency in General

Author	Measure	N	% BR[a]	N	% SR[b]	N	RIOC[c]	Outcome	Age	% RIOC
Feldhusen, Thurston, & Benning (1973)	Aggressiveness (teacher rating)	273	295	27.8	766	216	44.2	1550 Select	31.6	36.7 Police record	9-17 12-20 15-23	30.3
Kirkegaard-Sorensen & Mednick (1977)	Easily angered (teacher rating)	13	50	20.0	201	18	58.1	282 Select	11.0	22.3 Conviction	(10-20)- (23-33)	25.2
Kirkegaard-Sorensen & Mednick (1977)	Violence & aggressiveness (teacher rating)	7	20	8.0	231	24	77.4	282 Select	11.0	9.6 Conviction	(10-20) -(23-33)	17.0

Prediction: Male Recidivism

Author	Measure	N	% BR[a]	N	% SR[b]	N	RIOC[c]	Outcome	Age	% RIOC
Osborn & West (1980)	Self-reported aggression	15	8	36.4	14	6	28.6	43 Delinquents	48.8	53.5 Persisting vs. temporary recidivism	18-23	38.5
Magnusson, Stattin, & Duner (1983)	Aggressiveness 6+ (teacher rating)	25	34	10.3	296	57	69.5	412 Unselected	19.9	14.4 Two or more offenses	(10-13)-26	28.1
Mulligan, Douglas, Hammond & Tizard (1963)	Aggressiveness (teacher rating)	22	31	24.8	94	27	55.1	174 Delinquents	66.7	30.5 Reconviction	13-15	38.3

[a]% BR = percent base rate; [b]% SR = percent selection rate; [c]RIOC = Relative Improvement Over Chance.

TABLE 12.2. Drug Use as Predictor of Later Delinquency

Study	Predictor	Valid Positives	False Positives n	%	Valid Negatives	False Negatives n	%	N	% BR[a]	% SR[b]	Criterion	Prediction Interval	RIOC[c]
Prediction: Male Delinquency in General													
Robins, Darvish, & Murphy (1970)	Adolescent drug use other than marijuana (self-report)	40	4	4.2	92	86	68.3	222 Stratified random black	56.8	19.8	Adult non-traffic offenses	(−20)–(c.33)	79.0
Farrington (1979)	Drug use (self-report)	45	77	25.8	222	45	50.0	389 Normal/ inner city	23.1	31.4	Conviction	18–21	27.0
Prediction: Male Recidivism													
Osborn & West (1980)	Drug taking in past year	15	7	31.8	15	6	28.6	43 Recidivists	48.8	51.2	Persisting vs. temporary recidivism	18–23	41.6

[a]% BR = percent base rate; [b]% SR = percent selection rate; [c]RIOC = Relative Improvement Over Chance.

Truancy

As shown in Table 12.3, the four studies that measured truancy as a predictor of delinquency in general yielded a median RIOC of 25.5 percent (range = 20.4 − 26.3 percent). Truancy was related to later serious delinquency in children referred to a child guidance clinic (RIOC = 27.8 percent; Nylander, 1979) as well as in young delinquents (RIOC = 65.1 percent; Glueck & Glueck, 1940). In the latter study, 77.2 percent of all subjects were truant compared to an average of 12.5 percent for all the subjects in the nondelinquent samples in Table 12.3. Those delinquents that were not truant turned out to engage largely in minor, rather than serious offenses. One interpretation is that unsupervised time created by truancy gives children the opportunity to practice delinquency and develop the skills and attitudes necessary for a more sustained career in crime (see also Chapter 8).

Lying

Lying is an almost necessary accompaniment to a delinquent career because delinquents often need to verbally conceal their criminal behavior. Since the ability to lie is usually acquired much earlier than delinquent behavior, lying is thought to be a precursor of delinquency. The predictive power of lying in relation to later delinquency has not often been measured, however. Table 12.4 shows that in about one-third of the delinquents and in about 50 percent of the recidivists, lying was noted as a precursor of later delinquency. The median RIOC for the two studies relating parent or peer reports of the youngster's lying to later official delinquency was 22.4 percent (range = 22.0 − 22.7). In addition, Mitchell and Rosa (1981) found that children's lying, reported by parents *and* teachers, identified recidivists within a group of delinquents (RIOC = 31.0 percent).

Stealing

The studies summarized in Table 12.5 all refer to unofficial reports by parents and teachers of children's stealing. To a large extent these reports consisted of acts of theft that had not come to the attention of the police. Early theft can be expected to be a good predictor of later delinquency since most official delinquency consists of property crimes. Only two studies reported on early stealing as a predictor for later delinquency in general, and their RIOCs differ greatly. Mitchell and Rosa's (1981) study on children with behavior problems resulted in a RIOC of 57.8 percent, whereas Nylander's (1979) study with children seen in child guidance clinics yielded a RIOC of 17.1 percent. However, early pilfering or theft in the latter study also was predictive of serious crime (RIOC = 37.5 percent). In addition, parent and teacher reports of stealing also predicted recidivism in a small group of delinquents (RIOC = 60.5 percent; Mitchell & Rosa, 1981). It should be noted that the subjects in these

TABLE 12.3. Truancy as Predictor of Later Delinquency

Study	Predictor	Valid Positives	False Positives		Valid Negatives	False Negatives		N	% BR[a]	% SR[b]	Criterion	Prediction Interval	RIOC[c]
			n	%		n	%						
Prediction: Male Delinquency in General													
Robins & Hill (1966)	Truancy	44	83	37.7	137	32	42.1	296 Black	25.7	42.9	Police or court record	(6–12)–17	26.2
Nylander (1979)	Truancy	57	97	8.0	1110	262	82.1	1526 Clinic	20.9	10.1	Criminal register	(1–20) 20 years later	20.4
Farrington (1981)	Truancy	16	23	7.0	304	68	74.7	411 Normal/inner city	20.8	9.5	One or more adjudicated offenses	(8–10)–17	26.3
Mitchell & Rosa (1981)	Wandering (parent report)	15	23	8.9	235	48	76.2	321 "Deviant group"	19.6	11.9	Court appearance for indictable offense	(5–15) to 20+	24.7
Prediction: Male Serious Delinquency													
Nylander (1979)	Truancy	47	107	7.7	1285	87	64.9	1526 Clinic	8.8	10.1	Serious delinquency	(1–20) 20 years later	27.8
Glueck & Glueck (1940)	Truancy	185	113	61.1	72	16	8.0	386 Delinquent	52.1	77.2	Serious vs. minor offenses	13–28	65.1

[a]% BR = percent base rate; [b]% SR = percent selection rate; [c]RIOC = Relative Improvement Over Chance.

TABLE 12.4. Lying as Predictor of Later Delinquency

Study	Predictor	Valid Positives	False Positives		Valid Negatives	False Negatives		N	% BR[a]	% SR[b]	Criterion	Prediction Interval	RIOC[c]
			n	%		n	%						
Prediction: Male Delinquency in General													
Mitchell & Rosa (1981)	Lying (parent report)	22	37	14.3	221	41	65.1	321 "Deviant group"	19.6	18.4	Court appearance for indictable offense	(5-15)-20+	22.0
Farrington (1981)	Dishonest (peer report)	33	55	16.8	272	51	60.7	411 Normal/inner city	20.4	21.4	One or more adjudicated offenses	10-17	22.7
Prediction: Male Recidivism													
Mitchell & Rosa (1981)	Lying (parent & teacher report)	14	8	26.7	22	13	48.1	57 Delinquents	47.4	38.6	Two or more court appearances	(5-15)-20+	31.0

Note: [a]BR = percent base rate; [b]SR = percent selection rate; [c]RIOC = Relative Improvement Over Chance.

TABLE 12.5. Stealing as Predictor of Later Delinquency

Study	Predictor	Valid Positives	False Positives n	%	Valid Negatives	False Negatives n	%	N	% BR[a]	% SR[b]	Criterion	Prediction Interval	RIOC[c]
					Prediction: Male Delinquency in General								
Mitchell & Rosa (1981)	Stealing (parent report)	12	6	2.3	259	51	81.0	312 "Deviant group"	19.0	18.4	Court appearance for indictable offense	(5–15)–20+	57.8
Nylander (1979)	Pilfering/theft (staff)	96	155	12.8	1052	223	69.3	1526 Clinic	20.9	16.4	Criminal register	(1–20) 20 years later	17.1
					Prediction: Male Serious Delinquency								
Nylander (1979)	Pilfering/theft (staff)	59	192	13.8	1200	75	56.0	1526 Clinic	8.8	16.4	Serious crime	(1–20) 20 years later	37.5
					Prediction: Male Recidivism								
Mitchell & Rosa (1981)	Stealing (parent & teacher report)	11	3	9.7	28	15	57.7	57 Delinquents	45.6	24.6	Two or more court appearances	(5–15)–20+	60.5

Note: [a]% BR = percent base rate; [b]% SR = percent selection rate; [c]RIOC = Relative Improvement Over Chance.

studies were already deviant in some respect, and that it is not known how well early frequent stealing predicts later delinquency in normal populations.

General Problem Behaviors

Table 12.6 contains a variety of predictors such as antisocial referral, poor socialization, and troublesomeness, as well as more specific categories of behavior such as destructiveness, daring, and disruptive behaviors at school. The median RIOC for male delinquency in general was 30 percent (range = 4.0 − 64.2 percent). As can be seen, most of the RIOCs were in the 20 to 30 percent range. There were, however, several notable outliers. Youths referred for antisocial behavior to a clinic were much more likely to have nontraffic arrests as adults than the nonclinic controls (Robins, 1966), yielding an RIOC of 64.2 percent for males and 82.9 percent for females (for further support for the higher predictiveness of delinquency in females, see Werner, in press; Robins, in press). At the other extreme, hyperactivity, which has been asserted by some to be related to later delinquency (Hechtman, Weiss, & Perlman, 1984; Mendelson, Johnson, & Stewart, 1971) was found to have a RIOC of only 4 percent (Nylander, 1979). In terms of serious delinquency and recidivism as outcomes in males, early problematic behavior led to median RIOCs of 66.3 percent (range = 9.2 − 91.8 percent) and 52.5 percent (range 26.0 − 89.0 percent) respectively, but here, as before, hyperactivity was a poor predictor (RIOC = 9.2 percent). What appears to be important is whether the hyperactivity occurred together with aggressiveness or not (RIOC = 45.3; Stattin & Magnusson, 1984; see also Loney, Kramer, & Milich, 1982; Loney, Whaley-Klahn, Kosier, & Conboy, 1983; Milich & Loney, 1979; Schachar, Rutter, & Smith, 1981).

Other characteristics that cannot be called strictly conduct problems, and consequently are not included in Table 12.6, relate to the economic situation of older adolescents. Farrington (1979) reported that unstable job history and absence of savings were related to later convictions (RIOCs = 30.0 and 35.4 percent, respectively). Moreover, prolonged unemployment was a factor that differentiated persisting and temporary recidivists (RIOC = 28.1 percent; Osborn & West, 1980).

Low Educational Achievement or IQ

Low educational achievement has been consistently linked to delinquency in many cross-sectional studies (Hirschi & Hindelang, 1977; Menard & Morse, 1984 see also Chapters 4 and 6). Table 12.7 shows the results of longitudinal studies on educational achievement and IQ as predictors of later delinquency. The median RIOC of male delinquency in general was 22.9 percent (range = 11.1 − 46.1). Most of the studies used official delinquency as outcome. However, a low vocabulary by the age of 10 and later poor school performance were also related to high self-reported delinquency (RIOCs = 27.4 and 18.3

TABLE 12.6. Various Conduct Problems as Predictors of Later Delinquency

Study	Predictor	Valid Positives	False Positives		Valid Negatives	False Negatives		N	% BR[a]	% SR[b]	Criterion	Prediction Interval	RIOC[c]
			n	%		n	%						
Prediction: Male Delinquency in General													
Robins (1966)	Antisocial referral	185	75	58.1	54	15	7.5	260 Antisocial & 69 controls	60.8	79.0	Nontraffic arrests	(−18)−(−48) (1−20)	64.2
Nylander (1979)	Hyperactivity (staff)	100	335	27.8	872	219	68.7	1526 Clinic	20.9	28.5	Criminal register	−20 years later	4.0
Simcha-Fagan (1979)	Delinquency (mother report)	32	54	8.5	581	62	66.0	729 Normal/ city	12.9	11.8	Police contact	(7−16)−(12−21)	28.2
Mitchell & Rosa (1981)	Destructiveness (parent report)	12	14	5.4	244	51	81.0	321 "Deviant group"	19.6	8.1	Court appearance for indictable offense	(5−15) to 20+	31.8
Farrington (1981)	Daring (peer rating)	38	62	19.0	265	46	54.8	411 Normal/ inner city	20.4	24.3	One or more adjudicated offenses	10−17	27.5
Farrington (1981)	Daring (peer & parent rating)	42	79	24.0	250	38	47.5	409 Normal/ inner city	19.9	29.6	21 or more self-reported acts	(8−10)−(14−16)	32.6
Huesmann, Eron, Lefkowitz, & Walder (1984)	Aggression (peer rating)	19	63	22.4	218	32	62.7	332 Non-random	15.4	24.7	Conviction	8−30	16.7

Study	Predictor						Sample			Outcome	Age	
Janes, Hesselbrock, Myers, & Penniman (1979); Janes (1982)	Poor socialization (teacher report)	24	34.4	61	21	47.6	138 Clinic	32.6	40.6	Ever in trouble with the law	(4–15)–(16–30)	21.5
Nylander (1979)	Disruptive at school (staff)	80	11.1	1073	239	74.9	1526 Clinic	20.9	14.0	Criminal register	20 years later	20.8
West & Farrington (1973)	Troublesome (teacher & peer rating)	41	15.6	276	43	51.2	411 Normal/inner city	20.4	22.4	One or more adjudicated offenses	(8–10)–17	34.1
Farrington (1979)	Troublesomeness (teacher & peer rating)	31	18.2	269	49	61.3	409 Normal/inner city	19.6	22.2	21 or more self-reported acts	(8–10)–(14–16)	21.1

Prediction: Male Delinquency in General

Study	Predictor						Sample			Outcome	Age	
Mitchell & Rosa (1981)	Problem behavior (parent & teacher report)	30	28.4	179	30	50.0	310 "Deviant group"	19.3	32.6	One or more adjudicated offenses	(5–10)–20+	25.7

Prediction: Female Delinquency in General

Study	Predictor						Sample			Outcome	Age	
Robins (1966)	Antisocial referral	21	68.1	29	1	4.5	83 Antisocial & 29 controls	19.5	73.5	Arrest	(–18)–(–48)	82.9

Prediction: Male and Female Delinquency in General

Study	Predictor						Sample			Outcome	Age	
Robins & Ratcliff (1979)	Three or more antisocial behaviors	34	29.9	122	15	30.6	223 Clinic	22.0	38.6	Adult crime	(–18)–(–48)	50.2
Kirkegaard-Sorensen & Mednick (1977)	School disciplinary problem	10	5.9	236	21	67.7	282 Select	11.0	8.9	Conviction	(10–12)–(20–23)	32.3

(cont.)

341

TABLE 12.6. (continued)

Study	Predictor	Valid Positives	False Positives		Valid Negatives	False Negatives		N	% BR[a]	% SR[b]	Criterion	Prediction Interval	RIOC[c]
			n	%		n	%						
		Prediction: Male Serious Delinquency											
Robins (1966)	Antisocial referral	114	146	68.5	67	2	1.7	260 Antisocial & 69 controls	35.3	79.0	Major crime	(−18)−(−48)	91.8
Nylander (1979)	Hyperactivity (staff)	47	388	27.9	1004	87	64.9	1526 Clinic	8.8	28.5	Serious delinquency	20 years later	9.2
Craig & Glick (1968)	Problem behavior in Grades 1, 2, & 3 (teacher rating)	35	70	27.2	187	9	20.5	301 High del area	14.6	34.9	"Serious and/or persistent"	(6−9)−16	66.3
		Prediction: Male Recidivism											
Robins (1966)	Antisocial referral	127	133	66.8	66	3	2.3	260 Antisocial & 69 controls	39.5	79.0	Three or more nontraffic arrests	(−18)−(−48)	89.0
Robins & Ratcliff (1980)	Five or more deviant behaviors	39	18	8.2	202	72	64.9	331 Black	33.5	17.2	Three or more adult arrests	(−18)−(30−35)	52.5
Mitchell & Rosa (1981)	Problem behavior (parent & teacher report)	17	13	39.4	20	10	37.0	60 Problem	45.0	50.0	Two or more court appearances	(5−15) to 20+	26.0

Note: [a]% BR = percent base rate; [b]% SR = percent selection rate; [c]RIOC = Relative Improvement Over Chance.

percent respectively; Farrington, 1979). West and Farrington (1973) related IQ to recidivism, resulting in a RIOC of 42.9 percent.

It is not clear from the data in Table 12.7 which factors mediated the effect of IQ and educational achievement on delinquency. One school of thought has focused on the child's reaction to the educational system and his/her own performance, and considers educational failure as a precursor of delinquency (Hirschi & Hindelang, 1977). Another line of thinking has seen the child more as a victim of specific institutional responses to low IQ and poor educational performance (Hawkins & Doueck, in press; Menard & Morse, 1984). A third hypothesis postulated that early conduct problems tend to precede poor educational performance. At this point, a number of longitudinal studies, not shown in Table 12.7, have found support for the latter hypothesis (McMichael, 1979; Richman, Stevenson, & Graham, 1982; Spivack, 1983; Stott, 1981). For instance, Spivack (1983), after an extensive analysis, concluded that "for both sexes, early academic achievement is only minimally implicated in the at-risk picture, and in those few instances where it is, its effect are indirect, operating through at-risk aberrant behavior and/or subsequent misconduct that may lead to delinquency" (p. 163). McMichael (1979) also came to the conclusion that an "antisocial form of classroom deviance would appear to precede later reading difficulties in a considerable number of cases" (p. 230). However, these studies concerned poor educational performance in elementary school. Whether the same is true for delinquency in high school is not clear from the studies mentioned in Table 12.7 (Kirkegaard-Sorensen & Mednick, 1977; Polk, 1975).

Prediction Indices

Several prediction indices have been formulated on the basis of children's behavior (see Table 12.8). Two consisted of a teacher nomination of potential delinquency (Reckless & Dinitz, 1972; Scarpitti, 1964), and led to high RIOCs (64.4 and 78.0 percent, respectively). In addition, Stott and Wilson (1968) used a teacher rating scale to predict delinquency, but the RIOC of this composite score was only 27.8 percent. Finally, Spivack (1983, 1985; Spivack & Cianci, in press) have formed a high-risk profile for children in the early elementary grades. This profile includes such behavior as being over-socially involved, impatience, disrespect/defiance, external blaming, and irrelevant responsiveness. A high score on this profile predicted chronic offending with a RIOC of 87.0 percent. However, the false positive rate was high. We will come back to this important study when discussing the prediction of chronic offenders.

A word of caution should be inserted here about the use of nomination techniques such as those used by Reckless and Dinitz (1972) and Scarpitti (1964). One cannot be sure that the teachers based their nominations only on the children's behavior and excluded other factors, such as socioeconomic status, sibling behavior, or parent behavior. To some extent this criticism is true for all ratings, but the risk increases when the task is not well specified.

TABLE 12.7. Educational Performance as Predictor of Later Delinquency

Study	Predictor	Valid Positives	False Positives		Valid Negatives	False Negatives		N	% BR[a]	% SR[b]	Criterion	Prediction Interval	RIOC[c]
			n	%		n	%						
	*Prediction: Male Delinquency in General*												
Robins & Hill (1966)	School retardation before age 15	22	72	28.1	184	18	45.0	296 Nonwhites	13.5	31.8	Police or Court record	(−15)–17	34.1
Farrington (1979)	Low vocabulary at 10	40	87	26.4	242	40	50.0	409 Normal/ inner city	14.7	31.0	21 or more self-reported acts	(8–10)–(14–16)	27.4
Farrington (1979)	Poor school leaving results	30	66	20.1	263	50	62.5	409 Normal inner city	19.6	23.5	21 or more self-reported acts	11–(14–16)	18.3
Polk (1975)	Grade point average below C	30	26	19.8	105	46	60.5	252 Normal/ small town	30.2	10.3	One or more contacts with police-adult criminality	15–(28–30)	33.5
Rutter, Maugham, Mortimer, & Ouston (1979)	Verbal reasoning	266	553	67.5	266	46	14.7	1131 Normal/ city	27.6	72.4	Cautioned or found guilty	12–18	46.1

Study	Predictor						Sample	%BR	%SR	Outcome	Range	%RIOC
Wolfgang, Figlio, & Sellin (1972)	Low achievement level in school	486	368	65.2	196	157	24.4	1207 Normal/ City/ Black	53.3	70.7	Police arrest	(6–12)–18	16.4
Wolfgang, Figlio, & Sellin (1972)	Low achievement level in school	242	320	16.4	1632	448	64.9	2642 Normal/ city/whites	26.0	21.3	Police arrest	(6–12)–18	22.9
Kirkegaard-Sorensen & Mednick (1977)	Attended special education	12	24	21.8	86	19	61.3	102 High risk / 39 controls	22.0	25.5	Conviction	(10–20)–(23–33)	29.7
Wadsworth (1979)	Attitude toward school work (teacher rating)	68	262	16.9	1290	178	72.3	1798 Normal	13.7	18.3	Court appearance or cautioned by police	10–20	11.2

Prediction: Male Recidivism

Study	Predictor						Sample	%BR	%SR	Outcome	Range	%RIOC
West (1973)	IQ of 90 or lower	51	52	19.2	219	89	63.6	411 Normal/ inner city	34.1	25.1	Police contact	(8+10)–17	14.0
McCord & McCord (1959)	IQ of 90 or lower	32	36	22.5	124	61	65.6	253 Control/ city	36.8	26.9	Conviction	(10–15)–(20–23)	11.1
West & Farrington (1973)	IQ of 90 or lower	21	82	21.9	292	16	43.2	411 Normal/ inner city	9.0	25.1	Recidivism	(8+10)–17	42.9

Note: [a]% BR = percent base rate; [b]% SR = percent selection rate; [c]RIOC = Relative Improvement Over Chance.

345

TABLE 12.8. Preciction Indices of Later Delinquency

Study	Predictor	Valid Positives	False Positives n	%	Valid Negatives	False Negatives n	%	N	%BR[a]	%SR[b]	Criterion	Prediction Interval	RIOC[c]
					Prediction: Male Delinquency in General								
Reckless & Dinitz (1972)	Likelihood of future delinquency (teacher nomination)	213	881	59.5	600	32	13.1	1726 Experimental contr/comp.	14.2	63.4	Police contact	13–16	64.4
Scarpitti (1964)	Potential delinquent (teacher nomination)	27	43	31.0	99	4	12.9	173 Select/inner city	17.9	40.5	Court contact	12–16	78.0
Stott & Wilson (1968) Marsh (1969)	Delinquency prediction scale (teacher rating)	29	53	7.2	683	53	64.6	818 Maladjusted, unsettled or stable	10.0	10.0	Conviction	18–21	27.8
					Prediction: Male Recidivism								
Spivack (1983)	Problem profile (teacher rating)	21	111	60.3	73	1	4.5	206 High risk	10.7	64.1	Four or more police contacts	7–18	87.0

Note: [a]%BR = percent base rate; [b]%SR = percent selection rate; [c]RIOC = Relative Improvement Over Chance.

Early Delinquency

How well does current delinquency predict later delinquency? Because of the similarity of predictor and criterion, the predictive relationship should be relatively strong (Monahan, 1981). Table 12.9 shows several studies that used self-reported delinquency as a predictor for either continued self-reported delinquency or reconviction. The median RIOC for males was 34.5 percent (range = 30.4 − 41.2 percent). Elliott, Dunford, & Huizinga (1983) used self-reported delinquency for predicting self-reported chronic offending in boys and girls over a two-year period. The RIOC was 33.6 percent, with most of the errors in prediction being false negative errors, that is, youths who were not predicted to become career offenders. Five studies used official delinquency as a predictor for later recidivism. The median RIOC was 45.5 percent, with a range of 32.0 to 81.3 percent.

Opinions have been divided as to whether seriousness of offense is a predictor of chronic offending. For example, Elliott et al. (1983) concluded that "the seriousness of the arrest offense was not predictive of a career status" (p. 29). Other researchers reported similar findings (e.g. Holland & McGarvey, 1984; Wolfgang, Figlio, & Sellin, 1972). On the other hand, some investigators have found that the seriousness of juvenile offenses was predictive of continuing rather than temporary delinquent involvement (Knight & West, 1975; Shannon, 1978). For instance, Knight and West (1975) found that conviction by the age of 17 for a serious offense was a strong predictor of reconviction in early adulthood, yielding a RIOC of 81.3 percent. Remarkably, the proportion of errors were relatively low: 27.3 percent false positives and 6.3 percent false negatives (see Table 12.9). However, in a later analysis of these data, the seriousness of the first juvenile offense did not predict well chronic offending (Blumstein et al., 1985). Shannon (1978) used a multiple regression analysis to predict the seriousness of offending and found that of all variables seriousness of offense scores between ages six and seventeen contributed most to the prediction of seriousness of offenses between ages 18 and 20; in turn, the seriousness of offenses in the latter period contributed most to the prediction of the seriousness of subsequent offenses.

Another aspect of juvenile delinquency is whether first arrest in childhood or early adolescence is a better predictor of later delinquency than arrest in late adolescence. Farrington (1983) found that *all* of the 23 youths who had became chronic offenders by age 25 (i.e., those convicted six or more times), had been first convicted at least once by their 16th birthday. To turn it around, 32.3 percent of those convicted before that age became chronic offenders, compared with *none* who were convicted after that age. Similarly, Robins and Ratcliff (1979) found that arrest before the age of 15 predicted adult offenses (RIOC = 36.5). This predictability probably rests on the fact that those who start earlier have a higher rate of offending and nondelinquent problem behavior than those who start later (Cohen, 1986; Farrington, 1986; Loeber, 1982). A recent reinterpretation of the early onset effect postulated that it

TABLE 12.9. Delinquency as Predictor of Recidivism

Study	Predictor	Valid Positives	False Positives n	%	Valid Negatives	False Negatives n	%	N	% BR[a]	% SR[b]	Criterion	Prediction Interval	RIOC[c]
					Prediction: Male Recidivism								
LeBlanc (1980)	Average & high delinquency (self-report)	55	61	38.9	96	21	27.6	233 Normal	32.6	49.8	Average & high delinquency (self-report)	(14–16)– (16–18)	41.2
LeBlanc (1980)	High delinquency (self-report)	29	51	28.0	131	22	43.1	233 Delinquent	21.9	34.3	High delinquency (self-report)	(14–16)– (16–18)	34.5
Osborn & West (1978)	Self-reported delinquency	31	17	31.5	37	21	40.4	106 Delinquents	49.1	45.3	Reconviction	(14–16)– (19–23)	30.4
Polk (1975)	Delinquent	31	19	10.8	157	45	59.2	252 Normal/ small town	30.1	19.9	Adult criminal record	(15–16)–28	45.5

348

Prediction: Male and Female Recidivism

Study	Variable						N / Sample			Criterion	Age range	RIOC
McCord (1979)	Juvenile delinquent record	19	18	16.4	92	23	56.1	152 Select	27.6	24.3	Adult conviction for serious crimes	(5–17)–(18–40)	35.4
Wolfgang (1977)	Offense before age 18	138	214	27.1	576	47	25.4	975 Normal	19.0	36.1	Rearrest	(–17)–(18–30)	60.0
Knight & West (1975)	Conviction for serious offense	45	9	27.3	24	3	6.3	81 Most delinquent	59.3	66.7	Continued delinquency	(–17)–(18–20)	81.3
Osborn & West (1978)	Prior convictions	37	15	33.3	30	24	39.3	106 Delinquents	57.6	49.1	Reconviction	(8–18)–(19–23)	32.0
Elliott, Dunford, & Huizinga (1983)	Composite self-report index	67	343	35.4	625	47	41.2	1082 Probability	38.5	35.6	Career offender (self-report)	(11–17)–(15–22)	33.6
Robins & Ratcliff (1979)	Arrest before age 15	25	23	15.5	125	23	47.9	196 Clinic	24.5	24.5	Adult crime	(–18)–(–48)	36.5

Note: [a]% BR = percent base rate; [b]% SR = percent selection rate; [c]RIOC = Relative Improvement Over Chance.

represents individual differences between subjects not only in the rate at which they commit offenses, but also the rate of engaging in, at least for them, new conduct problems or new forms of delinquency (Loeber, 1986).

Summary of Exponential Predictors

Table 12.10 provides an overview of the studies summarized in Tables 12.1 through 12.9, and compares the predictive power of different categories of child behavior. It should be kept in mind, however, that the studies that are being compared have many dissimilarities in terms of samples, predictors, criteria, and ages of assessments. Second, the range of values per category is often large, whereas the number of studies is usually small. Therefore, the following conclusions are tentative at best. Table 12.10 shows that for almost all behavior categories, serious delinquency and recidivism were better predicted than delinquency in general. The median RIOC for all studies with delinquency in general as outcome was 27.0 percent (range = 4.0 − 79.0 percent), compared to 65.7 percent (range = 9.1 − 91.8 percent) and 38.5 percent (range = 26.0 − 89.0 percent) for serious delinquency and recidivism, respectively. Furthermore, it seems that for boys' aggression (median RIOC = 45.3 percent), stealing (median RIOC = 37.4 percent), and drug use (median RIOC = 53.0 percent) were better predictors than truancy and lying (median RIOCs = 25.5 and 22.4 percent, respectively). This conclusion corresponds with Robins's (1966) finding that boys referred for theft, and to some extent those referred for aggression, were more likely to receive a later diagnosis of sociopathy than boys referred for any other reason (see also Loeber & Schmaling, 1985). Averaged over all the studies in Tables 12.1 through 12.9, delinquency in girls was equally well predicted as delinquency in boys. However, in some studies the predictability was highest for girls.

Turning to recidivism, it was surprising that earlier offending usually was not a better predictor than stealing, general problem behavior, drug use, or aggression. Finally, prediction scales, consisting of either teachers' judgments or a combination of variables outperformed predictions based on single variables.

The conduct problems, dichotomized in Tables 12.1 through 12.9, represent continua from less to more frequent/serious acts. Several studies based on more than two categories showed the behavior stability of individuals initially most extreme in deviant behavior, those intermediate in that respect, and those who were least deviant. These studies invariably revealed that those who were most deviant and those who were most nondeviant were more likely to retain their position on the deviancy-nondeviancy continuum over time, whereas the most change took place in the intermediate group of subjects (Cline, 1980; Ghodsian, Fogelman, Lambert, & Tibbenham, 1980; Loeber, 1982). This finding is concordant with personality research indicating that temporal consistency is not the same for all individuals within a population, but that some are more consistent than others (Bem & Allen, 1974).

TABLE 12.10. Summary of Youth Behaviors as Predictors of Later Delinquency

Predictor	Sex	General Delinquency			Serious Delinquency			Recidivism		
		#[a]	Median RIOC	Range	#[a]	Median RIOC	Range	#[a]	Median RIOC	Range
Aggression	B	5	45.3	16.4–51.4				3	38.3	28.1–38.5
	B+G	3	25.2	17.0–30.3						
Drug use	B	2	53.0	27.0–79.0				1	41.6	
Truancy	B	4	25.5	20.4–26.3	2	46.5	27.8–65.1			
Lying	B	2	22.4	22.0–22.7				1	31.0	
Stealing	B	2	37.4	17.1–57.8	1	37.5		1	60.6	
General problem behavior	B	12	26.6	4.0–64.2	3	66.3	9.1–91.8	3	52.5	26.0–89.0
	G	1	82.9							
	B+G	2	41.3	32.3–50.2						
Educational achievement	B	11	22.9	11.1–46.1				1	42.9	
Prediction scales	B	3	64.4	27.8–78.0				1	87.0	
Delinquency	B							8	38.3	30.4–81.3
	B+G							2	35.1	33.6–36.5

[a]Number of studies.

351

CIRCUMSTANTIAL PREDICTORS

Circumstantial variables refer to conditions in the child's environment. Details of longitudinal studies that revealed circumstantial predictors of delinquency have been recently reviewed in Loeber and Stouthamer-Loeber (1986) and will only be summarized here.

Family Variables

As we have seen in Chapter 8, there is ample evidence for the role of family variables in delinquency, and most circumstantial variables in available studies concern the family. Table 12.11 shows the summary of studies relating family variables to later delinquency. For each family variable the median RIOC and the number of analyses is reported. Again, the findings should be interpreted with caution as the number of studies in each outcome category is small. The first four variables (poor supervision, poor discipline, lack of parent involvement, and parent's rejection of the child) reflect the interaction between parents and their children. Of these, poor supervision tended to predict best delinquency in general (median RIOC = 51.0; range 21.2 to 80.8 percent), but this is based on two studies. Parents' lack of involvement with the child, and their rejection of him/her predicted delinquency moderately well, while poor discipline was the weakest predictor (RIOC = 17.6 to 22.6 percent). However, this could be because discipline practices are notoriously difficult to measure (Patterson & Stouthamer-Loeber, 1984).

The next five variables in Table 12.11 concern the child's family environment. Poor marital relations predicted relatively strongly serious delinquency in the offspring (RIOC = 26.2 to 42.6 percent). Parental criminality and aggressiveness predicted general delinquency (median RIOC = 31.0 percent) better than serious delinquency (median RIOC = 19.5 percent). In comparison, parental absence was a weaker predictor for delinquency in general, both in samples of boys and boys and girls (median RIOCs 20.8 and 18.6 percent, respectively). Also weak was poor parental health (median RIOC = 14.2 percent).

Composites of Family Variables

Circumstantial predictors based on composites of family variables usually outperformed those based on single variables. Prediction on the basis of composite factors had its start with the Gluecks (1950) who devised a prediction table consisting mainly of parent-child interaction variables such as discipline, supervision, and affection. Since that time their table has been modified by successive researchers. Even though these studies have been criticized on various grounds (Prigmore, 1963; Reiss, 1951), they consistently showed that the parents' childrearing practices highly predicted delinquency in children. An-

TABLE 12.11. Summary of Family Variables as Predictors of Delinquency (from Loeber & Stouthamer-Loeber, 1986)

Predictor (Studies)	Sex	General Delinquency			Serious Delinquency			Recidivism		
		#[a]	Median RIOC	Range	#[a]	Median RIOC	Range	#[a]	Median RIOC	Range
Poor supervision (1,2,3)	B	2	51.0	21.2–80.8	1	29.2				
Parent uninvolvement (6)	B+G	1	31.0							
Poor discipline (4,5)	B	1	22.6		1	17.6				
Parent rejection (7)	B				2	38.7	33.7–43.8			
Parent criminality and aggressiveness (1,7,8,9)	B	2	31.0	24.4–37.6	5	19.5	10.8–34.4	1	26.4	
Marital problems (7)	B				2	34.4	26.2–42.6			
Parent absence (10,11,12)	B	2	20.8	11.5–30.2	1	8.5				
(13,14,15)	B+G	3	18.6	7.4–25.1						
Poor parent health (4)	B	6	14.2	5.7–22.9						
Composite family handicap (24,19, 20,21,4,22,8,25)	B	5	56.4	45.7–86.7				3	72.3	46.9–81.9
(24,23,6)	B+G	3	58.5	49.5–86.7						
Socioeconomic status (1,6,10,16,17,18)	B	6	17.7	10.5–30.9				3	14.0	11.7–49.3
Deviant peers (1)	B	1	32.5							

[a]Number of studies.

Studies: 1: Farrington, 1979; 2: Wilson & Herbert, 1978; 3: Farrington, 1978; 4: West & Farrington, 1973; 5: McCord, 1981; 6: Wadsworth, 1979; 7: McCord, 1984; 8: Osborn & West, 1978; 9: Robins, West, & Herjanic, 1975; 10: Robins & Hill, 1966; 11: Gregory, 1965; 12: McCord, 1982; 13: Wadsworth, 1980; 14: Simcha-Fagan, Langner, Gersten, & Eisenberg, 1975; 15: Ensminger, Kellam, & Rubin, 1983; 16: Wolfgang, Figlio, & Sellin, 1972; 17: Rutter, Maughan, Mortimer, & Ouston, 1979; 18: Knight & West, 1975; 19: Thompson, 1952; 20: Voss, 1963; 21: McCord, 1979; 22: Craig & Glick, 1968; 23: Trevvett, 1972; 24: Tait & Hodges, 1972; 25: Blumstein et al., 1985.

353

other set of studies used composites based on family and exponential variables (McCord, 1979; Osborn & West, 1978; Wadsworth, 1979; West & Farrington, 1973; Farrington & Tarling, 1985). The results for either category were about the same: The median RIOCs were 56.4 and 58.5 for the prediction of delinquency in general in male and mixed samples, respectively, and 72.3 percent for the prediction of recidivism. This is a substantial improvement over the average median RIOC for single predictors.

Socioeconomic Status

A number of literature reviews have appeared on the relationship of social class and delinquency (Braithwaite, 1981; Hindelang, Hirschi, & Weiss, 1979; Tittle, Villemez, & Smith, 1978). The most thorough review is by Braithwaite (1981), who concludes that social class is related to official delinquency and serious self-reported delinquency, and to a lesser extent to self-reported delinquency in general. Most of the studies in the reviews are concurrent studies and thus do not show a true predictive relationship. However, socioeconomic status is relatively stable and might be hypothesized to have existed before the delinquent behavior started. The longitudinal studies reporting on the relationship between socioeconomic status and delinquency have been reviewed in Loeber and Dishion (1983) and are here only summarized in Table 12.11. Socioeconomic status, like most of the other family contextual variables, had only a modest predictive relationship with delinquency in general and with recidivism (median RIOCs were 17.7 and 14.0, respectively). On the other hand, there is evidence from self-reported delinquency studies that lower socioeconomic strata are overrepresented among the chronic offenders (Elliott et al., 1983).

Peers

We were able to locate only one longitudinal study on the influence of deviant peers on later delinquency. Farrington (1979) found that involvement with antisocial peers at the age of 18 led to a RIOC of 32.5 percent. As deviant peer influences play a pivotal role in several theories of delinquency, and in the conceptualization of the Socialized Aggressive subgroup discussed in Chapter 5, it is curious to see that its temporal relationship to delinquency has not yet been sufficiently clarified (but see Elliott et al., 1983).

Comparisons Between Exponential and Circumstantial Predictors

Despite the emphasis by sociologists on more circumstantial variables, others have thought that exponential variables predict later delinquency better than circumstantial variables (Monahan, 1981). A comparison of Tables 12.10 and 12.11 generally bears this out. Children's own behavior predicted later delinquency better than contextual variables such as parent absence, parent health, or socioeconomic status. However, several of the interactional variables such as poor supervision and parental rejection tended to be equally strong predictors as children's own behavior.

The use of children's individual problem behaviors or family variables improved the prediction of delinquency by about 25 to 35 percent. Although this improvement is considerable, there is still ample room for misclassification. In contrast, combinations of variables, either through prediction scales or through composite family scores, performed better as predictors, doubling the improvement in prediction of the individual variables.

THE EARLY IDENTIFICATION OF CHRONIC OFFENDERS

Several studies reporting on chronic offenders all agree that these offenders are recognizable before they enter high school. As mentioned, in the Spivack (1983; 1985) study (Table 12.8), the eventual chronic offenders (four or more offenses) in elementary school were characterized by being over-socially involved, and showing impatience, disrespect/defiance, external blaming, and irrelevant responsiveness. These youngsters became already optimally recognizable in grade 2, but 68 percent of the eventual chronic offenders were already distinguishable from other children in kindergarten. In the analyses by Farrington (Blumstein et al., 1985; Table 12.11), the chronic offenders (six or more offenses by age 25, all of whom had already been first convicted by age 15) scored at or before the age of 13 high on three out of the following seven factors: troublesomeness, conduct disorder, acting out, social handicap, criminal parents, poor parental childrearing behavior, and low IQ.* The two studies have in common a relatively low false negative rate: 4.5 percent and 13.0 percent. A third study by Craig and Glick (1968), mentioned in Table 12.6, also produced relatively few false negative errors (20.5 percent). This study measured children's problem behavior in grades 1 to 3, and highly predicted serious and/or persisting delinquency (RIOC = 66.3). Finally, Pulkkinen (1983) studied multitype offenders, that is, those who had by age 20 already committed at least one alcohol, theft, and violent offense. This group of serious offenders, compared to other groups of offenders, had the highest number of police contacts. The longitudinal data showed that the multi-type offenders (almost all were males) already differed on peer nominations at age eight from other offenders because of their high score on a factor called ag-

---

*The study showed that of 55 youths scoring four or more out the seven criteria, 15 became chronic offenders (out of 23), 22 became nonchronic offenders, and only 18 were unconvicted.

gressive/short-spanned (likely a combination of the Undersocialized and Attention-Deficit patterns discussed in Chapter 5).

The first three studies provided the clearest data indicating that early behavior patterns of two-thirds to almost all of the chronic delinquents are recognizable in the elementary school age period.* This conclusion agrees with the finding by Robins (1966) that about four out of five of the antisocial children referred to a child guidance clinic by age 10 later became adult sociopaths. Our summary on chronic delinquents and the work by Robins (1966) point in the same direction, that serious antisocial behavior rarely emerges *de novo* in adulthood, and instead starts much earlier (Robins & Ratcliff, 1979). Given that many chronic offenders commit both property and violent forms of crime, it is likely that early aggressiveness is among their premorbid characteristics (see also Petersilia et al., 1977; Pulkkinen, 1983).

It should be noted that a high proportion of those initially thought to be at risk do *not* become chronic offenders, at least within the limits of the follow-up studies. This may indicate that a number of individuals desisted from chronic delinquency to a degree or perhaps went undetected by the police. Another possibility is that more chronic delinquents would emerge in these studies when the follow-up periods were longer. At this stage, the presence of false positive errors would affect the efficiency of potential screening instruments based on the above predictors. However, even when screening does not take place, arguments for early intervention are still in place.

In an important early intervention program, the Perry Preschool Program, preschoolers from low-income families were randomly assigned to intervention and control groups (Berrueta-Clement, Schweinhart, Barnett, Epstein, & Weikart, 1984). By the ages of 19 to 24, the intervention subjects had incurred about half the number of arrests as those in the control group. Given the sample sizes in the groups, it is difficult to statistically demonstrate that the program affected chronic offenders, but the results certainly are in the right direction (see also Chapter 13).

Aside from early onset, the above findings reflect several dimensions of child behavior, not immediately evident from Tables 12.1 to 12.11, that appear to be of importance for the identification of those at risk for chronic offending (Loeber, 1982). First, many of these children apparently show a *variety* of early rather than single problem behaviors (see also Loeber, 1982; Robins & Ratcliff, 1979). Judging from other studies, it is likely that these youngsters display these problem behaviors in *multiple settings,* and that those who do so in single settings are less at risk for delinquency or other maladjustment (Loeber, 1982; McGee, Silva, & Williams, 1983; Mitchell & Rosa, 1981; Schachar et al., 1981).

---

*Kraus (1973), in a study of child problem behaviors up to grade 6, found that all but three of problematic children had already been identified by the end of grade 3. Problematic status was defined as the high ratings by three different teachers from kindergarten onwards. The study did not relate these ratings to later delinquency.

THE PREDICTION OF SPECIFIC TYPES OF CRIME

Opinions have been divided as to whether early conduct problems are equally predictive of all forms of crime, or whether particular conduct problems are indicative of particular offense categories (e.g., Buikhuisen & Jongman, 1970; Kohlberg et al., 1984; Loeber, 1985; Robins, 1966). Some investigators have discounted specific links, as for example Kohlberg et al. (1984), who concluded that "The predictive power of antisocial behavior does not appear to depend on specific types of antisocial behavior . . . " (p. 140). Also, Robins and Ratcliff (1980) came to the conclusion that "With the exception of early drug use . . . we find no childhood behavioral predictors of particular types of offenses" (p. 362).

On the other hand, as Reiss (1951) and Buikhuisen (1979) have pointed out, one cannot assume that delinquency is a homogeneous phenomenon, and that there are no subgroups within a delinquent population who practice particular types of crimes. Analyses of official records have often failed to find specific subgroups of those committing particular crimes (Gibbons, 1975; Petersilia, 1980; Rojek & Erickson, 1982), but exceptions should be noted (Buikhuisen & Jongman, 1970; Smith, Smith, & Noma, 1984; see also Chapter 5). It is thought that delinquency prediction might be improved if variables could be identified that differentially predict offense-related subgroups of delinquents. We have been unable to find studies on predictors of offense-specific subgroups of offenders. Instead, available studies focused on categories of offenses— violence, property, drug or alcohol offenses—and then tried to link each category to particular precursors. One rationale for such specific relationships over time is the similarity between early and later problem behaviors, such as early and later theft, or early aggression and later violence (Patterson, 1982; Loeber, 1985). Some less obvious links that have been hypothesized are the triad of enuresis, pyromania, and cruelty to animals as precursors of adult violence (Hellman & Blackman, 1966).

The verification of the specific links has practical and theoretical implications. Such knowledge is essential for focused preventive efforts. Moreover, if early problem behavior can be linked to particular forms of later crime, this will have considerable implications for our theoretical conceptualization of developmental tracks that lead to some but not to other outcomes (Loeber, 1985, 1986).

Table 12.12 summarizes relevant studies based on "normal" samples, that is, those not based on extreme groups or on clinic-referred children. Two of the three studies on lying/cheating revealed that this behavior was more related to property than to person crimes (McCord, 1977; Wadsworth, 1979). One study showed that teacher reports of theft were more related to person crimes and alcohol offense than to property crime (Pulkkinen, 1983). However, as mentioned before, early theft is highly predictive of delinquency in general, which mostly consists of property offenses. This finding is also supported by a follow-up study of youths involved in theft (as identified by their

TABLE 12.12. The Relationship Between Early Predictors and Specific Forms of Delinquency in Studies with Normal Samples

Study	Sample	Predictor	Property Crime/ Vandalism	Criterion Drug Use/ Alcohol Offense	Person Crime/ Aggression	Prediction Interval
McCord, 1977	466M	Lying (teacher rating)	+		−#	(6–8)–(40+)
Pulkkinen, 1983	196 M 173F	Lying/exagerating (peer nomination)	−	+	+	8–20
Wadsworth, 1979	c. 2196 M	Cheating or cribbing	+*		−	10–20
Pulkkinen, 1983	196 M 173 F	Takes other children's possessions (teacher rating)	−	+	+	8–20
Johnson, O'Malley, & Eveland, 1978	1994 M	Drug use (self-report)	+		−	15–23
Magnusson, Stattin, & Duner, 1983	412 M	Aggressiveness (teacher rating)	−		+	(10–13)–26
Pulkkinen, 1983	196 M 173 F	Attacks without reason (teacher rating)	−	+	+	8–20

+ = predictor related to criterion.

− = predictor less or not related to criterion.

Includes a combination of person and property crimes.

* The relationship is with less serious offenses (i.e., with nonviolent forms of delinquency).

parents), many of whom later became delinquent (Moore, Chamberlain, & Mukai, 1979), while Farrington (1973) found that many youths who admitted to frequent theft later started committing burglaries.

One study found that drug use was more related to later self-reports of vandalism than to aggression (Johnston et al., 1978). Other studies not mentioned in Table 12.12 further indicate that early drug use was predictive of later drug use (Jessor, Donovan, & Widmer, 1980; Robins et al., 1970), and that drug use together with multiple arrests for nondrug offenses was predictive of arrest for drug use (Robins and Ratcliff, 1980).

The results in Table 12.12 also show that early aggressiveness was more related to later person crimes than to property crimes (Magnusson, Stattin, & Duner, 1983; Pulkkinen, 1983).* This agrees with a number of other studies showing high stability of aggression over time (Olweus, 1979; but see also Ahlstrom & Havighurst, 1971; Farrington, 1978; Gersten, Langner, Eisenberg, Simcha-Fagan, & McCarthy, 1976; Havighurst et al., 1962; Huesmann et al., 1984; it should be noted that the latter study also included nonaggressive acts). The findings also correspond with the extensive review of relevant studies, interviews, and 1055 case histories by Justice, Justice, and Kraft (1974), who concluded that the *joint* occurrence of fighting, temper tantrums, school problems, truancy, and inability to get along with others "indicate a strong possibility of violent behavior in adulthood" (p. 458). However, they found little or no evidence for the aforementioned triad of precursors hypothesized by Hellman and Blackman (1966.)[†] Moreover, even when low-base-rate behavior such as firesetting and cruelty are used as predictors, they are bound to produce many false negative errors.

An important question is whether or not the majority of those who committed violent acts in adulthood had been aggressive as youngsters. In prediction terms, this would be evident from a low rate of false negative errors. Robins (1966; 1978) concluded on the basis of her study of children seen in an child guidance clinic that "Violent and aggressive behavior patterns do not appear in adults if they have been absent in childhood except of course in the context of specific physical or psychiatric disorder like mania, drug intoxication, or temporal lobe epilepsy" (Robins, 1978, p. 668). Along that line, Farrington (1978) found that aggression rated between ages 12 and 14 predicted violent offenses by age 21. The false negative error rate was 29.6 percent, indicating that seven out of 10 highly aggressive youths eventually were convicted for violent crime. The data presented by Magnusson et al. (1983) showed that nine out of each 10 individuals who had committed a violent offense by age 26 had been rated highly aggressive at ages 10 to 13.

In sum, the findings lend support to the hypothesis that overt antisocial

*It should be noted that in the Magnusson et al. (1983) study robbery was classified as a property crime.
†Robins (1966) found that enuresis after the age of six was one of the few nonantisocial symptoms that was related to the diagnosis of sociopathic personality in adulthood.

behavior (Undersocialized Aggression—see Chapter 5) is associated with later violent offenses, and that to some extent lying, and perhaps theft, and drug use (Socialized Aggression—see Chapter 5) are associated more with property than with violent offenses. However, the evidence is far from complete.

It has been postulated that these specific links between problem behavior over time are less evident for those whose early problem behavior was extreme and/or led to referral to a clinic (Loeber, 1985). This would also help to account for the fact that there is a group of juvenile and adult offenders who commit property *and* person crimes at relatively high rates (Chaiken & Chaiken, 1984; Loeber & Schmaling, 1985; Petersilia, 1980; Wolfgang et al., 1972). The presence of such "generalist" offenders in study populations is bound to weaken observed links between subgroup membership and later offenses. For that reason, Table 12.13 separately summarizes the studies on highly deviant youngsters and their later offending. It shows that for this category of children a number of specific early problem behaviors, such as lying, theft, destructiveness, and truancy, are *not predictive* over time of specific forms of crime (Mitchell & Rosa, 1981; Pulkkinen, 1983). Another study, not shown in Table 12.13, that was undertaken with underprivileged black youngsters, showed that high scores on aggressiveness *and* shyness (withdrawal would probably be a better term) predicted heavy marijuana use nine years later, but only marginally so (RIOC = 17.1; Kellam, Brown, & Fleming, 1982). On the other hand, as shown in Table 12.13, early less serious behaviors such as hyperactivity (without aggression), wandering away from home, smoking, and use of alcohol did not predict all categories of crime.* These findings should be accepted with caution, for most of the studies lack replication. However, the data suggest that extremely deviant children are more likely to become "generalist" offenders, whereas there is more evidence for some forms of specialization when more normal samples are followed up.†

METHODOLOGICAL LIMITATIONS

Several factors can affect the outcome of prediction studies (Ohlin & Duncan, 1949; Gottfredson, 1967). Lack of independence of measurement may occur in retrospective studies where the outcome is already known to the person who is asked to judge behavior or circumstances in the past. Lack of independence of measurement may also take place when the assessment of one particular category of child or parent behavior is colored by knowledge of other child

---

*The data support the speculation by Patterson (1982, p. 39) that hyperactivity is related to later theft (see also Hechtman, Weiss, Perlman, & Amsel, 1984, for serious theft during the high school years).

†Another reservation is the fact that the prediction of specific forms of crime is often hampered by the very low base rate of, for instance, violence in the general poulation. This sets a limit to predictive efficiency (Meehl & Rosen, 1955).

TABLE 12.13. The Relationship Between Early Predictors and Specific Forms of Delinquency in Studies with Select Samples

Study	Sample	Predictor	Criterion			Prediction Interval
			Property Crime/Vandalism	Drug Use/Alcohol Offense	Person Crime/Aggression	
Mitchell & Rosa, 1981	321 MF "deviators"	Lying (parent rating)	+		+	(5–15)–(17–28)
Loney, Whaley-Klahn, Kosier & Conboy, 1983	65 M clinic referred	Hyperactivity without aggression	+		–	(4–12)–(21–23)
Mitchell & Rosa, 1981	321 MF "deviators"	Theft	+		+	(5–15)–20+
		Destructiveness	+		+	
		Wandering away from home (all parent rating)	+		–	
Pulkkinen, 1983	77 M 77 F select	Truancy	+	+	+	14–20
		Smoking	–	+	–	
		Taking alcohol	–	+	+	

\+ = predictor related to criterion.

– = predictor less or not related to criterion.

361

or parent behaviors. For instance, parents may judge truancy as a problem when they know that the child has gone shoplifting during school hours, whereas they otherwise might have ignored the truancy. Also, parents may be judged to be poor supervisors on the basis of the child's antisocial behavior rather than on evidence of the parents' behavior. To some extent this can be circumvented by judicious phrasing of the questions, for example, asking for frequencies rather than judgment of seriousness, and by using multiple data sources. In this context, it may also be important to exclude data from subjects that are known to respondents as already delinquent at the initial assessment.

In longitudinal studies with delinquency as outcome variable, selective attrition may cause important changes in the results, since the groups most at risk for delinquency usually have the highest attrition rate (Polk & Ruby, 1978). In the present review, where the outcome was mainly official records, presumably the attrition was not that important given that these records remained available. However, when self-reported delinquency was the outcome variable, it can be expected that high attrition would affect the predictive efficiency of precursors. We have already mentioned the psychometric weakness of many predictor variables. Unreliable measurement of these variables will lead to an underestimate of predictive relationships with outcome variables (Nunnally, 1978).

As was already alluded to earlier, the larger the mismatch between the cutting score of the predictor and the base rate of the criterion, the larger the reduction in the maximum number of possible correct predictions. Since the base rate of the criterion is usually fixed as delinquent or not delinquent, one may adjust the cutting score of the predictor variable, in order to optimize the match with the eventual base rate of delinquency (Dunn, 1981; Loeber & Dishion, 1982). This requires an estimate of the base rate years hence, which can be best gauged from existing data on comparable subject populations. However, concomitant with an increase in prevalence or base rate of delinquency over time, the proportion of false negatives will increase, while a decrease in prevalence will result in an increase in false positives (Dunn, 1981; Loeber & Dishion, 1982). Knowledge of this phenomenon will help to anticipate the amount and the type of prediction errors that can be expected in longitudinal studies.

CRITICAL PERIODS

The average percentage of subjects initially thought to be at risk who turned out to be nondelinquent in Tables 12.1 to 12.9 (calculated as (b/ (a + b) in Figure 12.1), was about 50 percent. This indicates that a substantial number of children who initially seemed at risk did not become delinquent (see also Robins & Ratcliff, 1979). One way of conceptualizing this development is that behavior patterns in children "crystallize" in particular periods, leading to some becoming deviant and others becoming nondeviant. The picture is obviously simplistic but if "crystallization" were to take place, then children's problem behavior could be expected to become predictive of criminality around certain age ranges. The identification of such developmental periods are important for several reasons. Youth at risk can best be assessed at the time of such peaking of predictors. Moreover, it seems likely that there is a *critical period* prior to the peaking in predictability, during which the "crystallization" takes place.

We have already pointed to the emergence in the elementary school years of behavior patterns that are predictive of chronic offending. The question is whether there are any other critical periods and age-specific manifestations discernable from the available data. For instance, it is probable that many young would-be chronic offenders are characterized by highly aggressive behavior. Given that many aggressive children outgrow their aggressiveness (Loeber, 1982, 1985), the question is *when* high aggressiveness becomes optimally predictive of later aggressiveness. Loeber (1982) reanalyzed data from the large number of studies reviewed by Olweus (1979), and found that, on the average, aggressiveness measured at the age of 13 accounted for about two and one-half times more of the variance in explaining later aggression than when measured at age eight.* Further evidence was provided by Roff and Wirt (1984), who reported that aggressiveness predicted adult delinquency better for 5th and 6th graders than for 3rd and 4th graders. Additionally, Stattin and Magnusson (1984) found that aggressiveness by the age of 10 predicted delinquency less well than when measured by the age of 13 for girls but not for boys. Similarly, Farrington's (1978) data show that aggression at ages eight to ten did not as well predict later conviction for violent offenses as did aggression measured at ages 12 to 14 (the false negative errors decreased from 51.9 percent to 29.6 percent). Whereas these pieces of evidence are few in number, they point to the same direction, that is, that early adolescence probably is a time when aggressiveness has crystallized and becomes highly predictive of aggression and delinquency. McCord's (1981) study linking early aggressiveness to alcoholism in adulthood came to a similar conclusion (see Jones, 1968, and Livson & Peskin, 1967, for further support based on composites of predictors). Of course, these data also indicate the general finding that predictions made temporally closer to the criterion are more accurate.

We do not know of data on critical periods for other child conduct problems, but Kohlberg and his associates found a similar trend for children's moral reasoning. Colby, Kohlberg, Gibbs, and Lieberman (1983) reported that moral scores at age 10 were poor predictors of scores at ages 24 to 26 or 26 to 30 (r = .20; −.25). Scores at ages 13 to 14, however, were significant and strong predictors of later states: r = .70 at ages 24 to 26, and .67 at ages 28 to 30. The scores at later ages remained highly correlated with subsequent outcomes.

*Only two studies mentioned by Olweus (1979) provided data on aggressiveness measured after age 13, which prevented a similar analysis for the older age groups.

A second study further supported these findings (Snarey, 1982, cited in Kohlberg et al., 1984).

It is thought that intervention and prevention probably are most effective when focused on each group during the critical period, compared to after a critical period, when child problem behavior is usually more entrenched. In that sense, we agree with Gersten et al. (1976) who concluded, on the basis of the stability data of juvenile conduct problems and delinquency, that intervention can best occur in the preschool and in the elementary school periods. It should be stressed that information about critical periods invariably refers to the characteristics of groups of subjects rather than of individuals. As illustrated by the early emergence of a subgroup of youths at risk for chronic offending, it is quite likely that for some youths antisocial behavior patterns have stabilized at an age below the median for a population, whereas for others this stabilization takes place over longer periods of time.

THE PREDICTION OF NONDELINQUENCY AND DESISTANCE

Errors in prediction can arise from a number of conditions. Some of these can be anticipated and can therefore be reduced. We will highlight two sources of error: (1) there is weak relationship between the predictor and delinquency, and many subjects are not seen at risk who actually later appear to be at risk (false negatives); and (2) a group of subjects initially thought to be at risk do not become delinquent (false positives). In the first instance, a researcher's choice is to search for other predictors to better discriminate between those at risk and those not at risk. In the second case, prediction can be improved by systematically forecasting who will remain nondelinquent.

The Reduction of False Negative Errors

The best way of reducing false negative errors is to use better predictors. Children's aggressiveness as a predictor of delinquency can serve as an example (see Table 12.1). The rate of false negative errors in these studies averaged 53.9 percent, with a range from 28.6 percent to 74.4 percent, indicating that about half of the delinquents formerly were either observed as nonaggressive or low aggressive. These errors rates are also about 50 percent for the prediction of serious delinquency and recidivism. We interpret these findings to show that separate risk factors are needed to identify subgroups at risk (Reiss, 1951). As was noted in Chapter 5, studies of conduct problems have suggested that overt antisocial behavior (Undersocialized Aggression) and covert antisocial behavior (Socialized Aggression) form distinct behavior patterns that only overlap in a minority of children (see also Loeber & Schmaling, 1985). Therefore, it is likely that multiple rather than single predictors will more exhaustively identify future delinquents. We expect that future research will identify other multiple sets of precursors that optimize predictions and reduce false negative errors.

Another way to reduce false negative errors lies in improving the prediction of valid negatives. The majority of the efforts in prediction have been aimed at finding predictors that forecast *deviance* at a later point in time. Whereas this has advanced the field immensely, the question of whether predictions can be optimized by more precise information about predictors of *nondeviance* needs to be raised. One can conceptualize predictors of deviance and nondeviance as each having their own distributions that usually overlap to some extent (Wiggins, 1973). The larger the overlap the poorer the predictive efficiency. The function of a prediction instrument is to discriminate between the two distributions and optimally allocate subjects with respect to a future criterion. The traditional predictive approach in criminology has been to use the high-risk indicators to identify those most at risk to be maladjusted later, while taking the absence or low degree of these indicators as the criterion for those least at risk. Such one-sided discriminations are best for the subjects on the most extreme positions on the prediction dimension. However, the approach is least successful for the middle range of subjects, some of whom may become delinquent. Translated into errors of prediction, a group of these middle range subjects is bound to become false negatives.

In criminology, the reduction of false negative errors is potentially feasible since the risk of delinquency for at least one group of youths tends to be *lower than chance*. Several researchers have commented on the fact that children with "emotional problems" without conduct disorder have a reduced risk of becoming antisocial, maladapted, or delinquent (Cass & Thomas, 1979; Graham & Rutter, 1973; Kohlberg et al., 1984; Mitchell & Rosa, 1981; Rutter, Tizard, & Whitmore, 1970; Wickman, 1928). For instance, Mitchell and Rosa (1981) noted that certain of these children's behaviors such as food fads, worrying, and being afraid of the dark were significantly negatively related to criminality. In a follow-up of the Isle of Wight subjects, Graham and Rutter (1973) found that "children who had suffered from emotional disorders when younger *never* [emphasis added] developed an antisocial disorder" (p. 1228). This also is evident from the Cambridge-Somerville study, where shyness and lack of self-confidence is preadulthood predicted delinquency at a rate much lower than chance (RIOC = −23.1 and −33.3, respectively).* Note however, that as pointed out in Chapter 5, there is an anxious subgroup well represented among adjudicated delinquents. We postulate that the prediction of delinquency may very well be improved by including catagories of predictors of nondelinquency. It is quite possible that future research will further uncover other categories of such predictors.

---

*West and Farrington (1977) found a nonsignificant trend that children's nervousness was negatively related to later delinquency. However, Blumstein et al. (1985), in a further analysis of that data, showed that nervousness at age eight significantly distinguished convicted offenders from nondelinquents.

The Reduction of False Positive Errors

False positive errors in prediction can be caused by several factors. For instance, they can result from less-than-perfect predictors or from subjects' desisting from deviant behavior. The question can be raised whether it is possible to forecast which subjects will desist over time.

A number of potential predictors of desistance have emerged from the literature. First, in line with what has been said about emotional problems, several researchers have found that when early conduct problems co-occur with emotional problems, the outcome of later maladjustment tends to be lower compared to conduct problem youths without emotional problems (Glueck & Glueck, 1940; Graham & Rutter, 1973; Mitchell & Rosa, 1981; Rutter et al., 1970). Turning to desistance in delinquency, amazingly little work has been done since the pioneering work by Glueck and Glueck (1940). They found that good to fair compared to bad parental discipline was a marginal predictor of desistance by known juvenile delinquents before the age of 21 (RIOC = 13.2 percent). Other predictors were absence of school misconduct and starting delinquency after the age of 12. More recent work by Buikhuisen and Hoekstra (1974) and Osborn (1980) revealed that leaving town affected desistance rates. Other factors reported by Osborn and West (1980), such as committing crime for "enjoyment" rather than financial gain, and committing crime in the company of peers rather than alone an indicator of the Socialized subgroup (Knight & West, 1975; Petersilia et al., 1977), differentiated between nonpersisting/intermittant delinquents and persisting/intensive delinquents. These variables probably are good candidates to differentiate desisters or low-rate offenders from persisters and high-rate offenders. Increasing research on "protective" factors in youths at risk for later maladjustment may further shed light on other potential differentiators (e.g., Werner, in press; Werner & Smith, 1982).

Whereas some studies on desistance have focused on the cessation of arrest, there is an obvious need to assess whether factors predicting desistance also apply to the cessation of self-reported delinquency (see LeBlanc, 1980). The further study of factors predicting desistance might not only optimize predictive accuracy, but should further shed light on the processes that influence individuals' rates of offending over time.

PREDICTION OF DELINQUENCY PROCESSES

The preceding comments suggest that in the area of predictive modeling of delinquency processes, merely linking the assessment of individuals' behavior at one time with that of a decade or more later is too simplistic an approach. Instead, repeated measurements at small intervals are more likely to capture these processes and allow more precise predictions. This requires the tracing of the chains of intervening variables that link early independent variables to later delinquent outcomes. We postulate that the developmental process of conduct problems can be best captured by the following assumptions: (1) that predictors do not necessarily predict equally well the onset of delinquency in different periods (as e.g., adolescence or adulthood); (2) that developmental processes of delinquency can be best modeled by describing the relationships between early precursors, intervening variables, and intermediate, and long-term outcomes; and (3) that some factors may predict delinquency better over long than short periods of time.

The Prediction of Delinquency Onset at Different Periods

In the longitudinal studies by McCord (1983) and by West and Farrington (1977), the onset of official delinquency (and possibly high rate of self-reported delinquency) is distributed throughout a period, although it usually peaks in middle adolescence (Farrington, 1983). It is questionable whether predictors are equally operative irrespective of the age of onset of delinquency over, for instance, adolescence and adulthood. West and Farrington (1977) found that troublesomeness at school and conduct disorders were predictive of juvenile convictions (up to age 17), but did not predict those who were first convicted in young adulthood (ages 18 to 21). On the other hand, some precursors can be predictive of convictions in both periods, as for example, aggressiveness, critical attitude toward the police, and self-reported delinquency (see further Farrington, 1979; Osborn & West, 1980). Other researchers have similarly documented different predictors for juvenile and adult crime (McCord & McCord, 1959; Robins & Wish, 1977).

Stepwise Predictions

Three issues can be raised that relate to stepwise predictions. First, given that the data support the notion that early conduct problems are antecedents to serious and/or repeated forms of delinquency many years later, it has been posed that developmental progressions exist from less serious nonantisocial behaviors to serious delinquency, and that individuals differ in the extent and speed at which they progress (Loeber, 1986). From this it would follow that predictions can be improved by constructing a stepwise sequence such as from chronic disobedience to lying, and from lying to stealing. A second issue is whether it is possible to conceptualize youngsters' drift into delinquency as a gradual process, characterized on the one hand by sets of relatively stable risk factors, and punctuated on the other hand by the occurrence of other, "novel" risk factors that accelerate the delinquent involvement. Examples of the latter are entry into a deviant peer group, moving into a high-crime neighborhood, and school failure. Few researchers have systematically explored the temporal sequence of stable as well as "novel" risk factors in delinquency (for conduct problems, see Cohen & Brook, 1984). A third issue involves the need to disentangle the colinearity of predictors, which tends to blur their unique contribution. Farrington (1986), using logistic regression, partialled out the contribution of each risk variable independent from other risk variables. For instance, he found that convictions by ages 10 to 13 were best predicted by (child's age at the time of measurement is indicated in parentheses): troublesomeness (8 to 10), poor housing (8 to 10), low IQ (8 to 10), and Catholic family (8). Convictions between the ages of 14 and 16 were best independently predicted by convictions in the earlier period, daring behavior (8 to 10), convicted parent (10), and dishonesty (10). In comparison, convictions between the ages of 17 and 20 were best independently predicted by convictions (14 to 16), delinquent friends (14), low social class (14), truancy (12 to 14), and convicted parent (10). Further analyses for older age groups show similar results. Some predictors reappear for the onset of convictions in subsequent periods, other predictors appear unique. These findings should be interpreted with caution for not all variables were measured at each assessment. However, the results support the notion that the delinquency process can be best modeled and interpreted by stepwise predictions, that help to explain the onset, continuity, and desistance of offending for different groups of individuals. In that sense, we agree with Buikhuisen (1979) who advocated a "probabilistic model" of the explanation of crime, in which the future likelihood of crime is a function of the presence of predisposing factors, the presence of facilitating factors, and the absence of inhibitory factors (see also the discussion of reward and inhibitory processes in Chapter 5).

Sleeper Effects

Some risk factors may initially have a relatively low correlation with delinquency, but, in certain cases, the correlation can increase in magnitude over time. It is thought that such sleeper effects can occur when youngsters are exposed to the cumulative effects of particular risk factors over long rather than short periods of time. To our knowledge, sleeper effects have not been highlighted in delinquency studies, probably primarily because most delinquency theories have been based on concurrent rather than longitudinal data (e.g., Hirschi, 1969). However, the comparison between these two survey methods allows us to identify potential sleeper effects.

   Loeber and Stouthamer-Loeber (1986) in their meta-analysis of familial factors affecting juvenile conduct problems and delinquency, found some indications of sleeper effects. Specifically, they postulated that sleeper effects were evident for interactional variables within the family, such as lack of supervision and rejection. In comparison, nonsocialization variables such as family size and socioeconomic status did not show such sleeper effects. However, the proof of sleeper effects is only possible in studies that measure the dependent variables at different points in time. An example is the five-year follow-up of youths in the Manhattan longitudinal study. Simcha-Fagan et al. (1975) reported on parent-child relationship variables such as parents being cold and punitive, and mothers being excitable-rejecting. The concurrent correlation of these variables with delinquency averaged .15, while the average correlation five years later was .23. Expressed in variance accounted for, the value was twice as high for the follow-up than for the concurrent data. The role that familial influences play is also evident from the study by Richman et al. (1982) showing that the majority of the children who developed behavior problems by age eight and who were without these at age three had family relationships that were tension-ridden. Given the relative stability of these family relationships in this study, the finding supports the notion that enduring deficits in the family have a sleeper effect and are associated with the emergence of aggravation of later problem behavior in children.

In summary, the data provide some inklings that sleeper effects exist in delinquency, and serve to emphasize that such effects need to be more systematically studied, for they may be more prevalent than we have indicated here. Knowledge of these effects is not only critical for the identification of risk groups, but also for the evaluation of interventions. In the latter case, ideally one would like to eliminate or reduce especially those risk factors that have a cumulative effect over time.

STEPWISE SCREENING METHODS

Given that delinquency patterns develop over time, it follows that stepwise screening methods that sample different risk factors at different points in time would be more optimal than "single stage" screening procedures, a fact already illustrated by those studies that have identified risk groups of children on the basis of repeated teacher ratings over two or more years (Craig & Glick, 1968; Kraus, 1973; Magnusson et al., 1983). These studies have much merit, but have been confined to exponential risk factors. We see great promise in a more systematic use of multiple screening methods, especially those that are theory-based and would allow the successive assessments of parental, peer, and school influences.

Stepwise screening metods have also been conceptualized in other ways. Usually, the cost of "single stage" assessments is commensurate with the number of risk factors that are measured. The cost is usually prohibitive if assessments of early conduct problems, various aspects of family functioning, peer influences, academic performance, and moral development are all measured in thousands of youngsters, especially when this is repeated over time. An alternative procedure is to use stepwise screening methods that have successfully been applied in the field of personnel selection (Wiggins, 1973).

The few systematic, stepwise screenings of juvenile delinquents that have been simulated in the past, lacked empirical justification for why certain risk factors were included and others not (for exceptions see Briggs, Wirt, & Johnson, 1961; Havighurst et al., 1962). In contrast, Loeber, Dishion, and Patterson (1984) simulated a multiple gating procedure on existing data, and based it on two principles: economy and a combination of best known predictors. The predictors used were multiple and frequent conduct problems as noted by teachers and parents, and the parents' child-rearing practices. In a first gate, teachers rated the 7th and 10th grade boys. A low score on positive behaviors was used to identify a risk group. Only this group formed the basis for the next gate, which was five telephone calls to the mother about the child's problem behavior in the last 24 hours, family organization, and the mother's knowledge of the child's whereabouts. Only families with youths at risk identified by this second gate formed the basis for the final assessment consisting of an interview with the mother on child-rearing practices. Thus, the smallest numbers of families would be exposed to the most expensive assessment. The results of the multiple gating procedure are based on a follow-up of the subjects in court records over a period of three years (Loeber and Dishion, in press). The procedure correctly identified 80 percent of the multiple offenders (i.e., with three or more police contacts). However, 67 percent of those thought to be at risk did not incur a police record. Given that most of the youngsters had not reached the peak in their offending, only a longer follow-up (now underway) will show the ultimate effectiveness of this stepwise screening procedure. In terms of cost, the multiple gating was 58 percent less expensive than a single-stage screening procedure.

CONCLUSIONS

The following are the most important conclusions from our survey of predictors of delinquency:*

1. Early conduct problems—aggression, stealing, truancy, lying, drug use—are not only predictive many years later of delinquency in general, but especially of serious delinquency, and in certain cases, of recidivism. These results are virtually consistently replicated across studies on subject samples from different places and countries. The data, although less available for girls than for boys, indicate considerable consistency between the sexes.
2. Children who have not outgrown their aggressiveness by early adolescence appear to be at high risk for delinquency and aggressiveness later.
3. Although juvenile arrest or conviction is a predictor of arrest or conviction in adulthood, the seriousness of the juvenile offense appears to be a better predictor of the continued, serious delinquency in adulthood.
4. Individual family variables predicted moderately well subsequent delinquency in offspring. Particularly strong predictors were poor supervision and the parents' rejection of the child, while other child rearing variables such as lack of discipline and lack of involvement were slightly less powerful. In addition, parental criminality and aggressiveness, and marital discord were

---

*Although delinquency was the focus in the present chapter, these predictors are also ominous in forecasting other forms of later maladjustment such as alcohol and drug abuse, chronic unemployment, poor interpersonal relationships, poor health status, and so forth (Janes, Hesselbrock, Myers, & Penniman, 1979; Robins, 1966; in press).

moderately strong predictors. Parent absence, parent health, and socioeconomic status were weaker predictors of later delinquency. The strongest predictors were multiple family handicaps.

5.   Poor educational performance predicted later delinquency to some extent, but available evidence suggests that the effect is mostly mediated through accompanying conduct problems.

6.   A majority of eventual chronic offenders can be recognized in the elementary school years on the basis of their conduct problems and other handicaps.

7.   A majority of the later violent delinquents appear to have been highly aggressive as children.

8.   Similar offense-specific precursors were observed for other categories of crime: early theft predicting later theft and burglary, and early drug use predicting later drug use.

The results of our survey of predictors should be interpreted with caution. First, the number of studies per category of predictor was often small, making it hazardous to generalize to other populations. Second, as prospective and retrospective studies have been included, the results are not immediately transferrable to future prospective studies. Third, some of the studies that we reviewed concerned special groups of children, such as those referred to clinics, first-time offenders, or otherwise designated as deviant. The predictability of early precursors tends to be higher for these groups as compared to the same precursors derived from more normal populations. Fourth, we compared the efficacy of predictors on the basis of the Relative Improvement over Chance index. As yet it is unclear whether the observed ranking of predictors would be different when other indicators of predictive efficiency are used, such as, for example, Mean Cost Rating (Duncan, Ohlin, Reiss, & Stanton, 1953; Simon, 1971). Fifth, there was a lack of studies on the prediction of self-reported delinquency. In the Cambridge Study on Delinquent Development, convictions were easier to predict than self-reported delinquency, as predictors for the first were more numerous than predictors for the latter (Farrington & Tarling, 1985). We found only one study that attempted to predict serious self-reported delinquent involvement (Elliott et al., 1983). Sixth, although the prediction results show considerable replicability in different settings and populations, there still is a paucity of information on risk factors in particular segments of our society. Notably, there is an amazing scarcity of risk studies within black or other minority populations. Finally, it should be stressed that predictors of delinquency cannot be equated with causal factors without further proof of the direction of causal influences. For instance, whereas it has been postulated that inadequate parenting underlies children's conduct problems and delinquency, virtually all parents have difficulty raising a temperamentally difficult child.

We have mentioned that combinations of powerful predictors tend cumulatively to improve predictive efficiency of a screening instrument (Robins &

Wish, 1977; Rutter, 1978). There are several methods that can be used for the optimal combination of predictors, such as the ones developed by Burgess, Glueck, and others (Farrington & Tarling, 1985; Simon, 1971; Wilbanks, 1985). Systematic comparisons between simple unit methods and more sophisticated weighting procedures, as in multiple regressions, has shown that simple unit analyses generally lead to less shrinkage in cross-validation (Farrington, 1985). Copas (1985) has shown ways to calculate expected shrinkage in prediction studies. Farrington (Farrington & Tarling, 1985), after reviewing predictors of delinquency, concluded that predictive efficiency "will not be improved by devising and using more sophisticated mathematical methods of selecting and combining variables into a prediction instrument, at least with our present methods of measurement. . . . " Instead, he opined, "advances in predictive efficiency will only follow the development of more valid, reliable, and sensitive measurement techniques" (p. 171).

To this we would add that the identification of better predictors will further augment predictive efficiency in future studies. There are several possibilities, including improvements in the identification of valid positives (and a reduction in false negatives) by means of more efficient predictors. Another possibility is the improvement of prediction of valid negatives (and a reduction in false negatives), by means of the more accurate prediction of those who will *not* become delinquent. Lastly, predictions can be improved by the more accurate forecasting of those who will desist in problem behavior over time (the false positives).

Although the construction of composite risk factors is useful for the identification of groups of youths at risk for delinquency, we have pointed out that sometimes delinquency processes can best be modeled by stepwise predictions over time rather than by combining all the most powerful predictors at time one and relating these to a much later outcome. On the other hand, it should be kept in mind that the impact of some predictors (such as lack of socialization within the family) probably becomes stronger the longer youngsters are exposed to unfavorable circumstances. Being poorly supervised by parents for a few months may not be as good a predictor of delinquency as lack of supervision for several years.

Virtually all of the studies that provided data for our review followed the performance model of behavior rather than a model accounting for aptitudes. We argue that advanced delinquent behavior reflects an aptitude, or in other words, skills that have been acquired over time. Examples of such skills are casing opportunities for crime, gathering partners, planning the crime, developing a new identity, not to mention the skills involved in breaking of safes, elaborate schemes of fraud, and so on (Petersilia et al., 1977). In performance models the concern is with whether the behavior occurs or not, whereas in an aptitude model the concern is whether the behavior has been acquired, and what the factors are that determine the absence or presence of its performance. The study of delinquency is largely that of performance, and rarely addresses whether aptitudes learned early in life are connected with law breaking even after long periods of law-abiding behavior. What may count is the initial practice in cheating, bullying, or scheming. Along this line, the findings reported by Chaiken and Chaiken (1984) and Osborn and West (1980) are relevant. After interviewing incarcerated convicts and males in a community sample, these researchers noted that some men, after a two- to five-year crime-free interval, again engaged in delinquent activities. Theories on delinquency need to be able to account for both aptitudes and the reasons why performance occurs in some and not in other instances.

ACKNOWLEDGMENTS

This chapter is partly a revision of a review by the senior author and Tom Dishion of predictors of male delinquency, published in *Psychological Bulletin* in 1983. The chapter was written during the senior author's membership on the panel on Criminal Career Research, sponsored by the National Academy of Sciences, where he found much inspiration from his fellow members. The present authors are grateful for the comments of David Farrington and Charles Lidz on an earlier draft. Danette Waller efficiently assisted in the data analysis, while Celia Eatman helped with the preparation of the chapter.

REFERENCES

Ahlstrom, W. M., & Havighurst, R. J. (1971). *400 losers*. San Francisco: Jossey-Bass.

Bell, R. Q., & Pearl, D. (1982). Psychosocial change in risk groups: Implications for early identification. *Journal of Prevention in Human Services, 1,* 45–59.

Bem, D. J., & Allen, A. (1974). On predicting some of the people some of the time: The search for cross-situational consistencies in behavior. *Psychological Review, 81,* 506–520.

Berrueta-Clement, J. R., Schweinhart, L. J., Barnett, W. S., Epstein, E. S., & Weikart, D. P. (1984). *Changed lives: The effects of the Perry Preschool Program on youths through age 19*. Ypsilanti, MI: High/Scope Press.

Blumstein, A., Farrington, D. P., & Moitra, S. (1985). Delinquency careers: Innocents, desisters, and persisters. In M. Tonry & N. Morris (Eds.), *Crime and Justice* (Vol. 6, pp. 137–168). Chicago: University of Chicago Press.

Braithwaite, J. (1981). The myth of social class and criminality reconsidered. *American Sociological Review, 46,* 36–57.

Briggs, P. F., Wirt, R. D., & Johnson, R. (1961). An application of prediction tables to the study of delinquency. *Journal of Consulting Psychology, 25,* 46–50.

Buikhuisen, W. (1979). An alternative approach to the etiology of crime. In S. A. Mednick & S. G. Shoham (Eds.), *New paths in criminology* (pp. 27–43). Lexington, MA: Lexington Books.

Buikhuisen, W., & Hoekstra, H. A. (1974). Factors related to recidivism. *British Journal of Criminology, 14,* 63–69.

Buikhuisen, W., & Jongman, R. W. (1970). A legalistic classification of juvenile delinquents. *British Journal of Criminology, 10,* 109–123.

Cass, L. V., & Thomas, C. B. (1979). *Childhood pathology and later adjustment: The question of prediction.* New York: Wiley.

Chaiken, M. R., & Chaiken, J. M. (1984). Offender types and public policy. *Crime and Delinquency, 30,* 195–226.

Cline, H. F. (1980). Criminal behavior over the life span. In O. G. Brim & J. Kagan (Eds.), *Constancy and change in human development* (pp. 641–674). Cambridge, MA: Harvard University Press.

Cohen, J. M. (1986). Research on criminal careers: Individual frequency rates and offense seriousness. In A. Blumstein, J. Cohen, J. A. Roth & C. A. Visher (Eds.), *Criminal careers and "career criminals"* (pp. 292–418). Washington, D.C.: National Academy of Sciences.

Cohen, P., & Brook, J. (October, 1984). *Family factors related to the persistence of psychopathology in childhood and adolescence.* Paper presented to the Society for Life History Research in Psychopathology, Baltimore.

Colby, A., Kohlberg, L., Gibbs, J., & Lieberman, M. (1983). A longitudinal study of moral judgment. *Monographs of the Society for Research in Child Development, 48,* No. 1–2, Monograph 200.

Copas, J. B. (1985). Prediction equations, statistical analysis, and shrinkage. In D. P. Farrington & R. Tarling (Eds.), *Prediction in Criminology* (pp. 232–255). Albany: State University of New York Press.

Craig, M. M., & Glick, S. J. (1968). School behavior related to later delinquency and nondelinquency. *Criminologica, 5,* 17–27.

Duncan, O. D., Ohlin, L. E., Reiss, A. J., & Stanton, H. R. (1953). Formal devices for making selection decisions. *American Journal of Sociology, 58,* 573–584.

Dunn, C. S. (1981). Prediction problems and decision logic in longitudinal studies of delinquency. *Criminal Justice and Behavior, 8,* 439–470.

Elliott, D. S., Dunford, F. W., & Huizinga, D. (1983). *The identification and prediction of career offenders utilizing self-reported and official data.* Unpublished manuscript, Behavioral Research Institute, Boulder, CO.

Emmerich, W. (1964). Continuity and stability in early social development. *Child Development, 35,* 311–332.

Empey, L. T. (1982). *American delinquency—Its meaning and construction* (rev. ed.). Homewood, IL: The Dorsey Press.

Ensminger, M. E., Kellam, S. G., & Rubin, B. R. (1983). School and family origins of delinquency: Comparisons by sex. In K. T. Van Dusen, & S. A. Mednick (Eds.), *Antecedents of aggression and antisocial behavior* (pp. 73–98). Boston: Kluwer-Nijhoff.

Farrington, D. P. (1973). Self-reports of deviant behavior: Predictive and stable? *The Journal of Criminal Law and Criminology, 64,* 99–110.

Farrington, D. P. (1976). *Statistical prediction methods in criminology.* Paper presented at the NATO Advanced Institute on Computer Assisted Decision Making in Parole. Cambridge, England.

Farrington, D. P. (1978). The family background of aggressive youths. In L. A. Hersov, M. Berger & D. Shaffer (Eds.), *Aggression and antisocial behavior in childhood and adolescence* (pp. 73–93). Oxford: Pergamon Press.

Farrington, D. P. (1979). Environmental stress, delinquent behavior, and convictions. In I. G. Sarason & C. D. Spielberger (Eds.), *Stress and anxiety* (Vol. 6, pp. 93–107). Washington, DC: Hemisphere.

Farrington, D. P. (1981). The prevalence of convictions. *The British Journal of Criminology, 21,* 173–175.

Farrington, D. P. (1983). Offending from 10 to 25 years of age. In K. T. Van Dusen & S. A. Mednick (Eds.), *Prospective studies of crime and delinquency* (pp. 17–38). Boston: Kluwer-Nijhoff.

Farrington, D. P. (1985). Predicting self-reported and official delinquency. In D. P. Farrington & R. Tarling (Eds.), *Prediction in criminology* (pp. 150–173). Albany: State University of New York Press.

Farrington, D. P. (1986). Stepping stones to adult criminal careers. In D. Olweus, J. Block, & M. R. Yarrow (Eds.), *Development of antisocial and prosocial behavior* (pp. 359–383). New York: Academic Press.

Farrington, D. P., & Tarling, R. (Eds.). (1985). *Prediction in criminology.* Albany, NY: SUNY Press.

Feldhusen, J. F., Thurston, J. R., & Benning, J. J. (1973). A longitudinal study of delinquency and other aspects of children's behavior. *International Journal of Criminology and Penology, 1,* 341–351.

Gersten, J. C., Langner, T. S., Eisenberg, J. G., Simcha-Fagan, O., & McCarthy, E. D. (1976). Stability and change in types of behavioral disturbances of children and adolescents. *Journal of Abnormal Child Psychology, 4,* 111–127.

Ghodsian, M., Fogelman, K., Lambert, L., & Tibbenham, A. (1980). Changes in behavior ratings of a national sample of children. *British Journal of Social and Clinical Psychology, 19,* 247–256.

Gibbons, D. C. (1975). Offender typologies—two decades later. *British Journal of Criminology, 15,* 140–156.

Glueck, S., & Glueck, E. T. (1940). *Juvenile delinquents grow up.* New York: Commonwealth Fund.

Glueck, S., & Glueck, E. T. (1950). *Unraveling juvenile delinquency.* Cambridge, MA: Harvard University Press.

Gottfredson, D. M. (1967). Assessment and prediction methods in crime and delinquency. In the President's Commission on Law Enforcement and Administration Task Force Report, *Juvenile Delinquency and Youth Crime.* Washington, DC: U.S. Government Printing Office.

Gottfredson, S. D., & Gottfredson, D. M. (1984). *Accuracy of prediction models.* Paper presented to the National Research Council's Panel on Research on Criminal Careers, National Academy of Sciences, Woods Hole, MA.

Graham, P., & Rutter, M. L. (1973). Psychiatric disorders in the young adolescent: A follow-up study. *Proceedings of the Royal Society of Medicine, 66,* 1226–1229.

Greenwood, P., & Abrahamse, A. (1982). *Selective incapacitation.* Report to the National Institute of Justice. Santa Monica, CA: Rand Corporation.

Gregory, I. (1965). Anterospective data following childhood loss of a parent: I. Delinquency and high school dropout. *Archives of General Psychiatry, 13,* 99–109.

Havighurst, R. J., Bowman, P., Liddle, G., Matthews, C., & Pierce, J. (1962). *Growing up in river city.* New York: Wiley.

Hawkins, J. D., & Doueck, H. (in press). Social development and the prevention of antisocial behavior among low achievers. In D. H. Crowell (Ed.), *Childhood aggression and violence.* New York: Plenum.

Hechtman, L., Weiss, G., & Perlman, T. (1984). Young adult outcome of hyperactive children who received long-term stimulant treatment. *Journal of the American Academy of Child Psychiatry, 23,* 261–269.

Hechtman, L., Weiss, G., Perlman, T., & Amsel, R. (1984). Hyperactives as young adults—initial predictors of adult outcome. *The Journal of the American Academy of Child Psychiatry, 23,* 250–260.

Hellman, D. S., & Blackman, N. (1966). Enuresis, firesetting and cruelty to animals: A triadic predictive of adult crime. *American Journal of Psychiatry, 122,* 1431–1435.

Hindelang, M. J., Hirschi, T., & Weis, J. G. (1979). Correlates of delinquency: The illusion of discrepancy between self-report and official measures. *American Sociological Review, 44,* 995–1014.

Hirschi, T. (1969). *Causes of delinquency.* Berkeley: University of California Press.

Hirschi, T., & Hindelang, M. J. (1977). Intelligence and delinquency: A revisionist review. *American Sociological Review, 42,* 571–587.

Holland, T. R., & McGarvey, B. (1984). Crime specialization, seriousness, progression, and Markov chains. *Journal of Consulting and Clinical Psychology, 52,* 837–840.

Huesmann, L. R., Eron, L. D., Lefkowitz, M. M., & Walder, L. O. (1984). Stability of aggression over time and generations. *Developmental Psychology, 20,* 1120–1134.

Janes, C. L. (1982). Unpublished data.

Janes, C. L., Hesselbrock, V. M., Myers, D. G., & Penniman, J. H. (1979). Problem boys in young adulthood—Teacher ratings and 12-year follow-up. *Journal of Youth and Adolescence, 8,* 453–472.

Jessor, R., Donovan, J. E., & Widmer, K. (1980). *Psychosocial factors in adolescent alcohol and drug use: The 1980 National Sample Study, and the 1974–78 Panel Study, Final Report.* Institute of Behavioral Science, University of Colorado, Boulder.

Johnston, L. D., O'Malley, P. M., & Eveland, L. K. (1978). Drugs and delinquency: A search for causal connections. In D. B. Kandel (Ed.), *Longitudinal research on drug use.* New York: Wiley.

Jones, M. C. (1968). Personality correlates and antecedents of drinking patterns in adult males. *Journal of Consulting and Clinical Psychology, 32,* 2–12.

Justice, B., Justice, R., & Kraft, I. A. (1974). Early warning signs of violence: Is a triad enough? *American Journal of Psychiatry, 131,* 457–459.

Kagan, J. (1971). *Change and continuity in infancy.* New York: Wiley.

Kellam, S. G., Brown, C. H., & Fleming, J. P. (1982). The prevention of teenage substance use: Longitudinal research and strategy. In T. J. Coates, A. C. Peterson,

& C. Perry (Eds.), *Promoting adolescent health: A dialog on research and practice* (pp. 171-200). New York: Academic Press.

Kirkegaard-Sorensen, L., & Mednick, S. A. (1977). A prospective study of predictors of criminality. In S. A. Mednick & K. O. Christiansen (Eds.), *Biosocial bases of criminal behavior* (pp. 229-243). New York: Gardner Press.

Knight, B. J. & West, D. J. (1975). Temporary and continuing delinquency. *British Journal of Criminology, 15,* 43-50.

Kohlberg, L., Ricks, D., & Snarey, J. (1984). Childhood development as a predictor of adaptation in adulthood. *Genetic Psychology Monographs, 110,* 91-172.

Kraus, P. E. (1973). *Yesterday's children: A longitudinal study of children from kindergarten into adult years.* New York: Wiley.

LeBlanc, M. (1980). *Développement psycho-social et évolution de la delinquance au cours de l'adolescence.* Unpublished manuscript. University of Montreal, Groupe sur l'Inadeptation Juvenile. Montreal, Quebec.

Lemert, E. M (1951). *Social pathology.* New York: McGraw-Hill.

Livson, N. & Peskin, H. (1967). Prediction of adult psychological health in a longitudinal study. *Journal of Abnormal Psychology, 72,* 509-518.

Loeber, R. (1982). The stability of antisocial and delinquent child behavior: A review. *Child Development, 53,* 1431-1446.

Loeber, R. (1985). Patterns and development of antisocial child behavior. In G. J. Whitehurst (Ed.), *Annals of Child Development* (Vol. 2, pp. 77-116). Greenwich, CT: JAI Press.

Loeber, R. (1986). *National histories of juvenile conduct problems, substance use, and delinquency: Evidence for developmental progressions.* Unpublished manuscript. University of Pittsburgh, Pittsburgh, PA.

Loeber, R., & Dishion, T. J. (1982). *Strategies for identifying at-risk youth.* Unpublished manuscript, Oregon Social Learning Center, Eugene, OR.

Loeber, R., & Dishion, T. J. (1983). Early predictors of male delinquency: A review. *Psychological Bulletin, 94,* 68-99.

Loeber, R., & Dishion, T. J. (in press). Antisocial and delinquent youths: Methods for their early identification. In J. D. Burchard & S. Burchard (Eds.), *Prevention of delinquent behavior.* Beverly Hills: Sage.

Loeber, R., Dishion, T. J., & Patterson, G. R. (1984). Multiple gating: A multistage assessment procedure for identifying youths at risk for delinquency. *Journal of Research on Crime and Delinquency, 21,* 7-32.

Loeber, R. & Schmaling, K. B. (1985). The utility of differentiating between mixed and pure forms of antisocial child behavior. *Journal of Abnormal Child Behavior, 13,* 315-336.

Loeber, R., & Spyrou, S. (1986). *The advantages and limitations of a prediction index called Relative Improvement Over Chance.* Unpublished manuscript, Western Psychiatric Institute and Clinic, University of Pittsburgh.

Loeber, R., & Stouthamer-Loeber, M. (1986). Family factors as correlates and predictors of juvenile conduct problems and delinquency. In M. Tonry & N. Morris (Eds.), *Crime and Justice* (Vol. 7 pp. 29-149). Chicago: University of Chicago Press.

Loney, J., Kramer, J., & Milich, R. S. (1982). The hyperactive child grows up: Predictors of symptoms, delinquency, and achievement at follow-up. In K. D. Gadow & J. Loney (Eds.), *Psychosocial aspects of drug treatment for hyperactivity* (pp. 381–415). Boulder, CO: Westview Press.

Loney, J., Whaley-Klahn, M. A., Kosier, T., & Conboy, J. (1983). Hyperactive boys and their brothers at 21: Predictors of aggressive and antisocial outcomes. In K. T. Van Dusen & S. A. Mednick (Eds.), *Prospective studies of crime and delinquency* (pp. 181–208). Boston: Kluwer-Nijhoff.

Magnusson, D. (1984). Early conduct and biological factors in the developmental background of adult delinquency. Paper presented at Henry Tajfel Memorial Lecture, Oxford.

Magnusson, D., Stattin, H., & Duner, A. (1983). Aggression and criminality in a longitudinal perspective. In K. T. Van Dusen & S. A. Mednick (Eds.), *Antecedents of aggression and antisocial behavior* (pp. 277–302). Boston: Kluwer-Nijhoff.

Marsh, R. W. (1969). The validity of the Bristol Social Adjustment Guides in delinquency prediction. *British Journal of Educational Psychology, 39,* 278–282.

McCord, J. (1977). *A longitudinal approach to understanding crime.* Paper presented at the American Society of Criminology, Atlanta, GA.

McCord, J. (1979). Some child-rearing antecedents of criminal behavior in adult men. *Journal of Personality and Social Psychology, 9,* 1477–1486.

McCord, J. (1981). A longitudinal perspective on patterns of crime. *Criminology, 19,* 211–218.

McCord, J. (1982). A longitudinal study of the link between broken homes and criminality. In J. Gunn & D. Farrington (Eds.), *Abnormal offenders, delinquency, and the criminal justice system* (pp. 113–128). London: Wiley.

McCord, J. (1983). A longitudinal study of aggression and antisocial behavior. In K. T. Van Dusen & S. A. Mednick (Eds.), *Antecedents of aggression and antisocial behavior* (pp. 269–276). Boston: Kluwer-Nijhoff.

McCord, J. (1984, July). *Family sources of crime.* Paper presented at the International Society for Research on Aggression, Turku, Finland.

McCord, W., & McCord J. (1959). *Origins of crime.* Montclair, NJ: Patterson Smith.

McGee, R., Silva, P. A., & Williams, S. (1983). Parents' and teachers' perceptions of behavior problems in seven-year-old children. *The Exceptional Child, 30,* 151–161.

McMichael, P. (1979). "The hen or the egg?" Which comes first—Antisocial emotional disorders or reading disability? *British Journal of Educational Psychology, 49,* 226–238.

Meehl, P. E., & Rosen, A. (1955). Antecedent probability and efficiency of psychometric signs, patterns, or cutting scores. *Psychological Bulletin, 52,* 194–216.

Menard, S., & Morse, B. J. (1984). A structuralist critique of the IQ-Delinquency hypothesis: Theory and evidence. *American Journal of Sociology, 89,* 1347–1378.

Mendelson, W., Johnson, N., & Stewart, M. A. (1971). Hyperactive children as teenagers. A follow-up study. *Journal of Nervous and Mental Disease, 153,* 273–279.

Milich, R., & Loney, J. (1979). The role of hyperactive and aggressive symptomatology in predicting adolescent outcome among hyperactive children. *Journal of Pediatric Psychology, 4,* 93–112.

Mitchell, S., & Rosa, P. (1981). Boyhood behavior problems as precursors of criminality: A fifteen-year follow-up study. *Journal of Child Psychology and Psychiatry, 22,* 19–33.

Monahan, J. D. (1978). The prediction of violent behavior in juveniles. In *The serious juvenile offender.* Washington, DC: U.S. Department of Justice.

Monahan, J. D. (1981). *Clinical prediction of violent behavior.* Washington, DC: U.S. Government Printing Office.

Moore, D. R., Chamberlain, P., & Mukai L. (1979). Children at risk for delinquency: A follow-up comparison of stealing and aggression. *Journal of Abnormal Child Psychology, 7,* 345–355.

Mulligan, G., Douglas, J. W. B., Hammond, W. H., & Tizard, J. (1963). Delinquency and symptoms of maladjustment. *Proceedings of the Royal Society of Medicine, 56,* 1083–1086.

Nunnally, T. (1978). *Psychometric Theory* (2nd ed.). New York: McGraw-Hill.

Nylander, I. (1979). A 20-year prospective follow-up study of 2164 cases at the child guidance clinics in Stockholm. *Acta Paediatrica Scandinavia, 68,* (Supplement 276), 1–45.

Ohlin, L. E., & Duncan, O. D. (1949). The efficiency of prediction in criminology. *American Journal of Sociology, 54,* 441–452.

Olweus, D. (1979). Stability of aggressive reaction patterns in males: A review. *Psychological Bulletin, 86,* 852–857.

Osborn, S. G. (1980). Moving home, leaving London and delinquent trends. *British Journal of Criminology, 20,* 54–61.

Osborn, S. G., & West, D. J. (1978). The effectiveness of various predictors of criminal careers. *Journal of Adolescence, 1,* 101–117 [authors' updated and corrected version].

Osborn, S. G. & West, D. J. (1980). Do young delinquents really reform? *Journal of Adolescence, 3,* 99–114.

Patterson, G. R. (1982). *A social learning approach, Vol. 3: Coercive family process.* Eugene, Oregon: Castalia Publishing Company.

Patterson, G. R., & Stouthamer-Loeber, M. (1984). The correlation of family management practices and delinquency. *Child Development, 55,* 1299–1307.

Petersilia, J. (1980). Criminal career research: A review of recent evidence. In N. Morris & M. Tonry (Eds.), *Crime and delinquency: An annual review of research* (Vol. 2, pp. 321–379). Chicago: University of Chicago Press.

Petersilia, J., Greenwood, P. W., & Lavin, M. (1977). *Criminal careers of habitual felons.* Santa Monica: Rand Corporation.

Polk, K. (1975). Schools and the delinquency experience. *Criminal Justice and Behavior, 2,* 315–338.

Polk, K., & Ruby, C. H. (1978). *Respondent loss in the longitudinal study of deviant behavior.* National Council on Crime and Delinquency, San Francisco.

Prigmore, C. S. (1963). An analysis of rater reliability on the Glueck scale for the prediction of juvenile delinquency. *Journal of Criminal Law, Criminology and Police Science, 54,* 30–41.

Pulkkinen, L. (1983). Search for alternatives to aggression in Finland. In A. P. Goldstein & M. Segall (Eds.), *Aggression in global perspective* (pp. 104-144). New York: Pergamon.

Reckless, W. C., & Dinitz, S. (1972). *The prevention of juvenile delinquency.* Columbus, OH: Ohio State University Press.

Reiss, A. J. (1951). The accuracy, efficiency, and validity of a prediction instrument. *American Journal of Sociology, 56,* 552-561.

Richards, P., Berk, R. A., & Forster, B. (1979). *Crime as play—delinquency in a middle class suburb.* Cambridge, MA: Ballinger.

Richman, N., Stevenson, J., & Graham, P. J. (1982). *Pre-school to school: A behavioural study.* London: Academic Press.

Robins, L. N. (1966). *Deviant children grow up: A sociological and psychiatric study of sociopathic personality.* Baltimore: Williams & Williams.

Robins, L. N. (1978). Longitudinal methods in the study of normal and pathological development. In K. P. Kisker et al. (Eds.), *Psychiatrie der Gegenwart* (Vol. 1). Heidelberg: Springer-Verlag.

Robins, L. N. (in press). Changes in conduct disorder over time. In D. C. Farren & J. D. McKinney (Eds.), *Risk in intellectual and psychosocial development.* New York: Academic Press.

Robins, L. N., Darvish, H. S., & Murphy, G. E. (1970). The long-term outcome for adolescent drug users: A follow-up study of 76 users and 146 nonusers. In J. Zubin & A. M. Freedman (Eds.), *The psychopathy of adolescence.* New York: Grune & Stratton.

Robins, L. N., & Hill, S. Y. (1966). Assessing the contribution of family structure, class and peer groups to juvenile delinquency. *Journal of Criminal Law, Criminology and Police Science, 57,* 325-334.

Robins, L. N. & Ratcliff, K. S. (1979). Risk factors in the continuation of childhood antisocial behavior into adulthood. *International Journal of Mental Health, 7,* 96-116.

Robins, L. N. & Ratcliff, K. S. (1980). Childhood conduct disorders and later arrest. In L. N. Robins, P. J. Clayton, & J. K. Wing (Eds.), *The social consequences of psychiatric illness* (pp. 1-12). New York: Brunner/Mazel.

Robins, L. N., West, P. A., & Herjanic, B. L. (1975). Arrests and delinquency in two generations: A study of black urban families and their children. *Journal of Child Psychology and Psychiatry, 16,* 125-140.

Robins, L. N. & Wish, E. (1977). Childhood deviance as a developmental process: A study of 223 urban black men from birth to 18. *Social Forces, 56,* 448-473.

Roff, J. D., & Wirt, R. D. (1984). Childhood aggression and social adjustment as antecedents of delinquency. *Journal of Abnormal Child Psychology, 12,* 111-126.

Rojeck, D. G., & Erickson, M. L. (1982). Delinquent careers: A test of the career escalation model. *Criminology, 20,* 5-28.

Rutter, M. (1978). Family, area and school influences in the genesis of conduct disorders. In L. A. Hersov, M. Berger & D. Shaffer (Eds.), *Aggression and antisocial behavior in childhood and adolescence.* Oxford: Pergamon.

Rutter, M., Maugham, B., Mortimer, P., & Ouston, J. (1979). *15,000 hours—second-*

ary schools and their effects on children. Cambridge, MA: Harvard University Press.

Rutter, M., Tizard, J., & Whitmore, K. (1970). *Education, health and behavior.* New York: Wiley.

Scarpitti, F. R. (1964). Can teachers predict delinquency? *The Elementary School Journal, 65,* 130–136.

Schachar, R., Rutter, M., & Smith, A. (1981). The characteristics of situationally and pervasively hyperactive children: Implications for syndrome definition *Journal of Child Psychology and Psychiatry, 22,* 375–392.

Shannon, L. W. (August 1978). *A cohort study of the relationship of adult criminal careers to juvenile careers.* Paper presented at the International Symposium on Selected Criminological Topics. University of Stockholm, Sweden.

Simcha-Fagan, O. (1979). The prediction of delinquent behavior over time: Sex-specific patterns related to official and survey-reported delinquent behavior. In R. G. Simmons (Ed.), *Research in community and mental health: An annual compilation of research.* Greenwich, CT: JAI Publishing Co.

Simcha-Fagan, O., Langner, T. S., Gersten, J. C., & Eisenberg, J. G. (1975). *Violent and antisocial behavior: A longitudinal study of urban youth.* (Report NO. OCD-CB-480). Unpublished report of the Office of Child Development. Washington, DC.

Simon, F. H. (1971). *Prediction methods in Criminology.* London: HMSO.

Smith, D. R., Smith, W. R., & Noma, E. (1984). Delinquent career-lines: A conceptual link between theory and juvenile offenses. *Sociological Quarterly, 25,* 155–172.

Spivack, G. (1983). *High risk early behaviors indicating vulnerability to delinquency in the community and school—A 15-year longitudinal study.* Report to the Office of Juvenile Justice and Delinquency Prevention. Philadelphia: Hahnemann University.

Spivack, G. (1985). Personal communication.

Spivack, G., & Cianci, N. (in press). High risk early behavior pattern and later delinquency. In J. D. Burchard & S. Burchard (Eds.), *Prevention of delinquency and antisocial behavior.* Washington, DC: U.S. Government Printing Office.

Stattin, H., & Magnusson, D. (May, 1984). The role of early aggressive behavior for the frequency, the seriousness, and the types of later criminal offenses. *Reports from the Department of Psychology,* University of Stockholm.

Stott, D. H. & Wilson, D. M. (1968). The prediction of early-adult criminality from school-age behaviors. *International Journal of Social Psychiatry, 14,* 5–8.

Tait, C. D. & Hodges, E. F. (1972). Follow-up study of Glueck Table applied to a school population of problem boys and girls between the ages of five and fourteen. In S. Glueck & E. Glueck (Eds.), *Identification of predelinquents* (pp. 49–59). New York: Intercontinental Medical Book Co.

Tannenbaum, F. (1938). *Crime and Community.* New York: Columbia University Press.

Thompson, R. E. (1952). A validation of the Glueck Social Prediction Scale for proneness to delinquency. *Journal of Criminal Law, Criminology, and Political Science, 43,* 451–470.

Tittle, C. R., Villemez, W. J., & Smith, D. A. (1978). The myth of social class and criminality: An empirical assessment of the empirical evidence. *American Sociological Review, 43,* 643–656.

Toby, J. (1961). Early identification and intensive treatment of predelinquents: A negative view. *Social Work, 6,* 3–13.

Trevvett, N. B. (1972). Identifying delinquency-prone children. In S. Glueck & E. Glueck (Eds.), *Identification of pre-delinquents* (pp. 60–66). New York: Intercontinental Medical Book Co.

Tuchfeld, B. S., Clayton, R. R., & Logan, J. A. (1982). Alcohol, drug use and delinquent and criminal behaviors. *Journal of Drug Issues, 12,* 185–198.

Voss, H. T. (1963). The predictive efficiency of the Glueck Social Prediction Table. *Journal of Criminal Law and Criminology, 54,* 421–430.

Wadsworth, M. E. J. (1979). *Roots of delinquency, infancy, adolescence and crime.* Oxford: Robertson.

Wadsworth, M. E. J. (1980). Early life events and later behavioral outcomes in a British longitudinal study. In S. B. Sells, K. Crandell, M. Roff, J. S. Strauss, & W. Pollin, (Eds.), *Human functioning in longitudinal perspective* (pp. 168–180). Baltimore: Williams & Wilkins.

Werner, E. E. (in press). Vulnerability and resiliency in children at risk for delinquency: A longitudinal study from birth to young adulthood. In J. D. Burchard & S. Burchard (Eds.), *Prevention of delinquent behavior.* Beverly Hills, CA: Sage.

Werner, E. E., & Smith, R. S. (1982). *Vulnerable, but invincible: children and youth.* New York: McGraw-Hill.

West, D. J., & Farrington, D. P. (1973). *Who becomes delinquent?* London: Heinemann.

West, D. J., & Farrington, D. P. (1977). *The delinquent way of life.* London: Heinemann.

Wickman, E. K. (1928). *Children's behavior and teacher's attitudes.* New York: Commonwealth Fund.

Wiggens, J. S. (1973). *Personality and prediction: principles of personality assessment.* Reading, MA: Addison Wesley.

Wilbanks, W. L. (1985). Predicting failure on parole. In D. P. Farrington & R. Tarling (Eds.), *Prediction in criminality.* (pp. 78–94). Albany: State University of New York Press.

Wilson, B. J., & Reichmuth, M. (1985). Early screening programs: When is predictive accuracy sufficient? *Learning Disability Quarterly, 8,* 182–188.

Wilson, H., & Herbert, G. W. (1978). *Parents and children of the inner city.* London: Routledge & Kegan Paul.

Wolfgang, M. E. (1977, September). *From boy to man—From delinquency to crime.* Paper presented at the National Symposium on the Serious Juvenile Offender, State of Minnesota, Minneapolis, MN.

Wolfgang, M. E., Figlio, R. M., & Sellin, T. (1972). *Delinquency in a birth cohort.* Chicago: University of Chicago Press.

CHAPTER 13

Prevention

RAYMOND P. LORION
University of Maryland

PATRICK H. TOLAN
DePaul University

ROBERT G. WAHLER
University of Tennessee

As has been documented in earlier chapters, antisocial and delinquent behaviors are a significant social problem whose resolution should be a major national priority. Such a resolution can be justified solely in economic terms. Each year, billions of dollars are spent to repair the tangible consequences of such acts as vandalism, "joyriding," and shoplifting. Additional billions are invested in responding to the legal, correctional, educational, and psychological needs of those youth whose behavior is both recognized and determined to warrant intervention. Other costs may be less easily calculated but are equally real. For example, serious involvement during adolescence may reduce an individual's educational and occupational opportunities. As a consequence, lifetime earnings may be significantly reduced. In some cases, what could have been productive lives are spent in unemployment and dependency on public welfare. In yet other cases, earning potential is reduced by premature death, disability, or educational limitations resulting from delinquent behavior.

Alone or in unison, these multiple economic consequences argue strongly for increased attention to existing levels of antisocial and delinquent behavior among youth. An even more compelling argument, however, involves the *human* costs of such involvement. Such activities separate youth from families and friends, negatively modify self-concept and future expectations, and often trigger a series of increasingly serious deleterious experiences. The human costs are especially important for several reasons. First, the "casualties" of youthful delinquency are not merely the youth themselves and their immediate victims but also their families and friends. Second, early involvement can have long-term consequences (see Chapter 12) for all involved, only some of which can be anticipated. Finally, these costs appear to escalate and presumably increase in their resistance to reversal or control over time.

It is this "snowballing" characteristic of youthful involvement in antisocial and delinquent behavior with respect to the human costs that most concerns us and has stimulated our ongoing interest in its scientific study. As clinical researchers, we share the assumption that genuine progress in responding to the multiple impacts of these behaviors depends on systematic efforts to understand, control, and predict their occurrence (see Chapter 12). The results of such efforts will undoubtedly inform the design of future diagnostic and treatment approaches which in turn will hopefully improve our effectiveness in responding to the needs of those actively engaging in such activities.

We must, however, acknowledge our reservations about the ultimate value of diagnostic and treatment advances for solving the "problem." However effective such advances might be, their application cannot occur until *after* many of the aforementioned costs have already been incurred. Although future generations of affected youth may be better served, their numbers will not be reduced. This limitation of after-the-fact intervention has long been recognized by public health practitioners who argue that no condition or disorder has ever been controlled by treatment, but only by prevention. It is the application of that dictum to the problem of juvenile delinquency that is the focus of this chapter.

From the outset, we acknowledge that the behavioral sciences have yet to identify demonstrably effective and disseminable prevention strategies which noticeably reduce incidence or prevalence rates of antisocial and delinquent behavior. In our view, however, progress has been at least partially impeded by the lack of a common paradigm within which to conceptualize the planning, design, and interpretation of programmatic prevention research. We concur with Kuhn (1970) that preparadigmatic research, heuristically valuable though it may be, cannot produce the systematic buildup of knowledge that defines scientific progress. Furthermore, we believe that such a systematically developed foundation is necessary for the design and implementation of effective prevention. For that reason, this chapter begins with articulation of a developmental model within which to conceptualize prevention research.

A PARADIGM FOR PREVENTION

Basic Definitions and Other Issues

Thus far we have used the terms "antisocial and delinquent behavior" and "prevention" generically. Since each of these terms has multiple referents (e.g., Loeber & Dishion, 1983; Cowen, 1983), it is important to clarify their use in this chapter. The former term refers to a continuum of behaviors which transgresses social norms in ways that have resulted or could result in serious disciplinary (e.g., school suspension) or adjudicatory (i.e., legal conviction) consequences. Included along the continuum is behavior that is simply socially unacceptable (e.g., disrupting the classroom), status offenses that are illegal/problematic by virtue of the age of the offender (e.g., truancy, running away, alcohol use), and criminal acts whose illegality is independent of the offender's age (e.g., assault, robbery, rape). In referring to a continuum we intend to communicate to the reader our perception that these acts are progressive and hierarchical with increasingly negative consequences for the perpetrator, the victim, and the community. As will become evident in the section on outcome definition which follows, the notion of a continuum is central to understanding and ultimately preventing this category of youthful maladjustment. Since considerable attention will be given to definitional aspects of antisocial and delinquent behavior in that section, further discussion of the issue is deferred at this point.

The second major concept which must be defined is prevention. Long a central element of the public health movement, the application of prevention concepts to mental health in recent times is typically attributed to Caplan (1964) who argued persuasively that public health's classic triad of intervention (i.e., primary, secondary, and teriary prevention) offered significant new strategies for the then recently initiated community mental health movement. It is important to understand the distinction among these alternatives for the prevention of any disorder, including delinquency. To do so, however, one must first recognize the difference between the epidemiological indices of prevalence and incidence. The latter term refers to the number of new cases of a disorder which have their onset during a specified time. Typically, this index is reported as a rate per some fixed unit of the population (e.g., n cases/100,000 people) per unit of time (e.g., one year). By contrast, prevalence refers to the total number of cases in a given population at a given point in time. Prevalence thus depends on both incidence and duration.

Understanding the interrelatedness of these indices is important for selecting among alternative prevention strategies. For example, assuming either rapid recovery or complete lethality and hence brief duration, both indices would reflect essentially the occurrence of new cases in the population. As a consequence, clear emphasis should then be placed on primary preventive efforts intended to avoid the onset of the disorder. Classic public health models argue that this goal can be achieved by altering one of the three essential components for disease/disorder occurrence. In effect, one could eliminate the *agent* or cause of the disorder, one could render immune or resistant the *host* or victim, or one could alter the environment or conditions necessary for the disease/disorder to occur.

Clearly, primary prevention represents the ideal accomplishment for those interested in reducing morbidity and mortality. If onset can be avoided, symptoms will not occur, nor will their sequalae (i.e., related consequences) need to be addressed. The design of such interventions, however, necessarily depends on the availability of certain information. For example, it is essential that criteria exist that reliably and clearly distinguish between the presence and absence of the disease/disorder. In the absence of such criteria, onset cannot be determined, and consequently the impact of preventive efforts on incidence rates cannot be assessed. Whereas such criteria frequently exist for physical disorders, their availability for psychopathological disorders, and in particular, antisocial and delinquent behavior, is unfortunately limited.

Assuming, however, that onset can be determined, the initiation of primary prevention efforts also depends on knowledge of the relative contributions of the aforementioned triad of factors necessary for such onset. Thus, causal factors must be known before they can be systematically eliminated; relevant characteristics of individuals which increase or decrease their vulnerability must be known before they can be systematically influenced; and situational conditions necessary for the pathological process to be initiated and to continue must be identified before they can be systematically controlled. Without knowledge of these factors, the bases for selecting the components of a primary prevention strategy must be questioned (Lorion, 1983a, 1983b). As will be proposed later, the importance of a paradigm is that it defines both the characteristics of such information and the procedures for its acquisition.

As argued elsewhere (Lorion, 1985a, 1985b), an important source of information relevant to primary prevention is available through the systematic application of other prevention strategies. Specifically, secondary and tertiary efforts can inform us about the natural course of the disease/disorder, its sequelae, and its long-term effects. As described as follows, such interventions provide important opportunities to study significant developmental aspects of such diseases/disorders. By attempting to change the pathogenic processes which produce such diseases/disorders, we will learn about their evolution.

Tertiary efforts involve strategies to minimize the consequences of an established disorder. Tertiary efforts are appropriate for those conditions whose onset cannot be (or has not been) avoided, whose duration is significant, and/or whose sequelae are themselves problematic. Tertiary efforts do not prevent disorder. They can, however, reduce prevalence rates to the extent that they limit duration and avoid related sequelae. Thus, tertiary strategies involve effective treatment methods which minimize disability and chronic distress. Their effectiveness depends on knowledge about the long-term course of the disorder and on the availability of methods for assessing the presence/absence of sequelae. Careful assessment of the differential effectiveness of treatment procedures can provide important insights into individual and situational factors that contribute to resistance to such consequences and responsiveness to treatment. As treatments are introduced increasingly earlier in the course of a disorder's development, opportunities will arise for even greater understanding of the disorders' course. In turn, such insights can provide the knowledge base on which to establish secondary prevention strategies.

In our view (Lorion, 1983a, 1985b; Lorion, Work & Hightower, 1984), secondary prevention represents the most promising approach for the behavioral sciences in general, and for delinquency research specifically *at this time*. The qualifier is appended to reflect the assumption that the ultimate goal of all preventive efforts is the avoidance of onset. That goal may however need to be deferred pending the acquisition of requisite knowledge. Thus, secondary prevention can serve as an important interim step in reaching the ultimate goal. Based on the systematic development and application of early detection and intervention procedures, secondary efforts can reduce prevalence by interrupting further development of the disorder as soon after its onset as possible. Ideally, such procedures will allow for the identification of individuals with incipient manifestations of disorder who in many cases may not even be aware of these manifestations or of their diagnostic implications. Compared with traditional treatment approaches, secondary interventions are typically less intense, have fewer iatrogenic consequences, and have a higher probability of success (Cowen, 1973; Lorion, 1985b). By focusing on disorder early in its development, opportunities arise for gaining insight into risk-factors which contribute to onset. Moreover, as argued elsewhere:

> secondary efforts offer both an opportunity for immediate reduction in rates of disorder and the potential for highlighting promising routes for primary preventive efforts. Logistically, secondary efforts involve technologies that are closely related to those available to most traditionally trained mental health professionals (i.e., screening, diagnosis, and treatment). Moreover, those served by secondary efforts are deemed by the general public to be appropriate for the receipt of publicly funded services. Although they are less intense and debilitating than those of traditional clientele, the needs of secondary prevention target populations can be documented and, in a world of increasingly limited human service resources, justified for both humane and economic reasons. Secondary preventive efforts reduce human suffering at minimal cost (Cowen, 1973; Dorr, 1972). Overall, the advantages of active secondary preventive efforts are clear. We can carry out such efforts *now* and, in the process, gain both information and . . . important credibility for the concept of prevention. (Lorion & Lounsbury, 1982, pp. 28–29.)

Thus, in thinking about preventive interventions and their application to antisocial and delinquent behavior, one must appreciate the multiple avenues available for reducing the prevalence of the disease or disorder of interest. Reductions achieved either through the avoidance of onset or the abbreviation of duration are both valuable. However, one must proceed cautiously and methodically since attaining the goals of either primary or secondary intervention requires a considerable knowledge base firmly rooted in solid epidemiological findings. At a minimum, onset cannot be avoided without a basis for its detection and justifiable hypotheses about related factors. Moreover, interventions to reduce onset cannot be evaluated in the absence of reliable data about the base rate at which the outcome to be avoided occurs in the population of interest. As discussed as follows and in Chapter 12, this knowledge is central to planning preventive interventions in view of the influence of base rates on predictive validity (Cronbach & Meehl, 1955), and the longstanding controversy about the prevalence of delinquency (see Chapter 2).

An equally demanding, albeit different knowledge base is essential for the design of interventions which attempt to reduce duration either soon after onset (i.e., secondary efforts), or following development of an established diagnosable condition (i.e., tertiary efforts). In each of these instances, the pathogenic course must be known in order to establish prodromal forms as targets for early detection and intervention or rehabilitation efforts. Base rates are also important here, but in a somewhat different way. Multiple base rates must be determined to reflect the fact that at each step along the pathogenic course, some portion of those manifesting prior indices may *not* display subsequent indices (Gold & Petronio, 1980). A form of natural attrition may be involved and consequently be relevant to both the design and assessment of interventions to limit duration. Specifically for delinquency and antisocial behavior, the goal of preventive intervention is not just the absolute reduction of delinquency rates, but the reduction to a level *lower* than would occur without intervention.

At this point one may question the applicability of existing disease-derived preventive models to deviant social behavior. After all, as currently understood, these phenomena do not result from causal factors in any way analogous to a virus or a bacterium (Albee, 1982; Gordon, 1983). In fact, most are presumed to be multiply determined from a complex interaction of causes whose outcomes can at best be predicted categorically. Moreover, their occurrence is rarely either simply present or absent but is typically a matter of severity and chronicity (Tolan, in press). These problems have led some (e.g., Bloom, 1984; Albee, 1982; Gordon, 1983) to propose replacement of the public health/disease concept of prevention with "nonmedical/nondisease" oriented models which emphasize the unique characteristics of behavioral phenomena. We would argue, however, that without a paradigmatic framework within which to consider this alternative there is a danger that selection among them will be based on semantic rather than scientific considerations. For that reason, we will defer consideration of these alternatives until after presentation of our proposed paradigmatic orientation.

Paradigmatic Issues

In his now classic essay, Kuhn (1970) examined factors that he believed contributed to the acquisition of scientific knowledge. Central among these was the availability of a paradigm, that is, an overarching model of how the phenomenon of interest is to be defined, studied, and explained. To be scientifically valuable, that model must be shared by a number of investigators who generally agree on which questions to ask and when and how to ask them. The advantage of shared paradigms, according to Kuhn, is that they allow for, indeed enable, the acquisition of incremental knowledge that permits the progressive understanding of natural phenomena or processes. Kuhn labeled this incremental process as "the work of normal science."

In effect, a paradigm allows for a shared understanding of what is already known about the phenomenon and relatedly identifies what remains to be learned. To illustrate the advantages of paradigmatic research, Kuhn differentiates "problems" and "puzzles" by comparing the tasks of "drawing a picture" and "solving a picture puzzle." The first of these, in Kuhn's terms, represent a "problem," that is, a generic question without identifiable guidelines for determining the acceptability of proposed solutions. By contrast, a "puzzle" has the advantage of assuming that *a* solution exists and that there are rules that both limit the nature of acceptable solutions and the procedures for obtaining such solutions. Unlike the task of "drawing a picture" which provides no information about what product will meet that demand, a picture puzzle has *a* solution (i.e., the completed picture) which can only be achieved if: (1) all pieces are used; (2) their plain sides are turned down; (3) they can be interlocked without force or alteration; and (4) no gaps remain. Not unlike paradigmatic research, which Kuhn argued allows for the articulation of problems into solvable puzzles, work on picture puzzles is incremental since a given solution also provides one with insights which facilitate the solution of similar, albeit distinct, puzzles.

Thus, a paradigm reflects an overarching model or view of what a phenomenon is and how it works. The necessary knowledge accrues by means of three relatively sequential, albeit overlapping, research directions. Applied to the prevention of antisocial and delinquent behavior, these directions would be as follows: First, their descriptive characteristics would be identified and procedures developed for determining their presence/absence. Through taxonomic and instrument development procedures the defining criteria and developmental pathways of delinquency would become known and identifiable. Through observational and measurement procedures, information would be obtained about the relative presence/absence of such behavior in certain individuals and under certain conditions.

In turn, such information would lead to hypotheses about causal factors and pathogenic courses. This category of research would systematically examine assumptions about how delinquency begins, evolves, is maintained, and is dissipated. Relevant mechanisms would become known, their operative processes understood, and their consequences predicted. Each new finding would refine and potentially extend the scientific understanding of processes relevant to antisocial and delinquent behavior. Increasingly, the elements necessary and sufficient for their appearance/disappearance would be identified and the likelihood of their control determined.

Such information would at some point spur researchers to examine the applicability of the identified mechanisms and processes to understanding other behavioral disorders. Thus, the third stage of paradigmatic activity is the pursuit of its limitations across individuals, situations, and conditions. Through such work, the paradigm's explanatory breadth is maximized and its capacity to explain, predict, and control other behavioral phenomena is understood.

Throughout this process, the existence of a community of researchers who operate from a shared perspective allows for the systematic comparison and incrementation of knowledge. Through this process, Kuhn argued, scientific progress occurs. By contrast, in the absence of an overarching model:

> all of the facts that could possibly pertain to the development of a given science are likely to seem equally relevant. As a result, early fact-gathering is a far more nearly random activity than the one that subsequent scientific development makes familiar. Furthermore, in the absence of a reason for seeking some particular form of more recondite information, early fact gathering is usually restricted to the wealth of data that lie ready to hand. The resulting pool of facts contains those accessible to casual observation and experimentation together with some of the more esoteric data retrievable from established crafts. . . . But though this sort of fact-gathering has been essential to the origin of many significant sciences . . . it produces a morass. One somehow hesitates to call the literature that results scientific. (Kuhn, 1979, pp. 15–16.)

Few would deny that available knowledge relevant to the prevention of antisocial and delinquent behavior is at a preparadigmatic stage. For example, as has been noted in earlier chapters, little agreement exists as to the definition, prediction, and control of delinquency. Competing theoretical models disagree on the relative contributions of constitutional, environmental, and familiar factors. In sum, we lack an integrated psychological theory of antisocial and delinquent behavior. Consequently, few criteria are currently available for determining the applicability of disparate findings to selecting among available conceptual options.

The general prevention literature offers little assistance in this respect. As Bloom (1984) has noted, the public health model which Caplan (1964) originally offered for consideration by the mental health professions has limited value for understanding behavioral dysfunctions. According to Bloom, the three components of this model are as follows:

> 1. identify a disease of sufficient importance to justify the development of a preventive intervention program. Develop reliable methods for its diagnosis so that people can be divided with confidence into groups according to whether they do or do not have the disease;

> 2. by a series of epidemiological and laboratory studies, identify the most likely theories of the path of development of that disease;

> 3. mount and evaluate an experimental preventive intervention program based on the results of those research studies (Bloom, 1984, p. 198).

Unquestionably, the prevalence and costs (economic and human) of delinquency are sufficient "to justify the development of a preventive intervention." The reliability of its "diagnosis," however, is less certain. Additional operationalization of the behavior of interest is necessary if agreement on its presence/absence is to be achieved. Further, it may be that even with such agreement, the ubiquitous nature of such behavior among adolescents renders the distinction of presence/absence moot (Gold & Petronio, 1980). The relevant operationalization issue then becomes the differentiation of types and levels of such behavior.

Given the very low probability of adjudication (Williams & Gold, 1972), we would argue that criteria which define the behaviors *per se* independent of their legal consequences are needed. For example, substance abuse should be included independent of society's response to that abuse. Similarly, vandalism and assault should clearly be included. In effect, what is proposed is that a concept of "a disease or state of delinquency" be abandoned. Rather than considering it as something which one *has*, it must be recognized as something which one *does*. Also, rather than considering it as something that one *does or doesn't do,* it must be recognized as something that is *done more or less* (Tolan, 1984).

From that perspective, Bloom's (1984) second component must also be reconsidered. Rather than seek to understand the "path of development" of a disease, epidemiological and laboratory studies should be conducted to determine which individuals and situational factors relate to the occurrence of the clusters of behaviors of concern. Specifically, information must be obtained which describes the nature, and most importantly, the mechanisms whereby they develop, are maintained, and can be altered. Since prevention efforts are directed to the avoidance of, rather than response to, such behaviors, emphasis must be placed on understanding the *processes* which lead to them. In fact, their developmental processes rather than their results should be the foci of preventive interventions.

As explained elsewhere (Lorion, 1985a, 1985b) this view leads to the conclusion that preventive interventions must be conceptualized within a theoretical framework which is oriented toward dynamic processes rather than static conditions. As we suggested earlier, antisocial and delinquent behavior would be understood as points along a continuum characterized by increasing social inappropriateness and individual maladjustment and representing increasing levels and degrees of disturbed behavior. The developmental progression along this continuum becomes the process of interest. What must be understood is the sequence whereby an individual initiates, continues, and escalates involvement in delinquency.

If, as we suggest, understanding developmental processes is the *sine qua non* of effective preventive interventions, then the relevant guiding paradigm must necessarily be a developmental one. Such a paradigm would both view antisocial and delinquent behavior as evolving across the multiple developmental periods which constitute youth, and understand that *each* behavior represents the product of a developmental sequence. In effect, for any behavior, one should be able to identify its precursors, the antecedents to those precursors, the precedents to those antecedents, and so forth. Presumably each step taken along that continuum represents an increasing probability that the final step will occur. At the same time, however, each behavioral step also represents both an indication that the initiated process is ongoing, and, once a preventive intervention is initiated, a potential index (through its absence) that the process has been interrupted. Once the developmental analysis of the continuum has been completed, it may be possible to identify one or more "triggering behaviors" whose elimination reduces significantly the likelihood that the sequence will occur.

The identification of such sequences even for the major categories of antisocial and delinquent behavior will require considerable scientific "work" (according to Kuhn's (1970) definition of the "work of normal science") by investigators operating from a common paradigm. We would propose that serious consideration be given to use of the transactional perspective offered by Sameroff and Chandler (1975) to understand a variety of early childhood disorders. This perspective simultaneously consideres both constitutional and environmental factors. In fact, Sameroff and Chandler have argued that these factors relate to each other synergistically and thereby can increase, decrease, or mitigate the potential of each succeeding influence. Evidence for this synergistic relationship has been reviewed at length by Sameroff and Chandler (1975) who have documented that significant individual vulnerabilities can often be mitigated by a supportive environment. Similarly, significant negative environmental conditions can be resisted by "invulnerable" individuals with adequate temperamental, cognitive, and emotional resources.

Thus, the proposed paradigm seeks to understand delinquency as the product of a synergistic transaction between individual constitutional factors impacting environmental conditions, which in turn impact the individual who in turn effects the situation, and so on. As Sarason and Doris (1979) have explained:

> From the transactional perspective, heredity and environment are never dichotomous. It can even be misleading to say they "interact" because that is more often than not interpreted in terms of effects of heredity on environment just as for so long we have paid attention to the effects of parents *on* children and virtually ignored the influence of children on parents. The transactional approach is always a two-way street. There is nothing in the transactional formulation that denies the existence and influence of genetic processes or the existence of a socially structured context populated by diverse people. (p. 25).

Sameroff and Chandler's developmental model has paradigmatic qualities. It proposes that behavioral analysis consider the unique and synergistic contributions of individual/constitutional and social/environmental factors. It argues that changes in either of these factors can alter the other factors and thereby the subsequent developmental course. It presents a model for understanding prior limitations in the identification of risk for antisocial and delinquent behaviors (discussed in detail later in this chapter) and for translating unanswered questions about these behaviors into solvable "puzzles." Among the most immediate puzzles to be addressed are the following:

1.   Clarification of the outcomes that are the focus of our preventive efforts and articulation of their defining characteristics

2.   Identification of salient triggering marker behaviors along the identi-fied developmental sequences

3.   Identification of critical timing issues, including age at which onset is most likely, the temporal rate at which an individual progresses from one marker behavior (or developmental step) to the next and relatedly from onset to the manifestation of the behavior of concern

4.   Identification of salient individual and environmental contributors to the onset, continuance, and interruption of the developmental sequences lead-ing to specific behavior or categories of antisocial and delinquent behavior.

Were such information available, it would enable those interested in the prevention of delinquency to determine which individuals were most at risk, under specified conditions, to become delinquent. It would also aid in selec-tion among prevention alternatives. If knowledge of the processes related to onset were available, then it would be possible to design, implement, and eval-uate primary prevention strategies. If instead, the identities of salient markers were known, then secondary interventions could be designed which hopefully would abort continuation of the initiated sequence. In all cases, knowledge of the salient temporal characteristics of antisocial and delinquent behavior is essential if the preventive intervention is to be introduced at the right time and for the proper duration. By understanding the meaning of early occurrence of markers which normally occur further along the sequence, the preventive in-tervention's effects can be assessed both immediately and at the point at which the focal behaviors are to occur.

By proposing that the transactional developmental perspective be adapted to understanding antisocial and delinquent behavior, we certainly do not in-tend to imply that existing knowledge about them must be replaced. Rather we believe that its careful review will reveal considerable application to the proposed model. In effect, we believe that the transactional developmental perspective will allow for the synthesis of much of what is currently known, while providing a means for considering the interactive effect of each step in the developmental process in a way which is both heuristically and program-matically valuable. We believe this to be especially true with respect to prior work on identifying the risk factors for delinquent behavior. Rather than view-ing evidence of one indicator (e.g., constitutional factors) as opposing the rel-evance of another (e.g., social-environmental) factor, we propose that much can be gained by examining the relative explanatory contribution and syner-gistic effect of both of these elements.

THE DEFINITION OF OUTCOME

The first "puzzle" to be addressed in examing the relevance of prior research to a transactional developmental approach to preventing delinquency, is the clear definition of the outcome to be prevented. As in any preventive effort, outcome measurement can be elusive since the desired effect is reflected in the *absence* of the target behavior or disorder. Yet, thus far, reliable criteria for distinguishing the presence and absence of delinquency have been difficult to establish. Solving this problem remains challenging for several reasons. As noted in earlier chapters of this book, investigators disagree widely in how they define delinquency. Delinquency has been defined in terms of assignment to a residential school, membership in a juvenile gang, "conviction" by a juvenile court, appearance in juvenile court, arrest by police, reports of behavior by parents and self-reports. To add to the confusion, terms such as "antisocial behavior," "aggressiveness," "delinquency-prone activities," and "predelinquency" are often used interchangeably with "delinquency." Such inconsistency in definition seriously limits the possibility of cross-study comparisons of results and thereby the systematic incrementation of knowledge.

As we have seen, there is also disagreement about the relative advantages and disadvantages of archival indices (e.g., police arrest records, juvenile court records, or assignment to a juvenile correctional facility) versus behavior measures (e.g., reports by self and others), as definitional criteria. West and Farrington (1973) have concluded that archival records are best for distinguishing serious and repeat offenders, the group in clear need of our attention, from the rest of the population. However, Hindelang (1974) has contended that significant information about delinquent behavior is lost when relying on official records since: "1) some unknown number of offenses committed by the sample are never discovered, 2) of those discovered, some are not reported to the authorities, 3) of those reported some are not recorded, 4) the offense categories used are very broad (e.g., robbery) and very dissimilar acts can fall into the same category, 5) the definitions of offense categories vary from time to time and from jurisdiction to jurisdiction, and 6) procedures for handling multiple offenses and multiple victims in an incident have not been worked out in a detailed and standard way."(p. 72)

We find Hindelang's argument compelling. We concur that reports of behavior provide more immediate and direct indicators of delinquency. In our view, such reports are potentially more sensitive to actual incidence and prevalence patterns. After all, preventive interventions are presumably concerned with differentiation of risk for delinquent behavior rather than risk for legal prosecution. The former represents a behavioral problem that can be empirically studied in and of itself, whereas the latter is primarily a sociopolitical issue (e.g., who should and should not be prosecuted).

For these reasons, we suggest that researchers focus on delinquent behavior per se. Further, we suggest adoption of the following lexicon for describing outcomes in delinquency prevention. First, "delinquency" should be used only as a general descriptor indicating concern with some aspect of the general phenomenon. Prevention studies should use more specific terms to indicate their outcome. "Delinquent behavior" should be used to refer to the performance of an act by a minor who transgresses some law and therefore places himself at risk for arrest and or prosecution. "Official status" should be used to refer to the legal status of a delinquent due to a recording of an arrest, conviction, and/or adjudication. Further, we suggest that legal status indicators be specified (e.g., arrest versus conviction rather than referring to both as official status only), since each step in the legal process correlates differently with delinquent behavior.

Terms such as "delinquent prone" or "predelinquent" should be used to refer to behavior or states that have been empirically demonstrated to relate *sequentially* and predictably to delinquency. Finally, as has been discussed earlier (see Chapter 5), there is considerable evidence to suggest that delinquent behavior and antisocial behavior are highly related, albeit different problems. Yet, as noted, delinquent behavior necessarily involves legal liability whereas antisocial behavior may or may not have legal consequences.

Even if behavior is accepted as focal and antisocial and delinquent behavior are considered as distinct points on a continuum, the definition of delinquency for prevention remains complicated because of the episodic nature of delinquent behavior. Unlike the diseases targeted by many public health prevention programs, involvement in antisocial and delinquent behaviors is not a continuous state for most adolescents. For many, the issue is not whether the behavior will occur, but rather, in what form, to what extent, how serious it will become, and how long it will continue. For this reason, prevention efforts should be targeted toward one of several aspects of delinquency. In addition to efforts to prevent occurrence, we should consider steps to curtail increasing seriousness, diminish frequency, or redirect developmental pathways leading to delinquent behavior.

Thus, multiple preventive goals can be used to direct efforts to reduce specific "delinquent" risks. For example, delinquent behavior varies in frequency with common and logical distinctions made between single and repeat offenders and between those frequently and infrequently delinquent. Second, delinquents differ in the variety or types of acts they exhibit. Relative specificity (or lack there of) has been related to chronicity (Wolfgang, Figlio, & Sellin, 1972); and type of act (against property versus against person) has been related to outcome prognosis (Moore, Chamberlain, & Mukai, 1979). Third, acts can be differentiated by their seriousness, ranging from mild transgressions of social convention (e.g., staying out too late) to very serious offenses (e.g., mayhem, rape, murder). Similarly, acts can be differentiated in terms of legal seriousness, with the most common distinctions made between status offenses (illegal because of the offender's age—e.g., alchohol use) and criminal offenses (illegal no matter what the age of the offender—e.g., robbery), and within criminal offenses between misdemeanors and felonies (and at times, between the most serious felonies and other felonies). Although these aspects of delinquency are highly interrelated ($r = .72$ to $.81$; Tolan, 1984; in press), prevention researchers may find it useful to specify which dimension is being used to scale delinquency.

The other three "immediate puzzles" outlined previously can now be addressed. Two primary types of research activities can shed light on these puzzles: studies of correlates to delinquency (risk identification), and evaluations of intervention outcomes.

THE IDENTIFICATION OF RISK OF ANTISOCIAL
AND DELINQUENT BEHAVIOR

Two primary strategies have been employed in delinquency risk studies. Each provides important information for delinquency prevention. The first strategy focuses on aggressive and antisocial behavior patterns as a way to identify the precursors to and developmental pathways of delinquent behavior. This type of research assumes that delinquent behavior is a point in a "developmental stream" of behavior and is an adolescent outgrowth of the social aggression and antisocial behaviors typical of behavior-disordered children (see Loeber, 1982; Mulvey & LaRosa, 1984; Patterson, 1982; Wahler, 1976; and Chapter 8). The second strategy focuses instead on the psychosocial characteristics which relate and/or contribute to the onset, course, and diminution of delinquent behavior. This line of research assumes that risk for, type, and extent of delinquent behavior relates to differences in individual and environmental characteristics, and that identification of such characteristics can both aid in prediction and eventually serve as targets for interventions. We will consider research employing each strategy in turn.

Behavioral Patterns

Two types of research are relevant to delinquency risk identification. The first strategy seeks to identify behavioral indicants related to risk. This research has produced two credible indicants to date.

As has been pointed out in Chapters 5 and 12, numerous studies have reported that early behavior problems are associated with later antisocial and delinquent behavior. For example, West and Farrington (1973) reported that the best indicator of later delinquency was the occurrence of behavior problems during the primary grades. By contrast, Simcha-Fagan (1979) found that the earlier presence of behavior problems was an important contributor to explaining observed differences in levels of delinquent behavior for both males and females. Although the absolute level of correlations has varied from study to study, the finding that early behavior problems are a significant and often the most powerful discriminant of the appearance of delinquent behavior is consistent across studies.

The second promising behavioral indicant is age of onset. Documentation of early appearance of delinquent behavior substantially increases our ability to distinguish levels of chronicity of delinquent behavior. For example, Petersilia (1980) reported that 45 percent of the variance in number of arrests was accounted for by age of onset. Similarly, Farrington (1979) reported that those who began committing crimes between ages 10 and 12 continued to do so at a higher rate throughout adolescence and had conviction rates twice that of those starting later. In our own research, we found similiar results in a recent survey of a normative sample of males. Age of first offense was the single best predictor (explaining 27 to 35 percent of the variance) observed from a series of psychological variables of frequency, variety, and seriousness of delinquent behavior (Tolan, 1984, in press).

The consistency of this finding has led some to consider social aggression (and in its later form of delinquent behavior) as a stable individual trait, which is identifiable in early childhood (Olweus, 1979; Robins, 1978). If so, very early identification of risk for antisocial and delinquent behavior might be possible. However, in practice such identification may be far too inaccurate given the number of intervening variables which could potentially influence behavior between the time of prediction and the outcome age. Patterson (1982) has presented an alternative to viewing social aggressiveness as an inherent and stable trait. He has argued that clinically significant aggressiveness exhibits all of the definitional properties associated with the concept of a character trait. Thus, it is displayed at relatively consistent rates across settings, appears in several forms, and, despite developmental changes in its expression across childhood and adolescence, individuals tend to retain their relative ranks compared to peers across these age spans. However, rather than defining antisocial and delinquent behavior as a fixed individual characteristic, Patterson has suggested viewing social aggression as a behavioral tendency that is minimized or enhanced by its social context (especially the family interaction patterns). In turn, this tendency synergistically affects its social context (Wahler, Leske, & Rogers, 1977). In effect, Patterson proposes that what distinguishes this "tendency" from a "trait" is its dependence on environmental factors for its manifestation.

The consistency of support for early behavior problems and age of onset across studies and their level of explanatory and discriminative ability stands out in comparison to other predictors. At present, they represent our two best predictors of the occurrence (early behavior problems) and extent (age of onset) of delinquent behavior. However, we caution readers that even these "best" indicators leave unexplained most of the variance related to the occurrence and extent of delinquent behavior. Other variables must also be considered to predict antisocial and delinquent behavior at an acceptable level.

The second strategy that focuses on behavioral patterns attempts to identify behaviors which mark transitions toward or away from delinquency. This strategy views delinquency as the product of a developmental course. Consequently, identification of relevant variables related to onset, course, and reduction can increase our ability to determine risk (Mulvey & LaRosa, 1984). Unfortunately, this strategy has only been employed recently and little information about the developmental course(s) of delinquent behavior thus far has been accumulated. That which is available, however, is most promising.

As was noted in Chapter 8, studies by Patterson (1982) his colleagues (Loeber, 1982; Moore et al., 1979) and Wahler (1976) have contributed to constructing a developmental schema for the appearance and maintenance of antisocial behaviors in which family interaction provides reinforcement for "coercive behaviors." Such behaviors are defined as social acts having an aggressive command as their message. As the child develops and the behaviors generalize beyond family interactions to other social situations, a likely outcome is involvement in delinquent behavior. The extent and specific type of antisocial or delinquent behavior which occurs depends on the interaction over time among the child's behavioral tendencies, the family's interactional habits, and its social context.

As discussed in Chapters 8 and 12, Patterson has argued for the development of maps of the chains of behaviors which constitute a developmental track. Having done this, one could determine "conditional probabilities" for the occurrence of any behavior in terms of preceding behaviors. Ideally, at any point in development, the presence of marker behaviors would allow for determining the probability of each subsequent step in the developmental sequence. Predicting the risk for and the nature of delinquent behavior would then be defined as a function of the probability for a given sequence of intermediary behaviors and environmental contexts. Preliminary determination of the conditional probabilities of serious offenses based on the occurrence of less serious offenses suggests that his method has promise (Tolan, in press).

It is important to understand that most delinquents discontinue their illegal behavior with age. For most individuals, involvement in delinquent activities is a transient state, limited to their adolescent years (Tolan, in press). Given this fact, we and others (Gold & Petronio, 1980) have concluded that "transient" delinquents need to be differentiated from those for whom delinquent behavior is "prodromal" to chronic and very serious adult criminal activity. The former's delinquency seems more linked to resolution of adolescent developmental tasks, whereas the latter's seems to follow Patterson's (1982) aforementioned developmental schema. It is likely that different predictor variables will be necessary to distinguish subjects at risk for transient delinquent behavior versus those at risk for chronic-serious delinquent behavior.

Although the cessation of delinquency is quite common, information about what initiates it is sparse. Fortunately, it has begun to receive attention. For example, Mulvey and LaRosa (1984) found that factors contributing to decreased involvement in delinquency reported by subjects included the onset of a heterosexual relationship, vocational opportunity, and decreased involvement with peers. These results were also observed by Osborn and West (1975) who reported that adolescents who continued delinquent behaviors reported more unemployment, were less likely to be married, and spent more time with male peer groups. Tittle, Villemez, and Smith (1978) reported that discontinuing delinquent activity was typically preceeded by an increase in "spheres of social activities," especially those involving vocational and heterosexual interests. This research suggests that the *absence* of normal adolescent concerns may reflect continuing delinquency risk.

In sum, focusing on behavioral patterns seems promising for delinquency risk identification research. Substantive findings are beginning to emerge. However, the state of this research is such that the promise still exceeds the substance. In addition to the caution noted previously (i.e., that the majority of the variance is left unexplained by these "best" predictors), behavior patterns have limited utility as risk indicants for another reason. Their manifestation is, in part, dependent on the characteristics of the psychosocial context. Identifying the combinations of individual and environmental characteristics which are related to the emergence of these behaviors is thus necessary for risk assessment.

Psychosocial Variables

The research literature relating psychosocial factors to delinquency reviewed in detail in earlier chapters is massive, of varying quality, and most difficult to integrate. For our purposes, psychosocial functioning can be understood in terms of four elements: (1) individual factors; (2) school factors; (3) family factors; and (4) social factors. We will briefly examine each separately before discussing their overall meaning.

Individual Characteristics

The available literature on individual characteristics, to date, has limited relevance to predicting delinquency risk. In part, this reflects the predominance of descriptive studies which precludes the systematic integration of findings. Moreover, much of the available research is directed toward differentiating psychological subtypes within delinquent populations rather than identifying the individual characteristics that increase or decrease delinquency risk within the general population (see Chapters 5 and 6.) Three research foci within the psychosocial area have particular relevance to our present concern.

As noted in Chapter 6, it appears that characteristics such as self-control and social conformity are only moderately related to delinquent behavior. Overall, general emotional adjustment does not appear to be a good predictor of antisocial and delinquent behavior. It is possible that emotional adjustment reflects the consequence of, rather than acting as contributor to, involvement in delinquent activities. Longitudinal research is needed to determine whether emotional adjustment as indicated on psychological tests is an antecedent to, a concurrent of, or a consequence of delinquent behavior.

As was also discussed in Chapter 5, delinquents consistently evidence lower levels of social skills than their nondelinquent peers. Thus, level of social skills development cannot be ruled out as a potentially useful variable for assessing delinquency risk. What is now needed is research which tracks simultaneously the development of social skills and delinquent behavior to determine if change in one precedes change in the other.

Finally, as discussed in Chapter 4 and 6, cognitive functioning, especially the ability to direct one's own behavior by verbal mediation, may contribute to the prediction of risk. This relationship holds for both involvement in delinquent behavior and legal status. Understanding the meaning of this relationship is complicated, however, since higher order cognitive functioning as a risk factor is not specific to delinquency but instead applies to a range of behavioral and emotional problems (Hogan & Quay, 1984). Thus, research on individual characteristics indicates that summary indicators such as cognitive abilities, social skills level, or emotional adjustment are not likely to provide enough power by themselves to be useful risk predictors. At best, given our present knowledge, they appear to have some potential as risk factors when combined with other psychosocial factors.

School Factors

A second psychosocial variable often linked to risk for delinquent behavior relates to the school setting. For purposes of discussion, we shall examine separately academic performance and social functioning in school.

ACADEMIC PERFORMANCE. Academic difficulties have long been related to delinquency both theoretically and statistically (see Chapters 4 and 12, and Loeber & Dishion, 1983; Robins & Hill, 1966). The relationship is thought to reflect the effects of limited verbal abilities and perhaps, learning disabilities. Such limitations are assumed to result in poor general adaptation, which in turn increases delinquency risk. Reciprocally, such limitations may be the direct cause of academic difficulties which are mislabeled by school personnel as disciplinary rather than intellectual problems. Little support currently exists for either of these hypotheses. However, the evidence has been consistent in showing that ratings of academic competence, aspirations, and attitude are significantly related to delinquent behavior. For example, Elliot, Huzinga, and Ageton (1985) carried out an extended investigation of the interrelationships of educational aspiration, academic capability, and self-reported delinquent behavior. They report that neither academic skills nor level of aspiration per se was related to delinquent behavior. Rather, such behaviors relate to the combination of either very low or very high educational aspirations and certain academic skill levels. Thus, it may be that effects of academic or intellectual deficiencies on delinquency risk are more directly attributed to attitude and aspiration toward academic achievement. Direct consideration of these variables may therefore provide significant explanatory power. Clarifying the mechanisms that promote or diminish such attitudes and aspirations presumably will require consideration of the school as a social environment.

SOCIAL BEHAVIOR WITHIN SCHOOL. One of the most consistent findings in delinquency research is that social difficulties in school relate to later or ongoing delinquent behavior. A study of this relationship by Elliot & Voss (1974) revealed that delinquent behavior relates to problems in social functioning *within* the school rather than poor attendance or academic difficulties. Elliot and Voss also found that a majority of dropouts reported that they left school for social rather than academic reasons. On follow-up, it appears that quitting school actually decreased their rate of delinquent behavior (Elliot,

1976). In our own research, we included measures of number of disciplinary actions and absenteeism in the previous school year. Although neither measure correlated highly with delinquent behavior, number of disciplinary actions correlated significantly but very modestly with frequency of delinquent behavior ($r = .17$; Tolan, 1984). This variable was not, however, a significant predictor in a multiple regression analysis of factors relating to reported delinquent activity (Tolan, in press).

Yet unanswered is the question of whether the school as a social context is particularly influential regarding the development of such characteristics as aggressiveness, self-control, and social conformity. A related question is whether obtained school functioning difficulties are attributable to individual differences, or are best understood as reflecting organizational factors which exacerbate individual tendencies. If the latter is the case, then the salient risk factor is the combination of individual characteristics and the school environment.

A recent study by Rutter, Maugham, Mortimor, Ouston, and Smith (1979) provides some insight into these questions. They concluded that the "ecology" of the school (e.g., proportion of low-income students in the school, teachers' morale, organizational style of the school) was a more important contributor to delinquent behavior than individual capabilities or specific academic programs. In addition, they observed that the environment's influence affected the school population as a whole rather than specific subgroups. Their findings suggest that it is the "ecology" of the setting rather than individual adjustment characteristics which must be considered in assessing risk for delinquent behaviors.

Overall, it appears that behavioral adjustment in school reflects the combined effects of personal adjustment and the school as a social environment. It is becoming increasingly clear that the school's organizational atmosphere and the makeup of its student population can catalyze or moderate individual risk factors. This conclusion provides further support for our proposition that delinquency and its prevention is best understood within a transactional-developmental model.

Family Factors

Unquestionably, family variables have received the most attention to date by those attempting to identify factors contributing to delinquent behaviors. Admittedly, examination of family characteristics represents one of the more complex areas of delinquency research. An extended review of this research area has already been provided in Chapter 8. For that reason, we will focus on two aspects of families that appear to be most pertinent to delinquency risk identification: family demographics and family systemic functioning.

FAMILY DEMOGRAPHICS.   Family "demographics" refer to such "framework" characteristics of the family as the marital status of the parents, the presence (or lack there of) of both parents in the household, sibling birth order, and family size. It is evident that a child from an intact family is less at risk for delinquent behavior than a child from one that is not intact. Yet, the consequences often attributed to parents' martial status are quite complex. As has been noted earlier, multiple variables appear to mediate the influence of parents' marital status on delinquency risk, including gender of the child, recency of the father's departure, the reason for the father's departure, the family's socioeconomic status, and the age of onset of delinquency.

The need for similar precision becomes apparent in reviewing the effects of birth order and family size on delinquency risk. Although early studies suggested that children in the middle birth order position and those from large families were at increased risk for delinquency, it now appears that the most parsimonious explanation for the reported relationship relates to decreased parental supervision in large families and the exposure of middle children to modeling of delinquent behavior by older siblings. In our own research, neither birth order nor family size related to reported delinquent behavior (Tolan, 1984; in press). In our view, there appears to be little justification for continued emphasis on these family characteristics.

Further research on the links between delinquency and parents' marital status is still needed. Simply considering parents' marital status is insufficient. Two refinements in research design are important to the assessment of its links to delinquency. First, the investigator must specify the exact dimensions of marital status which are being studied. Among those factors which should be defined are clarification of the reason for the marital dissolution (e.g., death versus divorce), measurement of the permanence of the parent's absence and documentation of the recency of the marital dissolution. Admittedly, such refinements will complicate the selection of samples and the analysis of the data. In turn, however, the resulting information is likely to be useful for both explaining and predicting delinquency risk.

Family Systemic Functioning

As noted elsewhere (Tolan Cromwell & Brasswell, in press), considerable empirical and conceptual support exists for focusing on family systemic characteristics in delinquency research. Reviewing family interaction research, Jacob (1975) documented five trends that differentiated the family interactions of delinquents from nondelinquents. These are as follows: (1) families of delinquents tend to have a greater frequency of parental disagreements during their interactions; (2) delinquent families are characterized by less differentiation between parents' and children's influence on family decisions (with families of delinquents having child-skewed power distributions); (3) delinquent families are characterized by less expression of positive affect and more expression of negative affect; (4) families of delinquents tend to experience more misperceived communication; and (5) families of delinquents tend to be relatively less willing to compromise.

Tolan (1984) found that several dimensions measured by the Moos Family Environment Scale (Moos & Moos, 1981), including cohesion, conflict, organization, and intellectual and moral-ethical orientation, related to level of self-reported delinquency. Moreover, family systemic functioning variables were the most important contributors to a multiple regression analysis of psychosocial predictors of reported involvement in delinquent behaviors (Tolan, in press).

Research findings that support focusing on family systemic functioning, despite their consistency, are to date limited. The majority of studies have involved concurrent measures of delinquent behavior and family systemic functioning. Clearly, prospective studies are necessary if causal links are to be uncovered. Admittedly, observed correlations between family systemic variables and reported delinquent behavior are at low to moderate levels. Nevertheless, their promise as significant predictors leads us to urge their continuing study and analysis. At present, indices of family systemic functioning represent the second set of most useful risk predictors, next to measures of individual aggression.

Sociological Factors

The influence of sociological factors as contributors to delinquency has been discussed at length in Chapters 2 and 3. Three specific sociological variables have received substantial attention in delinquency research, namely, socioeconomic status, racial/ethnic differences, and involvement in peer groups. As we have seen earlier in this volume, most studies show negligible differences or no differences in overall rates of deviant behavior across ethnic groups. Those differences which have been found appear to reflect interactional effects of race and socioeconomic status (Elliot & Ageton, 1980). Thus, it appears that consideration of racial and ethnic differences adds little to our ability to predict delinquency risk.

The influence of peer group membership on delinquency risk has, to date, been minimally assessed (Tittle et al., 1978). What work has been carried out reflects the assumption that the peer group's influence was only negative (Youniss, 1980). However, recent research suggests that peer group contribution to delinquency is significant (Truckenmiller, 1982), situationally specific (Larson, 1972), and, depending on the quality and strength of bonds to specific peers, may vary in the direction of its influence (Smith, 1976; Truckenmiller, 1982). Thus, peer influences may be important determinants of delinquency risk. However, until the dimensions of their influence are examined systematically, their contribution to the design of delinquency prevention programs will be limited. At present, consideration of the adolescent's entire social network is likely to provide a better understanding of delinquency risk than focusing specifically on the effects of peer delinquency.

Implications of Psychosocial Research

Of the many psychosocial variables reviewed, only family functioning has consistently been shown to relate to risk of delinquency. Further research on this variable, with specific focus on the dimensions listed by Patterson (1982) and

Patterson and Stouthamer-Loeber (1984) appears to be highly promising. Further investigation of these dimensions and examination of other dimensions (e.g., those outlined by Jacob, 1975) seem likely to provide some direction for risk identification based on family systemic characteristics.

With respect to many of the other psychosocial variables considered, the majority of hypothesized relationships with deliquency risk have not been borne out (e.g., socioeconomic status). The meaning of observed relationships cannot be clarified because of the method of measurement (e.g., social skills). For some (e.g., marital status) the link seems more indirect than direct. Those variables correlated directly with delinquent behavior are, for the most part, linked only at low to moderate levels and thus have only limited explanatory power.

In fact, we doubt that any single psychosocial variable can distinguish risk for delinquent behavior strongly enough to guide identification efforts adequately. Only when they are combined do these factors explain enough variance in delinquent behavior to be predictively useful (Bry, McKeon, & Pandina, 1982). Thus, their effect seems to be a summative one. Studies that use multivariate models have shown that in combination, individual, school, and family factors can explain substantial portions of the variance in delinquent behavior (Simcha-Fagan, 1979; Tolan, in press). Application of this method therefore seems necessary if social variables are to be considered in delinquency prediction.

Conclusions About Risk Identification

Our summary and the detailed discussions in earlier chapters generally supports the conclusion that little is presently known about factors leading to delinquency which can be translated into specific elements of preventive interventions. The methodological limitations of the field, the absence of a common theoretical perspective, and the wide diversity of approaches to the issue overshadow any specific results. We are clearest about what areas of study seem futile, rather than what areas promise significant insights. The conclusion that more research is needed is appropriate but inadequate. What is specifically needed is research that operationalizes delinquency outcomes and examines systematically relevant behavioral and psychosocial variables. Such research, we believe, should be theoretically based and incremental in nature. The field does not need additional isolated findings.

With this in mind, we suggest that current findings can be logically interpreted within the transactional developmental paradigm. None of the variables studied correlates with or predicts delinquent behavior at a level that allows its exclusive use for risk identification. Even the relatively large predictive ability of behavioral indicants does not preclude the need to consider other variables. As we have suggested elsewhere (Tolan, 1984; in press), a model of delinquency risk identification which allows for consideration of the interaction of several variables is theoretically and empirically advantageous over one that considers each variable in isolation or aims to identify the single best predictor. By examining the interactions between individual characteristics and behavioral tendencies and familial and environmental factors across the major developmental stages of childhood and adolescence, we may be able to develop an adequate enough explanation of delinquent behavior to permit meaningful prediction.

Several tentative conclusions can be made about which factors merit emphasis. It is evident that childhood antisocial behavior is the best predictor of the onset of delinquency and should therefore be central to any predictive model. Age of onset as a predictor of the extent and chronicity of delinquent behavior also merits inclusion in any predictive equation. Family functioning appears to be the only psychosocial variable that is related to delinquent behavior at a level that distinguishes it from other psychosocial variables. Psychosocial factors other than family functioning are best considered nonspecific risk factors, with only minor individual or specific impact on risk. Their influence seems to be as moderator variables within a multivariate model. Admittedly, their total contribution to predictive accuracy remains questionable at this time. Further empirical study is needed to clarify whether some variables are even correlated (e.g., social skills), and whether other previously unconsidered variables (e.g., unemployment and reliance on welfare rather than socioeconomic status) are rich veins to mine.

Thus, as demonstrated here and in Chapter 12 the current status of delinquency risk identification is quite primitive. Based on current knowledge, we encourage pursuit of two identification models that consider the interaction of behavior indicants and psychosocial variables. Research can provide theoretically and empirically based models on which to base intervention strategies by systematically refining our definitions of delinquent states, identifying behavioral patterns that relate to various outcomes, and determining how the predictive and contributing variables interact.

Interventions to Prevent Delinquency

The identification of delinquency risk is obviously a formidable task. Equally challenging is the development of intervention programs designed to prevent delinquency. From the outset, we think it is fair to say that preventive treatment approaches with troubled children have yet to prove their merit. The majority of studies of such interventions are so flawed by measurement and design problems as to render their outcome data vaguely interpretable, of unknown value, or at best, promising. In those few studies where unequivocal interpretations are possible, the *preventive* value of the interventions was either nonexistent or, again, somewhat "promising" in that slightly positive differences were documented. Because the following review is limited to empircially sound studies it has an obvious pessimistic attitude toward currently used therapeutic packages. At the same time we believe that a reasonable case can be made for the continued development and field testing of new prevention strategies. Independent of currently available data, we believe that there is reason for optimism regarding future approaches to prevention.

Our survey of the literature identified two broad categories of preventive interventions which differed in their emphasis on "imposed" versus "natural" sources of behavior change. The former procedures, typified by the residential and institutional programs reviewed in Chapter 9, were based on the expected benefits of radical environmental change for troubled children. Ideally, a new course of behavioral development can be instigated within these special environments. Presumably, that course will then be nurtured through the systematic involvement with appropriate transition steps in which the child is gradually reintroduced into the regular environment.

By contrast, "natural" prevention programs attempt to retain the troubled child in the normal environment by utilizing resources indigenous to that environment. Such community-based programs (see Chapter 10) tend to be focused on the families, school settings, and peer groups of troubled children. Not surprisingly, different theoretical perspectives are represented in both intervention categories. In effect, some (e.g., psychodynamic) are geared toward the alteration of within-child hypothetical processes, and others (e.g., social learning) emphasize the child's relationship to other people. Our analysis, however, did not suggest that theory was a particularly useful means of differentiating what was *actually done* in the intervention program. In part, this ambiguity reflected the generally poor quality of evaluation procedures across studies. In addition, there were many instances in which procedures based on different theories (e.g., transactional analysis versus social learning) were, in fact, quite similar. Quite significant procedural differences, however, separated "imposed" versus "natural" interventions.

Imposed Strategies

In general, as noted in Chapter 9, individuals assigned to residential programs are at greater risk than those assigned to community-based programs. It is understandable that parents and juvenile justice and social welfare officials are unlikely to remove a child from the natural environment unless that child's behavior is seriously deviant and/or the natural community (typically the family) is seriously deficient in its capacity to care for the child. In actuality, residential programs should be viewed as quantitatively rather than qualitatively distinct from community programs, in the sense that "removal from the community" comprises interventions varying from complete separation of the child from the community (e.g., placement in a state institution) to simply requiring the child's attendance at an "alternative" school. Although the latter separation from the natural community does not actually belong in the "residential" category, the child nevertheless experiences a setting which is quite different from the typical public school. In a similar vein, community-based group homes represent contrived family settings, yet oftentimes the children who enter such residential programs continue to be enrolled in their natural public schools.

The intervention logic behind "imposed" programs is fairly clear. Certain troubled children are perceived as so deficient in prosocial skills and so disruptive in their maladaptive actions as to preclude successful childrearing by some parents, teachers, and peers, or the environment is so poor as to preclude social development. By placing the child in a more appropriate and prosocial environment, the development of necessary but absent skills and the modification of misapplied skills presumably can occur. Obviously, the prediction of the undesired consequences of maintaining the child in the natural setting reflects a negative judgement about the competence and motivation of relevant people in the troubled child's natural community. It is expected that parents, teachers, and peers are unlikely to comply with an intervention strategy because of competing motivational issues and/or their profound lack of prosocial skills. In cases of marked child deviance and the absence of workable support within the child's natural groups, residential placement would appear to be the only reasonable alternative. Ideally, one would make the above judgments based on assessments of the troubled child's behavior within the context of the three natural group settings: family, school, and peers. In effect, these settings can provide important diagnostic insights into the severity of the child's developing disorder. As the child's antisocial behavior becomes increasingly problematic in multiple settings, and as responsible people in these settings demonstrate a lack of response to suggested change, the necessity of residential treatment becomes clear (Loeber, 1982).

In contrast to what may have become demonstrably unworkable community settings for child behavior intervention, residential settings can contribute significantly to two important therapeutic targets: social skill development and the fostering of prosocial values. As has been described in detail in Chapter 9, changes in both areas have been demonstrated in a segment of some residential treatment programs. In these settings the skill factor in youth adaptive development is highlighted to a greater extent by virtue of the school's focus on academic and/or vocational tasks. Since it is also true that changing school task performance is related to changes in delinquency (Jensen, 1976), this focus makes considerable therapeutic sense. According to Hirschi's (1969) interpretation of these correlations, an antisocial child's failure in school will duplicate that child's prior family experiences, namely, rejection of adult authority and an orientation toward peers.

As is true with residential environments, creating an optimal school environment for antisocial children should be possible given the potential for control inherent in any residential setting. The popular notion of "alternative schools" clearly represents this strategy (see Gold, 1978; Stallings, 1980; Slavin, 1980). These special schools can either be part of an institutional program or located within the community. The teaching and learning atmospheres within these schools are markedly different for the typical public school in several respects: (1) In part because of more favorable student-teacher ratios, alternative school teachers are expected to be more consistent in their contingent use of praise, the firmness of their limit setting, and the avoidance of arguments with students. This strategy is much like that shown to promote good adult-child relationships in natural family settings (see Baumrind, 1968). (2) The likelihood of student mastery of learning objectives is also presumably increased, because those objectives are prescriptively "tailored" to each student (Block, 1971; Peterson, 1972). Thus, unlike public schools, grades are not based on group norms. (3) Students work in "teams" or small groups which require cooperative learning among the individual members (Slavin, 1980). Since each student's success is at least partly dependent on other group members, peers ought to support student achievement (O'Leary & Becker, 1967).

A review of outcomes in the evaluations of alternative school programs indicates that antisocial and delinquent children do, in fact, make greater gains in achievement than they do in public schools (Gold, 1978). At the same time, there is little evidence that the intended "bonding" occurs between these children and the alternative school staff (Reckless & Dinitz, 1972). Nevertheless, academic skill mastery is presumed to serve an important delinquency prevention function in its own right (e.g., Hirschi, 1969).

Natural Programs

Most community programs have evolved from one or both of the following operating assumptions: (1) some environmental conditions, suspected of supporting the antisocial child's deviance, can be altered; and (2) there are untapped sources of corrective child guidance in any community. Examples of the first assumption primarily include educational and clinical programs aimed at increasing the management skills of the parents, peers, and public school teachers of antisocial children. In addition, what might be called "environmental design" intervention, has appeared, which focuses on altering the more material elicitors of antisocial actions (e.g., availability of frequently stolen items). The second assumption involves novel utilizations of mental health, medical, and juvenile justice personnel, the use of volunteers in the guidance of children, and diversionary programs that attempt to shift a youngster's attention away from delinquency-tempting settings. As detailed in Chapter 10, it is apparent that periodic interventions involving the troubled child and clinicians or educators, even when implemented over multiple years, have accomplished little in the way of delinquency prevention. (McCord, 1978). On the other hand, somewhat more encouraging results have been reported when interventions have included the natural caretakers of these youth as well as the youngsters themselves. Thus, Alexander and Parsons (1973), and Alexander, Barton, Schiavo and Parsons (1976) established improved communication exchanges and formal contingency contracts between parents and their antisocial children. Compared to no-treatment controls, the 18-month follow-up results were favorable. A similarly designed, but more strictly contingency-managed approach designed by Forehand, King, Peed, and Yoder (1975) and Patterson (1974) produced equally favorable 12-month follow-up comparisons. Unfortunately, when later investigators included measures of family stressors (e.g., marital conflict, socioeconomic disadvantage), it was found that the more seriously stressed families did not respond to these parent-child interventions (Dumas & Wahler, 1983; Webster-Stratton, 1985).

The somewhat encouraging strategies just described have an emerging parallel form within public school classrooms. Several investigators, notably, Hawkins and Lam (in press), have created and measured some major shifts in the quality of teacher-student styles in junior high school classrooms. These shifts are much the same as those described earlier in reference to alternative schools (i.e., individualized instruction, contingent use of praise and discipline, and cooperative peer learning). However, these newer applications are intended to encompass *all* children within a school district and, thus have the potential of achieving primary prevention goals as well. The encouraging preliminary outcomes in the Hawkins and Lam (1983) large scale study document the links between teacher use of "alternative" teaching methods and increases in on-task work behavior of all pupils. In addition, teacher use of these methods correlated inversely with official disciplinary actions and days of student suspension from school. We concur with Hirschi's (1969) speculation that such a school environment will eventually compete with a child's inclination toward delinquency. As such, primary prevention outcomes consistent with findings from alternative schools may result. There is, however, no evidence of improved student "bonding" with teachers who use these more effective methods. When such procedures are adopted in preschool programs, however, substantial increments in both achievement and youth commitment to school are observed years later (Schweinhard & Weihart, 1980). Once again, such findings justify optimism about school based prevention programs.

We have argued thus far that preventive interventions which hold the most promise are characterized by continuous exposure of the children at risk to the presumed effective programmatic components. If parents and public school teachers are taught to apply behavioral contingencies which compete with the suspected environmental factors contributing to delinquency, participating children appear to respond quite positively. A similar emphasis on environmental restructuring is represented in diversionary programs already reviewed in Chapter 10. Clearly, one must conceptualize remediation and prosocial development as a task requiring major environmental restructuring rather than the offering of periodic special experiences. We turn now to a speculative picture of such future prevention programs.

An Ecological Perspective on Prevention

In a survey of delinquency problems (Twentieth Century Fund Task Force on Confronting Youth Crime, 1978) an interesting review is presented with reference to two time honored and clashing views on delinquency. One of these, the "welfare model" subsumes a psychological and/or sociological perspective on causality. In this case we see the general presumption that delinquency is symptomatic of adverse family and community influences. Following this presumption, one would prevent delinquency by altering these environmental problems.

On the other hand, the "justice model" views child development as a process of free will and, therefore, considers the child's deviant actions as a matter of reasoned choice. Should this presumption yield guidelines on prevention, they would largely be concerned with making the child accountable for his or her actions. In essence, the Task Force report urges a better balance between the models, which is tantamount to moving the conceptual pendulum toward the justice model or a community's exercise of sanctions and controls over youth behavior. While some might fear a return of the nineteenth century punitive orientation toward child care, there is another more benevolent aspect of this position. We have repeatedly voiced our contention that truly effective therapeutic programs for antisocial children must alter the day-to-day lifestyles of these children. In other words, the family, peer, and school settings in which these children live must be "fine tuned" to respond to the children's chronic behavior deficits and excesses. The children must become accountable for their actions in such a way that they expect *predictable* outcomes for their prosocial efforts as well as for their rule-violating actions. The justice model, stressing a child's accountability in this fashion, could lead to some highly significant developments in community life.

The justice model also gains credibility in reference to present-day ambiguities in our understanding of delinquency development. Certainly the welfare model is gaining ground in promoting our understanding and prediction of antisocial delinquent behavior. However, since we cannot presently identify causal factors with the precision necessary to construct specific interventions, the notion of comprehensive environmental restructuring does not make sense. Regardless of whether or not delinquency is caused by a combination of genetic (see Chapter 7) and environmental factors, the deficits and rule-violating excesses of children can be modified by painstaking, time consuming, and expensive attention to their natural environments. Leitenberg's (in press) proposal on "proactive" programs for entire communities is a good example of the justice model translated into direct action. According to Leitenberg, we already know enough about child-rearing principles to educate parents and teachers on ways to develop good working relationships between themselves and troubled children. But the implementation of these principles will ultimately require political as well as psychological strategies. For example, his proposal to require high school courses in child rearing and some sort of premarriage examination of parenting skills presumes some drastic rethinking of community values. Should a community put these child-rearing principles to their systematic test, we would expect beneficial outcomes with respect to delinquency.

An obvious drawback to the justice model has to do with its presumption about the delinquent's "free choice" between prosocial and antisocial options. Behavioral science has yet to provide clear answers as to the cause of delinquency, yet the complexity implied in some of the answers now available suggests that there is deceptive simplicity to the application of the justice model. Free choice, as a conceptual variable, views the troubled child as responsive to stimulus conditions in immediate proximity to their behavior (e.g., consequences). While the bulk of empirical research supports this viewpoint, there are also data to show that children will behave in accordance with more remote stimulus conditions (e.g., Fowles & Baer, 1981; Baer, Williams, Osnes, & Stokes, 1984). In essence, these studies suggest that children may respond to the "demand characteristics" of a social setting and these characteristics are not tied functionally to the consequences of child behavior. Thus, Fowles and Baer (1981) taught preschool children to share with peers when sharing was reinforced by points. As long as the teachers provided instructions on the importance of sharing and the children received point reinforcers at the end of each day, the children would continue their sharing even though the "reinforcers" for this behavior were *randomly* presented. Therefore, the children were sharing even though the consequences of the behavior were irrelevant. This is hardly "reasoned choice" by the children since their receipt of points occurred regardless of how often they shared. Studies of this sort indicate that children can and will behave in ways that have little bearing on the immediate outcomes of their behavior. Research which identifies the factors which actually maintained the desired behaviors may provide important insights into how antisocial behavior arises and continues.

An ecological perspective on delinquency prevention must recognize the irrational nature of human behavior as well as its more reasoned quality. The justice model can provide some useful guidelines in our formulation of proactive and reactive strategies of child guidance. We must, however, use the welfare model as a thrust toward the refinement of such strategies. For example, parents on the road to rearing an antisocial child could become responsive to a parenting program geared to their immediate responsibilities as parents. But these people might also be influenced by environmental events little connected to their problems in childrearing (e.g., contextual conflicts with extended family). Therefore, a well-informed prevention agent would look to the larger picture as well as the more molecular and familiar picture of parent-child coercive exchange. There are commonly accepted guidelines for this enlightened agent. Without a doubt, this agent must lead others to create accountability-conscious environments for the troubled child. In addition, the agent must look to indirect or contextual factors in the child's problems. As researchers who follow the welfare model continue to gain ground on identifying the nature of these factors, the well-informed agent will construct progressively more fine-tuned interventions.

FINAL COMMENTS

We hope that readers of this chapter will interpret its contents as justification for optimism about the future of delinquency prevention efforts. Admittedly, much work remains to be done before the definitional, conceptual, methodological, and progammatic challenges of this goal are resolved. The position echoed throughout this chapter is that achievement of significant incremental progress in these areas will be enhanced by adoption of Sameroff and Chander's (1975) transactional-developmental model as the paradigmatic base of scientific work on delinquency. As stated earlier, the field is not likely to profit from the continued accretion of isolated findings. Rather, it will profit from shared agreements among investigators as to operationalizing relevant independent (i.e., delinquency) and dependent (e.g., onset, severity, or consequence) variables, and identifying the questions which need to be addressed. Undoubtedly, reasonable people will disagree about the specific sequence in which these questions should be addressed. Nevertheless, if the pool of questions can be reduced somewhat, some agreement reached on the relative priority of sets of questions, and a common framework adopted for consideration of answers, the likelihood of accelerated progress seems quite high. Naively, perhaps, we believe that the time is right for this to occur.

Readers, we hope, will also gain from this chapter a sense of the seriousness with which we take prevention research. Such research is extraordinarily challenging and, we believe, will force the behavioral and mental health sciences to explore new approaches to research design, data analysis, and involvement in social policy and programming. To maximize the opportunities presented by this challenge, we urge prevention researchers to exploit the conceptual and empirical benefits offered by all forms of prevention intervention. This position in no way implies that the goals of primary prevention, in other words, the avoidance of the onset of delinquent processes, should be replaced, only that the available options for its achievement be appreciated and used!

Thus, we urge readers to pursue as vigorously as possible preventive strategies for delinquency reduction. We believe that the goals are attainable and the necessary scientific conceptual and political resources are available. If the moment is seized, we expect that a revision of this chapter a decade from now will bear witness to the promise we see.

REFERENCES

Albee, G. W. (1982). Preventing psychopathology and promoting human potential. *American Psychologist, 37,* 1043–1050.

Alexander, J. F., Barton, C. Schiavo, R. S., & Parsons, B. V. (1976). Systems-behavioral intervention with families of delinquents: Therapist characteristics, family behavior and outcome. *Journal of Consulting and Clinical Psychology, 44,* 656–664.

Alexander, J. F., & Parsons, B. V. (1973). Short-term behavioral intervention with delinquent families: Impact on family process and recidivism. *Journal of Abnormal Psychology, 81,* 219–225.

Baer, R. A., Williams, J. A., Osnes, P. G., & Stokes, T. F. (1984). Delayed reinforcement as an indiscriminable contingency in verbal/nonverbal correspondence training. *Journal of Applied Behavior Analysis, 17,* 429–440.

Baumrind, D. (1968). Authoritarian vs. authoritative parental control. *Adolescence, 3,* 225–272.

Block, J. J. (1971). *Mastery Learning: Theory and Practice.* New York: Holt, Rinehart and Winston.

Bloom, B. L. (1984). *Community mental health: A general introduction.* Monterey, CA: Brooks Cole.

Bry, B. H., McKeon, P., & Pandina, R. J. (1982). Extent of drug use as a function of a number of risk factors. *Journal of Abnormal Psychology, 91,* 273–279.

Caplan, G. (1964). *Principles of preventive psychiatry.* New York: Basic Books.

Cowen, E. L. (1973). Social and Community interventions. *Annual Review of Psychology, 24,* 423–472.

Cowen, E. L. (1983). Primary prevention in mental health: Past, present, and future. In R. D. Felner, L. A. Jason, J. N. Moritsugu, & S. S. Farber (Eds.), *Preventive Psychology: Theory, research and practice* (pp. 11–25). New York: Pergamon.

Cronbach, L. J., & Meehl, P. F. (1955). Construct validity in psychological Tests. *Psychological Bulletin, 52,* 281–302.

Dorr, D. (1972). An ounce of prevention. *Mental Hygiene, 56,* 25–27.

Dumas, J. E., & Wahler, R. G. (1983). Predictors of treatment outcome in parent training: Mother isularity and socioeconomic disadvantage. *Behavioral Assessment, 5,* 301–313.

Elliot, D. S. (1976). Delinquency, school attendance and dropout. *Social Problems, 13,* 306–318.

Elliot, D. S., & Ageton, S. S. D. (1980). Reconciling race and class differences in self-reported and official estimates of delinquency, *American Sociological Review, 45,* 95–110.

Elliot, D. S., Huzinga, D., & Ageton, S. S. (1985). Explaining *delinquency and drug use.* Beverly Hills: Sage Publications.

Elliot, D. S., & Voss, H. L. (1974). *Delinquency and dropout.* Lexington, MA: Lexington Books.

Farrington, D. P. (1979). Longitudinal research on crime and delinquency. In N. Morris & M. Tonry (Eds.), *Crime and justice: An annual review of research* (Vol. 1, pp. 289–348). Chicago: University of Chicago Press.

Forehand, R., King, H., Peed, & Yoder, P. (1975). Mother-child interaction: Comparison of a non-compliant clinic group and a non-clinic group. *Behavior Research and Therapy, 13,* 79–84.

Fowles, S. A., & Baer, D. M. (1981). "Do I have to be good all day." The timing of delayed reinforcement as a factor in generalization. *Journal of Applied Behavior Analysis, 14,* 14–24.

Gold, M. (1978). Scholastic experiences, self esteem, and delinquent behavior: A theory for alternative schools. *Crime and Delinquency, 24,3,* 290–308.

Gold, M., & Petronio, R. J. (1980). Delinquent behavior in adolescence. In J. Adelson (Ed.), *Handbook of adolescent psychology.* (pp. 495–535). New York: Wiley.

Gordon, R. (1983). An operational definition of prevention. *Public Health Reports, 98,* 107–109.

Hawkins, J. D., & Lam, T. (in press). Teacher practices, social development and delinquency. In J. Burchard (Ed.), *Vermont Conference on the Primary Prevention of Psychopathology.*

Hindelang, M. J. (1974). The Uniform Crime Reports revisited. *Journal of Criminal Justice, 2,* 1–18.

Hirschi, T. (1969). *Causes of delinquency.* Berkeley, CA: University of California Press.

Hogan, A. E., & Quay, H. C. (1984). Cognition in child and adolescent behavior disorders. In B. B. Lahey & A. E. Kazdin (Eds.), *Advances in Clincal Child Psychology.* (Vol. 7, pp. 1–34) New York: Plenum.

Jacob, T. (1975). Family interaction in disturbed and normal families: A methodological and substantive review. *Psychological Bulletin, 82,* 33–65.

Jensen, G. F. (1976). Race, achievement and delinquency: A further look at delinquency in a birth cohort. American Journal Sociology, 82,2, 379–387.

Kuhn, T. (1970). *The structure of scientific revolutions.* Chicago: University of Chicago Press.

Larson, L. E. (1972). The influence of parents and peers and during adolescence: The situational hypothesis revisited. *Journal of Marriage and the Family, 34,* 67–74.

Leitenberg, H. (in press). Primary prevention of delinquency. In J. Burchard (Ed.), *Vermont Conference on the Primary Prevention of Psychopathology.*

Loeber, R. (1982). The stability of antisocial and delinquency child behavior. A review. *Child Development, 53,* 1431–1446.

Loeber, R., & Dishion, T. (1983). Early predictors of male delinquency: A review. *Psychological Bulletin, 94,* 68–94.

Lorion, R. P. (1983a). Research issues in the design and evaluation of preventive interventions. In J. P. Bower (Ed.), *Education for primary prevention in social work.* (pp. 7–23). New York: Council on Social Work Education.

Lorion, R. P. (1983b). Evaluating preventive interventions: Guidelines for the serious social change agent. In R. D. Felner, L. A. Jason, J. N. Moritsugum, & S. S. Farber (Eds.), *Preventive psychology: Theory, research and practice.* (pp. 251–268). New York: Pergamon.

Lorion, R. P. (1985a). Environmental approaches to prevention: The dangers of imprecision. *Prevention in human services,* 1985, *4* (#1–2), 193–205.

Lorion, R. P. (1985b). *The prevention of mental disorders: Bases for optimism.* Invited address to the XXth Interamerican Congress of Psychology. Caracas, Venezuela, July.

Lorion, R. P., & Lounsbury, J. W. (1982). Conceptual and methodological considerations in evaluating preventive interventions. In W. R. Tash & G. Stahler (Eds.), *Innovative approaches to mental health evaluation.* (pp. 23–57). New York: Academic Press.

Lorion, R. P., Work, W. C., & Hightower, A. D. (1984). A school-based, multi-level preventive intervention: Issues in program development and evaluation. *Personnel and Guidance Journal, 62,* 479–484.

McCord, J. (1978). A thirty year follow-up of treatment effects. *American Psychologist, 33,* 284–289.

Moore, D. A., Chamberlain, P. & Mukai, L. H. (1979). Children at risk for delinquency: A follow-up comparison of aggressive children and children who steal. *Journal of Abnormal Child Psychology, 1,* 345–355.

Moos, R. J., & Moos, B. S. (1981). *Family Environment Scale Manual.* Palo Alto, CA: Consulting Psychologist Press.

Mulvey, E. P., & LaRosa, J. F. (1984). *Targeting delinquency policy on developmental processes. Preliminary data.* Paper presented at the Annual Meeting of the American Psychological Association. Toronto.

O'Leary, J. O., & Becker, W. C. (1967). Behavior modification of an adjustment class: A token reinforcement program. *Exceptional Children, 33,* 637–642.

Olweus, D. (1979). Stability of aggressive reaction patterns in males: A review. *Psychological Bulletin, 86,* 852–875.

Osborn, S. G., & West, D. H. (1975). Temporary and continuing delinquency. *British Journal of Criminology, 15,* 43–50.

Patterson, G. R. (1974). Interventions for boys with conduct problems: Multiple settings, treatments and criteria. *Journal of Consulting and Clinical Psychology, 43,* 471–481.

Patterson, G. R. (1982). *Coercive family process.* Eugene, Oregon: Castalia Publishing Co.

Patterson, G. R., & Stouthamer-Loeber, M. (1984). Parental monitoring and child antisocial behavior. *Child Development, 55,* 1299–1307.

Petersilia, J. (1980). Criminal career research: A review of recent evidence. In N. Morris & M. Tonry (Eds.), *Crime and Justice: An annual review of research* (Vol. 2, pp. 321–379). Chicago: Chicago University Press.

Peterson, P. (1972). *A review of research on mastery learning strategies.* Unpublished manuscript. Stockholm: International Association for the Educational Achievement.

Reckless, W., & Dinitz, I. (1972). *The prevention of juvenile delinquency.* Columbus, OH.: Ohio State University Press.

Robins, L. (1978). Sturdy childhood predictors of adult antisocial behavior: Replications from longitudinal studies. *Psychological Medicine, 8,* 611–622.

Robins, N., & Hill, S. Y. (1966). Assessing the contributions of family structure, class, and peer groups to juvenile delinquency. *Journal of Criminal Law, Criminology, and Police Science, 57,* 325–334.

Rutter, M., Maugham, B., Mortimor, P., Ouston, J., & Smith, A. (1979). *Fifteen thousand hours: Secondary schools and their effects on children.* Cambridge, MA: Harvard University Press.

Sameroff, A. J., & Chandler, M. J. (1975). Reproductive risks and the continuum of caretaking casualty. In F. D. Honowitz, M. Hetherington, S. Scarr-Salapatek, & G. Siegel (Eds.), *Review of child development research* (pp. 87–244). Chicago: University of Chicago.

Sarason, S. & Doris, J. (1979). *Educational handicap, public policy, and social history: A broadened perspective on mental retardation.* New York: Free Press.

Schweinhard, L. J., & Weihart, D. P. (1980). *Young Children Grow Up: The Effects of the Preschool Program on Youths Through Age 15.* Monograph High/Scope Education Research. Foundation No. 7, Upsitante, Michigan: The High/Scope Press.

Simcha-Fagan, O. (1979). The prediction of delinquent behavior over time: Specific patterns related to official and survey-reported delinquent behavior. In R. G. Simmons (Ed.), *Research in community and mental health* (pp. 163–177). Greenwhich, CT: JAI Press.

Slavin, R. E. (1980). Cooperative learning. *Review of Educational Research, 50,* 315–342.

Smith, T. E. (1976). Push versus peer-group variables as possible determinants of adolescent orientations toward parents. *Journal of Youth and Adolescence, 8,* 5–26.

Stallings, J. (1980). Allocated academic learning time revisited, or beyond time or task. *Educational Researcher, 9, 11,* 11–16.

Tittle, C. R., Villimez, W. J., & Smith, D. H. C. (1978). The myth of social class and criminality: An assessment of the empirical evidence. *American Sociological Review, 43,* 643–656.

Tolan, P. H. (1984). Multivariate identification of delinquent behavior in males (Doctoral dissertation University of Tennessee, 1983). *Dissertation Abstracts International, 45,* 368B.

Tolan, P. H. (in press) Implications of age of onset for delinquency risk identification. *Journal of Abnormal Child Psychology.*

Tolan, P. H., Cromwell, R. E., & Brasswell, M. (in press). The application of family therapy to juvenile delinquency: A critical review of the literature. *Family Process.*

Truckenmiller, J. L. (1982). Delinquency, bread, and books. *Behavioral Disorders, 7,* 82–85.

Twentieth Century Fund Task Force on Sentencing Policy Toward Young Offenders. (1978). *Confronting youth crime.* New York: Holmes and Meier.

Wahler, R. G. (1976). Deviant child behavior within the family: Developmental speculations and behavior change strategies. In H. Leitenburg (Ed.), *Handbook of behavior modification and behavior therapy.* (pp. 516–543). Englewood Cliffs, NJ: Prentice-Hall.

Wahler, R. G., Leske, G., & Rogers, E. S. (1977). The insular family. In E. Mash, L., Hamerlynck, & L. Handy (Eds.), *Behavior modification* (pp. 102–107). New York: Brunner/Manzel.

Webster-Stratton, C. (1985). Predictors of treatment outcome in patent training for training for conduct disordered children. *Behavior Therapy, 16,* 223–243.

West, D. J., & Farrington, D. P. (1973). *Who becomes delinquent?* London: Heinemann.

Williams, J. R., & Gold, M. (1972). From delinquent behavior to official delinquency. *Social Problems, 20,* 209–229.

Wolfgang, M. E., Figlio, R. M., & Sellin, T. (1972). *Delinquency in a birth cohort.* Chicago: University of Chicago Press.

Youniss, J. E., (1980). *Parents and peers in social development: A Sullivan-Piaget perspective.* Chicago: University of Chicago Press.

CHAPTER 14

Research Methods

LEE SECHREST and ABRAM ROSENBLATT
University of Arizona

As is evident from the reviews and discussions of the myriad interventions in Chapters 9, 10, and 11, there remain doubts about the efficacy of all of them. There are three ways of looking at this seemingly dismal situation: (1) there really is no good way to rehabilitate juvenile offenders; (2) there may be good ways to rehabilitate juvenile offenders, they have just not been found; or (3) owing to methodological problems in earlier research, we really don't know much of anything about which approaches to rehabilitation work or don't work. We believe that this last option best describes the true state of affairs.

This Chapter thus attempts to lay out the methodological issues involved in evaluating juvenile delinquency intervention programs. The critical problem with most of the studies which have evaluated such programs can be traced to a failure to distinguish process evaluations from outcome evaluations. This failure leads to difficulties in interpreting and ensuring the strength and integrity of the treatment (the rehabilitation program) as well as difficulties in pinpointing the exact problems with the treatment. One such problem that has received some attention (see Chapters 5 and 9) involves the classification of offenders for treatment programs (Edelman and Goldstein, 1984; Sechrest, 1985). It appears that certain different "types" of treatment programs may only be effective with certain "types" of juvenile delinquents. Applying one treatment to all juvenile delinquents may result in a "no-effect" conclusion even though some delinquents may have benefitted by the treatment. A good process evaluation can draw attention to just this type of situation and thus help considerably to strengthen the treatment.

We will begin by examining the distinction between process and outcome evaluation. We will then look at issues involved in conducting process evaluations designed to determine and ensure both the strength and integrity of the program. We will identify the appropriate independent and dependent variables and provide examples of independent variables specific to certain types of programs. Finally, we will discuss outcome evaluation, problems in linking the independent and dependent variables, and the various methodologies available to the researcher. While much of our discussion will necessarily be idealized (we are all too aware of the considerable difficulties involved in conducting evaluations of real-world programs), we hope it will at least encourage researchers to consider these issues before embarking on the difficult endeavor of determining whether anything really "works" in the rehabilitation of juvenile offenders.

We are focusing on problems in program evaluation for the sake of organization of our discussion and to provide some integration with respect to research examples. We believe, however, that the discussion that follows has broad relevance to the methodological issues that arise in work on delinquency, most especially with respect to measurement and intervention studies. Research problems associated with determining the etiology of delinquency, although seemingly of a different nature, still depend upon our ability to assess variables of interest in an accurate and meaningful way and to substantiate the reasonableness of causal relationships between those variables. This chapter is addressed to those fundamental research problems.

PROCESS AND OUTCOME

Complex programs are not easy to translate from conceptualization into implementation, and implementation is, itself, a hazardous process. Programs usually develop and change in many ways before ever reaching a steady endpoint. Traditionally, studies that evaluate the developmental phases of a program have been called *process* (after Cronbach, 1964) or *formative* evaluations (Scriven, 1967). Studies that evaluate the change from some initial state to an endpoint have been called *outcome* (after Cronbach, 1964) or *summative* (Scriven, 1967) evaluations. More recently, Tharp, and Gallimore (1979) applied the terminology of ecology to social programs. Basically, they have described programs as moving through a set of "seral" stages, composed of relatively transitory associations of elements, that culminate in a stable condition called "climax." They noted that not all programs reach a climax stage, described as "an association of program elements, organized for and producing a defined social benefit, which will continue to exist, and in which there will not be a replacement by other element types, so long as social values, goals and supporting resources remain constant" (Tharp & Gallimore, 1979, p. 43).

They have further described four external conditions necessary for a program to reach climax. These include: (1) longevity—the climax condition usually can not be reached quickly; (2) stability of values and goals—a program must be designed to meet a stable value; (3) stability of funding—a program obviously must remain stable in its funding if it expects to survive; and (4) power of the evaluator—the influence of the evaluator must be maintained in a way that ensures the integrity of research and development. It is highly unlikely that many rehabilitation programs for delinquency even begin to meet these conditions, and programs funded on a "prove your effectiveness in so many days" basis are especially likely to be in the early stages of development.

The person who evaluates a program in its initial stages of development is putting the cart before the horse; he or she will likely use incorrect methodologies and will likely as not confirm the null hypothesis owing to the weakness of his or her independent variable (the program).

PROCESS EVALUATION AND JUVENILE DELINQUENCY

Far too often, research in the delinquency area has indeed put the cart before the horse. Most evaluations that have been conducted have been outcome evaluations of programs still in their initial stages of development. This prematurity has led to evaluations of weak programs. A weak program can be defined as one that lacks strength or integrity (Quay, 1977; Sechrest and Redner, 1979). Process evaluation serves to improve the strength and integrity of the program. With such an evaluation we can test each program element at each stage of its development from conceptualization to formulation to implementation. These program elements can be viewed as independent variables (requiring strength and integrity in their own right) and, in this case, strength and integrity of treatment can be viewed as conceptual dependent variables. Tharp and Gallimore (1979) described an approach to process evaluation called "evaluation succession." A key feature of this model involves using the results of each test of each element to guide further development of the program element. Implemented elements may be tested in association with other elements to determine how separate elements work together in achieving program goals.

We will begin by discussing the independent variable(s) in research, a much neglected topic. Most research focuses on results and seems to take the intervention for granted. We think that this is a wrong approach; strength and integrity of interventions must be assured before it makes sense to think of outcomes.

Evaluating the Strength of the Intervention

It is appropriate to begin a discussion of research methods with the topic of strength of interventions because so many methodological problems depend on the strength of the treatment and, consequently, the size of the effect that can be anticipated. But even more fundamentally, it makes sense to ask before undertaking any research project whether there is, in fact, a phenomenon to be studied. If careful consideration of the nature of an independent variable leads to the conclusion that it is not likely to have any important effects, then no effort should be wasted in studying it. The same question needs to be asked about variables in correlational studies, namely, whether there is sufficient variability to make it likely that an interesting correlation will be found.

Although the strength and integrity of the independent variable are especially pertinent to evaluating juvenile offender rehabilitation programs, in virtually all evaluations too little attention is paid to this (Sechrest and Redner, 1979). Strength of the treatment refers to the *a priori* likelihood that a treatment will have the intended outcome (Yeaton and Sechrest, 1981), or to the amount of treatment provided (Sechrest, West, Phillips, Redner, & Yeaton, 1977; Yeaton and Sechrest, 1981). The evaluator needs to be aware of the need to evaluate the strength of any independent variable (see Sechrest & Redner, 1979; Sechrest et al, 1977; and Sechrest, Ametrano & Ametrano 1982 for specific methods). Fairly elaborate and detailed discussions of the issues of strength and integrity of treatment of rehabilitation studies are available (Sechrest and Redner, 1979; Yeaton and Redner, 1980) and a summary of this discussion will suffice here. We agree with Yeaton and Redner (1980) in their assertion that inadequacies of strength and integrity of treatment can serve to explain why nothing works.

The basic idea of "strength of treatment" is applicable to any other representation of an independent variable, even if the variable is what is often known as a "subject" variable. For example, if one wanted to study the effect of fathers' education on delinquent behavior, it would make a difference over what range of education the relationship were studied. If one tried to study the phenomenon in a group of boys whose fathers were predominantly unskilled workers, the almost inevitable conclusion would be that there is no relationship between fathers' education and the delinquency of their sons. It is surprising how little attention is paid to the problem of restricted range when assessing the effects of variables on each other. The problem is, we repeat, quite analogous to that of assessing treatments implemented at very low strength.

In human services, we generally simply do not know very much about what constitutes a "weak" or a "strong" treatment. As a counterpoint, it is often possible in medicine to determine with considerable precision the strength of treatment. If a patient is given a dose of aspirin for a headache, and the headache remains, then we would be unlikely to simply say that "aspirin does not work." We would want to know if the dose was strong enough, that is, how much aspirin the person took and how often, before drawing any conclusions as to the efficacy of aspirin as a pain reliever.

At this point the question becomes: (1) how do we create or ensure a strong treatment?; and (2) how do we assess whether a treatment has been strong? The answers to both questions lie in process evaluation. A well-conducted "evaluation succession" effort will eventually lead to as strong a program as possible. In the course of conducting such an evaluation, data are accumulated that (if reported) make it easier to assess, *a posteriori,* the strength of the treatment. The data should also allow the program director and researchers to determine which program elements are useful and which are not, something that is not always possible in an outcome evaluation.

We warn, however, that in many areas of the social and behavioral sciences, knowledge about the workings of our interventions is extremely limited. Certainly that is true in juvenile delinquency. We do not know the "dosage" represented by our treatments, and we do not, consequently, know how to adjust the dosage to match it to the requirements at hand. In an as yet unpublished study of expert judgments about strengths of criminal offender rehabilitation programs, West and Sechrest (1986) found very little agreement concerning which program elements are critical and how they might be adjusted or enhanced to improve effectiveness. The discussion that follows can only be taken as illustrating the possibilities for manipulating the strength of interventions.

The Independent Variables

A wide variety of independent variables potentially influence the strength of virtually any given rehabilitation program. When designing a program, researchers need to make *a priori* decisions regarding the strengths of these variables as well as build in mechanisms that will allow for *a posteriori* assessment of the contribution of each element to program strength. This latter process is analogous to that frequently used in traditional social-psychological experimentation, in which each independent variable is chosen for its potential impact (i.e., strength), and manipulation checks are included to allow an *a posteriori* assessment of the actual strength of the manipulation (Aronson & Carlsmith, 1968, Carlsmith, Ellsworth, & Aronson, 1976). Discussing specific independent variables for rehabilitation programs in general is difficult; different types of programs will comprise different types of independent variables. Nonetheless, it is possible to identify some variables likely to be applicable to most programs. We will note some of these and will provide illustrations of independent variables that are specific to certain types of programs. The list of independent variables that follows is by no means meant to be exhaustive. The list does, however, provide guidelines as to the types of variables requiring some consideration by most planners and most evaluators of most rehabilitation programs.

THE THEORY.   Most delinquency programs are either explicitly or implicitly based on some type of theoretical premise. Greenberg (1975) has noted that many of these theories "border on the preposterous," (p. 141), and Glaser (1977) has posited the failure to employ adequate theory as a major deficiency in criminal justice evaluation research. Basic theory needs to be carefully linked to proposed interventions and outcomes as well as to the types of offenders to which it will be applied. For example, Fitzpatrick (1967) found that prisoners released from forest camps showed no lower levels of recidivism than prisoners released from other facilities. There was no mention as to why prisoners released from these camps should have lower recidivism rates, in short; there was no obvious theory. Evaluating the quality of the theory is important for several reasons that may contribute to the strength of the program. For one, if a theory is weak and expectations about the effect of the treatment are not met, there is no good way to interpret the basis for the failure of the treatment. Simply saying that psychotherapy should reduce recidivism does not allow for further hypotheses should the null hypothesis be confirmed.

However, if one assumes that a certain type of psychotherapy will improve self-esteem, which will lead to a reduced need to succumb to peer pressure to commit criminal acts, then if the desired effect is not found, the researcher can explore a variety of important hypotheses, make necessary changes in the intervention, and reintroduce the improved psychotherapy element into the program.

Theory and the treatment plan stemming from it may be evaluated by some group of "expert" judges in terms of the treatment's likelihood of producing the desired change. The variety of possible "experts," including counselors, corrections officials, and offenders, is great. Which types of experts can render the best opinion is an empirical question, but it is possible that judgments of experts could be used to increase the likelihood of a treatment's succeess. At the least, this type of scrutiny would help ensure a sound link between theory and implementation.

QUALIFICATIONS OF STAFF. That qualifications of treatment staff are important is often assumed: "better qualified" staff produce better outcomes. Until some standards are established for qualifications of staff, obtaining useful judgments of their qualifications will be difficult. Even if standards existed, for example, for qualifications of instructors in vocational training, it might be very difficult to obtain and present the information necessary to judge whether staff met the standards. Nonetheless, if sufficient information were presented, it would seem likely that qualified persons could rate staff on something like a five-point scale ranging from "not at all qualified" to "highly qualified." Then, testing the effects of the "nonqualified" as opposed to the "qualified" staff on the program or placing a given program on some continuum with respect to the variable of staff qualifications would be possible.

INTENSITY. The amount of treatment per unit time, say per week in the case of vocational, educational, or counseling programs, may be taken to reflect to intensity of treatment. In the case of parole supervision, intensity might refer not only to number of hours of contact per month, but to the overall level of supervision made possible by access to various sources of information such as reports from employers, from family members, and from personal observation. Again, at present, it might not be possible to do much more than rate some treatments on a simple scale ranging from low- to high-intensity treatment. Degree of probable involvement of staff and clients on the treatment process could also be assessed. Intensity may be critical for some treatments such as therapy (see Kassebaum, Ward, & Wilner, 1971) but less critical for other treatments such as parole (e.g., Greenberg, 1975).

LENGTH. The time span over which treatment is carried out is another important variable, the standards for which would obviously differ from one treatment to another. Ordinarily treatments extended over time would be considered stronger than briefer treatments, but there could be a point of maximum benefit before reaching some type of ceiling effect (e.g., as appears the case for psychotherapy; Howard, Kopta, Krause, & Orlinsky, 1986). It would be possible to vary systematically the lengths of treatments to determine where any point of diminishing returns might lie for the type of treatment.

INTENSITY X LENGTH.   Totality, or at least optimality, of treatment may not be completely reflected in the separate factors of intensity and length. There is probably some optimal level of total treatment for some interventions that reflects a combination of intensity of treatment and length of treatment. As a classic example, psychoanalysis can be expected to be a strong treatment only if both the intensity and length of the treatment are fairly great. Some behavioral interventions, however, are probably not any more effective past a certain degree of intensity or length.

FOCUSED TREATMENT.   Generally speaking, a treatment would likely be considered stronger if it were focused on one or a few problems or outcomes than if it were diffuse. For example, 24 counseling sessions devoted to alcohol problems may be a stronger treatment than 24 counseling sessions devoted to a variety of problems. Six months of training on reading may be a stronger treatment than six months of general school experience, at least if reading is the problem of interest. Determining what to focus on and how much to focus are matters for process evaluation.

CLARITY OF TREATMENT PLAN.   A treatment with a well-developed protocol to back it up would almost certainly be considered stronger than one lacking such a protocol, presumably because the treatment would be better grounded in theory, more focused, and so on. However, what constitutes a well-developed protocol and which of several well-developed protocols is likely to yield the best results for specific programs need to be considered and tested.

DIFFERENTIAL ASSIGNMENT.   A treatment plan involving assessment of the suitability of different candidates and assigning them according to suitability would be considered a stronger treatment. Classifying offenders for specific treatments is, however, is no simple task (see Sechrest, 1985), and just which types of offenders are suitable for which types of programs is by no means an answered question (see also Chapter 9).

Strength of Treatment as a Summarizing Variable

Strength of treatment is a construct that summarizes the separate and possibly interactive effects of independent treatment variables, for example, those just listed. We do not know how best to combine these variables, even if we had good measures of them. Careful study of our interventions and how they may be quantified is an item that should rank high on our agenda for methodological developments. Outcome variables must be chosen that will both adequately represent the domain expected to be affected by the intervention, *and* be sensitive to the intervention.

Assessing the Integrity of Interventions

The extent to which an element is delivered as planned constitutes the integrity of treatment. Although conceptually separate from strength of treatment, a program that lacks integrity will almost certainly be reduced in strength. The only exception would be a failure to adhere to plans that actually resulted in a more effective treatment, something that should be rare if we know at all what we are doing. Critical problems in assessing treatments may arise in that there may be discrepancies between the treatment as described in a plan, the treatment that was intended, and the treatment that is actually delivered. Conclusions about the outcome of a treatment should be linked only to the delivered treatment. Assessing treatment integrity is a classic problem of process evaluation and nicely illustrates how the "evaluation succession" model of program evaluation can work. At the basic level, we would assume that any program that wishes to maximize integrity should provide some sort of feedback on how well staff is following the treatment plan. Such feedback could be used to initiate measures that would insure some type of corrective action, allowing the program to mature. Steps need to be taken (e.g., monitoring implementation of the element, clearly describing the treatment or element, ensuring staff commitment to implementing the element) to ensure the integrity of implementation of any independent variable.

Integrity in the treatment of juvenile offenders appears often to have been lacking (Sechrest and Redner, 1979). An example, detailed originally by Quay (1977), serves well to illustrate our point even though it involved adult offenders. As was briefly noted in Chapter 9, Kassebaum et al. (1971) tested group therapy as a treatment for adult offenders. Their study is rare in having provided a fairly detailed picture of the actual treatment. It is clear from their description that most counselors were not professionally trained and were not committed to the treatment program. Inmates were also dubiously committed to the program, many participating only so as to improve their records. The therapy groups did not follow an explicit protocol and met for only one to two hours per week, generally in large groups. These factors combine to suggest a weak treatment. Furthermore, the integrity of treatment seemed to be undermined by considerable turnover in group leadership. The absence of any data on the attendance of inmates, the behaviors and techniques used by counselors, and the compliance of counselors with the treatment program, all point to problems with the integrity of the treatment. Again, we will try here to identify some independent variables relating to integrity of treatment that are likely to be applicable across a number of programs, saving our discussion of specific programs for later.

Enhancing Integrity of Interventions

Some measures can be taken in the planning and implementation of research to enhance the probability of high integrity of treatment implementation.

THE TREATMENT PLAN. The first element to be examined is the treatment plan itself. As Quay (1977) noted, a conceptually sound and clear treatment plan is more likely to be delivered with integrity than is a vague or poorly described plan. It is possible that the failure to delineate in any clear way the treatment to be delivered is more a failure of communication than of concept and protocol. Certainly a very well conceived and sharply defined treatment could be concealed by dense, imprecise, or careless verbiage. Nonetheless, when a treatment plan is not clearly spelled out and comprehensible, those responsible for a program should immediately make some type of change. A program is almost bound to fail if a detailed treatment plan is not available and if the plan has not undergone some type of process evaluation to ensure its clarity, utility, and practicality. For example, the plan should at least be tested with those who will be responsible for implementing the treatment.

Some common sense guidelines exist for such treatment plans. For one, the conceptual basis for a treatment should make clear the assumptions about the target behaviors on which the treatment is predicated and the links by which the processes involved in the treatment are expected to result in behavior change. For example, if as posited by Kassebaum et al. (1971) the effects of group counseling on recidivism are thought to be mediated by weakening the commitment of inmates to a criminal value system, the mechanisms or processes in counseling that produce that weakening should be spelled out, and the way in which weakening of commitment to the value system is to reduce criminality at remote times in the future should also be specified. If reduced parole-officer case loads are thought to lead to more intensive surveillance and hence to reduced opportunities for criminal behavior, that chain of actions and consequences should be made explicit; for one reason, so as to enhance the prospect that the original action of reducing case-load size would actually lead to closer surveillance.

There are many elements that might be important to an adequate treatment plan; just which elements should be listed would differ depending on the type of treatment. Still, some should almost always be present: (1) the methods used to select persons for treatment(s) and how any matching of persons to treatment occurs; (2) the frequency, length, and circumstances of any intervention with individuals or groups; (3) a description of the total services to be delivered, including the elapsed time in treatment; and (4) the identities, experiences, and training of the staff who are to deliver treatment. Once a plan is judged as adequate, it can be tested with the staff who will implement it to determine whether it is understandable, as well as to garner any staff reactions to the plan.

SUPERVISORY PLAN. Despite the best of plans and intentions, programs can fail for want of adequate supervision. A satisfactory proposal for evaluation of a treatment should include a specific plan for supervision of delivery of treatment to ensure that delivery conforms to plan. For example, the supervisory plan should provide for monitoring of training of personnel, for checking on adherence to treatment protocols, for verification of staff activities, and the like. To some extent an adequate program of supervision may seem to cast doubt on the qualifications and dedication of staff, but with a well-motivated and committed staff, supervision can be seen as a valuable method of verification and accountability rather than as an intrusion. Without a good plan for supervision, a project is always open to a charge of inferior treatment, especially if the treatment proves to have minimal or equivocal effects. Again, supervisors and staff can be shown the supervisory plan for comment, and a plan based on these comments can then be implemented on a trial basis, with provisions made to collect data on the effectiveness of the plan.

COMPLEXITY AND DIFFICULTY OF TREATMENT.   Generally speaking, we can expect that the more complicated or difficult a treatment is to administer, the greater the likelihood that its integrity will suffer. Were it possible on *a priori* grounds to surmise that a treatment will be complex and difficult, concern for integrity of treatment should be sharpened, and demands for protections of integrity should be increased. Unfortunately, the more complex the treatment, the more difficult it is to establish its integrity. When a treatment is as apparently simple as delivering a monetary subsidy to parolees for a period of time, it should not be difficult to document that the treatment was carried out as planned. Even with such simple treatment, it is reasonable to ask how parolees will be kept in contact with the staff and how there can be assurance that parolees receiving the subsidy are in fact unemployed. When the treatment is more complex, as in vocational training, counseling, and so forth, there are many more possibilities for shortcomings, and anticipations of problems in maintaining treatment integrity will be greater. When programs are very complex, for instance, when they require delivery of a wide variety of services by diverse agencies, as in the UDIS (Murray, Thompson, & Israel, 1978) study, apprehensions become even stronger. Patton (1978) provided an example of an intervention that was evaluated even though it never took place at all. Some treatments may also raise doubts about probable integrity because of the likelihood of resistance within the corrections community or even the community at large. Resistance might occur, for instance, with ambitious plans for community placements or because of seemingly excessive resources required to implement the program.

The fact that complex or otherwise difficult programs are suspect from the beginning may seem unfair, an indictment of treatments before they have had a chance to be tried. However, the history of treatment efforts in many fields justifies greater doubts for more difficult innovations. What is required in such cases is that investigators who propose to test the efficacy of unusually complex interventions propose correspondingly careful and thorough devices to ensure that departures from the treatment plan are minimized and that when departures do occur, they are detected and assessed. The more complex the treatment, the more detailed should be the plan for protecting treatment integrity by appropriate treatment protocols, supervision, monitoring, and motivation of staff. Similarly, the more complex the treatment, the more the need to evaluate the integrity (and strength) of individual elements before they are implemented into the program as a whole. If this is not done, it can be virtually impossible to assess where the breakdown in integrity occurs, making modifications of the program difficult.

Questions concerning "integrity" of treatment may also be raised by analogy concerning any variables analyzed as independent variables in research. The questions may seem to pertain more to some rather vague notions about the "validity" of measures, but they reflect the same concerns that arise with respect to manipulated variables. For example, if one wanted to compare rates and types of delinquency between boys raised in single-parent and two-parent families, questions ought to be asked about the "integrity" of family types as treatments. If one could do an experiment and assign boys to the family types, surely one would want to be certain that single-parent families really did only have a single parent present and that two parents were really present in two-parent family types. To the extent that two-parent families might be unstable, with one or the other parent often absent or uninvolved, the conceptual integrity of the family-type variable is impaired. Unfortunately, whether we think of the problems as those of validity or integrity, they are very often quite ignored.

Integrity and Strength of Interventions: After the Fact

Integrity of treatment is an easier conceptual variable to operationalize than strength of treatment. We can at least specify certain necessary ingredients in a treatment that would signify a high level of integrity. For example, we can specify the number of times offenders attend group therapy sessions, we can gather data on deviations from the treatment protocol, and we can document staff qualifications and staff commitment. We will examine one of these, staff commitment, in more detail as follows. A very first step is to ensure that treatment actually took place; that services were delivered as planned.

DOCUMENTATION OF SERVICE DELIVERY.   Fundamental to assessment of integrity of treatment is documenting that the treatment as described did take place. Every research proposal needs to include a specific plan by which it can be documented that services were delivered according to the plan as described in the proposal. The plan should include mechanisms for establishing that treatment sessions took place, that those to be treated attended, that the treatment protocols were adhered to, and that the total amount of treatment can be estimated with confidence. Proposals to evaluate treatments should include such appendices as forms on which dates and places of sessions could be recorded, along with the names of those in attendance, provisions for tape or video recording of sessions to be analyzed later for conformance to requirements of treatment, spot-checking of treatment sessions by supervisors, interviews or questionnaires with subjects of treatment, and so on. Reputable survey research firms regularly do checks to determine that their interviewers perform according to instructions, that interviews actually take place, and so on, and it does not seem less important that such quality-control mechanisms should be applied in evaluations of treatments.

STAFF COMMITMENT. Once documentation of service delivery has been assured, researchers need to identify the appropriate conceptual dependent variables. For most treatment interventions, the commitment of the staff to the treatment program is vital. Investigators have found (e.g., Jesness, Allison, McCormick, Wedge, & Young, 1975; Kassebaum, et al., 1971; see also Chapter 10) that if staff are not committed to a treatment program, it is unlikely to be well implemented and delivered. In fact, it is difficult enough to deliver many treatments even with a completely committed staff; a half-hearted commitment, let alone outright resistance, is likely to be disastrous. Ideally the description of a proposed treatment program should include positive evidence of staff commitment. Such evidence might come in the form of questionnaire responses, interview data, or even unsolicited testimonials.

Some Specific Examples

So far, we have spoken of delinquency programs in the generic sense and have tried to make a case for, and demonstrate how process evaluations of such programs can be conducted. However, as we have seen in earlier chapters, programs designed to rehabilitate offenders are diverse and varied. Some specific examples may be helpful for further illustrating the need for assessing strength and integrity of treatment and just how this can be accomplished within different types of programs.

In order to assess strength of treatment, one must first know exactly what it is and be able to describe it well. The evaluation of juvenile diversion by Palmer and Lewis (1980) was accompanied by a reasonably clear specification of what they meant by diversion, and an evaluation of vocational rehabilitation of delinquents by Johnson and Goldberg (1983) presented a good description of the program. The latter study does, however, somewhat unaccountably neglect to indicate the kinds of jobs that the male delinquents were being trained for. It is a fairly straightforward matter to assess the probable strength of a vocational rehabilitation effort. It is not so easy to determine whether a diversion program is "strong." Palmer and Lewis did present evidence that 51 percent of the youth in their study would ordinarily have been processed by the juvenile justice system; on the other hand, 49 percent would not have been processed and could be regarded as victims of a "widening net." Diversion is an example of an intervention that we may not understand well enough to quantify in any satisfactory way.

Some reports provide information about interventions in quantitative form. A report on structured learning therapy reported that sessions were 60 minutes long, conducted twice per week for six weeks. Presumably one could compare that amount of therapy with other implementations or ask experts to judge the likely adequacy of that amount of treatment, for instance, on a 10-point scale. A study of community treatment of delinquents (Lerman, 1975) was intended to be implemented in the form of "intensive treatment services" defined as two to five contacts per week between each juvenile and the case worker. Certainly one could, again, relate that amount of treatment to other intervention plans, to expert judgments of need, to an abstract ideal, or whatever.

By contrast, a review of "group treatment" of juvenile delinquents by Julian and Kilman (1979) did not provide descriptions of the treatments, in some instances because the original studies provided no information. Without information about just what was done and in what amount, however, it is difficult to know what to make of any conclusions. The study of vocational rehabilitation by Johnson and Goldberg (1983) did not find any evidence of effectiveness of the program, but that finding is to be understood in the perspective of a comparison study by Shore and Massimo (1966) that had shown positive findings for a similar intervention. In the latter study, however, the vocational counselors had caseloads of only 10 boys apiece, presumably permitting as much as four hours per week of contact. In the Johnson and Goldberg study, caseloads were as high as 50 per counselor, and individual contacts ranged from perhaps three per month to only two per year.

One cannot be sure just what was intended in the Johnson and Goldberg study, but other studies raise issues concerning the integrity of treatments, that is, whether they are actually carried out as planned. The community treatment study reported by Lerman (1975), which was to have provided "intensive" services, did not do so. Unfortunately, the treatment plan, which specified two to five contacts per week, did not specify how long those contacts would last, nor did the plan specify how the counselors would allocate their time to their various activities. The result was that counselors spent an average of only about 20 percent of their time with their wards, and probably averaged no more than an hour a week or so with each one. One outcome of the study that was probably related to a general failure of treatment was that far more youth ended up being placed in foster homes or in temporary confinement than was intended as the program was conceived.

Many other examples could be brought to bear on these issues, but we will merely reiterate that a good research protocol must provide for adequate description, including as much quantitative information as possible about the intervention, for assurance that the intervention will be delivered as intended, for monitoring to see that the intervention is delivered, and for quantititative information about what was done in fact.

COMPLEX TREATMENTS AND RESEARCH STRATEGIES.   Most "programs" of intervention consist of two or more, often many, conceptually separate elements. For example, a school absenteeism prevention program (Werner & Paladina, 1984) included working with teachers to help them to recognize children's problems, self-esteem-enhancing exercises for the children, contacts with parents, resolving such mundane problems as lack of suitable clothing, and so on. The approach was, in fact, "clinical" in many respects in that it depended upon the expert judgment of a specialist concerning just what was needed to reduce absenteeism in individual cases. Such treatments are global in nature, the "global X" as Campbell and Stanley (1966) call them. Global treatments can be described and evaluated; in the case of the absenteeism program, evidence indicated considerable effectiveness. They may be difficult to replicate insofar as they depend upon clinical skills of a special sort, but that does not make them either suspect nor unevaluable.

On the other hand, treatments that are global and complex are often expensive and conceptually confusing; as already suggested in Chapter 10, we want to know just which aspects of the treatments are critical. One general strategy to developing and understanding interventions, adapted from classical approaches to experimentation, has been that of *combining* elements. We try to identify potentially important elements and then combine them, often incrementally, in order to build up an effective intervention or program. This approach is slow and tedious and runs the risk of failure because important interactions or synergisms may be missed in the process of testing isolated elements. The individual elements may be so disappointing and the process of combining them so tedious that discouragement sets in and the whole process is abandoned before any success is achieved.

The alternative strategy is to try on the basis of the best thinking available to develop a strong intervention, one that has the best chance of working if anything will. If a test of a strong, complex intervention proves successful, the subsequent strategy for identifying critical elements is one of dismantling the intervention (Kazdin and Wilson, 1978). That is, one makes some guesses about which program elements may be less essential, preferably based on process-evaluation data, and then one tries the complex treatment in a reduced form, that is, with one or more elements omitted. One can selectively omit elements and repeat testing until an irreducible form of the intervention is identified.

In general we favor the dismantling strategy, for, although it may be tedious, it starts with the flush of success. The initial impetus of success is a better basis for sustaining a research effort than is incremental hope, and the research enterprise is maximally efficient if it turns out, as we expect is usually the case, that a complex intervention is required. There is no contradiction between our recommendation and the evaluation succession model proposed by Tharp and Gallimore (1979). Although they describe the process of program development, they also recommend beginning with the best-conceived intervention possible and building on that base.

OUTCOME EVALUATION AND JUVENILE DELINQUENCY

The idea of combining interventions with proven outcomes leads us to outcome evaluation of juvenile delinquency programs. Most evaluations have been outcome evaluations of programs that have not reached a climax condition.

Of course, a great many outside pressures may make early outcome evaluations necessary (e.g., demands of sponsors), and repeated outcome assessments as the program continues to change are desirable. Consider that when we are discussing outcome evaluation of a program, the program itself becomes the independent variable. Consequently, issues of strength and integrity of treatment apply to the program as a whole.

Outcome Measures

The conceptual dependent variable in outcome evaluations of juvenile delinquency programs is the obvious one of stopping the delinquent behavior, usually operationalized in terms of recidivism rates. Recidivism is defined variously, though, and may be taken to include continued involvement in delinquent activity determined by self-report. It is possible that delinquency programs should also be concerned with reducing the costs to the community and to the state of delinquency, and dealing with offenders. Our focus, and that of most studies, however, has been on rehabilitation. We cannot take space here to detail all the problems involved in selecting appropriate outcome measures. Suffice it to say that the task is critical. We do want to call attention to the powerful need of investigators to pay more attention to the psychometric properties of outcome measures.

Social and behavioral scientists are unaccustomed to thinking in psychometric terms about outcome variables. The psychometric properties of dependent variables are, however, of exceptional importance. It is true by definition that one cannot predict or dependably influence an unreliable measure. Or to put it conversely, our ability to detect influences of interventions depends critically on the dependability of our outcome measures. If, for example, rearrest is essentially a random event and is used as an index of recidivism, we will surely find no effects of interventions designed to change likelihood of rearrest. It is, in our experience, rare to find a study making any attempt to assess recidivism measures psychometrically, although, as with the weather, complaints abound. We note in passing that psychometric problems are usually couched in terms of reliability and validity, but the alternative of *generalizability theory* (Cronbach, Gleser, Nanda, & Rajaratnam, 1972) is likely to be more useful and deserves to be better known.

A second major potential problem involving inadequate outcome measure lies in differential reliability of an outcome measure for different populations. Both Sutcliffe (1980) and Bejar (1980) have shown how very misleading results may ensue from outcome measures that are differentially reliable across groups. If some recidivism measure of outcome is chosen, and that measure is less reliable in one group than another, then a program would appear to be less effective with the group for whom the measure is least reliable. For example, if recidivism is less reliably measured for girls than for boys, that is, if repeat offenses are less dependably reported, then an intervention might seem to work with boys but not with girls. The same sort of problem can occur if separate measures are differentially reliable. If self-reported offenses are less reliably measured than official offenses, an intervention might appear to reduce official offenses without reducing self-reported offenses. Major problems stem from the fact that very little attention is usually given to the characteristics of dependent outcome measures.

DESIGN ISSUES

When one sets out to do an outcome evaluation, design issues come to the fore. In part, perhaps in large part, that is because there is likely to be an important change in audience between process and outcome phases of an evaluation. Process evaluation is most often done for project insiders; it is for the purpose of guiding development of an intervention. Outcome evaluation is done for outsiders: funding sources, policymakers, the general public, and the most critical audience of all, journal editors. Attention must, therefore, be paid to questions about the plausibility of the research to these more critical audiences. Unfortunately, we actually know very little about the standards of evidence held by these audiences, and very little about how to do research that will be plausible to them. We do know enough, however, to indicate that the quality of our research designs can loom large as a factor (Holland, 1984; Weiss and Bucuvalas, 1980).

Causality

We take for granted the likelihood of establishing a dependable empirical relationship (correlation) between phenomena of interest. Problems arise in evaluation, or just about any field, when we attempt to insist that a causal relationship is involved (see Sechrest, 1984 for examples of causal and not so causal relationships in the health-care arena). The problem of inferring causality is a long-standing one in the social sciences (see Babbie, 1983 for a brief summary; Hirschi and Selvin, 1973 for an example of causation within the context of a particular research finding). As in any other field, the issue can not be ignored in evaluating juvenile delinquency programs. Most important questions are ultimately causal in nature; we are not satisfied with description. We want to know, for example, does counseling result in (cause) decreased recidivism?; does improving physical condition produce (cause) an increase in self-esteem?

Traditionally, the most straightforward and compelling evidence for causality is achieved by means of a randomized experiment. Cook and Campbell (1979) have provided a cogent discussion of problems of inferring causality and thinking in causal terms. Many of these problems result from the presence of a third variable that may plausibly explain why the variables of interest are related. A well-implemented experiment can usually resolve these problems. The advantage of the randomized experiment, if properly done, is that research cases assigned to different conditions can be assumed to be equivalent in all ways save exposure to the experimental variable (treatment), with the consequence that any final differences would be unequivocally attributable to the treatment itself.

Unfortunately, things are not that simple. True randomization is rarely achieved even in the laboratory. The moment any single case is lost from a group or there is any variation in procedure, the groups are no longer strictly equivalent. Generally, we do not concern ourselves with these relatively small perturbations in protocol. However, in an action setting such as a delinquency program, random assignment to groups may be well nigh impossible, and even if randomization is initially achieved, it may not be possible to maintain it. It may be ethically or practically difficult to withhold treatment from certain groups. The "subjects" are, in this case, persons with certain rights. Delinquents are, however, unlike most persons in settings sometimes truly "captive" making random assignment possible on occasion. Drop-out rates may be controllable with this population, but the consequences of forced participation can be manifest in the offender's attitude and commitment to the treatment. Moreover, as we have noted, mental health care providers and corrections officers alike are not research assistants and may have reactions to having to withhold certain treatments (e.g., Borgatta, 1955), or to having their effectiveness questioned.

In short, a wide variety of factors (see Weiss, 1972 for a summary) make the experiment an often difficult option in evaluating a living, breathing program. Thus, a great deal of our discussion will involve a variety of quasi-experimental methods that may, with the proper cautions, produce useful, if not completely persuasive, causal data.

Plausibility

One would assume that the better the methodology used in evaluating a program, the more plausible the findings would be. Yet, this connection remains an unknown empirical question. The audiences for a study evaluating a delinquency program differ from editors and referees of scientific journals. Congressmen, businessmen, program heads, corrections officials, and the public are not necessarily as likely as editors and journal referees to be swayed by methodological rigor. Weiss and Bucuvalas (1980) did find that the judged utility of research was related to its perceived quality, but the quality judgments included variables beyond methodological rigor, for example, lack of bias in conclusions. Furthermore, Holland (1984) found that a group of mental health service providers did not distinguish between "usefulness" and "truthfulness" of findings concerning the effectiveness of programs. The first question the researcher needs to ask in considering the plausibility of his or her research is "to whom does this need to be plausible?" In terms of process evaluations, the likely answers include program participants, directors, and perhaps funding sources, including their surrogates and agents, like grant reviewers. The second question becomes, given one's audience, how does one make research plausible as a basis for policy?

Researchers who want to influence policy must attend to issues of external validity. External validity refers to the generalizability of the study. It has been clearly demonstrated that different methods, done properly and addressing the same issue, can lead to very different results (Konecni and Ebbeson, 1979). To illustrate the case, consider the evaluator who wants to know how length of treatment affects delinquent behaviors in juveniles. So the evaluator constructs a true (randomized), internally valid causal experiment in which college students (18 years of age or younger so as to qualify as "delinquent") are given the MMPI Pd (see Chapter 6) scale or some other measure of "anti-social" tendencies. These individuals are then randomly assigned to either 0, 1, 5, or 10 hours of a specific, highly controlled therapy designed to reduce antisocial tendencies. The results may be causally interpretable, but they would not be plausible as a basis for any policy. "Real" delinquents are certainly different in a number of ways from high Pd college students. Whatever the results of such a study they would be unlikely to influence any real world criminal justice system. A well done quasi-experiment conducted in the system might be far more convincing.

Although the example is certainly exaggerated, we want to consider the possibility that under some circumstances quasi-experimental research may be at least equal to randomized experimentation in its overall impact. Much of the variance in the impact of research findings may depend on how the findings are couched. There is only one universal code for expressing research findings, and that is in terms of statistical significance. Unfortunately, for a great many reasons, statistical significance does not convey much useful information about a research finding, particularly information that might be useful to a policy maker (Sechrest and Yeaton, 1981a). Policymakers need to know how large an effect is produced by some intervention or how much difference it makes when one is considering one group or another. There is simply not a good generally agreed upon metric for expressing effect sizes. Sechrest and Yeaton (1981a, 1981b) have, however, suggested some approaches that should be useful (see also Chapter 10).

Plausible Rival Hypothesis

For any relationship between two variables there is always at least one alternative, or rival, hypothesis to any that might be put forth. That means that in any instance in which we may have a favored causal hypothesis, there is at least one other possible explanation. Some rival hypotheses we are likely to consider implausible. For example, supernatural explanations are always possible, but we reject them out of hand as implausible. Other rival hypotheses may be considerably more plausible, and much of the art of research design is in creating arrangements that render most or all rival hypotheses implausible. To begin with, for example, chance is always a rival hypothesis, and we must do our research in such a way that the operations of chance come to seem implausible as an explanation for our findings.

The issue of plausible rival hypotheses arises most often in relation to internal validity, although it can arise with respect to any other feature of a research project. By their very nature, most plausible rival hypotheses have limits on their plausibility. One limit is Bayesian in character. That is, our inclination to accept a research outcome as real will depend in part on our prior expectations about the likelihood of finding it. We will, and should, therefore, have a bias in favor of research findings that make theoretical sense.

Plausible rival hypotheses also very often involve rather subtle effects, and presumably nuances, in findings. We might believe that if an intervention is likely to produce large effects, even a relatively weak design might be impervious to most rival hypotheses. Unhappily, those occasions when we might trust weak designs to reveal truth are not frequent in research, but the possibility should not be ignored.

Ethics and Practicality

Ethical issues may present a threat or conflict in research design. One common ethical dilemma raised in evaluation studies on treatment programs involves the possibility of withholding potentially beneficial treatment elements from some of the patients of the program. This dilemma is tempered by the possibility that untested treatments may not prove beneficial or may even prove harmful. Under such circumstances withholding the treatment may actually be the more ethical option. Borgatta (1955) argued, for example, that providing an ineffective treatment may prevent a client from receiving an effective treatment.

In the case of delinquency programs, ethical problems involving withholding of treatment are likely to be major. If a treatment exists that may keep a potentially dangerous offender from committing crimes to person or property, withholding the treatment poses some real ethical dilemmas in terms of cost to society. It may be useful to assign patients to one type of treatment or element as opposed to a similar type of treatment or element, so it is possible the evaluator will not need to assign patients to a "no treatment" condition. Ethical problems are likely to be decided as much by politics as by any absolute ethical standards. Practitioners and corrections officials may disagree with the ethics, and in the cases of inmates, threats to security, of many interventions. In this, as well as many other areas of the evaluation, researcher and practitioner or correction official are likely to clash. Such problems are common in evaluation research (Aronson and Sherwood, 1967; Weiss, 1971, 1972), and are to be expected in evaluating delinquency programs and implementing program elements. Regardless of the cause, such clashes almost always threaten the strength of the treatment in some way. Solutions to these problems include: getting the necessary support from administrators; involving practitioners in the evaluation; minimizing disruption; emphasizing theory and benefits; providing information useful to the program; and clearly defining roles and authority structures (Weiss, 1972).

Careful selection of research design may also serve to minimize ethical and practical problems in evaluation. A delayed treatment design (Weiss, 1972) may, for example, get around problems of withholding treatments from certain groups. This design, similar to that used for waiting list control studies, could be especially useful in cases where services were limited and only a part of the population could be served at any one time. Scriven (1967) proposed another option for dealing with this problem by offering controls weaker versions of the treatment rather than placebos. Such a strategy does, however, reduce the chances of finding any advantage in the experimental condition (Baum et al., 1981). The researcher must, as in any setting, judge the value of the work against any potential harm the work may produce. Valueless, poorly conducted work can not justify putting subjects through even minimal discomfort or risking any social cost in terms of safety of the community.

Experimentation

When properly conducted, experimentation leads to the most causally unambiguous results of any method. Experimentation is the only design that allows one to eliminate alternate explanations of the results (Campbell and Stanley, 1966). To achieve its power, the experimental method relies on: (1) random assignment of cases to groups; (2) one or more control groups assumed equal to the experimental groups in every way except for receiving the treatment. All other designs allow for one or more rival hypotheses to remain plausible, and thus fail to ensure internal validity. True experimental designs have the additional advantage of being very efficient (more powerful) and thus more able to detect small effects (Gilbert, Light, & Mosteller, 1977). The advantages of well done, true experiments are such that they should be used whenever possible.

A word or two of caution about randomized experiments is, however, in order. Conducting a true, tightly controlled experiment is a tricky task; things will likely go wrong, all of which will serve to weaken the causal interpretation of any results. Things never get better during the course of an experiment. For example, persons assigned to different groups may become aware of the presence of the other groups and may talk to these groups or seek other treatments. Randomization itself can break down in many places (for example, see Lerman, 1975). Those responsible for randomization may subvert the process because they do not like its consequences. Persons within treatment groups may be differentially likely to drop out, or the nature of the treatment itself may result in better tracking of persons so that attrition is not equal.

In addition, experiments provide only a very specific service in the formative evaluation of the program. They can evaluate the probable value of isolated elements in a program. An experiment (or quasi-experiment), cannot, however, accurately predict the value of the element when it is implemented in the program and combined with other elements (Tharp & Gallimore, 1979). For example, an experiment might prove that a certain supervision plan is effective and that a certain treatment plan is effective. However, we can not be sure whether the two in combination will be effective. The two plans might be incompatible. In a broader sense, we can not be sure if proven effective counseling program combined with a proven effective job training program will still be effective.

Quasi-Experimental Designs

Since experimental designs are not always feasible in an action setting such as a delinquency program, the evaluator must possess full knowledge of various "quasi" experimental designs (Campbell and Stanley, 1966; Cook and Campbell, 1979). In choosing one of the following designs, which we think particularly useful in delinquency research, the researcher must carefully consider which design provides the strongest evidence of causality, given the circumstances. When conducted properly, many of these alternatives provide data that approach experiments in causality and plausibility.

NONEQUIVALENT CONTROL-GROUP DESIGNS.   Nonequivalent control group designs are probably among the most frequently used quasi-experimental designs. They vary from experimental designs in that cases get into the comparison groups on a nonrandom basis. Nonrandom "assignment" creates a variety of methodological problems (summarized by Judd & Kenny, 1981; Reichardt, 1979), owing to the possibility that cases ending up in different groups were different in ways that affected the outcome measures. Thus, if differences are found between the experimental (treatment) group and the control group, the researcher cannot be sure whether outcome differences were due to the manipulation or to preexisting differences between the two groups. For this reason, it is usually advisable to have the two groups be as similar as possible. Finding groups that weaken potential plausible rival hypotheses constitutes much of the work in nonequivalent control group designs. The researcher needs to identify plausible rival hypotheses and select the comparison groups in a way as to eliminate these sources of error. If multiple plausible confounding hypotheses exist, it might be possible to select more than one comparison group, each designed to eliminate an alternate hypothesis and thus strengthen the conclusiveness of the results.

Two other ways of equating controls seem intuitively useful but must be viewed with caution. Matching seems as though it would reduce the variance between the groups, but serious problems with this tactic make it almost always undesirable. Offenders, for example, are often matched by type of crime. Matching may have serious negative consequences for making causal inferences. All the relevant variables cannot be matched for; matching for some variables may result in opposite mismatching for others, and the likelihood of regression effects, which usually do not pose a threat in nonequivalent comparison group designs, is greatly increased. Studies that use matching must be looked upon with skepticism (Campbell and Stanley, 1966; Cook and Campbell; 1979; Neale and Liebert, 1973).

A second approach to dealing with nonequivalence between groups is through statistical means (e.g., analysis of covariance). Much as is the case with matching, it is likely that allowances for initial differences are wrong in unknown, or even unknowable, degrees (Sechrest, 1984). Thus, nonequivalence remains a problem in these designs, especially when the differences in outcomes between groups are small.

TIME SERIES.   Interrupted time series designs are a fairly attractive quasi-experimental technique capable of yielding high-quality data and defensible conclusions (Judd & Kenney, 1981). These designs involve a series of measures taken at periodic intervals before an intervention begins (a baseline phase), followed by a series of measures taken after the intervention starts. These designs are similar to the designs frequently used in assessing the efficacy of behavioral interventions in individual subjects (See Kazdin, 1974 for a summary). They are different, however, in that they may be used with a large sample size and are formulated around complex statistical tests (Gottman and Glass, 1978; McCleary and Hays, 1980) that ensure that changes in data are due to the treatment and not to some general trend. A time series may show that the mean levels of some phenomena are different before and after treatment, that the slope of change over time is different, or that there is a change at the time of treatment that is of an abrupt nature. For example, a new treatment plan might be implemented in an attempt to ensure staff commitment to the treatment. The researcher can take a series of measures assessing staff commitment, introduce the new plan, and take a further series of measures assessing commitment. The subsequent analysis might show that commitment increased after the new plan was introduced; or they might show that commitment was generally increasing, but increased more rapidly after the plan was introduced. Or, it might show that commitment quickly increased after the introduction of the plan, but eventually declined to former levels.

Other factors such as history (e.g., a new supervision plan may have been implemented at the same time as the treatment plan) or maturation (e.g., staff simply began to enjoy working together more as they became friends and thus felt more committed to the workplace and the plan), can explain the results of a simple time-series design. To control for these problems, a researcher can use an elaborated version of a time-series design called a multiple time-series design. These designs usually combine a time-series design with a non-equivalent comparison group design. Referring to the previous example, a second, similar treatment team could have served as a nonequivalent control group, receiving the same measures as the treatment group over the same period of time without receiving the new treatment plan. Much like nonequivalent control group designs, multiple comparison groups may be used to eliminate multiple confounding hypotheses. When conducted properly, multiple time-series designs can provide information that approaches that of an experiment in terms of causality and plausibility.

There are, however, some practical problems with these designs, the main one being that they often take considerable time. They require a long series of observations, which may mean a considerable delay before results of the intervention are known. This delay is ethically problematic if there are potential negative outcomes of the intervention, for instance, if patients are at risk for termination of services. Delay in availability of results may also provide considerable practical problems if a program element is unlikely to be implemented without immediate data as to its effectiveness. In our criteria example, peer reviewers would likely not respond favorably to having to try a new, more difficult set of criteria for a long period of time without evidence as to its effectiveness.

THE REGRESSION-DISCONTINUITY DESIGN.   It often happens that decisions about persons or cases must be or may be made on the basis of some numerical indicator, a cutting score, so that persons with a score at some level or above are to be treated one way while persons below the critical score are to be treated another way. For example, youth of age 16 years plus 364 days or less may be treated as juvenile offenders, while youth of 17 years or older are treated as adult offenders. Or, delinquents with a reading test score of 74 or less may be assigned to a remedial reading class, while those with 75 or greater are not assigned to remedial reading. Or youth with a probation index score of 12 or less may be given probation, while those with a score of 13 or greater may be denied probation. We assume that in the absence of intervention there is a smooth function relating score on the decision measure to any outcome measure. Thus, we would probably assume that in the absence of any intervention, the relationship between initial reading test score and a subsequent reading test, say after one year, would be linear and with a positive slope (see Figure 14.1). Or in the absence of any intervention the relationship between age at the time of comission of a given offense and the likelihood of any later offense would be linear, perhaps with zero slope (see Figure 14.2).

If, however, there is an intervention at some particular point along the range of scores or other numerical indicators, and if that intervention had an effect, it should result in a discontinuity in the relationship (regression) between the two variables. Let us suppose, for example, that a youth processed as an adult offender has an increased likelihood of being involved in later criminal activity, perhaps because of damage to self-image, being placed with bad companions, and the like. In that case, rather than the aforementioned relationship portrayed, we would expect something like that shown in Figure 14.3. Or, in the case of reading scores, if remedial reading had a good effect on later reading scores, we would expect something like Figure 14.4.

The phenomena sketched out here fall into the general category of regression-discontinuity effects (Trochim, 1984). When decisions about persons are made on the basis of sharp cutting scores, and in some cases even relatively sharp cutting scores, the opportunity exists to make some assessment of the effects of that decision. The regression-discontinuity design can, in fact, be a fairly powerful design, often providing quite persuasive evidence for a causal effect of the intervention examined. The statistics for detecting regression-

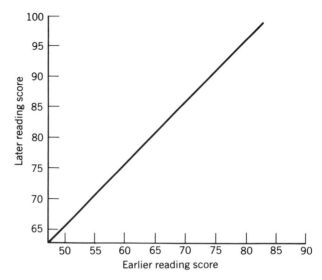

Figure 14.1.

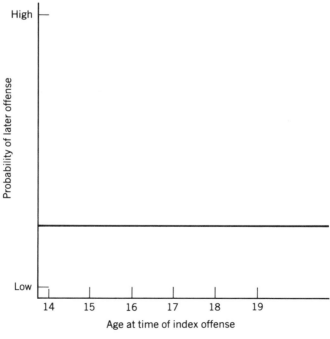

Figure 14.2.

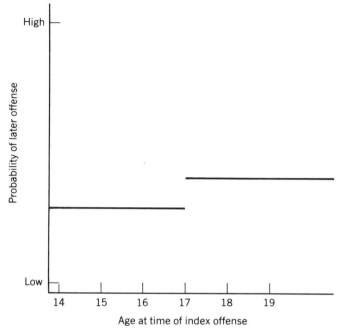

Figure 14.3.

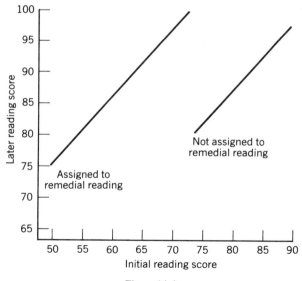

Figure 14.4.

discontinuity effects are reasonably well worked out, although further improvements are likely, especially for the case where the cutting score may be somewhat "fuzzy." Juvenile delinquents probably are fairly often exposed to some intervention based on a criterion score, and advantage should be taken of the opportunity to learn something about interventions applied on that basis. Trochim's (1984) book is the standard for the field.

META-ANALYSIS AND DATA SYNTHESIS.   Resolution of any issue by means of a single experiment, however well done, is infrequent. For some topics, a large number of studies are available and relevant. Whenever more than one study or piece of information exists with respect to a problem, the question that arises is how to put things together and sythesize the findings so as to arrive at an overall conclusion. For most of the history of the social and behavioral sciences, methods of data synthesis were subjective and often fairly haphazard, the most typical example being the "review of the literature." A later development was the "boxscore" approach of counting how many studies produced results on each side of an issue. More recently the National Institutes of Health have developed a fairly standard procedure for conducting "consensus panels" to resolve complex and sometimes controversial issues (Vinokur, Burnstein, Sechrest, & Wortman, 1985; Wortman, Vinokur, & Sechrest, 1982). Essentially, consensus panels consist of "neutral" experts convened to hear presentations of findings and arguments and then to formulate a conclusion. National Academy of Sciences panels have operated in much the same way, for example, a NAS panel was formed to consider whether it is indeed true that in relation to rehabilitation of criminal offenders "nothing works" (Sechrest, White, & Brown, 1979).

A more recent development in methods of data synthesis has been the quantitative approach known as meta-analysis (see Light & Pillemer, 1984, for an excellent presentation). This method requires a systematic search of the literature and coding of both findings and characteristics of studies. Outcomes are transformed by statistical procedures into a common metric, so that, for example, whether an outcome has to do with recidivism, vocational skills, or self-esteem, the results from study to study can be added together and an average effect computed. Effect sizes can be related to characteristics of the intervention, the sample studied, the nature of the study, and so on. For example, a study of the effects of "psychoeducational interventions" on length of postsurgical hospital stay (Devine & Cook, 1983) indicated that such interventions reduce hospital stay by about $1\frac{1}{4}$ days, and that the reduction is unrelated to whether the study was published, whether the physician discharging the patient was aware of the patient's experimental condition, or whether the study had a strong (internally valid) design. The effects were also smaller for more recent studies.

Meta-analyses are growing in frequency and complexity, but they are not a cure-all for our problems. For one thing, a good meta-analysis usually requires a fairly large data base that is well documented. Such data bases are not to be found everywhere. There is disagreement about whether studies should be screened for adequacy of initial methodology, but one should not expect by some act of statistical legerdemain to transform the junk studies of science into a sound foundation for action. Considerable expertise may be required for accurate coding of studies. Finally, meta-analyses are complex and difficult to do properly, and no one should labor under the misapprehension that they can be done by following some manual and by persons not trained in the method.

CAUSAL MODELING.   One additional analytic approach to the attempt to strengthen causal interpretations is causal modeling. Although, strictly speaking, causal modeling is an approach to analysis of data rather than to research design per se, effective causal modeling almost always requires a sound research design (Bentler, 1980). To be a bit more exact, effective causal modeling demands a fairly precise plan for measurement and collection of data. Selection of measures is crucial, for causal modeling, especially by way of the more sophisticated procedures involved in structural equations, which require multiple measures of variables. Moreover, causal modeling involves no magic, and good results are unlikely to be achieved from poor data. It is necessary that the measures chosen be highly reliable and have high validity if results are to be interpretable and persuasive.

Another limitation on causal modeling is that sample size must ordinarily be fairly large because of the large number of estimates that must be made in most analyses. Sample size will, in fact, be a prohibitive limitation in most applications to program evaluation since only rarely will one have access to appropriate data sets involving hundreds of cases.

Many approaches to causal modeling are possible, but the most common at present involves the use of complex statistical procedures, most frequently LISREL (Joreskog & Sorbom, 1984), to develop estimates of standardized partial regression coefficients. These coefficients can be compared to assess the reasonableness of different causal models for the phenomena of interest. As an example, Aneshensel and Huba (1983) showed by means of causal modeling of longitudinal data that it is likely that depressed persons may try, in the short run, to alleviate their problems by using alcohol but that, in the long run, use of alcohol increases depression. In contrast, depression and cigarette smoking are seemingly unrelated in any causal way. Causal modeling, even with the most sophisticated sets of structural equations cannot demonstrate causality; certainly not with the same degree of persuasiveness as can be achieved in a good randomized experiment. Causal modeling can be regarded as a method of argumentation, of arguing for one causal interpretation rather than another. One of the difficulties it poses is that it may be either over- or underpersuasive to those not familiar with its nature and assumptions. Determining just how much faith one ought to have in the outcome of a LISREL analysis is not easy. Unfortunately, Gottfredson (1979) and Berk (1977) have produced data suggesting that the results of efforts at causal modeling may be substantially unstable.

Nonetheless, used cautiously with data of good quality and with sizable samples, causal modeling may produce useful information. Good descriptions of the processes involved may be found in Judd, Jessor, and Donovan (1986).

No Difference Findings

Although the classical problem in research design and statistical analysis has been to devise things so as to be able to reject the null hypothesis, it often happens in research that we want very much to be able to accept, in essence to "prove" the null hypothesis, if that is at all possible. For example, we would not need to show that a juvenile diversion project actually reduces recidivism beyond the level achieved by incarceration; we would be pleased to discover that diversion simply does not differ from incarceration. We would be pleased to be able to demonstrate that the null hypothesis is tenable. In other cases, we may not set out to demonstrate no difference between two interventions, but we would be satisifed to accept a null finding and subsequently to act on it. Thus, we might suppose that a particular intervention would have different effects on different types of delinquents, but if the evidence indicated otherwise, that is, if it pointed toward the null, we might well accept the seeming fact of no difference and discontinue trying to treat the delinquent types differently.

Coming to the position of accepting a finding of no difference (or no relationship, for instance, between a personality variable and involvement in delinquent activity) is not something that should be done lightly. We have already noted that weak and poorly implemented treatments may result in mistaken conclusions that they are ineffective. In addition, poor research design, unreliable measures, small samples, and careless implementation of research procedures can all lead to a mistaken conclusion of no difference. Just as we should err on the side of caution in concluding that an intervention is effective when it may not be, we ought to err on the side of caution in concluding that an intervention is not effective.

We cannot take the space here to detail the problems involved in concluding that "no difference" is the preferred interpretation of findings (see Yeaton and Sechrest, in press a, in press b for such a discussion). We can say that demonstration of the null hypothesis seems to require even stronger methodology than is required to support a conclusion that a difference exists. Only with the best designs, measures of proven quality, and procedures of great precision well documented, are we likely to be able to persuade doubtful audiences that we have succeeded in showing that the conclusion of no difference is correct.

Power Analysis

Ignored for many years was the fact that the likelihood that one can detect an effect of an intervention and detect a relationship between two variables, is strongly determined by sample size. Small samples may cause us to miss important relationships. Fortunately, there are methods available to determine in advance the sample sizes that are required to detect effects or relationships of whatever magnitude are expected or reasonable (Cohen, 1977). Power analyses should by now be routine in virtually all social science research, whether program evaluation or any kind, but they are still regrettably infrequent in research on juvenile delinquency.

Qualitative Methods and Personal Knowing

Although not really representing a methodology per se, it is important to call attention to the role of qualitative methods and personal knowing in understanding the developing program (Campbell, 1974). As outlined in the evaluation succession model, personal knowledge ranges from intuition to systematic ethnography. Tharp and Gallimore (1979) noted that personal knowing is not a substitute for other methods. Rather, it may serve the function of understanding and interpreting the results gleaned from other methods, of providing ideas translatable into variables, and of complementing more quantitative methods. Especially in the developing program, data without interpretation and variables without ideas are bound to lead to dead ends and frustration. Patton, (1980) has made the case for qualitative evaluation, but we believe with Cook and Reichardt (1979) that a combination of qualitative and quantitative methods is required: There is no substitute for knowing *what* you are doing and *how much* you are doing of it.

CONCLUSION

Conducting effective process and outcome evaluations for juvenile delinquency programs is a matter of identifying the independent variables, identifying the dependent variables, and applying the appropriate methodology to relate them. Owing to practical and ethical limitations, application of the experimental method will likely be difficult or impossible in many cases. Researchers will be forced to use quasi-experimental methods such as nonequivalent control group designs, time-series analyses, causal modeling, power analyses, and regression-discontinuity designs in an attempt to yield causal and plausible results. If these designs are precisely and appropriately used in process evaluations, then the difficulties with strength and integrity of treatment will, as a matter of course, no longer pose an overriding threat to research conducted in this area.

Until that time arrives, we can only view the "no-result" findings in juvenile delinquency research with some skepticism. Only when the considerable methodological difficulties in this field have been effectively dealt with, can we reach any well-informed conclusions as to the efficacy of these programs.

Methodological problems abound in program evaluation, and they are particularly troublesome because the stakes are so high. The problems are not, however, different in kind from those in other types or arenas of research in juvenile delinquency. The problems grow from the need to get beyond simple descriptive levels to inferences of cause-effect relationships. Methodological problems may frustrate attempts to be confident in cause-effect inferences, and we may have to operate more in a mode of argumentation than proof. Proper attention to methodology, though, and use of the best methods we have available, will put us on stronger grounds in our arguments about causes and what to do about them.

REFERENCES

Aneshensel, C. S., & Huba, G. J. (1983). Depression, alcohol use, and smoking over one year: A four-wave longitudinal causal model. *Journal of Abnormal Psychology, 92,* 134–150.

Aronson, E., & Carlsmith, J. M. (1968). Experimentation in social psychology. In G. Lindzey & E. Aronson (Eds.), *Handbook of social psychology* (Vol. 2, 2nd ed., pp. 1–79). Reading, MA: Addison-Wesley.

Aronson, S. H., & Sherwood, C. C. (1967). Researcher versus practitioner: Problems in social action research. *Social Work, 12,* 89–96.

Babbie, E. (1983). *The practice of social research.* Belmont, CA: Wadsworth.

Baum, M. L., Anish, D. S., Chalmers, T. C., Sacks, H. S., Smith, H., & Fagerstrom, R. M. (1981). A survey of clinical trials of antibiotic prophylaxis in colon surgery: Evidence against further use of no-treatment controls. *New England Journal of Medicine, 305,* 795–799.

Bejar, I. I. (1980). Biased assessment of program impact due to psychometric artifacts. *Psychological Bulletin, 87,* 513–524.

Bentler, P. M. (1980). Multivariate analysis with latent variables: causal modeling. *Annual Review of Psychology, 31,* 419–456.

Berk, R. (1977). The vagaries and vulgarities of "scientific" jury selection. *Evaluation Quarterly, 1,* 143–158.

Borgatta, E. (1955). Research: Pure and applied. *Group Psychotherapy, 8,* 236–277.

Campbell, D. T., & Stanley, J. C. (1966). *Experimental and quasi-experimental designs for research.* Chicago: Rand McNally.

Carlsmith, J. M., Ellsworth, P. C., & Aronson, E. (1976). *Methods of research in social psychology.* Reading MA: Addison-Wesley.

Cohen, J. (1977). *Statistical power analysis for the behavioral sciences.* New York: Academic Press.

Cook, T. D., & Campbell, D. T. (1979). *Quasi-experiments: design and analysis issues for field settings.* Chicago: Rand McNally.

Cook, T. D., & Reichardt, C. S. (Eds.) (1979). *Qualitative and quantitative methods in evaluation research.* Beverly Hills: Sage Publications.

Cronbach, L. J. (1964). Evaluation for course improvement. In R. W. Heath (Ed.), *New Curricula* (pp. 231–248). New York: Harper & Row.

Cronbach, L. J. (1975). Beyond the two disciplines of scientific psychology. *American Psychologist, 30,* 116–134.

Cronbach, L. J., Gleser, G. C., Nanda, H., & Rajaratnam, N. (1972). *The dependability of behavioral measurements: Theory of generalizability for scores and profiles.* New York: John Wiley.

Devine, E. C., & Cook, T. D. (1983). A meta-analytic analysis of effects of psychoeducational interventions on length of postsurgical hospital stay. *Nursing Research, 32,* 267–274.

Edelman, E., & Goldstein, A. P. (1984). Prescriptive relationship levels for juvenile delinquents in a psychotherapy analog. *Aggressive Behavior, 10,* 269–278.

Fitzpatrick, J. J. (1967). *An analysis of recidivism among inmates released from the forestry camps.* Massachusetts Department of Corrections.

Gilbert, J. P., Light, R. J., & Mosteller, F. (1977). Progress in surgery and anesthesia: Benefits and risks of innovative therapy. In J. P. Bunker, B. A. Barnes, & F. Mosteller (Eds.), *Costs risks and benefits of surgery* (pp. 124–169). New York: Oxford University Press.

Glaser, D. (1977). Concern with theory in correctional evaluation research. *Crime and Delinquency, 23,* 173–179.

Goldstein, A. P., Glick, B., Reiner, S., Zimmerman, D., & Coultry, T. (1986). *Aggression replacement training.* Unpublished Manuscript.

Gottfredson, G. D. (1979). Models and muddles: An ecological examination of high school crime rates. *Journal of Research in Crime and Delinquency, 16,* 307–331.

Gottman, J. M., & Glass, G. V. (1978). Analysis of interrupted time series experiments. In T. R. Kratochwill (Ed.), *Single-subject research: Strategies for evaluating change.* (pp. 197–235) New York: Academic Press.

Greenberg, D. F. (1975). The correctional effects of corrections: A survey of evaluations. In D. Greenberg, (Ed.), *Corrections and punishment* (pp. 111–148). Beverly Hills, CA: Sage.

Hirschi, T., & Selvin, H. (1973). *Principles of survey analysis.* New York: Free Press.

Holland, R. S. (1984). *Perceived truthfulness and perceived usefulness of program evaluations by direct services staff.* Unpublished doctoral dissertation, University of Michigan.

Howard, K. I., Kopta, M., Krause, M. S., & Orlinsky, D. E. (1986). The dose effect relationship in psychotherapy. *American Psychologist, 41,* 159–164.

Jessness, C., Allison, T., McCormick, P., Wedge, R., & Young, M. (1975). *Cooperative behavior demonstration project.* Sacramento: California Youth Authority.

Johnson, B. D., & Goldberg, R. T. (1983). Vocational and social rehabilitation of delinquents: A study of experimentals and controls. *Journal of Offender Counseling, Services and Rehabilitation, 6,* 43–60.

Joreskog, K., & Sorbom, D. (1984). *LISREL: Analysis of linear structural relationships by the method of maximum likelihood.* Chicago: SPSS, Inc.

Judd, C. M. Jessor, R., & Donovan, J. E. (1986). Structural equation models and personality research. *Journal of Personality, 54,* 148–159.

Judd, C. M., & Kenny, D. A. (1981). *Estimating the effects of social interventions.* New York: Cambridge University Press.

Julian, A., & Kilman, P. R. (1979). Group treatment of juvenile delinquents: A review of the outcome literature. *International Journal of Group Psychotherapy, 29,* 3–37.

Kassebaum, G., Ward, D. A., & Wilner, D. M. (1971). *Prison treatment and parole survival.* New York: John Wiley.

Kazdin, A. E. (1974). Methodological and interpretive problems of single-case experimental designs. *Journal of Consulting and Clinical Psychology, 4,* 629–642.

Kazdin, A. E., & Wilson, G. T. (1978). *Evaluation of behavior therapy: Issues, evidence, and research strategies.* Cambridge, MA: Ballinger Publishing Co.

Konecni, V. J., & Ebbesen, E. B. (1979). External validity of research in legal psychology. *Law and Human Behavior, 3,* 39–70.

Lerman, P. (1975). *Community treatment and social control.* Chicago: University of Chicago Press.

Light, R. J., & Pillemer, D. B. (1984). *Summing up: The science of reviewing research.* Cambridge, MA: Harvard University Press.

McCleary, R., and Hays, R. A., Jr. (1980). *Applied time series analysis for the social sciences.* Beverly Hills: Sage Publications.

Murray, C. A., Thompson, D., & Israel, C. B. (1978). *UDIS: Deinstitutionalization of the chronic juvenile offender.* Washington, DC: American Institutes for Research.

Neale, J. M., & Libert, R. M. (1973). *Science and behavior: An introduction to methods of research.* Englewood Cliffs, NJ: Prentice-Hall.

Palmer, T., & Lewis, R. V. (1980). *An evaluation of juvenile diversion.* Cambridge, MA: Oelgeschlager, Gunn and Hain Publishing.

Patton, M. Q. (1978). *Utilization-focused evaluation.* Beverly Hills, CA: Sage.

Patton, M. Q. (1980). *Qualitative evaluation methods.* Beverly Hills: Sage.

Quay, H. C. (1977). The three faces of evaluation: What can be expected to work. *Criminal justice and behavior, 4,* 341–354.

Reichardt, C. S. (1979). The statistical analysis of data from nonequivalent group designs. In T. D. Cook & Campbell (Eds.), *Quasi-experimentation: Design and analysis issues for field settings.* (pp. 147–205). Skokie, IL: Rand McNally.

Scriven, M. (1967). The methodology of evaluation. In R. W. Tyler, R. M. Gagne, & M. Scriven (Eds.), *Perspectives of curriculum evaluation, AERA monograph series on curriculum evaluation, No. 1.* (pp. 39–83). Chicago: Rand McNally.

Sechrest, L. (1984). *Evaluating Health Care.* Unpublished Manuscript, University of Arizona.

Sechrest, L. (1985). *Classification for treatment.* Paper presented at National Institute of Justice Working Conference on Prediction and Classification Research, Old Town Alexandria, Virginia.

Sechrest, L., Ametrano, I. M., & Ametrano, D. A. (1982). Program evaluation. In J. R. McNamara & A. G. Barclay (Eds.), *Critical issues, developments and trends in professional psychology* (pp. 190–226). New York: Praeger Publishers.

Sechrest, L., & Redner, R. (1979). *Strength and integrity of treatments in evaluation studies.* Washington, DC: National Criminal Justice Reference Service, National

Institute of Law Enforcement and Criminal Justice, Law Enforcement Assistance Administration, U.S. Department of Justice.

Sechrest, L., West, S. G., Phillips, M. A., Redner, R., & Yeaton, W. (1977). Some neglected problems in evaluation research: Strength and integrity of treatments. In L. Sechrest, S. G. West, M. A. Phillips, R. Redner, & W. Yeaton (Eds.), *Evaluation studies review annual* (Vol. 4, pp. 15–35) Beverly Hills, CA: Sage Publications.

Sechrest, L., White, S., & Brown, E. (1979). *Rehabilitation of criminal offenders: Problems and prospects.* Washington, DC: National Research Council.

Sechrest, L., & Yeaton, W. H. (1981a). Empirical bases for estimating effect size. In R. F. Boruch, P. M. Wortman, & D. S. Cordray (Eds.), *Reanalyzing program evaluations* (pp. 212–213). San Francisco: Jossey-Bass.

Sechrest, L., & Yeaton, W. H. (1981b). Assessing the effectiveness of social programs: methodological and conceptual issues. In S. Ball (Ed.), *New Directions for Program Evaluation* (pp. 41–56). Beverly Hills: Sage Publications.

Shore, M. F., & Massimo, J. L. (1966). Comprehensive vocationally oriented psychotherapy for adolescent delinquent boys: A follow up study. *American Journal of Orthopsychiatry, 36,* 609–615.

Sutcliffe, J. P. (1980). On the relationship of reliability to statistical power. *Psychological Bulletin, 88,* 509–515.

Tharp, R. G., & Gallimore, R. (1979). The ecology of program research and evaluation: A model of evaluation succession. In L. Sechrest, S. G. West, M. A. Phillips, R. Redner, & W. Yeaton (Eds.) *Evaluation studies review annual* (Vol. 4, pp. 39–60) Beverly Hills, CA: Sage Publications.

Trochim, W. M. K. (1984). *Research design for program evaluation: The regression-discontinuity approach.* Beverly Hills: Sage Publications.

Vinokur, A., Burnstein, E., Sechrest, L., & Wortman, P. M. (1985). Group decision making by experts: Field of study of panels evaluating medical technologies. *Journal of Personality and Social Psychology, 49,* 70–84.

Weiss, C. H. (1971). Organizational constraints on evaluation research. New York: Bureau of Applied Social Research.

Weiss, C. H. (1972). *Evaluation research: Methods of assessing program effectiveness.* Englewood Cliffs, NJ: Prentice-Hall.

Weiss, C. H., & Bucuvales, M. J. (1980). Truth tests and utility tests: Decision makers frames of reference for social science research. *American Sociological Review, 45,* 302–313.

Werner, K., & Paladina, A. M. (1984). *Community College of Beaver County Prevention Project.* Monaca, PA: Community College of Beaver County.

West, S. G., & Sechrest, L. (1986). *Expert judgments of strength of intervention in offender rehabilitation programs.* Unpublished manuscript.

Wortman, P. M., Vinokur, A., & Sechrest, L. (1982). *Evaluation of NIH consensus development process: Final report.* Ann Arbor, MI: University of Michigan, Center for Research on the Utilization of Scientific Knowledge, Institute for Social Research.

Yeaton, W. H., & Redner, R. (1980). *Strength and integrity of treatments in rehabilitation studies.* Unpublished manuscript, University of Michigan.

Yeaton, W. H., & Sechrest, L. (1981). Critical dimensions in the choice and maintenance of successful treatments: Strength, integrity and effectiveness. *Journal of Consulting and Clinical Psychology, 49,* 156–167.

Yeaton, W. H., & Sechrest, L. (in press a). Use and misuse of no difference findings in eliminating threats to validity. *Evaluation review.*

Yeaton, W. H., & Sechrest, L. (in press b). No difference findings in medical research. *Medical Care.*

Author Index

Numbers in *italics* refer to bibliographic references.

Abe, M., 142, *170*
Abrahamse, A., 325, *375*
Abrahamsen, D., 25, *28*
Achenbach, T. M., 35, *58,* 122–123, *135*
Adams, S., 292, *317*
Ageton, S. S., 37, 39, 44, 46, 49, 55–56, *58,*
    93–94, 99–100, *102,* 153, *170,* 218, 223,
    224, 226, 230, *239,* 269, *284,* 400, 403, *413*
Agg, B., *286*
Ahlborn, H. H., 302, *319*
Ahlstrom, W. M., 359, *373*
Aichhorn, A., 70, *101*
Ajzen, I., 156, *170*
Akamatsu, T. J., 129, 131, *135,* 300, *324*
Akers, R., 23–24, *29*
Albee, G. W., 388, *412*
Alexander, F., 20, *28*
Alexander, J. F., 229, *238,* 268, *284, 286,*
    288, 310–312, 314, *317, 320–321,* 408, *412*
Alexander, P. S., 167, *181*
Alexander, R. N., *286*
Alkire, A. A., 229, *238*
Allen, A., 350, *373*
Allison, T., 428, *447*
Alterman, A. I., 111, *117*
Altus, W. D., 108, *115*
American Correctional Association, 244, *262*
American Psychiatric Association, 1, *28,* 126,
    135
Ametrano, D. A., 420, *448*
Ametrano, I. M., 420, *448*
Amini, F., 152, *171*
Amrung, S. A., 132, *138*
Amsel, R., 360, *376*
Anderson, A. C., 143
Andrew, J. M., 112, *115,* 268, *284*
Aneshensel, C. S., 443, *446*
Anish, D. S., 436, *446*
Anson, W. B., *28*

Anthony, H. S., 167, *170*
Arbuthnot, J., *159,* 160–161, 163–164, *170,*
    176, 301–303, 311, 314, *317, 319*
Ariès, P., 13, *28*
Armstrong, J. S., 152, *170*
Arnkoff, D. B., 297, *321*
Arnold, J., 308, *317*
Arnold, K. D., 161, *174,* 302, *319*
Aronson, E., 421, *446*
Aronson, S. H., 434, *446*
Ash, P. M., 231, *242*
Asu, M. E., 151, *182*
Atkins, J. W., 152–153, *170*
Attorney General's Task Force on Violent
    Crime, 38, *58*
Atwater, J. D., 255, *263,* 288
Aultman, M. G., 167, *170*
Ausnew, H. R., 268, *286*
Austin, J., 266–267, *285*

Babbie, E., 432, *446*
Bachman, J., 154, *171*
Bacon, J. G., 147, 149, *180*
Baer, D., *176, 288*
Baer, D. M., 411, *413*
Baer, R. A., 411, *413*
Bailey, W., 269, *284*
Bakal, Y., 167, *182*
Baker, J. W., II, 144, *171*
Bakkestrom, E., 192, *214*
Bandura, A., 70, *101,* 208, *209*
Bangert-Drowns, R. L., 245, *262*
Bank, L., 221, 231–232, *242*
Banks, C., 166, *181*
Bannatyne, A., 113, *115*
Bardwell, R., 132, *136*
Barkwell, L. J., *286*
Barnett, A., 43, *58*
Barnett, W. S., 356, *373*

451

Krisberg, B., 266–267, *285*
Kuhn, T. S., 92, *103,* 384, 388–390, 392, *414*
Kulik, J. A., 146, 167, *177, 182*
Kumchy, C. I. G., 151, *177*
Kunce, J. T., 112, *116*
Kushler, M., 266, *285*

La Greca, A. M., 134, *137*
Lahey, B. B., 131, *135*
Lam, T., 409, *414*
Lambert, L., 350, *375*
Landau, S., 56, *60*
Landau, S. F., 146–147, *177*
Lander, B., 86–87, *103*
Landman, S., 302, *322*
Langan, P. A., 188, *211*
Lange, J., 187, *211*
Langner, T. S., 220, 224, 229, 236, *243,* 353, 359, 364, 368, *375, 381*
Lanyon, R. I., 142, *177, 181*
LaRosa, J. F., 396–398, *415*
Larson, L. E., 403, *414*
Latané, B., 197, *213*
Laufer, W. S., 141, 143, *177*
Lautt, M., 40, *59*
Lavik, N. J., 148, *177*
Lavin, M., 331, 356, 366, 372, *379*
LeBlanc, M., 200, *210,* 348, 366, *377*
Lee, P., 262, *265*
Lee, R., *288*
Lefkowitz, M. M., 142, *176,* 340, 359, *376*
Leibert, R. M., 437, *488*
Leipciger, M., 142, *174*
Leitenberg, H., 410, *414*
Lemert, E. M., 327, *377*
Lerman, P., 429, 436, *448*
Le Roux, J. A., 162, *175*
Leske, G., 397, *416*
Levander, S. E., 200, 202–204, 207, *211, 213*
Levine, A., 308, *317*
Levine, R., 146, *178*
Levinson, R. B., 127, *137,* 253, *263*
Levitt, E. L., 267, 269, 283, *285*
Levy, L., 90, *103*
Levy, R. H., 111, *116*
Lewis, A., 236, *240*
Lewis, J., *287, 289*
Lewis, M. A., 254, *263, 288*
Lewis, R., *288*
Lewis, R. G., *286*
Lewis, R. V., 428, *448*
Liberman, R. P., *289,* 308
Lidberg, L., 200, 202–204, 207, *211, 213*
Lidberg, Y., 200, 202–204, *211*

Liddle, G., 332, 359, 361, *376*
Lieberman, M. A., 158, 160, *171, 177,* 363, *374*
Lieberman, R. P., *323*
Light, N. B., 316, *319*
Light, R. J., 436, 442, *447–448*
Liker, J. K., 222, 231, *239*
Lindgren, S. D., 114, *117*
Lippert, W. W., 199, *210–211*
Lipsey, M. W., *288,* 316, *320*
Lipton, D., 245, 256, *263,* 267, 269, 283, *285*
Little, V. L., 164, *177,* 297, 301, *320*
Littman, D. C., 221, *240*
Livson, N., 363, *377*
Lobitz, G. K., 221, *240*
Lockhart, R. A., 204, *211*
Lockwood, A. L., 302, *321*
Loeb, J., 201, *211–212*
Loeber, R., 46, 52, *60,* 122, *136,* 218, 221–223, 226–227, 232–233, 236, *238–241, 243,* 326, 328–331, 347, 350, 352, 354, 356–357, 360, 362–364, 367–370, *377,* 384, 396–397, 400, 407, *414*
Lofaso, A., 43, *58*
Logan, J. A., 331, *382*
Lombrosco, C., 19, *30*
Loney, J., 339, 361, *378*
Long, B. H., 152, *177*
Lorion, R. P., 386–387, 391, *414*
Lott, L. A., 307–308, *323*
Lounsbury, J. W., 387, *414*
Love, C. T., 128, *137,* 166, *179, 288*
Lovibond, S. H., 200, *212*
Lozes, J., *289*
Lubeck, S. G., 92, *102*
Ludwig, F. L., 7–9, *30*
Lund, N. L., 152, *177*
Lundsteen, C., 192, *214*
Lykken, D. T., 202, 206, *212*
Lynch, J. P., *288–289*

McAuley, R., 308, *321*
McCarthy, E. D., 359, 364, *375*
McCleary, R., 438, *448*
McCleary, R. A., 208, *212*
McClemont, W. F., 192, *211–212*
Maccoby, E. E., 52, *60,* 89, *103*
McColgan, E. B., 160–161, *178*
McConaghy, N., 200, *209*
McCord, J., 217, 220–222, 224, 226–229, 231, 233, 236, *241,* 245, *263,* 295, *321,* 345, 349, 353–354, 357–358, 363, 367, *378,* 408, *414*
McCord, W., 295, *321,* 345, 367, *378*

Subject Index

364.36 H236

Handbook of juvenile
delinquency /
c1987.

DATE DUE

DE 05 '91			
SEP 2 5 1999			
AP 18 '01			

Demco, Inc. 38-293

Please remember that this is a library book,
and that it belongs only temporarily to each
person who uses it. Be considerate. Do
not write in this, or any, library book.